MODERN
SOFTWARE ENGINEERING

FOUNDATIONS AND CURRENT
PERSPECTIVES

MODERN SOFTWARE ENGINEERING

FOUNDATIONS AND CURRENT PERSPECTIVES

Edited by

Peter A. Ng

Institute for Integrated Systems Research
Department of Computer and Information Science
New Jersey Institute of Technology
Newark, NJ

Raymond T. Yeh

International Software Systems, Inc.
Austin, TX

 VAN NOSTRAND REINHOLD
_____ New York

Printed in the United States of America

Van Nostrand Reinhold
115 Fifth Avenue
New York, New York 10003

Van Nostrand Reinhold International Company Limited
11 New Fetter Lane
London EC4P 4EE, England

Van Nostrand Reinhold
480 La Trobe Street
Melbourne, Victoria 3000, Australia

Nelson Canada
1120 Birchmount Road
Scarborough, Ontario M1K 5G4, Canada

16 15 14 13 12 11 10 9 8 7 6 5 4 3 2 1

Library of Congress Cataloging-in-Publication Data

Modern software engineering: foundations and current perspectives
   edited by Peter A. Ng and Raymond T. Yeh.
      p.   cm.
   Includes index.
   ISBN 0-442-26695-2
   1. Software engineering. I. Ng, Peter A. B. 1941– II. Yeh, Raymond
Tzuu-Yau, 1937–
QA76.758.M63   1989
005.1—dc20   89-8907
                                                        CIP

Preface

During the last 30 years, there has been a phenomenal proliferation of computers in the business world. This is partly due to the cost/performance ratio of computer hardware, which has improved dramatically, and to the microcomputer revolution, which has made it possible not only for businesses but also for individuals to have computers. This growth is expected to continue at the rate of 25% each year.

As computers became more accessible, the demand for information that increased business opportunities and provided better management practices also grew. People became interested in using the PC to build and execute business applications similar to the large and often complex systems designed for mainframe computers.

This growing demand for computer solutions, coupled with increasingly complex environments, far exceeds the supply of new programmers. According to a recent study, the average application backlog in large development shops has increased from 19 months to 27 months in just three years. Adding to the backlog problem is the fact that software is in a constant state of change due to new requirements. The manual development process simply cannot respond to changes fast enough. Often, the software is already obsolete upon delivery because requirements have changed.

It seems that a solution to this (labor and capital) imbalance is to automate the software development and maintenance processes, such as manufacturing has done in CAD/CAM. Indeed the term Computer Aided Software Engineering (CASE) has received significant attention in recent years. However, it is generally recognized that the traditional software development process, being complex, lengthy, labor-intensive, and unpredictable, is currently deemed to be inadequate to satisfy user demands. Furthermore, studies have indicated that automating the current process would not provide the necessary improvements in productivity. In the editors view, CASE must be approached by considering the following factors: process model, language, and methodology. The process model defines the framework for developing any software systems. One or more languages are used to describe and analyze the process. The methodology provides guidelines/procedures for carrying out the process. Finally, computer-aided tools are used to support the process/methodology.

The purpose of this book is to provide a broad perspective of the emerging

CASE field. In Part I, the editors have collected a set of papers which are concerned with the foundation of CASE; namely, process model, languages, and methodology. Chapter 1 begins with the discussion of an alternative paradigm for software evolution. The discussion refers to a new process model, the importance of high-level specification/design language, a methodology that is geared towards prototyping, reuse, incremental delivery, and environmental support centered on objected-oriented database management systems (DBMS). Subsequent papers in this part were selected to highlight issues discussed in Chapter 1.

First generation CASE tools can be broadly classified into three groups; information generators or 4th generation language (4GL), front-end design/ analysis tools, and application generators.

The variety of 4GL products includes the following: report generators, query languages, DBMS front-ends, and modeling languages. Most suffer from short-comings: they are tied too closely to a proprietary database system thereby offering a very restricted solution; they are functionally too weak to be more than a building block in a larger application solution, or they are not easily integrated with existing production systems and data.

Design tools help a user to draw "blueprints" or design diagrams based on some preselected methodology. Typically, high-level design documentation is provided automatically. The obvious flaw in these tools is that they are stand-alone, and their results are not easily integrated into the subsequent phases of the life cycle.

The base technology of application generators is usually a set of precoded COBOL shells. Precoded shells permit less sophisticated users to access the tool. However, because these pre-existing code segments cannot cover the entire spectrum of applications requirements, a large percentage of coding needs to be done manually. Furthermore, use of precoded shells produces loss of flexi-bility and efficiency.

A major shortcoming of these first generation CASE products is their inability to bridge the gap between design and application generation.

The second generation CASE tools evolved into two major categories: life cycle automation and solution software. The first category of tools is aimed at data-processing professionals to provide general solutions to their problems. The second category of tools is aimed at analyst or application specialists, in a restricted domain of application, to provide fast solutions to the end user. Electronic spread sheets represent such a tool in the very restricted domain of financial analysis.

Part II of this book provides a sample set of second generation CASE tools. Because it is not possible to describe every single tool, a survey of many existing commercially available CASE tools presented in Chapter 10 provides a general view of what is available. Chapters 11 through 15 present a set of tools based on life cycle automation; i.e., requirements, prototyping, design, and code generation. Chapter 16 describes how a set of tools is integrated and used effectively for producing large commercial systems. It should be noted, however, a software factory as described by Dr. Matsumoto, takes years to evolve. Finally a business application domain specific CASE tool, called MicroSTEP, is discussed in Chapter 17. This tool is an example of solution software. This type of tool increases productivity in two ways: first the user is more productive and, second, it creates an option of allowing more people to build applications without the need of programming.

Part III of the book provides a glimpse into major software projects around the world. With software expenditure skyrocketing, CASE has become a competitive edge for both major corporations and nations. Considering the fact that software expenditures in the U.S. will be 12% of GNP in 1990, and the U.S. DOD alone is projected to spend more than $32 billion in software by then, a 50% reduction in cost means billions of savings each year. Chapters 18 through 24 cover the major projects in the U.S., Japan, Europe, Brazil, and China. It is interesting to observe that each project is taking a different CASE strategy to sharpen their competitive edge.

Where are we now? And where are we going in the future? The editors will attempt to answer these questions in the forthcoming book, *Computer-Aided Software Engineering: Strategies and Practices.* Currently CASE products are classified into upper CASE and lower CASE: upper CASE tools support the front end of the development life cycle; lower CASE tools support the back end of the development life cycle. Many of the tools are designed to support a particular methodology. One approach is to integrate these tools to cover more of the development life cycle. Another is the development of a CASE shell, which is an environment that provides advanced facilities for the user to build his/her own tools. In this forthcoming book, the editors will introduce current CASE practices and evolution strategy in the near future.

This book is directed to those not satisfied with the traditional software development paradigm and for those interested to know what new development is coming. It directly addresses those issues on central repository, language and methodology. The book can also be used as a textbook for an advanced graduate seminar course in software engineering or as one of two or three books in an advanced software engineering course.

The editors understand that any technical book can soon become outdated, especially in a field that evolves as quickly as CASE. They believe that the language issues, methodology, and environmental support in this book are necessary to achieve long-term development in the field.

Contents

MODERN SOFTWARE ENGINEERING

FOUNDATIONS AND CURRENT PERSPECTIVES

Part I

Foundation

The effectiveness of a computer-aided tool is dependent upon the environment of the user, in particular, the process model, the language, and methodology that the user is using or with which the user is familiar. These factors are the foundation of CASE.

In Chapter 1, Raymond T. Yeh discusses an evolutionary model for software that provides an alternative process model for developing requirements and specifications of software systems. This model assumes that code is mostly synthesized automatically and that maintenance is done at the specification level. The foundation of the model emphasizes early validation and evaluation via various kinds of prototypes to minimize risk. This model is very similar to Barry Boehm's spiral model,[9] although it is presented in a different way and with a different emphasis.

The remainder of Part 1 explores issues discussed by Yeh in subsections of language, methodology, and environment. Clearly, it is not possible to include all the ideas relevant to these titles: the editors supplement the selected papers with references for those interested.

The language section consists of three chapters. They cover graphics language, nonprocedural language, specification, design language, and prototyping language. In the past, graphics language did not receive the same attention as now, due to processability. With the increased use of computers, diagrammers are becoming more common. It is clear that iconographic notations will be the common user interface for any CASE products. Thus, in Chapter 2, Felicia Cheng and Peter A. Ng present a survey of commonly used diagramming techniques of CASE today. Most of the techniques are widely used in the commercial market or in military applications. Others, such as Greenprint, are not as commonly used, but the essential feature of language appears in some commercial products. While the list provided by both authors may not be complete, it provides the reader with a glimpse at the alternative graphics languages. Also discussed are the essential features that are necessary to be included in the tools, such as consistency checking. However, it in no way provides what the future will hold in regard to the tremendous research effort in this area in recent years. An example of what could come of it in the next generation CASE product is hypermedia.

Nonprocedural language, or fourth generation language (4GL), enables non-data processing (DP) professionals, such as managers, to become competent in building and solving problems, retrieving information, and predicting performance in an interactive manner. In Chapter 3, Pieter R. Mimno provides a survey of high productivity language and a set of very effective productivity tools developed over the last decade. The author categorizes high-productivity languages into the following: 1) a decision support system, 2) application generators for end-users, 3) application and code generators for the DP professional, 4) computer-aided software engineering (CASE) tools, and 5) expert system tools. A detailed description of the tools, a comprehensive checklist of the features, and a comparison of the products are presented. It is the editors belief that 4th generation language (4GL) will eventually be totally replaced by the next generation CASE tools. However, many of the language features of 4GL will survive and will be incorporated into CASE products.

Chapter 4, by Valdis Berzins and Luqi, discusses the differences and characteristics of specification, design, and prototyping languages, illustrated with examples. To achieve a high level of automation, both authors propose that a formal notation be used. Specification language, design language, and prototyping language should have different characteristics because of the different functionalities. For example, specification language should be precise while a design language should support description, with a controlled degree of incompleteness so that detail of the design can be filled in later in the development process. Prototyping language, aside from being executable, is expected to precess the expressive power of the specification language and design language. The authors use a specific Prototyping System Description Language (PSDL) as an example in illustrating principles of software prototyping.

The editors believe these languages are of critical importance in the next generation of CASE products. Several other language chapters covering functional, object-oriented, and algebraic languages, etc. could have been included, but to compensate for their omission, a supplementary reading or reference list was added after each chapter.

The methodology section contains four chapters. In Chapter 5, Roland Mettermeir, *et al.*, provide a survey of different approaches to requirements analysis and integrates these approaches with the role of those involved during this phase of activity. The authors propose an objective analysis phase, which should precede the requirement analysis. An objective analysis phase is required to investigate the real need of the people involved and to identify design alternatives. It consists of context analysis, object and problem analysis, and problem definition. In the context analysis phase, all personnel involved are identified. Objective and problem analysis are concerned with resolving the differences among the group. Finally, problem definition investigates the definition of the system and its environment, as well as the boundary between the system and its environment. With the goal structure of the customer's organization and a set of alternative solutions, the system analyst can obtain a better and more stable solution. This chapter is an important contribution not only because it encompasses the most difficult aspect of the software development process, but it also segments the approaches over the last decade. It is important to know that different approaches can be used in combination to solve different problems.

Design methodology was of great research interest in the 1970s. There have been few discussions on design methodology geared toward the CASE paradigm. Of the three approaches: top-down functional design, data-driven design, and object-oriented design, the authors only discuss object-oriented design in this section. References are provided for a discussion of other design methodologies. In Chapter 6, Grady Booch presents the concepts of object-oriented design. Four sets of notation are introduced; namely, hardware diagram, class structure, object diagram, and architecture diagram. All are used to capture the design decision. An example is presented to demonstrate the differences between object-oriented design and functional design. Although not widely tested, the object-oriented design approach has received a great deal of attention in recent years. Because the editors are fairly certain that the next generation CASE products will have object-oriented interfaces, the exploitation of such design techniques is urgently needed. Grady Booch has done a superb job presenting his concepts in Chapter 6.

To effectively generate code from high-level specification as suggested by R. T. Yeh in Chapter 1, reuse of code, specification/design, and rules (policy rules, design rules, etc.) are paramount to any future CASE products. In Chapter 7, Roland Mettermeir and Wilhelm Rossak give an in-depth discussion of reusability and all of its ramifications. The different areas of application of software reuse are discussed, showing the limitation of writing software based on some existing design methodologies, and an object-oriented approach in software design is suggested. The authors also suggest that verification cost and maintenance cost should also be taken into consideration when deciding to reuse. The chapter describes the overall organization of software archiving, and how reuse can be structured to support retrieval.

One of the key characteristics of Yeh's model is to have a built-in evaluation/ validation model during the development process so that quality of the design can be monitored at all times. In Chapter 8, Jerry W. Baker, *et al.* provide a methodology specific to performance evaluation through the design process. The authors propose an alternative approach to software development. It is an approach that successively refines and evaluates a working model of the desired system. A detailed discussion of the design structure model, the system structure model, and the evaluation model are included. An interaction of the three models form the desired model. They conclude by proposing a set of tools that helps designers to refine their prototypes.

The environmental support section consists of only Chapter 9 by Bob Strong. Any future CASE environments must provide a mechanism for the integration of various tools. It is commonly recognized that the management of all CASE objects, from requirement analysis data to domain/application specific knowledge, can no longer be adequately handled by traditional DBMS. The object manager is the ideal candidate at this point. In Chapter 9, the author reviews some critical characteristics of current management systems and discusses the appropriateness of using an object-oriented Data Manager to support CASE applications. The data models of several types of DBMS are explored and their capabilities are compared to the context of the requirements of CASE application. Also discussed are the detailed technical issues which provide the requirements for a design DB. There are several commercial and research products already available, such as the European community's Portable Common Programming Environment (PCPE), and Aston Technology's Backplane. However, the editors believe presenting the requirements is more suitable at this time.

A reference list for language and methodology follows as additional reading material.

READING LIST (METHODOLOGY)

1. Agresti, W. W., *New Paradigms for Software Development*, Washington, D. C.: IEEE Tutorial, IEEE Computer Society Press, 1986.
2. Berzins, V. and Luqi, *Software Engineering with Abstractions: An Integrated Approach to Software Development with Ada*, Reading, MA: Addison-Wesley, 1989.
3. Bernstein, P. A., "Database System Support for Software Engineering," *Proc. Ninth Int'l Conference on Software Engineering*, IEEE Computer Society Press, Los Alamitos, California, March 1987, pp. 166–178.
4. Bigelow, J., "Hypertext and CASE," *IEEE Software*, March 1988; pp. 23–29.
5. Blum, B. I., "The Life-Cycle—A Debate Over Alternative Models," *ACM Software Engineering Notes*, 7, October 1982, pp. 18–20.
6. Boar, B. H., *Application Prototyping*, New York: John Wiley & Sons, 1984.
7. Boehm, B. W., *Software Engineering Economics*, Englewood Cliffs, NJ: Prentice-Hall, 1981.
8. Boehm, B. W., "Improving Software Productivity," *IEEE Computer*, Vol. 20, No. 9, September 1987, pp. 43–57.
9. Boehm, B. W., "A Spiral Model of Software Development and Enhancement," *IEEE Computer*, Vol. 21, No. 5, May 1988, pp. 61–72.
10. Brooks, F., *The Mythical Man-Month*, Reading, MA: Addison-Wesley, 1975.
11. Chikofsky, E. J., "Software Technology People Can Really Use," *IEEE Software*, March 1988, pp. 8–10.

12. Cleaveland, J. C., "Building Application Generators," *IEEE Software*, July 1988, pp. 25–33.
13. Davis, A., *Software Requirements: Analysis and Specification*, Englewood Cliffs, NJ: Prentice-Hall, 1989.
14. Frenkel, K. A., "Toward Automating the Software-development Cycle," *Communications of the ACM*, Vol. 28, June 1985, pp. 578–589.
15. Goldberg, A. and D. Robson, *Smalltalk-80: The Language and Its Implementation*, Reading, MA: Addison-Wesley, 1985.
16. Hartley, D. J. and I. A. Pirbhai, *Strategies for Real time System Specification*, New York: Dorset House, 1987.
17. Mills, H., *Software Productivity*, Little, Brown, and Company, 1983.
18. Pressman, R., *Software Engineering: A Practitioner's Approach*, 2nd Edition, New York: McGraw-Hill, 1987.
19. Vick, C. R. and C. V. Ramamoorthy, *Handbook of Software Engineering*, New York: Van Nostrand Reinhold, 1984.
20. Wegner, P., "Capital-Intensive Software Technology," *IEEE Software*, July 1984, pp. 7–45.
21. Yeh, R. T., *Current trends in Programming Methodology*, Vol. I and Vol. II, Englewood Cliffs, NJ: Prentice-Hall, 1978.
22. E. Yourdon and L. L. Constantine, *Structured Design*, New York: Yourdon Press, 1978.

READING LIST (TOOLS)

1. Acly, E., "Looking Beyond CASE," *IEEE Software*, March 1988, pp. 39–45.
2. Ambras, J. and V. O'Day, "MicroScope: A Knowledge-Based Programming Environment," *IEEE Software*, May 1988, pp. 50–58.
3. Basset, P. G., "Frame-Based Software Engineering," *IEEE Software*, July, 1987, pp. 9–16.
4. *Computer* (special issue on visual programming) Grapton, R. B. and T. Ichikawa, guest eds., Vol. 18, No. 8, August 1985.
5. *Computer* (special issue on requirements engineering environments), W. Rzepka and Y. Ohno, guest eds., Vol. 18, No. 4, April 1985.
6. *Computer* (special issue on seamless systems), P. B. Henderson and D. Notkin, guest eds., Vol. 20, No. 11, November 1987.
7. Feiler, P. H., and Medina-Mora, R., "An Incremental Programming Environment," *IEEE Trans. Software Engineering*, Vol. SE-7, No. 5, September 1981, pp. 472–482.
8. Leblang, D. B. and R. P. Chase, "Parallel Software Configuration Management in a Network Environment," *IEEE Software*, November 1987, pp. 28–35.

9. Manley, J. H., "CASE: Foundation for Software Factories," *COMPCON Proceedings*, IEEE, September 1984, pp. 84–91.
10. Martin, C. F., "Second-Generation CASE Tools: A Challenge to Vendors," *IEEE Software*, March 1988, pp. 46–49.
11. McClure, C., "CASE Product Categories," *CASE Symp. Workbook*, Digital Consulting, Andover, MA, 1987.
12. Puncello, P. P., P. Torrigiani, F. Pietri, R. Burlon, B. Cardile, and M. Conti, "ASPIS: A Knowledge-Based CASE Environment," *IEEE Software*, March 1988, pp. 58–65.
13. Partsch, H. and R. Steinbruggen, "Program Transformation Systems," *ACM Computing Surveys*, Vol. 15, No. 3, September 1983, pp. 199–236.
14. Shriver, B. D., *Special Issue on Seamless Systems, IEEE Software*, Vol. 4, No. 6, November 1987.
15. Symonds, A. J., "Creating a Software-Engineering Knowledge Base," *IEEE Software*, March 1988, pp. 50–57.
16. Wasserman, A. I. and P. A. Pircher, "A Graphical, Extensible Integrated Environment for Software Development," Proceedings ACM SIGSoft/SIGPlan Software Engineering Symposium on Practical Software Development Environment, *SIGPlan Notices*, January 1987, pp. 131–142.

Chapter 1

An Alternative Paradigm for Software Evolution

RAYMOND T. YEH
International Software Systems, Inc.
Austin, TX

1.0. INTRODUCTION

Projections show that the demand for software applications outweigh our society's ability to produce them at this time. The software tools applied to assist users, including programmers, in developing solutions are improving slowly. One solution to keep pace with this rapidly growing demand is to increase the productivity of the individuals developing computer solutions. Another solution is to enhance the ability of individuals, with varying degrees of computer sophistication, to directly solve a wide range of problems. To do so, software development must become a problem definition process rather than a detailed coding process. Users must be able to interact with a system that possesses some degree of knowledge of the user's problem domain—the solution environment.

The U.S. software industry is charged with more than $300 billion worth of inventory of ill-structured, difficult-to-maintain software. The inertia created by this huge inventory has a tremendously negative impact on the industry: not only has the cost for fixing post-development errors become prohibitively expensive, but the "fixing" itself has usually introduced additional errors. There exist large systems which are so complex that, due to a history of continued patch work, their reliability can no longer be improved. The software maintenance process must be made simpler and more productive. One solution is to maintain the system at the highest level of system description rather than at the code level.

The "double squeeze" just mentioned creates a tremendous bottleneck, which prevents the timely automation of various segments of our society as we move into an information age. A jump into a new technology is needed to achieve vast improvements in software productivity in order to break through this bottleneck. In this chapter, an alternative paradigm for programming is discussed that may lead to the required productivity improvement.

2.0.   AN ALTERNATIVE PARADIGM FOR SOFTWARE EVOLUTION

The predominant model for current software development is the phased refinement approach. In this approach, all system functionality is specified in the first step of development, and subsequent implementation phases add proscribed design details. This approach is criticized for its high cost of maintenance, poor motivation of system developers doing abstract tasks in early phases of development, and complication of system integration. Therefore, evolutionary enhancement such as incremental development strategy has been added to the phased approach. However, the added evolution strategy has been criticized for producing poorly structured software which can lead to problems in error-handling, project management, and errors from modification. The author proposes an evolutionary approach that seeks to avoid these pitfalls.

The author predicts an evolutionary software development paradigm in which a number of nonstandard concepts work together to achieve effective software evolution. To describe this paradigm, it is necessary to discuss a process model and its associated languages, methodologies, and tools as depicted in Figure 1-1.

The process model of this paradigm is depicted in Figure 1-2. It supports both the traditional phased approach and the evolution incremental development approach. However, a validation and evaluation process is part of the development process rather than an afterthought, after completion of the development depicted in Figure 1-3.

Central to this approach is the expression of software system functionality specification in a form that is precisely interpretable and yet does not over specify

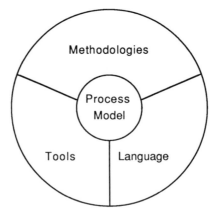

Figure 1-1. Components of a Software Evolution Paradigm.

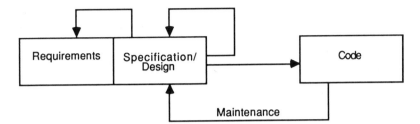

Figure 1-2. New paradigm for Software Evolution.

the form of system design and implementation. This can be achieved by abstraction, whereby the functionality specification expresses constraints on the multiple possible embodiments, which would achieve different objectives in cost, performance, error-tolerance, etc.

There are three types of abstractions that are essential in characterizing the functional attributes of any software system; namely, (1) data, (2) control, and (3) function. Data abstraction is used to hide certain properties of the organization of a set of data structures. It is expressed at the level of the database schema, showing acceptable operations on data objects. Control abstraction is used to hide certain properties of the order of executions among a set of operations. Generally, it shows precedence, sequencing, and synchronization constraints. Function abstraction is used to hide certain properties of some algorithms that perform certain transformations.

Given a precise statement of functionality, a set of evaluation and validation processes can be coupled closely with the design/development process. As shown in Figure 1-3, rapid functional prototyping, performance modeling, and

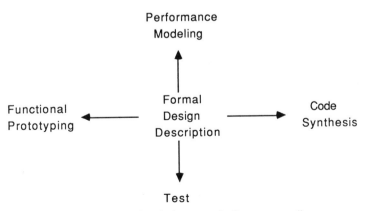

Figure 1-3. Interactive design steps in the new paradigm.

design testing are all part of this evaluation process. Rapid functional proto-typing is the direct generation of executable code from the functional statement. This permits the initial user to review the proposed system capabilities. It also helps users to better understand and express their needs. This early evaluation of the development services eliminates many of the causes for later system maintenance. Performance modeling at different stages of design helps to examine the performance issues before the system is completed so as to exchange different design approaches. Design testing will help to rule out bad designs early by checking interfaces, coupling strength between modules, etc.

The code synthesis arrow in Figure 1-3 also implies that in this evolution paradigm, code is synthesized at the highest level of specification via direct transformation or utilizing previously developed component and subsystem designs. It avoids a common barrier for reusing code; namely, even if the functionality is correct the implementation details might not fit. The reusable component is described in terms of its functionality abstraction. With this strategy, extensive reuse should become possible.

This paradigm incorporates two kinds of evolution: incremental delivery and maintenance. With the functionality structure directly determining the system implementation structure, it is convenient to add functional capability incre-mentally. It is valuable to put into use an early implementation having limited capabilities. This achieves early usage of the system as an alternative to check on specification errors. It also achieves an early pass at system integration, defective design, and interface errors.

The paradigm foresees system design occurring as a set of functionality-preserving transformations applied to the original functionality descriptions, with the choice of transform determined by objectives in target performance, error handling, etc. In this paradigm, maintenance is done by modification to the original specification with reimplementation by application of the transforma-tions to the revised description. This approach minimized the opportunity for new errors to be introduced during modification and assures error minimization as the system evolves in response to changing user circumstances.

To summarize the discussion above, it is concluded that in order to support the process model depicted in Figure 1-2, it is necessary to have an executable specification and design language based on abstractions. The supporting methodology must incorporate an evaluation process into the development process as suggested in Figure 1-3. Finally, a cohesive set of tools is required to support the evolution. Ideally, each tool is independent of the other tools and can be inserted into or removed from the system without impacting other tools. These tools will typically be closely integrated with a database, and they all should exhibit a consistent user interface.

The following sections provide more details on the various issues associated with the proposed paradigm; namely, language, methodology, and tools.

3.0   THE GENERAL METHODOLOGICAL FRAMEWORK

The key differences between the author's approach and the traditional waterfall process is as follows:

- Risk management orientation vs. document management orientation. The authors approach centers on the desire to minimize development risks. Therefore, an evaluation and validation process is built into the design process. System design is continuously evaluated as the design unfolds through testing, prototyping, performance modeling, etc. Other management risks, such as cost and scheduling, can also be factored in through the evaluation of alternative designs, reuse, etc.
- Mixed-level representation vs. single-level representation. Traditional paradigm centers on a phased approach, hence documentation evolves from one representation (e.g., requirements document) to another (e.g., architecture design). However, in the new paradigm a system's design may be in various phases simultaneously—some part is being prototyped whereas another part is in the design stage.
- Evolution vs. maintenance. Traditional paradigm lumps all changes or enhancements into maintenance, which should only be conceived with "repair." Those activities are part of the evolving development effort in the new paradigm.
- Automatic code synthesis vs. manual development. The authors approach emphasizes automatic code synthesis via reuse or functionality-preserving transformations.

In the following section, the author discusses the evaluation and validation problems, particularly the prototyping and performance modeling aspects. Reusability is also discussed because it plays a major role in both a design and prototyping technique.

Validation of a system implies testing for correctness in the system. Consistency and completeness must be tested at each level of the system design along with the correctness of transformations between levels. Evaluation of the system, on the other hand, is a trade-off analysis function. At any stage of development, there may be several valid and correct representations. The evaluation at that stage will select the host representation based on the evaluation criteria applied to the system at that stage. The problem of evaluation and validation, (E & V), is multidimensional. In building large systems, it is necessary to treat each dimension as independently as possible to minimize analysis complexity at any one point in the design process. The E & V process has not previously been made part of the design process, so new concepts and techniques are needed to match E & V to the dimensions of the design. Each dimension will have its own evaluation criteria, metrics, and tools. In this section the author discusses two primary techniques for E & V, namely, prototyping and performance evaluation.

3.1   Prototyping

Prototyping is the process of developing and exercising models of a proposed system early, to gain insight into what the requirements and design of the system should be, before committing major development resources. To be effective, prototyping must offer this insight but at a relatively modest cost. The following are two types of prototyping activities:

- Functional prototyping. The logical capabilities of a proposed system are modeled and exercised. Such activity permits debugging of the requirements and design. For example, in firming up requirements, functional prototyping may illustrate how the system would process a user's input information, how it would deal with erroneous cases, etc. Whereas during design validation, such activity can demonstrate that required functionality of a certain component is feasible or that the interface mechanism between components is correct.
- Behavioral or Human interface prototyping. Where human interface factors are studied in terms of screen layout, icons used, how easily one could insert and retrieve information from the system, etc.

3.2   Performance Modeling

Performance modeling is used to provide accurate timing analysis and resume utilization profiles of the proposed system. Discussed here is a brief description of a performance evaluation; techniques center around the construction of a Hierarchical Performance Evaluation Model (HPEM).[1]

The HPEM is developed in parallel with the system design and is, likewise, hierarchically structured. As the design unfolds, new levels are added to the HPEM, each reflecting increased knowledge about the implementation of the system and the resulting effects upon system performance. Thus, the HPEM allows the designer to derive as much information as possible about the potential performance characteristics of the current design. Constant interaction with the HPEM enables the designer to "guide" the system through an appropriate design path with minimum redesign and backtracking.

The addition of each level to the HPEM consists of three distinct phases:

(1) parameterization,
(2) construction of an analytical model, and
(3) construction of a simulation model.

Parameterization. The parameterization of the i-th level of the HPEM is concerned with specifying those aspects of the system design at level i, which are important to system performance. The designer has complete freedom in choosing the performance parameters and, hence, design aspects may be represented explicitly or not at all in the HPEM. The parameterization is modular with respect to the system design; that is, for each data abstraction of system level i, a performance parameter specification is developed—this specification reflects the properties of the data abstraction relevant to system performance.

Analytical Model. The analytical model consists of analytical equations that define the cost of a particular design (completed through level i) in terms of time expressions for the operations of level i and estimates of storage requirements.

Using an approach similar to that used by B. Wegbreit,[14] it is possible to analyze a program module at level i in order to derive a cost expression in terms of the model performance parameters at level $i + 1$. Such analysis enables the designer to evaluate a cost expression at each design step in terms of the parameters of the most recently completed level.

Simulation Model. Many aspects of complex systems cannot be captured by an analytical model. Thus, it is sometimes necessary to simulate the operation of the system design.

The basis for the simulation process is a queuing network model constructed by the designer. It differs, however, from typical queuing models in that it attempts to model contention for *abstract resources* (relations, files, directories, indices, etc.) defined in the software rather than hardware resources, such as CPUs, disks, and I/O devices. The structure of the model reflects that of the system itself, that is, a hierarchy of queuing networks is constructed, each of which models the performance characteristics of the system design at a particular level of abstraction. Thus, successive networks in the hierarchy represent increasingly detailed models of the system performance. Moreover, adjacent networks are "connected" in that the solution of each network can be used to parameterize the immediately preceding one.

3.3 Reusability

Software reuse can be applied to every phase of a software development life cycle. A piece of software is reusable when it is interpretable, incorporable, or portable. Interpretable meaning information can be obtained to understand the software's functionality, operational environment, and all other required attributes. Incorporable meaning the software will be usable in building larger software systems. Portable meaning the software can be used in different environments with different machines.

One can divide the current state of software reuse into three categories: (1) reuse of program parts, (2) reuse of systems, and (3) reuse of design. Reuse of program parts is to incorporate a software module into many different application programs. Examples of program parts reuse consist of subroutine library, data abstraction, and generic program units.

Generic program units are the most flexible reuse of program parts. A generic program unit is a template of program units. It can be instantiated to a family of similar program units. For example, one can write a generic sorting function for a list. The type of the elements can be generic. The precedence rule used in sorting can also be generic. This generic function can then be instantiated to sort a list of integers in ascending order or to sort a listing of strings in lexical order. Thus, generic units increase the modifiability of a program unit allowing a program part to be adapted to many slightly different applications.

The difference between a program part and a system is that a part is a subunit within a system. It cannot be executed by itself, while a system can. Because the functions that can be performed by a system are usually fixed, it is much harder to adapt them to work with a slightly different situation than to modify or extend a part of the function. On the other hand, being the final products, these offer many more benefits toward their successful reuse.

Reuse of program parts or reuse of systems are dependent on programming languages and implementations. However, design uses a higher level of abstraction and thus provides more flexibility than the other two forms of software reuse. Further, design reuse is practiced only in limited areas such as compiler, data base, operating system, etc.

There are three natural levels of reusability. The first level consists of components that can be reused during run time; namely, parts and systems as described above. The second level consists of various levels of design (abstractions). The highest level should consist of ''rules,'' which can modify or create designs or systems, the higher the level, the more flexible the reuse.

4.0 LANGUAGE ISSUES — EXECUTABLE SPECIFICATION AND DESIGN DOCUMENTATION

The iterative process of design depicted in Figure 1-2 usually results in a sequence of specifications precisely describing the functionality at each level of design. For this paradigm, it is required that a specification be executable in the sense that it describes an exact computational behavior. As such, it differs from conventional specifications and from conventional programs in ways that significantly influence system structure. Some of these differences are noted as follows:

- *Functionality*—Specifications describe only the logical system behavior, e.g. describing output values as functions of input sequences. This omits specification of such design parameters as performance, reliability, software structure, memory management, etc. The execution of a specification should be useful for the results it achieves and not for its internal sequence of events nor its performance.

- *Precision*—To be executable, a specification cannot be ambiguous, because a repeatable execution must result. This places a significant burden on the specification writer and is the greatest barrier to widespread usage. For example, a specification may call for a sort function, leaving many detailed parameters ambiguous about interfaces, exceptional handling, etc. An actual execution has to use some specific sort, however, and must resolve all details.
- *Completeness*—Specifications are incomplete, so many aspects of functions and data structures will be left undefined. This is necessary both to allow freedom in implementation and to permit implementation to begin prior to completion of the specifications. Execution of incomplete specifications is required, so that critical logic functions can be prototyped before too much effort is spent on details.
- *Simplicity*—A desirable characteristic of a specification language is simplicity. A graphical syntax for representing functions and data structures is best, because it simplifies variable naming and also supports the natural tendency of people to describe system structures graphically. The language should provide abstraction mechanisms for data, control and functional definitions, so that the specifications can be free of design information as much as possible.

Functional specification language is not sufficient in capturing all the design decisions made during the design process. Therefore, a design documentation language, which is to be an integral part of the design process, is needed. Such a language should contain the following three features for describing global properties of system designs.

- *Specification of alternative designs*—Consider the implementation of level i in the hierarchical design process. There may exist a large number of modules, which may be combined in various ways to produce alternative designs for level $i - 1$. The designer may document in the language a) modules that must appear together in designs, b) modules that represent alternatives to other modules, and c) modules that are optional in the design.
- *Specification of modules interconnections*—To specify the interconnections between modules of a system design, the following different relationships are considered: the *has access* relationship, where one module has access to instances of another module because it created that instance or has access to another module that has access to it; the *uses* relationship, which indicates the means by which one module may use an instance of

another module to which it has access. These uses include reading from and writing to modules and creating new instances of modules.
- *Specification of level structure*—To describe the structure of a particular design level, specify the hierarchical relationships (if any) between modules of the level and partition the level into subsystems, which may be partially ordered within the level.

5.0 ENVIRONMENT FOR SUPPORTING THE METHODOLOGY

This section outlines key requirements for an integrated environment consisting of a set of tools to support the evolutionary methodology described in the previous sections. The fundamental components required for this environment are the following:

- a collection of tools for building, modifying, testing, and documenting components of the target system;
- a user interface through which the designer can create, modify, and view components of the target system; and
- a database system which manages all components that make up the target system.

The following subsections expand upon these three areas of requirements.

5.1 Software Tools Capability

The environment must support all software tools required for the complete development. This tool set should have the following minimum requirements:

- Orthogonality—each tool is independent of other tools and can be inserted or removed from the environment without impacting other tools.
- Common interface—all tools should exhibit a consistent user interface.

The following outlines a sample of the capabilities that should be supported by tools. This organization is provided by capability, not by specific tool. For example, functional and performance prototyping are two separate capabilities, but the interactive editing for these two capabilities may be provided by the same tool.

The tools that support each of the following capabilities can be viewed as being independent; however, they are integrated because the user support system provides a seamless interface in moving from one tool to another.

Editing. A graphical editor for each diagramming technique provided (e.g., dataflow diagram, structure diagram, etc.) so that each editor will understand

and enforce the syntax for the particular type of diagram being constructed enabling movement from one editor to another without conflicting interfaces.

Functional prototyping. To support the development of functional prototypes such as an editor for generating dataflow-like diagrams representing the functional specification, a type definition language for defining user datatypes and database schemas, a high-level expression language for defining operations to be applied to data types, an interpreter for directly executing the prototype, and a translator for translating the prototype into a high-level language.

Performance modeling. Tools for building performance models (e.g., prototypes that address timing analysis, synchronization issues, queue management, etc.) should be similar to the tools for functional prototyping. One difference is that the performance prototype editor includes special capabilities for handling events and for associating timing with components. Additionally, special simulators (e.g., a discrete event simulator) are required for performing different types of performance analysis.

Behavioral Prototyping. For handling behavioral (i.e., human interface) prototyping, these tools include a what-you-see-is-what-you-get editor for building screens (slide shows) simulating the displays that will be presented to end users, a tool for specifying the actions to be performed as the result of actions the user performs, and tools for relating the user interface prototype to functional and performance prototypes. With these tools, the user interface prototype can be exercised as an independent activity, or it can be exercised in conjunction with the functional and performance prototypes.

Creating/tailoring reusable components. To support reuse of both designs and code modules, these include database tools to assist the user in locating useful modules from a library, tools to help the user understand the functionality of a candidate module, and tools to help the user customize the module and insert it into the target system.

Query and browsing. A query language allowing the user to locate groups of objects that meet certain criteria; and a browser to allow the user to view individual objects from a selected group.

Diagraming capability. Capabilities to interact with the data model through special diagrams. Possible examples include data flow diagrams, data structure diagrams, entity-relationship diagrams, decision table and decision tree diagrams, state transition diagrams, etc.

Tool tailoring capabilities. One or more tools to tailor the user interfaces provided by other tools. For example, the ability to change text fonts and icons, or to add new menu options, possibly using a macro language to attach functionality to the options.

Design rules (integrity constraints). The database must allow specification and enforcement of rules regarding data items (e.g., allowable ranges for attributes) and relationships among different data items.

Data management capabilities. To allow traditional data management features including transaction control, access control, backup and recovery, etc.

5.2   User Interface Capability

The fundamental goal of a support environment is to make users more productive in solving complex problems. A critical requirement is to provide a user interface that is "transparent," or an interface should give users the feeling that they are working directly on the problem to be solved with minimal attention being paid to the details of the support tools.

The following user interface capabilities are necessary:

- *Graphical design*—design languages should have a graphical syntax, such as providing a syntax directed diagram editor for creating a functional prototype, similarly, a what-you-see-is-what-you-get editor for prototyping a user interface.
- *Direct manipulation of objects*—system viewing should be one of direct manipulation of database objects. Any object can be selected for depiction on the screen, and presented with a list of actions that can be performed on that object (or at least all actions given the current operational context). When one of the available actions is performed, the action is applied directly to the database.
- *Multiple windows*—support a multi-window display that can simultaneously display any collection of information about the system being developed. Different windows can contain different views of the database (e.g., a graph display and a textual display), or they can contain one view of different data (e.g., two different subsets of a graph structure).
- *Multiple pictorial representations*—the support system maintains a single integrated model for the target system being developed; however, the user must have the ability to view the data from a variety of different perspectives. For example, when performing functional prototyping, the user may initially want to view the target system as a high-level data flow diagram, then later view the system through a diagram that accurately depicts control flow for the program.
- *Seamless movement between tools*—movement between tools without changing the current context; for example, the ability to edit a dataflow diagram representing a prototype, then running a functional simulator on the prototype system using the existing diagram as the user interface to the simulator. Alternatively, the system should be able to depict a control flow view of the prototype, then run the functional simulator using the control flow diagram as the user interface to the simulator.
- *Animated simulation*—provide a variety of capabilities for animating the execution of simulations of the target system.

5.3   Database System

The database system is responsible for maintaining a complete model for the target system throughout the software lifecycle and for providing appropriate views of this model to each of the software tools used to construct, modify, and view the target system. It is key to tool integration and, therefore is of great importance to the support environment.

A multi-tool design environment must support frequent updates to design data, because a designer often uses one tool to modify a design and then a succession of other tools to check the modification, display it, etc. The continual editing of designs and the sharing of those modifications across tools is a principal test of a Database Management System (DBMS) for a design environment. Thus, the choice of a database system for such an environment should be based on the following two criteria:

- Develop a data storage format which best simplifies the development of individual tools while permitting them to share data.
- High performance in database retrieval of complex design objects in large databases.

An object oriented DBMS or object manager is the most suitable choice for the support environment discussed here.[15] The underlying assumption that promotes the use of object management is that system descriptions are compositions of subsystems or language primitives with specified interrelationships. This presents the option of a parsing (textual) description to find the subsystem and relationships, or maintaining that parsed information in an object format. The advantage of an object manager over a relational DBMS is that an object manager can have a hierarchically structured attribute, but a relational system allows this only by construction using multiple ''joins.''

The key features which should be provided by an object manager are as follows:

Data Model. The object manager manages a group of objects. Associated with each object is a schema, methods and assertions. The schema defines the structure of an object instance and includes a unique identifier, class (type), and attributes. The class of an object is described by another object (whose class is ''class''), whose attributes describe the domain information for each attribute of the instance object. Attributes have values which may be compared, edited, calculated, printed, etc. Attributes can be simple (e.g., integer, character, etc.) records which are made up of simple attributes or records. Attributes can also be references to other objects thereby allowing one to define objects that are complex collections of other objects.

Each object class has an associated collection of methods (i.e., functions) that can be applied to members of the class. For example, all classes include methods for creating and deleting instances of objects. Assertions which include constraints objects of a given class must meet (e.g., maximum and minimum values for attributes, access control rules, etc.) and rule governing relationships between this class and other classes of objects. A class can inherit attributes, methods and assertions from its parent class. For example, the method for creating an instance of a particular class typically invokes the method for creating the parent for this class. Similarly, the set of assertions an object must meet can include the set of assertions its parent must meet.

Object Definition Language. The data to be stored in developing a target system is diverse. The object types include different types of diagrams representing design (e.g., graphs representing dataflow diagrams and hierarchical structures representing hierarchical decomposition), arbitrarily complex data types required by the target system (e.g., a model for a target system workstation) including icons and other graphic, textual descriptions of designs, source code fragments, object code, test cases, etc. There are also complex relationships among the data types. For example, graphs can contain other graphs and different object types may be related by rules or assertions.

An Object Definition Language should allow end users or programmers to define new object classes by defining attributes for the instances of the class and relationships between this class and other classes. The user also defines methods associated with the class and assertions that objects of the class must satisfy.

Viewing Mechanism. The target system model should be maintained as a single integrated model that can be viewed from different perspectives. For example, a design was displayed using a dataflow diagram, and at a later time the same design was displayed from a control perspective. Each of these perspectives can be viewed as an object that includes data from a common underlying model plus a method for displaying the object from the desired perspective. The single model approach is taken to ensure that the different representations of a design are totally consistent.

Query Facilities. The choice of a good query strategy for an object-oriented database is currently the subject of extensive research. Two capabilities are required: 1) a query language that assists in the selection of sets of objects based on the values of attributes for the objects, and 2) a browser that sequentially scans members of selected sets or that navigates through a more complex structure by following references to parent or child objects.

Data Dictionary. Since the schema and other information that define a new class of objects is in itself a collection of objects, the object manager includes an integrated data dictionary that describes all object classes in the database. This "dictionary" is used by the browser and query language, and is available to other tools that need access object class definition information.

Versioning, Configuration Control, and Change Management. Using the object manager, multiple versions of a given object can exist simultaneously.

A configuration is a collection of object versions. The object manager is responsible for keeping track of different users of the system, working with different configurations. Change management software is responsible for notifying a user when updates made by others might have rendered his/her current configuration obsolete.

Multiuser Environment. Allow for support of multiple users in a distributed workstation environment. For example, a team can have a central database that contains the "approved" state of the target system model. Any individual can extract a subset from this central database and move the subset into a local database on a workstation. The user can then work with this database locally and after completing modifications, can check the updates back into the central database. These check-out and check-in features are actually part of the change management system mentioned above.

Standard DBMS Features. These features include tools for backup and recovery, transaction management capabilities, tools for mapping data to and from character files to allow for movement of data to or from a foreign system, data base administrator tools for defining the physical organization of data, tools for generating reports, etc. Much of the contents of this chapter were derived from ongoing research being conducted by the author and his colleagues at International Software Systems, Inc. More specifically, Dr. Terry Welch has been guiding the development of a very high level language for prototyping and design, and Dr. Don Hartman has been managing the development of an object manager and graphical user interface manager as the backbone for integrating tools. This development is being done on UNIX workstations (SUN and Apollo). The author is especially indebted to Terry Welch and Don Hartman in deriving the contents of this paper.

REFERENCES

1. Baker, J., D. Chester, and R. T. Yeh, "An Integrated Methodology and Tools For Software Development," SDBEG-20, *Computer Science Technical Report*, University of Texas, Austin, Texas, 1978.
2. Balzer, R., *et al.*, "RADCO Requirements Engineering Testbed Research and Development Program Panel Recommendation," *Tech. Report*, International Software Systems, Inc., Austin, Texas, 1985.
3. Bauer, F. L., "Programming As An Evolutionary Process," *Proc. Second International Conference on Software Engineering*, pp. 223–324. October 1976, pp. 223–324.
4. Boehm, B. W., "A Spiral Model of Software Development Enhancement," IEEE Computer, Vol. 21, No. 5, May 1988, pp. 61–72.
5. Doberkat, E., E. Dubinsky, and J. T. Schwartz, "Reusability of Design for Complex Programs: An Experiment with the SETL Optimizer," *Proc. Workshop on Reusability in Programming*, October 1983.
6. Guttag, J., "Abstract Data Type and the Development of Data Structure," *CACM*, Vol. 20, No. 6, 1977, pp. 396–404.
7. Konard, M., *et al.*, "VHLL System Prototyping Tool User Manual," International Software Systems, Inc., Austin, Texas, 1987.

8. Luckenbaugh, G., "The Activity List: A Design Construct for Real-Time Systems," Master's Thesis, University of Maryland, December 1983.

9. Martin, J., *Application Development Without Programmers*, NJ: Prentice-Hall, Inc., 1982.

10. Neighbor, J. M., "The DRACO Approach to Constructing Software From Reusable Components," *Proc. Workshop on Reusability in Programming*, October 1983, pp. 167–178.

11. Royce, W. W., "Healing the Software Crisis: An Rx for Knowledge-based Technology", LOKTEK IX, Lockheed Missiles Space Company, Inc., 1987.

12. Shaw, M., "Abstraction Techniques in Modern Programming Languages," *IEEE Software*, October 1984, pp. 10–27.

13. Special Issue on Seamless Systems, *IEEE Software, IEEE Computer*, November 1987.

14. Wegbreit, B., "Verifying Program Performance," *JACM* 23, 4, 1976, pp. 691–699.

15. Welch, T., "Data Base Requirements for Multi-Tool Development Environment," *Tech. Report*, International Software Systems, Inc., Austin, Texas, 1988.

16. Yeh, R. T., R. Mittermeir, N. Roussopoulos, and J. Reed, "A Programming Environment Framework Based on Reusability," *Proc. Computer Data Engineering Conference*, April 1984, pp. 24–27.

17. Yeh, R. T., N. Roussopoulos, B. Chu, "Management of Reusable Software," *Proc. COMPCON*, September 1984, pp. 311–320.

18. Yeh, R. T., and P. Zave, "Specifying Software Requirements," *Proc. IEEE*, Vol. 68, No. 9, September 1980, pp. 1077–1085.

19. Yeh, R. T., "Software Engineering," *IEEE Spectrum*, November 1983, pp. 91–94.

20. Zelkowitz, M., R. T. Yeh, R. Hamlet, J. Gannon, and V. Basili, "A Survey of Software Practices in Industry," *IEEE Computer*, June 1984, pp. 57–66.

Chapter 2

Diagramming Techniques in CASE

FELICIA CHENG AND PETER A. NG
Institute for Integrated Systems Research
Department of Computer and Information Science
New Jersey Institute of Technology
Newark, NJ

1   INTRODUCTION

The computer industry is projected to grow rapidly in the next decade. Among the dollars spent in the industry, software development accounts for 80% of a new system development, and the remaining 20% to hardware development.[25] Each year, the number of positions available in the software development industry exceeds the number of graduates. The demand for experienced software engineers and the development of automated hardware design are a few reasons why software development costs are increasing while hardware development costs are decreasing. The situation is made worse by the huge amount of software backlog waiting to be changed. A study by Musa[17] indicated that in the years between 1965 and 1985 the demand for software increased one hundredfold, while programmer productivity increased twofold. In order to meet the demands of the coming decade, to dispose of existing backlog, and to eliminate the ''productivity crisis,'' it became necessary to develop tools that would increase the productivity of software designers.

Recognizing the importance to increase programmer productivity, the issue of software development environment has drawn attention from the software research community[28] and, the impact of the software development environment on productivity was studied.[37] The concept of software factory[11, 12] and workbench[9, 10, 13] was introduced. The study by Boehm[37] and the establishment of a software factory did not only focus on providing software development tools to programmers but also studied the effect of the physical environment and managerial decisions on productivity. A survey by Boehm[37] showed that software tools were the programmers major need for improving software productivity. It is evident that automation of the software development process can improve productivity and reduce software development costs.

However, software development is considered a team effort. If the computer were used as a software development aid, computer usage could cause a bottle-

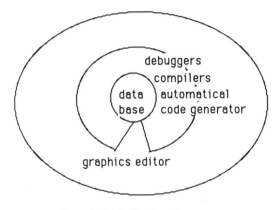

Figure 2-1. A CASE environment.

neck. The current state of hardware development helps to encourage the development of CASE tools. The advent of hardware technology has made graphics workstations commonly available and, networking of computers allows database projects to be shared by engineers. CASE tools are not only available in the research environment[23, 31, 35, 36] but are increasingly common in the commercial market.[14, 30]

What are CASE tools? CASE tools are an integrated set of tools designed to support the entire software life cycle and developed with an aim to automate much of the software development process. CASE tools increase the productivity of software engineers. With the help of CASE tools, drawing and redrawing of a design, as well as the development of a program, can be perceived as a "point and click" exercise. A CASE environment, in its simplest form, can be expressed by the diagram as shown in Figure 2-1.

An important characteristic of a CASE environment is its ability to provide any information a user[1] might need at any time.[28] Therefore, the innermost layer of the CASE environment is a database that contains all information associated with the various projects. It contains managerial as well as technical data, such as budget, personnel, schedule requirements, design and program code. These data are accessible by the tools in the middle layer. Examples of such tools are compilers, debuggers, pretty-printers, operating system utilities, consistency checkers, and automatic code generators. The outer layer consists of the interface components that directly interact with end users, such as graphics editors and diagrammers. Ideally, a user interacts with the environment via the outer layer, and the system should be able to generate a skeleton of the problem after the specification of the problem is detailed. The interface between a user and the environment chosen is vital to the success of the system. Basically, the

---

[1]Users (in this chapter) include customers of a software project, analysts, and programmers.

choice of an interface falls into two main categories: graphics and textual. Graphics (or diagrams), are a better choice than text, because when borrowing properties from the physical world such as shape, size, color, texture, direction and distance, graphics provide a multidimension of information,[20] which is richer than the single-dimension stream of words, making it easier to grasp the content.

The concepts of using diagrams to express program logic and design is not a new idea. In the 50s and 60s, flowcharts were commonly used as a technique to express program logic.[13] But, as computing power increased and demands changed, sophisticated software had to be developed and flowcharts became obsolete. Some criticism of flowcharting is that it leads programmers to write unstructured programs that are difficult to maintain, because the technique cannot handle large complex programs. In the 70s, structured chart and data flow diagrams were popular diagramming techniques that were developed to combat the "software crisis." The increasing magnitude and complexity of software products in the 70s also brought about an engineering approach for the development of software. The major contribution of this approach was the introduction of the life cycle concept. In general, there are three phases[(2)] in the software development life cycle: definition, development, and maintenance.

Definition refers to the software engineer communicating with his/her client(s) to understand the problem domain and the requirements of a system. Development refers to developing the structure of the problem: it consists of identifying the major components of the problem (architectural design) and establishing the interface between the components. The components are then broken down into units, which are given to programmers to code (detailed design and coding). After a software product has been tested and found to be acceptable, it is shipped to the customers. Most of the work is done in the maintenance phase. During the last 15 years, many design methodologies[2, 3, 6, 7, 8, 18, 19, 21, 22, 23, 24, 26, 32, 33] were developed to assist in one or two phases of the software life cycle. Most incorporate diagrams to help a designer conceptualize his idea and understand the problem domain and incorporate software design principles, such as information hiding and stepwise refinement in their methodologies. Many CASE tools that are developed commercially are able to support a variety of the methodologies.

The authors present an introduction to some diagramming techniques that are currently available. It is not the intent of this chapter to detail the methodologies; however, the diagramming techniques based on the software life cycle into which they fit is introduced. Table 2-1 gives a representative listing of the methodologies based on this categorization.[29] In the following section, an introduction to some diagramming techniques that are currently available is presented.

---

[2]Different authors have proposed different sets of phases.

Table 2-1.   A Representative Listing of Methodologies

Definition	Architectural Design	Detailed Design
Data flow diagram		
HIPO	HIPO	
SADT	SADT	
R-NET	R-NET	R-NET
	Structured chart	
	Object-Oriented diagram	
	Entity-relationship diagram	
	Jackson diagram	Jackson diagram
	Warnier-Orr diagram	Warnier-Orr diagram
		Greenprint
		N-S Chart

2 DIAGRAMMING TECHNIQUES

People tend to relate easily to pictures, which is why software developers use diagrams to communicate with their clients and among themselves. The multi-dimensional nature of a diagram provides a clear and concise picture of the problem that not only allows a user to pinpoint the error easily but also helps the designer to visualize the problem. The phrase ''a picture is worth a thousand words'' also explains why researchers in the software community often use diagrams to enforce the methodologies which they have developed.

It is commonly acknowledged that methodologies for software development should be based on software engineering principles. A methodology can be realized by a diagramming technique. On the other hand, diagramming techniques can incorporate software engineering principles and reinforce the methodologies. Figure 2-2 depicts this interaction.

In the remainder of this section, the authors describe the diagramming techniques listed in Table 2-1. When appropriate, a brief description of the underlying methodology is given.

2.1 Data Flow Diagram

The data flow diagram was developed to specify the flow of data in a system. There are two major schools of data flow diagram: Gane[8] and Yourdon.[32] The two methodologies are very similar but differ somewhat in the symbols used. Figure 2-3 shows a comparison of the symbols.

2.1.1 Diagrammmatic Notations

The four basic symbols used in a data flow diagram are shown in Figure 2-3. A data flow diagram consists of: entities which indicate the sources or desti-

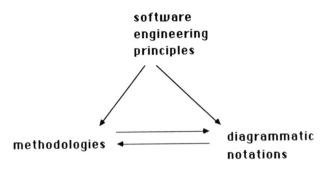

Figure 2-2. Interaction between software-engineering principles, methodologies, and diagrammatic notations.

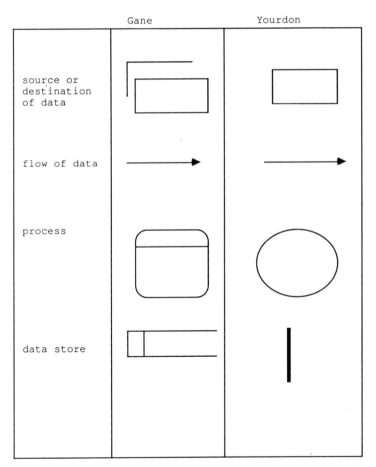

Figure 2-3. Basic symbols of dataflow diagram introduced by Gane and Yourdon.

nations of data, data flow which describe the flow of data, processes which are transformation centers that transform data from one form to another, and data stores which are anything that hold data for pickup or deposit by processes.

2.1.2 Discussion

Data flow diagrams are used by system analysts as thinking aids. To understand a problem domain, a system analyst first identifies the input and output of the system. He/she then constructs processes that transform the input to the output. Processes are linked together via arrows which indicate the direction of data flow. At this stage, processes do not need to be defined, they are viewed as "black boxes" which perform certain functions. As the analyst understands the system more, individual processes are then "exploded" to a finer level. This procedure repeats until the processes are at their finest details. Figure 2-4 is an example of a data flow diagram—an airline schedule system. The system allows different airline ticket agents to have different privileges in updating flight schedules. These privileges depend on the password entered. Figure 2-5 is a level 2 data flow diagram of the problem in which the request process has been "exploded."

At the lowest level, the functionality of a process is described by pseudocode or "Structured English" which consists of the three basic control structures: sequence, selection, and iteration. A data dictionary, which describes the information of the data flowing through the system, is also included.

The data flow diagram has been successful in portraying a snapshot of a system. It has been widely used in the data processing environment as a documentation tool. It is especially useful in the system definition phase when system requirements and functions need to be specified. Due to its simplicity, the system is easily understood and can provide feedback to the analysts. When combined with a structure chart, it allows the software developer to design a hierarchical structure of the modules. However, evidence suggests that when

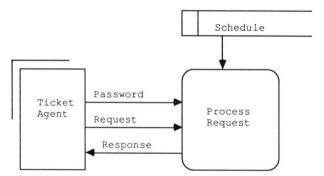

Figure 2-4. Level 1 dataflow diagram of an airline schedule system.

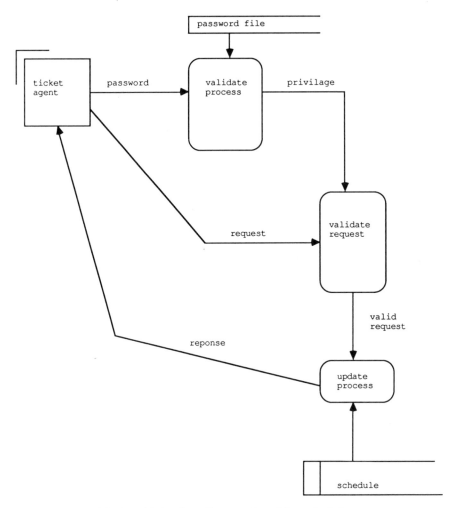

Figure 2-5. Level 2 dataflow diagram of an airline scheduling system.

applied to complex systems, it can produce a very messy diagram. A common criticism of the technique is its inability to show the logical order in which the processes take place. For the design to be useful, it must be able to be transformed to other diagrams.

2.2 Structure Chart

The structure chart was first developed by Stevens, Meyers, and Constantine[44] to specify the overall architecture of the system.

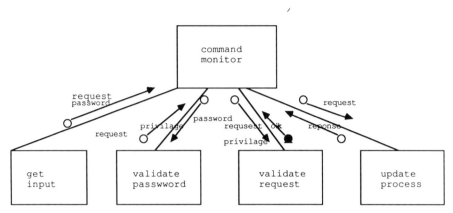

Figure 2-6. An example of a structure chart.

2.2.1 Diagrammatic Notations

A design tree is the fundamental component of a structure chart. The three basic symbols used are: rectangles which represent modules; lines with arrow heads, which specify the interconnection between modules; and small arrows with circular tails, which represent the transfer of control or data between modules. Figure 2-6 is an example of a structure chart of the airline schedule system.

2.2.2 Discussion

The design starts with a main module that is broken into submodules. Any of these submodules can be further refined into sub-submodules. To develop a structure chart, submodules of any given module are drawn as "children" of the given module. A child module is connected to its parent via an arrow which specifies the interface between the modules. In a structure chart, a submodule can be shared by different modules and can only be invoked by its parent modules.

Advocates of the structure chart claim that it reinforces software engineering principles, such as information hiding, step-wise refinement, and decomposition.[34] It has since appeared in different forms in various methodologies. Gane[8] included the use of a structure chart as a second step in his structured system analysis. In structured system analysis, a designer first constructs a data flow diagram, then, based on the data flow diagram, he/she identifies those components that can be combined together to form a module. Smaller modules can then be combined together to form a larger module. When transformed to a structure chart, a smaller module inside a larger module becomes the child of the larger module. An alternate way of grouping the modules allows software developers to see a different perspective of the design.

The structure chart had been used extensively in the data processing environment. Most often, it is used in combination with data flow diagrams. The hierarchical structure imposed in the design and the clearly specified interface make it an attractive candidate for methodologies that will ultimately lead to structured programs. This methodology is also designed for the problem specification phase of the software life cycle. Its major drawback is its incapability to show the order of execution among modules.

2.3   Hierarchy Plus Input-Process-Output Chart

Hierarchy Plus Input-Process-Output (HIPO) chart was developed by IBM[24] as a design and documentation aid. A HIPO chart consists of a hierarchy chart and an input-process-output chart (IPO).

2.3.1   Diagrammatic Notations

The hierarchy chart shows the decomposition of a module. Associated with each module is an input-process-output chart which describes the input, output, and functions to be performed within the module. The input-process-output chart is represented by three vertical boxes which depict the input, process, and output. The order in which subprocesses appear inside the process box implies the sequence of execution. Figure 2-7 is a HIPO chart of the airline schedule system.

2.3.2   Discussion

The hierarchy chart and input-process-output chart are developed concurrently. The procedures for establishing a HIPO chart are summarized as follows: (1) at the highest level, a hierarchy chart consists of a single module (represented by a rectangle), its input and output are then identified; (2) in the second step, the processes that transform the input of the module to the corresponding output are identified and an input-process-output chart is constructed; (3) modules that correspond to the processes inside an IPO chart are drawn on the next level of the hierarchy chart; (4) the refinement steps repeat until the processes cannot be further decomposed.

HIPO was also designed as a tool for documentation. It has been used extensively to state the requirements and specifications of a problem. However, its capability of specifying the interface between modules and order of execution between modules is not immediately obvious.

2.4   Structured Analysis Language

Structured Analysis[3] (SA)[21] was developed by SofTech. It is the diagramming language of Structured Analysis and Design Technique (SADT)[4]—a technique

---

[3]It has slightly different meaning in different context, here the authors explicitly mean the diagramming language of SADT.
[4]SADT is a trademark of SofTech.

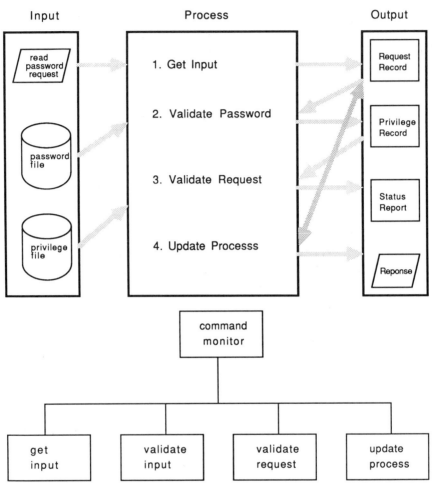

Figure 2-7. An example of a HIPO chart.

that is used for defining and analyzing systems. A detailed description of SADT is beyond the scope of this chapter.

2.4.1 Diagrammatic Notations

The basic symbols in SA consist of boxes and arrows. The direction in which an arrow is pointing when entering an SA box represents the direction of flow through the system. Figure 2-8 is an example of an SA box.

2.4.2 Discussion

In SA terminology, a diagram is made up of boxes and arrows. A system is modelled by a collection of diagrams. The rationale is that very complex systems

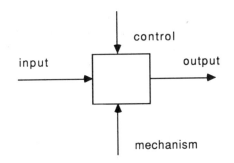

Figure 2-8. An SA box.

can be broken down into smaller, more understandable and more manageable subsystems: each subsystem can be represented as an SA box. In SADT every system or subsystem must have a purpose. In understanding the system and answering why, how, and what of a system, a designer can specify the input, output, control and mechanism of the system. Together, they represent the constraints and define the boundaries of a SA box. The designer can then work within those boundaries to solve the subproblem, which may mean further decomposition. SADT allows multiple models; i.e., an activity model and a data model to coexist within a system. In an activity model, the boxes are processes of the system, and arrows are used to denote the thing in a system. The opposite applies to a data model. A complete model can be created by combining the activity model and the data model for the problem.[21, 19] Figure 2-9 is an example of a SA diagram.

SADT was initially introduced as a documentation methodology for large, complex systems. It has proven useful in many applications.[21] The design is

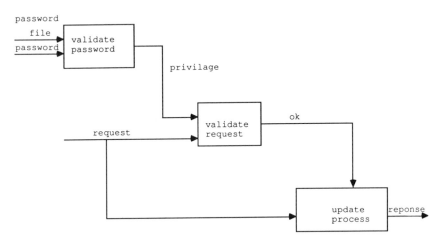

Figure 2-9. An SA diagram.

mainly applicable to the problem definition phase. To be applied to other phases of the software life cycle, it must interface with other methodologies. SA has more graphics symbols than shown.[19] This many symbols is a drawback, because it may be difficult for a client to understand and interpret the diagram and to pinpoint any errors.

2.5   Requirement Network

Requirement Network (R-Net) was developed as part of the Software Requirements Engineering Methodology (SREM),[2, 4] a research project sponsored by the U.S. Army Ballistic Missile Defense Advanced Technology Center in an attempt to formalize and automate techniques for specifying software requirements for a given system. It was designed because a hierarchical model does not adequately show the sequence of operations.

2.5.1   Diagrammatic Notations

R-Net consists of three kinds of nodes; ALPHA, subnet, and structured nodes. ALPHA nodes, represented by rectangles, specify processing operations; and subnet nodes, represented by ovals, are a refinement of ALPHA nodes. Structured nodes are AND, OR, SELECT, and FOR-EACH nodes. Except for the FOR-EACH node, which is a rectangle, all other structure nodes are represented by circles with the appropriate symbol inside. AND nodes specify operations that can be executed in parallel, OR nodes allow the execution of one of several operations, SELECT nodes specify the condition for selecting a node, and FOR-EACH nodes allow each element of a list to be executed. Arcs are used to connect these nodes.[4] Figure 2-10 is a diagram using R-Net.

2.5.2   Discussion

R-Net is the graphical form of the Requirements Statement Language (RSL) that is used in SREM to state requirements. In addition to RSL, SREM also consists of the Requirements Engineering and Validation System (REVS), which is an automated tool system. In SREM, R-NET is used to show the sequence of operations performed on a given input message. It is outside the scope of this chapter to describe SREM.

As the name suggests, R-Net was designed for the requirement analysis phase of a software cycle, and is applicable in different areas.[2] In order to support the life cycle, it has to be integrated with other tools.

2.6   Warnier-Orr Diagram

The Warnier-Orr Diagram was invented by Jean-Dominique Warnier in France. It was introduced in the Structured System Design Method by Kenneth Orr.[33]

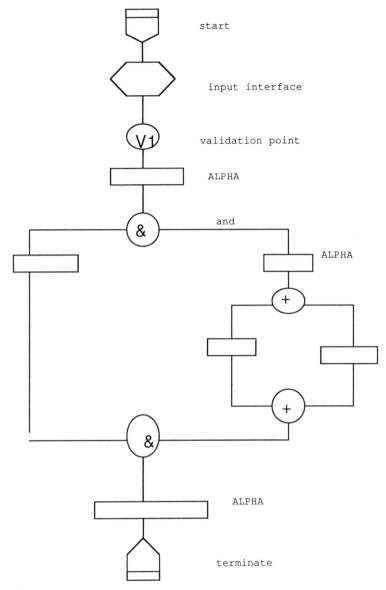

start

input interface

validation point

ALPHA

and

ALPHA

Figure 2-10. An example of R-net.

The Warnier-Orr method (or Logical Construction of System—LCS) is a technique that "sees" the data structure as input and output and derives the program structure from this. The methodology is applied by successfully decomposing modules into submodules.

2.6.1   Diagrammatic Notation

The Warnier-Orr diagram uses brackets as its major symbol. It allows the three basic control constructs: sequence, iteration, and decision to be specified in the diagram. A notation (1,N) under a process indicates that specified steps are to be performed N times. The symbol ⊕ represents an exclusive OR situation. Processes are to be executed sequentially if there are no operation symbols included between them. Basic notations of the Warnier-Orr diagram are shown in Figure 2-11. Figure 2-12 is an example using the Warnier-Orr diagram.

2.6.2   Discussion

The following design steps of the Structured System Design Method are summarized from Orr:[33]

- Identify the problem.
- Identify the structure of the output, particularly the frequency of occurrence.
- Identify the logical database for the system.
- Place the systems requirement into a basic flow hierarchy.
- Check if the data already exists.
- Identify real world events that will affect the logical database.
- Place logical updating actions into the basic system hierarchy.

An advantage of the Warnier-Orr diagram is its application in many areas such as, describing system activities, designing programs, and defining databases, also it is easy to understand. One drawback is that its application to complex problems is not immediately apparent.

2.7   Nassi-Shneiderman Chart

The Nassi-Shneiderman Chart (N-S Chart)[18] was named after its developers, I. Nassi and B. Shneiderman. It was designed to replace the traditional flowchart, aiming to produce a more structured flowchart.

2.7.1   Diagrammatic Notation

Similar to other diagramming techniques that are used to specify program logic, the N-S chart consists of basic control constructs, such as sequence, iteration, and decision. The basic building block of a N-S chart is a process symbol. The process symbol is represented by a rectangle. Sequential execution of processes is represented by a stack of process symbols. Repeating processes are represented by the iteration symbol as shown in Figure 2-13. The decision symbol

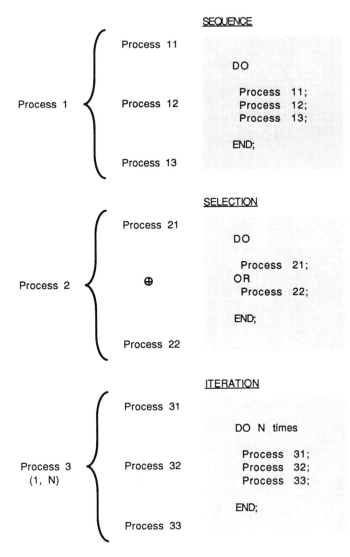

Figure 2-11. Basic symbols of the Warnier-Orr Diagram.

for an If-Then-Else construct is represented by a rectangle that contains five parts. The upper half consists of three triangles, and the lower half consists of two process boxes. The uppermost triangle contains the condition to be tested; the other two triangles represent the possible outcomes i.e., "true" or "false." The two process symbols represent the true clause and the false clause of the condition. In addition, the N-S chart also consists of a Do-Case symbol that is similar to an If-Then-Else symbol, except it has more than two conditions.

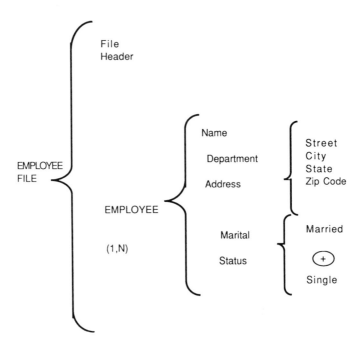

Figure 2-12. An example of the Warnier-Orr Diagram to depict data.

Figure 2-13 shows the basic notations of a N-S chart and Figure 2-14 depicts an example using a N-S chart.

2.7.2 Discussion

The N-S chart was developed to replace the traditional flowchart. It is developed at the same time the logic of a module is developed. The advantage of a N-S chart over a flowchart is that it encourages structured programming. Without including any arrows in the design, the N-S chart allows one entry point and one exit point into and out of any segment. Similar to a flowchart, it is used as a tool for detailed design. Its advantages are that it is easy to understand and its ability to be translated into structured code. Its drawback is that it is difficult to use in high level design, and the interface between segments (or modules) is not clearly specified. If not supported by automated tools, a change in the algorithm may require the diagram to be redrawn.

2.8 Greenprint

Greenprint was named after the color of certain CRT displays and parallels the term blueprint. It was designed by Belady, et al.[3] and aimed at producing graphics diagrams that could be drawn parallel to a program.

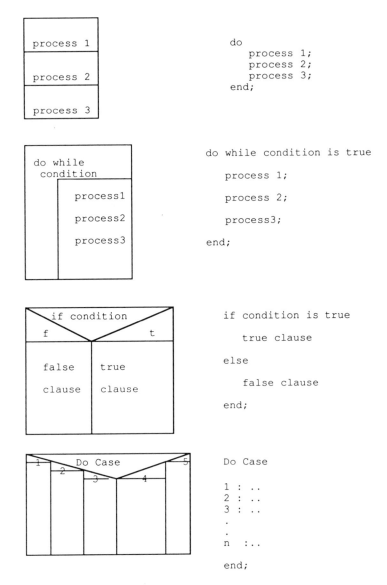

Figure 2-13. Basic notations of N-S chart.

2.8.1 Diagrammatic Notations

The components of Greenprint consist of two types of symbols—blocks and boxes, and auxiliary control lines. Blocks are either procedure, selection, or iteration: boxes are either processor or gate. The processor box consists of

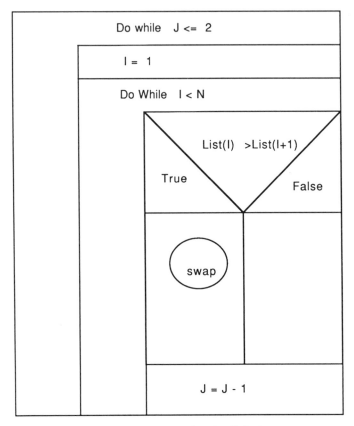

Figure 2-14. An example using N-S chart.

sequential statements, and the gate box consists of decision statements. Each box consists of a pillar and at least one gate box on top of the pillar. The structure of a Greenprint diagram is similar to that of a program; for example, the inclusion of some statements inside a loop is represented by a loop block drawn on the left of a processor box. The auxiliary control lines are used to define nonstructured control flow. The basic notations are shown in Figure 2-15, and Figure 2-16 depicts its usage.

2.8.2 Discussion

Two applications of Greenprint are described in Belady's[3] paper: (1) it can be used to produce graphics from text, allowing the software maintainer to capture the concept of complete programs, and (2) it can be used as a design tool to express a program's logic.

Greenprint is able to highlight a program's structure. The use of auxiliary control lines may lead to the development of unstructured programs. Although

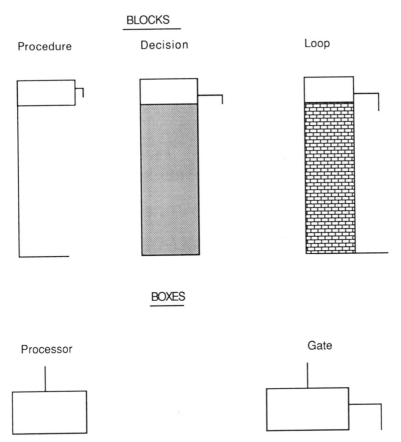

Figure 2-15. Basic notations of Greenprint.

it can be used in the detailed design level, it is difficult to apply to high level design.

2.9 Object-Oriented Design Notation

Object-oriented design notation consists of the graphics symbols used in object-oriented design, a methodology described by Booch.[6, 7] Object-oriented design is a methodology that is applied by decomposing a system based on the concept of the object.

2.9.1 Diagrammatic Notations

Booch[7] classifies the graphical notations into four parts: hardware diagram, class structure, object diagram, and architecture diagram. As Booch also contributes a chapter to this book, please refer to Chapter 6 for an example.

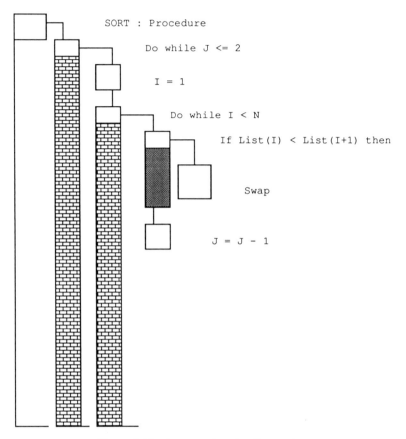

Figure 2-16. An example using Greenprint.

2.9.2 Discussion

The major components of object-oriented design are the objects and their associated set of operators. The following steps are summarized from Booch:[6]

- definition of the problem;
- development of an informal strategy for the problem domain; and
- formalization of the strategy;
    - identification of the objects and their attributes.
    - identification of the operations performed on the objects.
    - definition of the interfaces.
    - decision on the operations.

This methodology allows a designer to consider the structure of an application as he/she would see it if only looking at the abstract objects and their associated operators that make up the application. Therefore, when using this methodology, all he/she needs to detail is the specification of the objects. A common criticism is that the methodology is only applicable to small and medium scale applications. For it to be applied to larger applications, a designer must supply another methodology that breaks the application into smaller parts.

The graphics notations and the design principles tie the design closely to the programming language, Ada. In Ada, programming units, such as packages, tasks, and subprograms consist of two parts, a specification and a body. The specification provides the information necessary for the correct use of the programming unit; the body provides the encapsulated local variables and subprogram definitions. Thus, objects and operators can easily be implemented as packages, tasks, or subprograms.

2.10   Jackson Diagram

A Jackson diagram is the graphics notation used in both Jackson Structured Programming (JSP)[40] and Jackson System Development (JSD).[38] JSP, a technique developed by Michael Jackson, is intended for developing programs for data processing applications. JSD, a methodology developed by Michael Jackson and John Cameron, is designed to cover the requirements analysis, design and programming phases of the software life cycle. Both are widely used in Europe and are applicable to any information processing system, and both use a similar set of diagrammatic notations. Since JSD covers a longer period of the software life cycle, JSP is not covered in the remaining discussion.

2.10.1   Diagrammatic Notations

There are essentially two sets of graphic symbols used in JSD: first, in modeling and second, in specifying the system (system specification diagram). In modeling the real world, JSD requires a software developer to construct a model of real world entities. In JSD terminology, an entity is a noun that performs or allows actions in a significant time-ordering. Its basic structure is a tree. The rectangles inside the tree represent actions, a rectangle containing a star represents an iterative action, and a rectangle containing a circle represents a selected action. Rectangles on the same level are assumed to be executed from left to right. The basic notations and their corresponding meanings are shown in Figure 2-17.

Figure 2-18 is an entity structure for an EMPLOYEE entity.[41] It computes the length of time an employee has worked at various jobs within a company. The problem assumed that: "the career path of all employees is; start as office-boy or as messenger, get promoted to clerk, get promoted to manager, get demoted to clerk, and retire."[41]

In specifying the requirements of the system, JSD requires the software

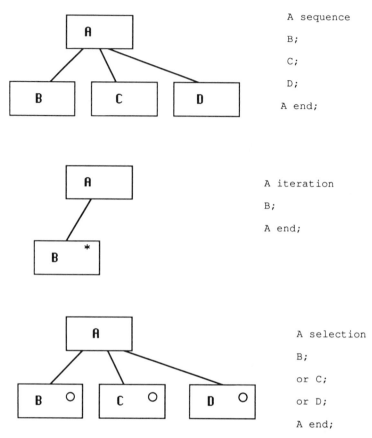

Figure 2-17. Basic symbols of Jackson Diagram.

developer to "map" a real world process to a computer process (i.e., develop a system specification diagram). In the system specification diagram, a rectangle represents a process, a circle represents a data stream, and a diamond represents a state inspection. An arrow is used to link a process and a data stream or a process and a vector inspection. Figure 2-19 depicts an example that maps the real world abstraction of the employee process to the corresponding abstraction of the computer process.

2.10.2 Discussion

JSD does not begin the development process with the requirement analysis process phase. Instead, it starts by creating a model of the real world. The end product is a compilable source code. The major steps used in JSD are summarized as follows:

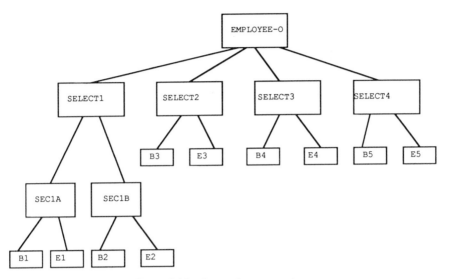

Figure 2-18. An employee structure.

- Modeling the real world, excluding the functions required of the system.
- Inserting the required functions to the real world and picking up time constraints.
- Implementing the system.

The JSD approach to real world modeling provides an implementation that parallels real world problems. The implementation step is considered to be mechanical, consisting of transforming the design from structured text to compilable source code. This has a very important implication; it means that any modification of the system can be achieved by changing the design. However, the development process can be very time-consuming: it claims that it can support the complete life cycle, but it does not provide any guideline to analyze a problem.

2.11   Entity-Relationship Diagram

The entity-relationship diagram was introduced by Peter Chen[42] to define the logical relationship between data.

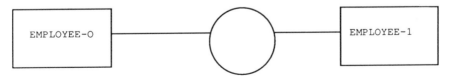

Figure 2-19. A system specification diagram.

Figure 2-20. An example of an Entity-Relationship diagram.

2.11.1   Diagrammatic Notations

Basic notations of the entity-relationship diagram consist of rectangles which represent entity types and diamonds which represent relationship types. Entities are objects that can be uniquely defined. Relationships are conceptual links that exist between objects. Figure 2-20 is an entity-relationship diagram that depicts a manager-employee relationship.

2.11.2   Discussion

Using the entity-relationship approach, an analyst first identifies the entities and their corresponding relationships in a system. Relationships between two entity types are shown by joining a relationship type symbol to the two entity type symbols. The notation, 1 and n shown, in Figure 2-20, indicates that every employee can have only one manager, but every manager can have any number of employees.

The entity-relationship diagram is widely used in the data processing environment to define the logical view of data.

3   REQUIREMENTS

It is evident that a single set of diagrams from existing design methodologies cannot support the requirements of CASE tools. Can the combination of the diagramming techniques from existing design methodologies adequately support the requirements of today's development? If the answer is yes, then what is the criteria for choosing a set of diagram techniques? In order to have some insight to the question, the authors first address the requirements of CASE tools. In the midst of the "productivity crisis," CASE products have received much appeal due to their promise of automating the development process and, hence increasing programmer productivity.[14, 15] In order to carry out its promise, the following development processes should be supported by CASE products.

Rapid prototyping. Rapid prototyping emerged as a discipline under the observations that some problems cannot be properly defined, and a system can best be determined incrementally.

"Building a system that the user really wants and needs is one of the greatest challenges facing the developers of programming systems" as stated by Scharer.[45] With the complexity of the problem domain of todays software, there are user's problems that do not admit "quick" solutions, or the nature of the problem cannot be clearly stated. In both cases, rapid prototyping provides a solution. Often, a user's demand of the system can be better specified, or the problem domain can be better understood when the user's experience with the system grows. In the past, rapid prototyping was rarely performed because the problem domain was easier to understand, computing power was expensive, and prototypes were considered to be expensive commodities. But with the complexity of today's software and the availability of hardware, it is both necessary and practical to develop tools that can quickly generate a working model of a system. In papers by Yeh[27] and Agresti,[1] both suggested that in the new paradigm of software development, rapid prototyping should be considered as an integral part of the software life cycle. Yeh states that "it is a norm rather than an exception." Rapid prototyping, in fact, can contribute to tremendous savings in time and effort. By observing a working model of the system, a user can be sure of the accuracy of the system; this ability to pinpoint errors early in the design phase can save a significant amount of man hours at the later stages of development.

Maintenance. It is acknowledged that maintenance accounts for over 60% of the dollars spent on software. To be cost-effective, a better scheme of software maintenance is required. In the past, maintenance was performed on the executable code, which meant that after several modifications the initial design was lost. Later maintenance required an extra amount of time from programmers. Yeh[27] and Balzer, et al.[5] both suggested that maintenance be performed at the specification level. Balzer, et al.[5] suggested that "In the new paradigm, maintenance is performed on the specification rather than the implementation and the revised specification is then implemented with computer assistance." Yeh proposed that in the new paradigm "maintenance should be folded into the entire evolution framework and, hence is done at the highest suitable level of system description." One of the goals of a CASE product is to develop automated tools that can transform a specification to its corresponding executable code. Therefore, modification of a system is likely to be achieved by modifying the specifications.

Reuse of existing components. Mittermier[16] states "Automating software implies the concept of software reuse." Reusability of software contributes to the cost-effectivity of the software. If a designer develops and validates a module, it is a legitimate expectation to be able to reuse the module when necessary. Reusability, using CASE tools, may mean storing the design (or code) of a module in a library and retrieving it when required. Much of the automation process requires the existence of modules.

Automated generation of code. The main problem associated with productivity is the lack of software engineers. This shortage can be obviated if the system can generate code automatically from specifications. Automatic code generation enables the system engineer to concentrate on more sophisticated work, such as optimization of code. Automatic code generation can also enhance the applicable likelihood of the previously stated development processes—maintenance and rapid prototyping. Allowing a system to automatically generate code encourages rapid prototyping: this not only gives customers a better ability to specify the input requirements of the system, it also encourages designers to try alternative designs. Automatic code generation also makes maintenance at the highest level of the design possible. If a system is capable of automatically generating code from the design level, any change made to the system can be accomplished by modifying the design specifications. Automatically generating code also allows software developers to validate the software during various points of development.

Diagrams, as the front-end of CASE tools, interact directly with users; therefore, it is important that the diagrams minimally support the above mentioned development processes. There are two fundamental requirements for any set(s) of diagramming techniques: user friendliness and life cycle coverage.

User friendliness. User friendliness is an important and fundamental requirement. If a diagramming technique is not user friendly, it will eventually be abandoned by the user and fail in the market. There are two aspects of user friendliness: ease of use and ease of learning. Ease of use can be supported by existing technologies, such as icons, pop-up menus, and other pointing devices. Ease of learning means that a user should not have to spend too much time learning the system; it is not practical to expect a customer to understand the technical language of the computer industry. Spending the time to learn a system always poses a problem for users, especially non-technical personnel, and teaching the system requires the availability of trained personnel. On-line help, which includes explanation and examples, should always supplement a written manual. Diagrams should be simple and direct to bridge the gap between the conceptual model of a problem and the program.

Full life cycle coverage. Software development is an ever-evolving process. Diagrams, which are another way of representing the software, should always reflect the changes of the system. It is not easy with all graphical representations because some of them are developed to assist a specific phase of the development process, and some combinations of diagramming techniques may be required. It is not easy to do manually due to the ripple effect caused by the changes—diagrams created for other phases need to be modified or redrawn. CASE products are designed to support the complete software life cycle. Therefore, the set of diagramming techniques used should be able to cover the complete lifetime of the software. Diagramming techniques that cover the full life cycle also enhance the likelihood of automatic code generation, and maintenance can be achieved by modifying the specifications at a high level.

4 BEYOND GRAPHICS

As previously noted, CASE tools are an integrated set of tools that were developed to support the complete software life cycle and aim to automate much of the software development process. It is outside the scope of this chapter to provide a detailed description of CASE tools.[30] In order to provide a full life cycle coverage, existing CASE tools fall into two categories. They include several methodologies, often including a user-defined symbol, to allow users to choose from or provide their own set of diagrams that are able to cover the complete life cycle.

The former approach provides flexibility as well as constraints. It is flexible because software designers are free to choose from any set of diagrams with which they are familiar. At the same time, it imposes certain constraints because different groups of the software development team use different diagrams to communicate. Diagrams designed by one group have to be converted to diagrams used by another group. At the very best, this conversion can and should be done automatically. Most of the design methodologies were developed by different researchers, therefore, they emphasize a different aspect of the life cycle and may not be compatible with each other. It is difficult to provide a smooth transition from one set of diagrams to another; for example, it is hard to automatically transform a structure chart to pseudocode or to generate executable code from a structure chart without an intermediate step that specifies the logic of the system. Most often, CASE products using this approach cannot support the complete life cycle or automate much of the development process. Nevertheless, for this kind of system to be useful, it should provide as much integration and automation as possible. For methodologies that are ''compatible,'' such as data flow diagrams and structure charts, modifications done on one set of diagrams (for example, data flow diagram) should be reflected on the other set of diagrams (for example, structure chart). This system can automatically generate the structure chart once the root node is identified.

CASE products adopting the later approach are available commercially and in the research environment. To support the complete life cycle, some products modify existing design methodologies, and some develop new sets of diagrams. In most cases, they share the common characteristics providing a combination of control flow and data flow in their design methodologies: they allow the control flow of the system to be specified at an early stage of the design process and decompose the components of the system at some later stage. This approach brings about two unconventional concepts: first, it distinguishes itself from the traditional design methodologies, which emphasize separating the ''what'' of the specification from the ''how'' of the design and are commonly believed to be analytical; second, it deviates from Parnas's concept of decomposition, which suggests that one should begin the design from a list of difficult design decisions or design decisions that are likely to change. Refutation to the above arguments are: first, it is shown in Swartout, et al.[39] that discussing the ''what'' of the system in any useful sense demands that design and implementation be addressed; second, given the computing power of today, efficient implementation is not a major concern. The benefits of such an approach are that it allows a working model of the system to be generated quickly.

The approach that uses a single set of diagrams throughout the development process presents a more compact appearance; it implies that users at various levels can communicate by using the same language. It also increases the likelihood of automation, and it is probable that a change of the specification can directly change the executable code; therefore, it encourages rapid prototyping.

Regardless of any set of diagramming techniques used, the graphics tools should go beyond automating the drawing of diagrams, which would otherwise be drawn manually. To realize the computing power of today, a graphics tool should be able to support consistency checking in the process and data flow if an earlier or later part of the diagram is modified. It should also be able to check that requirements do not conflict with one another.

5 CONCLUSION

"Graphics techniques should have a very high payoff in a software environment that supports the whole life cycle," states Grafton.[43] Diagrams used in CASE, analogous to architectural blueprints, are the major medium of communication and criticism. A clear and concise diagram can uncover errors early and, hence reduce development cost. A representation method that covers the full life cycle provides a common medium of communication within the software development community. If more than one set of representation methods have to be used, they should cover the complete life cycle, since automation and rapid prototyping are an integral part of a development process. Full life cycle coverage of a diagramming technique enhances the likelihood of automation.

In this chapter, the authors surveyed some diagramming techniques that are currently available. Some claim to cover the whole development process, i.e. be suitable for high- and low-level design, and for defining the logical relationship between data. Most have been adopted in CASE products. Whether or not any combination of the techniques can work well depends on the application as well as the integration of the set of underlying tools. Nevertheless, graphics tools should be more than mere drawing tools; they should reinforce software engineering principles and provide consistency checking in the software development life cycle.

REFERENCES

1. Agresti, W. W., "IEEE Tutorial: New Paradigms for Software Development," IEEE Computer Society, 1986.
2. Alford, M., "SREM at the Age of Eight: The Distributed Computing Design System," *IEEE Computer*, Vol. 18, No. 4, April 1985, pp. 36–46.
3. Belady, L. A., C. J. Evangelist, and L. R. Power, "Greenprint: A Graphic Representation of Structured Program," *IBM System Journal*, Vol. 19, No. 4, 1980, pp. 542–553.
4. Bell, T., D. Bixler, and M. Dyer, "An Extendable Approach to Computer-Aided Software Requirements Engineering," *IEEE Transactions on Software Engineering*, Vol. SE-3, No. 1, January 1977, pp. 49–60.

5. Balzer, R. and T. E. Cheatham, "Software Technology in the 1990's: Using a New Paradigm," *IEEE Computer*, Vol. 16, No. 11, November 1983, pp. 39–46.
6. Booch, G., *Software Engineering with Ada*, Menlo Park, CA: Benjamin/Cummings Publishing, 1983.
7. Booch, G., "On the Concepts of Object-Oriented Design," *Modern Software Engineering: Foundations and Current Perspectives* (ed. P. A. Ng and R. T. Yeh), New York: Van Nostrand Reinhold, 1989, pp. 165–204.
8. Gane, C. and T. Sarson, "Structured System Analysis," Englewood Cliffs, NJ: Prentice-Hall, 1979.
9. Gutz, S., *et al.*, "Personal Development Systems for the Professional Programmer," *IEEE Computer*, April 1981, pp. 45–53.
10. Ivie, E. L., "The Programmer's Workbench—A Machine for Software Development," *CACM*, October 1977, pp. 746–753.
11. Matsumoto, Y., "Software Factory: An Overall Approach to Software Production," in *Software Reusability*, (ed. by P. Freeman), *IEEE Computer Society*, 1987.
12. Matsumoto, Y., "Toshiba Fuchu Software Factory," *Modern Software Engineering: Foundations and Current Perspectives* (ed. P. A. Ng and R. T. Yeh), New York: Van Nostrand Reinhold, 1988, pp. 479–501.
13. McClure, C., *Spring 1987 Computer-Aided Software Engineering Symposium*, Digital Consulting Inc., Andover, MA, 1987.
14. Mimno, P. R., *Computer-Aided Software Engineering* (Ed. P. R. Mimno) The James Martin Productivity Series, High Productivity Software Inc., Marblehead, MA, 1987.
15. Mimno, P. R., "High-Productivity Languages," *Modern Software Engineering: Foundations and Current Perspectives* (ed. P. A. Ng and R. T. Yeh), New York: Van Nostrand Reinhold, 1989, pp. 53–82.
16. Mittermier, R. T., and W. Rossak, "Reusability," *Modern Software Engineering: Foundations and Current Perspectives* (ed. P. A. Ng and R. T. Yeh), New York: Van Nostrand Reinhold, 1988, pp. 205–235.
17. Musa, J. D., "Software Engineering: The Future of a Profession," *IEEE Software*, January 1985, pp. 55–62.
18. Nassi, I. and B. Shneiderman, "Flowchart Techniques for Structured Programming," ACM *SIGPLAN Notices*, 8, 1973, pp 12–26.
19. Ross, D. T., "Application and Extension of SADT," *IEEE Computer*, April 1985, pp. 25–34.
20. Raeder, G., "A Survey of Current Graphical Programming Technique," *IEEE Computer* August 1985, pp. 11–25.
21. Ross, D. T. and K. E. Schoman, Jr., "Structured Analysis for Requirements Definition," *IEEE Transactions of Software Engineering*, Volume SE-3, Number 1, January 1977, pp. 69–84.
22. Scheffer, P. A., A. H. Stone, and W. E. Rzepka, "A Case Study of SREM," *IEEE Computer*, Vol. 18, No. 4, April 1985, pp. 47–54.
23. Sievert, G. E. and T. A. Mizell, "Specification-Based Software Engineering with TAGS," *IEEE Computer*, April 1985, 56–65.
24. Stay, J. F., "HIPO and Integrated Program Design," *IBM System Journal*, Vol. 15, No. 2, 1976, pp. 143–154.
25. Suydam, W., "CASE Makes Strides Toward Automated Software Development," *Computer Design*, January 1987, pp. 49–70.
26. Wasserman, A. I., "The User Software Engineering Methodology: An Overview," *Information Systems Design Methodologies: A Comparative Review*, (T. W. Olle, H. G. Sol, and A. A. Verrijn-Stuart, editors), 1982, pp. 591–635.
27. Yeh, R. T., "An Alternative Paradigm for Software Evolution," *Modern Software Engineering: Foundations and Current Perspectives*, (ed. P. A. Ng and R. T. Yeh), New York: Van Nostrand Reinhold, 1989, pp. 7–22.

28. Osterwel, L., "Software Environment Research: Direction for the Next Five Years," *IEEE Computer*, April 1981, pp. 35–43.
29. Martin, J. and C. McClure, *Diagramming Techniques for Analysts and Programmers*, Englewood Cliffs, NJ: Prentice-Hall, 1985.
30. Mimno, P. P., "Survey of CASE Tools," *Modern Software Engineering: Foundations and Current Perspectives* (eds. P. A. Ng and R. T. Yeh), New York, Van Nostrand Reinhold, 1989, pp. 323–350.
31. Schulz, A., "CASE: A Tool for the Interactive Program Design," *Conference on Software Tools*, 1985, pp. 131–137.
32. Yourdon, E. and L. L. Constantine, *Structured Design, Fundamentals of a Discipline of Computer Program and Systems Design*, Englewood Cliffs, NJ: Prentice-Hall, 1979.
33. Orr, K. L., *Structured System Development*, New York: Yourdon Press, 1980.
34. Paranas, D. L., "On the Criteria to be used in Decomposing Systems into Modules," *CACM*, Vol. 15, No. 12, December 1972, pp. 1053–1058.
35. Rosene, A. F., "A Software Development Environment Called Steps," *Conference on Software Tools*, 1985, pp. 154–160.
36. Blum, B. I., "A Life Cycle Environment for Interactive Information Systems," *Conference on Software Tools*, 1985, pp. 198–206.
37. Boehm, B. W., *et al.* "A Software Development Environment for Improving Productivity," *IEEE Computer*, June 1984, pp. 30–44.
38. Jackson, M. A., *System Development*, Englewood Cliffs, NJ: Prentice-Hall, 1983.
39. Swartout, W. and R. Balzer, "On the Inevitable Interwining of Specification and Implementation," *CACM*, July 1982, pp. 438–440.
40. Jackson, M. A., "Constructive Methods of Program Design," *Proceedings of the First Conference of the European Cooperation in Informatics*, Vol. 44, 1976, pp. 236–262
41. Cameron, J. R., "Two Pairs of Examples in the Jackson Approach to System Development," *Proceedings of the 15th Hawaii International Conference on System Sciences*, January, 1982.
42. Chen, P., "The Entity-Relationship Model—Toward a Unified View of Data," *ACM Transactions on Database Systems*, Vol. 1, No. 1, March 1976, pp. 9–36.
43. Grafton, R. B., and T. Ichikawa, "Guest Editors' Introduction," *IEEE Computer*, August 1985, pp. 6–9.
44. Stevens, W., G. Meyers, and L. L. Constantine, "Structured Designs," *IBM Systems Journal*, Vol. 13, No. 1, May 1984, pp. 115–139.
45. Scharer, L., "The Prototyping Alternative," *ITT Programming*, Vol. 1, No. 1, 1983, pp. 34–43.

Chapter 3

High Productivity Languages

Pieter R. Mimno
High-Productivity Software, Inc.
36 Bessom Street
Marblehead, MA

HIGH-PRODUCTIVITY LANGUAGES

3.1 Rapid Changes in Technology

Major changes now occurring in hardware and software technology are permanently altering the way computers are used. These changes include a shift toward end-user computing, the availability of powerful desktop workstations, and the growing integration of micro and mainframe facilities. Significant advances in software technology include the availability of PC-based high-productivity application development systems, computer-aided software engineering (CASE) tools, improved development life-cycle processes, and the introduction of practical artificial intelligence techniques.

These improvements, in both hardware and software technology, enhance the advantages of high-productivity tools over third-generation languages, such as COBOL. With the introduction of PC-based versions of fourth-generation languages, (4GL), many of these high-productivity tools have become available to non-DP end users.

High-productivity tools for DP professionals will improve more rapidly with the introduction of powerful front-end CASE design tools tightly coupled with efficient back-end code generators. These new CASE-oriented application development tools are likely to replace the current generation of high-productivity tools for DP professionals. Major additional improvements in high-productivity tools are expected through the application of more effective development life-cycle processes, embedded methodology aids, and the incorporation of expert system techniques.

The net effect of these changes is a broader range of applicability of high-productivity tools relative to COBOL. It is increasingly difficult to justify the use of costly, error-prone, manual coding techniques for the development of applications when more efficient high-productivity tools are available. As a result, many organizations are reassessing the role of high-productivity tools within their application development processes and are looking for high-productivity tools that will provide both better access to information and support for an overall corporate information processing strategy.

This chapter examines the applicability range of several categories of high-productivity tools, relative to the use of traditional programming languages such as COBOL. Categories of high-productivity languages that are evaluated in this chapter include the following:

- decision support systems;
- application generators for end users;
- application and code generators for DP professionals;
- computer-aided software engineering (CASE) tools; and
- expert system tools.

3.2 Decision Support Systems

Decision support systems (DSS) are high-productivity tools designed to increase the efficiency and effectiveness of decision makers. as shown in Figure 3-1, there are four distinct categories of decision support systems; i.e., executive information systems, spreadsheets/financial modeling systems, decision support generators, and statistical analysis systems. Each category of DSS tools is oriented toward a specific class of end user, such as senior executives, group managers, business managers, and business analysts.

3.2.1 Proper User/Tool Match

Representative DSS tools in each category are listed in Figure 3-1. It is important to match DSS tools to the appropriate class of end user; i.e., a top executive should be supported by an executive information system, not by a financial modeling tool, a financial analysis tool, or a full-function decision support generator. Many attempts to interest top management in direct on-line interaction with computers have failed due to the selection of an inappropriate DSS tool.

Decision support systems differ greatly from production-oriented information systems. In general, prior to implementation, the functionality to be supported by a DSS is not well-defined. DSS functionality tends to evolve as the user learns more about the application. Decision support systems are used to spot trends and project business performance for a given set of assumptions. As a result, DSS applications require ad-hoc access to time-series data; i.e., current, historic, and future information. Decision Support System data bases are dynamic structures, often consisting of large multidimensional arrays.

In contrast, traditional, production-oriented systems tend to be well-defined, and their detailed functionality can be specified before development. Produc-

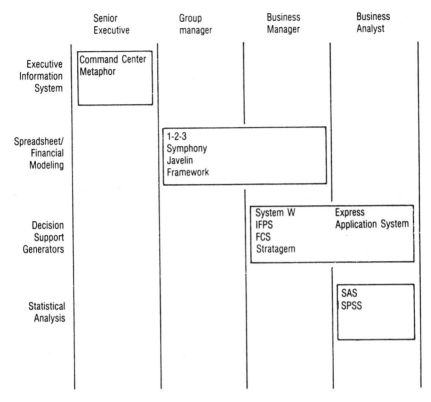

Figure 3-1. Representative DSS products.

tion-oriented systems provide structured access to data files, and their data bases are organized as relatively static, relational, inverted, or hierarchical structures.

3.2.2 Decision Support Prototyping Methodologies

For the development of systems that cannot be precisely specified in advance, a rapid iterative prototyping methodology is highly appropriate. Decision support systems are ideal candidates for such implementation. Initial user-provided functional requirements are rapidly translated into a working proto-type, which is then demonstrated to the end user. Based on end-user feedback, the prototype is either discarded or refined. As the user learns more about the application, the prototype evolves, stage-by-stage, into the final end-user system.

The methodology's success depends on its ability to build prototypes rapidly, at low cost. High-productivity DSS tools, such as Application System, EXPRESS, Metaphor, Stratagem, and System W are ideally suited for such applications and, in most cases, the prototype system can evolve directly into the released system.

Traditional programming languages such as COBOL are not suitable for use in a rapid prototyping development environment. It is expensive, both in time and in resources, to build and evolve multiple prototype applications using third-generation languages such as COBOL. High-productivity languages are a better choice for building DSS applications.

3.3   Application Generators for End Users

Application generators, specifically designed for non-DP end users, are a rapidly growing segment of the computer software market. The increasing accessibility of computers to a broad range of business professionals and non-DP end users is a significant trend in the computer industry. Representative high-productivity tools for end users are listed in Figure 3-2. These tools are well-suited for information center applications or for applications that do not have heavily loaded, on-line transaction processing requirements.

3.3.1   What to Look For in a 4GL for End Users

Due to the many competing products, the selection of suitable high-productivity end-user tools can be confusing. However, the selection process can be simplified by identifying the critical factors that differentiate appropriate from inappropriate tools for a specific computing environment.

For an end-user computing environment, these critical factors include the following:

- support for an effective end-user computing strategy;
- compatibility with a hardware/software architecture for end-user computing (i.e., an integrated micro/mainframe environment, PC implementation of the mainframe 4GL product, and an open PC environment providing support for standard PC software products);
- high productivity (at least a 10:1 improvement in productivity over COBOL);
- high degree of integrated functionality (i.e., support for data base query, report generation, graphics, decision support, project management, application generation, procedural language, etc.);
- interface to standard data base management systems, (DBMS), including DB2 and SQL/DS;
- superb human factoring including elimination of alien syntax, provision of deci-second response rate, and support of multiple front-end interfaces oriented to different classes of end users;

Application System	IBM
CA-UNIVERSE	Computer Associates International
FOCUS	Information Builders, Inc.
FUSION	Pansophic Systems, Inc.
INGRES	Relational Technology, Inc.
MAPPER System	Unisys Corporation
NOMAD2	MUST Software International
ORACLE	Oracle Corporation
POWERHOUSE	Cognos Corporation
RAMIS II	On-Line Software International
SAS	SAS Institute, Inc.
TIF	IBM

Figure 3-2. Representative application generators for end users.

- incorporation of a CASE front end to convert user-oriented graphical specifications directly into operational code;
- use of expert systems and embedded methodology aids to guide the user, step-by-step, through the development of computable specifications for an application.

Features to look for in end-user products that support well-designed human interfaces are summarized in Figure 3-3.

Well-designed languages for end users offer the following:

- Avoidance of alien syntax, i.e., commands that require the user to remember an unnatural, "computerese" syntax.

- Use of natural languages or menu structures that do not require the memorization of any command sequences or codes.

- Intuitive interaction with the computer, requiring little training or dependence on reference manuals.

- Choice of multiple command interfaces geared to different levels of user experience (e.g., choice of natural language, two-dimensional menu structures, near-English command languages, icons, graphical diagrams, report-by-example, etc.).

- User-seductive interaction with the computer at a high business level, requiring little or no disruption of the interaction to solve low-level syntax problems.

- Adequate menus, prompts, Help and self-teaching facilities.

- Rapid, on-line interaction at a deci-second response rate.

- Two-dimensional display dialog.

- Use of the widely-understood Lotus 1-2-3 interface, incorporating use of the "/" key, pull-down menus, pop-up windows and one-key menu selection sequences.

- Use of graphic symbols (icons).

- Use of a mouse or other pointing device to select commands, menus, options, data items, etc., and to control scrolling, scaling and graphical editing functions.

- Minimal keyboard interaction.

- Intelligent default options and smart editors.

- Simple subset of operations that can be learned by business professionals in one or two hours.

- Use of an intelligent-assistant mode of operation that guides the user in the application of the tool.

Figure 3-3. Features to look for in application generators for end users.

3.3.2   End-User Computing Strategy

To avoid selecting inappropriate products for end users, it is advantageous to evaluate tools top-down, based on their support for an overall corporate information processing strategy, rather than bottom-up, based on a detailed functionality analysis. The objective of an information processing strategy is to utilize information as a strategic corporate resource to improve the decision making process and to sharpen the competitive edge of the organization.

An effective end-user computing strategy should target those end users making high-dollar value decisions and provide them with better, easily accessed information. The aim is to get the right information to the right decision makers in order to make better decisions. Ideally, the strategy will be determined jointly— and only after a thorough survey of both end-user needs and application requirements—by business and MIS professionals.

The end-user computing strategy leads to the definition of an appropriate hardware/software architecture. Figure 3-4 illustrates a typical end-user computing architecture that supports networks of PCs tightly integrated with departmental processors and/or mainframes. Desirable components of an end-user computing architecture include the following:

- Integrated 4GL tool on the mainframe.
- Industry-standard mainframe DBMS. (DB2 and SQL/DS from IBM are rapidly becoming the standard DBMS's for end-user applications).
- Integrated, transparent, micro-to-mainframe data communication capability, supporting a network of distributed workstations.
- Industry-standard workstation. (The IBM PC, supported by MS/DOS, is the current industry standard. The IBM Personal System/2, coupled with the proprietary IBM operating system OS/2, is likely to become the new standard for high-productivity tools.)

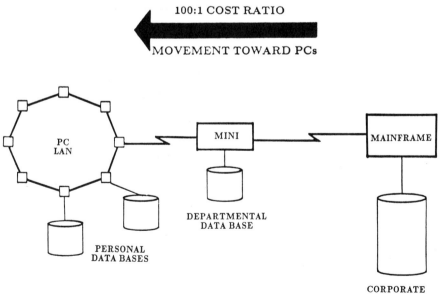

Figure 3-4. End-user computing architecture.

- PC version of the same 4GL tool installed on the mainframe.
- Open PC environment providing support for standard PC tools, such as 1-2-3 from Lotus Development Corporation and dBASE III from Ashton-Tate.

3.3.3 Micro/Mainframe Versions

An important development is the increased availability of both PC and mainframe versions of leading 4GL products for end users. Access to data on the mainframe is simplified through the use of compatible 4GL tools on both the mainframe and the PC. As shown in Figure 3-4, this software structure permits PC users to query and extract data from the mainframe, transmit the data transparently to the PC, and perform customized processing of the data on the PC. The PC version of the 4GL tool can be used to support local information processing, such as data query, report generation, graphics generation, decision support, and application development. Applications developed on the PC may be run on the mainframe without reprogramming.

3.3.4 Comparison of Products for End Users

Figure 3-5 shows a matrix which compares the functionality of application generators for end users that are reviewed in *Computer-Aided Software*

Products	ENVIRONMENT					APPLICATION-GENERATION FUNCTIONS														HUMAN FACTORING				DATA-BASE SUPPORT			
	IBM Environment	DEC Environment	Tool Available Only on PC	Micro-to-Mainframe Link	Full PC Implementation	Query Language	Report Generator	Screen Painter/Data Entry	Graphics Generator	Decision-Support Tools	Subset for End Users	Primarily for DP Professionals	Procedural Language	Interface to Action Diagrams	Well-Structured Code	Provable Specifications	Heavy-Duty Computing	Full COBOL Replacement	Recommended for Info. Centers	Human Factoring (scale of 1-5)	HELP Facility	Computer-Aided Instruction	Computer-Aided Thinking	Support of Data-Base Management	Standard DBMS Package	Data Dictionary	Data-Modeling Tool
FOCUS	■	■	□	■	■	■	■	■	■	■	■	□	■	□	■	□	■	■	■	4	■	■	■	■	■	■	□
MAPPER System	□	□	□	■	■	■	■	■	■	■	■	□	■	□	□	□	□	□	■	3	■	□	□	■	□	□	□
NOMAD 2	■	□	□	■	■	■	■	■	■	■	■	□	■	□	■	□	■	■	■	3	■	■	□	■	■	■	□
RAMIS II	■	□	□	■	□	■	■	■	■	■	■	□	■	■	□	■	■	■	■	4	■	■	□	■	■	■	□
SAS System	■	■	□	■	■	■	■	■	■	■	■	□	■	□	□	□	□	□	■	3	■	■	■	□	□	□	□
TIF	■	□	□	□	□	■	■	■	■	□	■	■	■	□	□	□	□	□	■	3	■	□	□	□	■	□	■	□

Figure 3-5. Functionality matrix for end-user application generators.

Engineering, Volume 4 of **The James Martin Productivity Series,** published by High-Productivity Software, Inc., Marblehead, MA. Each row of the matrix summarizes the functionality of a specific product. Columns of the matrix show the availability of a particular function, such as hardware environment, integrated functionality, human factoring, and data base support functions, across all products. The functional categories included in the matrix are specific to the product category "Application Generators for End Users."

Categories of functions that are presented in the functionality matrix include the following:

- Hardware: Type of hardware supported by the product.
- Integrated Functionality: Integrated functions that are available directly to the end user in the environment of the product; for example, data base query, report generation, screen painter, graphics generator, etc.
- Human Factor Considerations: Functions that affect the human interface to the product; for example, HELP facility, computer-aided instruction, embedded methodology, etc.
- Data Base Support: Functions that relate to the support of either internal or external DBMSs.

Each entry in the functionality matrix indicates whether or not a particular function is available in a specific product; for example, function is available, function is partially available, and function is not available.

The functionality matrix provides a useful "first cut" in determining whether a product meets the needs of a potential user. The matrix provides answers to the following:

- Does the tool run on an IBM mainframe computer or a DEC VAX computer?
- Is a compatible version of the mainframe tool available for an IBM PC?
- Does the tool support a micro-to-mainframe communication link?
- Does the tool support a range of integrated functions, such as data base query, report generation, screen panel painting, graphics, etc?
- Does the tool support a proprietary DBMS as well as external DBMS's, such as DB2 and SQL/DS?

3.3.5 Desirable Product Features

To greatly increase end-user productivity across a broad range of end-user experience, managers should look for products that support most of the following features:

- availability for a major end-user **hardware environment,** such as IBM or DEC;

- **compatibility** with an IBM PC or equivalent; first choice—full PC implementation, and second choice—micro-to-mainframe link;
- **distributed communications** capability permitting the interconnection of multiple workstations and facilitating access to corporate mainframe data bases; first choice—peer-to-peer communications strategy using SNA or OSI communication standards, and second choice—dumb terminals using 3270 emulation communication strategy;
- **open architecture**, including MS-DOS compatibility to make use of the thousands of MS-DOS-compatible support programs available for the workstation environment;
- closely integrated **family of functions** with a common command syntax, including:
  - query language,
  - report generator,
  - screen painter,
  - graphics generator,
  - decision support tools,
  - financial modeling and statistical analysis tools, and
  - project management tools,
- well-structured, very high-level, **procedural language**;
- efficient **performance** in a heavily loaded, transaction-processing environment;
- ability to **replace COBOL** for all business applications;
- **support of business professionals** within an Information Center environment;
- **support for the entire development life cycle**, including the early phases of requirements analysis and design;
- **automatic documentation** of functional specifications;
- superb **human factoring**, including deci-second response to on-line interaction, elimination of complex command mnemonics, on-line diagnostic and HELP facilities, elimination of the need for user reference manuals, and incorporation of an imbedded life-cycle process within the tool;
- **support for standard DBMS's** including Read/Write interfaces to DB2 and SQL/DS;
- utilization of integrated data base analysis and **data modeling** tools.

3.3.6 PC Versions of Mainframe Products

The best features of a hardware/software architecture for end users are shown in Figure 3-6. Products that support this architecture include FOCUS, NOMAD2, ORACLE, and INGRES.

FOCUS was the first full-function application generation tool available for both mainframe and PC, PC/XT, or PC/AT. Without conversion, users of PC/

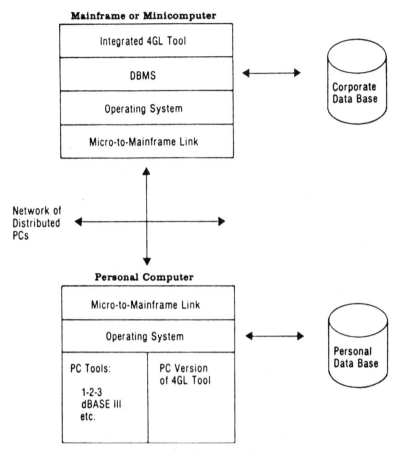

Figure 3-6. Components of typical end-user architecture.

FOCUS can gain direct access to a wide variety of corporate data from files created by QSAM, VSAM, ISAM, IMS/VS, DB2, SQL/DS, IDMS/R, TOTAL, ADABAS, MODEL 204, System 2000, DOS/DL/I, and FOCUS files. The user of the mainframe FOCUS product has a choice of three query interfaces to access mainframe data; i.e., a menu interface called TableTalk, a command language interface, and a natural English interface. The user at a PC has a choice of a menu interface (TableTalk) and a command-level interface. Mainframe data that has been extracted by a PC user via the query interface can be downloaded transparently to the PC for processing by PC/FOCUS. Alternately, the data format can be converted automatically for use by standard PC tools.

PC versions of mainframe 4GLs are also available for NOMAD2, ORACLE, and INGRES. The PC version of NOMAD2 offers syntax compatibility with mainframe NOMAD2 but has been completely redesigned and rewritten to suit the unique features of the PC; e.g., it is written in "C" language (for portability) and provides a relational DBMS designed specifically for the PC. Additional features include an active data dictionary, elimination of alien syntax, and support for user-oriented PC screen handling techniques.

3.3.7 Integrated Environment

An important selection criterion for end-user languages is the provision of a highly integrated development environment that is easy to learn and that supports a wide variety of end users. Many leading 4GL products provide support for multiple application categories within a single integrated environment. With an integrated tool, it is necessary to learn only one command language rather than multiple languages. All integrated functions are available within a common command environment.

Highly integrated application generators for end users, such as Application System, FOCUS, NOMAD2, RAMIS II, and SAS provide a wide range of integrated functionality within a single environment. Integrated functions supported by many of these languages include a query language, report generator, graphics generator, screen generator, decision support system, financial analysis functions, application generator, procedural language, integrated PC interface, a PC version of the product, a variety of front-end interfaces, a data dictionary, a DBMS, a read/write interface to DB2, and other facilities.

3.3.8 Data Base Management Systems (DBMS)

Many highly integrated 4GL products incorporate their own proprietary DBMSs. Most vendors of these products have attempted to establish their own DBMS as an industry standard but now recognize that it is necessary to provide at least read-only interfaces to other file management and DBMSs. Some vendors support read/write interfaces to external data base systems, such as IMS/DL/I and VSAM. In addition, most vendors are aware of the rapidly accelerating trend toward the use of IBM's DB2 and SQL/DS relational DBMSs as an industry standard. In response to this trend, many integrated 4GL products will incorporate read/write interfaces to DB2 and SQL/DS. Application generators for end users that currently provide these interfaces include Application System, FOCUS, and NOMAD2.

3.3.9 10:1 Advantage over COBOL

Most 4GL tools routinely demonstrate about a 10:1 improvement in productivity relative to COBOL for business applications which do not require a large amount of complex procedural logic. Large productivity gains are achieved by the non-procedural components of the tools; i.e., the ability to support very rapid specification of data dictionary entries, data views, edit criteria, display screens, menus, reports, graphics, and simple prototypes. Many users report productivity gains in the range of 10-20:1 relative to COBOL for on-line, transaction processing applications involving large numbers of screens, transactions, and reports.

Lower productivity gains, however, are reported for applications requiring extensive amounts of procedural logic. Productivity gains in the range of 3:1 relative to COBOL are closer to the norm for the specification of complex procedural logic, using integrated application generators.

The use of high-productivity tools within an information center environment permits business professionals to access data and solve business problems with minimal support from Information Systems (IS). This degree of accessibility would be impossible to achieve with third-generation languages such as COBOL.

3.4 Application and Code Generators for DP Professionals

3.4.1 Representative Tools for DP Professionals

Application generators, specifically oriented toward DP professionals, incorporate a substantially wider range of procedural and data base management capabilities than end-user-oriented products. Tools such as NATURAL, IDEAL, ADS, MODEL 204, and MANTIS are appropriate for the development of heavy-duty applications characterized by high transaction processing rates and the management of large, complex data bases.

Tools for DP professionals can be divided into the following three general categories:

• fully-integrated application generators,
• partially-integrated application generators, and
• COBOL code generators.

Representative products in each category are shown in Figure 3-7.

3.4.2 Fully-Integrated Application Generators

Fully-integrated application generators for DP professionals provide a very wide range of functionality within a single, integrated environment. Supported functions generally include the following:

• internal DBMS,
• interfaces to widely-used external DBMSs,
• data dictionary,

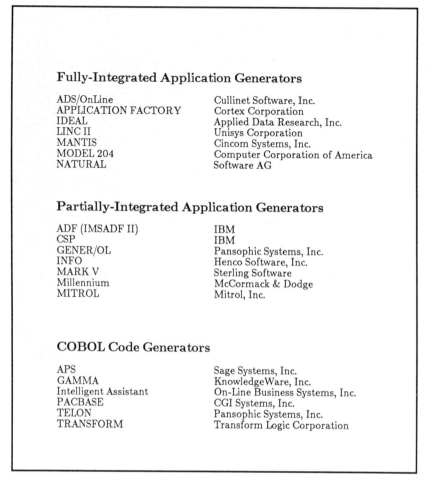

Fully-Integrated Application Generators

ADS/OnLine	Cullinet Software, Inc.
APPLICATION FACTORY	Cortex Corporation
IDEAL	Applied Data Research, Inc.
LINC II	Unisys Corporation
MANTIS	Cincom Systems, Inc.
MODEL 204	Computer Corporation of America
NATURAL	Software AG

Partially-Integrated Application Generators

ADF (IMSADF II)	IBM
CSP	IBM
GENER/OL	Pansophic Systems, Inc.
INFO	Henco Software, Inc.
MARK V	Sterling Software
Millennium	McCormack & Dodge
MITROL	Mitrol, Inc.

COBOL Code Generators

APS	Sage Systems, Inc.
GAMMA	KnowledgeWare, Inc.
Intelligent Assistant	On-Line Business Systems, Inc.
PACBASE	CGI Systems, Inc.
TELON	Pansophic Systems, Inc.
TRANSFORM	Transform Logic Corporation

Figure 3-7. Representative application generators for DP professionals.

- security features,
- restart/rollback capability,
- query language,
- report generator,
- screen painter,
- menu generator,
- graphics generator,
- decision support and financial modeling tools,
- multiple end-user interfaces,
- high-level procedural language,
- data definition language,

- distributed processing facilities, and
- micro-to-mainframe communications link.

Representative functions necessary for leading fully-integrated application generators for DP professionals are listed in Figure 3-8.

None of the major fully-integrated application generators currently provide a

---

- data base query and reporting

- screen and dialogue generation

- graphics

- decision support

- financial modeling and statistical analysis

- project management

- subset of functions for end users

- COBOL generator

- interpretive or compile option

- multiple user interfaces, including:

  - natural language
  - menu-driven interface to all product functions
  - near-English command language
  - procedural language
  - graphical languages for design automation

- automatic documentation

- data dictionary and integrated data base management system

- Read/Write interface to DB2 and SQL/DS

- Read-only interface to DL/I, IMS/VS, IDMS/R, TOTAL, SUPRA, ADABAS, DATACOM/DB, MODEL 204, System 2000

- good on-line performance relative to hand-generated COBOL

- integrated micro/mainframe environment

- open PC environment supporting standard PC products

- PC implementation of the mainframe 4GL product

- front-end CASE tool with automatic design analyzer

- expert systems

- embedded methodology (intelligent assistant mode)

Figure 3-8. Features to look for in application generators for DP professionals.

compatible version of the mainframe tool for a personal computer. Several of them incorporate a proprietary DBMS; e.g., ADS/OnLine (IDMS/R), IDEAL (DATACOM/DB), MANTIS (SUPRA), MODEL 204 (MODEL 204), and NATURAL (ADABAS). These proprietary DBMSs were developed primarily to compete with IBM's IMS data base management system and, although they have offered a viable alternative to the use of IMS, they are highly vulnerable to competitive pressure from IBM's DB2 and SQL/DS relational DBMSs. IBM is positioning DB2 as the standard DBMS for end-user applications in the MVS/ TSO or MVS/XA environments. In addition, the IBM SQL language is evolving as the standard data base query language used to access data in either DB2 or SQL/DS. As the performance of DB2 improves with successive releases of the product, it will become increasingly attractive to utilize DB2 as a common facility to support both production and end-user applications. The use of a single DBMS for all classes of applications greatly simplifies application support requirements and promotes the sharing of data across all computer architectures that support SQL.

Vendors now recognize that it is necessary to provide at least read-only interfaces to other file management and DBMSs. Some support read/write interfaces to external data base systems, such as IMS/DL/I and VSAM. In addition, they are aware of the accelerating trend toward the use of IBM's DB2 and SQL/DS relational DBMSs as an industry standard. In response to this threat, many integrated 4GL products will incorporate read/write interfaces to DB2 and SQL/ DS.

3.4.3 Partially-Integrated Application Generators

Partially-integrated products (e.g., ADF, GENER/OL, INFO, MARK V, etc.) are limited data management systems that do not provide the range of integrated functionality supported by products such as ADS/OnLine, IDEAL, MANTIS, MODEL 204, and NATURAL. Many of these products do not support functions, such as an integrated DBMS, query language, graphics generator, decision support facilities, financial analysis functions, or a very high-level procedural language.

Products such as CSP, GENER/OL, MARK V, Millennium, and UFO simplify the definition, testing, generation, documentation, and maintenance of programs executed within a CICS communications environment. These systems provide menu-driven interfaces that make it easy for analysts to define data structures, data items, screen maps, variable fields, interactive dialogues, report generation, and application processes without requiring detailed knowledge of transaction processing within a CICS environment.

3.4.4 COBOL Code Generators

Code generators, such as APS, GAMMA, PACBASE, TELON, and TRANS-FORM automatically generate COBOL code from user-supplied specifications.

System components include a data dictionary, librarian, documentation manager, and application generator.

These tools incorporate an interactive screen menu interface for specifying design level information, such as edit criteria, screen layouts, data base descriptions, data access, and control procedures. Constructs, which cannot be specified using the design facility, must be implemented with custom COBOL code.

COBOL code generators do not support the degree of integrated functionality or data base management capability provided by the leading fully-integrated application generators. They are complex products that do not accommodate a user-friendly interface. Their primary strength is that they generate efficient COBOL code, which does not impose a significant performance penalty at run time.

The combination of a CASE front end coupled with a COBOL generator back end could pose a serious competitive threat to more traditional 4GL products, such as IDEAL, NATURAL, ADS, CSP, MANTIS, and MODEL 204. Such a combination provides support for the entire life-cycle process and does not exact a significant run-time performance penalty.

3.4.5 Run-Time Performance

Performance in an on-line transaction processing environment is an important issue in evaluating the applicability of a high-productivity tool. Several tools, including MODEL 204 and NATURAL, have earned reputations for relatively high performance in relational data base management operations. However, all full-function application generators exact a run-time performance penalty relative to hand-generated COBOL code. Production-oriented applications produced by application generators run about twice as slowly than applications coded by hand. This performance penalty is offset by the fact that applications can generally be developed 7 to 10 times faster with an application generator than with hand code.

As noted above, COBOL code generators, such as APS, GAMMA, PACBASE, TELON, and TRANSFORM cause a smaller run-time performance penalty than application generators. However, they are more difficult to use and provide smaller improvement in productivity relative to hand-coding in COBOL.

Over 90% of most applications are built using an application generator, and applications that have severe on-line performance requirements are developed using a combination of an application generator and hand-coded COBOL. Only the highest speed loops or most critical transaction processing bottlenecks still warrant hand-coding.

3.4.6 Development Productivity

Most 4GL tools demonstrate about a 10:1 improvement in productivity relative to COBOL for business applications that do not require large amounts of complex procedural logic. Large gains in productivity are achieved by the non-procedural components of the tools; i.e., the ability to support very rapid specification of data dictionary entries, data views, edit criteria, display screens, menus, reports, graphics, and simple prototypes. Productivity gains are reported in the range of 10–20:1, relative to COBOL for on-line transaction processing applications involving large numbers of screens, transactions, and reports.

Lower productivity gains are reported for applications requiring extensive amounts of procedural logic. Productivity gains in the range of 3:1 relative to COBOL are closer to the norm for the specification of complex procedural logic using integrated application generators.

3.4.7 Reluctance to Use High-Productivity Tools

Many IS organizations have been reluctant to utilize high-productivity tools to implement large, complex applications. They are concerned with issues such as run-time efficiency, detailed functionality, and retraining their staff. Unfortunately, COBOL is still widely regarded by IS organizations as the preferable language for building production systems.

Properly used, high-productivity tools for DP professionals can provide substantial strategic advantages to corporations. Using these tools, new applications can be implemented much faster than with COBOL. In addition, the corporation can react more rapidly and effectively to competitive pressures. Improvements in the technology of high-productivity tools for DP professionals, such as CASE front ends, COBOL generator back ends, expert systems, and embedded methodologies, will greatly expand their ranges of applicability.

3.4.8 Automated Development Techniques

A primary advantage of application generators for DP professionals is their ability to replace manual development techniques with automated processes. Automated techniques have major advantages relative to manual techniques as follows:

- Manual techniques are incapable of providing the 10:1 productivity increase that is required and should be replaced by automatic techniques wherever possible.
- Automation of manually-oriented conventional or structured techniques is not productive and should be avoided. Tools that are based on automated procedures are inherently much more productive than tools that attempt to automate a manual process.
- Automated tools require entirely new methodologies (such as information engineering) that are based on automated techniques.

Automatic code generation is an integral part of automated development techniques. The non-procedural (i.e., non-coding) components of full-function 4GLs make it easy to specify to the computer what is to be done. Using most leading full-function application generators, it is relatively easy to use non-procedural functions to formulate a data base query, specify a report, plot a graph, or analyze data using statistical tools. Most of these tools contain user-friendly interfaces to define data variables, data attributes, edit criteria, screen layouts, menu sequences, and interactive dialogues.

These non-procedural components of 4GLs can be used effectively by non-DP professionals to access data, generate simple data entry, edit transactions, and produce reports or graphs. These same non-procedural components can be used by experienced systems analysts in building prototype systems for demonstration to an end user in a rapid prototyping development life-cycle process. All these tasks can be performed without writing one line of procedural logic.

The procedural component of full-function 4GLs is used to specify the procedural logic required in most applications. The procedural language used by 4GLs is a high-level programming language that includes input/output statements, loops, conditions, control statements, arithmetic and assignment statements.

A typical fourth-generation procedural language is similar to COBOL but operates at a much higher level. In some 4GLs such as NATURAL, IDEAL, MODEL 204, and APPLICATION FACTORY, the procedural language is functional enough to replace COBOL for most business applications. Other less procedural languages require usage of COBOL, FORTRAN, PL/I, APL, or assembler to implement specialized procedural logic.

For all 4GLs, the problem exists that specification of procedural logic is a slow process compared with the specification of non-procedural functions, such as the generation of screens, reports, graphics, and on-line transaction dialogues. Applications requiring only a relatively small amount of specialized procedural logic are developed 10 to 15 times faster with a 4GL than with COBOL.

Unfortunately, most real-world applications developed by DP professionals require a great deal of procedural logic. The logic is used to specify detailed processing functions, utility functions, error handling conditions, highly customized, formatted reports, specialized interfaces, etc. In one large application, for example, 15% of the total effort was devoted to the non-procedural specification of screens and reports, however, 35% of the total effort was in coding utility routines using the fourth-generation procedural language.

In general, if an application requires a substantial amount of procedural logic, the overall productivity improvement provided by the 4GL will be lessened.

To minimize the time required to specify procedural logic, various techniques are employed by different 4GL products. Both ADS/OnLine and APPLICATION FACTORY encourage specification of small modules of logic tied directly to specific events in the application. (In APPLICATION FACTORY, logic modules can be attached to screen events, report events, data base access events, menu events, or data entry events.) This is to eliminate the need for large blocks of procedural code and to simplify maintenance.

Action diagrams have been used by products, such as NATURAL and APPLICATION FACTORY, to simplify the specification of procedural logic. These clearly show the logical structure of the procedural code.

Major improvements in the specification of complex, production-oriented systems will be achieved by a new technology based on CASE tools, expert system techniques, and advanced development methodologies.

3.4.9 Trends in DP Professional Computing

Several technological trends are converging that will have a major impact on the evolution of high-productivity tools for DP professionals. These trends include the following:

- introduction of powerful, desk-top **workstations** based on the Intel 80386 microprocessor (e.g., the IBM Personal System/2, Model 80);
- incorporation of **CASE technology** as a graphically-oriented frontend to application and code generators;
- utilization of **expert systems** to analyze specifications for logical consistency and correctness and to implement an embedded life-cycle process within the tool;
- adoption of **advanced development methodologies**, such as information engineering, interactive JAD and Timebox, to improve the communication process between end users and analysts and to speed up the development of applications.

The impact of these trends on the future evolution of application generation tools for DP professionals is summarized as follows.

3.4.10 Trends in Intelligent Workstations

One important change now occurring is the rapid acceptance of the IBM PC as a key component of the hardware/software architecture for both end users and DP professionals. The pending introduction of 80386-based workstations, such as the IBM Personal System/2, Model 80, will create major developments in the applicability of desktop workstations. It is already possible to purchase PC-compatible workstations supporting the following features:

- 3 MIPS processing rate,
- 16 MB RAM,
- 130 MB hard disk,
- 500 MB CD-ROM, and
- high-resolution graphics display terminals (1000 by 1000 pixels).

Within two years, workstations of this power will be available for between

$5,000 and $6,000 and be widely used. Their capabilities will include the following:

- provide CAD-type workstation power at PC cost;
- use of specialized chips to implement software layers, such as virtual memory, multi-tasking, multi-users, high-resolution graphics, data base management, communications interfaces, etc;
- use of CASE technology to support graphically-oriented front-end analysis, design and specification functions;
- incorporation of expert system techniques;
- major improvements in human factors;
- built-in life-cycle development processes.

Figure 3-9 illustrates the rapidly dropping cost of a MIPS (millions of instructions per second) of processing power. The new Compaq 386 microcomputer

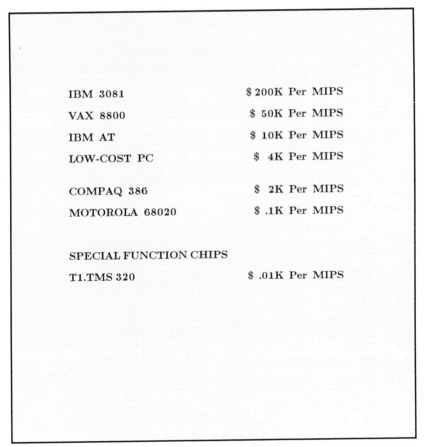

Figure 3-9. Cost of MIPS.

costs only about $2000 per MIPS, while an IBM 3081 costs about $200,000 per MIPS (one hundred times more than a Compaq 386!). Although only a small fraction of current available workstation MIPS are being utilized, this percentage will rise as the computational workload is shifted toward low-cost, but powerful, desktop workstations.

The great disparity in the cost/performance ratio of mainframes to micros will cause many to switch from mainframes to desktop workstations. It will become hard to justify the development of applications or the manipulation of information in the mainframe environment. The desktop workstation is the ideal environment to solve business problems, process information, and specify new applications.

The rapid proliferation of PCs is causing significant changes in the hardware/ software architecture required to support both end users and DP professionals. As discussed, the hardware architecture for many organizations is evolving into a multi-level hierarchy consisting of networked PCs, departmental minicomputers, and corporate mainframes. Within this architecture, individuals at PCs access and extract information from departmental or corporate data bases. The extracted data is downloaded transparently to the PC in a standard format, ready to be processed directly via standard PC utilities, such as Lotus 1-2-3, dBASE III, Javelin, etc. Alternatively, the data can be processed by specialized applications developed using PC-based application generation systems.

In accordance with strict data upload controls, any data, process models, and application specifications prepared at the PC level may be uploaded for consolidation within departmental or corporate data bases. To transfer data efficiently between elements of homogeneous or heterogeneous architectures, peer-to-peer communications (rather than 3270 emulation) should be used. Within this architecture, the mainframe is primarily for storaging of the corporate data base and for batch processing. The corporate data base is the central repository for corporate-wide process and data definitions, as well as for data that has been consolidated from all operational units of the organization.

To promote compatibility between disparate computer architectures, a variety of standards are being adopted that will govern the future evolution of hardware, software, data bases, file formats, and communication interfaces. Evolving standards in hardware and software are summarized in Figure 3-10.

3.4.11 Comparison of Product Functionality

Figure 3-11 shows a matrix that compares the functionality of application generators for DP professionals, reviewed in *Computer-Aided Software Engineering*, Volume 5 of **The James Martin Productivity Series**. Each row of the matrix summarizes the functionality of a specific product. Columns of the matrix show the availability of a particular function, such as hardware environment, integrated functionality, human factoring, and data base support functions, across all products.

- open hardware architecture based on the IBM PC;

- establishment of the Intel 80386-based IBM PS/2 Model 80 as the standard high-performance desktop workstation;

- open software architecture based on dual support for both MS-DOS (low-level applications) and OS/2 (high-level applications operating within an integrated, windowed, multi-user, multi-tasking environment);

- DBMS standard based on DB2 and SQL/DS;

- SQL language standard for data base query and reporting;

- communication standards based on peer-to-peer communications utilizing SNA or OSI protocols. Within SNA, standards include use of DIA and DCA formats, LU 6.2 interconnection protocol, SNADS and DISOSS for office communications, the token-ring baseband standard for exchanging information between distributed systems and the use of the OS/2 communications monitor to control PC LAN communications.

- increasing utilization of the evolving SAA (Systems Application Architecture) to provide a standard software environment supporting a diverse, multi-vendor hardware environment.

Figure 3-10. Evolving hardware/software standards.

3.5   Computer-Aided Software Engineering—CASE

Major improvements in application and code generation systems for DP professionals will result from the integration of (CASE) techniques with application generators. CASE tools are described in *Computer-Aided Software Engineering*, Volume 6 of **The James Martin Productivity Series**. An important objective of CASE products is to generate complete application code automatically from consistent design specifications.

Computer-Aided Software Engineering techniques enforce a disciplined engineering approach to the design and development of systems, and their introduction will allow substantial improvements in application generation systems for DP professionals. Though CASE products emphasize the design and analysis

Products	ENVIRONMENT					APPLICATION-GENERATION FUNCTIONS														HUMAN FACTORING				DATA–BASE SUPPORT			
	IBM Environment	DEC Environment	Tool Available Only on PC	Micro-to-Mainframe Link	Full PC Implementation	Query Language	Report Generator	Screen Painter/Data Entry	Graphics Generator	Decision-Support Tools	Subset for End Users	Primarily for DP Professionals	Procedural Language	Interface to Action Diagrams	Well-Structured Code	Provable Specifications	Heavy-Duty Computing	Full COBOL Replacement	Recommended for Info. Centers	Human Factoring (scale of 1-5)	HELP Facility	Computer-Aided Instruction	Computer-Aided Thinking	Support of Data-Base Management	Standard DBMS Package	Data Dictionary	Data-Modeling Tool
ADS/OnLine	■	□	□	■	□	■	■	■	□	□	■	■	■	□	■	□	■	■	□	3	■	□	□	■	■	■	□
APPL. FACTORY	□	■	□	■	□	■	■	■	■	□	■	■	■	■	□	■	■	■	□	4	■	□	■	■	■	■	■
CSP	■	□	□	□	■	■	■	■	■	□	■	■	□	■	□	□	■	□	3	■	□	□	■	□	□	□	
IDEAL	■	□	□	■	■	■	■	□	□	■	■	■	□	■	□	■	□	3	■	■	□	■	■	■	■		
LINC II	□	□	□	■	■	■	■	■	■	■	■	□	■	□	■	■	□	4	■	■	□	■	■	■	■		
MANTIS	■	■	□	■	□	■	■	■	■	■	■	■	■	■	■	■	□	3	■	■	□	■	■	■	■		
MODEL 204	■	□	□	■	□	■	■	■	□	■	■	■	□	■	□	■	■	■	3	■	□	□	■	■	■	□	
NATURAL	■	■	□	■	□	■	■	■	■	□	■	■	■	■	■	□	■	■	4	■	■	□	■	■	■	□	

Figure 3-11. Functionality matrix for representative application generators for DP professionals.

phases of the development life cycle, they provide processes and tools for every phase of the life cycle. CASE technology promises software development the same benefits CAD/CAM has brought to manufacturing.

3.5.1 Components of CASE Products

Figure 3-12 illustrates key components of leading CASE products. These include: front-end diagramming tools, used to create specifications in graphical form; and a central repository (or Encyclopedia), used to store and maintain the components of the system specification. A design analyzer is used to detect logical inconsistencies and incompleteness in the design specifications. Expert system techniques are beginning to be used to build a knowledge base of specifications and rules that is processed by the design analyzer. With few tools, application specifications can be converted automatically into code using an integrated code generator.

Components of technically advanced CASE products include the following:

- **CAD/CAP Diagramming Techniques:** Most CASE tools utilize computer-aided design and programming techniques to create diagrams of

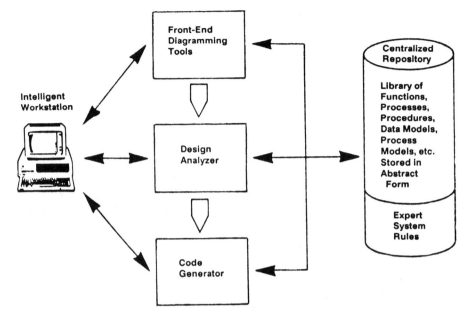

Figure 3-12. Key components of CASE products.

the system design. Analysts are able to create, verify, and revise drawings on an interactive screen. CASE tools support diagramming techniques associated with a variety of development methodologies, including modern, information engineering techniques and older, manually-oriented, structured engineering techniques such as Yourdon-DeMarco, Gane & Sarson, Jackson, Warnier-Orr, and others.

- **Design Analyzer:** The function of the design analyzer is to detect internal inconsistencies, ambiguities, and incompleteness in the design specifications. To provide rigorous consistency and completeness checks, it is important for the analyzer to be based on an underlying formal information model. Design analyzers in current CASE tools are being improved to incorporate smart editors, intelligent assistants, and expert systems.

- **Code Generator:** Many CASE tools integrate with a code generation module that automatically generates code from consistent design specifications. The CASE tool serves as a front end to either a fully-integrated application generator for DP professionals (e.g., ADS/OnLine, APPLICATION FACTORY, IDEAL, MANTIS, MODEL 204, or NATURAL) or a COBOL code generator (e.g., APS, GAMMA, PACBASE, TELON, or TRANSFORM).

- **Methodologies:** CASE tools incorporate a disciplined methodology that guides the analyst, step-by-step, in the application of the tool. The specification of a comprehensive, well-defined development process brings a more standardized approach to the design and systems implementation and enables management to gain better control over the development process.

3.5.2 Code Generators

COBOL generators, such as APS from Sage Systems, Inc., GAMMA from KnowledgeWare, Inc., PACBASE from CGI Systems, Inc., TELON from Pansophic Systems, Inc., and TRANSFORM from Transform Logic Corporation have been used to increase the productivity of DP professionals. Although these tools are approximately 2 to 3 times more productive than COBOL programming, they lack completeness and do not incorporate front-end design tools; they provide support for only a portion of the development life-cycle process. In addition, COBOL generators do not produce all COBOL code automatically—significant portions of an application must be coded by hand—and the lack of powerful dictionaries and front-end design tools severely limits the usefulness of COBOL generators for complex applications.

3.5.3 Limitations of 4GL Products

Highly-integrated 4GLs, such as ADS/OnLine from Cullinet Software, Inc., APPLICATION FACTORY from Cortex Corporation, IDEAL from Applied Data Research, Inc., MANTIS from Cincom Systems, Inc., MODEL 204 from Computer Corporation of America, and NATURAL from Software AG were introduced to aid DP professionals in the development of complex systems. Each provides a wide variety of integrated functions, including a DBMS, nonprocedural functions (screen and report generation, data base queries, decision support, graphics, etc.), as well as a high-level procedural language. Many organizations demonstrated that 4GL tools can be used effectively to achieve major improvements in productivity—in many cases, a 10:1 improvement in productivity over COBOL.

Despite their potential for productivity improvements, 4GL tools designed for use by DP professionals have not replaced COBOL as the language of choice for the implementation of complex systems. This is attributed to many factors, including the following:

- Perceived lack of performance in an on-line transaction-processing environment. 4GLs impose a performance penalty in machine resources and processing speed relative to hand-generated COBOL programs. Although it varies greatly, this performance penalty is around 100%. For many applications, particularly heavily loaded, on-line transaction-processing applications, a performance penalty of more than 10% is unacceptable. However, for many organizations, the ability to generate applications 5 to 10 times faster than with hand-coding techniques is more important than run-time performance.

- Lack of support for the entire development life cycle process, particularly the critical analysis and design phases.
- Reluctance on the part of DP professionals to use a tool that appears to lack flexibility and functional capabilities of third-generation languages such as COBOL.
- Lack of well-documented life-cycle process for 4GLs.

3.5.4 I-CASE—An Integrated CASE Environment

CASE tools, which are not linked to code generators and support only the analysis and design phases, do not overcome the limitations of current 4GL products. They are used to enter specifications in graphical form and check the logical consistency and completeness of the specifications.

The resulting set of specifications must then be converted by hand into program code. Due to the inefficiency of the programming process, some current CASE tools offer only limited gains in productivity.

A major challenge for all vendors of CASE products is to implement an integrated architecture that provides a tight linkage between a CASE tool and an associated code generator. I-CASE (integrated CASE) describes such an environment where the CASE product and the code generator are closely coupled. An I-CASE architecture incorporates an integrated family of tools that supports the entire life-cycle process. These tools include the following:

- planning tools,
- analysis tools,
- design tools,
- tightly integrated code generator capable of generating highly efficient code,
- data base generator,
- documentation generator, and
- project management aids.

Several vendors (KnowledgeWare, TI, Cortex, Index Technology and CGI) have taken steps to develop tightly integrated interfaces between their CASE products and an associated code generator. The objective is to generate code automatically from logically consistent and complete graphical specifications.

An alternative approach, pursued by Index Technology and other vendors, is to provide flexible linkages between CASE tools and a variety of code and application generators. This approach would be facilitated through the adoption by the industry of a standard electronic data interchange format, governing the transmission of text and graphic data. In the near future, CASE products will be interfaced to a wide variety of code generators and 4GL application generators.

CASE tools, coupled with COBOL generators (e.g., APS, GAMMA,

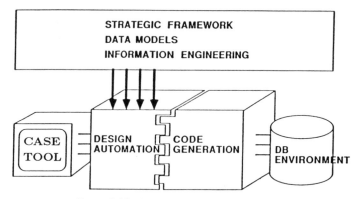

Figure 3-13. Integrated CASE environment.

PACBASE, TELON, or TRANSFORM), offer the potential of overcoming the limitations of current 4GL products. Figure 3-13 illustrates the use of a front-end CASE tool to enter and check specifications, while a back-end generator converts these specifications directly into COBOL code. Initial products may use import/export file facilities to link the CASE tool's repository to the data dictionary facilities of the code generator on the mainframe. It is unlikely that a simple import/export file facility will be an adequate interface between a CASE product and an associated code generator: much tighter coupling between these components may be necessary in order to generate efficient code.

The combination of a front-end CASE tool and a back-end COBOL generator supports the entire life-cycle process and generates highly efficient code that may be used without performance penalty in a heavily loaded, transaction-processing environment. Some IS organizations that are committed to COBOL choose to skip over current 4GL technology and move directly to the next generation of tools—CASE front ends coupled to efficient code generators.

Many CASE products will provide a generalized and customizable interface to a variety of code generators. These products will support the entire life cycle and balance the investment made in mainframe code generation facilities. CASE tools can be interfaced to more traditional 4GL products, such as ADS/OnLine, APPLICATION FACTORY, IDEAL, MANTIS, MODEL 204, and NATURAL APPLICATIONS FACTORY from Cortex Corporation is the first traditional 4GL application generator to be interfaced to a CASE front end.

Figure 3-14 illustrates a work-group specification environment, supported by the Excelerator product from Index Technology Corporation. In a work-group environment, application specifications generated by an individual analyst at a PC are checked locally for consistency and completeness. Periodically, the specifications from all analysts are consolidated on the host computer, where they are checked for consistency and completeness at the project level.

CASE tools, in combination with existing COBOL generators or application

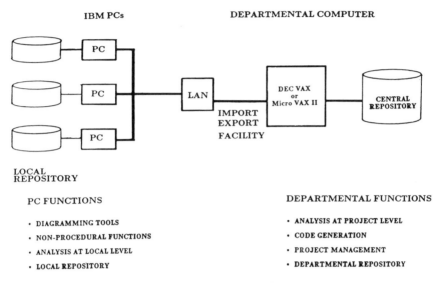

Figure 3-14. Work group environment.

generators for DP professionals, offer potential support of the entire life-cycle process. These tools apply rigorous engineering principles to the development and analysis of software specifications. They convert specifications in graphical form directly into code. CASE technology represents a new approach to the implementation of complex systems. The tools automate all phases of the life-cycle process and tie application development more closely with the strategic operations of the business.

As noted above, the combination of a CASE front-end tool and a back-end COBOL generator poses a serious competitive threat to the current generation of 4GL products such as NATURAL, IDEAL, ADS, CSP, MANTIS, and MODEL 204. CASE tools provide improved support for the early phases of the life-cycle process, while the COBOL generator produces highly efficient code. This combination of products may be attractive to IS organizations that avoid use of current 4GL products due to a perceived lack of run-time performance or lack of coverage of the entire life-cycle process.

3.6 Expert System Tools

A small number of tools are beginning to incorporate rule-based expert system techniques to aid the systems analyst in designing and implementing applications. The Information Engineering Workbench from KnowledgeWare is the first CASE tool to apply expert system techniques to the development of computable specifications in a CASE workbench environment. The tool uses approximately 1200 expert system rules to enforce design constraints.

CASE tools, incorporating expert system techniques, offer the potential of a highly effective front-end analysis and design facility for application generators oriented toward DP professionals (e.g., ADS/OnLine, APPLICATION FACTORY, CSP, IDEAL, LINC II, MANTIS, MODEL 204, and NATURAL) or for COBOL generators (e.g., APS, GAMMA, PACBASE, TELON, and TRANSFORM). In the future, expert systems will be used extensively as part of advanced prototyping methodologies to develop logically consistent, computable specifications.

Chapter 4

Languages for Specification, Design, and Prototyping

VALDIS BERZINS and LUQI
Computer Science Department
Naval Postgraduate School
Monterey, CA

INTRODUCTION

This chapter discusses how specification, design, and prototyping languages support new paradigms for software development. The languages used in the Computer Aided Software Engineering (CASE) paradigms differ from languages used in traditional software development because they must support a higher level of automation at the early stages. The traditional software life cycle consists of a series of phases sometimes called requirements analysis, functional specification, architectural design, module design, implementation, testing, and evolution (Figure 4-1). The result of each phase is a document serving as the starting point for the next phase or an error report requiring reconsideration of the earlier phases. Traditionally, the phases before implementation were carried out by manual processes, and the resulting documents expressed in informal notations. The implementation phase produces a document expressed in a programming language. Programming languages are formal notations processed by a variety of automated tools, such as compilers, static analyzers, debuggers, execution profilers, etc. Most computer-aided design in traditional software development environments is applied in the implementation and later phases.

A formal language is a notation with a clearly defined syntax and semantics. Formal languages are critical components of a CASE environment because they must achieve significant levels of computer-aided design with current technologies. Automated tools are capable of detecting structure in a notation if the structure is formally defined, and responds to aspects of its meaning, only if the meaning of the aspect has been formally defined. The tools applicable to informal notations usually treat them as uninterpreted text strings, limiting the tools to bookkeeping functions such as version control. Notations with a formally defined syntax but an informal semantics can support tools sensitive to the structure of the syntax, such as pretty printers and syntax-directed editors.

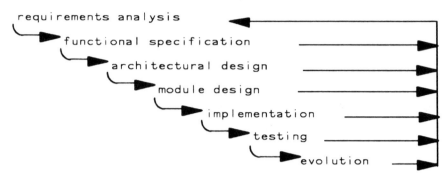

Figure 4-1. Traditional software life cycle.

If both the syntax and semantics of a special purpose language are fixed and clearly defined, it becomes possible to create automated tools for analysis, transformation, or execution of the aspects of the software system captured by the language and its conceptual model.

The new software development paradigms are a solution to problems with traditional development methods, requiring great effort to produce systems that do not meet the user's needs. These problems are largely caused by labor intensive tasks at the early stages of development. Currently there are several ways to approach these problems. One is to automate some tasks in the early stages of the traditional life cycle. Examples of this approach are to work on executable specification languages and formal verification. Another CASE approach introduces the prototyping software life cycle.

A software prototype is an executable model or a pilot version of a proposed system. The prototype is a partial representation of the proposed system, used as an aid in requirements analysis and system design through an iterative negotiation process between the systems analyst and the customer. The construction activity leading to such a prototype is prototyping. The customer describes the requirements, while the analyst interprets them and builds a prototype. The analyst then demonstrates the execution of the prototype to the customer. Requirements are adjusted based on feedback from the customer, and the prototype is modified until both customer and analyst agree on the requirements: this process is illustrated in Figure 4-2.

Formal languages for the specification, design, and prototyping of software systems are required to support the new CASE paradigms, since they involve computer-aided analysis and design from the earliest stages of software development. In the new paradigm, the goals and functions of the intended system are negotiated in the context of a computer-aided analysis of the customer's problem.

A CASE environment with knowledge-based assistants for each phase of development starting with requirements analysis is an example of this approach. The computer-aided aspects of the process include completeness and consist-

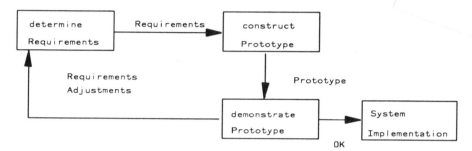

Figure 4-2. The prototyping life cycle.

ency checking, displaying descriptions of the system from various viewpoints, demonstrations of prototypes, concurrency and configuration control for the design data, and information retrieval functions. The CASE tools in such an environment depend on each other and must be integrated together to meet this goal. Such integration depends both on formal languages and emerging technologies for managing engineering databases.[27-29,38]

A specification language records a specification. A specification is a black-box description of the behavior of a software system or one of its components. The black-box description explains a software component in terms of the data that crosses the boundary of the box, without mentioning the mechanism inside the box. A specification language provides simple abstract descriptions of complex behaviors that can be easily understood and mechanically analyzed.

A design language records a design. A design is a glass-box description of a software system or component. The glass-box description gives the decomposition of a component into lower level components and defines their interconnections in terms of both data and control. A design language provides simple abstract descriptions of system structure that can be easily understood and mechanically analyzed.

A prototyping language defines an executable model of a system, using both black-box and glass-box descriptions. Some meta-programming and functional programming languages have similar properties. However, a prototyping language is not required to give detailed algorithms for all components of the system as long as it is descriptive and executable. Prototyping language allows an analyst to create and modify a working system quickly, while a programming language is optimized to allow a programmer to produce a time and space efficient implementation. A prototyping language supports simple and abstract system descriptions, locality of information, reuse, and adaptability at the expense of execution efficiency. It should facilitate recording specification and design information, subject to the constraint that the final product must be executable.

The difference between specification and design languages is the difference between interface and mechanism: a specification says what is to be done, and a design says how to do it. They serve as a precise medium of communication between the members of a development team working on a large system. The evaluation criterion for both specification and design languages is their ability to support simple, concise, and understandable descriptions of complex processes. They should be executable but simplicity of expression takes precedence when the two considerations conflict. It is important to determine the properties of a specification and to certify that a design "realizes" a specification. Execution can help attain these goals, but it is not the only way to do so and not necessarily the most effective way.

Prototyping languages are used in requirements analysis for requirements validation by early demonstrations to the customer. They evaluate competing design alternatives, validation of system structure, and feasibility studies. Prototypes can demonstrate the feasibility of real-time constraints and record and test interfaces and interconnections. Specification languages are used for recording external interfaces in the functional specification stage and for recording internal interfaces during architectural design at the highest levels of abstraction. They verify the correctness and completeness of a design or implementation. Design languages are used for recording conventions and interconnections during architectural design and module design.

It is useful to briefly examine the history of language development, because the terminology for describing languages has been changing dramatically along with implementation technology. Originally any compiled programming language was a very high level language. As systems became more complex, the meaning of the term shifted towards design languages that describe system structure without introducing low level implementation details and generalized components, which can be adapted to many different situations. Eventually technology improved so programming languages could support abstraction and generalization (for example, Ada and Smalltalk). As systems became larger, the meaning of the term shifted again, towards languages describing what a system is supposed to do, without specifying how the system is to accomplish its goals. Technology is advancing to the point where some languages in these categories are executable as well (for example, Prolog, Refine, and PSDL). The concept of a very high level language is always changing and depends on the current state of compiler technology and the speed, memory capacity, and cost of available hardware.

This chapter presents languages for specification, design, and prototyping. The authors discuss these classes of languages one at a time to simplify the presentation. Many of the existing languages for the software development described combine aspects from several of these categories. The authors describe the characteristic properties and restrictions for the languages in each category, examine ways to use the languages, and compare them with other languages. This chapter is limited to general purpose languages that span a range of applications. Application specific "fourth generation" languages (4GL), are discussed in Chapter 3.

1 SPECIFICATION LANGUAGES

A specification language describes the interfaces of a software system or component. It is used for formulation, analysis, communication, and retrieval. A specification language provides a set of concepts and notations which allows the analyst or designer to formulate an interface for a system or component. Notations are important for inventing large systems because the user is limited in the number of items they can consider at the same time. Considering each aspect of a system in isolation and recording the result before proceeding to the next overcomes this limitation. The language used is important because it influences the analyst's thinking and determines what is easiest to express and what is impossible or impractically difficult. A specification language should help the analyst to construct a simpler conceptual model for the intended system and establish and maintain its conceptual integrity.

A formal specification language allows the proposed interface to be analyzed with respect to many different properties. At a structural level, the language can help the analyst organize his/her thoughts and determine which pieces of information are missing. At a semantic level, the language can determine properties of the description and the behavior of the proposed interface. Examples of such properties include type consistency, correctness of a particular response for a particular input, the set of correct responses for a particular input, freedom from deadlock for multistep protocols, coverage of all possible input values, satisfiability, uniqueness of outputs, and consistency with a proposed design. These semantic properties cannot be determined without a precise specification.

The specification language is a medium for communication between the analysts, the development team, and the customers. The specifications form part of the contract agreement governing a development project and act as a primary source of information about what the designers and implementors are supposed to accomplish. Large systems involve many users over a long period of time. In large organizations, oral communication is ineffective, and decisions have to be written down and circulated. Written specifications avoid repeating the same information to different audiences, getting everyone together at the same time, or relying on imperfect memories. The information in the specification is also the basis for customer review, although it may be necessary to paraphrase the information[25,52] and provide summaries and simplified views.

Specifications also have an important role in retrieving reusable software components. To find an existing component that can perform a given task, it is necessary to describe the required behavior and match it to descriptions of the behavior of existing components. For large component libraries, this is a major task that can benefit from mechanical assistance,[37,38] suggesting reusable components be stored with formal specifications. The CASE tool performing this function is known as a software base management system.[55]

The primary benefits of using a formal specification language are precision and the potential for automation, which lead to better software products. The consequences of not using a formal specification language are miscommunication, a manual work style, and software that is hard to use and understand. Miscommunication is caused by ambiguity and incompleteness, allowing an author to have a different interpretation than the readers. It also leads to system faults. Manual processing leads to a larger number of faults because users make more errors than programs do and do not have enough time and patience to do exhaustive error checking. Because informal languages do not guide the analysts' thinking or support simplifying transformations very well, systems developed without a formal specification language are more complex than they have to be.

A specification language should have the following properties:

- Precision—each statement should have a single, well defined meaning.
- Abstractness—to completely define interface behavior without considering mechanisms and low level details.
- Expressiveness—allow brief descriptions of common system behaviors, which are understandable. Abbreviations that must be expanded before they can be understood are not expressive in this sense. Brief descriptions must be constructible by users in a natural way.
- Simplicity—rules describing the meaning of the language should be simple, without exceptions or interactions between multiple components. This is important both for easy learning and easy automation. It is also important to avoid misunderstandings, because situations where extensive reasoning is required to determine the meaning of a statement provides opportunities for errors of interpretation.
- Locality—support localized description units with limited interactions and the dependencies between the units should be mechanically detectable. This reduces the amount of information needed to understand or modify a given aspect of a specification to a manageable level and supports mechanical aid in assembling and displaying the information needed for a single specification step.
- Tractability—to implement a variety of automated aids for analyzing, transforming, and implementing subsets of the specification language. While subsets of the language that can be handled by the tools should be large, it may not be possible to cover the entire language without compromising the abstractness and expressiveness of the language.
- Adaptability—support the description of general purpose components and the adaptation of those components to particular situations. Generic modules and inheritance mechanisms are two well known ways to support adaptability.

Specification languages are designed for CASE paradigms following the traditional software life cycle. A specification language is used in functional specification to define external interfaces of the system and in architectural design to define internal interfaces of the system.

The relation between requirements and specifications is controversial, and there has been no clear agreement on the distinction between the two.[30] The authors found the following formulation useful.

A specification defines a set of disjoint interfaces. Formally, an interface is a predicate on a subset of the possible observable behaviors of a system indicating which behaviors are acceptable and which are not.

Requirements consist of functional goals for the system and constraints on its development. These constraints include limits on schedule and budget. Formally, a goal is a function from interfaces to a set of utility values. In the simplest case the utility set consists of two values, **acceptable** and **not acceptable,** in which case goals become predicates on interfaces. This corresponds to the view of a goal as an acceptance test, which does not completely capture current practice in requirements analysis. It is more realistic to view the utility set as an ordered interval of values which indicate the relative usefulness of different interfaces. This corresponds to the view of a goal as an objective function in an optimization problem.

From this standpoint, requirements analysis is the process of determining the constraints and the objective function, while functional specification is the process of solving the optimization problem. The solution to the optimization problem is an interface, represented in the specification language.

In current practice, developers have only informal and approximate descriptions of the goals that are used to guide intuitive design tradeoff decisions, producing an approximate solution to the optimization problem. Requirements analysis and functional specification often overlap in time, because the design tradeoff decisions being made require more information about some aspects of the goals, in the form of more accurate approximate descriptions. It is a matter of research whether this optimization process can be usefully automated and whether classical results from optimization theory can be applied. One difficulty is calculating accurate estimates of the budget and schedule required to implement a particular interface or class of interfaces. Another is that the descriptions of the goals available at any given time are incomplete and uncertain.

A validation step is required to demonstrate that the proposed interface, resulting from the functional specification effort, meets the user's requirements, given that it optimizes the formal model of the constraints and goals resulting from requirements analysis. This step is necessary because of the uncertainty associated with the formal model, which is incompletely understood by the user. To carry out the validation step, it is necessary to demonstrate the characteristics of the proposed interface. Because most interfaces are capable of many behaviors, such demonstrations are inherently incomplete, with statistical rather than absolute conclusions.

The relation between specifications and programs is more traditional. A program determines a set of algorithms and data structures to be used to calculate the responses of a software system or component. The correctness of a program, with respect to a given interface, can be demonstrated by showing that all possible behaviors of the proposed mechanism are acceptable with respect to the interface (proof of correctness) and it can be refuted by exhibiting a particular behavior of the mechanism that is not acceptable with respect to the interface (testing). The specification also tells the programmer and the program generation tools what is to be accomplished (implementation). In the current state of CASE technology, it is reasonable to expect that implementation will not be entirely manual or entirely automatic but the result of the cooperation between skilled programmers and a set of computer-aided design tools. This imposes a dual burden on specification languages—effective communication with both user and programs.

Specification languages are used in specification-based software design.[7] The goal of architectural design is to decompose a system into a set of simpler modules. Specification languages define the interfaces of these modules. Decomposition into simpler tasks is necessary for implementing large systems whether the design is created by the user or CASE tools. Precise specifications are required to guide implementation, especially if the process is computer-assisted.

There has been increasing interest in executable specification languages, motivated by two main considerations:

(1) automated prototyping for validating requirements and specifications, and
(2) automated implementation of production quality software.

The main distinction between the two versions of the problem is that the first version relaxes performance constraints while the second does not. However, both versions of the problem are algorithmically unsolvable in the general case. The practical impact of an "executable" specification language can be judged by considering the expressiveness of the entire language, the expressiveness of its executable subset, and the relative difficulty of transforming simple but non-executable specifications into executable equivalents.

1.1   Approaches to Specifications

Many specification languages use a form of predicate logic to describe the constraints and properties of input and output of a black box in the system, independent of the algorithms and data structures used for calculating the outputs of the box. This has both advantages and disadvantages. Quantifiers are convenient to use because they allow many problems to be specified in a simple, compact and natural way. This allows the system specifier to work at the black box level, concentrating on behaviors of the system rather than on the mechanisms of implementing the system. Quantifiers can lead to implementation difficulties. Specification languages that include unrestricted integers and quantifiers can specify functions that are not computable. Such functions are impossible to implement perfectly, because any partially correct implementation will have some input values where execution will fail to terminate even though the specified function has a well defined value. An implementation is partially correct if it never produces an output that conflicts with the specification. While a plausible response to this difficulty is that customers will not specify non-computable functions in practical projects, there are related difficulties that are less easily avoided.

Consider a function with an output y subject to the following specification.

if for all (x: integer :: f(x) = g(x)) then y = 0 else y = 1

This is an example of a conditional with a universal quantifier in the test predicate, in the syntax of Spec 87.[6,7] The output y is to be zero if functions f and g have the same value for all integer arguments and one otherwise. Any compiler that handles all specifications of this form solves the equivalence problem for recursive functions, which is well known to be undecidable. According to Rice's theorem, examples of specification forms with this property are plentiful.[48] This means any specification compiler will have many specifications for which compilation will fail to terminate or will produce an implementation that either produces incorrect results or fails to terminate for some inputs. An example of the first case is an implementation strategy where the compiler tries to prove both theorems "$f = g$" and "$f \neq g$" in parallel, producing the constant 0 or the constant 1 as an implementation if the corresponding goal succeeds and taking forever to compile if it cannot decide. An example of the second case is an implementation strategy where the compiler produces a program that tries the equivalence of f and g on particular integers until it discovers a difference and produces a 1 and fails to terminate if there are no differences.

Neither alternative is very appealing. More practical approaches either impose a time limit and report failures for compilations that are too difficult, or restrict the specification language to forms that can be successfully compiled. The second alternative is less attractive because it is difficult to impose syntactic restrictions that will guarantee successful compilation without damaging the abstractness, expressiveness, and simplicity of the specification language. Under the first alternative, the designer can initially work with the simplest formulation and later help the specification compiler over difficult spots by adding annotations or giving interactive advice. The annotations can be removed in a mechanically produced summary when the specifications are used for communication rather than execution, thus regaining the initial simplicity.

1.2   Different Approaches to Specification Languages

One well established category of specification languages is based on heterogeneous algebras. Some of the specification languages in this category include

Larch[19,20] and Clear.[8] The languages in this class are geared towards specifying abstract data types, and many of them support correctness proofs for programs written using the data types.[45] In the algebraic approach data types are specified by giving axioms for the primitive operations of the type in the form of conditional equations. By adding restrictions on the form of the axioms, algebraic specifications can be made executable.[12,17]

One set of restrictions that will suffice to make a set of algebraic specifications executable is the following:

- The axioms must be orientable so that the right hand side of each equation is strictly less than the left hand side with respect to some well founded ordering on symbolic terms.
- The oriented axioms must be confluent.[22]
- The set of axioms must be sufficiently complete.[17]
- The left hand side of each axiom must contain at least one instance of a constructor operation.

These conditions allow the axioms to be treated as rewrite rules. The first condition ensures that all rewrite sequences terminate, so that each expression has a normal form. The second condition ensures that the result of a rewrite sequence is independent of the order in which the axioms are applied, so that all equivalent expressions have the same normal form. The Knuth-Bendix algorithm can be used to check for confluence and to transform some sets of axioms without the property into equivalent sets with the property.[22] The third condition ensures every non-constructor operation applied to variable-free terms is provably equivalent to a constant of another type with respect to the axioms. An operation is a constructor if its range is the type being defined. Because a constant of another type contains no constructor operations, it must be in normal form, and since the normal form is unique, all rewrite sequences for a non-constructor expression must result in a constant. This ensures that all variable free terms of other types can be evaluated by applying the rewrite rules.

An example of an algebraic specification with these properties is given as the following:

```
type set[t]
  empty(): set[t]
  add(t, set[t]): set[t]
  in(t, set[t]): boolean
  subset(set[t], set[t]): boolean
  equal(set[t], set[t]): boolean
axioms
  in(x, empty) = false
  in(x, add(y, s)) = equal(x, y) or in(x, s)
```

```
    subset(empty, s) = true
    subset(add(x, s1), s2) = in(x, s2) and subset(s1, s2)
    equal(s1, s2) = subset(s1, s2) and subset(s2, s1)
  end
```

The free variables in each equation are implicitly universally quantified. Equations in this form are equivalent to recursive definitions of the non-constructor operations, if values of the type are represented as symbolic expressions in terms of the constructor operations. Consequently, writing specifications in the restricted form is much like programming. Sometimes it is necessary to introduce auxiliary operations to define the operations in which one is interested.[42] In the example, it is difficult to define the "equal" operation on sets in terms of the "in" operation without introducing an auxiliary operation such as "subset". If the problem does not require a "subset" operation, then introducing one complicates the specification by adding unnecessary details.

Another approach to specifications is based on logic and the event model. Some languages in this class are MSG 84[4] and Spec 87. This approach uses predicate logic to define the responses to an event, where an event consists of the arrival of a message at an interface boundary. The major emphasis of these languages has been on abstractness and expressiveness. Both MSG 84 and Spec 87 have facilities for defining functions, state machines, and iterators as well as abstract data types. Experience in a series of software engineering courses[5] indicates that MSG 84 is useful in practice on software developments of appreciable size (five people teams working twenty weeks). The languages support consistency checking of many kinds, and tools for automating the checking are under investigation.

Spec 87 is more advanced than MSG 84 with respect to expressiveness and simplicity. An example of a Spec 87 fragment defining the equal operation on sets is shown below.

```
MESSAGE equal(s1 s2: set{t})
REPLY (b: boolean)
WHERE b ⟺ FOR ALL(x: t :: in(x, s1) ⟺ in(x, s2))
```

This states that two sets are equal if they have the same elements. The definition is simpler than the corresponding algebraic definition, since three axioms have been replaced by one, and the auxiliary concept "subset" has been eliminated. This axiom cannot be expressed in the conditional equation form used by the algebraic techniques because its prenex normal form contains an existential quantifier, and the conditional equation form admits only universal quantifiers. The definition is not executable as is because the bound variable x ranges over a potentially infinite type t, but it is subject to the following meaning-preserving transformations.

WHERE b ⇔ FOR ALL(x: t :: in(x, s1) ⇨ in(x, s2))
         & FOR ALL(y: t :: in(y, s2) ⇨ in(y, s1))

WHERE b ⇔ FOR ALL(x: t SUCH THAT in(x, s1) :: in(x, s2))
         & FOR ALL(y: t SUCH THAT in(y, s2) :: in(y, s1))

The first transformation expands the equivalence into a conjunction of two implications and decouples the universal quantifiers on the two conjuncts. The second transformation turns the implications into restricted range quantifications. The resulting specification is executable by enumeration because the bound variables x and y have been restricted to finite sets. Informally, the transformed specification states that two sets are equal if all of the elements of the first are contained in the second and vice versa.

The Gist language follows a different approach to specifications.[1,24] Gist is based on an extended entity-relationship model of a global state, and the behavior of a system is viewed as a sequence of states. This choice is motivated by the philosophy that the functions of a proposed system should first be defined in a global model and should be allocated to particular internal or external subsystems in a later step. Unlike the entity-relationship model common in database work,[10] the version of the model used in Gist allows relations with infinitely many tuples. Relationships are treated as predicates and are defined using a first order logic with unbounded quantifiers and modal operators for time references. The behavior of the system can be characterized by state invariants and demons that can trigger state changes when stated conditions are met. The language has facilities for introducing boundaries which can be used for creating black-box descriptions. It also allows global references and imperative statements that can be used to describe mechanisms.

The tools associated with Gist include a paraphraser, which generates English narrative texts from the formal specifications.[52] The paraphraser was originally motivated by the need to support review sessions with customers who could not read the formal notation. The paraphraser is also useful for locating faults, because it presents the specifications from a different viewpoint than the formal text. Both symbolic and concrete execution tools are under development for subsets of the language. The symbolic execution facility describes sequences of states resulting from a given situation using predicates, while the concrete execution facility works with particular data values.

An approach for generating production quality implementations from specifications is embodied in the Psi project,[14,15,26] Chi project,[16,50] and the Refine language. This work concentrated on ways to automatically implement behavior specified in first order logic and on choosing efficient algorithms and data structures for some common general purpose data types, including sets, sequences, Cartesian products, mappings, and relations. This approach has been influenced by work on implementing the SETL language.[49]

These problems have been attacked by assembling sets of rules for transforming logical specifications of behavior into algorithm fragments for realizing the behavior. The work has been done using a wide spectrum language with capabilities for describing both specifications and programs. Such a language is necessary for the approach, because the transformations produce intermediate results where logical specifications are mixed with program fragments. A specification becomes executable when it is transformed into a program without any specification fragments. The goal of efficiency is pursued by using performance estimates as a guideline for choosing between data representations and algorithms in cases where more than one transformation is applicable.[13] Work on extending the approach to a wider variety of data types is in progress. An active research direction in this area concerns application of the technology to user-defined abstract data types.

Specification languages are useful for simplifying the conceptual design of large systems and for certifying the correctness of critical properties of such systems. Many people are working on automating aspects of the process of producing working systems from formal specifications. Much progress has been made, and it is reasonable to expect the future work in the area will lead to practical benefits that include higher quality software and more efficient software development. Progress on increasing the size and expressive power of the executable subsets of specification languages is possible, and useful results are expected from future work in this direction.

The most powerful specification languages available should be used in the analysis and design of large systems to control conceptual complexity. Such specification languages do not have computable compilation functions, making it unlikely that implementation of large software systems can be completely automated. A more realistic goal is implementation by creating and refining annotations for high level specifications. Many practitioners are currently reluctant to accept formal specification languages because they see extra work: an additional language must be learned and a formal document must be produced that does not contribute directly to the program they have to write. They are reluctant to spend much effort on a document that will be produced and discarded. This will change if a specification can be made automatically executable by adding pragmas containing only irredundant compiler directives, especially if pragmas are not needed for the easy but tedious parts of the implementation. Other potential paths to acceptance are automatically producing documentation or automatically generating and evaluating test data by means of tools based on the specifications. Even if the pragmas have the effect of choosing between correctness-preserving transformations, testing will still be needed because the transformations may depend on potentially incorrect assumptions about the actual operating environment.

2 DESIGN LANGUAGES

The purpose of a design language is to describe the architecture or internal structure of a software system or component. The architecture of a software system consists of a hierarchically structured set of components. The description of a system architecture involves both a design language and a specification language. The design language is used to define the structure of the hierarchy and to describe the interconnections between the components. The specification language is used to define the interface of each component.

The difference between a design and a program is the difference between a plan and a finished product: a design records the early decisions that determine an implementation strategy, while a program contains all the details necessary to get an efficiently executable system. The primary goal of a design is documentation rather than execution. Designs should describe justifications, assumptions, and conventions as well as algorithms and data structures.

Design languages are used for formulation, communication, analysis, and planning. A concise and powerful notation is important for inventing, recording, and communicating designs as well as specifications. The design language is an important medium of communication between the designers, the managers of the project, the implementors, and the CASE tools supporting implementation. A design language can be analyzed with respect to many different properties, such as correctness, performance, and development cost.

Managers are interested in estimating, planning, and tracking a development project. Each software component determines a number of tasks that must be scheduled, such as the design, implementation, and verification of the component. All these tasks must be identified before accurate estimation, planning, and task assignments become possible. The managers and the CASE tools for supporting management functions are concerned with extracting task descriptions from the system design and estimating the effort required to do each task.

A design language should have the following properties.

- Expressiveness—the language should allow brief and natural descriptions of implementation strategies and justifications. The most powerful known control and data structuring concepts should be included.
- Abstractness—it should be possible to determine the essential properties of algorithms, data structures, and subtasks without going into the low level details.
- Incompleteness—the language should support descriptions with a controlled degree of incompleteness. Details that must be filled in later should be sufficiently clear to be locatable by a mechanical procedure.
- Correspondence—a design language need not be executable, but it should have an executable subset that can be automatically mapped into the implementation language. The non-executable features should be subject to automatic transformations into the implementation language if augmented by pragmas explaining how to implement them in each case. There should also be an automatic mapping from the specification language to the design language for generating the interface description part of the design.

A traditional idea is that design languages should be extensible.[31] This idea should be re-examined in the context of a CASE paradigm. It is desirable to incorporate powerful new ideas in control and data structuring as they come along, since new ideas are rare and it is easier to extend the design language than it is to convert to a new programming language. However, since CASE tools depend on the language, it is desirable to limit language changes. If a new design language is to be designed for the CASE environment, it should include currently known types of constructs for defining program objects, with emphasis on those that are powerful enough to cover open-ended sets of applications. Examples of such mechanisms include user-defined abstract data types, user-defined loop sequencing abstractions, generic modules, multiple inheritance, parallel loops, atomic transactions, nondeterministic wait (for responding to the first observed instance of a set of asynchronous events), and demons (processes activated whenever a specified predicate becomes true). The mechanisms chosen should be orthogonal or nearly so. Including variations on a theme can increase rather than decrease the designer's intellectual burden. A single more general mechanism should be sought if a language appears to be sprouting a whole family of similar mechanisms with small variations.

Another traditional justification for extensible design languages is supporting application specific constructs while allowing the aspects of the design language common to all applications to be standardized. With the advent of the powerful and flexible mechanisms listed above, application-specific constructs can be supplied by standard libraries of specialized operations, data types, looping constructs, generic modules, and inheritable generalized module fragments without changing the design language. The desire to simplify the language by dropping the constructs that are not needed in a particular application is consistent with this approach and can be supported by tools providing simplified subset views of the underlying general purpose language. Some subsets of the language can be certified to have special properties. For example, the CASE tools may know that the functional subset of the design language is side-effect free, so that unsynchronized and unprotected concurrent references can be used in the implementation mapping for the subset language. The remaining advantage in changing the language is to allow the use of special syntactic forms familiar in an application domain. Such advantages are cosmetic, and can be provided by preprocessors or structure editors that support multiple concrete syntactic forms for the same abstract syntax without affecting the structure of the language as seen by the CASE tools.

Another consequence of the CASE paradigm is that design languages should be formal. Informal descriptions can be included as comments, which are not interpreted by the tools. Informal descriptions have been used in the past for two main purposes: to support abstraction and to make it easier to express designs. Abstraction in this context is the ability to capture the essential elements of a design without getting into low level details. Some formal ways to achieve this capability depend on predicate logic and on shared community knowledge. For example, a predicate with quantifiers can describe a complex condition on a data structure serving as the test in a conditional or loop statement. State changes can be described either by explicitly introducing and specifying a black-box component for a lower-level component, or by a transition predicate, which specifies the relation between the initial and final states of a transition without describing the details of how to implement the transition. An example of the use of shared community knowledge is a reference to a ''sort'' function with a pragma ''use quicksort.'' In such a case, ''sort'' refers to a general class of modules described in a design library, and ''quicksort'' refers to a specialization of that class with a particular algorithm known by the designer to have the properties needed in a particular context.

Formal notations are used to gain the advantage of automated processing, possibly at the expense of some extra effort in formulation. One approach to design has been to start from natural language descriptions and to transform them into more formal designs. Such an approach is based on the premise that either detailed natural language descriptions of the processes to be performed are already available from the customer, or that the system designer can sketch an implementation strategy in natural language more quickly than in more formal notations. The process of transforming the natural language descriptions into a formal design language can be partially automated. Some of the more interesting tools attempt to identify abstractions by locating repeated phrases in the natural language text and to identify data types and program objects by locating common noun phrases. A detailed description of this approach and references to related work can be found in Reference 3.

The idea that designs should be accompanied by justifications is motivated by the desire to make changes easier when the system must evolve to meet changing requirements. Some justifications are easiest to record as informal comments, but doing so implies checking will be done manually, perhaps at a design review meeting. Examples of some kinds of justifications and conventions that are important to record are preconditions, data invariants, loop invariants, bounding functions, and termination orderings.

Preconditions are assumptions on the inputs to a module that must be met for a limited implementation to produce correct results. Preconditions in the design usually come from the specification, because they are black-box properties. However, sometimes resource constraints motivate the implementors to introduce stronger preconditions in the design than were originally specified. Such stronger preconditions have to be reflected back to the specification,[47] and the places in the design where the module is used must be checked to make sure they respect the stronger precondition, or adjustments must be made in case they do not. Mechanical aid for such checking is desirable.

Data invariants are restrictions on data structures that must be respected by all programs creating or modifying its instances. Data invariants usually apply to the implementation structures for abstract data types, serving as hidden internal properties specified in the design of a type module. Many of the well known data structures for efficiently implementing common data types gain their efficiency from elaborate data invariants that have been designed to avoid recomputation of various properties of the data structure. The data invariants constitute the assumptions shared by the implementations of all operations of a type. Since they are not local to a single procedure they can be a vehicle for unwanted interactions, especially for types so large that it is not practical for the same person to implement the operations. Bugs caused by procedures damaging invariants are common and are difficult to diagnose based on fault symptoms, because they involve interactions between pieces of code that are separated both spatially and in execution time: this justifies expending a fair amount of effort on documentation and checking.

Loop invariants are properties of the state variables of a loop that hold both before and after every execution of the loop body. Many of the more efficient algorithms depend on carefully constructed loop invariants to achieve their efficiency. While loop invariants are local to a single procedure, they should also be documented to avoid inadvertent damage when the code has to be modified due to a requirements change. Loop invariants as well as data invariants are often difficult to reconstruct from the code so they should be recorded as they are introduced in the design process. This is especially important for implementations of critical functions whose correctness will be subject to correctness proofs, because there are automatic procedures for constructing the required theorems that will operate without designer interaction if the loop invariants are given along with the desired preconditions and postconditions.

Bounding functions and termination orderings are justifications for knowing that the loops and recursions in the program will terminate. A bounding function gives an upper bound on the number of loop iterations still left for given values of the state variables of the loop, or an upper bound on the depth of any remaining recursive calls for given values of the formal parameters of a recursive subprogram. A terminating program will strictly reduce the bounding function after each execution of the loop body or upon each recursive call. Checking the termination of a program becomes easy if the bounding functions are given. The bounding functions are also useful for performance analysis, because they give worst case estimates of the running times. Termination orderings are useful for establishing termination in some cases where bounding functions yielding natural numbers are difficult to construct. The range of a bounding function can be any well founded set. Some well known termination orderings are the lexicographic and multiset orderings on sequences. These orderings can be used to construct sequence-valued bounding functions for loops or recursive functions whose progress is governed by the interaction of several different parameters.

The kinds of justifications described above can be used in the process of formally or informally verifying the correctness of a design with respect to a given specification. Other kinds of justifications include priorities for different design goals, such as "optimize space."

Design languages are used by experienced and highly skilled people to determine the overall system architecture and to make the key design decisions. Traditionally the more mundane decisions are performed by less experienced and less skillful people. As CASE technology improves, a larger fraction of the software engineering community will be concerned with architectural design, which will become less tedious with mechanical aid, and the routine aspects of programming will be gradually taken over by automated tools. This trend will be driven by demands for larger and more sophisticated computer systems.

3 PROTOTYPING LANGUAGES

The purpose of a prototyping language is to support rapid prototyping. Rapid prototyping is a promising approach to evolutionary software design that was proposed in the early 1980s to solve problems with productivity and reliability in software development.[54] More specifically, prototyping is a method for rapidly constructing executable models of software systems. Such models are known as software prototypes.

Prototyping was distinguished from simulation to emphasize that it should be applied to the early stages of software development and that its goal should be quickly accomplished by an environment containing state-of-the-art software tools. Simulation can be used at any level, including assembly language. The goal of simulation is to determine the properties of a specific program or system. Rapid prototyping refers to the activities of constructing software prototypes using CASE design tools at the requirements analysis, functional specification, and architectural design stages of software development. The goal of prototyping is to design, tailor, define, test, document, and implement a system (Figure 4-3). The prototyping life cycle has two stages, prototyping and system

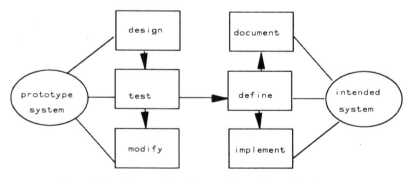

Figure 4-3. The use of prototypes for software development.

generation. In the prototyping stage, a prototype version of the system is designed and repeatedly tested and modified until the customer is satisfied with it. In the system generation stage, the prototype defines and documents the architecture of the intended system. The system is implemented by filling in missing details and reworking key modules as needed to achieve adequate performance. Prototyping is most useful for systems that are difficult to built directly, quickly, and correctly, such as software systems with hard real-time constraints and systems large enough to require multiple man-years of design effort.

As shown in Figure 4-2, the prototyping process integrates the early stages of the traditional life cycle (Figure 4-1) and the evolution stage into the prototyping cycle, which tests the evolving prototype system through execution. The programming level details of the system can be completed after the analyst and customer are satisfied with the functional performance of the prototype. The capability for rapid prototyping can best be realized in the context of a high level prototyping language. A prototyping language should have the properties of both a specification language and a design language. The algorithmic level characterizing most current programming languages is not appropriate for supporting rapid prototyping, because too many details must be specified. A high level view aids the prototype developer to cope with the complexity of typical software systems, and supports more effective computer-aided systems; for example, reasoning from a design data base or retrieving reusable software components. A prototyping language containing constructs for expressing descriptions of specifications and designs is crucial as well as an automated support environment. An example of such an environment and the associated prototyping methodology is described in References 35, 38, and 39 respectively.

3.1 Requirements for Prototyping Languages

A language for supporting rapid prototyping has different requirements from a general purpose programming language or a specification language. In addition to being executable, the language must support the specification of requirements for the system and functional descriptions for the component modules. Because rapid prototyping involves many design modifications, the language must make it easy for the system designer to create a prototype with a high degree of module independence,[51] and to preserve its good modularity properties across many modifications. The prototyping language should be sufficiently easy to read in order to serve as design documentation and also should be formal enough for mechanical processing in the rapid prototyping environment.

The design of a prototyping language should be motivated by the above reasons and the following requirements:

- A prototyping language should be executable so that the customer can observe the operation of the prototype.
- It should be simple and easy to use. The language should be based on a simple computational model and be integrated with a computer-aided prototyping method. It should support a good designer interface with graphical summary views.
- The language should support hierarchically structured prototypes, to simplify prototyping of large and complex systems. The descriptions at all levels of a prototype should be uniform. The underlying computational model should limit and expose interactions between modules to encourage good decompositions. The language should harmoniously support data abstraction, function abstraction, and control abstraction.
- A prototyping language should apply at both the specification and design levels to allow the designer to concentrate on designing the prototype without the distraction of transforming one notation into another.
- It should be suitable for specifying the retrieval of reusable modules from a software base, to avoid creating multiple descriptions of each module.
- A prototyping language should support both formal and informal module specification methods, to allow the designer to work in the style most appropriate to the problem.
- A prototyping language should contain a set of abstractions suitable for the problem area for which the prototyping language is designed; for example, timing for real-time and embedded systems.

When looking for a language meeting such a set of requirements, the designer or analyst may find his choices are limited. It is not hard to convince someone that high level abstractions and brief and powerful language structures are necessary to simplify the design at a conceptual level. Many requirements specification and conceptual modeling languages are at a suitable high level, but unfortunately most of them are not executable. Many existing programming languages are too inflexible and too difficult to use. Various coupling problems between modules of a system are not preventable in a programming language, because conventional programming languages are required to execute efficiently on conventional machines. Strong coupling can make a rapid prototyping effort fail because modifications get progressively more difficult and error prone, so conventional programming languages cannot be adequate for prototyping. Consequently, the design of a special purpose language for rapid prototyping has to be considered.

A prototyping language must have the characteristics of a good design language, because the structure of a prototype must be understandable and easy to modify. Early design languages[31,33,51] were not executable, although more recent work has promise in this direction.[9] Some design languages work at the design and specification levels but are not executable.[2] Other work on executable specifications[34] has taken the automatic transformation of specifications into running systems as a distant long term goal, and has concentrated on generating run-time checks from the specifications in the short run. These approaches are not sufficiently well developed to produce results applicable to rapid prototyping in the near future.

Many informal versions of data flow diagrams have been used extensively to model the data transformation aspects of software systems. Data flow diagrams are easy to read, revealing the internal structure of a process and the potential parallelism inherent in a design, making dataflow attractive to designers. A language based on dataflow makes it easier for a prototyping environment to provide graphical capabilities for displaying and updating the structure of the prototype. However, data flow diagrams or other informal notations do not provide a unified mechanism to represent the relevant attributes of software systems and are not sufficient to be executable. A more precise model of a dataflow computation has been developed in the context of hardware design.[11] LUCID[53] is a good dataflow based programming language. These models and languages support execution but not specification and design. The languages are not sufficient for specification, design and prototyping in a CASE environment, because requirements are more complex.

A language supporting both good modularity and good control is needed to support system decomposition.[46] System decomposition is a central issue in the design of any large system. Good modularity is a key factor for increasing productivity, since it reduces the debugging effort for producing a correct executable system, and improves the understandability, reliability, and maintainability of the developed system. A powerful set of control abstractions are required for simple glass-box descriptions. These features are especially important in rapid prototyping.

Each method for decomposing a software system is associated with a family of computational models. Two well known system decomposition methods are based on data flow and control flow. The components of a data flow decomposition are independent sequential processes that communicate via buffered data streams, while the components of a control flow decomposition are procedures that are called by and return to a main procedure with a single thread of control. Neither of these decomposition methods offers both good modularity and good control.

Iwamoto, *et al.*[23] suggest circumstances in which each of the two kinds of decomposition is preferable and give some restrictions sufficient to guarantee that computed results are independent of scheduling decisions. However, this system is subject to many confusing restrictions and is not sufficient as a base for a CASE prototyping environment. The authors use a data flow decomposition in cases where there is a mismatch between the structures of the input data stream and the output data stream of an operator, introducing an intermediate data stream of lower level data elements to resolve the structure clash. A control flow decomposition is applied in cases where the data stream forks into several branches and is rejoined or where the operators on the branches influence each other's results by means of state changes, because in these cases a data flow decomposition will result in computations whose results can depend on the unpredictable behavior of the process scheduler. An example of the first case is a decomposition with a dispatch operator that recognizes several alternative kinds of inputs and routes them to the appropriate special purpose operator. A data flow decomposition for such a structure requires an extra purpose operator. A data flow decomposition for such a structure requires extra sequencing information in the data elements to make sure that the result streams do not get out of order when they are merged, since the relative speeds of independent processes are not predictable under the usual interpretation of dataflow. An example of the second case is a transaction with multiple updates to a shared database, where the final state of the database may depend on the arbitrary order of the updates performed by operators on parallel branches of the dataflow graph.

To avoid the problems with data flow decompositions mentioned above, the authors of this chapter have developed a new underlying model of computation for PSDL,[35,40] which is based on dataflow and guarantees that the results of a computation do not depend on undetermined properties of the schedulers. Control constraints are combined with the dataflow model to achieve the best modularity with sufficient control information. Dataflow is used to simplify the interactions between modules, eliminating direct external references and communication via side effects. The first problem with data flow decompositions mentioned above does not arise in our model because of a rule in PSDL, which states that a composite operator cannot fire again until all of the internal activity associated with the previous firing is complete. This rule provides a kind of mutual exclusion that prevents interference between successive actions by the same operator without preventing concurrent execution of the components of a composite operator. The second problem with data flow decompositions does not arise in PSDL prototypes, because there is no implicitly shared mutable data.

3.2 Execution of Prototyping Languages

There are two approaches to making a prototyping language executable, one based on meta-programming and the other on executable specifications. The meta-programming approach views the prototyping language as a means for adapting and interconnecting available software components. The processor for such a language generates the skeleton of an implementation, with empty places for component modules. These empty places can be filled in with reusable components drawn from a software base, with stubs for roughly simulating the expected behavior of a module, or by hand-crafted code. The prototyping language PSDL described in Section 3.3 uses this approach.

The executable specification approach uses black-box specifications in the executable subset of a specification language for realizing the behavior of a system. For expressive notations, this amounts to implementation by enumeration, since this is one of the few known implementation techniques powerful enough to realize arbitrary computable specifications. These techniques can produce slow implementations, even with sophisticated approaches, such as the one taken in logic programming. The execution mechanism of a logic based programming language such as Prolog is a symbolic version of enumeration. This is more efficient than enumeration by brute force, because each logical step considers a potentially unbounded class of individuals rather than a single individual. However, the number of classes to be considered can still be unbounded and is often very large if the logic program contains only the abstract essence of a specification, without any extra information to help narrow down the search. Since executable specifications run slowly without special implementation guidance, this approach must be strengthened to be applicable to prototyping very large systems. One way to strengthen the approach is to add annotations for speeding up execution to the pure specifications. Another way is to combine executable specifications with the first approach, and use them to realize only small and simple components of a larger system in cases where efficient implementations for the components are not already available.

3.3   PSDL: An Example of a Prototyping Language

In this section, the concepts and constructs of the prototyping language PSDL (Prototype System Description Language)[40] are used for explaining and analyzing the design principles for prototyping languages mentioned in Sections 3.1 and 3.2. Other languages being used for rapid prototyping include SETL, Prolog, Refine, and Kodiyak.[21] These languages are suited for prototyping, because they are capable of executing abstract descriptions of processes.

PSDL supports the prototyping of large systems with hard real-time constraints.[43,44] The language is based on a simple computational model that is close to the designer's idea of real-time systems. The model integrates operator, data, and control abstractions and encourages hierarchical decompositions based on both dataflow and control flow. More details are described below.

3.3.1   Computational Model

The PSDL computational model contains operators that communicate via data streams. Each data stream carries values of a fixed abstract data type.[32] Each data stream can also contain values of the built-in type "exception." The operators may be either data driven or periodic. Periodic operators have traditionally been the basis for most real-time system design, while the importance of data driven operators for real-time systems is recognized.[41]

To provide a small and portable syntax with clear semantics it is necessary to have a mathematical model behind the language constructs. Formally the computational model is an augmented graph

$$G = (V, E, T(v), C(v))$$

where V is the set of vertices, E is the set of edges, $T(v)$ is the maximum execution time for each vertex v, and $C(v)$ is the set of control constraints for each vertex v. Each vertex is an operator, and each edge is a data stream. The first three components of the graph are called the enhanced data flow diagram.

An **operator** is either a function or a state machine. When an operator fires, it reads one data object from each of its input streams and writes at most one data object on each of its output streams. The output objects produced when a function fires depend only on the current set of input values. The output values produced, when a state machine fires, depend only on the current set of input values and the current values of a finite number of internal state variables. Operators of these two types are useful for prototyping real-time systems.

Operators are either atomic or composite. Atomic operators cannot be decomposed in the PSDL computational model. Composite operators have realizations as data and control flow networks of lower level operators. If the output of an operator A is an input to another operator B, then there is an implicit precedence relationship between the two, which says that A must be scheduled to fire before B. A composite operator whose network contains cycles is a state machine. In such a case, one of the data streams in each cycle is designated as the state variable controlling the feedback loop, and an initial value is specified for the state variable. State variables serve to break the circular precedence relationships among the operators which would otherwise be implied by the data flow relationships.

A **data stream** is a communication link connecting exactly two operators, a producer and a consumer. Communication links with more than two ends are realized using copy and merge operators. Each stream carries a sequence of data values. Streams have the pipeline property: if a and b are two data values in data stream Y and the data value a is generated by op-1 before the data value b is generated then it is impossible for a to be delivered to op-2 after b is delivered.

There are two types of data streams—**dataflow** streams and **sampled** streams. A dataflow stream guarantees that none of the data values is lost or replicated, while a sampled stream does not make such a guarantee. A dataflow stream can be thought of as a FIFO queue, while a sampled stream can be thought of as a cell capable of containing just one value, which is updated whenever the producer generates a new value. Since real-time systems must often operate within a (small) bounded memory, the finite queue length imposes a restriction on the relative execution rates of two operators communicating via a dataflow stream. A sampled stream imposes no such constraint, since it can deliver a value more than once if the consumer demands more values before the producer has provided a new value, and it can discard the previous value if the producer provides a new value before the consumer has used the previous one.

Dataflow streams must be used in cases where each data value represents a unique transaction or request that must be acted on exactly once. For example, the transactions in a system for electronic funds transfer would be transmitted along a dataflow stream. Sampled data streams are often used for simulating continuous streams of information, where only the most recent information is meaningful. For example, an operator that periodically updates a software estimate of the system state based on sensor readings would use a sampled stream. In PSDL the stream type is determined from the activation conditions for the consumer operator, rather than being explicitly declared.

3.3.2 Abstractions

Abstractions are an important means for controlling complexity,[5] which is especially important in rapid prototyping because a system must appear simple to be built or analyzed quickly. PSDL supports three kinds of abstractions: operator abstractions, data abstractions, and control abstractions.

An **operator abstraction** is either a functional abstraction or a state machine abstraction. Both functional and state machine abstractions are supported by the PSDL constructs for operator abstractions. PSDL operators have two major parts: the SPECIFICATION and the IMPLEMENTATION. The specification part contains attributes describing the form of the interface, the timing characteristics, and both formal and informal descriptions of the observable behavior of the operator. The attributes both specify the operator and form the basis for retrievals from a reusable component library or software base. The size and the content of the set of attributes may vary depending on the specific usage, underlying language, or the type of the modules specified; e.g., GENERIC PARAMETERS, INPUT, OUTPUT, STATES, and EXCEPTIONS.

A PSDL operator corresponds to a state machine abstraction if its specification part contains a STATES declaration, otherwise it corresponds to a functional abstraction. The STATES declaration gives the types of the state variables and their initial values. The state variables of a PSDL state machine are local, in the sense that they can be updated only from inside the machine. This restriction prevents coupling by means of shared state variables and is one of the features of PSDL that leads to good modularization. It is also important for making the correctness of distributed implementations independent of the number of processors.

The implementation part determines whether the operator is atomic or composite. Atomic operators have a keyword specifying the underlying programming language followed by the name of the implementation module

implementing the operator. Composite operators have the attributes COMMU-
NICATION GRAPH, INTERNAL DATA, CONTROL CONSTRAINTS, and
INFORMAL DESCRIPTION.

Data abstractions are an important concept for language design. Data
abstractions decouple the behavior of a data type from its representation. This
is especially important in prototyping because the behavior of the intended
system is only partially realized, capturing only those aspects important for the
purposes of the prototype. The behavior of the prototype data is also a partial
simulation of the data in the intended system, so that the data representations
in the prototype and the intended system are likely to be different. Data abstraction allows the data interfaces to be described independently of the representation of the data, so that the interfaces for the operations on the data can be
the same in the prototype and in the intended system. Aspects of the data not
included in the prototype will be reflected in extra operations on the type, which
appear in the intended system but not in the prototype. It is important to have
common interfaces between the prototype and the intended system, because it
makes comparisons easier during the validation of the intended system, and it
enables the structure of the prototype design to be reused in the intended system
where appropriate.

All PSDL data types are immutable, so that there can be no implicit communication via side effects. Both mutable data types and global variables have been
excluded from PSDL to help prevent coupling problems in large prototype
systems. If many modules communicate implicitly through a shared data structure or global variable, then it is easy to inadvertently interfere with a module
by making an apparently unrelated change to another module. Repairing such
faults is too time consuming in a rapid prototyping effort.

The PSDL data types include the immutable subset of the built-in types of
the underlying programming language, user-defined abstract types,[18] the special
types i.e., time and exception; and the types that can be built using the immutable type constructors of PSDL. The PSDL type constructors were chosen to
provide data modeling facilities with a small set of semantically independent
structures.[40] For example, finite sets, sequences, tuples, mappings, and relations
correspond to the usual mathematical concepts.

The definition of an abstract data type in PSDL contains two parts: SPECI-
FICATION and IMPLEMENTATION.

Control abstractions are important for simplifying the design of real-time
systems, because much of the complexity of such systems lies in their control
and scheduling aspects. The control abstractions of PSDL are represented as
enhanced data flow diagrams augmented by a set of control constraints. As a
common property of real-time systems, periodic execution is supported explicitly. The order of execution is only partially specified and is determined from
the data flow relations given in the enhanced data flow diagrams, based on the
rule that an operator consuming a data value must not start until after the operator

producing the data value has completed. This constraint applies only if the operators have the same period or if neither is periodic. If the order of execution for two operators is not determined by this rule, then both can run concurrently if sufficient processors are available. Conditional execution is supported by PSDL triggering conditions and conditional outputs.

3.3.3 Control Constraints

The control aspect of a PSDL operator is specified implicitly, via control constraints, rather than giving an explicit control algorithm. There are several aspects to be specified: whether the operator is PERIODIC or SPORADIC, the triggering condition, and output guards. The stream types for the data streams in the enhanced data flow diagram are determined implicitly, based on the triggering conditions.

PSDL supports both **periodic** and **sporadic** operators. Periodic operators are triggered by the scheduler at approximately regular time intervals. The scheduler has some leeway: a periodic operator must be scheduled to complete sometime between the beginning of each period and a deadline, which defaults to the end of the period. Sporadic operators are triggered by the arrival of new data values, possibly at irregular time intervals.

A PSDL operator is periodic if a period has been specified for it and otherwise it is sporadic. A period can be specified explicitly, or it can be inherited from a higher level of decomposition in a hierarchical prototype.

There are two types of **data triggers** inside PSDL operators:

- OPERATOR p TRIGGERED BY ALL x, y, z; and
- OPERATOR q TRIGGERED BY SOME a, b.

In the first example, the operator p is ready to fire whenever new data values have arrived on all three of the input arcs x, y, and z. This rule is a slightly generalized form of the natural dataflow firing rule,[11] since in PSDL a proper subset of the input arcs can determine the triggering condition for an operator, without requiring new data on all input arcs. This kind of data trigger can be used to ensure that the output of the operator is always based on new data for all of the inputs in the list and can be used to synchronize the processing of corresponding input values from several input streams.

In the second example, the operator q fires when any of the inputs a and b gets a new value. This kind of activation condition guarantees that the output of operator q is based on the most recent values of the critical inputs a and b mentioned in the activation condition for q. If q has some other input c, the output of q can be based on old values of c, since q will not be triggered on a new value of c until after a new value for a or b arrives. This kind of trigger can be used to keep software estimates of sensor data up to date.

Every operator must have a period, a data trigger, or both. If a periodic operator has a data trigger, the operator is conditionally executed with the data trigger serving as an input guard.

A **timer** is a special type of abstract state machine whose behavior is similar to a stopwatch. Timers are used to record the length of time between events, or the length of time the system spends in a given state. This facility is needed to express sophisticated aspects of real-time systems, such as timeouts and minimum refresh rates. The state of a timer can be modeled as a time value and a boolean run switch. The value of the timer increases at a fixed rate reflecting the passage of real-time when the run switch is on and remains constant when the run switch is off.

There are four primitive operations for interacting with timers: read, start, stop, and reset. The read operation returns the current value of the timer without affecting the run switch. The start operation turns the run switch on without affecting the value of the timer. The stop operation turns the run switch off without affecting the value of the timer. The reset operation turns the run switch off and sets the value of the timer to zero.

Timers are treated specially in PSDL because they provide a nonlocal means of control for hard real-time systems. The PSDL declaration TIMER t creates an instance of the generic state machine described above, with the fixed name *t*. The name of a timer can be used like a PSDL input variable, whose value is the result of the read operation of the timer. The value of a timer can be affected by PSDL control constraints of the forms

START TIMER t,
STOP TIMER t, and
RESET TIMER t.

These control constraints can appear anywhere the name *t* is visible, with the effect of invoking the start, stop, and reset operations of the abstract timer *t*.

PSDL supports two kinds of **conditionals:** (1) conditional execution of an operator, and (2) conditional transmission of an output. These constructs handle the controlled input and output of an operator.

PSDL operators can have a TRIGGERING CONDITION in addition to or instead of a data trigger for **conditional execution.** The following are two examples of operators with triggering conditions:

OPERATOR r TRIGGERED BY SOME x, y IF x: NORMAL AND y: critical
OPERATOR s TRIGGERED IF x: critical

The first example shows the control constraints of an operator with both a data trigger and a triggering condition. The operator *r* fires only when one or both of the inputs x and y have fresh values, x is a normal data value, and y is an exceptional data value with the exception name "critical." This example illustrates exception handling in PSDL.

The second example shows the control constraints of an operator s with a triggering condition but no data trigger. In this example s must be a periodic operator with an input x since sporadic operators must have data triggers, and triggering conditions can only depend on timers and locally available data. In this case the value of x is tested periodically to see if it is a "critical" exception, and the operator s is fired if that is the case. Both of these examples illustrate ways of using PSDL operators to serve as exception handlers.

In general, the triggering condition acts as a guard for the operator. If the predicate is satisfied, the operator fires and reads its inputs. If the predicate is not satisfied, the input values are read from the input data streams without firing the operator. If a periodic operator has a data trigger or a triggering condition, then the guard predicate is tested periodically, and if found true, the operator is fired. The guard predicate of an operator can depend only on the input values to the operator and on the values of timers. The predicate can make use of the operators of the abstract data types carried by the input streams, allowing a structure similar to a guarded command, where different operators handle an input depending on some computable properties of the input value.

An example of a control constraint specifying a **conditional output** is the following:

OPERATOR t OUTPUT z IF 1 < z AND z < max

This example shows an operator with an output guard, which depends on the input value max and the output value z.

In general, an output guard acts as if the corresponding unconditional output had been passed through a conditionally executed filtering operator with the same predicate as a triggering condition. The filtering operator passes the input value to the output stream unchanged if the predicate evaluates to TRUE. If the predicate evaluates to FALSE, the filter removes the value from its input stream without affecting its output stream. An output predicate can depend only on the input values to the operator, the output values of the operator, and values of timers.

Output guards are convenient, but they do not strictly increase the expressive power of the language, since they can be simulated by adding an explicit filter operator, at the cost of some additional output streams to the original operator since the output guard can depend on the INPUTS of an operator as well as on its outputs.

PSDL **exceptions** are values of a built in abstract data type called exception. This type has operations for creating an exception with a given name, for detecting whether a value is an exception with a given name, and for detecting whether a value is normal (i.e., belongs to some data type other than exception). PSDL provides a shorthand syntax for the latter two operations, as illustrated in the following example of a PSDL predicate

x: overflow AND y: NORMAL

which is true if the input value x is the exception value with the name "overflow" and the input value y is normal, as indicated by the PSDL keyword "NORMAL."

Values of type exception can be transmitted along data streams just like values of the normal type associated with the stream. Exceptions are encoded as data values in PSDL to decouple the transmission of an exceptional result from the scheduling of the actions for handling the exception and to provide a programming language independent interface between atomic operators. This makes it possible to use atomic operators realized in several different programming languages in the same PSDL prototype.

Exceptions can be produced and handled in PSDL. For example, the control constraint

OPERATOR f EXCEPTION e IF x > 100

transmits the exception value named e on all output streams of f instead of the values actually computed by f whenever the input value x is greater than 100. Exceptions can be handled by operators with triggering conditions selecting only input values of type exception, as illustrated in a previous example. Exceptions can be suppressed either by a PSDL output guard of the following form

OPERATOR g OUTPUT Y IF Y: normal

or a PSDL input guard of the form

OPERATOR h TRIGGERED IF Y: normal.

The data trigger of an operator determines the **stream types** of its input streams by the following two rules:

(1) If a stream is listed in an ALL data trigger, then it is a **dataflow stream.**
(2) All streams not constrained by the first rule are **sampled streams.**

These rules are motivated by the fact that an operator must be executable whenever its triggering conditions are satisfied. In particular, values of streams that are not mentioned at all, or are mentioned in SOME data triggers can be demanded at arbitrary times, which is inconsistent with the fact that dataflow streams cannot allow the consumer to read more values than the producer has written. Consequently, rule (1) captures the most general situation where dataflow streams make sense.

In the following example, the operator op has the input streams x, y, z and the output stream w.

```
              x ---->  ┌ ─ ─ ─ ─ ┐
input streams y ---->  │   op    │ ------> w output stream
              z ---->  └ ─ ─ ─ ─ ┘
```

Under the following control constraint

OPERATOR op TRIGGERED BY ALL x, y

x, y are data flow streams while z is a sampled stream. Under a different control constraint

OPERATOR op TRIGGERED BY SOME x, y

x, y, z are all sampled streams. In either case, the stream type of w is not affected by the control constraint associated with its producer operator op.

3.3.4 Timing Constraints

Timing constraints are an essential part of specifying real-time systems. The most basic timing constraints are given in the specification part of a PSDL module, and consist of the MAXIMUM EXECUTION TIME, the MAXIMUM RESPONSE TIME, and the MINIMUM CALLING PERIOD. The maximum execution time is an upper bound on the length of time between the instant when a module begins execution, and the instant when it completes. The maximum execution time is a constraint on the implementation of a single module, and does not depend on the context in which the module is used.

The last two constraints are important for sporadic operators. The maximum response time for a sporadic operator is an upper bound on the time between the arrival of a new data value (or set of data values for operators with the natural dataflow firing rule), and the time when the last value is put into the output streams of the operator in response to the arrival of the new data value. The maximum response time for a periodic operator is an upper bound on the time between the beginning of a period, and the time when the last value is put into the output streams of that operator during that period. The maximum response time includes potential scheduling delays, while the maximum execution time does not.

The minimum calling period is a constraint on the environment of a sporadic operator, consisting of a lower bound between the arrival of one set of inputs and the arrival of the next set. In a PSDL specification every sporadic operator with a maximum response time constraint must have a corresponding minimum calling period constraint.

3.3.5 Hierarchical Constraints

PSDL operators are defined in a hierarchical structure, which induces some consistency constraints on the language. The most fundamental constraints are concerned with interface consistency. Every input stream of a component of a composite operator must either be an input of the composite or be produced by a component of the composite. Similarly, every output stream of a component operator must also be an output stream of the composite operator if it is consumed by an operator that is not a component of the composite. Every components. If the consumer of a data stream is a composite operator, then both the composite and all of its components consuming the same data stream induce constraints on the stream type. PSDL timing constraints also impose some consistency requirements between the various levels of a hierarchical design. The maximum execution time and the maximum response time of a subnetwork must be no larger than those of the composite operator realized by the subnetwork. The minimum calling period of a composite must be no larger than the minimum calling period of any of its components.

3.3.6 Execution of PSDL Prototypes

The prototyping language PSDL uses the meta-programming approach for execution (see Section 3.2). PSDL prototypes are executable if all required information is supplied, and the software base contains implementations for all atomic operators and types. To simplify the design of the PSDL translator, Ada is used for implementing both the PSDL reusable components in the software base and the PSDL execution support environment.[36] The PSDL execution support system contains a static scheduler, a translator, and a dynamic scheduler. The static scheduler produces a static schedule for the operators with real time constraints. The translator augments the implementations of the atomic operators and types with code realizing the data streams and activation conditions, resulting in a program in the underlying programming language that can be compiled and executed. Execution is under the control of a dynamic scheduler, which schedules the operators without real-time constraints and provides facilities for debugging and gathering statistics. More details can be found in Reference 35.

4   CONCLUSIONS

As compiler and hardware technology improves, the distinctions between proto-typing languages, specification languages, design languages, and programming languages are getting smaller and may eventually disappear. Programming languages are getting more expressive and more flexible and are supporting more abstract descriptions of the processes to be carried out, while specification and design languages are beginning to have larger executable subsets. A proto-typing language must have the capabilities of both a specification and a design language, while still remaining executable. In the short run, these four kinds of languages will remain distinct to more effectively support different classes of powerful CASE tools. Programming languages will support optimizing compi-lers whose main objective is to produce efficient implementations. Specification and design languages will support CASE tools for requirements analysis and for proving the correctness of designs and implementations. Prototyping languages will support tools for prototype demonstrations and implementation planning.

Because the completely automatic and correct implementation of powerful specification languages is an algorithmically unsolvable problem, research on CASE technology should investigate ways that people can most effectively guide tools for computer-aided implementation. A promising approach for applying CASE technology to rapid prototyping is augmenting abstract specifications with annotations or pragmas giving hints about ways to implement them. An impor-tant problem is finding concepts and notations that can naturally express such information in an abstract and orthogonal way. Abstractness is desired to simplify the problem of guiding the tools by avoiding as many details as possible. Orthogonality is desired to avoid repeating information that is already contained in or implied by the abstract specification. It is desirable to keep the abstract specification separate or easily mechanically separable from the annota-tions to provide simplified views of large system models.

Progress on automatically generating prototypes or efficient implementations from abstract specifications will depend on a knowledge-based approach. The size of the required knowledge bases depends on the range of problems the language is attempting to address. For this reason, the most powerful systems appearing in the near future will be those with narrow application areas, because such tools can be built with smaller knowledge bases. For a general purpose system, the knowledge base will have to include a large fraction of currently available knowledge about classes of efficient algorithms and data structures, along with the restrictions on their use and measures of their performance. This part of the knowledge is known as the software base. Other forms of knowledge that may turn out to be necessary include knowledge about ways of adapting and combining the structures in the software base, properties of the application domain and properties of the CASE environment.

REFERENCES

1. Balzer, R., "A 15 Year Perspective on Automatic Programming," *IEEE Trans. on Software Eng. SE-11*, 11, November 1985, pp. 1257–1267.
2. Beichter, F. W., O. Herzog, and H. Petzsch, "SLAN-4 A Software Specification and Design Language," *IEEE Trans. on Software Eng. SE-10*, 2, March 1984, pp. 155–162.
3. Berry, D. M., N. Yavne, and M. Yavne, "Application of Program Design Language Tools to Abbott's Method of Program Design by Informal Natural Language Descriptions," *Journal of Software and Systems*.
4. Berzins, V., and M. Gray, "Analysis and Design in MSG.84: Formalizing Functional Specifications," *IEEE Trans. on Software Eng. SE-11*, 8, August 1985, pp. 657–670.
5. Berzins, V., M. Gray, and D. Naumann, "Abstraction-Based Software Development," *Comm. of the ACM 29*, 5 May 1986, pp. 402–415.
6. Berzins, V. and Luqi, "Specifying Large Software Systems in Spec," Tech. Report submitted to *IEEE Software*, 1987. Also NPS 52-87-033, Computer Science Department, Naval Postgraduate School.
7. Berzins V. and Luqi, *Software Engineering with Abstractions: An Integrated Approach to Software Development using Ada*, Reading, MA: Addison-Wesley, 1989.
8. Burstall, R. M. and J. A. Goguen, "An Informal Introduction to Specifications using Clear," in *The Correctness Problem in Computer Science*, R. S. Boyer and J. S. Moore (eds.), New York: Springer Verlag, 1981, pp. 185–213.
9. Cheatham, T., J. Townley, and G. Holloway, "A System for Program Refinement," in *Interactive Programming Environments*, New York: McGraw-Hill, 1984, pp. 198–214.
10. Chen, P. P., "The Entity-Relationship Model—Toward a Unified View of Data," *Trans. Database Systems 1*, 1 March 1987, pp. 9–36.
11. Dennis, J. B., G. A. Boughton, and C. K. C. Leung, "Building Blocks for Dataflow Prototypes," in *Proc. Seventh Symposium on Computer Architecture*, La Baule, France, May 1980.
12. Goguen, J. A. and J. J. Tardo, "An Introduction to OBJ: A Language for Writing and Testing Formal Algebraic Specifications," in *Proceedings of the Conference on Specifications of Reliable Software*, IEEE, April 1979, pp. 170–189.
13. Goldberg, A., "Technical Issues for Performance Estimation," in *Proc. Second Annual RADC Knowledge-based Assistant Conference*, RADC(COES), Grifiss AFB, N.Y., 1987.
14. Green, C., "The Design of the Psi Program Synthesis System," in *Proceedings of the Second International Conference on Software Engineering*, 1976.
15. Green, C., and D. Barstow, "On Program Synthesis Knowledge," *Artificial Intelligence Journal*, November 1978.
16. Green, C., and S. Westfold, "Knowledge-Based Programming Self-Applied," in *Machine Intelligence*, Vol. 10, New York: J. Wiley & Sons, 1982.
17. Guttag, J. V., "The Specification and Application to Programming of Abstract Data Types," CSRG-59, Ph. D. Thesis, University of Toronto, 1975.
18. Guttag, J. V., E. Horowitz, and D. R. Musser, "Abstract Data Types and Software Validation," *Comm. of the ACM 21*, 12 (1978), pp. 1048–1063.
19. Guttag, J. V. and J. J. Horning, "A Larch Shared Language Handbook," *Science of Computer Programming 6* (1986), pp. 135–157.
20. Guttag, J. V. and J. J. Horning, "Report on the Larch Shared Language," *Science of Computer Programming 6* (1986), pp. 103–134.
21. Herndon, R. and V. Berzins, "The Realizable Benefits of a Language Prototyping Language," to appear in *IEEE TSE*, SE 14-6, June 1988, pp. 803–809.
22. Huet, G., "Confluent Reductions: Abstract Properties and Applications to Term Rewriting Systems," *J. ACM 27*, 4 October 1980, pp. 797–821.
23. Iwamoto, K., and O. Shigo, "Unifying Data Flow and Control Flow Based Modularization Techniques," in *Proceedings of the Fall COMPCON Conference*, IEEE, 1981, pp. 271–277.

24. Johnson, L., "Overview of the Knowledge-Based Specification Assistant," in *Proc. Second Annual RADC Knowledge-based Assistant Conference*, RADC(COES), Grifiss AFB, NY, 1987.
25. Johnson, L., "Turning Ideas into Specifications," in *Proc. Second Annual RADC Knowledge-based Assistant Conference*, RADC(COES), Grifiss AFB, NY, 1987.
26. Kant, E., "On the Efficient Synthesis of Programs," *Artificial Intelligence Journal*, 1983.
27. Ketabchi, M. and V. Berzins, "Generalization Per Category: Theory and Application," *Proc. Int. Conf. on Information Systems*, 1986. Also Tech. Rep. 85-29, Computer Science Dept., University of Minnesota.
28. Ketabchi, M. and V. Berzins, "Modeling and Managing CAD Databases," *IEEE Computer 20*, 2 February 1987, pp. 93–102.
29. Ketabchi, M. and V. Berzins, "Mathematical Model of Composite Objects and its Application for Organizing Efficient Engineering Data Bases," *Transactions on Software Engineering*, IEEE, January 1988.
30. Leite, J. C., "A Survey on Requirements Analysis," RTP-070, Department of Information and Computer Science, University of California at Irvine, 1987.
31. Linger, R. C., H. D. Mills, and B. I. Witt, *Structured Programming: Theory and Practice*, Reading, MA: Addison Wesley, 1979.
32. Liskov, B. and S. Zilles, "Programming with Abstract Data Types," *Proc. of the ACM SIGPLAN Notices Conference on Very High Level Languages 9*, 4 April 1974, pp. 50–59.
33. Luckenbaugh, G., "The Activity List: A Design Construct for Real-Time Systems," Master's Thesis, Department of Computer Science, University of Maryland, 1984.
34. Luckham, D. and F. W. Henke, "An Overview of Anna, a Specification Language for Ada," *IEEE Software 2*, 2 March 1985, pp. 9–22.
35. Luqi, "Rapid Prototyping for Large Software System Design," Ph. D. Thesis, University of Minnesota, 1986.
36. Luqi and M. Ketabchi, "A Computer Aided Prototyping System," in *Proceedings of ACM First International Workshop on Computer-Aided Software Engineering*, Vol. 2, Cambridge, Massachusetts, May 1987, pp. 722–731.
37. Luqi, *Normalized Specifications for Identifying Reusable Software*, Proc. of the ACM-IEEE 1987 Fall Joint Computer Conference, Dallas, Texas, October 1987, pp. 46–59.
38. Luqi and M. Ketabchi, "A Computer-Aided Prototyping System," *IEEE Software 5*, 3 March 1988, pp. 66–72.
39. Luqi and V. Berzins, "Rapidly Prototyping of Real-Time Systems," *IEEE Software 5*, 9 September 1988, pp. 25–36.
40. Luqi, V. Berzins, and R. Yeh, "A Prototyping Language for Real-Time Software," *IEEE Transactions on Software Engineering*, SE-14, 10, October 1988, pp. 1409–1423.
41. MacLaren, L., "Evolving Toward Ada in Real Time Systems," *Proc. ACM SIGPLAN Notices Symp. on the Ada Programming Language*, November 1980, pp. 146–155.
42. Majster, M. E., "Limits of the 'Algebraic' Specification of Abstract Data Types," *SIGPLAN Notices Notices 12*, 10 (1977), pp. 37–42.
43. Mok, A. K., *The Design of Real-Time Programming Systems Based on Process Models*, IEEE, 1984.
44. Mok, A. K., "The Decomposition of Real-Time System Requirements into Process Models," *IEEE Proc. of the 1984 Real Time Systems Symposium*, December 1984, pp. 125–133.
45. Musser, D., "Abstract Data Type Specification in the AFFIRM system," *IEEE Trans. on Software Eng. SE-6*, 1 June 1980, pp. 24–31.
46. Parnas, D., "On the Criteria to be Used in Decomposing a System into Modules," *Comm. of the ACM 15*, 12 December 1972, pp. 1053–1058.
47. Parnas, D. L., and P. C. Clements, "A Rational Design Process: How and Why to Fake It," *IEEE Trans. on Software Eng. SE-12*, 2 February 1986, pp. 251–257.
48. Rogers, H., "*Theory of Recursive Functions and Effective Computability*," NY: McGraw Hill, 1967.

49. Schonberg, E., J. Schwartz, and M. Sharir, "An Automatic Technique for the Selection of Data Representations in SETL Programs," *Trans. Prog. Lang and Systems 3*, 2 April 1981, pp. 126-143.

50. Smith, D., G. Kotik, and S. Westfold, "Research on Knowledge-Based Software Environments at Kestrel Institute," *IEEE Trans. on Software Eng.*, November 1985.

51. Stevens, W., G. Meyers and L. Constantine, "Structured Design," *IBM Systems Journal 13*, 2 May 1974, pp. 115-139.

52. Swartout, W., "GIST English Generator," in *Proceedings of the National Conference on Artificial Intelligence*, AAAI, 1982.

53. Wadge, W. W., and E. A. Ashcroft, *LUCID, the Dataflow Programming Language*, NY: Academic Press, 1985.

54. Yeh, R. T., R. Mittermeir, N. Roussopoulos, and J. Reed, "A Programming Environment Framework Based on Reusability," *Proc. Int. Conf. on Data Engineering*, April 1984, pp. 277-280.

55. Yeh, R. T., N. Roussopoulos, and B. Chu, "Management of Reusable Software," *Proc. COMPCON*, September 1984, pp. 311-320.

Chapter 5

An Integrated Approach to Requirements Analysis

ROLAND T. MITTERMEIR
Institut f. Informatik
Universitaet Klagenfurt
Austria

NICHOLAS ROUSSOPOULOS
Department of Computer Science
University of Maryland
College Park, MD

RAYMOND T. YEH
Syscorp International
Austin, TX

PETER A. NG
Institute for Integrated Systems Research
Department of Computer and Information Science
New Jersey Institute of Technology
Newark, NJ

ABSTRACT

Requirements Analysis is the earliest phase in most of the methodologies for developing software systems. Usually, it begins with a needs statement which is already expressed in fairly technical terms. There are inadequate efforts for gaining some basic understanding of the organization that plans to have a new system and the objectives for developing a proposed system. In this chapter, an objectives analysis phase that precedes the requirements analysis is introduced. Combining both analyses, an integrated approach to software requirements analysis is proposed.

1 INTRODUCTION

There exists a variety of software development life cycle models. In general, the software development process can be divided into six consecutive phases:

119

requirements analysis, specification, design, coding, testing, and operation and maintenance.[40,41] Of these phases, the specification phase, which produces a document of functional systems specification, is considered one activity of the requirements analysis phase.[14,27] In another well-known version of the software life cycle the requirements analysis is broken down into system requirements and software requirements; the design phase is split into preliminary design and detailed design; and, most importantly, validation is an activity to be considered within each phase.[3] For other phase models, a distinct installation phase is proposed:[9] the validation and verification activities are tied into the respective analysis or construction activities;[4] and the whole development process is divided into an analytical-constructive portion and an integrated-examinative portion, such that each phase in the first analytical-constructive part has its image in the integrated-examinative part.[7,14] Common to these phase models is their concentration on technical aspects of system development.

There are phase models that begin with considering managerial aspects of system development.[5,8,32] The initial phase of these models is to investigate the feasibility of alternative concepts as conceived by those who initiated the project, to evaluate the alternative concepts, and to select a superior concept from them. This is done by estimating the expected benefits and costs in terms of manpower, equipment, financial resources, and time for both the development and the operating phase.

However, current methodologies are not able to answer the questions "Why does this organization need what its people have expressed by needs statements?" or "Do they really want what they are stating?" Because these questions are of fundamental importance for the success of a project that has long lasting life, the authors propose the objectives analysis phase, which precedes the requirements analysis phase of the system development life cycle. It helps analysts to clearly define the purposes that the new system should serve. The information collected during this phase is obtained from multiple sources within the hierarchy of the organization that plans to get a new system. The prospective users of the target system thus become more active in its perception and development. This reduces fear about the new system and, therefore, contributes to its acceptance.

This chapter deals with the objective analysis and its integration with the requirements analysis. Furthermore, we want to stress that both verification and validation activities, as well as the feasibility study need to be addressed during all phases of the system development life cycle. Similarly, configuration management is a task to be considered during the whole product lifetime.[5] Its significance for the requirements specification, which is an intermediate product, must not be underestimated.

2   THE EARLY PHASES OF SYSTEM DEVELOPMENT

The authors believe that development of software systems should not begin with the requirements analysis. At this phase, a number of unnecessary and possibly restricting assumptions are made due to misconceptions, management politics, technical ignorance, mistrust, established practices, personnel resistance, and so forth. Many management decisions are made to accommodate personal objectives rather than the organization's objectives. For the most part task, process, and personnel assignments are given in the requirements specification without understanding their explicit relationships to the organization's objectives. Thus, some unnecessary constraints for the software development may arise. The addition of an objectives analysis phase preceding the requirements analysis allows us to undertake the study of the organization's objectives, and constraints against full achievement of the objectives, and their influences, interactions and degrees of freedom. Therefore, an advantage of the objective analysis is that the new system can be built in such a way that it will accomplish the organization's objectives even when certain modifications to the system are made to account for changes in the environment.

Generally, it is important that analysts are not mislead by the problems and the constraints of the current system. The solution for solving a problem may be different, depending on whether one talks to the corporate president, a senior manager, a department head, or a clerical staff, who is actually performing some related activity. The difficulty is that the opinion of the people involved in the daily operations is biased by the level of abstraction from which they conceive the problem, their planning horizon, their detailed acquaintance with the application, personal preconceptions, goals and responsibilities. Therefore, the true picture of ''the problem to be solved'' can be obtained only from collecting information from all parties concerned. Unfortunately, it is a time consuming process, but the advantage resulting from this process is that the system can be used effectively by the users because of their participation during the system development.[24]

2.1   Fundamentals of Objectives Analysis

The term ''objectives'' refers to a fundamental, long lasting and stable purpose of an organization or a human being. The term ''goal'' means a shorter term achievement pertinent to a given objective. Thus, an objective contains goals, which in turn contain subgoals. Goals and subgoals pertinent to a given objective may interact in a positive or negative way. These goals which are pertinent to an objective and the associated interactions are called an ''objectives structure.''

2.1.1   Activities of Objectives Analysis

Assume that a person always has an outline for a potential solution for a problem within the organization. The statement expressing the need of a system and its justification is the point of departure for the analysis effort. It serves to identify the part of the organization that will be affected by the development effort. The major activities of the objectives analysis phase are context analysis, objectives and problem analysis, and problem definition.

Context Analysis.   The objectives analysis phase begins with the determination of the preliminary scope of the development effort. It helps the analysts gain some basic understanding of the system and its immediate environment. In other methodologies, similar analysis is undertaken in an investigation phase[23] or "1st-Analyse."[33]

In context analysis, the analysts should learn about the basic functions to be performed by the target system, the environment of the target system, and the boundaries between the target system and its environment. They must also identify the major quantitative characteristics of the system and its environment.[1,28] Examples of the quantitative characteristics are number of employees, number of items produced or sold, and so forth.

When all this information is collected, the persons who are effected by the development effort can be identified. These include the users of the new system, their managers, supervisors, and other personnel who will be effected by the results of the target system. The list of persons obtained will be used as the basis for selecting the informants to be questioned during the following activities.

Objectives and Problem Analysis.   A problem can be defined as the difference between an original goal set and the actual goal attainment on a certain objectives dimension. For this reason, the problems expressed may be good indicators of objective dimensions. However, when solving a problem it is important not to forget about those aspects of the organization's goals, which are well enough attained, so that they would not be mentioned in connection with problems. Since the ultimate solution must continue to accommodate these aspects, one cannot obtain a complete view of the organization using a mere problem analysis but must rather find the major objectives that lead the activities of the organization.

After structuring the obtained objective dimensions into goal-subgoal relationships, the analysts must determine whether there are complementary or adversary relationships between various goals and/or subgoals (i.e., the magnitude of inter-goal dependencies). The analysts are required to identify the objectives of adverse groups (e.g., competitors) which have the possibility to hinder full goal achievement (i.e., the level of current attainment versus the desired attainment). These "negative" objectives will serve as restrictions in the later analysis and during the process of selecting the best alternative solution.

This activity follows the integration of objectives structures of the different groups within the customer organization by resolving the differences through negotiation and arbitration. Finally, the objectives structure of the organization, which is relevant to the current development effort, should be formally agreed upon and accepted.

Problem Definition.   This activity investigates the definition of the system, its environment, the boundary between the system and its environment, the problem areas that need to be addressed, and the constraints under which solutions need to be sought.

2.1.2   Input and Output of the Objectives Analysis Phase

Input—a statement of needs with justification and the authorization to start the analysis.

Output:

- a formally agreed upon objectives structure,
- a list of problems,
- the scope of the development (analysis) area and the restrictions for the new solution,
- some basic understanding of the organization (kind of enterprise, kind of products or services, macrostructure and history of the organization, management policies) and its environment (associated industrial world, local laws, cultural background, state of the associated markets, share of market),
- main tasks of the system, and
- available resources;

Byproduct:
- a list of potential informants for the requirements analysis phase, and
- a set of alternative solutions to be considered.

2.2   Fundamentals of Requirements Analysis

In the objectives analysis, the scope of the development effort and the goals of the customer organization are identified. These goals have been refined to a point where actual operations and required resources to achieve them have been identified. During the process of analyzing and refining objectives, the analysts formulate ideas about how to reach those objectives. Therefore, at the end of the objectives analysis phase, the analysts have obtained the goal structure of the organization and a set of alternative ideas for solutions, proposed on the basis of their own experience or a detailed study of the problems at hand. As shown in Figure 5-1, the requirements analysis includes the alternatives evaluation, system requirements analysis, medium definition, and software requirements analysis subphases.

2.2.1   Tasks to be Performed

Major tasks to be performed by the subphases of the requirements analysis follow.

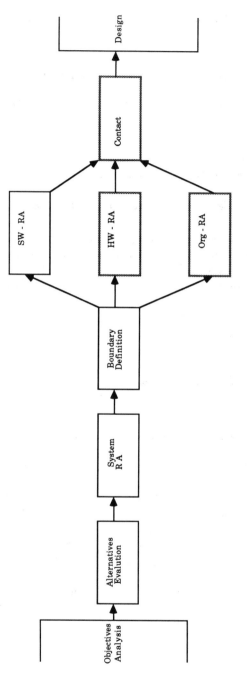

Figure 5-1. Subphases during Requirements Analysis.

Alternatives Evaluation Subphase:
- determine the schedule and resources for this phase
- refine the individual alternative to a point where a meaningful selection can be done
- define the evaluation criteria (on the basis of the goal structure)
- evaluate the alternatives in terms of their feasibility and desirability
- obtain a decision about whether the project should proceed and which alternative should be undertaken for further study in detail
- appoint a project manager to be responsible for the project

System Requirements Analysis Subphase:
- determine the schedule and resources for this phase
- refine requirements to be fulfilled by the chosen alternative to the degree that the boundary between the software, hardware, and organizational components of the system can be defined
- verify the requirements model
- validate the requirements in terms of the technical, operational, and economical feasibilities, and the feasibility of the schedule
- refine (redefine if necessary) the evaluation criteria and determine testing criteria for an acceptance test
- decide whether the project is to be continued

Medium Definition Subphase:
- determine which tasks or operations are to be performed by hardware, software, or the people within the organization
- validate the technical and economical feasibility of this assignment, and check the feasibility of the established schedule
- decide whether the project is to be continued

Software Requirements Analysis Subphase:
- refine the functional software requirements and associated nonfunctional aspects, such as quantitative, performance, availability, human engineering, documentation, and so forth
- refine testing criteria, and establish software testing criteria
- prepare the requirements specification (contract)
- validate the functional and nonfunctional aspects of the specification and the testing criteria

In this context, the term ''hardware'' refers to the major architectural hardware components of a system. Hardware requirements analysis will therefore, mainly investigate the workload characteristics expected for the future system.

The authors define ''organization'' as the organizational aspects of the application system that need to be redesigned in line with the design of the new information processing system. For example, the changes induced if a company replaces manual procedures by a computerized information processing system or if it switches from a batch system to an interactive system.

The decision about whom to award the development contract may have been made before the requirements analysis. If the hardware and software subsystems are contracted to different partners, the respective contracts should be given only after the requirements specification has been agreed upon by the partners.

2.2.2 Input and Output of the Alternatives Evaluation Subphase

Input:
- the formal agreement on goal structure and a list of current problems
- an inventory of available resources
- a set of alternative ideas about how current problems might be solved and how organizational objectives can be better achieved
- a list of informants from whom the analysts or developers can get further information in their search to broaden the set of alternative ideas

Output:
- a decision whether the project should continue and which alternative is to be pursued further during the requirements analysis
- relationships of chosen alternatives to objectives
- scope of further investigations
- appoint the project manager if not already appointed earlier
- appoint the steering committee

Byproduct:
- global evaluation criteria for the project
- rough cost and benefit analyses
- rough feasibility estimates
- better understanding of the working environment among members of the organization

2.2.3 Input and Output of the System Requirements Analysis

Input:
- description of the selected alternative, and
- a revised list of informants

Output:
- full requirements model (system specification) including functional and nonfunctional aspects, data and flow representations, testing considerations and anomalies description as well as the interface requirements to other systems in the immediate environment
- rough life cycle estimates and schedules
- refined and/or revised evaluation criteria

- revised cost and benefit analyses
- decision about the validity of the expressed requirements

Byproduct:
  - draft operator manuals
  - overall feasibility considerations
  - final list of informants

2.2.4 Input and Output of the Medium Definition Subphase

Input:
  - requirements specification, including special financial or organizational constraints

Output:
  - rough design of which functions (aspects of the solution) are to be realized in hardware and software or should be covered by the organization (system concept)
  - interface specification between software, hardware, and the organization
  - decision about the acceptability of this solution

Byproduct:
  - more reliable results of feasibility study, revised schedule and cost estimates, benefit estimates, and revised or refined operator manuals

2.2.5 Input and Output of Software Requirements Analysis

Input:
  - system requirements specification
  - system concept and task assignment to the software portion of the system
  - proposed software and hardware interface, and software and operators interface

Output:
  - detailed software requirements specification
  - developmental constraints
  - draft software development contract
  - test and acceptance criteria
  - full life cycle estimates (cost, time, manpower)
  - precise cost and benefit analyses
  - decision on whether the project is to be continued

Byproduct:
  - partial validation of the interface specification between the software subsystem and the other components

3 METHODOLOGICAL ASPECTS OF OBJECTIVES ANALYSIS

In this section, the authors consider the following issues: in the objectives analysis phase, what are the basic activities, what information is needed, and who plays which role during the individual steps of the phase. With the content and sources of information defined, the authors suggest approaches for getting this information, how to document it, how to analyze it and what to look for, how to evaluate the obtained result, and what the criteria are for judgment about the further process of the project.

3.1 Personnel

During the objectives analysis phase, each of the following organizational groups will play an important role:

- High level management within the customer organization—those at the organizational level and/or above who endorse the initiation of objectives analysis and eventually authorize the whole project.

- The steering committee—the committee serves to relieve the rest of management from the task of continually supervising the efforts of the analysis team and the project management. The committee contains members of those departments which will be concerned about the project and which are closer to the actual operations to be carried out in achieving the objectives of the organization. However, because conflict of interest is possible, neither a representative from the project team nor its manager should become members of the steering committee. If there is some lack of technical knowledge, a representative from the project team may be consulted occasionally.

- The project manager—this position will be created at the end of the objectives analysis phase. Once appointed, he/she will be the administrative head of the analysis team (project team). It is important that the project manager has sufficient power and status compared to the rest of the permanent organization with which he has to deal.[11]

- End-users—those who will ultimately use the target system. These users will state the problems to be solved during the current effort, and therefore, they must be asked about their objectives and hopes concerning the new system.

- The analysis team—main actor throughout the objectives and requirements analysis phases. Not only members of the organization are included: independent consultants and/or developers of the new system may also be on this team. It is possible that its composition changes over time and between the objectives and requirements analysis phases.

- The system developing organization—because different sources of information from the developers side are required, we further distinguish the developing organization into the manager of the development effort, designers, and experts in programming, testing and maintenance.

- Experts—for special information will provide advice on organizational matters, finance, business administration, law, etc.

3.2 What Information is Needed?

Through analysis, existing problems in the customer organization are found. Problems between a desired value and the actual value within one or several objectives dimensions can be viewed differently: this desired value will be referred to simply as an objective or goal. The important point of the objectives analysis phase is that it is insufficient to provide solutions to problems at surface level; these problems arise when the target system investigation begins. There may be problems of deeper levels which are important to consider; also objectives dimensions that are not currently problematic, but are important to consider in any large scale reorganization or redevelopment effort.

Objectives should not only come from people who authorize the project of developing a system but also from representatives working in the organization and those who will work with the new system. These various levels of management and operational personnel can express their views about the new system and suggest alternative ideas of potential solutions for their problem.

Frequently, there may be conflicts among the objectives, and more frequently there are constraints against full achievement of the objectives. Constraints may also come from facts inside the customer organization (e.g., physical operations, personnel structure, financial resources, etc.), from the environment of the organization (e.g., customers, competitors, laws, or government regulations, etc.), and finally (though usually only during the later phases) from the developers (e.g., current technology, constraints within the developing organization, etc.).

During the process of establishing relationships among the objectives, constraints, and ideas for solutions, one realizes that the objectives expressed by the organization are at different levels of abstraction. For example, they may range from "increase corporate profit by 20%" to "reduce error rate in the order entry procedure." These objectives form a hierarchy from abstract to operational goals of which, the relationships on a hierarchy are of the type goal-subgoals. In fact, this is a partially ordered set because there may be several goals at the highest level, which cannot be related to each other, and a given subgoal may be instrumental to more than one super goal.

Several authors call this goal–subgoal hierarchy a goal-means hierarchy.[13,16,34] The authors of this chapter do not follow this terminology and rather distinguish between means and subgoals. Subgoals are conceptual possibilities (alternative solutions) to reach a particular goal. On the next lower level of analysis, subgoals will be considered as goals. Means on the contrary are the actual resources spent to achieve goal attainment.

A given goal, in most cases, can be achieved by pursuing a large number of combinations of subgoals, which can be interpreted as different solutions to reach the goal. Therefore, the ordering of abstraction of goals also applies to the alternative ideas for solutions. With means, a different hierarchy exists. The means and objectives meet at the task level. There, an assignment of resources is made to accomplish a given objective by performing a certain task. Therefore, it is only on the task level that conflicts between objectives can arise because of limited resources. All conflicts within the objectives structure itself are not due to resource limitations. They are rather of ontological nature or due to some conflict of interest among those expressing these objectives.

To allow for a selection among the alternative ideas for achieving the overall objectives of the organization, the relationships between objectives (or between objectives and constraints) should be weighed by the impact one has upon the other, and each objective (or constraint) itself needs to be weighed according to its importance.

On the basis of the above, the objectives structure can be reduced to retain only those goals that are relevant to the current investigation. Further refinements will be made with representatives of those departments in the organization, who ultimately will carry out the operations attached to those subgoals of the selected high level goals. This refinement process terminates when the level of actual tasks or resources has been reached.

3.3 Who is Involved?

A project can be initiated by people at management level who express their objectives, constraints, and ideas with respect to the company, the organizational subunits, and people involved. Ideally, this information is obtained through a process of interviewing people involved at all organizational levels. With a large organization, an intermediate reduction in the scope of study, and the number of informants to be interviewed can be achieved by tracing those organizational subunits that are responsible for carrying out the subgoals (or subfunctions). The interviewing requires intermediate structuring and a selection process. At the end of the process, all objectives should be brought together into one objectives-constraints structure.

Figure 5-2 shows how the boundary in the scope of the analysis may fluctuate when proceeding down the hierarchy. After all users contribute their objectives, the scope of the analysis must be defined. This definition and selection process should be based on a consensus of all persons involved (giving enough consideration to the different power and responsibility of different echelons). Ample time should be provided for negotiations to reach this consensus.

On the basis of the final objectives structure, the set of alternative ideas,

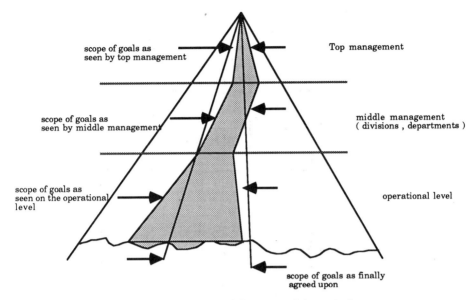

scope of goals as
seen by top management

Top management

scope of goals as
seen by middle management

middle management
(divisions , departments)

scope of goals as
seen on the operational
level

operational level

scope of goals as finally
agreed upon

Figure 5-2. Definition of the scope of the analysis.

which should be subject to a more detailed evaluation in the requirements
analysis, can be chosen. An a-priori selection may be necessary because too
many alternatives were discovered for a detailed study.

Figure 5-3 shows what roles should be played by the various parties during
the objectives analysis phase. We consider roles according to the following:
those of the main actor (A), the main information source (I), those who should
further support this step by either contributing information on demand or doing
certain supportive analysis (S), those who verify the correctness of the results
of a step if no thorough analysis can be done (J). The individual parties are
listed as row labels. The column labels define the steps of the phase, which are
ordered according to their sequential application from left to right. Sometimes
this order may be changed by iterations over subsets of the columns. For
example, one may iterate over columns 2 and 3, over columns 2 through 5, and
2 through 7.

Initially, the main actor is someone from higher level management (in most
cases he/she acts on an initiative of middle management), but an analysis team
will become the main actor, once it is created. During this phase, a steering
committee is formed as early as possible. Its members are usually the first
informants for the analysis team. But one also needs to get information from
other management at all levels before the actual users of the system are reached.
To account for these repetitions, the respective role symbols are given with
indices in Figure 5-3. However, more than three iterations for any large organization will be needed.

	start process	find objectives, constraints and related measures	structure objectives and constraints	determine importance of objectives and constraints	define alternatives to reach objective	determine impact of each alternative	select set of alternatives
High level management	A	I_1, V_1, J_3	I	I,V,J	I	(J)	I,J,V
steering committee		$I_1, V_1/J_1, J_3$	S	A,I		V,J	I,J,V
other management levels	I	$I_2, V_2/J_2, J_3$	I	I,V	I	(I)	I,J,V
end users		I_3, V_3, J_3		I,V	I	S	I,V
project manager			does not yet exist				
analysis team		A	A	(A) S(V) (A)	A,I	A	A,I V
developer management syst. designer programmer tester maintenance					S or I	S I,V	S,V
experts of organization business physical system			S S	S S	S S	I,V I,V I,V	V S V V
other sources		I		I			

A ... actor
I ... information source
S ... support
V ... verifier
J ... judge

Figure 5-3.   Role/activity relationship during the objective analysis phase.

The developers will not be involved at the beginning of this process, but the closer the analysis approaches the operational (end-user) level, the higher the likelihood that consultation with the potential developers is necessary to assess a broad range of possible alternatives. Experts of various areas inside the organization will support the goal structuring, but other sources are often required to provide information, such as information about the environment of the organization and the constraints within this environment, which work against the objectives of the organization.

Owing to the fact that the analysis team may also contain people from outside the organization and that the consideration of goals is a delicate operation, a role shift of the main actor of the task to the steering committee, leaving the analysis team as a supporting role results.

3.4 How to Get the Necessary Information

In the process of gathering information, one concern is the means used to find information within the organization or environment. The other concern is related to techniques for broadening the perspective of the organization to find a sufficient number of subgoals and finally, operational alternatives to accomplish these goals.

For the first concern, information gathering, interviewing, questionnaires, documents analysis, observation, and brainstorming can be used. Among these, the interview is most common. It can be conducted in a free format (open interview), guided by a set of questions, or an outline about what strategies should be used to get the information and what items should be covered by the interview. Although the interview consumes a large amount of the analysts' (the analysis team) time, the advantages of the interview over the other techniques are its flexibility and the opportunity for the interviewer to stimulate motivation, clarify uncertainties and adjust the frame of references of the conversation.

To overcome the amount of analysts' time required, a questionnaire can be used. The questionnaire can be considered as an extension of the interview if the number of respondents is large or if the respondents are spread over a wide geographical area. Questionnaires not only refer to standardized multiple-choice type questions: a letter with a set of detailed questions is also considered as a form of (open) questionnaire, if it requires written communication for a response. In both cases, the fact that the interviewer is not present at the time when the response is given may distort the response and limit the respondent's cooperation. An approach using partly structured forms filled in by the respondent may be an adequate compromise between these two.

In many cases, observation is an important method. During the objectives analysis phase, observation can be used to detect certain constraints that may result from the organization, the scheduling of activities, or the personnel structure of the organization. However, the main method used in this phase is the interview, primarily because it is the most effective technique to discover the goals of the organization. Although these goals may not appear in the corporate charter, they may decide the ultimate success or failure of the project.

Confidentiality is an important factor during the interview process, but its assurance is difficult, especially when the interviewers are members of the organization itself. Either way, a more detailed discussion of information gathering techniques can be found in References 10 and 18.

The second concern is the refinement of goals into operational subgoals. Besides interviews, techniques stimulating creativity can be used to broaden perspectives. Some of these techniques are brainstorming or brainwriting, synectics, morphological methods, or the delphi method.[31] Finally, in every application area, the "rule of thumb" technique has been advantageous.

Further clues about the refinement of objectives can be derived from the measure of goal attainment. Sometimes, one can assign numerical values to the current state of the goal attainment. The rule for computing the values can conform to the structure of the problem. For example, "profit = income − expense" implies that profit increases by increasing income, reducing expenses, or a combination of both. Goal attainment is not directly measurable, and one needs some indicators for assessing the level currently reached. Similarly, working with the indicators will help find subgoals if the indicators are valid. For example, happiness: a person is happy if . . . ; she is unhappy if . . . Looking at positive and negative aspects is helpful in this context.

3.5 Documentation

Natural language alone is not sufficient for formally analyzing and documenting the relationships between objectives and between objectives and constraints. A matrix specification should be used. In the matrix shown in Figure 5-4, a column header is a current level goal, and a row header is a subgoal or constraint. The ratings of the impact is the matrix element. In addition to the impact, this matrix may also contain entries for specifying the importance of each goal, level of desired goal attainment and actual goal attainment, and various relationships to constraints. This additional information could also be recorded in special goal or constraint matrices.[22]

Besides the matrices, an objectives structure diagram is a method for documentation. The basic components of the diagram are shown in Figure 5-5. It shows the goals as circles and a top to bottom relationship between high level goals and operational goals. The relationship of subgoals supporting an objective can be indicated by upward-pointing broken arrows. If there is a mutually supportive relationship between objectives of the same level of abstraction, a double-headed arrow between these two circles is added. If this relationship is negative or exclusive, an inverse arrow is used.

The measure for importance and impact can be written into the goal circles

OBJECTIVES SUB- OBJECTIVE	importance	increase earnings	increase number of customers	increase price	increase service	increase quality of personnel
importance		1	(.9)	(.1)	(.5)	(.5)
increase earnings		---	0	0	0	0
increase number of customers		.5	---	(-0.7)	0	0
increase price		.5	(-0.7)	---	0	0
increase service		0	.8	0	---	(.6)
increase quality of sales personal		0	.2	0	(.6)	---
CONSTRAINTS	importance					
size of market	.8	0	(-0.2)	0	0	0
elasticity of market	.9	0	0	(-0.8)	0	0
current personnel	.6	0	0	0	0	(-0.9)
structure of labor market	.4	0	0	0	0	(-0.3)

Figure 5-4. Goal/sub-goal and goal/constraint matrix.

or to the relationship arrows. Importance can also be highlighted by the relative size of the goal circles. The strength of a relationship can be indicated by the width of the arrow.

Constraints are represented as diamonds. In a large objectives structure, as shown in Figure 5-6, the addition of constraints to the structure may lead to clutter. Therefore, we propose to draw a separate constraint diagram for each goal.

3.6   Consistency and Completeness Verification

The analysis steps of the phase involve formal reasoning about the information collected. The consistency and completeness of the objectives structure is checked. One approach for detecting consistencies is to analyze the objectives structure for cyclic substructures. Another approach is to check whether the importance of the subgoal equals the respective supergoals and the impact ratings they have on their supergoals, taking the constraints or negative relationships to other goals into consideration. Eventually, inconsistencies must be resolved among those who provided the objectives structures.

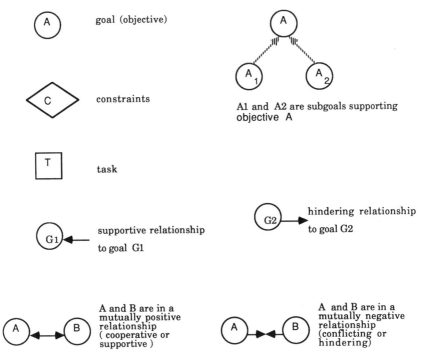

Figure 5-5. Symbols of goal (constraints) structure diagrams.

In a completeness check, it is difficult to show that a goal has been completely decomposed into all its possible subgoals. It is possible to explicitly rule out several theoretical subgoal alternatives. Such a decision should be documented by showing each alternative as a constraint with an appropriately large and negative weight of importance.

Another completeness check is to determine the complete coverage of information sources at every iteration when going down the organizational hierarchy. There may be relationships on the operational level that are not fully conforming to the hierarchical structure of the organization and will go unnoticed if an organization chart is used as the only means for finding the task assignment. A means for finding such additional information sources is to combine the organization chart with a network of dynamic work relationships (e.g., flow of control, information, etc.). An example of such an approach has been presented in Reference 12.

3.7   Evaluation

Verification determines whether the facts expressed in the objectives-constraints structure match with reality. Verification can best be done by reviews with the

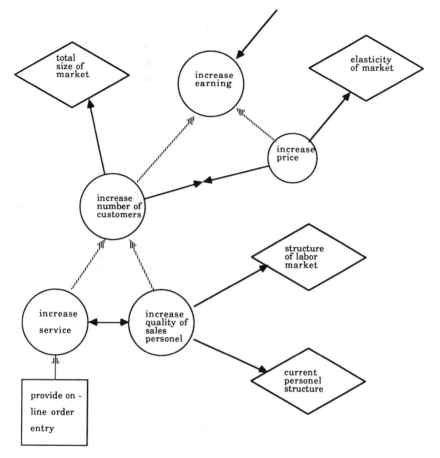

Figure 5-6. Example of a goal/constraint structure diagram.

information sources. Validation will come mainly from the theory about the application area and from past experience. It should not be confused with judgement or authorization of legitimacy of goals.

3.8 Decision Criteria About Whether to Proceed

This phase determines the main objectives structure of the organization and translates the objectives into a set of possible actions. The transition to the next phase can be done only after this translation process has been completed, that is, when the goals and subgoals are already at such a concrete level that they can be expressed in terms of processes, functions, tasks, data, or resources.

However, the complete translation into this operational level does not warrant the procedure to the next phase. The requirements analysis phase of the project should only be started after a consensus has been reached about the objectives structure and its refinement into tasks. This is indicated by the V's (verification) in the last column of Figure 5-3 for all persons involved in the effort. Reaching this consensus and acceptance of objectives takes time. Therefore, the schedule for the objectives analysis phase should provide ample slack for bargaining, explaining, and thought about this issue.

3.9   Tools

A key idea in the modeling approach is the distinction between behavioral and operational models. These two models complement one another at various stages of refinement. In the behavioral model, only the interactions of an object with its environment are described. The operational model explains how these interactions should be realized internally. In theory, the behavioral model should be constructed before the operational model. In practice, however, it is sometimes difficult to communicate with customer representatives at an abstract level. For this reason, modeling tools and methods should be flexible enough to express both behavioral and operational aspects of a component. The solution to this problem is to propose a conceptual schema definition language (CSDL),[30] which expresses both data and function oriented descriptions.[18,19] The language can easily be mapped into different notations, which are highly specialized for a particular type of analysis. These notations may form the outer shell of a system of requirements languages as shown in Figure 5-7. However, other requirements languages and tools can be used if one must overcome the particular shortcomings of these languages.

A basic and mandatory tool is a project data base where all information which is generated during the system life cycle is saved. In addition to adequate graphic support for drawing the goal structure chart and the goals-constraints relationships, simple matrix manipulation tools will help to derive the importance of subgoals and may also help to detect inconsistencies within the goal structure, (e.g., cyclic substructures, positive and negative relationships on parallel paths). For validating the subgoal refinement and subgoal weighing, simulation models of the application to be reorganized are helpful.

4   REQUIREMENTS ANALYSIS

The objectives analysis phase results in a set of alternatives that meet the various objectives of the organization. In the requirements analysis phase, the actual assessment of the requirements should be made. During the process of evaluating the set of alternatives, any alternative, which is less promising to meet the objectives of the organization, will be eliminated. After sufficient understanding of the system requirements for the chosen alternatives, the hardware configuration is selected and then the software requirements will be studied.

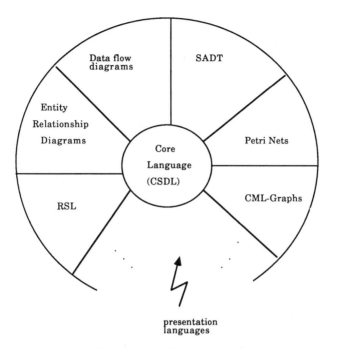

Figure 5-7. A system of requirements languages.

4.1 Alternatives Evaluation

During the objectives analysis phase, the whole organization and, to some extent, its environment is studied. The requirements analysis phase focuses directly on portions of the information processing system of the organization and those parts of the environment that interface with these parts. As shown in Figure 5-8, the environment can be distinguished as an inner environment and/ or an outer environment. An inner environment is the environment of the information processing system inside the organization (e.g., those parts of the organization that will use the information processing system). An outer environment is the environment of the customer organization (e.g., customers, competitors, etc.). After the objectives analysis, a sector of the physical system of the organization, which interfaces directly with the information processing system, is studied. For the assembly line or the warehouse, examples of a sector are order processing, production control, and a management information subsystem.

4.1.1 What Information is Required?

The author's attention is now restricted to the sector of the information processing system and its immediate environment. The sector includes its human

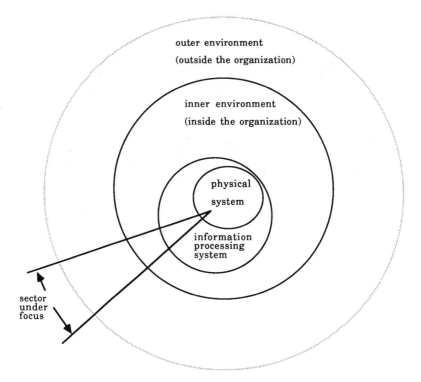

Figure 5-8. Scope of requirements analysis.

components and operations and its hardware and software components. Within the sector, both functional and non-functional system properties must be considered. The functional properties refer merely to the input-output transformations to be performed. Every qualification of these transformations, such as quantitative, temporal, qualitative, and economic aspects, refers to the non-functional properties. The functional properties may be specified either in behavioral or operational form. A checklist of what information should be contained in a requirements document is given as follows. This serves as a guideline for the system requirements study also, to a lesser extent, the evaluation and reduction of alternative ideas for solutions.

CONTENTS OF REQUIREMENTS DOCUMENT

General Remarks

Information about the document itself:
- date, version, author
- source of information

- degree of certification
  - person who verifies or approves it
  - method of verification
- portions that need further elaboration by the analyst (in terms of completeness or refinement)
- relationships with other documents.

Requirements Attached to Functional Aspects

Relationship to objectives:
- objectives related to this concept or task in a positive or negative way (e.g., primary and secondary purpose, detrimental affects)
- constraints or facilitation related to this task

Major functional and non-functional properties:
- intuitive description of the task
- data used by this function or task
  - distinguish data as "refer to (input)," "used up (input)," "produced (output)," and "change (input and output)"
  - when and from where does this data come, or where does it go (source, destination, circumstance)
  - where and when are the results ultimately required
  - how much data is to be processed (quantity and unit of measurement)
  - specify the context from which data is drawn or into which it is written (interface specification)
  - should the results be produced piecemeal or presented in their entirety when the task is complete. If piecemeal, what are the meaningful increments
  - is a copy of the results to be retained locally
- what are the actual data transformations performed (in a more formal way, behavioral description)
  - conditional input/output mapping
  - distinguish the transformations as normal and failure cases
  - what are the transformational invariants which should hold before and after execution of the task
  - in a distributed environment, where should the task be performed (if this is not a design decision)
- initiation of the task
  - how (by data flow, control flow, periodically)
  - when (time)
  - by whom (agent)
  - how often (frequency)

- under what conditions (e.g., internal conditions of the system)
- duration or termination of the task and performance requirements
- which factors determine the duration
- terminating condition
- are there any context dependencies (on data environment or system state)
- required accuracy
- consequences if required accuracy is not met
- reasons for inaccuracy (countervailing powers)

Other aspects:
- availability
  - required availability
  - required fallback operations in anomalous conditions
- security requirements
- diagnostic procedures to assess proper functioning of the system
- privacy requirements
- functional environment
  - which other functions does this function serve
  - which other functions does this function use
- functional core (operational specification of data transformation, indication whether this operational specification serves only as an example to ease comprehension of the function to be performed, or whether it is an actual requirement, such that the function must be implemented in that way
- demand on resources in terms of
  - computing power (time, processing rate, space needed for storing data, special equipment)
  - physical space
  - manpower
  - financial resources (during development and during operation)
- interface between present and future
  - maximum permissible time for system construction
  - procedure to change from present to future system (only the requirements, not the design aspects of this topic)
- further aspects of change in the future
  - expected modifications or changes in requirements (e.g., due to anticipated environmental changes)
  - portability aspects
- yardstick and method to assess degree of goal achievement by the proposed solution
- cost benefit analysis
- feasibility study
  - technical, operational, and economic feasibility

Data Oriented Requirements Aspects

- logical data structure
- volume (present, future, trend)
- present physical appearance (and whether it is a constraint for the future)
- where (in a functional sense) is the data
  - generated
  - stored/buffered
  - used (also includes slight transformation, e.g., value changes)
  - discarded (also includes substantial transformation, e.g., structural changes with necessity for generation of a new structure)
- from where (in a physical or geographical sense) is the data generated, stored, or used
- accuracy
- rules for consistency
- average (or actual) lifetime of data items and data values
- code system (if this should not be a design decision)
- security and methods for regenerating lost data
- privacy, ownership, responsibility, usage permissions
- transition from present to future system
  - is any new information required, if so can it be automatically derived or is manual data generation necessary
  - should the transition be gradual or instantaneous

4.1.2   Who is Involved?

Figure 5-9 is a role model for the evaluation phase in which the analysis team is the main actor. The project manager is responsible for scheduling and planning activities and supports the feasibility study as far as the economic or scheduling issues are concerned. If the position of the project manager is not filled, the steering committee and the analysis team will share the responsibility.

The evaluation process requires refining each individual alternative idea, and thus refining the evaluation criteria. New evidence shows that changes in the evaluation criteria are required but should be kept at minimum. Because such changes require endorsement from high level management, its participation is shown in parentheses. The end users are the main input source to be considered for refining individual alternatives.

In consultation with the steering committee, high level management should consider whether the selected alternative is sufficient and whether the project should continue to proceed with the detailed analysis of this proposed solution. If management does not give the endorsement to go ahead, the evaluation process can be repeated with new alternatives, or the project is halted.

	scheduling & planning	refinement of alternative solution ideas	refinement & redefinition of evaluation criteria	evaluation: in feasibility	evaluation: in desirability	evaluation: in economic justification	decide about: alternatives	decide about: project continuation
High level management	(I)	(I)	(I) (V,J)		(I)		J	J
steering committee	I A₁	(J for extension of scope)	I V,J		I		A J	A,I
end users (of system)		I,V	(I)		I,V			
analysis team	I	A, V	A	A,V	A,V	A,V	I	
project manager	A_2					S	S	
developer								
management		S		A I				
syst. designer		S		I				
programmer				S				
tester								
maintenance		S		S				
experts of organization		S	(I)		S			
business		S	(I)		S	I		
physical system		S	(I)		S			
other sources		S						

A ... actor
I ... information source
S ... support
V ...verifier
J ... judge

Figure 5-9. Role/activity relationship during the alternatives evaluation subphase.

4.1.3 How to Get the Necessary Information

As in the objectives analysis phase, interviews and documents analysis are the most effective means to gather information. The following system requirements for the selected alternative subphase will refine the information gathered from this phase. In this alternatives evaluation subphase, instead of gathering complete information details, the analysis team (analysts) should pursue a "most stringent requirements first" approach to speed up the screening process. The analysis requires a sequence of iterations yielding successive refinement of both the analysts' and customers' understanding of the solution space.

There have been many discussions about which approach is best suited to gain this understanding.[17,29,36,39] The analysts should select an effective approach based upon one of the following scenarios of the analysts' understanding of the investigated system:

- The analysts have a clear understanding of the environment of the problem domain, including a clear picture of what belongs to the system and what belongs to its environment. The environment is everything outside of what is currently perceived of as the system. But, the analysts do not fully understand the internal structure of the system and the interface between the system and its environment. In this situation, it will be most advantageous to use an OUTSIDE-IN approach to work from the system boundary towards the central system properties. Figure 5-10 is a scenario for outside-in analysis. Examples of this scenario are process control systems or machine systems. Usually, the interfaces (e.g., sensors and monitors) to the physical system are given. The initially perceived system boundary remains roughly the same throughout the whole development effort. The outside-in interaction analysis is also best suited for any system containing substantial human activities.
- The analysts have a well defined boundary of the system and a preliminary understanding about the core of the new system. However, the environment of the system and its interactions with the system are not clearly defined. It is also possible that the boundary between the system and its environment should include some portions of what is currently assumed to be within the environment. In this situation, an INSIDE-OUT interaction analysis can be used. This analysis begins from the currently perceived boundary of the system. A scenario of this type as shown in Figure 5-11 will usually occur at an intermediate stage of requirements analysis. For example, the problem, as seen initially, consists of automating a particular task. As the analysis progresses and the current system boundary is investigated, it becomes clear that an increase in scope seems desirable. Tasks which are peripheral to the main task should be investigated in detail, and the boundaries of the system and the environment are pushed outwards.

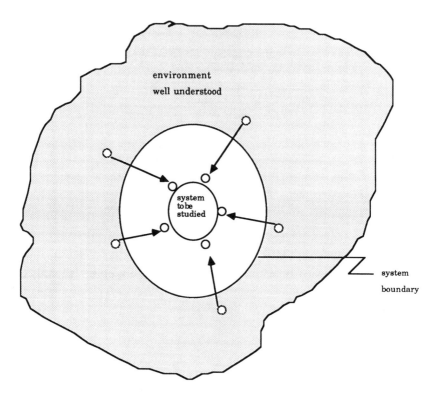

Figure 5-10. A scenario for outside-in analysis.

- The analysts have a description of a unique activity to be performed together with its input and output data. However, the details of this activity and the complete relationships between this activity and its environment are unclear. A TOP-DOWN approach is most suitable for this situation. It is our contention that this situation is rather rare in the initial phases of a project.
- Given a complete set of well defined operations and their relationships, the abstraction of these operations and their relationships to enhance understanding are unclear. A BOTTOM-UP approach is the best suited analysis for this situation. Situations requiring this approach will occur at intermediate steps of the analysis or after the main part of the analysis has been completed.

Both top-down and bottom-up approaches attempt to understand a system through the derivation of abstraction or refinement of the system. For outside-in (inside-out) approach, understanding of a complex system will be gained by partitioning the system into a set of layers inside (or outside) the currently perceived system boundary. These two approaches are conformant to our notion

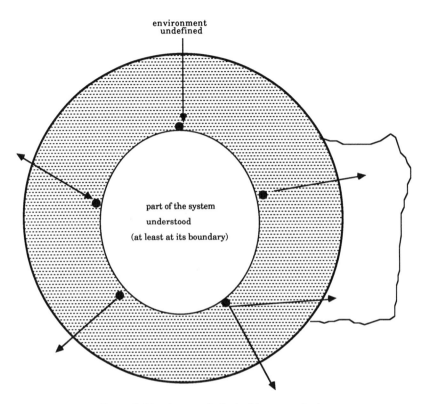

Figure 5-11. A scenario for inside-out analysis.

of behavioral system modeling, because in both approaches the interactions between the system and its environment are studied. The merit of using these two approaches in the requirements analysis is that they give a global perspective of the system, free from any implementation-oriented and operational considerations.

The notion of "system" is generic in this context. In the same way understanding the relationship between the total system to be developed and its environment by investigating the interactions on the system boundary, the interactions between system components and their local environment within the complete system can be studied.

For partitioning a system into components, one can unwrap the system, in a way similar to peeling an onion, by partitioning it into several moderately complex processes on the boundary and a central core, as shown in Figure 5-12. Refining the core of the system is proceeded by repetitive applications of the outside-in analysis until individual tasks are reached. For example, in an order processing system, "receive order," "receive inquiry," "answer to inquiry," "shipment order," and "shipment invoice" are the components at

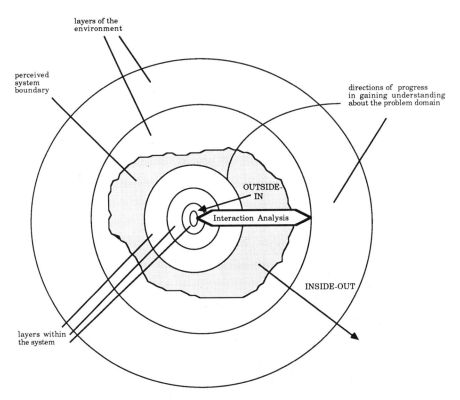

Figure 5-12. Different directions in understanding a system by behavioral modeling (interaction analysis).

the outer layer. At the next layer, we find "dispatch order," "collate items," and "produce invoice." Refining the remaining core of the system yields "fetch item in warehouse," "keep backorders," "maintain inventory," and "maintain price data."

The basic assumption of these scenarios is that at some well-defined level of abstraction, the analysts have a complete picture of the point of departure. In reality, this is not always the case. At the beginning of the requirements analysis phase, the analysts have bits and pieces of requirements that are neither on the same level of abstraction nor are they complete and fully consistent. The authors describe a STOP-GAPS approach, which is used to simply fill in the gaps that exist in the given description and then to elaborate the result until a situation where one of the approaches can be used, is obtained from bits and pieces of requirements.

There are two ways for obtaining a requirements model. One way is to begin by analyzing data until one comes to processes. The other is to follow the path of processes, and examine their data. The analysts may pick one for analysis, and use the other for verification.

Assume that the analysts begin with data analysis. The analysis starts with getting the description of existing permanent files, such as manuals, and information about existing temporal files, then determines which activities (processes) make use of these files and how these files are constructed, determines if any record elements are used, and if so, in which activity, and finally, determines all other relevant information about data, such as volume, trend, consistency rules, code system, etc. Further details are provided in Section 4.2.1. Unfortunately, at this point, one cannot assume that the set of activities derived from the data analysis is complete. Therefore, one may use the Stop-Gaps approach to organize the activities for completion.

In the remainder of this section, the authors discuss the Stop-Gaps, Outside-In, Inside-Out, Top-Down, and Bottom-Up approaches.

The Stop-Gaps Approach

Point of Departure—a set of processes or process sequences is given. Some processes may partially interface with the rest of the system (input, output, control) specified.

Analysis Steps:

1. Consider one of the processes in the given set. Define fully its interfaces with the rest of the system and with the environment, if any.

2. Trace the input, output, and control path of this process. If they lead to a process which is not yet known, add this process to the set of the given processes. Otherwise, check the respective interfaces of this process and continue.

3. If there is a process in the set of given processes that has not yet been analyzed, continue with step 1. Otherwise, an internally complete set of interacting processes has been found. Continue with step 4.

4. Organize the processes; then check whether they form a coherent system, and check whether the boundary of the current system is the desired system boundary. If the boundary should be extended, proceed Inside-Out. If some internal functions of the system are missing, use Outside-In. Then refine the processes. Repeat Stop-Gaps if necessary (repetition may be necessary if the levels of abstraction of the given processes did not match after the application of Top-Down or Bottom-Up).

If a complete and consistent definition of the system has been reached, proceed either Top-Down if further refinement is needed, or Bottom-Up for combining processes to higher level entities.

The Outside-In Approach

Point of Departure—a well defined system environment is given.

Analysis Steps:

1. Define interactions between the environment and the system in terms of data and control transfer and also in terms of other mutual influences and restrictions, which may come from the environment.

2. (Partitioning) Locate those processes that are dedicated to a specific inter-action with the environment or with a specific user group in the environment, those processes that are shared with certain limits (e.g., fixed communication pattern in the sense that user A provides input and user B receives output), and those processes which serve for communication with the central system. Identify the central system itself.

3. Analyze the input and output data for each process and the conditions under which this process is activated.

4. Analyze the central system aspects by repeating 1 through 3.

5. Check the partitioning by considering
   • environmental conditions:
     • common user category
     • common activating situation (state of environment, activation frequency such as yearly, daily, etc.) activation time such as end of month, 15th, etc.)
   • system situations (interface simplicity):
     • frequency of communication
     • amount of information transferred with each communication activity
     • kind of information transferred
     • other criteria of structured design.[37.25]

6. Get all other relevant information about each process (and about process abstractions if necessary).

7. If possible form generalizations (and aggregations) of the partitions.

8. Perform further refinement of individual processes as far as necessary.

9. Form process abstraction.

The Inside-Out Approach

Point of Departure—a well defined system kernel is given.

Analysis Steps:

1. Define the interactions between the already known system kernel and its environment. What are data transfer or other impacts across the system boundary which are currently perceived?

2. Identify the targets and the sources of the interactions with the environment. This step will lead to a partitioning of the environment.

3. Study the relevant aspects of all the environment objects identified in the preceding step.

The relevancy of an aspect is determined after a preliminary inspection of this object. The inspection classifies an object as an environmental object or a system component. For the environmental object, only the portions of the "system side" of this object need to be studied for a full understanding of the interface (e.g., form, frequency, and control of interaction). If the object is to be integrated into the system, it should be studied fully and another iteration, starting from step 1 in this approach, will be necessary. For example, in an order processing system, "sending remainders" could be initially perceived as a task of the accounting department and outside the scope of the system. After studying the boundary between the handling of orders and the accounting department, one may find that the handling of remainders may be easily integrated into the invoicing part of the order processing system. Therefore, one must not only study which data should be provided for the customer accounts but also how and under what conditions the remainders are sent.

4. Study interconnections between newly added components.

The Top-Down Approach

Point of Departure—the description of an unrefined object is given.

Analysis Steps:

1. Check the input, output, and control interfaces. Determine which additional interactions with the environment will exist.

2. Define the components of this activity.

3. Define the interconnection of these components in terms of data flow and control flow.

4. Check for completeness. Are there any undefined control and data flow? Are there any unresolved alternate branches of control or data flow?

5. Check for consistency. Is the input, output and control specification consistent with the interface specification? Can every activity be activated within finite time? Are the results produced by the activities used somewhere?

6. Check whether the partitioning into modules is meaningful. Check whether a different partitioning would better reflect the actual situation. In addition to the current partitioning, check whether other partitioning should be done for different viewpoints. If so, how are the resulting structures related to each other?

7. Define the interfaces of the components precisely.

8. Proceed with the next analysis iteration.

The Bottom-Up Approach

Point of Departure—a complete set of well defined operations is given.

Analysis Steps:

1. Search for identical operations. Examine any operations which have the same name and interface with the same data, which have the same name but interface with different data, or which have a different name but interface with the same data. If renaming must be done, repeat this step for the renamed item(s), and a reference between the old and new name must be kept in the project data base.

2. Perform abstraction: this can be in the form of generalization, collection, or aggregation.

For generalization, identify the objects that are not identical according to step 1 but are very similar. Identify their common properties, and form a generalization hierarchy; for example, order by mail, order by phone, and orders from a customer can be generalized to order.

For collection, identify objects that are identical in some sense but still exist as independent entities. Form these objects as a group with a higher level entity; for example, a file is a collection of records, a branch office has many workstations.

For aggregation, relate all those activities that serve a common purpose or are tightly coupled. The relationship of these activities shows the data, control, and time dependencies among them. Aggregate these activities as a new higher level entity with its input, output, and control relationships to its environment.

For example, availability check, the check for customer credit, and the price check are combined to "order acceptance checks." Then check whether the object formed in this way corresponds to the top-down partitioning rules mentioned beforehand.

3. Proceed to the next analysis iteration.

Figure 5-13 provides a summary of the analysis steps for each approach. The various checks listed for the outside-in approach should be done with any approach the analyst uses as a mainstream of the analysis. However, the authors propose the outside-in for the mainstream of the analysis, and the other approaches should play a supportive role whenever needed.

4.1.4 Documentation

Any external notations should be suitable for representing a particular aspect of the requirements model or for communication with a particular user group. Any graphical notations, which have the capability of information hiding and precisely representing details, are adequate. The layout of a well defined analysis form may be customized for particular applications and should provide some sections to include graphical notations. Compressing natural language state-

INTERACTION ANALYSIS			REFINEMENT/ABSTRACTION	
stop gaps	outside in	inside out	top down	bottom up
- define interface and analyze component			- check interface	
- trace data & control path	- define interaction	-define interaction		
	- parttition towards center	- expand system and partition environment	- define components	- analyze components
	- analyze data & control	- analyze components within expanded boundary		
		- study interactions	- define interconnections	
- check completeness			- check completeness	- check completeness
- sort				- sort/group
- check consistency	- check partitioning		- check consistency	- abstract
	- check sufficiency		- check partitioning	-generalize
	generalize/ aggregate			- aggregate
	refine			-collect
	aggregate			

Figure 5-13. Summary of analysis steps.

ments into portions of the analysis form will help in restricting the use of natural language.

For the internal representation of the conceptual model, a powerful and versatile language is required for having all the technical aspects of the conceptual model expressed in the same language. The conceptual schema definition language is a suitable candidate.[30] Integrating with various external notations, the language becomes user friendly for readers with only a moderate technical background.

If data oriented aspects are to be modeled, entity relationship diagrams will be a candidate for simplified presentations.[6,15,26] If activity related aspects should be presented, CML-graphs will serve the same purpose. For behavioral modeling, stimulus response graphs, event nets, state machines, or decision tables may be used as projections of the conceptual model.[35] The description of operational models can be expressed by applicative notations or RSL networks. For purely operational specifications, SADT and its derivatives, PSL, data flow diagrams, Petri nets, and PDL are candidates for external presentation. PAISLEY is a design language which allows precise specification and testing of process communication. A compromise between several of these languages is presented in Reference 23.

In the process of selecting a particular language, the analysts should bear in mind that it is desirable that this language should allow for the documentation of the analysis results, as well as the outline of the choosen alternative, and the procedure and criteria used to select this alternative.

4.1.5 Evaluation

Before the transition to the next phase, through review, the conceptual model built during the alternatives evaluation subphase is checked for completeness as far as the number of major functions and the most stringent requirements are considered. A further aspect worth considering is how far apart are the best two alternatives, the amount of risk involved with the leading alternative(s), and the degree they will contribute to goal achievement. The reviewers may not only look at the analysis results but also at similar cases from the past. Therefore, past experience and proper judgement about the future will be the most valuable evaluation criteria.

After this partial verification, the alternative ideas are evaluated in terms of their feasibility, their effectiveness to attain the desired objectives, and in terms of cost effectiveness. In later analysis activities, the cost and benefits for the entire life cycle should be considered. The complete life cycle cost includes the development cost, cost of system operation and potential system malfunction, cost of system maintenance and, in some cases, also the cost involved with abandoning the system. For these cost estimates, the complete man-machine system must be considered.

The potential benefits of the system can be estimated only if a thorough analysis of the system environment and the constraints and countervailing powers in the environment has been taken. Most of the necessary information for this analysis should have been obtained already during the objectives analysis.

Feasibility analysis should not only consider technical feasibility but also should look at feasibility in terms of the organizational environment both inside and outside the organization.

4.1.6 Tools

The tools can be divided into analysis and presentation tools. As a presentation tool, an intelligent editor for input into the project data base is most important. This intelligent editor may also be used to produce outputs of various degrees of refinement for presentation to either management or technical readers. Thus, it should allow for excerpt projections as well as selections from the data base. Both input and output should be partly possible in graphical form. If special notations are desired, they should be derivable from the data base by automated tools.

If a full project data base is not available, analysts should at least be provided with an automated data dictionary at this phase. This data dictionary supports numerous versions of any document. Therefore, a facility for version control would also be an important aid.

As an evaluation tool, an input and output checker is needed to examine whether and where there still are holes in the activity description. A cost data base and a configuration data base are also helpful. For certain types of quantitative analysis, tools for queuing network modeling are required.

4.2 System Requirements Analysis For the Chosen Alternative

This system requirements analysis subphase is a continuation of the previous subphase. In the subphase, a system alternative is studied in full detail; the resulting conceptual model should be complete and consistent, and the cost estimates and benefit analysis should be reasonable.

4.2.1 What Information is Needed?

From where and what kind of information is sought during the subphase, is similar to the previously described alteratives evaluation subphase. The only difference is that we are looking for detailed information to precisely refine system properties and economical aspects related to the proposed system.

4.2.2 Who is Involved?

Figure 5-14 depicts the role model for this subphase. The model for this subphase is similar to the one for the previous subphase. Because the alternative

	scheduling & planning	refinement of choosen alternative	verification	validation — technical feasibility	validation — economic justification	validation — schedule	refine and define evaluation criteria & testing criteria	decision about future of project
High level management		(I) (V)					I	
steering committee	J				(I)	J	J	A,J
end users (of system)		I V	I				I	I
analysis team	A	A		J	A,V	A,I	V	
project manager	I	A	A (I)	V			A	
developer / management / syst. designer / programmer / tester / maintenance		S	S	S; A,I	I; S	I; S	S; S S	
experts of organization / business / physical system		S S S			S I S			
other sources		S		S				

A ... actor
I ... information source
S ... support
V ... verifier
J ... judge

Figure 5-14. Role/activity relationship during system requirements analysis.

was selected, management is far less involved during this subphase. Only the refinement of evaluation criteria and the definition of testing procedures require some definite input or simple agreement from high level management. During this subphase, the main interactions will take place between the analysis team and the end users.

4.2.3 How to Get the Necessary Information

The system requirements analysis is a continuation of activity from the previous alternatives evaluation subphase. The subphase deals with a chosen alternative. Detailed information for refining the abstraction of the alternative is required. The approaches to gathering information, which are described in Section 4.1.3, will continue to be used.

4.2.4 Documentation

The documentation used in the search for the best alternative will continue to be used. However, in the language requirements, it is important that the language can describe in detail, for the user, a local view of his/her particular working place. A graphical notation for any pictorial presentation is desirable.

4.2.5 Evaluation

One of the important activities in the system requirements analysis is to check the conceptual requirements model for completeness and consistency. Besides all data used, the source and sink for the data should be defined for completeness. Every activity should have input and output data, and the activation rules for every activity must be specified. Consistency includes interface consistency, input and output consistency, consistency among various system hierarchies, and among activity and data descriptions, etc. Another aspect of consistency considered is the match between the behavioral and operational system specifications. For consistency checking, the analysts may apply the reverse of the approaches used for constructing the conceptual requirements model. For example, one may switch data and process view, switch outside-in to inside-out approaches, or switch top-down to bottom-up approaches.

During a review process, the conceptual requirements model will be checked to determine whether it is a valid representation of the actual requirements. Besides reviews, experiments may be used for evaluation of the requirements model.

4.2.6 Tools

The tools for the previous phase with special emphasis on the intelligent editor and a graphic display facility are adequate. Tools, which support formal completeness and consistency checks, are helpful. In addition, tools for fast prototyping or operational requirements testing are useful. Examples of such tools would be CS-4,[2] the form language HIBOL,[21] or the tools built around PAISLEY.[38,39]

4.3   Medium Definition

The objective of this subphase is to reduce the scope of analysis to the software portion of the information processing system to be developed. Therefore, the activity of this subphase is to determine the boundary between hardware, software, and human organization of the information processing system.

4.3.1   What Information is Needed?

To select an alternative of where the boundaries should be drawn, in close cooperation with the hardware designers who are responsible for hardware configuration, the software designer and experts for human engineering and organizational matters, the analysts should study any particular financial and organizational constraints for the system and the tasks or functions to be performed by hardware, software or human organization.

4.3.2   Who is Involved?

Figure 5-15 displays role and activity relationships during the medium definition subphase. Because most information of this subphase comes from the developers, many actions will take place outside the customer organization if the same supplier supplies both hardware and software for the system. If different suppliers are involved, then the analysts will be actively involved during the task assignment step. Most of the validation can be done by the developers. However, it is the customer and the steering committee who make the final decision about whether the project is to be continued, based on information supplied by the project manager and the analysis team.

4.3.3   Evaluation

Review is a method for evaluating the definition of these boundaries. However, quantitative aspects can be verified by using analytical models. Simulation and experiments will be used if the case is of extreme importance.

One of the main analysis activities in the subphase is feasibility assessments. The evaluation process of this subphase should include the validation of technical and economical feasibility of the proposed system, assessments about the suitability of the proposed solution under sociological aspects as well as aspects of human engineering, feasibility of the established schedules, and cost estimates. These are the decision criteria for further progress of the project.

	assignment of tasts to hardware, software human operation	Validation of technical feasibility	Validation of economic feasibility	Validation of schedule feasibility	decision about future of project
High level management					
steering committee					A,J
end users (of system)					S
analysis team					I
project manager	A	A	A	A	S
developer management	I,V	I	S	I	
syst. designer	I,V	I	S	I	
programmer					
tester maintenance	S				
experts of organization	I,V	I	S	I	
business physical system			I		
other sources					

A ... actor

I ... information source

S ... support

V ...verifier

J ... judge

Figure 5-15. Role/activity relationship during the medium definition subphase.

4.4   Software Requirements Analysis

After defining the boundaries of the human components, the hardware and software components of the information processing system, this subphase expands the result of the system requirements analysis subphase by considering the additional constraints and sometimes tasks, which were brought into the software subsystem.

4.4.1   What Information is Needed?

The information needed is mostly concerned with the intricacies of the particular hardware selected, its special capabilities and shortcomings. Most of these requirements are of nonfunctional properties, but, in some cases they lead to new functions close to the boundary between hardware and software components. Code checking and communication protocols are typical examples.

4.4.2   Who is Involved?

Figure 5-16 displays role and activity relationships during the software requirements analysis subphase. The customer organization takes part in most of the activities in this subphase, but any technical details involved in this subphase are still best resolved by the developing organization with the analysis team acting as mediator. For nonfunctional properties, end users may still play a supportive role. With the steering committee, the end users will define the acceptance and testing criteria.

The project manager has full responsibility for developing the life cycle plan. The steering committee validates both the life cycle plan, and the acceptance and testing criteria. The committee also prepares the materials that will be used for making decisions about further procedures and contractual activities. Preparation of contracts and validation of testing criteria will involve company lawyers.

4.4.3   How to Get the Necessary Information

Experienced software designers can provide most of the information needed for refinement and extension of the software requirements and information about the hardware components. Furthermore, information will come from document analysis and consultations with the hardware experts. The users participation is described in Section 4.1.3. Testing criteria is established by the analysis team through the guidance of the conceptual model as developed to date.

4.4.4   Documentation

The only difference from the documentation for the system requirements analysis described in Section 4.1.4 is that the documentation for the software require-

	refinement of functional software requirements	nonfunctional properties	acceptance criteria	testing criteria	preparation of requirements specification	Validation of — functional requirements	Validation of — nonfunctional properties	Validation of — acceptance & testing criteria	Life cycle — milestones	Life cycle — timing	Life cycle — staffing	Life cycle — budgeting	decision about future of project
High level management		(V)							V	(I) V	(I) V	I V	J
steering committee			I			A	A	A					I
end users		S V	I	S		S	S						(S)
project manager					V	I	I	I	A	A	A	A	I
analysis team	A	A	A	A	A	I	I	I	S	S	S	S	
developer — management	I V	I V	S	I					I	I	S	S	(S)
software designer	S	S	S	I					S	S			
hardware designer	S			I					S	S			
programmer									S	S			
tester									S	S			
maintenance													
experts of organization										S	S		(S)
business						S	S	S			S	I	(S)
physical system						S	S	S					(S)
other sources								S					

A ... actor   V ... verifier
I ... information source   J ... judge
S ... support

Figure 5-16. Role/activity relationship during the software requirements analysis subphase.

ments analysis emphasizes the precision and completeness of the modeling language. Quickly grasping intuitive concepts is no longer a primary concern.

4.4.5 Evaluation

Evaluation of this subphase will be concerned with details of managerial aspects rather than technical details. For example, the evaluation process will determine the suitability of testing and acceptance criteria, and validate the functional and nonfunctional aspects of the specification.

5 CONCLUSION

This chapter introduces an objectives analysis phase as the earliest phase of the system development life cycle. This phase substantially enlarges the scope of the analysis. There are several reasons for starting a large project with an objectives analysis phase instead of jumping right into the requirements analysis of the system. The arguments are quite analogous to those for doing requirements analysis instead of starting out with system design. This analogy holds because requirements are already expressed in technical terms, geared to the day-to-day operations, users may have been so overwhelmed by short term problems that they lose track of their own and their organizations long term objectives. Therefore, the real problems, their solutions and constraints for the solutions are very often not those initially expressed by the members of the customer organization. Objectives analysis helps to find a number of potential solutions that otherwise would have been lost in unduly required restrictions.

Corporate objectives are formalized and known to exist in organizations. Objectives of individuals or countervailing constraints always require identification in a very careful and time consuming process. Integrating them into a consistent and workable objectives structure is time consuming. However, the quality and stability of the solutions reached do warrant this effort.

By incorporating the objectives analysis into the system development methodology, it becomes possible to have users actively participating in the early phases of system development. The method proposed could, therefore, be called "participative requirements analysis" in contrast to "participative design."[24] End user participation will expand the effort of requirements analysis and, therefore, lead to overall better system solutions.

REFERENCES

1. Basili, V. R., "Tutorial on Models and Metrics for Software Engineering," IEEE Computer Society, 1980.
2. S. Berild and S. Nachmens, "CS4—A Tool for Data Base Design and Infological Simulation," *Tutorial: Software Methodology*, (ed. C. V. Ramamoorthy and R. T. Yeh), IEEE Computer Society, 1978, pp 8–32.

3. Boehm, B. W., "Software Engineering," *IEEE Transactions on Computers*, Vol. C-25, No. 12, December 1976, pp. 1226-1241.

4. Boehm, B. W., "Guidelines for Verifying and Validating Software Requirements and Design Specifications," *Proc. EURO-IFIP 79*, (ed. P. A. Samut), North Holland, 1979, pp. 711-719.

5. Boehm, B. W., "Software Engineering Economics," Englewood Cliffs, NJ: Prentice-Hall, 1981.

6. Chen, P. P., "The Entity-Relationship Model—Toward a Unified View of Data", *ACM Transactions on Database Systems* 1, 1, 1976, pp. 9-36.

7. Denert, E. and W. Hesse, "Projektmodell und Projekt-Entwichklung und Dokumentation," *Informatik-Spektrum*, Bd. 3, 4, Nov. 1980, pp. 215-228.

8. Donaldson, H., "A Guide to the Successful Management of Computer Projects," New York, NY: J. Wiley & Sons, 1978.

9. Endres, A., "Methoden der Programm—und Systemkonstruktion—Ein Statusbericht," *Informatik-Spektrum*, Bd. 3, 3, August 1980, pp. 156-171.

10. Gorden, R. L., "Interviewing—Strategy, Techniques and Tactics," Homewood, IL: Dorsey Press, 1975.

11. Gruen, O., "Projektorganisation," *PFA*, Zeitschriftenreihe der Polizei-Fuehrungsakademie, 6, 75, Duesseldorf, BRD, 1975, pp. 33-44.

12. Gutzwiler, S., "Trend—Eine Methode zur Gestaltung Optimaler Organizations—und Informationsstrukturen im Projekt—Management," *Angewandte Informatik*, Heft 6, June 1980, pp. 229-234.

13. Heinen, E., "Grundlagen betriebswirtschaftlicher Entscheidungen. Das Zielsystem der Unternehumung," 2. Aufl., Verlag Dr. Th. Gabler, Wiesbaden, 1971.

14. Hesse, W., "Das Projektmodell—Eine Grundlage Fuer die Ingenieurmaessige Software-Entwicklung," *Proc. GI—10*. Jahrestagung, Informatik-Fachberichte 33, Springer-Verlag, 1980, pp. 107-122.

15. Jajodia, S. and P. A. Ng, "Translation of Entity-Relationship Diagrams into Relational Structures", *Journal of Systems and Software*, Vol. 4, Nos. 2 and 3, July 1984, pp. 123-134.

16. Kirsch, W., "Einfuehrung in die Theorie der Entscheidungsprozesse," 2. Aufl., Verlag Dr. Th. Gabler, Wiesbaden, 1977.

17. Mittermeir, R. T., "Requirements Analysis Top Down or Bottom Up?" TR DA 02/02/80, Institut fuer Digitale Anlagen, Technische Universitaet Wien, Wien 1980.

18. Mittermeir, R. T. and R. T. Yeh, "Modelling Control Structures Using Semantic Nets," TR., Dept. of Computer Science, University of Maryland, College Park, MD., 1980.

19. Mittermeir, R. T., "Requirements of Requirements," TR DA 01/03/81, Institut fuer Angewandte Informatik und Systemanalyse, Technische Universitaet Wien, Wien, 1981.

20. Mittermeir, R. T., "An Objective-Directed Approach Towards System Specification" (working paper) Department of Computer Science, University of Maryland, College Park, MD., June 1981.

21. Mittermeir, R. T., "HIBOL—A Language for Fast Prototyping in Data Processing Environments," TR DA 01/09/81, Institute fuer Angewandte Informatik und Systemanalyse, Technische Universitaet Wien, Wien, 1981.

22. Mittermeir, R. T., "A Strategy for Treating Irregularities in Requirements Analysis," TR DA 01/01/82, Institute fuer Angewandte Informatik und Systemanalyse, Technische Universitaet Wien, Wien, 1982.

23. Miyamoto, I. and R. T. Yeh, "A Software Requirements and Definition Methodology for Business Data Processing," *Proc. 1981 National Computer Conference, AFIPS Conf. Proc.*, Vol. 50, 1981, pp. 571-581.

24. Mumford, E., "Participative Systems Design: Structure and Method," *Systems, Objectives, Selections*, 1, 1, 1981, pp. 5-19.

25. Myers, G. J., "Composite Structured Design," New York: Van Nostrand Reinhold Co., 1978.

26. Ng, P. A., "Further Analysis of the Entity-Relationship Approach to Database Design," *IEEE Trans. on Software Engineering SE-7, 1,* 1981, pp. 85–99.
27. Peters, L. J., and L. L. Tripp, "A Model of Software Engineering," *Proc. 3rd International Conference on Software Engineering,* Atlanta, May 1978, pp. 63–70.
28. Putnam, L. M., "A General Empirical Solution to the Macro Software Sizing and Estimating Problems," *IEEE Transactions on Software Engineering, Se-4, 4,* July 1978, pp. 345–361.
29. Ross, D. T., "Structured Analysis (SA): A Language for Communicating Ideas," *IEEE Trans. on Software Engineering, SE-3, 1,* 1977, pp. 16–33.
30. Roussopoulos, N., "CSDL: A Conceptual Schema Definition Language for the Design of Data Base Applications," *IEEE Trans. on Software Engineering, SE-5, 5,* September 1979, pp. 481–486.
31. Schlicksupp, H., "Idea-generation for industrial firms—Report on an International Investigation," *R&D Management,* 7, 2, 1977, pp. 61–69.
32. Surboeck, E., "Management von EDV-Projekten," Berlin: de Gruyer, 1978.
33. Wedekind, E., "Systemanalyse" Munchen: Carl Hanser Verlag, 1976.
34. Witte, E., "Entscheidungstheorie," Verlag Dr. Th. Gabler, Wiesbaden, 1977.
35. Yeh, R. T. and P. Zave, "Specifying Software Requirements," *Proc. of the IEEE,* Vol. 68, 9, September 1980, pp. 1077–1085.
36. Yeh, R. T. and R. T. Mittermeir, "Conceptual Modelling as a Basis for Deriving Software Requirements," *Proc. International Computer Symposium,* Taipei, Taiwan, Dec. 1980, pp. 1–14.
37. Yourdon, E. and L. L. Constantine, "Structured Design: Fundamentals of a Discipline of Computer Program and Systems Design," Englewood Cliffs, NJ: Prentice-Hall, Inc. 1979.
38. Zave, P., "The Operational Approach to Requirements Specification for Embedded Systems," *TR 976,* Department of Computer Science, University of Maryland, College Park, MD., Dec. 1980.
39. Zave, P. and R. T. Yeh, "Executable Requirements for Embedded Systems," *Proc. 5th Int. Conf. on Software Engineering,* San Diego, 1981, pp. 295–304.
40. Zelkowitz, M. V., "Perspectives on Software Engineering," *ACM Computing Surveys,* 10, 2 June 1978, pp. 197–216.
41. Zelkowitz, M. V., "Large-Scale Software Development," *Principles of Software Engineering and Design* (ed. Zelkowitz, Shaw, Gannon), Englewood Cliffs, NJ: Prentice-Hall Inc., 1979, pp. 1–44.

Chapter 6

On the Concepts of Object-Oriented Design

GRADY BOOCH
Director, Software Engineering Programs
Rational
Mountain View, CA

ABSTRACT

The fundamental concepts of object-oriented design are presented, with an emphasis upon the method's process and notation. The nature of an object is explored as is the canonical architecture of complex systems using objects as the essential criterion for decomposition. A study of the evolution of the object model in software engineering is offered, and the process of object-oriented design is contrasted with alternative design approaches. Two case studies are given.

1 FUNDAMENTAL CONCEPTS

Complexity and Software-Intensive Systems

Systems in which software is a major component are among the most intellectually complex human products. Unlike other artifacts, however, software is an intangible medium; it cannot be touched, smelled, or heard. Developers are generally unable to measure any of its characteristics precisely, short of counting the lines of code in a given program or producing a relative complexity measure. Also, software development involves the creation of many more products than just the source code itself. Therefore, for anything beyond a small system, the effort of a team of developers is required; this human factor further complicates the problem. Given the ever-growing capabilities of our hardware, along with an increasing social awareness of the utility of computers, there exists great pressure to automate more and more applications of increasing complexity. One cannot hope to reduce the complexity of these problems: as the tools become better and one's experience broadens, there continually opens up more complex—yet solvable—problem domains.

However, there are limits to a person's ability of dealing with complexity; it is when these limits are stressed that a person often ends up with software projects that are late, over budget, and deficient in their stated requirements. Fortunately, this situation is not hopeless. As Simon[2] suggests, "the fact that many complex systems have a nearly decomposable, hierarchic structure is a major facilitating factor enabling us to understand, describe, and even 'see' such systems and their parts."

As an industry, it is now recognized that issues of development-in-the-large are different from those of development-in-the-small. Indeed, since the 1970s, the field of software engineering has emerged as a well-defined discipline, and a number of principles that help manage the complexity of development-in-the-large have been identified,[3] namely:

- Abstraction
- Information hiding
- Modularity
- Localization
- Uniformity
- Completeness
- Confirmability

Of these seven fundamental principles, abstraction and information hiding provide the greatest leverage for our management of complexity. Simply stated, "the essence of abstraction is to extract essential properties while omitting inessential details"[4] and ". . . the purpose of hiding is to make inaccessible certain details that should not affect other parts of a system."[5] As the architecture of a software system evolves in the solution space, each module in the decomposition becomes a part of some abstraction from the problem space that builds upon abstractions at lower levels of the system.

The evolution of high-order programming languages reflects the drive towards higher and higher levels of abstraction. Wegner[5] has categorized some of the most popular high-order languages into generations arranged according to the features they introduced:

- *First-generation languages* (1954–1958)
FORTRAN I	mathematical expressions
- *Second-generation languages* (1959–1961)
FORTRAN II	subroutines, separate compilation
ALGOL 60	block structure, data types
COBOL	data description, file handling
LISP	list processing, pointers
- *Third-generation languages* (1962–1970)
PL/1	FORTRAN + ALGOL + COBOL
ALGOL 68	rigorous successor to ALGOL 60

Pascal   simple successor to ALGOL 60
SIMULA   classes, data abstraction
- *The generation gap* (1970–1980)
  Many different languages, but few endured

Another way we can categorize these same generations of languages is by noting the kinds of abstractions that each can best express:

- *First-generation languages* (1954–1958)
  mathematical abstractions
- *Second-generation languages* (1959–1961)
  algorithmic abstractions
- *Third-generation languages* (1962–1970)
  data abstractions

Since the 1970s, a number of other interesting languages have emerged, such as Ada, Smalltalk-80, LOOPS, Objective-C, C + +, and Object Pascal. These languages facilitate a fundamentally different abstraction mechanism, and so warrant the definition of a new generation of high-order programming languages:

- *Nth-generation languages* (1980–present)
  object-oriented abstractions

Evolution of the Object Model

The notion of an object plays the central role in object-oriented abstractions, but actually, the concept is not a new one. Indeed, as MacLennan suggests, "programming is object-oriented mathematics."[7] Lately, we have observed a confluence of object-oriented work from many elements of computer science. Levy reports that the following events have contributed to the evolution of object-oriented concepts:[8]

- Advances in computer architecture, including capability-based systems and hardware support for operating systems concepts
- Advances in programming languages, as demonstrated in SIMULA, Pascal, Smalltalk, CLU, and Ada
- Advances in programming methods, including modularization, information hiding, and monitors

The author adds to this list three more contributions to the advancement of object-oriented concepts:

- The work on abstraction mechanisms by various researchers
- Research in artificial intelligence
- Advances in data base models

Interestingly, the concept of an object has precedence in hardware. Work with tagged architectures and capability-based computer systems has led to a number of implementations that can be classified as object-oriented. For example, Myers reports on two object-oriented architectures, SWARD and the Intel 432.[9] The IBM System 38 is also regarded as an object-oriented architecture.[10]

Perhaps the first person to formally identify the importance of composing systems in levels of abstraction was Dijkstra.[11] Parnas later introduced the concept of information hiding.[12] which, as will be discussed later, is central to the nature of an object. In the 1970s a number of researchers, most notably Liskov and Zilles; Guttag, et al.; and Shaw pioneered the development of abstract data type mechanisms.[13,14,15] The late seventies and early eighties also saw the application of a number of software development methods, such as JSD, that were declarative, rather than imperative, in nature.

The greatest influence upon object-oriented concepts derives from a small number of programming languages. SIMULA 67 first introduced the class as a language mechanism for encapsulating data, but, as Rentsch reports, "the Smalltalk programming system carried the object-oriented paradigm to a smoother model." Indeed, the explicit awareness of the idea, including the term object-oriented, came from the Smalltalk effort."[16] Object-oriented languages, such as Object Pascal followed the more traditional path of SIMULA, but we also have seen a number of languages merge the concepts of LISP and Smalltalk; thus evolved languages such as FLAVORS, LOOPS, and ACTORS. It is also clear that LISP alone can be used effectively to apply object-oriented techniques.[17] More recently, there has been work to add Smalltalk constructs to C, resulting in languages such as Objective-C[18] and C++. Languages, such as Smalltalk have collectively been called actor languages, because they emphasize the role of entities such as actors, agents, and servers in the structure of the real world.[19]

As Stefik and Bobrow have observed, object-oriented concepts also derive from "a line of work in AI on the theory of frames (by Minsky) and their implementation in knowledge representation languages."[20] Also object-oriented concepts have emerged from data base technology, such as reflected in the work by Ross on entity modeling.[21]

Object-oriented Programming and Object-oriented Design

Rentsch predicts that "object-oriented programming will be in the 1980s what structured programming was in the 1970s.[22] Given that the phrase "object-oriented" shows up in so many segments of computer science, the question might be asked, what "object-oriented" means in this context. Cardelli and Wegner[23] suggest that "a language is object-oriented if and only if it satisfies the following requirements:

- It supports objects that are data abstractions with an interface of named operations and a hidden local state
- Objects may have an associated object type
- Types may inherit attributes from supertypes''

Thus, it can be said that languages, such as Smalltalk and Object Pascal are truly object-oriented, and languages such as Basic and FORTRAN are not. However, languages such as SIMULA and Ada fall into a middle ground, in that they support all of these requirements but with varying degrees of compliance. For this reason, object-oriented programming is viewed not as a binary issue, but rather as a spectrum that encompasses a number of languages.

Object-oriented programming is primarily concerned with language mechanisms. Just as structured programming concentrates upon the use of classical control structures, object-oriented programming concentrates upon mechanisms for defining abstractions from the problem space (objects), collections of such abstractions (classes), and relationships among objects and classes (through inheritance and other mechanisms).

Structured programming and object-oriented programming thus provide a vocabulary with which abstractions can be captured from the problem space; the former being most appropriate for expressing algorithmic abstractions, and the latter for expressing object-oriented abstractions. However, neither gives a systematic method for deciding what abstractions to express, nor what the boundaries of those abstractions should be. For this reason, the concepts of design and programming must be distinguished.

There exists a myriad of design approaches, which Sommerville[24] has divided into the following three categories:

- Top-down functional design—exemplified by Structured Design (Constantine and Yourdon) and stepwise refinement (Wirth).
- Data-driven design—exemplified by JSD (Jackson) and Warnier-Orr.
- Object-oriented design

Object-oriented design is fundamentally different from traditional functional methods, for which the primary criteria for decomposition is that each module in the system represents a major step in the overall process. The differences between these approaches become clear if one returns to the class of languages for which they are best suited.

Object-oriented programming languages require a different approach to design than the approach one typically takes with languages, such as FORTRAN, COBOL, C, and even Pascal. Well-structured systems developed with these older languages tend to consist of collections of subprograms (or their equivalent), primarily because that is structurally the only major building block available. Thus, these languages are best suited to functional decomposition techniques, which concentrate upon algorithmic abstractions. But, as Guttag and his colleagues observe, "unfortunately, the nature of the abstractions that conveniently may be achieved through the use of subroutines is limited. Subroutines, while well-suited to the description of abstract events (operations), are not particularly well suited to the description of abstract objects. This is a serious drawback."[25]

The subprogram (or its equivalent) is an elementary building block in many object-oriented programming languages. However, object-oriented programming languages additionally offer a mechanism as a major structural element, which gives us a facility for extending the language by defining new objects and classes of objects. One can, of course, develop systems using object-oriented programming languages, by applying the same methods as for the more traditional languages. However, such approaches neither exploit the power of the object-oriented programming language, nor help to manage the complexity of the problem space.

In general, functional design methods suffer from several basic limitations. They do not adequately address data abstraction and information hiding; they are generally inadequate for problem domains with natural concurrency; and they are often not responsive to changes in the problem space. With an object-oriented design approach, designers strive to mitigate these problems.

Designs for a simple real-time system (a car's cruise-control system) using functional and object-oriented techniques are compared.[26]

A cruise-control system maintains a car's speed, even over varying terrain. In Figure 6-1, a block diagram with several inputs of the hardware for such a system is shown. The inputs are the following:

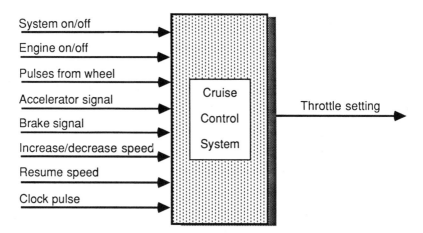

Figure 6-1. Cruise-control system hardware block diagram.

- *System on/off*—If on, denotes that the cruise-control system should maintain the car's speed.
- *Engine on/off*—if on, denotes that the car engine is turned on; the cruise control system is only active if the engine is on.
- *Pulses from wheel*—a pulse is sent for every revolution of the wheel.
- *Accelerator signal*—indication of how far the accelerator has been depressed.
- *Brake signal*—on when the brake is depressed; the cruise-control system temporarily reverts to manual control if the brake is depressed.
- *Increase/decrease*—increase or decrease the maintained speed; only applicable if the cruise-control system is on.
- *Resume speed*—resume the last maintained speed; only applicable if the cruise-control system is on.
- *Clock pulse*—timing pulse every millisecond.

And there is one output from the system:
- *Throttle setting*—digital value for the engine throttle setting.

How might the design of the software for this cruise-control system be approached? Using either a functional or object-oriented approach, one might start by creating a data flow diagram representing the behavior of the system, to capture our model of the problem space. In Figure 6-2, such a diagram is provided, using the notation by Gane and Sarson. According to their conventions, a double square represents a source or destination of data; a data store is represented by an open-ended rectangle. A directed line represents a flow of data, while a rounded rectangle represents a process that transforms such flows.

For example, as Figure 6-2 shows, the wheel of the car sends a pulse to the process labeled Calculate Current Speed. Together with the periodic pulse from the clock, this process can calculate the current speed of the car. Similarly, current speed flows into the process labeled Calculate Desired Speed. Whenever the driver issues a command to turn the cruise-control system on, this process takes the current speed and makes it the desired speed. Ultimately, the desired speed and current speed provide the data necessary for the process Calculate Throttle Setting to establish the next throttle setting. Basically, if the current speed is less than the desired speed, then the setting of the throttle must be increased. As Figure 6-2 indicates, this value may also be effected by the state of the engine as well as the state of the accelerator and the brake; if the cruise-control system is off or the brake is set, then the value of the accelerator is passed directly on to the throttle.

With a functional method, one would continue the design by creating a structure chart. In Figure 6-3, the techniques of Yourdon and Constantine[27] are used to decompose the system, using an input-process-output model, into modules that denote the major functions in the overall process. Thus, major functions

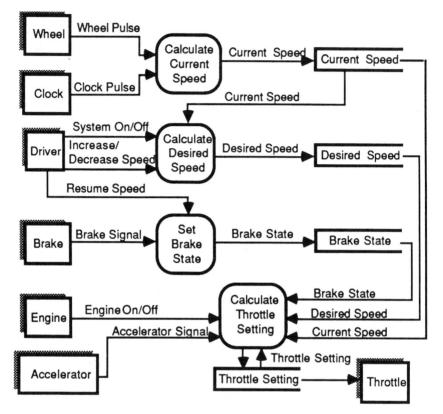

Figure 6-2. Cruise-control system data flow diagram.

that deliver the inputs of the system (Get Desired Speed, Get Current Speed, and Get Brake State) are given, next, a major function that processes this data (Calculate Throttle Setting), and finally, a function that denotes the output of the system (Put Throttle State).

Using an object-oriented approach, the design proceeds in an entirely different manner; indeed, by suggesting that structured design and object-oriented design are orthogonal views. Rather than factoring this system into modules that denote operations, it is structured around the objects that exist in the model of reality. By extracting the objects from the data flow diagram, the author generates the structure seen in Figure 6-4. The process and the notation used to generate this diagram will be explained more fully later. For the moment, simply accept that the amorphous blobs denote objects and that the directed lines denote visibility among the objects.

Immediately, it can be seen that the object-oriented decomposition closely matches the model of reality. On the other hand, the functional decomposition is only achieved through a transformation of the problem space; this design is

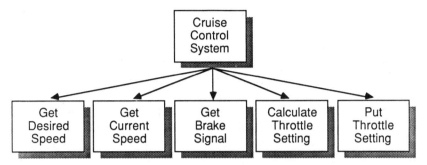

Figure 6-3. Functional decomposition.

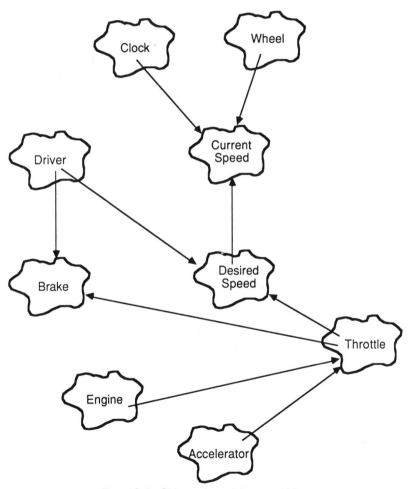

Figure 6-4. Object-oriented decomposition.

heavily influenced by the nature of the subprogram, and so emphasizes only the algorithmic abstractions. Hence one concludes that a functional decomposition is imperative in nature: it concentrates upon the major actions of a system and is silent about the agents that perform or suffer these actions.

The advantages of object-oriented decomposition are also evident when the effect of change (and change will happen to any useful piece of software) is considered. One side effect of functional decomposition is that all interesting data end up being global to the entire system, so that any change in representation tends to effect all subordinate modules. Alternately, in the object-oriented approach, the effect of changing the representation of an object tends to be more localized. For example, suppose one originally chooses to represent car speed as an integer value denoting the number of wheel revolutions per some time unit (which would not be an unreasonable implementation decision). Now, suppose one later adds a digital display that indicates the current speed in kilometers per hour, and for a variety of reasons, this internal representation for speed must be used throughout the system. In the functional decomposition, every part of the system that knows about the representation of speed must be modified. However, in the object-oriented decomposition, such a change effects only two objects (the inside view of the current speed and desired speed) and requires the addition of one more object that directly parallels the modification of reality.

Hypothesizing an even more fundamental change, suppose one chooses to implement the cruise-control system using two microcomputers, one to manage the current and desired speeds and the second to manage the throttle. Mapping the functional decomposition to this target architecture requires that the system design be split at the highest level. With the object-oriented approach, no modifications are necessary at this level of the design to take advantage of the physical concurrency.

The Meaning of an Object

Thus far, the term "object" has been used in an informal manner. Because the concept of an object is central to all object-oriented systems, and so that the process and notation of object-oriented design may be fully described, the common properties of an object can be extracted from the background introduced in an earlier section. An object may be defined as an entity that includes the following:

- has state;
- is characterized by the actions that it suffers and that it requires of other objects;
- is a unique instance of some (possibly anonymous) class;
- is denoted by a name;

- has restricted visibility of and by other objects; and
- can be viewed either by its specification or by its implementation.

The first and second points are the most important: an object is something that exists uniquely in time and space and can be affected by the activity of other objects. The state of an object denotes its value plus the objects denoted by this value. For example, in a multiple window user interface, the state of an individual window might include its size as well as the image displayed in the window (which is also an object). Because of the existence of state, objects are not input/output mappings as are procedures or functions. For this reason, the author distinguishes objects from mere processes. Thus, in a simplistic sense, state is data that persists over time. For any well-structured object-oriented system, each object encapsulates some state, and all state within the system is encapsulated in some object. Especially in the presence of multiple threads of control, maintaining the integrity and consistency of a system's state is essential. By encapsulating state within an object, ensuring that such state remains self-consistent is made much easier, even in the presence of some failure that may corrupt part of the state of the system.

From Smalltalk comes the concept of a method; a method denotes the response by an object to a message from another object. The activity of one method may pass messages that invoke the methods of other objects. Abstract data types deal with operations in a related way. Liskov and Zilles suggest that operations be divided "into two groups: those which do not cause a state change but allow some aspect of the state to be observed . . . and those which cause a change of state."[27] In practice, the author encountered one other kind of operation, iteration, which permits one to visit all subcomponents of an object. The concept of an iterator was formalized in the language Alphard.[28] For example, given an instance of a terminal screen, one may wish to visit all windows visible on the screen. Together, these operations can be classified as the following:

- *Constructor*—an operation that alters the state of an object.
- *Selector*—an operation that evaluates the current object state.
- *Iterator*—an operation that permits all parts of an object to be visited.

To enhance the reusability of an object or class of objects, all operations should be primitive. A primitive operation is one that can be implemented efficiently only if it has access to the underlying representation of the object. In this sense, the specification of an object or class of objects should define "the object, the whole object, and nothing but the object."

An object can be classified as an actor, agent, or server, depending upon how it relates to surrounding objects. An actor object is one that suffers no operations, but only operates upon other objects. Actors thus tend to be fairly autonomous entities. At the other extreme, a server only suffers operations and cannot operate upon other objects. An agent is an object that serves to perform some operation on behalf of another object and in turn can operate upon other objects.

It is this coupling of state and operations that distinguishes an object from mere data. Data are passive, and have no dynamic semantics; objects may be active and have a rich semantics. Indeed, an object exhibits both static as well as dynamic semantics. More precisely, the static semantics of an object are expressed by the existence of the operations it suffers or requires of other objects. The dynamic semantics of an object are expressed by the effect each operation has upon the state of the object. Such dynamic semantics can even include concurrency among objects, in the situation where the state of an object is a function of time, and the object is implemented using some multiprocessing construct provided by the underlying language (such as with tasks in Ada).

Another important characteristic of objects is that each object is a unique instance of some class. Put another way, a class denotes a set of similar but unique objects. The term class comes from SIMULA and Smalltalk; many traditional languages refer to the term class as the type of an object. A class serves to factor the common properties of a set of objects and specify the behavior of all instances. For example, there may exist a class named Window from which several instances (objects) are created. It is important to distinguish between an object and its class; operations are defined in a class but have effects only upon objects.

A class is characterized by a set of values and a set of operations applicable to objects of that class. Thus, the concept of constructors, selectors, and iterators applies here, as a way of categorizing the operations of a class. For example, Car might be envisioned as a class of items, with applicable operations such as starting, turning, stopping, and so on. For all instances of this class (this car, that car), these same operations apply. Thus, the class Car serves to factor all common car operations.

Of course, and this becomes somewhat complicated, one can treat a class as an object (forming a superclass), with operations such as creating an instance of the class. This strange loop in the definition is not only academically interesting but also permits some very elegant programs.

In some cases, the class of an object may be anonymous. Here the object does have a class, but the name of the class is not visible. The implication is that there can be only one object of the class (because there is no class name from which instances may be declared). In practice, such objects are implemented as abstract state machines instead of multiple instances of an abstract data type.

Some classes are primitive. For example, integers are a primitive class of numbers, because no further decomposition of this abstraction is useful. On the other hand, complex numbers are not necessarily primitive but rather are composite; they can be viewed as instances of a composite class that includes a real part and an imaginary part.

From Smalltalk comes the concept of inheritance, which permits a hierarchy of classes. In this sense, all objects are an instance of a class that might be a subclass of another class (and so on). For example, the class of a given object may be Bag, which is in turn a subclass of the more general class Collection, which in turn is a subclass of the more general class Object. An object is said to inherit the methods of this chain of classes. Thus, all objects of the class Bag have the same operations as defined by the class Collection, and for the Bag subclass, one can also add operations to, modify existing operations of, and hide operations from its superclass.

One may observe that inheritance is an important element of object-oriented programming, and a useful but not essential one for object-oriented design. It is but one specific language mechanism that allows the creation of hierarchies of objects and classes of objects. Other mechanisms that achieve a similar effect (such as generic mechanisms) are similarly useful in building hierarchies of objects and classes of objects. Inheritance is best suited to dynamic languages such as Smalltalk, while more static mechanisms are necessary for languages such as Ada.

On the spectrum of "object-orientedness," programming languages without inheritance still permit object-oriented design (assuming that there still is some mechanism to express hierarchies of objects and classes of objects). Still, object-oriented design is more than just programming with abstract data types, although abstract data types certainly serve as an important influence; indeed, the behavior of most objects can be characterized using the mechanisms of abstract data types. Whereas design with abstract data types deals with passive objects (that is, agents and servers), object-oriented design also concerns itself with objects that act without stimulus from other objects (call such objects actors). Another subtle difference between programming with abstract data types and object-oriented design is that in both cases the concern is with the operations suffered by an object, but in the latter case the concern is with the operations that an object requires of other objects. The purpose of this view is to decouple the dependencies among objects.

Another way to view the relationship between object-oriented design and programming with abstract data types is that object-oriented design builds on the concepts of the latter but also serves as a method that exposes the interesting objects and classes of objects from our abstraction of reality.

Another important consideration of any object-oriented system is the treatment of names. The rule is simple: objects are unique instances of a class, and names only serve to denote objects. As Liskov, *et al.* observe, "variables are just the names used in a program to refer to objects."[29] Thus, an object may be denoted by one name (the typical case) or by several names. In the latter situation, an alias can be used, such that operation upon an object through one name has the side effect of altering the object denoted by all the aliases. For example, there may be several variables in the window system that denote the same window object; operating upon an object (such as destroying the window) is independent of any alias chosen. This one object/many name paradigm is a natural consequence of the notion of an object, but, depending upon the manner of support offered by the underlying language, it is the source of most logical errors. The key concept to remember is that supplying a name to a constructor does not necessarily alter the value of the name but instead alters the object denoted by the name.

The names of objects should have a restricted scope. Thus, in designing a system, one establishes visibility among objects concerned with what objects see and are seen by another object or class of objects. In the worst case, all objects can see one another, and thus there is the potential of unrestricted action. It is better to restrict the visibility among objects, thus limiting the number of objects that must be dealt with to understand any part of the system and also limiting the scope of change. This is the essence of information hiding.

Finally, every object has two parts and so can be viewed in two different ways: there is an outside view and an inside view. Whereas the outside view of an object serves to capture the abstract behavior of the object, the inside view indicates how that behavior is implemented. One object can interact with another by seeing only the outside view, without knowing how the other is represented or implemented. When designing a system, the concern is first with the outside view.

The outside view of an object or class of objects is its specification. The specification captures all of the static and (as much as possible) dynamic semantics of the object. In the specification of a class of objects, several resources are exported to the rest of the system, including the name of the class and the operations defined for objects of the class. Ideally, the implementation language should enforce this specification, preventing violation of the properties of the specification.

Whereas the outside view of an object is that which is visible to other objects, the inside view is its implementation and so is not visible from the outside. In the body of an object or class, one of many possible representations that implement the behavior of the specification must be chosen. If the language permits it, the implementation of an object or class of objects can be replaced without any other part of the system being affected. The benefits of separation of interface and implementation should be clear: not only does this enforce the abstractions and, hence help manage the complexity of the problem space, but by localizing the design decisions made about an object, the scope of change upon the system is reduced.

Objects do not exist in isolation. For this reason, it is important to consider the canonical relationships among objects. To calibrate this discussion, Figure 6-5 illustrates the structure of a system that has been decomposed using functional design techniques. Note that the fundamental unit of decomposition is the subprogram, and hence the topology of this system is that of a tree, with all persistent data defined at the highest level of the system.

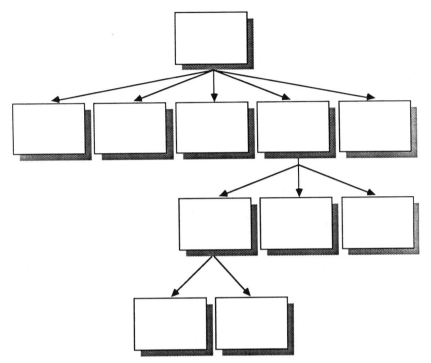

Figure 6-5. Topology of a system using functional decomposition.

By way of contrast, Figure 6-6 represents the structure of a small- to medium-sized system that has been decomposed using object-oriented techniques. Note that the fundamental unit of decomposition is the object, and hence the topology of this system is that of a DAG (directed acyclic graph), with all persistent data distributed throughout the system, and encapsulated within objects.

If we advance to a more complex system, distinct layering among objects appears, as illustrated in Figure 6-7. Here, the topology of the system is more hierarchic.

Interestingly, the topology of a software system as represented in Figure 6-6 and Figure 6-7 parallels that of complex systems that appear in nature. Courtois observes the following:[30]

- Frequently, complexity takes the form of a hierarchy, whereby a complex system is composed of interrelated subsystems that have in turn their own subsystems and so on, until some lowest level of elementary components is reached.
- In general, interactions inside subsystems are stronger and/or more frequent than interactions among subsystems.

Following the work of Rajlich, Seidewitz and Stark have examined these two

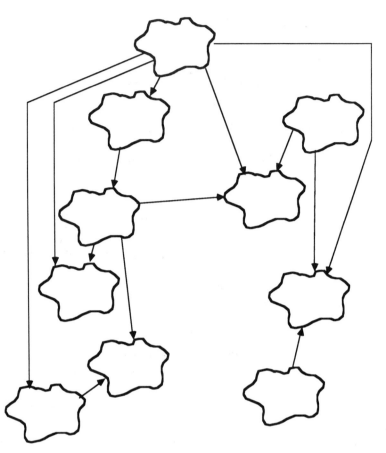

Figure 6-6. Topology of a small- to medium-sized system using object-oriented techniques.

orthogonal hierarchies. They note that[31] "the 'parent-child hierarchy' deals with the decomposition of larger objects into smaller component objects" and that "the 'seniority hierarchy' deals with the organization of a set of objects into layers."

2 THE METHOD

As we have already observed, object-oriented programming does not provide a systematic approach to the decomposition of complex systems, and hence does not constitute a design method. However, because there does exist a sound theoretic and engineering basis for object-oriented techniques, the author developed such a systematic approach called simply "object-oriented design." This method—in a variety of forms—has been in use since 1981 and has been applied

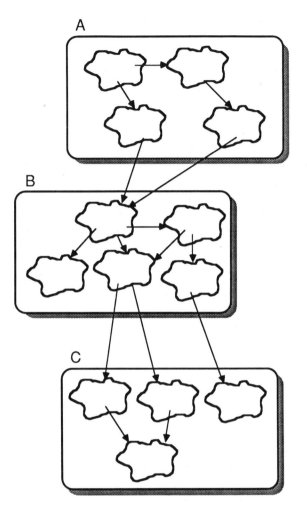

Figure 6-7. Topology of a complex system using object-oriented techniques.

to a broad spectrum of problem domains, for small as well massive software-intensive systems, some involving in excess of one million lines of code. In the evolution of this method, the author observed that for any method to be considered complete, it must address the issues of the following:

- logical and physical decomposition
- static and dynamic behavior

In addition, the author's method addresses the two dimensions of system structure that are peculiar to object-oriented systems, namely:

- parent-child and seniority hierarchies
- object and class decomposition

In dealing with a philosophy of design, the fundamental criterion should first be recognized for decomposing a system using object-oriented techniques: Each module in the system denotes an object or a class of objects from the problem space.

Abstraction and information hiding thus form the foundation of object-oriented design. Abstraction and information hiding are actually quite natural activities. People employ abstraction daily and tend to develop models of reality by identifying the objects and operations that exist at each level of interaction. Thus, when driving a car the accelerator, gauges, steering wheel and brake (among other objects) are considered, as well as the operations performed upon them and the effect of those operations. When repairing an automobile engine, lower-level objects are considered, such as the fuel pump, carburetor, and distributor.

Similarly, a program that implements a model of reality (and all of them should) can be viewed as a set of objects that interact with one another. Object-oriented design is founded upon this view. More precisely, the major steps in object-oriented design are the following:

1. Identify the objects and their attributes
2. Identify the operations suffered by and required of each object
3. Establish the visibility of each object in relation to other objects
4. Establish the interface of each object
5. Implement each object

These steps are evolved from an approach first proposed by Abbott.[32]

In any design method, there is a natural tension between rigidity and flexibility. On the one hand, the steps of the method (its process) in fine detail should be specified; on the other hand, degrees of freedom must be offered so that the method may be adapted to a variety of problem domains, constraints in the solution space, and realities of the using organization. The author does not believe that the discipline of software design is sufficiently mature to allow for any cookbook methods: designing software, or any physical system, for that matter, has always been and will remain a creative process. The best designers need a sound engineering foundation, simple guidelines, their own creativity, and their base of experience to proceed with the design of a new complex system. Less experienced designers need more guidance, but there must remain freedom of expression. For these reasons, the steps and the order that is offered should not be viewed as inviolate; rather, these steps should be viewed as an approach that adds value to the identification of objects and classes as the building blocks of complex systems.

The first step, identifying the objects and their attributes, involves the recognition of the major actors, agents, and servers in the problem space, plus their role in the model of reality. In the cruise-control system, concrete objects are identified, such as the accelerator, throttle, and engine, and abstract objects such as speed. Typically, the objects identified in this step derive from the nouns used in describing the problem space. It may be found that there are several objects of interest that are similar. In such a situation, a class of objects should be established, of which there may be many instances. For example, in a multiple window user interface, distinct windows may be identified (such as a help window, message window, and command window) that share similar characteristics; each object can be considered as an instance of some window class. The attributes of an object characterize its time and space behavior. For example, it may be desired to constrain the maximum and minimum size of a given window.

This first step embodies the hardest, yet most subtle, aspect of object-oriented design. Stated another way, this step involves the identification of the key abstractions in the problem space. The problem is not so much that of simply recognizing that the abstractions exist; rather, the fundamental challenge lies in drawing the boundaries of each abstraction so that the result is a set of abstractions that accurately captures the model of reality, is resilient to change, and expresses all interesting behavior—in short, abstractions that satisfy the properties of an object that were described in an earlier section.

The next step, identifying the operations suffered by and required of each object, serves to characterize the behavior of each object or class of objects. It is this step that draws concrete boundaries around the abstractions identified in the previous step. Here, the static semantics of the object is established by determining the operations that can be meaningfully performed on the object or by the object. It is also at this time that the dynamic behavior of each object is established by identifying the constraints upon time or space that must be observed for each operation. For example, it may be specified that there is a time ordering of operations that must be followed. In the case of the multiple window system, the operations of Open, Close, Move, and Size upon a window object should be permitted, and require that the window be open before any other operation is performed.

Clearly, the operations suffered by an object define the object's activity when acted upon by other objects. Why must a concern be with the operations required of an object? The answer is that identifying such operations enables decoupling objects from one another. For example, in the multiple window system, one might assume the existence of some terminal object is required for operations of Move Cursor and Put. The result is that objects can be derived that are inherently reusable, because they are not dependent upon any specific objects, but rather depend only upon other classes of objects.

In the third step, establishing the visibility of each object in relation to other

objects, the static dependencies among objects and classes of objects is identified (in other words, what objects or classes are seen by a given object or class).
The purpose of this step is to capture the topology of objects and classes from
the model of reality. It is during this step that patterns of objects may be found.
As such patterns are found, an engineering decision must be made whether to
create a new class that expresses the common behavior of all these objects, or
to continue managing individual, yet similar, objects.

Next, to establish the interface of each object (or class), the outside view of
each object (or class) is produced, using some suitable notation. This captures
the static semantics of each object or class of objects established in the previous
step. This specification also serves as a contract between the clients of an object
and the object itself. Put another way, the interface forms the boundary between
and object's outside view and inside view.

The fifth and final step, implementing each object, involves choosing a
suitable representation for each object or class of objects and implementing the
interface from the previous step. This can involve either decomposition or
composition. Occasionally an object is found to consist of several subordinate
objects (the parent-child hierarchy), in which case the method to further decompose the object is repeated. More often, an object is implemented by composition (the seniority hierarchy); that is, by building on top of existing lower-
level objects or classes of objects. As a system is prototyped, the developer
may chose to defer the implementation of all objects until some later time,
relying upon the specification of the objects (with suitably stubbed implementations) to experiment with the architecture and behavior of a system. Similarly,
the developer may chose to try several alternate representations over the life of
the object, in order to experiment with the behavior of various implementations.

It is difficult to design a solution to a complex system when one does not
have any previous models of experience; in such situations, design often
proceeds by discovery backed by sound engineering practice, using rapid prototyping to allow experimentation with alternate approaches. Only when one has
suitable experience in the problem domain can all the relevant abstractions, their
boundaries, and their canonical relationships to one another be confidently
identified. In either case, an object-oriented design approach is suitable. In the
former case, involving new complex systems, object-oriented design forces one
to concentrate upon these abstractions to understand such a system, independent
of any implementation. One is encouraged to build concrete abstractions of the
objects and classes derived from the analysis of the problem space and then,
coupled with a suitable implementation language, the abstractions can be
enforced, and made to be resilient to change. In the latter case, involving systems
for which one already has architectural models, object-oriented design encourages reuse of common abstractions, thus leading to development by composition—not decomposition—from rich libraries of reusable software components.

Stepping back from the details of these steps, it is observed that there is a clear distinction made between logical and physical design decisions. The first four steps are concerned with the identification of objects, classes, their behavior, and their relationships to one another: these are the elements of the logical design of a system. The final step centers upon the issues of physical design, that is, the packaging decisions regarding the collection of objects and classes into modules. In most cases, one may wish to have a one to one mapping from objects and classes to modules as provided by the underlying implementation language. Alternately, one may wish either to combine some objects and classes in the same module or to spread the implementation of some complex abstractions across several modules. Often, these decisions must be made for technical as well as non-technical reasons: reuse, security, geographical distribution of the development team, perceived implementation risk, and shear size are some of the reasons that must be considered in making such decisions.

Note that object-oriented design separates the issues of static and dynamic semantics. The static semantics of a design are expressed by the identification of all relevant objects, classes, their static relationships, and the existence of operations that statically describe the behavior of individual objects and classes of objects. Dynamic semantics are expressed by the meaning of individual operations, and the affect each has upon the state of the system. As shall be seen in the next section, there exist notations that allow the presence of concurrency among objects to be asserted, as well as the time ordering of operations for a given object.

Object-oriented design also supports the two dimensions of system structure that were introduced earlier. Parent-child hierarchies are denoted by objects that may be further decomposed into component objects, whereas seniority hierarchies are denoted by relationships among objects at the same level of abstraction. As present in the next section, there exists a notation to separately represent the issues of object hierarchies and class hierarchies.

3 THE NOTATION

The Products

In addition to the process of object-oriented design, the use of a suitable notation to capture design decisions along the way must be considered. The motivation for any such notation is two-fold. First, one must have a representation that is sufficiently rich so that all relevant details of the design are made visible; as in the process itself, one must capture logical and physical design decisions, static and dynamic semantics, and the aspects of both dimensions of systems structure (parent-child and seniority hierarchies, as well as object and class hierarchies). Second, it must be simple enough so that one can study the design, reason about its implications, visualize alternatives, and accurately communicate these decisions to other team members, who may be separated by time as well as space.

To support these goals, the author has developed a notation that consists of four parts; it is the generation of a set of these parts that constitutes the products of object-oriented design as follows:

- Hardware diagram
- Class structure
- Object diagram
- Architecture diagram

These diagrams are generally produced in their stated order. Depending upon the complexity of the system under development, it may be necessary to produce only one, or perhaps many more than one, of each diagram. Hardware diagrams serve to capture the organization of the underlying target hardware system; class structures and object diagrams form the logical design of the software system; architecture diagrams represent the physical software design. Together, these artifacts constitute what are called the project model. For any given system under consideration, there may be many versions of a project model (representing, for example, the design of a released version, versions in test, and versions under development). The only requirement is that each model be self-consistent.

The author stresses a notation consisting of parts developed that do not by themselves constitute object-oriented design. Rather, the emphasis in this method is upon the use of objects as the foundation for system design—this notation simply provides a powerful mechanism for capturing all design decisions.

Hardware Diagram

For any complex system, one does not generally create a single, isolated program for execution upon a monolithic processor. Rather, a more common requirement is to produce a set of programs that may run across a distributed collection of processors. For this reason, this notation begins with a hardware diagram, which asserts the existence of the following:

- *Processors*—which may run *N* number of programs;
- *Devices*—which are resources used by processors;
- *Networks*—which connect processors;
- *Connections*—which connect processors and devices, processors, processors, and processors and networks.

Figure 6-8 illustrates the symbols which may appear in a hardware diagram. A hardware diagram takes the form of a graph, in which processors, devices, and networks are vertices of the graph, and connections are undirected arcs.

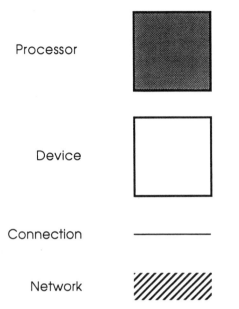

Processor

Device

Connection

Network

Figure 6-8. Hardware diagram symbols.

For each of these symbols, as text a name, its semantics, and design notes may be provided.

Hardware diagrams may be produced at anytime during the software design process, once a reasonably well-defined target hardware architecture has been selected. In the simplest of systems, one will have a single hardware diagram that contains exactly one processor symbol and no other. However, it is often the case that, for very complex systems, hardware development proceeds in parallel with, or even lags, software development. Thus, it may not be possible to generate a hardware diagram until the fifth step, when one begins to make hardware/software tradeoffs regarding the physical design of the system. At this time, based upon typical empirical evidence from prototypes, one can make intelligent decisions regarding the allocation of processes, the needed capacity of computational resources, and load balancing among processors.

Class Structure

Class structures denote the first dimension of the logical design of a system. From the perspective of static semantics, class structures are used to denote the relationships among classes of objects. In addition, these diagrams may be used to capture the dynamic behavior of individual classes. A project model may contain one or more class structures; multiple class structures may be used to group meaningful collections of classes. Each class structure may contain symbols that denote the following:

Class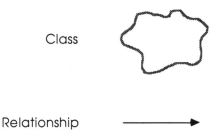

Relationship   ——————▶

Figure 6-9. Class structure symbols.

* *Classes*—which represent classes of objects;
* *Relationships*—which represent relationships among classes.

Figure 6-9 illustrates the symbols which may appear in a class structure. A class structure takes the form of a graph, in which classes are vertices of the graph and relationships are directed arcs.

For each class, one may provide as text a name, its semantics, and design notes. In addition, the static behavior of a class may be captured by recording the following items, each of which is a list of some textual information. These items express the resources exported by a class, or in other words, the abstraction that constitutes its outside view:

* constants,
* types,
* variables,
* constructors,
* selectors,
* iterators, and
* exceptions.

To complete the picture of the static semantics of a class, the author found it useful to denote the forms of the class,[33] any constraints upon the class that may be relevant, and the number of instances that may be made of the class. This last item is particularly helpful in capturing the design decisions regarding the allowable use of a class: it may be an anonymous class, there may be only one instance (in which case the object is simply an abstract state machine) or there may be multiple instances (in which case the class denotes an abstract data type).

To capture the dynamic semantics of a class, one may provide a finite state machine (which itself is another graph-like diagram); with this diagram, any allowable time ordering of operations, as well as the alteration of the state of any instances due to interactions among operations can be expressed.

For each relationship, the kind of relationship that exists between two classes must be described. The following five relationships were found to be typical among classes of a system:

- *Inherited*—there exists a superclass/subclass relationship
- *Instantiation*—one class is a parameterized instance of another class
- *Subtype*—one class is a constrained copy of another class; the two classes are effectively interchangeable
- *Derived*—one class is a constrained copy of another class; the two classes are not interchangeable, but are treated as distinct classes
- *Synthesis*—one class is a composite of several classes.

Class structures are generally produced during the second through fourth steps of the object-oriented design process. In practice, the author has found that one cannot typically populate a class structure immediately. Rather, once the major objects at any given level of abstraction have been identified and their boundaries chosen, a designer must look for patterns of abstractions. It is these patterns that become candidates for the introduction of new classes. In other cases, a designer may discover objects that are similar but not exactly so; this may suggest the introduction of a superclass that expresses much of the common behavior of the disparate abstractions and then the declaration of subclasses that express any differences.

It is important to note that the decision to generate a new class requires some engineering tradeoffs, since a class offers safety at the expense of flexibility. In addition, there is a non-zero cost to produce and generate multiple classes; on the other hand, classes offer a powerful vehicle for reuse of abstractions.

Object Diagram

Object diagrams represent the second dimension of the logical design of a system. Statically, object diagrams are used to express the visibility of each object in relation to other objects. Dynamically, object diagram may be used to express time and space constraints upon inter-object communication, in addition to the parallelism that might exist among a given collection of objects. A project model may contain one or more object diagrams; multiple object diagrams may be used to group meaningful collections of objects. Each object diagram may contain symbols that denote the following:

- *Objects*—which represent distinct objects
- *Visibility*—which represent visibility among two objects

For each object diagram, one may also provide a Petri Net, which may be used to express allowable patterns of concurrency among objects at the same level of abstraction.

Object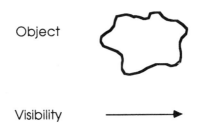

Visibility ⎯⎯⎯⎯⎯⎯➤

Figure 6-10. Object diagram symbols.

Figure 6-10 illustrates the symbols which may appear in an object diagram. An object diagram takes the form of a graph—representing the seniority hierarchy—in which objects are vertices of the graph and visibilities are directed arcs.

For each object, one may provide as text a name, its semantics, design notes and any relevant constraints upon the object. In addition, the static behavior of an object may be captured by recording its priority (in the case of an object that has its own thread of control) and a count (the number of instances of the same object).

Each object must have a class, which in effect is a reference to a specific class in a class structure; it is the definition of this class that provides the common behavior of all instances. In addition, to express the parent-child hierarchy, one may "explode" a single object to another complete object diagram, which represents the structure of all of its children.

Visibility, as a directed arc, denotes an asymmetric relationship between two objects: object *A* may see, but is not seen, by object *B*. For each visibility, one may supply a list of items which denote data or control flow; that is, the objects that may flow between two objects, or the operations that may be invoked by one object upon another. Each flow has its own set of design decisions, such as the operation to be invoked (which must match with an appropriate operation exported by the class of the designated object), the class of the objects that may travel along the flow, the direction of the flow (either with or against the direction of the visibility), and performance information, such as the frequency of the flow and manner of synchronization.

Object diagrams are generally produced during the second through fourth steps of the object-oriented design process. In fact, it is common to produce such diagrams incrementally. As objects are identified, they are included in an object diagram. Later, visibility decisions may be made, and only then is the graph decorated with arcs denoting visibility relationships. As with class structures, there exists an iterative element in the design process: one may choose to alter the boundaries of objects for a variety of technical and nontechnical reasons. Additionally, one may use object diagrams to visualize the relationships among objects and the implications of any restructuring.

Architecture Diagram

Architecture diagrams represent the physical design of a system, and thus primarily capture static information. A project model may contain one or more architecture diagrams; multiple architecture diagrams may be used to group meaningful collections of objects. Each architecture diagram may contain symbols that denote the following:

- *Components*—to represent structural elements provided by the underlying implementation language;
- *Dependencies*—to represent compilation dependencies among components.

The symbols for an architecture diagram are somewhat language specific, because not all languages provide the same packaging mechanisms, generic units, and tasks. The symbols which may appear in an architecture diagram used for Ada-based implementations are shown in Figure 6-11. In any case, an architecture diagram takes the form of a graph in which components are vertices of the graph, dependencies are directed arcs, and the topology of the graph satisfies the rules of separate compilation for the given implementation language.

For each component, one may provide as text a name, its semantics, and any relevant design notes. In addition, static design decisions may be captured by recording the kind of components (using the vocabulary of the underlying implementation language). Each component may reference a set of classes (from class structures of the same project model) or objects (from object diagrams of the same project model). This set of entities registers design decisions regarding the packaging of the implementation of individual classes and objects. Typically, there exists a one to one mapping of classes to components, and a many to one mapping of objects to components, although this is not always the case. For example, one may find some objects that exist as logically monolithic entities, yet must be implemented across physical boundaries. In this case, one may have a mapping of one object to many components. If the rules of the underlying implementation language allow it, some components may "explode" to unveil another complete architecture diagram. For example, if Ada is the underlying implementation language, the highest level architecture diagram may denote a hierarchy of libraries or subsystems. Zooming into any one of these elements, one finds a complete architecture diagram representing all of the separate compilation units that comprise the given subsystem.

Dependencies denote asymmetric relationships among components, according to the rules of compilation for the given implementation language.

Architecture diagrams are generally produced during the fifth step of the object-oriented design process. Producing such a diagram may motivate changes

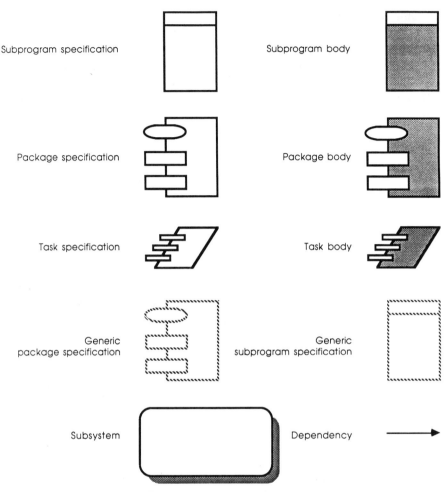

Subprogram specification

Subprogram body

Package specification

Package body

Task specification

Task body

Generic
package specification

Generic
subprogram specification

Subsystem

Dependency

Figure 6-11. Architecture diagram symbols.

in corresponding class structures and object diagrams, as the logical design is molded to conform to the physical constraints of the system. It is also at this time that one begins to assert a coupling between architecture diagrams and hardware diagrams. For very simple systems, it may have exactly one root thread of execution, which is mapped to a single processor in the one hardware diagram. In more complex cases, architecture diagrams may be used to identify the individual programs that must exist and their mapping to processors. Architecture diagrams therefore, facilitate representing the sharing of components among programs, even in the case where such programs execute in a distributed environment.

4 OBJECT-ORIENTED DESIGN IN THE SOFTWARE DEVELOPMENT LIFECYCLE

Coupling Analysis and Object-oriented Design

Object-oriented design is a partial life-cycle method; it focuses upon the design and implementation stages of software development. It is therefore necessary to couple object-oriented design with appropriate requirements and analysis methods, which help develop a model of the problem space. Jackson System Development (JSD) and the structured analysis techniques of Yourdon, Constantine, and DeMarco are promising matches; the real-time extensions to structured analysis by Ward and Mellor are especially suitable front-ends to object-oriented design.

Although a detailed discussion is beyond the scope of this current work, a mapping has been evolved between the products of structured analysis and object-oriented design. In simple terms, data flow diagrams can provide a model of the problem space, from which we can begin to derive candidate objects and classes, as the first step in the design process. Using the terminology of Ward and Mellor, the following is suggested:

- External entities
- Data and control stores
- Control transformations

Candidate classes of objects include:

- Data flows
- Control flows

This leaves data transformations, which one either assign as operations upon existing objects, or as the behavior expressed by individual objects that serve as agents responsible for the transformation.

Coupling Object-oriented Development and Programming Languages

The object-oriented design process may be used with virtually any high-order programming language, but the process is made easier when the given implementation language is powerful enough to allow expression of object-oriented abstractions and, more importantly, enforce these abstractions. At minimum, it is important to have some packaging mechanism in the underlying language. Next, the ability to separate specification from implementation minimizes the effects of changes, and permits many process steps to proceed in parallel.

Continuing, some ability to denote hierarchies of classes, either through a generic mechanism, inheritance, or both, greatly facilitates reuse.

In object-oriented design, the concerns of the implementation language begin to play a role primarily during the fourth and fifth steps, when interface and physical packaging decisions are made. If the given language is sufficiently rich, one can use it as a PDL (Program Description Language) to capture the design decisions made during these steps.

5 CASE STUDY

To bring together all of these concepts, consider the application of object-oriented design to a specific problem domain. For the purposes of this example, structured analysis is applied at the front end, using the notation of Ward and Mellor, assuming the use of Ada as the implementation language. In Figure 6-12, the context schema that defines the boundary of our problem is shown. The system under consideration is an automated gardener, responsible for monitoring the process of a large hydroponics farm. For a single greenhouse,

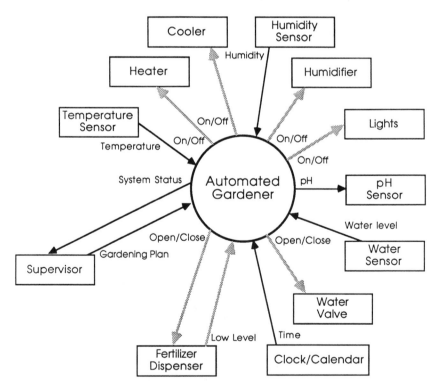

Figure 6-12. Automated gardener context schema.

a supervisor may establish a gardening plan; that is, he or she may assert the kind of crop to be farmed, set goals for production, and provide rules for the healthy production of the crop. Simply stated, the mission of the automated gardener is to carry out this plan with a minimum of human intervention. To carry out this goal, the automated gardener has, at each greenhouse, various sensors (for temperature, humidity, pH, water, and fertilizer) and actuators (for a heater, cooler, humidifier, lights, water valve, and fertilizer dispenser). Following the gardening plan (which is a function of time as well as the state of the crop), the automatic gardener must maintain a certain temperature, pH, humidity, and water level. In addition, the automatic gardener must periodically adjust the greenhouse lighting and follow a regular fertilization schedule. At any time, a supervisor may review the current status of a single greenhouse, as well as a log of all statuses over the past 180 days.

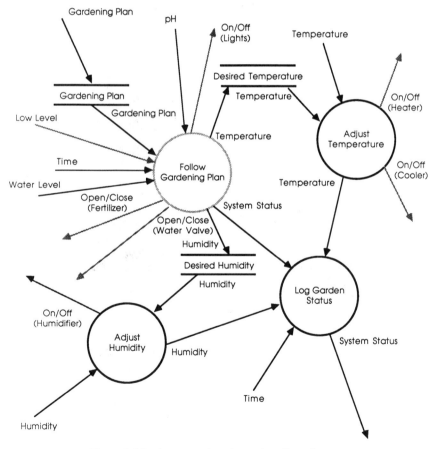

Figure 6-13. Automated gardener data flow diagram.

Also required is that this system be built to accommodate from one to ten greenhouses, with a single central supervisory function.

Figure 6-13 provides a top level data flow diagram for the automated gardener, based upon our analysis of the problem space. Here, we see that there is one primary control transformation (Follow Gardening Plan), two transformations for the primary functions of temperature and humidity maintenance, and a transformation that processes all system status.

Assume that the hardware engineers assigned to this project have decided to distribute the processing load of this system, by providing one microcomputer for the central supervisory function, connected to a microcomputer at each of up to ten greenhouses. As shown in Figure 6-14, each of these remote micro-computers is responsible for maintaining the gardening plan of a particular greenhouse (and plans may differ among greenhouses). Certainly, it is not necessary to make this hardware decision so early—indeed, as shall be explained, these hardware decisions do not effect any known software decisions until much later in the implementation phase. Through rapid prototyping of the software, a better hardware approach may be discovered. This is the kind of

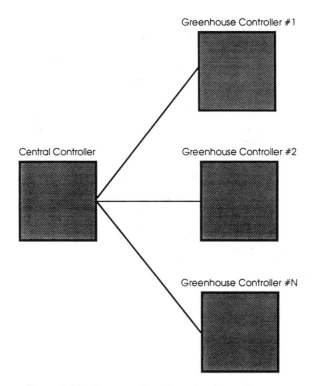

Figure 6-14. Automated gardener hardware diagram.

hardware/software tradeoff expected, by making the design decisions explicit in a notation that is sufficiently rich enough to study and reason about the model. Fundamental to the object-oriented design paradigm, the essential abstractions that exist in the problem space are identified—the objects and classes that are derived from the analysis of the real world. Think back to an earlier discussion of the problem itself, and additionally analyze the data flow diagram using the techniques described in the previous section, there are three basic classes in the domain to be discovered: sensors, actuators, and a single supervisory entity. All sensors have common attributes, although there are many kinds of sensors (temperature, humidity, water, and pH). Similarly, all actuators have common attributes, yet there are many kinds of actuators (humidifier, lights, water valve, fertilizer dispenser, heater, and cooler). These are all excellent class candidates, since in understanding the problem space, there may be several instances of each of these sensors and actuators (but only one supervisory entity) within the same system. To capture the design decisions regarding some initial boundaries around the basic abstractions that exist in the problem space, a class structure may be used (Figure 6-15). Notice that there are two disjoint classes (sensors and actuators) with subclasses for each.

The analysis also suggests that flows such as Time, Temperature, and System Status are candidate classes. These classes are not indicated in Figure 6-15, but they are certainly suitable for inclusion in a class structure so that we may capture our design decisions regarding their behavior.

Next, identify the basic actors, agents, and servers that exist at the highest level of abstraction of this system. Following the heuristics, candidate objects include the external entities, data stores, and control transformations. One may then ask: do all of these entities appear at the highest level of understanding of the system? The answer is that some of these entities appear at the boundaries of one's system, but it has been chosen to hide many details to provide a more abstract view in the solution space. For example, the data store, Desired Temperature, is certainly a candidate object, as are the external entities Heater, Cooler, and Temperature Sensor. However, it is also true that these entities are intimately related. Indeed, the existence of an agent that is responsible for managing all of these entities may be asserted. Upon considering the transformation named Adjust Temperature, it is found that this is a suitable activity that defines the basic behavior of the agent. For this reason, the existence of an object called Temperature Controller is asserted, which embodies the behavior of all these other objects and in fact hides their existence (which leads to a parent-child hierarchy). Similarly, the existence of a Humidity Controller may be asserted. The control transformation, Follow Gardening Plan, is also a candidate object which encompasses this transformation as well as the data store, Gardening Plan, and several other external entities. It should be noted that the state machine that one would create during analysis to define the semantics of this transformation is directly applicable to the state machine that defines the

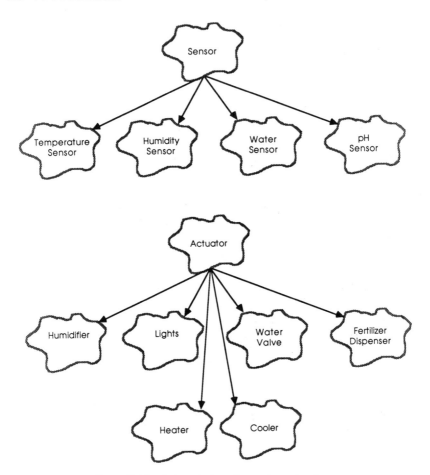

Figure 6-15. Automated gardener class structure.

behavior of this object's (anonymous) class, according to the conventions of the notation. Thus, traceability between the notation of object-oriented design and structured analysis can be achieved.

Revisiting the top level data flow diagram, one is left with the transformation, Log Garden Status, for which we generate another object as the agent responsible for this activity. Through this analysis, one must make an important point: there is not necessarily a one to one mapping from the items in a data flow diagram to the objects in an object diagram. More commonly, there is a many to one mapping; in some complex cases a one to many mapping may be found. The author's experience has been that one can analyze a data flow diagram at one level, plus one or two levels below, to establish a set of candidate objects. Given this set, either these objects exactly can be used or, collapse several of

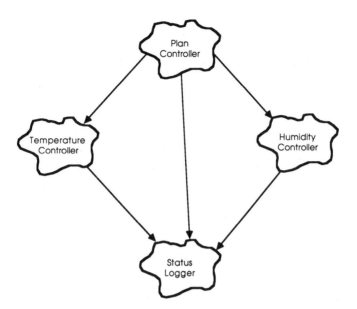

Figure 6-16. Automated gardener object diagram.

them into one object (as with Temperature Controller, to provide a more abstract view and hide unnecessary information), or even explode a very complex object (for greater understandability). As lower level data flows are analyzed, new objects that exist at lower levels of abstraction may be analyzed, or perhaps adjust the boundaries of objects at higher levels of abstractions to produce a more generalized mechanism. In any case, design decisions are made based primarily upon the notions of abstraction and information hiding.

Figure 6-16, provides this information in the form of an object diagram, one of the key products that results from steps one through four of the object-oriented design process. This diagram is generated by first writing the objects derived above as vertices of the graph. Next, consider the relationship among pairs of objects, and then added visibility arcs that captured these design decisions. Notice that the topology of this diagram clearly shows the seniority hierarchy at this level of abstraction: Plan Controller is the most senior object, and Status Logger is the least senior. Although not shown directly on this diagram (or the class structure), there would exist back-up information for each of the arcs and vertices, according to the notation described earlier. For example, for the visibility between the objects Plan Controller and Temperature Controller, the existence of a (desired) temperature objects, flowing in the direction of the visibility would be identified.

One might continue with the design process in one of two ways. First, further refine the design by analyzing lower level data flows and then generating additional class structures and object diagrams. This is fairly typical of the iterative nature of the object-oriented design process: as classes and objects are identified at one level of abstraction, the process is repeated to uncover entities at lower levels of abstraction. As such abstractions are uncovered, patterns of classes or objects are discovered that lead to the invention of more generalized mechanism, thus leading to greater reuse plus simplification of the entire architecture. Second, one might take a given level of class structure and object diagram, and immediately proceed to physical design by building a prototype, allowing experiment with the architecture, provide early feedback to users, and facilitate comparisons of alternate approaches.

In practice, both approaches used within the same project are found. In those segments of a system for which there is a base of experience, one can more confidently proceed with refinement of the logical design, mainly because one will have greater confidence that their choice of abstractions are sound. There may also be high risk elements of the system—elements involving complicated behavior, time and space constraints, or just sheer complexity because of unfamiliarity with key abstractions of the problem domain. In such cases, early prototyping is recommended, so as to facilitate understanding of the problem domain and early identification of tradeoffs among alternative solutions.

For the purposes of this example, the author proceeds with the physical design. As shown in Figure 6-17, the packaging decision of allocating the objects Plan Controller and Status Logger each to their own subsystem has been chosen. The author also has chosen to combine the objects Temperature Controller and Humidity Controller to the same subsystem, because these abstractions have great logical similarity.

Notice that this architecture preserves the seniority hierarchy of the object diagram in Figure 6-16. If one now zooms into the structure of the subsystem Environment Controller (an example of the parent-child hierarchy), one sees the design decisions made at this level in Figure 6-18. Here, are packages that provide the implementation of several objects identified earlier: the Cooler, Heater, Humidifier, Temperature Sensor, and Humidity Sensor. The objects Temperature Controller and Humidity Controller, from the object diagram in Figure 6-16 are also shown. The author also made the design decision to combine the objects representing the data stores Desired Temperature and Desired Humidity into one package, so as to unify the interface of this entire subsystem. In fact, notice a narrow interface between subsystems: the package Desired Temperature and Humidity is the only one made available to the using subsystem, Plan Controller, and the only resource this present subsystem needs is some (not yet described) package from the interface of the subsystem Status Logger. Indeed, the topology of the solution maps to the desired characteristics discussed earlier: there are distinct levels of abstraction, with narrow interfaces among subsystems arranged in a hierarchy; within subsystems, the topology is that of a DAG.

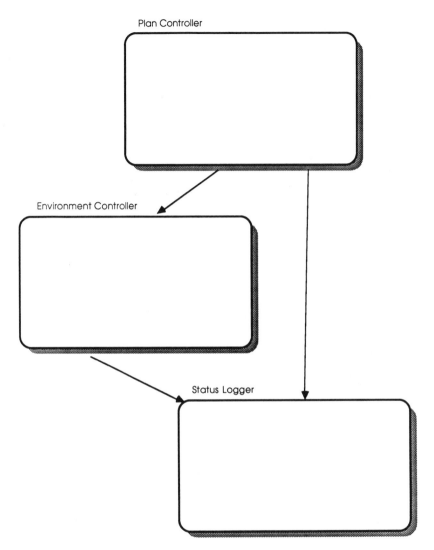

Figure 6-17. Automated gardener architecture diagram.

6   CONCLUSION

Having had the perversities of the real world intrude upon all too many software projects, designers remain pragmatic: their goal is to build useful systems that work, and as engineers, the methods and tools that enable building such systems are chosen in the presence of scarce resources. In that light, object-oriented design should not be viewed as the final word in design methods. Rather, as

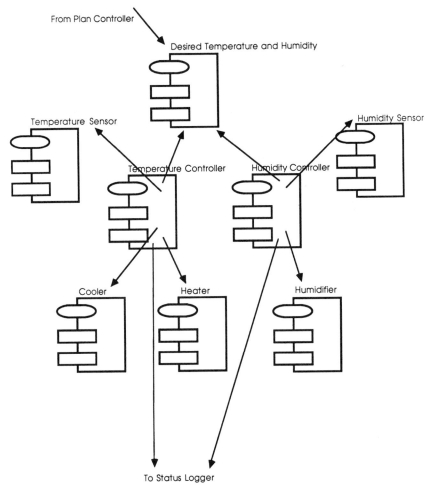

Figure 6-18. Environment controller architecture diagram.

just one approach that may be applied to help manage the complexity of a fairly broad set of problem domains. Object-oriented techniques have emerged from many unrelated disciplines of computer science, and indeed, the object model in software engineering may prove to be a powerful unifying concept. In this chapter, a process and notation for object-oriented design are defined, and therefore, are called an identifiable, legitimate method. As the method matures, there occurs the emergence of tool support; this will be an area of much future activity. Already, the method—in various forms—has been applied to a number of very complex problem domains. Although empirical studies are anticipated, it can be concluded that this method does indeed add value to the development of complex, software-intensive systems.

REFERENCES

1. G. Booch is Director of Software Engineering Programs at Rational, 1501 Salado Drive, Mountain View, CA 94043. This article is based upon work that appears in *Software Engineering with Ada*, Menlo Park, CA: Benjamin/Cummings, 1986 and *Software Components with Ada*, Menlo Park, CA: Benjamin/Cummings, 1987.
2. Simon, H., *The Sciences of the Artificial*, Cambridge, MA: MIT Press, 1969, pp. 218–219.
3. Ross, D., J. Goodenough, and C. Irvine, "Software Engineering: Process, Principles, and Goals," *IEEE Computer*, Vol. 8, No. 5, May 1975, pp. 17–27.
4. Ibid., p. 66.
5. Ibid., p. 67.
6. Wegner, P., "The Ada Programming Language and Environment," unpublished draft, June 1981.
7. MacLennan, B., "Values and Objects in Programming Languages," *SIGPLAN Notices*, December 1982, Vol. 17 (12), p. 75.
8. Levy, H., *Capability-Based Computer Systems*, Bedford, MA: Digital Press, 1984, p. 13.
9. Myers, G., *Advances in Computer Architecture*, New York: John Wiley & Sons, 1982.
10. Deitel, H., *An Introduction to Operating Systems*, Reading, MA: Addison-Wesley, 1983, p. 456.
11. Liskov, B., "A Design Methodology for Reliable Software Systems," *Proceedings of the Fall Joint Computer Conference*, AFIPS, 1972, pp. 191–199.
12. Parnas, D., "On the Criteria To Be Used in Decomposing Systems into Modules," *Communications of the ACM*, December 1972, pp. 1053–1058.
13. Liskov, B. and S. Zilles, "Specification Techniques for Data Abstractions," *IEEE Transactions on Software Engineering*, Vol. SE-1, No. 1, March 1975, pp. 7–19.
14. Guttag, J., E. Horowitz, and D. Musser, "The Design of Data Type Specification," *Current Trends in Programming Methodology*," Vol. 4., (ed. R. T. Yeh), Englewood Cliffs, NJ: Prentice-Hall, 1978, pp. 61–79.
15. Shaw, M., "Abstraction Techniques in Modern Programming Languages," *IEEE Software*, October 1984, Vol. 1 (4), pp. 10–26.
16. Rentsch, T., "Object-oriented Programming," *SIGPLAN Notices*, September 1982, Vol. 17 (9), p. 51.
17. Abelson, A., G. Sussman, and J. Sussman, *Structure and Interpretation of Computer Programs*, Cambridge, MA: MIT Press, 1985.
18. Cox, B., Message/Object Programming: "An Evolutionary Change in Programming Technology," *IEEE Software*, January 1984, Vol. 1 (1), pp. 50–62.
19. A Symposium on Actor Languages, *Creative Computing*, October 1980.
20. Stefik, M. and D. Bobrow, "Object-oriented Programming: Themes and Variations," *AI Magazine*, 1986, Vol. 6 (4), p. 40.
21. Ross, R., *Entity Modeling*, Boston, MA: Database Research Group, 1987.
22. Rentsch, T., "Object-oriented Programming," *SIGPLAN Notices*, September 1982, Vol. 17 (9), p. 51.
23. Cardelli, L., and P. Wegner, "On Understanding Types, Data Abstraction, and Polymorphism," *ACM Computing Surveys*, December 1985, Vol. 17 (4), pp. 471–522.
24. Sommerville, I., *Software Engineering*, Workingham, England: Addison-Wesley, 1985, p. 69.
25. Guttag, J., "Abstract Data Types and Their Development of Data Structures," *Programming Language Design*, Los Alamitos, CA: IEEE Computer Society Press, 1980, p. 200.
26. Adapted from an exercise provided at the Rocky Mountain Institute for Software Engineering, Aspen, CO, 1984.
27. Liskov, B., and S. Zilles, "An Introduction to Formal Specifications of Data Abstractions," *Current Trends in Programming Methodology*, Vol. 1, (ed. R. T. Yeh), Englewood Cliffs, NJ: Prentice-Hall, 1977, pp. 1–32.

28. Shaw, M., W. Wulf, and R. London, "Abstraction and Verification in Alphard: Iteration and Generators," *Alphard: Form and Content,* New York: Springer Verlag, 1981.

29. Liskov, B., R. Atkinson, T. Bloom, E. Moss, J. Schaffert, R. Schiefler, and A. Snyder, *CLU Reference Manual,* New York: Springer-Verlag, 1981, p. 8.

30. Courtois, P., "On Time and Space Decomposition of Complex Structures," *Communications of the ACM,* June 1985, Vol. 28 (6), pp. 590–604.

31. Seidewitz, E. and M. Stark, *General Object-oriented Software Development, Software Engineering Laboratory Series, SEL-86-002,* Greenbelt, MD., NASA Goddard Space Flight Center, August 1986, p. 43.

32. Abbott, R., *Report on Teaching Ada, Report SAI-81-312WA,* Science Applications, Inc., December 1980.

33. Booch, G., *Software Components with Ada,* Menlo Park, CA: Benjamin/Cummings Publishing Company, 1987.

Chapter 7

Reusability

ROLAND T. MITTERMEIR AND WILHELM ROSSAK
Institut f. Informatik
Universitaet Klagenfurt
Austria

ABSTRACT

This chapter provides an introduction to the topic of software reusability. It starts out asking the question why software reuse has become a major topic for the software industry and for researchers working in this field. Due to the importance of the theme, a variety of strategies has been proposed to tackle it. The first part of the chapter identifies them and gives an assessment about their relative merits. Further, it suggests a perspective on a software system that helps to isolate reusable components, and it discusses different purposes of reuse. The issue of reusability is then discussed with regard to the design of software aimed for later reuse. This perspective is complemented by reflections upon the effects of reuse on the life cycle cost for a system in which "old" components should be reused. Having thus set the tone that reusability is concerned with existing software as well as software yet to be written, the authors first concentrate on mechanisms to structure and retrieve old software. This is complemented by a section focusing on a mechanism that allows writing software in such a way that it can be highly parameterized for later reuse and supports the composition of systems out of such components. To show that reusability is not only concerned with tools, a glimpse on design decisions made with a particular software development environment is given.

1 INTRODUCTION

1.1 Motivation

Today, the edp industry has become a major economic factor. Besides providing the ability to perform calculations in the traditional sense, the ability to process information makes edp a critical factor of modern industrial nations.[73]

The rapid progress in hardware development provides users and developers with increased and less expensive processing power and storage capacity in relatively short periods of time. This renders new applications possible and thus leads to an increasing demand for reliable and functionally complete systems.

In this technology race, software has proven to be the bottleneck in the production process. There is a significant application backlog in domains that have used edp systems for a long time and no extra programmer capacity is left to solve the problems given by applications in new domains.

The reasons for this lie in the lack of highly qualified programmers and in a software production process which is, in most cases, on the level of pre-industrial craftsmanship, rather than on the level of industrial production. Thus, the production of software is still slow, costly, and error prone.

Some people are hoping for AI to solve all of these complicated problems.[63] But, the authors conjecture that a mere combination of software engineering and AI techniques for structuring and supporting software development will not be enough. They are just the necessary preconditions to apply other methods that improve productivity. Because almost any environment into which a software system might be placed changes with time, and because applying changes to systems is a primary source for introducing imperfections, sound development of software systems will be practicable only if a faster turn-around time between the initial expression of a needs statement and the use of the system can be achieved.

The following are three different major strategies to obtain this goal:

- automating software production as much as possible;
- delegating software production to expert systems; and
- reusing existing software as much as possible.

At the first glance, these are quite different approaches. But they tend to converge under the light of new developments in the areas of programming languages, applied AI, and conceptual modeling. Automating or delegating software production implies the concept of software reuse, if time constraints for the production process are critical. Reuse of existing software is not practicable without support given by appropriate languages, intelligent tools and application independent system structures. Thus, with regard to the goals mentioned above, software reuse turns out to be one of the key factors in enhancing the production process for edp systems.

1.2   Approaches of Reusing Software Development Effort[(1)]

Before suggestions are presented concerning software reuse, the various strategies are discussed to reutilize software development effort already expended.

[(1)]This chapter is an expanded version of the introductory chapter of Reference 48.

Any high level language supports simple forms of reusability by the subroutine concept. However, subroutines are confined in their applicability mostly to a single user and to a single project, because the mechanisms to precisely and succinctly communicate their contents to one's colleagues are not available. Only in restricted domains, such as statistical analysis or certain numerical problems, subroutine packages and libraries like SPSS or SSP have had a high impact. Nevertheless, such packages tend to become hard to manage with an increasing number of components enclosed, as no sufficient support structure or systematics is provided. They rely on the expert knowledge of the user: this implies that they are limited to a narrow application domain to be useful.

Reuse of low level components—near source code—can be found in nearly every environment where large and complex systems are being built. Modern programming languages, such as Modula-2 or Ada support this kind of reuse by the module- or package-concept. It allows the user to define data- and procedural-abstractions and to reuse them in different application systems. A further step forward is object-oriented languages like Smalltalk-80 and languages providing inheritance mechanisms.

So called 4-th generation languages (4GL) follow a different strategy to allow a dramatic speed up in software production. They are designed for particular application domains. However, at present these domains have been very narrow. Furthermore, 4GLs yield, in many cases, highly inaccessible and hard to read code, and they lack support to organize and retrieve the produced software in a structured way for later reuse.

All of the concepts mentioned above share one further disadvantage: they are programming language features—even though some of them are on a relatively high level. As language features, these concepts are confined to the level of source code, and do not take any other possible product of the development process into consideration.

Since coding is not the most expensive part of the development process, it will be necessary to look at more comprehensive concepts for software reuse. (Surveys of the state of the art are given in References 6, 23, 33, and 68.)

Some main directions of research can be identified as the following:

- prototyping;
- use of operating system features;
- knowledge based systems;
- transformation systems;
- generators; and
- reusable components.

The primary goal of prototyping is to support the requirements engineering phase. It helps to close the communications gap between clients and developers as well as to study the feasibility of certain architectural variants.[22,44,71] In the early 1980s, some people tended to define prototypes as throw-away versions of a system.[64] Nowadays, this discussion is overcome, and one generally recognizes that the executable code is not the core issue and that parts of the prototype or at least the concept, clarified by using it, can be reused or utilized.

Operating system features, such as pipes[34] can be used to support a certain degree of reusability.[25] The advantage is seen in providing a very simple and clear standard interface between software components at the source code level. Nevertheless, reuse of software is restricted to this level, and no further support is given to the user. This leads to problems similar to those mentioned for subroutine libraries and restricts the use of operating system features to a well known development environment.

With knowledge based systems, one has to distinguish between their architecture and their applications in software engineering.

As a result of their basic architecture, "knowledge" incorporated into a knowledge base is reusable under varying conditions. Chunks of knowledge are treated as complete entities and can be dynamically selected by the inference engine, dependent on the actual subproblem; but this reusability is confined within the problem domain modeled.

Nevertheless, knowledge based systems can be used as a tool to improve the engineering process of system development.[28] They allow a certain degree of automation by providing knowledge representation structures and fitting retrieval algorithms. They are well suited to control and support the development process and to give advice to the user by providing rules and integrity constraints. Some of these advantages are discussed in Sections 4 and 5.

Transformation systems and generators are also derived from AI concepts. Transformation systems, start with a software component similar to the one required and transform it to a fitting solution.[10,13] This transformation is normally done on the level of source code or on a very formal representation of the software component, thus narrowing its applicability.

Generators try to incorporate and thus reuse domain knowledge[14,51] or even certain design heuristics.[19] They are based on very high level languages (VHLL). Thus 4GLs can be considered a type of generator.[39] As mentioned for 4GLs, most generators lack support structures to deal with software components once they are generated and support no level of abstraction other than the VHLL.

As described above, composing systems out of reusable components was first done at the source code level, using programming languages and operating system features. Project libraries,[56] documentation systems[27] and configuration management systems[4] constitute a further step in the direction of involving levels other than source code and reutilizing the effort spent during different stages of development.

The concept of composing a system out of reusable components stems from the concept of Programming-in-the-Large.[18,37,38] It is based on a description of common features of modeled components[29,40,61,66] also on a higher level than source code and gives a functional description of the whole system with interface constraints.[43,47,48] The retrieval of components can be considered a type of classification problem.[26,57,59,60]

Looking at these different strategies, the concept of reusable components is the most comprehensive and practicable alternative. AI based methods, such as generators, transformation systems, knowledge representation techniques, and retrieval algorithms are merged with the idea of combining a system out of existing components. This leads to a concept which incorporates most of the basic ideas discussed in Section 1.1. This combined approach will allow further research and development to move one step further towards the goal of error free and rapid software development.

1.3 A Perspective for Reuse

In the previous sections, the unit of reuse was not defined in any detail. Only hints were given that it should not stop short on the level of program code. Here, the authors will expand on this by reviewing the system development process and its typical characteristics.[48,61]

Because coding contributes only a minor portion to the production cost for software, the unit of reuse should include other possible representational forms; i.e., some form of nonexecutable specification, thus allowing one to take advantage of the effort invested into earlier stages of system development.

Most system development methodologies recommend a top down approach and thus rely on a concept of dividing the system into smaller parts and adding details later. They start out with a crude but comprehensive description of the whole system and proceed to a fine grained level where transformation to a representation in a programming language will be appropriate. These approaches can be traced back to the notion of stepwise refinement, given in Reference 69, used to find an appropriate problem decomposition.

Thus, software production can be considered as a branching sequential decision process, resulting in a decision tree with software components on different levels of decomposition. The root of the tree is the system, its leaves are components at or near the source code level.

Components on a given level of decomposition are associated with each other if they have a common ancestor on the next higher level of aggregation/decomposition. Depending on the method followed, such an association may be used to define certain integrity constraints or dependencies, such as the calling sequence of dependent subroutines or I/O-relations between a dependent and its superior component.

Hence, a software system can be viewed as a cube spanned by the following dimensions: representation, decomposition, and association. This cube is referred to as the application cube (Figure 7-1).

In this cube, a component on a certain level of decomposition and represen-

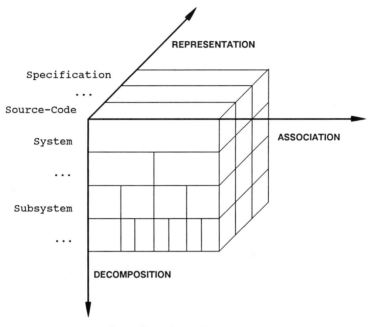

Figure 7-1. An application cube.

tation is embedded in an association structure. This association structure is based on the decomposition process and relates brothers derived from a common ancestor and refined by a given design decision. The individual components are referred to as design units.

Following the concept of an application cube, the unit of reuse will be such a design unit. It is not confined to a certain level of representation, and it can range in its comprehensiveness from anything between the whole system to a functional building block. Therefore, a design unit is not bound to a certain stage of development.

In reusing software at least two systems are involved. In analogy to the terminology used in the context of human organ transplantation, the authors refer to the system for which a component (to be reused) has been originally written for as the donating system. The system into which such a reused component is to be placed will be referred to as the receiving system. Donating and receiving systems can be considered different application cubes, sharing a common design unit.

1.4 Purposes of Reuse

The various strategies mentioned in the previous section should not only be evaluated from the vantage point of the software development process. Properties of the receiving system produced out of reusable components should also be considered in the reusability debate.

In general, a system will not be produced out of reused components only. On the contrary, usually components retrieved from the wealth of available software will be combined with newly written components, and this collection has to be bound together by code written for this particular application. With some of the modules of such a system, the developer will face the decision of whether to reuse and modify or to rewrite them.

The break-even-point for reusing or rewriting is in most cases determined by the usage pattern of the system to be built. To identify the extremes, one can distinguish here between the combination of reusable components for purposes of rapid prototyping, on the one hand and the reuse of components for integrating them into "final" operational systems for bulk usage, on the other hand.

In reality, this distinction is not as sharp as mentioned[22] and hence, the arguments raised should not be understood as binary recommendations but must be applied in the respective nuances.

For rapid prototyping purposes one can either follow the approach usually mentioned with such methodologies, i.e., use a very high level language to produce the prototypes and reuse then the knowhow about the application to (re)develop the final operational system, or one can construct the prototype by combining highly parameterized building blocks which yield the required functionality but would be far too inefficient to be used in an operational system. In both cases, the actual code of the operational target system is not reused but (re)produced. Only in the case of evolutionary prototyping[22] or prototyping with successive solidification of objects[35] VHLL code from the prototype will be reused within the final system.

With rapid prototyping by combination of reusable code, one strives to reuse existing software down to the code level. In these cases, the strategy of reuse will not necessarily aim for a perfect match between the application to be developed and the code to be reused in the prototype. One might rather work like builders constructing houses from prefabricated components where the buyer might make his own arrangements for certain details of the layout (user interface) but has to live with what he gets with respect to the basic structures. Considering a prototype as an experimental vehicle, this might be sufficient, since the user will raise his complaints in any way, and a system matching to a large degree might be as good as a system matching almost perfectly—provided that it can be produced at substantially lower costs. For psychological reasons, it might be even easier to "sell" the following full-fledged development process, if the prototype has not been presented to be a perfect solution to the clients demand.

An argument worth considering, is that composition of prototypes out of reusable components might yield a larger range of prototyping purposes than the fast-to-write/fast-to-execute/throw-away approach. For studying the technological risk (e.g., performance or security issues) the latter will hardly be applicable, while the former might serve these purposes as well as those of reducing the application risk.

Quite different arguments appear when a component is to be reused in a system destined to be eventually operational with this component included. In this case, a perfect fit is required at the completion. Hence, more severe constraints have to be placed on the retrieval mechanism. In analogy to information retrieval systems, one could state that in reuse for prototyping high recall would dominate the goal function of the search, but for reuse within a production version high precision at sufficient recall will become the determining factor.

It is worth mentioning in this context that descriptive information about a reusable design unit should be at a high enough level to use very early in the development process of the receiving system. Like mechanical engineers, who have books describing standard components to be used in an engine to be built, software engineers should eventually be provided with similar aids.[3] Consulting a reusable components library early in the design phase might solve the problem that a system component is specified (in all details), such that no reusable component would be available for reuse. If the specification would be less constraining, a very similar component available in the archive might have satisfied the given needs without corrupting the design goals. This means to look first at commonalities and only later determine any details, as proposed with the notion of "program families."[54]

2 DESIGN FOR REUSABILITY

As mentioned in Chapter 1, reusability can be targeted at various levels of software development. In certain prototyping cases, one would transfer only the knowledge about the true requirements of the client system. In other cases, it is the design of a system, which can be carried over to a new application, and in the supposedly most favourable case, even actual code can be copied into a new product. As donating systems for reusable components, one usually thinks of software written some time ago. However, one might also want to reuse the software which will be written tomorrow in projects in the distant future. Hence, one must ask, whether there are any factors the original producer of a design unit should keep in mind to make his/her product reusable at a level as high as possible, or is reusability only concerned with building a powerful retrieval mechanism over code modules (or design units) which were produced by somebody, somehow?

2.1 Reusing Existing Code

Reusing existing code is what most literature on reusability is concerned with.[4,6,23,25,26,37] In Reference 48, the authors extended this notion to the reuse of design units, acknowledging the fact that coding is not the most demanding portion within the software development process. But still, the implicit point of departure has been that whatever is to be reused already existed before somebody had the bright idea of "hasn't there been such a thing already in project X!"

This perspective is most valid, because reusing the wealth of software that is already available is definitely a major aim of the current debate on the issue. Further, if the previous project has been done well, the design units produced should be easily maintainable—if so, the chain of arguments continues; maintenance changes might not lead just to a new version of the same product but as easily to a new component in a totally new and different product.

The above statement might yield the conclusion that the authors try to address a non-issue. However, looking at design methodologies e.g., Structured Design[72], Jackson System Development (JSD)[32], and data encapsulation/information hiding[53] on one hand and the needs for easy composition of a neat (!) new system on the other hand, one might still find differences in the task at hand.

Structured Design

The basic principles of what came to be called Structured Design or the Constantine Method can be divided into the system-breakdown/packaging structure and an evaluation methodology.[50,65,73]

While the evaluation methodology will certainly help in terms of maintainability and, therefore, also in terms of reusability to the extent the two concepts overlap, recipies are considered for decomposing a data-flow diagram into a system structure as not particularly favoring reusability.

The reason for this negative attitude is because the data-flow diagram describes a system really at its very specifics. Hence, it tends to show that the given system with its particular data-flow is unique. Hence, chances are slim that one can reuse high level design units covering substantial portions of the data flow diagram (paths) in a new system with pragmatics not highly related to the pragmatics of the system one wants to draw from.

If the design of the donating system has been very neat, it might contain lots of functionally cohesive modules, and there should be nothing which speaks against reusing them. Just the granularity of reusage will be necessarily rather fine. Unfortunately though, real systems will also contain—for good reasons— modules of lesser cohesiveness or higher coupling than functional cohesion and data coupling. These components provide severe obstacles for the software builder aiming at reuse of readymade components. (For non-leaf modules, this argument will almost invariably apply.)

While these arguments center on data-flow oriented system decomposition, transform oriented decompositions will not do much better. Chances for reusability will highly depend on how neat the communications part of such a system was separated from the transaction-performing part. If a complete transaction-performing part can be reused, the builder of the system will be fine. If one needs to open it up and use only a part of it, and to modify and redo the rest, one ends up in most cases with the same difficulties one would have in reusing portions of a data-flow oriented design.

Information Hiding/Data Encapsulation

This principle builds on Parnas' articles in the Communications of ACM.[52,53,55] There is not really sufficient methodological advice in this proposal to allow for a widespread and disciplined use among software practitioners building large systems.[5] Only if one is directly aiming at an implementation in a language supporting data encapsulation similar to ADA or MODULA-2, sufficient impetus is present to make the data capsules true candidates for designing larger systems.

Even then, this approach tends to reduce reusability to a level very close to that of actual programming languages and, hence, the arguments raised with reusing functionally cohesive modules apply again.

Jackson Structured Programming (JSP)

As opposed to JSP,[31] Jackson System Development (JSD)[12,32] follows an object oriented trail in requiring that a software system is an accurate scale model of reality. Hence, we consider its potential of yielding reusable high level design units as rather high (see next subsection). On lower levels (after the implementation step), this does not necessarily hold any longer (notably if communication is achieved by low level inversion mechanisms).

To summarize, the authors admit that an excellent programmer can write highly reusable software with most methodologies. Even code written by an average programmer on an average work-day might be reusable with some pain. However, the system thus composed will most probably be far from what one would prefer to maintain.

2.2 Writing Software for Reuse

In light of the previous discussion, the authors conjecture that writing software for reuse requires more than writing easily maintainable software. While the latter goal helps to keep the system currently under construction clean, the former has to consider also the cleanliness of the yet unknown receiving systems.

Aiming for an orderly receiving system requires a firm basis for determining the independence of design units. The evaluation criteria of the Constantine method definitely point in the right direction. However, they are formulated on the level of executable code. With regard to reusability, such rules would be needed on any arbitrary level of representation a design unit might have.

Considering the data base field, normalization did provide the necessary separation of data from the particular application it had been collected and stored for originally. Hence, we could see in Codd's work[15] the crucial step towards making data "reusable."[15]

A similar type of normalization had been asked for, in the case of software design, which followed an object oriented approach.[46] The reason for tying normalization to object orientation will become more evident in Subsection 4.3. However, it can be stated that object oriented programming (see also Chapter 6 of this book) will greatly support reusability.[9,16]

Following an object oriented approach, reusability will not only become easier as a consequence of the correspondence between a real world entity-(class) and its software image. It will also become enhanced by the inheritance structures supported by object oriented methodologies and tools.

Writing software for reuse also documents special design decisions, which are crucial for the layout of the given design unit. Examining these decisions— e.g., represented by attributes of the unit—will allow one to trace back to a generalized design unit at higher levels of abstraction. This more generalized unit is—relative to the specialized one—more independent in terms of reusability and should also be documented.[54,55,61]

3 LIFE CYCLE CONSIDERATIONS OF REUSABILITY

Before going into a detailed discussion of various reusability strategies, the authors look briefly at when it would be beneficial to use a design unit from some donating system or from a software archive or software base as opposed to writing it from scratch.

It has been argued that the break-even-point of re-using versus redoing would be where the cost of search (plus modifications) exceeds the cost of reproducing the respective piece of software.[57]

This argument is definitely correct as a first approximation, and it might even hold for reusing design units for the purpose of rapidly producing a prototype. In finally assessing the merits of reusing software for incorporation within a supposedly long-living receiving system, one should be more careful. Here, one has to consider the whole spectrum of life cycle cost, which, in addition to whatever might be the degree of completeness of a reusable design unit, will also encompass verification and maintenance cost.

Concerning *verification cost,* one has to consider that the design unit to be incorporated into the receiving system supposedly was previously verified or tested for the purpose and within the context of the donating system (the reusability support system might indicate the degree of verification of the design units it manages). Hence, the substantial cost portion of software verification can be drastically reduced to the cost of determining whether a supposedly correct and self-consistent design unit would properly fit into the new environment (extended integration testing).[8,58]

It should be noted that this statement is somewhat biased towards reusing executable code. Obviously, in this case the leverage effect of reuse will be highest. It should be noted though, that verification is not just the last phase during software development. It has to take place in different forms within each major step of the production process.[7,8,42]

Considering *maintenance cost,* the assessment is less positive. Here, one has to evaluate, whether or not incorporation of a design unit from some donating system will have a negative impact on the overall system design. If so, one should carefully evaluate whether the current gain in time really warrants the (appropriately discounted) extra effort one might have later on during system maintenance.

Ideally there should be no difference between maintaining a system developed coherently in a single shot and a system glued together from reusable components. In practice though, one has to admit that software produced at different times by different people in different projects will simply exhibit many differences (naming space, naming conventions, style, documentation, etc.). Thus, at least understandability will suffer.

With clear cut designs one would still have the option of "let's use it now, we'll redo it later"—so to say, a kind of partial prototyping. This has the merit of reaping the benefits of the necessary system earlier than otherwise at almost no additional cost. The additional cost will be the higher, however, the idiosyncracies of the donated module must be accounted for in the design of the rest of the receiving system.

In opposition to the above statements, one could raise the argument that they are based on a binary world of reuse-as-it-is versus redo. Obviously, a reused design unit can be modified before incorporation in the receiving system. One possibility is to encapsulate the design unit in such a way that only the desired functionality will be visible on the outside of such a software cocoon—leaving any unneeded excess functionality as dead code. The other is to modify its internals in such a way that it yields the desired functionality while also fitting smoothly into the overall design of the new system (at least at the interface- and design-level). But in these cases, the software engineer definitely wants to maintain records about where such changes were applied and where the new version still matches the original one. Thus, help for version control is required with the additional constraint that it has to support maintaining multiple parallel versions.

Section 4.2 (The Software Archive) focuses on these problems. Its main theme is how the corporate software resource of a company can be structured to support software retrieval.

4 SUPPORT STRUCTURES

Section 1.3 gave a simplified model for an application system by defining the application cube. The building blocks of the cube, the design units, are embedded in a structure spanned by the following dimensions: representation, aggregation/decomposition, and association. The donating and the receiving systems are both applications and can be considered as application cubes.

The question is, whether or not an application independent structure can be found, which allows one to store and classify design units—taken from their donating system—independent from the application for which they were originally written. Later on, it should be able to retrieve these design units and to incorporate them into one or more receiving systems.

4.1 Dimensions of the Structure

Starting with the application cube, we re-evaluated the different dimensions with regard to their applicability in an application independent structure.[48]

The representation dimension against which a design unit can be classified allows one to include units from different stages of development (hence not only at the source code level) in such a classification and search structure. To classify a design unit according to its form of representation does not link this unit to a certain application system. Therefore, the representation dimension can be adopted to the needs of the search structure.

The level of decomposition gives a good indication of the comprehensiveness of a design unit. Knowing the required level of decomposition implies awareness of the most important attributes of this design unit. It drastically narrows the possible search space. Aggregation/decomposition alone, without the related association, is a very effective possibility for a first classification without binding the described unit to its donating system.

The classification dimension—as defined with regard to the decomposition abstraction—describes the result of system decomposition during the development process. Thus, it covers information about application-dependent links between modules. This information links the design unit and the donating system. Therefore, it is not useful in an application independent structure supporting reusability. However, association together with decomposition is the main structuring factor in the application cube, allowing one to treat a software system as a complete entity instead of the mere set of its components. To provide such a main structuring factor in an application independent way, a new dimension has to be introduced to be able to define a new kind of association based on this dimension. The resulting structure must have the following attributes:

- application independence;
- ability to build a taxonomy; and
- support search by hierarchically organizing information.

Generalization/specialization hierarchies as used in artificial intelligence fulfill these needs.[11,21] They are application independent, can be used to build taxonomies and allow hierarchical organization of knowledge by means of attribute inheritance. Furthermore, generalization structures have been used successfully to guide searching strategies.[41]

Regarding generalization, a new kind of association can be defined. The definition for associated components is the same as given in Section 1.3, the only difference is that the association dimension is related with generalization and not with aggregation/decomposition any more. Thus, two design units on a given level of generalization are associated by sharing a common ancestor on a higher level of generalization. This definition can be interpreted as two associated modules are similar to each other by being derived from the same general design unit. From this point of view, the association structure defines a hierarchical model of unit relationships based on the similarity between the design units and the degree of generalization of the single design unit.

Together with the dimensions taken from the application cube, an application independent structure is defined, which has the following dimensions:

- representation;
- generalization;
- association (with regard to generalization); and
- aggregation/decomposition.

This structure can be seen as (hyper-)cube, where design units are classified at each level of decomposition according to their representational form, their degree of generalization, and their place in the association structure (Figure 7-2).

4.2   The Software Archive

The software archive is a mechanism to support the storage and retrieval of design units for potential reuse.[48,61] It consists of a structure—as proposed for the classification structure in Section 4.1—containing the individual design units and the necessary retrieval algorithms to allow a guided search in the archive.

Design units are simply called modules. With respect to the definition of design units, the notion of "module" used in connection with the software archive differs from other definitions, insofar, as modules are not bound to a certain level of decomposition or to a representation at the source code level.[17,24,30]

4.2.1   Structure

The four-dimensional classification schema (Figure 7-2) defines the structure of the archive. The two most important structural components of the archive are aggregation, and generalization (association).

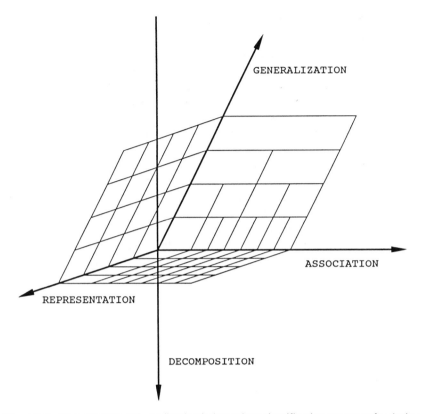

Figure 7-2. Four-dimensional, application independent classification structure for design units.

Modules in a highly abstract representational form—e.g., specifications—are normally on a high level of generalization with regard to the attributes they define. Modules on a low level of representation—e.g., source code programs—are automatically on a low level of generalization, or the other way around, are a very specialized form of design unit. Hence, representation is a special case of generalization/specialization and is merged with this dimension.

Aggregation/decomposition is implemented by a PART-OF relation between modules in the archive. This leads to a hierarchical structure, where modules at neighboring levels of decomposition can be linked together. Nevertheless, there is no aggregation-association defined anymore.

Modules having a common ancestor on a higher level of decomposition are related only by the fact that they can be interpreted as parts of the higher level design unit. There are no other dependencies implied by the PART-OF relationship, and there is no guarantee that all parts of a superior module will be listed on the next lower level of decomposition. Thus, different levels of aggregation are nearly independent from each other. Nevertheless, the linking of modules via a PART-OF relation allows certain searching strategies that would otherwise be impossible.

The generalization/specialization structure and its dependent association form hierarchies of modules on each different level of aggregation in the archive. Modules are linked together with the ISA relation, thus forming different levels of specialization.[11] Starting with very abstract module descriptions and going on to very specialized ones, a nearly tree shaped hierarchy is formed. This hierarchy reflects the possible design alternatives on the way from specification to code modules.

To define integrity rules for generalization and search, a tree-shaped structure of the hierarchy is forced. This can be done, without losing information, by allowing the coexistence of several—strictly tree-shaped—generalization hierarchies on one level of abstraction. Merged together, they constitute the original hierarchy. Here, association is simply given by the link of modules on a certain level of specialization to a superior module on the next higher level via the ISA relation. Using ISA relations, association refers to the similarity relationship between the modules involved.

All dependent modules on the next lower level of generalization inherit all attributes of their common ISA-ancestor. This allows a hierarchical organization of information in the generalization structure. To prevent this system of attribute organization from being damaged by exceptions from the inheritance mechanism, the strictest form of ISA relation.[11,61]

The structure of the archive, with its main factors aggregation/decomposition and generalization/specialization, can be seen as shown in Figure 7-3. On each level of aggregation, there exists at least one generalization hierarchy. Generalization is implemented by ISA relations, aggregation by PART-OF relations.

The description of a design unit is implemented as a frame. This allows one to link it easily into the given aggregation and generalization hierarchies.[23] It is defined as follows:

- type information;
- interface and placement/positioning description;
- contents definition, and
- search-related attributes.

Type information classifies the module with regard to its major functional pattern as follows:

- functional unit;
- data structure; or
- system resource.

This classification depends partially on the characteristics of the module and partially on its relation to the system under development. The distinction

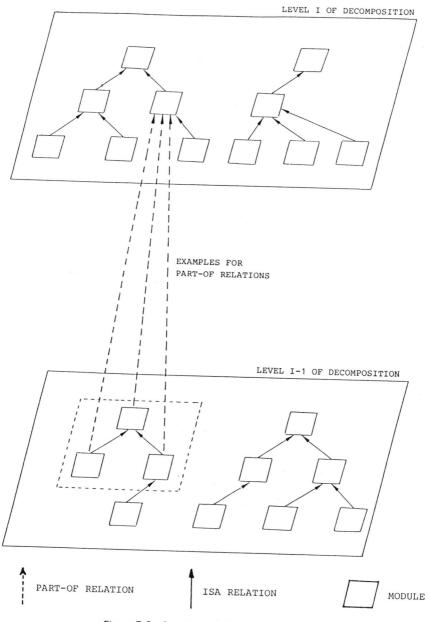

LEVEL I OF DECOMPOSITION

EXAMPLES FOR
PART-OF RELATIONS

LEVEL I-1 OF DECOMPOSITION

PART-OF RELATION   ISA RELATION   MODULE

Figure 7-3. Structure of the software archive.

between functional units and data structures depends on the state memory entailed with the module. Modules, which can be considered as part of the supporting environment, are classified as a system resource.

The module interface and placement description includes all information necessary to determine the modules' place in the structure of the archive and to give some details on necessary import/export relations (similar to Modula-2 definition modules[70]). It consists of information concerning the following:

- relations in the aggregation hierarchy;
- relations in the generalization hierarchy; and
- import/export definitions.

The contents definition includes the description of the body of the module and is divided into the following:

- internal description;
- module attributes;
- global restrictions; and
- comments.

The internal description is the description produced during the development process. Module attributes can be derived from the internal description. Global restrictions model characteristics of the module not as entity but on the conceptual level. Attributes and global restrictions are the parts of the module description which are hereditary in the generalization hierarchy.

Search-related attributes function as data stores for information needed during a retrieval in the archive. Comments can be seen as a place to make some remarks but have no further influence on the behavior or position of the module.

4.2.2 Formal Description of Design Units

Depending on the purpose of a description, the need for exactness and the knowhow of the persons involved, software can be described at various levels of detail and to various degrees of formality. The preceeding section was restricted to rather informal descriptions of software. These will be sufficient in most cases where reuse is confined within a narrow section of a company or application domain. There, most of the details can be communicated personally and internal conventions for naming and documentation might adequately support the location of a design unit.

When aiming for widespread reuse, however, more formality is necessary for communicating the contents of a design unit as well as for abstracting sufficiently from its original purpose. (Naming conventions do not protect from any descriptions which are closely application-dependent.) As application independent descriptions, mathematical specifications, such as used with abstract data types[36] or in wide spectrum languages come to mind.[1,2] Even though such notations would serve their purpose reasonably well, it is feared they would require too much mathematical training from an average programmer to actively use them in his/her daily work.[67] In some cases one might argue that there is not too much difference between programming in such mathematical languages as compared to programming in conventional programming languages.

Departing from these premises, the suggestion is to expand upon the informal type information as given by considering the state space of a module. To simplify the discussion, assume that an object oriented approach has been followed and that the design unit to be described is an image of a real world entity at some representational level. This keeps the discussion initially at the level of semantic (usually long living) states.

From this perspective, purely functional units can be considered as mere tool boxes, while anything else would carry a semantically meaningful state. Well designed toolboxes are, from the semantic point of view, memoryless. Only at the system level, one is able to distinguish between re-entrant toolboxes and those that are not re-entrant. With the former, the property of memorylessness is preserved, while the latter would have two states of which the using module should be aware—tool available and tool busy.

While toolboxes are special types of degenerated objects, full fledged objects would have to model the life history of their real world counterparts (compare steps 1 and 2 of JSD). This history is carried along by the semantic state of the object.

In most cases, the future behavior of an object depends only on its current state; i.e., it behaves as a first order Markovian process. In some instances though, an explicit life-time history of the object is required to be modeled. Fortunately, one does not have to be concerned with a two-dimensional state space for modeling the possible curricula (life history) of such objects. The relevant (finite) portions of such a history can be coded into a Göedel-number, which then uniquely describes an atomic state. Hence, one need not consider this as a special case from this point and no "tricks," such as synchronizing the role histories or treating marsupial entities, like in JSD, are necessary.[49]

A difference between our needs and the needs of JSD-modeling is that the descriptive information of a module in an archive must distinguish whether the concerned module describes a single instance object, or if it manages an entire set of members belonging to an entity class.

In the former case, the sheer number of states can serve as first glance information. Scrutinizing the module more closely requires identity of the state transition structure. In the case of sequential life histories, the state transitions can be described by a context free grammar. In most cases, the tree structures of JSD or regular expressions would suffice. If an object has to account for parallelism, the authors recommend describing its potential behavior by a Petri Net model rather than by the set of traces proposed by JSD. Incorporating this information in the formal description of a module is not too difficult, since the original designer should have made it explicit anyway. Thus, it should be within the intellectual scope of a well educated software developer. It is also at a sufficiently high level, such that a reasonably dense representation can be achieved.

Modules supporting an entity set (multi-instance objects) can be described along the same line by allowing a state vector with the elements of this vector describing the state of the respective real world instance. Tracking the behavior of the individual instances is not the main interest but also the potential behavior each instance might have: one need not store these vectors explicitly. It suffices to keep only the dimensionality of these vectors, which need not be a finite number, and the grammar (state machine) or petri net model describing the state transitions. If different instances would require different state transition models to describe their potential curriculum, this would be a clear indication that the design was not appropriately normalized.[46,49]

One could argue that language design is not a trivial task and determining the equivalence of grammars poses hard problems (unsolvable in the general case). However, it should be recognized that for reusability purposes it suffices if the developer of a design unit gives/obtains an approximate description of the modules which are too clumsy or too difficult to be described in a formally correct way.

The detailed description of the state transitions of these curriculum models will contain nothing additional to what is contained in the actual design unit. It consists of the function names and the parameter structure of the relevant procedures. Obviously, here again the problem arises that function names would be mnemonics for the original purpose in the original application. But it takes only a small program to reduce this to an application independent description which only considers the algorithmic pattern of function usage.

The descriptions mentioned can cover only the semantic states/state transitions of an object. Hence, they are sufficient if one aims at reusing the software model of such objects in their entirety. They are insufficient or of little help in cases where one aims at reusing only a specific function of such an object-abstraction or if one aims at reusing software which was not developed along an object oriented paradigm. In these cases, it will be necessary to perform a similar analysis of the implementation dependent transient states each program will pass during execution.

True functions (free from side effects) are simple in this context, since their behavior should depend only on the values of the parameters at the time of the function invocation. For procedures that perform communication with their environment, this perspective allows one to consider each process as a miniscule entity with its own internal state space. There will be a potential change in these transient states, with each interaction between the environment and this process. However, these interactions can be formally described by the grammar of the language describing the communication structure. Hence, the arguments raised previously would apply again at a lower level.

4.2.3 Search

When developing a new DP-system, there will be the usual process of decomposition, necessary to break down the first monolithic version of the system into smaller parts—the modules. At each level of decomposition, there is more than one way to do this job.[69] Therefore, it is necessary to evaluate possible alternatives.

With the goal of software reuse in mind, the system should be decomposed in such a way, that a maximum of modules in the archive can be reused directly or with minor modifications only. Therefore, the existence of reusable modules for a given decomposition can be made part of the evaluation algorithm for the decomposition. Thus, evaluating a decomposition against the criterion of reusability is to search in the archive for fitting modules.

The starting points for this search are modules on the level of decomposition reached in the development process. Independent of the level of decomposition, the search for a module in the archive will start on a very general (i.e., abstract level) in the generalization hierarchy to allow a maximum of possible results. Depending on the results and the target-level of generalization, the search may lead to a requirements or design document or to a piece of code, representing the module sought.

Having found a first order approximation in the archive, modules related via a specialization link to the given description allow a directed recursive search along the generalization/specialization-hierarchy. From a given module description, there are as many ways to continue the search as there are dependent modules. Each dependent module stands for a more specialized description of the current module, introducing more detail. Evaluating the alternatives given on each level of specialization, the user can determine the search path throughout the archive. The idea is to start with a vague description of the needed module and to add more and more details by selecting among the possible solutions given by the more specialized modules.

Sample algorithms for such a recursive search are presented in Reference 48 and with additional details in Reference 62.

A search in the archive can lead to the following three possible results:

- some fitting modules are found;
- an intermediate result (only a partial match) is found; and
- no usable result can be found.

Whether or not a module is a desired result can be determined by its description and by considering the information about its position in the archive relative to other modules. To find the best module among the search results, which are equivalent at first glance, means to evaluate the given module's characteristics.

An intermediate result is obtained, if the module description found is not a perfect solution for the problem at hand. There is neither an alternative left to find a better match, nor does there exist a more detailed solution in this archive. Starting from such a result there are the following two possibilities:

- To search for a module description at the desired level of specialization which is the most similar to the desired module and to transform this module into a fitting solution.
- To add another, better fitting module description to the successors of the given intermediate result and to take this module as a new intermediate result. This process is repeated until you have reached the desired level of refinement and a fitting solution.

In both cases, it is useful to incorporate newly generated modules into the archive to make them available for further use.

Finding no usable result can lead to the following three reactions:

- Search with an unaltered needs statement on another level of decomposition in the archive.
- Make another decomposition of the system under development, and start the search again with a new needs statement.
- Create the demanded module from scratch.

5   REUSABILITY AT THE LEVEL OF EXECUTABLE CODE

5.1   Software Bases

Section 4 described the overall organization of a software archive, notably how to conceive of software (at various levels of representation), how to describe it, and how to perform retrieval. This section focuses on the organization of actual code which was designed for reuse.

In abstracting from the representational level, the software archive can maintain documentation as well as complete executable computer programs. However, when seriously considering the demand for generalization hierarchies, one suddenly will see that it would be inefficient to describe software only according to the differentials between the variants of a more generalized design unit while keeping the complete variants in full coded versions in the archive's "basement." The software engineer will definitely not fall behind from the capabilities provided by update-libraries (in a slightly insecure way) as when programming was done on punched cards.

To fully account for the demands made by a reusability support system, one has to maintain the generalization hierarchies described previously, to support systems integration from the various modules found in the archive and to help in ensuring that modules may be integrated only according to some general integrity constraints. These requirements can be supported by a software base system.[47]

The support required from a software base, as shown in Figure 7-4, is mainly due to the property that it maintains software at two levels. This is accomplished by splitting software systems into task structures and by abstracting these task structures into task categories. For each task category a code skeleton, the program generic, is provided.

Related to a generic is a set of specialization rules which serves as prompts

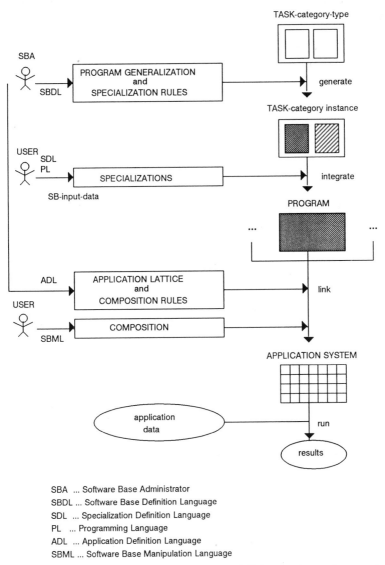

SBA ... Software Base Administrator
SBDL ... Software Base Definition Language
SDL ... Specialization Definition Language
PL ... Programming Language
ADL ... Application Definition Language
SBML ... Software Base Manipulation Language

Figure 7-4. Schematic description of the way from defining an abstraction to using a software base.

(and also as bounds) for the specification of specializations that will convert the program generic to a fully executable program when incorporated in a new system. Such refinements can be done with respect to data aspects (constants), procedural aspects (accounting for changes in detailed functionality), as well as aspects concerning the communication of parameters via module boundaries.

The 'programming-in-the-small' supported by refining program generics by their specializations is complemented by the 'programming-in-the-large' of application composition. Linkage of the various modules retrieved from the software base to obtain a full system is supported by an application lattice. It provides the overall control structure between those modules. If one has a particular application pattern in mind already, one can take advantage of the fact that the dichotomy between a generic and its specialization holds again on the application level.

The application lattice itself is a structure which pertains to a given class of applications, the application category. It can be refined by composition rules to adjust the control structure to the particular application at hand. Further, the composition rules allow one to specify which of a selection of refined programs may be used at a particular place of the lattice.

Apparently, the merits of such a lattice can be seen with prototyping or for the fast development of non-bulk DP applications as well as for the development of new versions of an application system. To support this last concern to the highest possible degree, a set of integrity constraints can be specified over the contents of a software base.[47]

5.2 HIBOL — An Example for Supporting Reusability

To show that the set of tools previously introduced has to be complemented by appropriate design heuristics to reach the desired reusability, the authors conclude this chapter by discussing some design decisions made when developing the HIBOL-system, a programming environment for developing high level business applications.[46]

The language HIBOL2 follows the paradigm of programming by specifying the formulas for computing the desired results at the actual place of a form template where those results would eventually appear. Layout and data type definitions are indicated by drawing an empty form template on a CRT-screen. As shown in Figure 7-5, the sequence of computing the individual instances of completed forms is controlled by a work rule which is bound to a desk. The desk also constitutes the operating environment of the blank form. Hence, it has slots for the various input-, update- and dialog-forms required to provide the data for completing an output form.

Considering the previous discussion of a software base, a HIBOL-desk can be seen as a special kind of an application lattice. The form itself is an object which communicates with its environment on the desk by requesting data in the

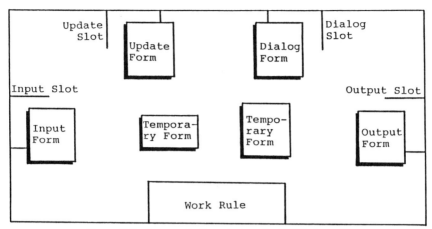

Figure 7-5. Schematic Description of a HIBOL-Desk.[20]

sequence and format required to fill in its blank fields. Since the set of form instances produced by a HIBOL-program corresponds structurally very closely to the form template, as in Figure 7-6, the template and the associated data can be considered as a data capsule if stored in conjunction.

Business forms are usually passed through various departments. Thus, an electronic form template is a highly reusable structure by itself. In an application involving passing along filled in forms, one has just to reuse layout and type descriptions inherent in the blank form template. The resulting specifications will be identities for those values which are not changed by the person at the desk for which this particular part of the application is relevant. Data entered by this person will be described by the equation(s) describing this person's work.

Paper forms are also long living organizational crutches. Whenever things change, one tries to preserve the form to which one is accustomed. The same applies if a form-layout is taken as a sample copy for designing the forms of an entirely new application or when changes in the form flow network require amendments.

All these considerations suggest using a form as a basic organizational unit of reuse. How did the authors approach this in the HIBOL project, and what was the rationale behind it?

While the HIBOL-environment is currently a conventional programming environment for a highly graphics-based language, it eventually should be complemented by an archive system which is highly comparable to the software base previously mentioned. Forms can be considered as a standardized type of program generic. The individual entries in such a form, notably the result specification, are a particular kind of procedural specialization of such a generic. (One could do similar things in terms of changing the layout of a form, the base type of items, or their internal representation.)

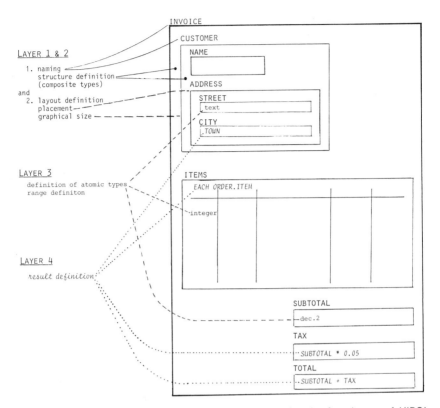

Figure 7-6. Structure of a HIBOL-form with examples for the four layers of HIBOL-programming.

Hence, the archiving system must account for a variety of ancestry relationships among forms to ensure that changes applied to some member of a subfamily of a form are applied in the correct way to all legitimate descendants of this particular form template instance.

Combining the various elements of a form and relating those forms via a desk, one obtains an executable HIBOL-program. In order to account for the reusability of code while observing semantic constraints, the internal design was done in a way that the structure of a totally empty form template serves as a skeleton to which the various form items and their properties (location, type, result specification, specification of internal representation) are bound. This information is kept in various relations, with each relation containing roughly the information provided by the HIBOL-programmer during a particular phase of writing or drawing of his/her program. According to this structure, not only the source code was provided in this way, but also the executable code pertaining to each form element was associated with it. It will be linked together whenever a HIBOL-program gets invoked.

This design would have allowed reusability on the target-code level (!) at a very fine granularity. However, after careful consideration the authors decided not to support this fine grained reusability of binaries but to limit the reusability of binaries to the comprehensiveness of complete forms. (Source code reusability is supported on the item level.)

What was reason for backing off from the extreme? It was to provide control of change and assurance of correctness/consistency (in the sense of secondary faults introduced during maintenance). Allowing reusability on a finer scale would have required maintaining version control at an extremely fine grained level and executing various (global) compiler functions at this level whenever a change occurred. It was concluded that this was too much a burden for the advantages thus obtained.

The authors decided that these concerns and conclusions extend over this particular system. A system supporting reusability of code should not be totally open for change. There have to be guards at the organizational level as well as in the software to ensure that whatever code (irrespective of the level of representation) is brought in, matches its description. The function performed by the compiler in the example of the HIBOL-system must be assumed in general by an elaborate reasoning and testing system. However, these issues are subject to further research.

6 SUMMARY

Out of various approaches towards making software reusable, recommendations have been made on how one can perceive the results of the various phases of software development to make them amenable for reuse. It has been shown that this approach is based on classical design perspectives, but essentially requires a transposition of the way one describes software. Further, it has been made clear that reuse must not be confined to the code level.

From these premises, suggestions have been made on how to provide a structure to support reuse of existing software.

For the code level, a system has been introduced which allows one to refine and combine modules under prespecified constraints and integrity rules. Finally, arguments have been raised that reuse requires strict discipline and configuration-management to be able to reap the desired benefits.

The authors acknowledge the work of their colleagues H. Wernhart and D. Lesjak on the HIBOL system as well as the many helpful comments by G. Springer and S. Hutt. The implementation of the HIBOL-environment has been made possible by a grant from the "Fonds zur Foerderung der wissenschaftlichen Forschung"; the implementation of the software archive mechanisms has been supported by Hewlett-Packard.

REFERENCES

1. Bauer, F. L., M. Broy, R. Gnatz, W. Hesse, R. Krieg-Brueckner, H. Partsch, P. Pepper, H. Woessner, "Towards a Wide Spectrum Language to Support Program Specification and Program Development," *SIGPLAN Notices,* Vol. 13, No. 12, December 1978, pp. 15–24.

2. Bauer, F. L., "Program Development by Stepwise Transformations—The Project CIP," in: BAUER and BROY: "Program Construction," *Lecture Notes in Computer Science,* New York: Springer-Verlag, 1979, pp. 237–266.

3. Belady, L. A., "Envolved Software for the 80s," *IEEE Computer,* Vol. 12, No. 2, February 1979, pp. 79–82.

4. Belkhatir, N., and J. Estublier, "Experience with a Data-Base of Programs," *ACM SIGPLAN Notices,* Vol. 22, No. 1, January 1987, pp. 84–91.

5. Bergland, G. D., "A Guided Tour of Program Design Methodologies," *IEEE Computer,* Vol. 14, No. 10, October 1981, pp. 13–37.

6. Biggerstaff, T. J., and A. J. Perlis, *Guest Editors Foreword to IEEE Trans. on Software Eng.,* Vol. SE-10, No. 5, September 1984, pp. 474–476.

7. Boehm, B. W., "Guidelines for verifying and validating software requirements and design specifications," Samet, P. A. (Ed.): *EURO IFIP 79, Proceedings of the European Conference on Applied Information Technology of the International Federation of Information Processing,* London, 25–28 September, 1979, pp. 711–719.

8. Boehm, B. W., *Software Engineering Economics,* Englewood Cliffs, NJ: Prentice-Hall, Inc., 1981.

9. Booch, G., "Object-Oriented Development," *IEEE Trans. on Software Eng.,* Vol. SE-12, No. 2, February 1986, pp. 211–221.

10. Boyle, J. M. and M. N. Muralidharan, "Program Reusability through Program Transformation," *IEEE Trans. on Software Eng.,* Vol. SE-10, No. 5, September 1984, pp. 574–588.

11. Brachman, R. J., "What IS-A Is and Isn't: An Analysis of Taxonomic Links in Semantic Networks," *IEEE Computer,* Vol. 16, No. 10, October 1983, pp. 30–36.

12. Cameron, J. R., "An Overview of JSD," *IEEE Trans. on Software Eng.,* Vol. SE-12, No. 2, February 1986, pp. 222–240.

13. Cheatham, Jr., T. E., "Reusability Through Program Transformations," *IEEE Trans. on Software Eng.,* Vol. SE-10, No. 5, September 1984, pp. 589–594.

14. Cheng, T. T., E. D. Lock, and N. S. Prywes, "Use of Very High Level Languages and Program Generation by Management Professionals," *IEEE Trans. on Software Eng.,* Vol. SE-10, No. 5, September 1984, pp. 552–563.

15. Codd, E. F., "A Relational Model of Data for Large Shared Data Bases," *CACM,* Vol. 13, No. 6, June 1970, pp. 377–387.

16. Cox, B. J., *Object-oriented Programming—An Evolutionary Approach,* Reading, MA: Addison Wesley, 1986.

17. Denert, E. and W. Hesse, "Projektmodell und Projektbibliothek: Grundlagen zuverlaessiger Software-Entwicklung und Dokumentation," *Informatik Spektrum,* Vol. 3, No. 4, 1980, pp. 215–228.

18. DeRemer, F. and H. H. Kron, "Programming-in-the-Large Versus Programming-in-the-Small," *IEEE Trans. on Software Eng.,* Vol. SE-2, No. 2, June 1976, pp. 80–86.

19. Doberkat, E., E. Dubinsky, and J. T. Schwartz, "Reusability of Design for Complex Programs: An Experiment with the SETL Optimizer," *Proc. Workshop on Reusability in Programming,* Newport, RI, September 1983, pp. 106–108.

20. Eder, J., R. Mittermeir, and H. Wernhart, "Induktive und deduktive Ermittlung des Informationsbedarfs," in: Wagner, Traunmueller, Mayr (Eds.): "Informationsbedarfsermittlung und -analyse fuer den Entwurf von Informationssystemen," *Informatik-Fachbericht* 143, Springer-Verlag 1987, pp. 89–118.

21. Fikes, R. and T. Kehler, "The Role of Frame-Based Representation in Reasoning," *Comm. ACM*, Vol. 28, No. 9, September 1985, pp. 904–920.

22. Floyd, Ch., "A systematic look at prototyping;" in Budde, *et al.* (Eds.): *Approaches to Prototyping*, New York: Springer-Verlag, 1984, pp. 1–18.

23. Freeman, P., "Reusable Software Engineering: Concepts and Research Directions," *Proc. Workshop on Reusability in Programming*, Newport, RI, September 1983, pp. 1–15.

24. Gannon, J. D., R. G. Hamlet, and H. D. Mills, "Theory of Modules," *IEEE Trans. on Software Eng.*, Vol. SE-7, No. 5, July 1987, pp. 820–829.

25. Garg, V. K., "Functional Composition—A Mechanism to Compose Programs," *ACM SIGSOFT Software Engineering Notes*, Vol. 10, No. 3, July 1985, pp. 37–39.

26. Gaube, W., P. C. Lockemann, and H. C. Mayr, "Wiederfinden zum Wiederverwenden: Rechnergestuetzter Modul-Nach-weis auf der Basis formaler Spezifikationen," *Proc. Software-Architektur und modulare Programmierung*, 26. Bericht des German Chapter of the ACM, B. G. Teubner, Stuttgart, 1986, pp. 66–80.

27. Geymayer, B. and H. Ranzinger, "Ein wissensgestuetztes System zur Erstellung techn. Dokumentation," in Pernul G., Tjoa A Min (Eds.): *Proc. of Berichte aus Informatikforschungsinstitutionen*, OCG-Schriftenreihe, Oldenbourg, Wien, 1987, pp. 173–183.

28. Goldberg, A. T., "Knowledge-Based Programming: A Survey of Program Design and Construction Techniques," *IEEE Trans. on Software Eng.*, Vol. 12, No. 7, July 1986, pp. 752–768.

29. Gougen, J., "Parameterized Programming," *IEEE Trans. on Software Eng.*, Vol. SE-10, No. 5, September 1984, pp. 528–543.

30. Hesse, W., H. Keutgen, A. L. Luft, and H. D. Rombach, "Ein Begriffssystem fuer die Softwaretechnik. Vorschlag zur Terminologie," *Informatik Spektrum*, Vol. 7, No. 4, November 1984, pp. 200–213.

31. Jackson, M. A., *Principles of Program-Design*, London: Academic Press, 1975.

32. Jackson, M. A., *System Development*, Englewood Cliffs, NJ: Prentice-Hall, 1982.

33. Jones, T. C., "Reusability in Programming: A Survey of the State of the Art," *Proc. Workshop on Reusability in Programming*, Newport, RI, September 1983, pp. 215–22.

34. Kernighan, B. W., "The Unix System and Software Reusability," *IEEE Trans. on Software Engineering*, Vol. SE-10, No. 5, September 1984, pp. 513–528.

35. Lichter, H., "Objektorientierte Sprachen und Rapid Prototyping," 8. Sitzung d. GI-Fachgruppe 4.3.1 *Requirements Engineering*, Freiburg i.B., September 1987.

36. Liskov, D. H. and S. N. Zilles, "Specification Techniques for Data Abstraction," *IEEE Trans. on Software Eng.*, Vol. SE-1, No. 1, 1975, pp. 7–19.

37. Lubars, M. D., "Code Reusability in the Large versus Code Reusability in the Small," *ACM SIGSOFT Software Engineering Notes*, Vol. 11, No. 1, January 1986, pp. 21–28.

38. Madhavji, N. H., "Operations for programming in the All," *Proc. 8th ICSE*, London, 1985, pp. 15–25.

39. Martin, J., *Fourth Generation Languages*, Vol. I to III, Englewood Cliffs, NJ: Prentice-Hall, 1985 (and 1986).

40. Matsumoto, Y., "Some Experiences in Promoting Reusable Software: Presentation in Higher Abstract Levels," *IEEE Trans. on Software Eng.*, Vol. SE-10, No. 5, September 1984, pp. 502–512.

41. Mitchell, T. M., "Generalization as Search," Webber B. L., Nilsson N. J. (Ed.): *Readings in Artificial Intelligence*, Palo Alto, CA: Tioga Publ. Co., 1981, pp. 517–542.

42. Mittermeir, R. T., N. Roussopoulos, R. T. Yeh, and P. A. Ng "An integrated approach to Requirements Analysis," in Ng, P. A. and R. T. Yeh (ed): *Modern Software Engineering: Foundations and Current Perspectives*, New York: Van Nostrand Reinhold, 1989, pp. 119–164.

43. Mittermeir, R. T., "Software Bases for Adaptive Maintenance of Complex Software Systems," *Proc. 7th International ADV-Congress*, Vienna 1983, pp. 483–492.

44. Mittermeir, R. T., "Requirements Elicitation by Rapid Prototyping," *Proc. Informatica 85,* Nova Gorica, 1985, pp. 105-108.
45. Mittermeir, R. T. and H. Wernhart, "Benutzerhandbuch zur Programmiersprache HIBOL-2," Institut fuer Informatik, Universitaet Klagenfurt, 1986.
46. Mittermeir, R. T., "Object-oriented Software Design," *International Workshop on Software Engineering Environments,* Beijing, China, August 1986.
47. Mittermeir, R. T., "Software Bases for the Flexible Composition of Application Systems," *IEEE Trans. on Software Eng.,* Vol. SE-13, No. 4, April 1987, pp. 440-460.
48. Mittermeir, R. T. and W. Rossak, "Software-Bases and Software-Archives—Alternatives to support Software Reuse," *Proc. of the FJCC 87,* Dallas, TX, October 1987.
49. Mittermeir, R. T., "A normalization theory for software components," Institut fuer Informatik, Universitaet Klagenfurt UBWI 88/1, 1988.
50. Myers, G. J., *Composite/Structured Design,* New York: Van Nostrand Reinhold, 1978.
51. Neighbours, J. M., "The Draco Approach to constructing Software from Reusable Components," *IEEE Transactions on Software Eng.,* Vol. 10, No. 5, September 1984, pp. 564-574.
52. Parnas, D. L., "A Technique for Software Module Specification with Examples," *Comm. of the ACM,* Vol. 15, No. 5, May 1972, pp. 330-336.
53. Parnas, D. L., "On the criteria to be used in Decomposing Systems into Modules," *Comm. ACM,* Vol. 15, No. 12, December 1972, pp. 1053-1058.
54. Parnas, D. L., "On the Design and Development of Program Families," *IEEE Trans. on Software Eng.,* Vol. SE-2, No. 1, March 1976, pp. 1-9.
55. Parnas, D. L., P. C. Clements, and D. M. Weiss, "Enhancing Reusability with Information Hiding," *Proc. Workshop on Reusability in Programming,* Newport, RI, September 1983, pp. 240-247.
56. Penedo, M. H., "PMDD—A Project Master Data-Base for Software-Engineering Environments," *Proc. of 8th ICSE,* London, 1985, pp. 150-157.
57. Prieto-Diaz, R. and P. Freeman, "Classifying Software for Reusability," *IEEE Software,* Vol. 4, No. 1, January 1987, pp. 6-16.
58. Putnam, L. M., "Software Cost Estimating and Life-Cycle Control: Getting the Software Numbers," *Tutorial at Compsac 80,* IEEE Computer Society Press, 1980.
59. Rescheleit, W. and L. Menner, "Klassifikationen—eine Fundgrube fuer die Wissensreprae-sentationsforschung?", Rundbrief des Fachausschusses 1.2 der GI, Nr. 42, July 1986, pp. 11-14.
60. Rich, C. and R. C. Waters, "Formalizing Reusable Software Components," *Proc. Workshop on Reusability in Programming,* Newport, RI, September 1983, pp. 152-158.
61. Rossak, W. and R. T. Mittermeir, "Structuring Software Archives for Reusability," *Proc. IASTED 5th International Symposium on Applied Informatics,* Grindelwald, Switzerland, 1987.
62. Rossak, W., "Software Development Reusing Existing Components. The Software Archive," Institut fuer Informatik, Universitaet Klagenfurt UBWI 88/2.
63. Simon, H. A., "Whether Software Engineering Needs to Be Artificially Intelligent," *IEEE Trans. on Software Eng.,* Vol. 12, No. 7, July 1986, pp. 726-732.
64. Squires, S. L., M. Branstad, and M. Zelkowitz, "Special Issue on Rapid Prototyping," Working Papers from the ACM SIGSOFT Rapid Prototyping Workshop, Columbia, Maryland 19-21 April 1982. *ACM SIGSOFT Software Engineering Notes,* Vol. 7, No. 5, December 1982.
65. Stevens, W. P., G. J. Myers, and L. L. Constantine, "Structured Design," *IBM Systems Journal,* Vol. 13, No. 2, 1974, pp. 115-139.
66. Volpano, D. M., "Software Templates," *Proc. 8th ICSE,* IEEE Computer Society Press, London, 1985, pp. 55-60.
67. Weber, J. H. and H. Ehrig, "Specification of Modular Systems," *IEEE Trans. on Software Eng.,* Vol. 12, No. 7, July 1986, pp. 784-798.

68. Wegner, P., "Capital-Intensive Software Technology," *IEEE Software*, Vol. 1, No. 3, July 1984, pp. 7-45.

69. Wirth, N., "Program Development by Stepwise Refinement," *CACM*, Vol. 14, No. 4, April 1971, pp. 221-227.

70. Wirth, N., *Programming in Modula-2*, vol. 3. Auflage, Springer, 1985.

71. Yeh, R. T., R. T. Mittermeir, N. Roussopoulos, and J. Reed, "A Programming Environment Framework Based on Reusability," *Proc. of Internat. Conference on Data Engineering*, Los Angeles, CA: IEEE Computer Society Press, 1984, pp. 277-280.

72. Yourdon, E. and L. L. Constantine, *Structured Design—Fundamentals of a Discipline of Computer Program and Systems Design*, Englewood Cliffs, NJ: Prentice-Hall, 1979.

73. Yourdon, E., *Nations at Risk—The Impact of the Computer Revolution*, New York: Yourdon Press, 1986.

Chapter 8

Software Design by Stepwise Evaluation and Refinement

JERRY W. BAKER, DANIEL CHESTER, AND RAYMOND T. YEH
International Software Systems, Inc., Austin, TX

1 INTRODUCTION

There are two well-established engineering practices in design that are just beginning to be included in today's software design methodologies. These two principles include the following:

- design evaluation; and
- the use of prototypes as a design aid.

Both of these principles are aimed at reducing the cost of system development by avoiding bad design decision. It is estimated by Boehm[5] that more than 60% of software errors are design errors. Thus, the high cost of software is primarily due to the high cost of maintenance because of redesign and reprogramming efforts. This is quite a contrast to the more established engineering disciplines where maintenance costs come mainly from wear and tear. The lack of these two previously mentioned engineering principles in software development is a major contributing factor to the high cost of software.

It is the authors' opinion that the incorporation of the philosophy of design evaluation is a necessity in the design of large software systems and would provide a solution for the most vexing problems in software development. These include the following:

- How to check the consistency between requirements and formal specifications of a system in a systematic fashion.
- How to incorporate performance evaluation as a design tool.
- How to provide users with early warnings of the inadequacies of the requirements.

In this chapter, the authors introduce an approach to software development in which the design process is consistently evaluated as the design unfolds. Such an approach provides information about a design in three ways. First, it provides system functionality and behavior information through direct and symbolic execution of specifications. Executable specification thus serves as a debugging tool for design specifications. Next, it provides system performance and cost estimates on the basis of various simulation and analytical methods. Finally, it provides for heuristic judgments on how the whole design is decomposed into parts. The information obtained in these three ways makes it possible to intelligently decide whether the design works as intended, what changes should be made, and with which of several designs one should proceed.

Using such a top-down design methodology, a family of designs (rather than a single design) will be generated and tested. However, the family of systems is not completely documented. A final system can be selected from the family and a complete formal documentation (such as, the generation of exception conditions for modules) can then be generated.

2   DESIGN METHODOLOGY: AN OVERVIEW

The principle of abstraction has been generally accepted as a principal mental tool to combat the complexity in software design. There are many design techniques based on the abstraction principle which lead to the design of hierarchically structured systems. These systems are easier to prove correct or modify. However, these techniques are inadequate for the following reasons:

- Performance is in general not a design consideration. Although it is claimed that performance can be considered as an item in the specification, there is no general provision to accommodate this type of specification in the design process.
- There is no provision for documenting the design process (e.g., why a designer picks a particular design from many possible alternatives). If developing evolutionary or portable systems, such a documentation is important.
- There is no provision for documenting the system structure. Although the system is hierarchical in structure, many hierarchies may coexist, each representing a different relationship between system components. It is also misleading to think of each level within the system hierarchy as flat. Indeed, it is sometimes advantageous to consider certain limited hierarchies within each ''abstraction'' level.

This chapter proposes to enhance the current methodology by adding additional models to alleviate the design problems mentioned previously. In current practice, the design model can be considered as both a model of the design structure and (primarily) as a model of the system structure. To allow explicit documentation of the design process, an evaluation model is proposed which should be refined along with the system structure at any given level. These three interacting models will form the design model as shown in Figure 8-1.

Current approaches to software development may be crudely modeled as a five stage process: statement of requirements, formal specification, formal design, coding, and testing (Figure 8-2). The statement of requirements, usually in natural language, is the document that those in authority (political, financial) give to those with the technical knowledge to produce the desired system. The designer's first task is to translate the informal requirements into a formal specification; i.e., a statement of the constraints on the desired system in terms of the parameters and concepts that the designers have been trained to use. Next, a formal design is produced or a plan for how the constraints can be satisfied. For the last two stages, the plan is implemented, thereby producing the system.

This model of the design process is admittedly crude; perhaps the largest error in the model is that it assumes a linear progression from the requirements to the final product. In practice, mistakes are made and the designers have to back-up to a previous stage and try an alternative path. If they have to back-up several stages, say from the testing to the formal specification, the time and energy spent in going down the wrong path can be very costly. This cost can be minimized if the designers have adequate feedback from their work so that errors can be detected as soon as they are made rather than later. Experience

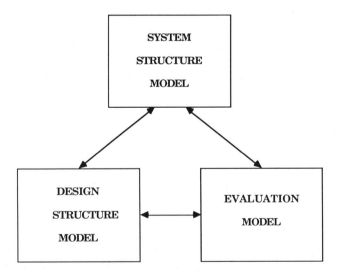

Figure 8 -1. A software design model.

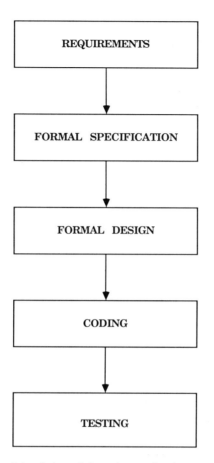

Figure 8-2. A traditional view of the software development process.

has shown, however, that too many of the early design errors go undetected until the last phases of a project—even as late as the final system installation!

An alternative approach to the software development process based on the design model that the authors are proposing is shown in Figure 8-3. At each stage, designers have a set of constraints describing the goals that they have yet to achieve and a model of their plans for achieving other goals. Initially, they have only the constraints given by the requirements. Their model is the ''null'' or empty model. Their first task is to make a model (model 1) of the required, functional behavior of the desired system without regard for other aspects, such as performance, hardware requirements, etc. Model 1 is the final system when seen at a very high abstract level. The constraints at this stage can be the performance and hardware requirements, etc., that still need to be met. Model 2 is another version of the final system, but seen at a lower abstract level. It is a

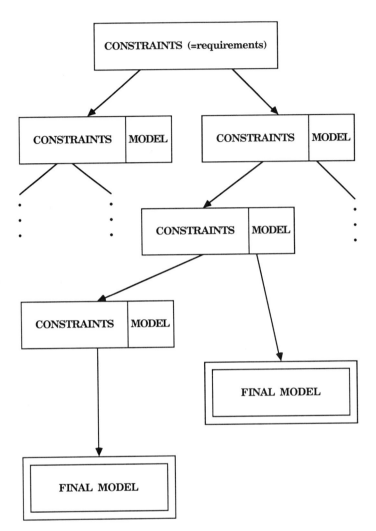

Figure 8-3. An alternative model of the software development process.

decomposition of model 1 into a combination of simpler modules whose functional behaviors are specified. At this level, some of the constraints at the previous levels are met. Part of the duty of the evaluation model is to see that upper level constraints are satisfied using lower level parameters.

It should be noted, however, that there may be many different ways to implement the upper level model. Hence, different alternative designs, each with its own set of constraints, may exist at this level. The evaluation model, then, is also used to aid the designers in choosing one or more of the alternatives for further development. This decomposition and selection process is repeated until all the constraints are met and the designers have the desired system.

The main difference between this proposed approach and the traditional approach to software development is the existence of *alternatives* at each decision point. Alternative designs come about from the following different sources:

- Different designers may choose to realize different parts of the constraints still present, and
- different realizations of the same constraints may exist.

Thus, as a result of the proposed design model, one would obtain *a family of designs* (Fig. 8-4), where each node in this tree represents a particular design at some level of abstraction. A complete system design then corresponds to a simple path emanating from the root of the tree.

It should be noted, however, that in general, the number of alternatives may be quite large and thus only a sub-family of designs will be maintained.

As a very simple example of this design methodology, suppose the designers

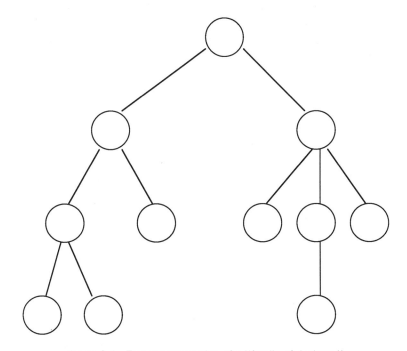

Figure 8-4. Tree representation of a "family of designs."

are given the task of designing a communication system between the bridge of a ship and its engine that meets the following requirements:

- The captain of the ship shall be able to transmit a signal to the engine room that will cause the engine to run at a desired speed.
- The engine shall not be caused to change speed faster than specified by the manufacturer.

The first model that the designers might develop is shown in Figure 8-5. This model is a single module that formally specifies the functional behavior indicated by the first requirement. The second requirement is not met, however, because nothing is said in the module about how the engine SPEED will be changed in response to the captain's COMMAND. To meet this requirement, model 1 is decomposed into model 2 (Figure 8-6). The LINK module in this module describes states and processes at a lower level than the module in model 1, and the B-to-ER module is an implementation of model 1 in terms of calls to the functions in LINK. The engine SPEED now increases or decreases at a controlled rate, so that the second requirement is satisfied. The designers cannot decompose the LINK module further until they have laid out a design for a combination of microprocessors (or relays or switches or levers) that will realize the desired communication link.

In this chapter, a framework for building the models in the alternative design methodology is discussed. It also provides ways to study these models to discover errors in their design, as will be shown later.

3   SYSTEM STRUCTURE

3.1   Abstraction, Stepwise Refinement And System Design

One of the most powerful tools in software development is abstraction. The use of abstraction allows a designer to initially express his/her solution to a problem in very general terms and with very little regard for the details of implementa-

```
Module: B-to-ER
Function: SPEED = X
INITIAL-VALUE: X = 0

Function: COMMAND(X) = nil
EFFECTS: SPEED = X

Constraints
Rate of Change in SPEED ≤ B.
```

Figure 8-5. Model 1 for Bridge to Engine Room Link and remaining constraints.

```
Module:  B-to-ER
procedure:  COMMAND(X)
definition:
  repeat
    if GETSPEED < X then UP els
    if GETSPEED > X then DOWN:
  until GETSPEED = X

Module:  LINK
function:  SPEED = X
INITIAL-VALUE:  X = 0

function:  GETSPEED = X
EFFECTS:  X = 'SPEED'

function:  UP = nil
EFFECTS:  SPEED = 'SPEED' + B

function:  DOWN = nil
EFFECTS:  SPEED = 'SPEED' - B
```

Figure 8-6. Model 2 for Bridge to Engine Room Link.

tion. This initial solution may be refined in a step by step manner, by gradually introducing more and more details of implementation.

The process continues until the solution is expressed within the framework of some appropriate target language. This combination of abstraction and stepwise refinement enables the designer to overcome the problem of complexity inherent in the construction of systems by allowing one to concentrate on the relevant aspects of the design, at any given time, without worrying about other details. An important result of this approach is the development of a hierarchically structured system (function abstraction) such that each level consists of a number of modules (data abstractions). Thus, the system is both horizontally and vertically modular.

The notion of abstraction is also important from the standpoint of protection. Through data abstraction, a designer may limit the access to a data object through a specified set of well-defined operations. Likewise, by hiding the implementation of a data abstraction from its users the designer protects them from any changes which might occur in that implementation.

The authors foresee the design of a system as a stepwise refinement process of functional abstraction which begins with the construction of a "top-level" abstract machine, M_n, satisfying the functional requirements of some high level requirements specification. This machine consists of a set of data abstractions represented by formal module specifications. Each module specification is self-contained in the sense that it specifies the complete set of operations which define the nature of the data abstraction.

In the next step of the process, another abstract machine, M_{n-1}, representing a "refinement" of M_n is designed. Its data abstractions are chosen in such a way that they can implement those of M_n. Basically, this implementation consists of *abstract program* modules (procedure abstractions), each of which defines operations of M_n in terms of accesses to functions of machine M_{n-1}. A verification process can then be used to ensure that the implementation is consistent with the specification of both machines.

This stepwise process of machine specification, implementation, and verification proceeds until, at some point, the data abstractions of the lowest level machine can be easily implemented on a specified "target" machine, which may be the data abstractions of some programming language, a low-level file management system, or the operations of some appropriate hardware configuration. This design process results in a structure consisting of a hierarchy of abstract machines, or levels, M_n, M_{n-1}, . . . , M_0 connected by a set of n programs I_n, I_{n-1}, . . . , I_1. Each machine, M_i, in the hierarchy represents a complete "view" of the system at a particular level of abstraction while the corresponding program $I_i(1 \leq i \leq n)$ represents the implementation of the view upon the next level machine M_{i-1}.

3.2 Module Specification

The method of module specifications used in this hierarchical approach is based upon the work of Parnas[21] and Robinson and Levitt[25] with slight modifications.[2] There are two kinds of modules. *Function modules* specify data abstractions, which are state machines.[12] The state transitions in these machines correspond to the operations specified by the modules. *Procedure modules* specify procedure abstractions, which are implementations of the operation of one abstract machine, M_i, in terms of the operations of the next abstract machine, M_{i-1}; i.e., an operation representing a single state transition in M_i may correspond to a *sequence* of state transitions (defined by the abstract program implementing the operation) in M_{i-1}. Thus, the function modules specify the operations at some level in the hierarchy, and the procedure modules specify the decomposition of high level operations into sequences of lower level operations.

The specification of each function module defines two types of access functions, state value (SV) and state transition (ST). The SV functions return values and the set of all SV functions of a machine is said to characterize the machine's abstract "state." The ST functions, on the other hand, produce a state change in the machine. The state change, which a function produces in a machine, is defined in an EFFECTS section of the module specification. Each "effect" is an assertion defining the change in the value of an SV function of the machine when the ST function is successfully invoked. The only observable change in the state of the machine produced by the execution of the ST function is that defined in the EFFECTS section.

The specification of each module also includes a set of *exception conditions*, each defining a condition about which the invoker of an operation must be notified. An exception condition definition consists of a name with a formal parameter list and a predicate, using the SV functions of the module and the formal parameters. The specification of each function in the module contains a list of exception conditions with the parameters of the function call appropriately substituted for the formal parameters of the exception condition list. If any predicate defining an exception condition in the list is *true* when the function is invoked, then a specified action is taken by the system. If the exception condition is "fatal" and the function is of type ST, then the effects specified in the function definition will not be observed, and the user is appropriately notified. If the function is of type SV, then the value(s) returned is (are) undefined. For a "non-fatal" exception condition, a simple warning message is issued.

The specification of each procedure module defines a set of procedures and mapping functions, which together form an implementation between two adjacent machines M_i and M_{i-1}. More formally, if $F = (f_{i1}, f_{i2}, \ldots, f_{ih})$ is the set of SV functions for M_i and $G = (g_{i1}, g_{i2}, \ldots, g_{ik})$ is the set of ST functions for M_i, then the implementation of M_i on M_{i-1} is defined by

$$I_i = \{m_{i1}, m_{i2}, \ldots, m_{ih}, p_{i1}, p_{i2}, \ldots, p_{ik}\}$$

where $m_{ij}(1 \leq j \leq h)$ is a mapping to f_{ij} from the SV functions of M_{i-1} and $p_{ij}(1 \leq j \leq k)$ is an abstract program which implements the ST function g_{ij} on machine M_{i-1}. The mappings $m_{i1}, m_{i2}, \ldots, m_{ih}$ together define a mapping function T_i which has the effect of "binding" each state of M_i to a state or set of states of M_{i-1}; i.e., if S_i and S_{i-1} are the state sets of M_i and M_{i-1}, respectively, then the mapping T_i is defined such that for every state s_i in S_i, we have $s_i = T_i(s_{i-1})$ for some state s_{i-1} in S_{i-1}.

The purpose of abstract program p_{ij} is to express the function g_{ij} of M_i in terms of the functions of M_{i-1}. Thus, the program is constructed using well-defined control constructs and the function set $F_{i-1} \cup G_{i-1}$. This implementation process must be consistent with the formal specifications of M_i and M_{i-1}; i.e., the commutative diagram must be satisfied as shown in Figure 8-7. Here s_i and s_i' are states of M_i and s_{i-1} and s_{i-1}' are states of M_{i-1}.

3.3   Verification

The verification of the implementation I_i requires a formal proof that the commutative diagram of Figure 8-7 is satisfied for every abstract program p_{ij}. This verification process is basically a standard inductive assertion proof[17] on p_{ij} and the authors, therefore, only give a brief description of it. However, the reader is referred to Robinson and Levitt,[25] which contains a detailed discussion of the hierarchical proof techniques used in the methodology.

In general, the precondition for each abstract program p_{ij} is *true* because the

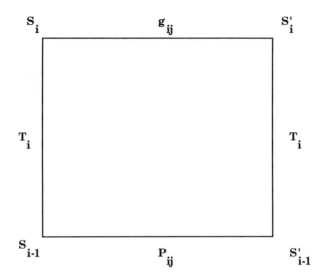

Figure 8-7. The state transition function of an abstract program.

program contains its own mechanisms for exception handling. The output assertions for p_{ij} are derived from the assertions in the EFFECTS section of the specification for function g_{ij} and from the mapping function T_i. Each output assertion is obtained by taking an EFFECTS assertion and replacing each reference to an SV function by the instantiation of the appropriate partial mapping function of T_i.

Inductive assertions for p_{ij} can be taken directly from the EFFECTS sections of the ST operations used to construct the program. Verification conditions can then be derived and used to establish the validity of these assertions. The verification of the output assertions then follows.

3.4 Design And Specification—An Example

The concepts discussed in the previous section can perhaps be best understood by looking at a data base system (DBS) designed using this hierarchical approach. A partial outline of such a system is shown in Tables 8-1 and 8-2. Table 8-1 contains a brief description of the nature of a few system modules, while Table 8-2 outlines the basic properties of the different level machines.

The UNIV module, shown at level 5, represents a specific application interface.

This module provides operations for recording and accessing information about university departments and professors. Specifically, the information represented includes the following:

- The name, social security number, age, salary, rank, and department of all professors employed by the university, and

Table 8-1. A descripton of the system modules. Only a partial list is given for each level.

Level 5		
UNIV -		Defines operations for recording and accessing information about university departments, professors, and related attributes. (This module represents an interface for a specific application.)
Level 4		
REL -		Defines the concept of a relation through relational algebraic operations.
INT -		Specifies operations for creating and enforcing "integrity assertions" which define allowable data values for relations.
AUTH -		Defines operations for creating and enforcing "authorizations" which specify allowable interactions for users.
Level 3		
RT -		Defines operations for creating, updating, and accessing logical "record tables."
RDIR -		Represents a directory of existing record tables.
FNT -		Defines tables containing information about field values for each existing record table.
TDS -		Specifies operations for creating and accessing sets of record identifiers. Used to implement the concept of a cursor (Astrahan[1]).
IMAGE -		Represents logical reorderings of records (Astrahan[1]).
IMCAT -		Defines a catalog of existing images.
SEL -		Specifies operations for creating, maintaining, and accessing partial indexes (selectors) to record tables.
SLCAT -		Represents a catalog of existing partial indexes.
LNK -		Defines operations for creating, maintaining, and using logical associations between records of different record tables.
LCAT -		Represents a catalog of defined associations.
Level 2		
BTR -		Defines the concept of a B-tree. Used to implement the IMAGE module of Level 3.
RBLK -		Represents fixed-length blocks of records. Used to implement the RT and LNK modules of Level 3.
RBDX -		Specifies operations for creating and using directories to RBLK structures.
RIDX -		Represents fixed-length blocks of record pointers. Used to implement the TS, SEL, and LNK modules of Level 3.
Level 1		
SEG -		Defines the concept of a segment of pages.
SEGDIR -		Represents a directory of existing segments.
VP -		Defines the concept of a page and bit and byte operations.
Level 0		
Machine hardware.		

- the chairman, number of professors, and average salary for each university department.

The ST operations of the module are semantically meaningful—each corresponding to a real world transition. They include "hire," "terminate," "promote," "raise-salary," and "change-chairman." The SV functions of the

Table 8-2. Summary of hierarchically designed DBMS.

Level	Visible Concepts	Operations	Concepts Hidden By Level
5	entities (university departments, professors, etc.), and their attributes	operations corresponding to real-world transitions ("hire", "terminate," etc.) and queries ("get_salary," "get_age," etc.)	logical structure of data
4	relations, tuples, cursors, authorization and integrity assertions	algebraic relational operations, creation and enforcement of authorization and integrity assertions, cursor creation and sequencing operations	access paths, record table structure, record identifiers.
3	record tables, records, images, partial indexes, record table associations, record identifier sets	creation, access, and maintenance of record tables, access paths, and record identifier sets	record block structures, implementation of access paths
2	fixed-length record and pointer blocks, B-trees, links between record blocks	record block access, B-tree operations	bit representation of information, segmentation of record blocks, B-trees, and directories
1	segments, pages	segment and page operations	distribution of segments in memory devices
0	machine architecture	paging operations, etc.	

module include "get-salary," "get-chairman," and "get-rank." At this level of interaction, a user is well-protected from organizational changes in the DBS because no physical (access paths, storage structures, etc.) structures are visible. Rather, the user is aware only of very abstract relationships and transitions which may occur in his applications.

The operations of the UNIV module are implemented on the next level machine, M_4, which represents an algebraic relational view of the DBS. The REL module, for example, defines the concept of a relation in terms of relational algebraic operations.

The two other modules shown, INT and AUTH, relate to the concepts of integrity and authorization. The authors note that at this level of interaction the concept of an access path is completely hidden from the user; i.e., the operations at this level provide no mechanisms for defining, deleting, or using any type of access path.

At the level of machine M_3, the DBS represents a somewhat different view. A user of this level can create and manipulate logical record tables (RT module) and a directory (RDIR module) to record information about existing record tables. Also, several modules—IMAGE, LNK, and SEL—make it possible to create fast access paths to records of existing record tables. The implementation of M_4 by M_3, of course, consists of programs which implement the module functions of M_4 in terms of the module functions of M_3. Thus, for example, the relational algebraic operations of the REL module are implemented in terms of record table operations and calls to the appropriate functions of the fast access path modules.

As the DBS is viewed at lower levels, the data abstractions become more "physically" oriented until the level of the machine hardware is reached. Missing is the sharp transition from logical to physical representation found in many systems. Rather, there is a gradual progression from a very abstract view to machine hardware occurring in a sequence of discrete steps.

4 DESIGN STRUCTURE DOCUMENTATION

The role of specifications in the development of large software systems is certainly an important one. Specifications are used not only as a means of communication between members of the design team, but also serve to enhance the understandability of the system. This is important both for users of the system and for future design teams who must perform modifications.

The previous sections have described certain "local" specifications which are required in the hierarchical design approach—module specification, abstract programs, and mapping functions. Each such specification describes in detail the nature of a very small part of the total system. Yet, these specifications are inadequate for purposes of understanding the system as a whole or for explaining why a particular design was developed.

There exists a requirement to document the system design and the design process at a much higher level of abstraction. Such documentation would suppress details—concentrating rather on the global properties of the system design and the design structure.

The following sections briefly describe a System Design Language (SDL) which can be used to document the design process and record information about the decision-making processes that occur during it. The features of the SDL include methods for the following:

- specifying the design alternatives at each level;
- the hierarchical relationships between system modules; and
- the structure of each system level.

4.1 Specification Of Alternative Designs

One aspect of the hierarchical design approach mentioned previously is developing alternative designs at each level. In general a module at level i may be implemented in many different ways and, therefore, at level $i - 1$ the designer may specify various alternative modules to accomplish this task. There exists the need, then, to document exactly how the various alternative modules for implementing the data abstractions of level i may be combined to form designs for level $i - 1$. The designer may then choose the most appropriate alternative design as part of the system (using the evaluation model).

Using the SDL the designer may accomplish this task of specifying the various alternatives through a process of constructing level *components*. The syntax of component specification is defined formally in the following Backus Normal Form (BNF) grammar:

```
⟨compname⟩::= C⟨integer⟩
⟨modlist⟩::= ⟨modname⟩ | ⟨modname⟩,⟨modlist⟩
⟨complist⟩::= ⟨compname⟩ | ⟨compname⟩,⟨complist⟩
⟨compdef⟩::= ⟨modlist⟩ | ⟨complist⟩ |
             ⟨compdef⟩,⟨modlist⟩ | ⟨compdef⟩,⟨complist⟩
⟨ctype⟩::= REQ | ALT | OPT
⟨cspec⟩::= ⟨compname⟩: (⟨ctype⟩,{⟨compdef⟩})
```

The simplest type of level component is a single module. However, more complex components can be constructed by combining modules or previously defined components.

Associated with each component constructed is a component *type specification* (⟨ctype⟩) which indicates how "members" of the component may be combined or used in any alternative design. The meanings of the three component types are as follows:

- REQ — each member of the component must be included in any design.
- ALT — exactly one member of the component must be included in any design.
- OPT — exactly one subset of the members of the component must be present in any design (this includes the null set).

Formation of alternative designs begins when the designer has developed all alternative modules for implementing each data abstraction of level i. The designer then begins to construct a hierarchy of components—each component being a composition of lower level components. This process of composition continues until a single component has been constructed which encompasses, directly or indirectly, every module of the initial set. This final component specification is then the starting point for the development of possible alternatives for level $i - 1$.

The process of component construction and alternative design formation for level 3 of Table 8-1 can be illustrated by the following example.

```
C1:   (R EQ, {IMAGE, IMCAT})
C2:   (R EQ, {LNK, LCAT})
C3:   (R EQ, {SEL, SLCAT})
C4:   (R EQ, {INDEX, INDCAT})
C5:   (ALT, {C1, C4})
C6:   (OPT, {C2, C3, C5})
C7:   (R EQ, {RDIR, FNT, RT, TDS, C6})
```

This specification indicates, among other things, the following:

- components RDIR, FNT, RT, TDS, and C6 must be in every alternative design for level 3.
- any subset of {C2, C3, C5} may be present in a design for level 3 (because C6 is of type "OPT").
- if C5 is chosen to be in an alternative design then exactly one of C1 or C4 is to be in the design, and
- if C1 is chosen to be in the design then both IMAGE and IMCAT must be in the design.

Each component of type "OPT" or type "ALT" represents a decision for the designer regarding the structure of the alternative design. Different alternative designs may thus be formed by following different decision pathways.

4.2 Specification Of Hierarchical Relationships

The next important aspect of the SDL is that of specifying *capability relationships* between modules of adjacent levels. These capability relationships define the hierarchy which exists between the different modules of the system. At least three types of relationships are of interest.

The *has access* relationship indicates the ways in which a module m can obtain access to instances of a module m'. Three different types of allowable access are the following:

- Creation access (C)—m obtains access to instances of m' by virtue of its ability to invoke operations to create such instances.
- Indirect access (I)—m obtains access to instances of m' indirectly by using another module m''.
- Global access (G)—the identification of each instance of m' is global to the definition of m.

The *uses* relationship indicates the means by which a module m may use instances of a module m' to which it has access. Three different types of usage are the following:

- Read (R)—m can invoke the SV operations of m'.
- Write (W)—m can invoke the ST operations of m' to modify instances in some way.
- Create (C)—m can use ST operations to create instances of m'.

The *provides* relationship indicates what types of module instances a module m may obtain by accessing another module m'.

Formally, a capability set for levels i and $i - 1$ is defined as a triple {A, U, P} where A, U, and P are sets of triples defined as follows:

```
A  is  a  subset  of  M_i  X  {C,G,I}  X  M_{i-1}
U  is  a  subset  of  M_i  X  {R,W,C}  X  M_{i-1}
P  is  a  subset  of  M_i  X  M_{i-1}  X  M_{i-1}
```

Figure 8-8 illustrates the capability relationships that exist between some modules of levels 3, 4, and 5 of the system design of Table 8-1.

A specification of capability relationships can be useful in enforcing restrictions on communication between modules. It can also aid the designer in assessing the impact of modifications to system design.

4.3 Specification Of Level Structure

The final aspect of the SDL is that of specifying machine structure. It may be useful to allow a limited hierarchy within a particular level and, hence, the SDL enables the designer to specify the global properties of such a hierarchy. The level structure specification of the SDL indicates, for any level design, the modules which form the level *interface* (those visible to users of the level),

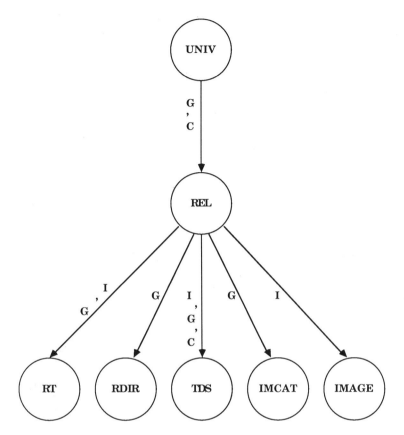

Figure 8-8a. The has access relationship between several modules of Table 8-1. The types of access are Global (G), Indirect (I), and Creation (C).

those modules which are *hidden* (from users of the level), and those modules which must use the interface of the next level (i.e., those modules which are not completely implemented within the level). The level structure specification also defines the hierarchical relationships which exist between modules of the level.

5 HIERARCHICAL PERFORMANCE EVALUATION

The success or failure of any system depends greatly upon the level of performance which it achieves during actual operation. Current approaches to performance evaluation rely heavily on *monitoring* a system after its design and implementation and then *fine-tuning* to achieve a desirable level of performance. In many cases, however, major redesign is required—an effort which may account for a large portion of the system development cost.

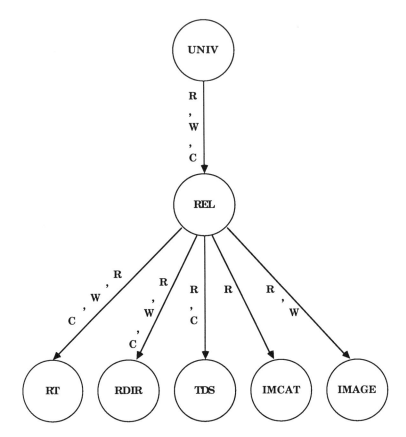

Figure 8-8b. The uses relationship between several modules of Table 8-1. These types of usages are Read (R), Write (W), and Create (C).

This section contains a very general description of a performance evaluation technique which can be used with the hierarchical design approach and which seems to have several advantages over current performance evaluation procedures. This technique involves the construction of a hierarchical performance evaluation model (HPEM). The purpose of this model is two-fold:

- to provide the designer with feedback at each step of the design process regarding the performance characteristics of the system; and
- to provide a basis for choosing between alternative designs at each level.

The HPEM is developed in parallel with the system design and is, likewise, hierarchically structured. As the design unfolds, new levels are added to the HPEM—each reflecting increased knowledge about the implementation of the system and the resulting effects upon system performance. Thus, the HPEM

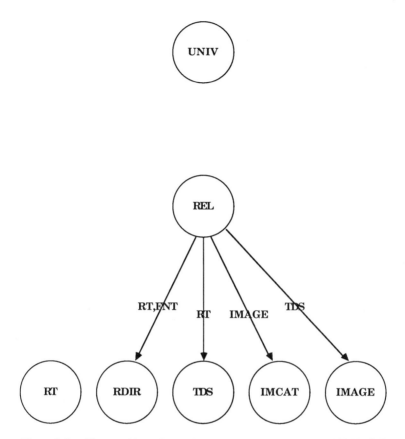

Figure 8-8c. The provides relationship between some modules of Table 8-1.

allows the designer to derive as much information as possible about the potential performance characteristics of the current design. Constant interaction with the HPEM enables the designer to "guide" the system through an appropriate design path with a minimum of redesign and backtracking.

The addition of each level to the HPEM consists of the following three distinct phases:

1. parameterization;
2. construction of an analytical model; and
3. queuing network simulation.

In the following sections, these processes are described in more detail using examples derived from the system design shown in Tables 8-1 and 8-2.

5.1   Parameterization

The parameterization of the i-th level of the HPEM is concerned with specifying those aspects of the system design at level i which are important with respect to system performance. The designer has complete freedom in choosing the performance parameters and, hence, design aspects may be represented explicitly, implicitly, or not at all in the HPEM. The parameterization is modular with respect to the system design; i.e., for each data abstraction of level i, a performance parameter specification is developed—this specification reflecting the properties of the data abstraction relevant to system performance.

The performance parameters of level i can be classified as *design* parameters or *implementation* parameters. The design parameters, representing aspects of the design which have been established, may be further classified as *scenario* parameters (S_i) or *control* parameters (V_i).

Scenario parameters represent aspects of the state of the system which are determined by the user application. The value of a scenario parameter at level N is determined by an expected workload specification. At level i ($0 \leq i \leq N$), the value of each scenario parameter is derived from a scenario parameter mapping function which defines the value of the parameter as a function of the performance parameters of level $i + 1$.

Consider, for example, levels 3 and 4 of the DBS design shown in Table 8-1. One scenario parameter for the REL module is NR which represents the number of defined relations in the system. In a similar manner, the scenario parameter NRT of the RT module specifies the number of existing record tables. The mapping function defined between these parameters is given by

$$NRT = NR$$

which indicates that, for a given application, the number of record tables seen at level 3 is the same as the number of relations seen at level 4. The scenario parameter mapping functions are thus used to transform a user application expressed in terms of level i ($0 < i \leq N$) concepts into a corresponding application expressed in terms of level $i - 1$ concepts.

At the top level, the scenario parameters are provided by the designer. Usually, a designer will provide a set of scenarios each with a different set of scenario parameters. These scenarios are based on the designer's intuition, experience, and whatever other information about the system he has in hand. A particular scenario may be inconsistent with specifications at some lower level as more detailed actual parameters come in. In this case, the designer will have to try a different scenario and start the whole evaluation process anew.

Control parameters represent those aspects of the system design which may be varied to enhance the performance of user applications. At level 3 (Table 8-1), for example, the boolean control parameter IMG(rt, f) takes the value *true* if an image structure is defined for record table rt on field f. Likewise, the boolean control parameter SEL(*rt*, *f*, *v*) is true when a selector structure exists for value *v*, in field *f*, of record table *rt*. During the evaluation process, the system designer may use different values of control parameters in order to determine the most appropriate configuration of the system for an application.

Implementation parameters represent aspects of the system design which have yet to be realized but which must be included in the model for proper evaluation of the system. Implementation parameters at level *i*, for example, would include the designer's estimates for the execution speeds of level *i* operations. The values of such parameters represent *constraints* on the design, which have yet to be satisfied.

5.2   The Analytical Model

The analytical model consists of analytical equations which define the cost of a particular design (completed through level *i*) in terms of time expressions for the operations of level *i* and estimates of storage requirements. A simplified example for illustrating this process of constructing this model is given as follows.

An abstract program (with error traps removed) implements the select (*R*, *d*, *v*) operation of the REL module of Table 8-1. The implementation of this operation requires the use of four operations at level 3: get—selector, image—exists, get—iptrs and create—selector.

Using an approach proposed by Wegbreit,[26] it is possible to analyze this program (in a manner similar to an inductive assertion proof) in order to derive a cost expression in terms of the model performance parameters of level 3.

```
relation procedure select(rt,f,v);

begin
    b:=get_selector(rt,f,v,tds);
    if b then   *selector exists*
          select:=tds;
        else  *selector does not exist*
          begin
              b:=image_exists(rt,f,image);
              if b then  *image exists*
              begin
                  b:=get_iptrs(image,v,ts,n);
                  if b then  *value v has an occurrence
                  in R*
                      select:=tds;
                  else
                      select:=null;
          end;
        else  *no image and no selector exists*
          select:=create_selector(rt,f,v);
        end;
end.
```

The following is a list of model parameters which are used in the analysis of this program.

Implementation Parameters (Time Expressions)

```
t₀ - simple assignment
t₁ - examination of simple boolean variable
t₂ - get_selector
t₃ - image_exists
t₄ - get_iptrs
t₅ - create_selector
```

Scenario Parameters

```
IMG(rt,f)   - true if an image structure is defined for
              field f of record table rt, false
              otherwise.
SEL(rt,f,v) - true if a selector structure is defined
              for value v in field f of record table rt,
              false otherwise.
PV(rt,f,v)  - probability that value v occurs in field
              f of record table rt.
```

Analysis of the program yields the following time expression for the select operation:

```
T(select) = (t₀ + t₂ + t₁) + (if SEL(rt, f, v) then t₀
     else [(t₀ + t₃ + t₂) + (if IMG(rt, f) then
     (t₀ + t₄ + t₂ + PV*t₀ + (1 - PV)*t₀)
     else t₅)]
```

Assuming that the execution of the abstract operations represents the limiting factor in performance, the expression reduces to:

```
t₂ + (if −SEL(rt, f, v) then [t₃ + (if IMG(rt, f)
then t₄ else t₅)])
```

The designer can thus evaluate the cost of executing this procedure for various values of the model parameters.

Performing such analysis on all procedures at each design step thus enables the designer to construct a cost expression for the design in terms of the parameters of the most recently completed level.

5.3 The Simulation Model

Unfortunately, many aspects of complex systems cannot be captured by an analytical model. In data base systems, for example, performance can be significantly affected by such things as contention for resources caused by multiple users, locking protocol, and creation of temporary data objects—factors which cannot easily be incorporated into an analytical model. Likewise, a simple time expression may not adequately characterize complex, parameterized operations.

The basis for the simulation process is a queuing network model constructed by the designer. The model differs from typical queuing models, however, in that it is used to measure contention for *abstract resources* in the system design. These may include software defined resources, such as relations, files, directories, and access paths as well as hardware resources.

The structure of the model constructed by the designer also reflects that of the system design itself—that is, the model consists of a hierarchy of queuing networks each of which models the characteristics of the system design at a particular level of abstraction. As each new level is added to the system design, a corresponding level is added to the simulation model. Thus, successive networks in the hierarchy represent increasingly detailed models of system performance. Moreover, adjacent networks are "connected" in that the solution of each network can be used to parameterize the immediately preceding one.

A queuing network in the model is represented by the following:

- a set of *resource queues*;
- a set of job (or transaction) sources which generate job requests to resources based upon a specified workload; and
- a method of job *routing*.

Each resource queue (Figure 8-9), moreover, consists of the following:

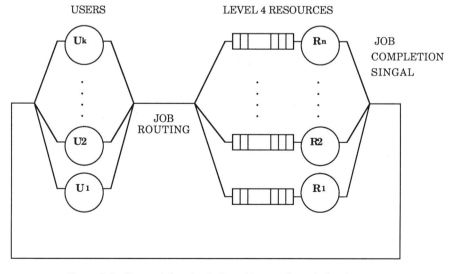

Figure 8-9. Network for simulation of interactive relational system.

- a set of job *classes*;
- a *queuing discipline*; and
- a set of one or more *servers*.

Each server in a resource corresponds to a particular abstract data object which is relevant to the level of design being modeled. Thus, each job class represents a particular operation or set of operations defined over the data objects represented by the resource. As jobs are received by the resource, they are placed into one of the defined classes and are removed for servicing according to the specified queuing discipline (e.g., first-come first-serve, priority, round-robin, etc.). Associated with each job class is a service time distribution (STD) which specifies information about the length of time the operations of the class will require for execution.

A very simple example, perhaps, can best illustrate how this simulation approach might be used to derive performance characteristics of system designs. The example is derived from a simplification of the design of levels 3 and 4 shown in Tables 8-1 and Table 8-2.

Figure 8-10 represents a view of the simulation model at level 4. The network at this level consists of k end-users $U_1, U_2, \ldots, U_k$ each representing a source of jobs and a set of n relations $R_1, R_2, \ldots, R_n$ representing the resources at this level (note that each resource has only a single server).

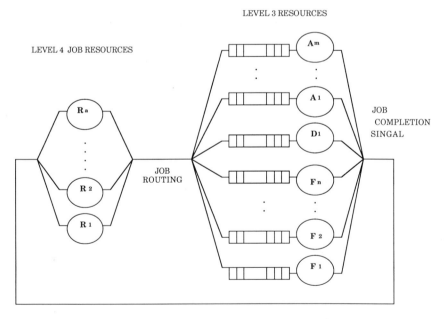

Figure 8-10. Network structure at level n-1.

The simulation of the model at this level proceeds somewhat as follows: users issue job requests in parallel according to a specified workload. Each job request is specified by a triple (op, pvals, uid) where *op* is a relation operation, *pvals* is a set of values for the parameters of the operation, and *uid* is the user requesting the operation. Based upon information in the request, the job is routed to the appropriate resource and is placed into one of the resource job classes— each class corresponding to a particular relational operation. Each job waits in the queue until its turn and is then processed by the resource (i.e., the operation is performed on the specified data object). The amount of time required for processing is determined by the STD specification for the job class. When processing is finished, a signal is sent to the user who requested the operation. The user may then submit a new job request after, perhaps, an appropriate think time.

At this level, then, the simulation is used to derive estimates to meaningful performance measures, such as response times and throughput. Also, computation of mean queue lengths provides some insight into contention for resources at this level.

After the design and implementation of level 3, a queuing network to model this level is constructed (Figure 8-11). This is similar to the network at level 4 except that the resources $R_1, R_2, \ldots, R_n$, which act as "sinks" at level 4 are now job sources. There are $m + n + 1$ resources at level 3: $F_1, F_2, \ldots, F_n$ corresponding to abstract record tables (files), D_1 representing a file directory, and $A_1, A_2, \ldots, A_m$ representing indexes to the records of certain record tables.

The simulation now proceeds as follows. As a job is received by a resource, say R_1 at level 4, it is transformed into a sequence of level 3 operations (e.g., file operations, directory operations, and index operations) according to the abstract program which implements the operation. These level 3 operations are submitted as job requests (one at a time) to the resources of level 3. The resources, of course, are simultaneously receiving job requests from the other relation sources. The actual sequencing of the operations as specified by the abstract program is ignored in the model (for the present time). Again, the service time required for each job is determined by a STD (provided by the designer) for the job classes of each resource. When the entire set of operations has been processed at level 3, then R_1 sends a completion signal to the appropriate user at level 4. New estimates for performance measures can thus be derived based upon the more accurate service time distributions predicted for level 3 job classes.

As each additional level is added to the model, the designer is able to specify with more certainty the STD of the level operations—hence increasing the accuracy of the modeling results. By varying the values of parameters at each level, the designer may determine the effects of different data base configurations and workloads upon total system performance. While the modeling results at each level would necessarily involve an amount of uncertainty, they might

LEVEL 4

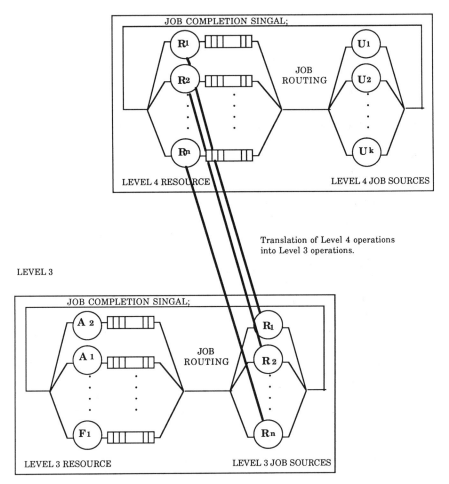

Figure 8-11. Hierarchical view of top two levels of the simulations.

nevertheless be useful for "guiding" the designer through the design space—providing a basis for choosing among alternative designs at each level or for backtracking when satisfaction of performance criteria seemed unlikely.

In the description of this approach to performance modeling, other aspects of the problem which must be explored in much more detail include the following:

1. *Formalization of locking protocol.* The notion of resource locking has not been fully developed in the model presented. In a DBS, for example, processes require exclusive locks on physical resources such as disks,

CPUs and I/O devices. Likewise, certain processes may be "blocked" by locks on "logical" components of the system, such as records, files, pages, etc. A realistic performance model should capture the interaction of these locking concepts. Hence, the model might be expanded to include the following:

- different types of locks (read, write, etc.),
- simultaneous locking of several resources by a user, and
- locking of a resource for several successive operations by the same user.

Such a model would hopefully provide some insight into the performance tradeoffs for locks of different "granularity" permitted on logical components of the system.

2. *Handling of nonshared, temporary data objects.* In an interactive environment users often create and use temporary (nonshared) data objects. The simulation approach described previously would allow dynamic creation and deletion of resources, but the approach needs to be formalized.

3. *Specification of system workload.* A framework for specifying workloads in terms of abstract operations must be developed.

4. *Specification of service time distributions.* Guidelines for specifying STD must be derived. It would be useful for the STD to be parameterized to depend upon values of the operation parameters. For example, the service time distribution for a relational JOIN operation might be a function of the number of tuples in the specified relations.

5. *Handling of operations over several data objects.* It is not immediately obvious how the model would handle operations like the JOIN or set union since more than one data object is specified.

6 AN APPROACH TO DEVELOPMENT OF SOFTWARE PROTOTYPES

A prototype is a model of some of the functional aspects of a proposed system. With suitable software tools, this model can become a working model, a computer simulation of the system being designed. With such a working model available, testing the logical design process can begin. Functions of the proposed design can be demonstrated to potential users to see if they meet their approval. One can become familiar with the dynamic behavior of the system before it is finished, and experiment with the design to "see" what effects various changes will have on the system's behavior.

The notion of a prototype fits naturally with the hierarchical design methodology discussed earlier. If a design has been refined into a hierarchy of abstract machines M_n, M_{n-1}, . . . , M_i with implementations I_n, I_{n-1}, . . . , I_{i+1}, the prototype 1 to level i consists of the procedure modules specifying I_n through I_{i+1}, together with the function modules specifying M_i. The prototype is, thus the hierarchy shown in Figure 8-12. A prototype can be made as a functioning simulation of the design by providing a suitable interpreter. Then, to perform an operation of M_n, the interpreter executes a program in I_n, which calls a program in I_{n-1}, and so on until a program in I_{i+1} is called, which finally calls an operation (ST function) of M_i. The values of the SV functions of M_i get changed, simulating the internal state changes that will occur when the operation is performed on the finished system.

6.1 Specification Language

The keystone to prototyping is a language for defining abstract models of proposed systems. This is the module specification language mentioned earlier, which is a combination of procedural and declarative statements that allow rigorous specfication of processes and structures to any level of detail and

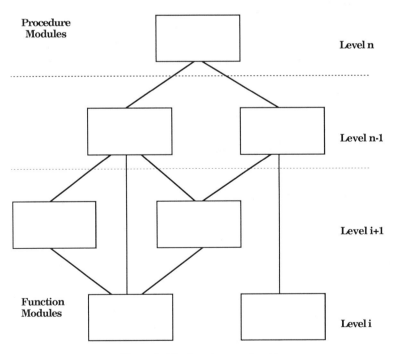

Figure 8-12. Prototype to level i.

completeness. It is designed to be perspicuous to both people and computers. Designers can sketch their ideas in this language, and the computer that interprets it can simulate their designs, provide performance estimates, and aid generally in the evaluation and further development of good designs. The following discussion is a brief overview of the specification language and its semantic concepts.

The specification of a function module consists of a set of function specifications. A function is specified in the language of the following grammar:

```
⟨function specification⟩::=<header⟩
                           ⟨declaration section⟩*
⟨header⟩::=function:⟨name⟩⟨parameter list⟩
           =⟨returned value⟩
⟨declaration section⟩::=⟨section type⟩
                        :⟨declarations⟩
⟨declarations⟩::=⟨declarative statement⟩
⟨declarations⟩::=⟨declarative statement⟩⟨declarations⟩
```

The section types that are allowed include EFFECTS, EXCEPTION-CONDI-TIONS, INITIAL-VALUES, and PURPOSE. Except for the PURPOSE section, which is a comment section written in English, the declarative statements in these sections are assertions in an augmented First Order Predicate Calculus notation. The augmentations include the following: the names of SV functions may be enclosed in single quotes, to signify function values before any changes have taken place, and finite sequences may be represented by an ellipsis notation as in "X(1), . . . , X(N)."

To understand more clearly what the specification language looks like, suppose one is designing a relational data base system. (This system is not the one discussed in Section 3; it has been kept small and simple so that attention can be focused on the specifications instead of the design.) The system must allow to insert n-tuples into a relation, delete them, define new relations in terms of other relations, and list all the n-tuples in a relation. The function module (named DBS) that describes this system contains the following functions:

SV Functions	ST Functions
data	define
defined	insert
definition	list
tempdata	remove
universe	undefine

The ST functions correspond to the five basic operations that the system will perform, while the SV functions store the relational information between operations (except for "tempdata," which stores information during the "list" operation).

The key distinction between SV function specifications and ST function specifications is that the former do not have an EFFECTS section and the latter do. The specification for the SV function "definition," for example, is the following:

```
function: definition(R,X)=Y
   PURPOSE: Relation R is the set of n-tuples X satisfy-
            ing well-formed formula Y.
   INITIAL-VALUE: Y=nil.
   EXCEPTION-CONDITIONS:
            NOT-A-LITERAL (R).
            NOT-A-LIST (X).
            NOT-A-WFF (Y).
```

The specification of ST function "define," on the other hand, is the following:

```
function: define (R, X, Y)=nil
   PURPOSE: The relation R is defined to be the set of
            n-tuples X satisfying Y.
            The undefined value ''nil''
            is returned by this function.
   EFFECTS: definition (R, X)=Y.
            defined (R)=true.
   EXCEPTION-CONDITIONS:
            ALREADY-DEFINED (R).
            NOT-A-LITERAL (R).
            NOT-A-LIST (X).
            NOT-A-WFF (Y).
```

The EFFECTS statements in this example state that the "define" operation causes the "definition" and "defined" functions to take on the values indicated. That is, what EFFECTS statements are: assertions that become true when the operation is performed.

Some EFFECTS statements describe complex state changes; these are usually quantified assertions about how new values of SV functions are related to old values. In the specification for the "list" operation, for example, there are EFFECTS statements that relate the values of a function called "tempdata" to the n-tuples in all relations in the data base. This function effectively enumerates the n-tuples in all of the relations. One statement in the definition of "list" is the following:

```
for all R, Y such that 'defined' (R)=nil:
tempdata (R, Y) = 'data' (R, Y).
```

This asserts that a relation R that is undefined contains exactly those n-tuples Y that are explicitly indicated by the values of the "data" function before the "list" operation was invoked.

If a relation R is defined as a projection of a relation S, then the EFFECTS statement becomes

```
for all R, X(1), . . . , X(I), S, Y(1), . . . , Y(J)
such that
'definition'
(R, (X(1), . . . , X(I1))) = S(Y(1), . . . , Y(J)):
   for all Z(1), . . . , Z(I):
   tempdata (R,(Z(1), . . . , Z(I)))=true
   if   for some U(1), . . . , U(J) such that
   for all K, L: if Y(K)=Y(L) then U(K)=U(L),
   and    if Y(K)=X(L) then U(K)=Z(L);:
   tempdata (S, (U(1), . . . , U(J))) = true
```

This guarantees that "tempdata" is true for the pair (R, Z) exactly when Z is an n-tuple satisfying R's definition. More specifically, assuming that "tempdata" is true of (S, U) exactly when U is an n-tuple in S, then it is true of (R, Z) if both Z and U can be substituted into the definition of R without conflict. (The restrictions on the substitution are given by that part of the above statement which is in the scope of variables K and L.) Other EFFECTS statements provide for the complement and joining of relations. Finally, there are statements asserting that when the "list" operation is applied to a relation name, the outcome is a list of all the n-tuples in that relation.

The intention of EFFECTS statements is that they describe what must be true after an operation has been performed. The SV functions describe a particular state of an abstract machine. After an operation is performed, a new set of SV functions (i.e., some values are different) describe the state of the machine. The EFFECTS statements corresponding to that operation are now satisfied by the SV functions. There may be more than one way to change the SV functions. To do this, however, the changes must be minimal; that is, none of them can be removed without ceasing to satisfy the EFFECTS statements. Otherwise, any set of changes is allowed. This non-determinancy reflects his/her desire to leave unspecified any details that are not crucial to the design. (In this relational data base example, for instance, the "list" operation is specified to return a list of n-tuples without repetition, but the order in which the n-tuples are listed is not specified.) The designer is free to refine a function module in any way that is consistent with the specifications.

Unlike Parnas,[21] "hidden" functions are allowed. These are SV functions which are not intended to be accessible by anything outside the module, but which are convenient, and sometimes even necessary for the definition of other functions. ("tempdata" is an example.) Not allowed are assertions that span more than a single state transition, as "PUSH(a); POP has no net effect," because this would greatly complicate the specifications interpreter.

The specification of a procedure module looks like a set of programs. The programs are the procedures that execute operations on one abstract machine in the proper order to implement an operation on a higher level machine. At present, a Pascal-like syntax for these procedures is used. Excerpts from a procedure module are shown in the upper half of Figure 8-13. This module implements the function module described earlier in terms of two lower level function modules, called "Files" and "Records." The programs in this module call other programs, which in turn eventually call on functions in the two function modules as if they were subroutines, thereby defining the hierarchy shown in Figure 8-14. As development continues, these function modules will be replaced by program modules until the lowest level machine corresponds to the hardware on which the system will be run. Note that the modules written in the specification language can be run as programs and analyzed as data to provide designers with the feedback necessary to correct their errors.

6.2   Execution

One way to know that a program contains an error is to run it on a test case and get the wrong result. This is the most common approach to debugging programs. The test case approach has one flaw, however, and that is that one may not try all the cases that produce errors. To get around this flaw, some developers propose symbolic execution (Hewett-Yonezawa[16] and King[18]) which is an attempt to prove that a program is error-free in all the cases concerned. In this section, symbolic execution tools, such as those developed for verifying programs that permit similar verification of module specifications is proposed.

The proposed interpreter provides for direct execution of modules as if they were programs. Procedure modules are interpreted in conventional fashion, since they are just collections of programs written in a language not too different from Algol or Pascal. Function modules, however, require a different kind of interpreter. In this case EFFECTS statements in the function specifications are taken to be constraints that must be satisfied by the interpreter. Programs that solve constraint satisfaction problems have been made for many years in areas of operations research and artificial intelligence, but those that come closest to the proposed interpreter are the programs of Lauriere[20] (a very close match), Elcock, et al.,[11] and Fikes.[13] When the constraints are satisfied, the interpreter has succeeded in changing a list of the old state function values into a list of new values. This simulates a state transition of the abstract machine that the function module represents. The sequence of function calls so simulated is controlled in the conventional way by the programs in the procedure modules.

As a brief illustration of how the proposed interpreter works on function modules, suppose that the function module DBS is to be executed. Initially, all the state functions return nil as their value (because there are no initial value statements) no matter what their arguments are. This state is represented by an empty list. Suppose now that one executes

```
''insert(employee-file,(Smith,ID#174,sales))''
```

```
Module: DBS
procedure: insert (R,(X(l),...,X(N)))
definition:
  include (R,(X(l),...,X(N)))
  for I : = l to N step 1 do
    increment (''universe,'' X(I))

procedure: list(R)
definition:
  X : = relations(R)
  until X = nil do
    begin
    makefile (head(X))
    X : = tail(X)
    end
  print(R)

procedure: relations(R)
 definition:
  [returns names of relations
   in order that they must be computed]

  [other procedures: remove, define, undefine, makefile,
   find, increment, decrement, include, exclude, project,
   complement, join, sort]

Module: Files

function: file(X) = Y
function: pointer(X) = Y
function: rewind(X) = nil
EFFECTS:
 pointer(X) = 'file'(X).

  [other ST functions: next, erase, replace,
   extend, rename]

Module: Records

function: current(X) = Y
function: head((X(1),...,X(N))) = Y
EFFECTS:
Y = X(1).
function: tail((X(1),...,X(N))) = (Y(1),...,Y(M))
EFFECTS:
(Y(1),...,Y(M)) = (X(2),...,X(N)).
  [other SV functions: oblist]
  [other ST functions: append, bind, startgen, nextgen,
   common, tooblist, fromoblist]
```

Figure 8-13. Model for a Data Base System.

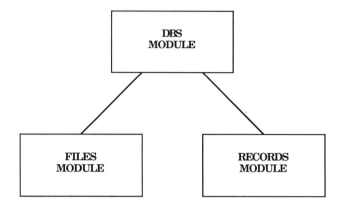

Figure 8-14. Hierarchy of modules in Prototype.

The interpreter looks up the specification for ''insert'' and matches the function pattern against the function call. Since the specification for ''insert'' is the following:

```
function: insert (R, (X(1), . . . , X(N))) = nil
PURPOSE: The n-tuple (X(1), . . . , X(N)) is inserted
  into the relation R.
EFFECTS: data(R, (X(1), . . . , X(N))) = true
  for all I such that 1 ≤ I ≤ N: universe(X(I)) = true
```

the interpreter assigns to variables $X(1)$ through $X(N)$ the values ''Smith,'' ''ID#174,'' and ''sales,'' respectively. (The value of N is now known to be 3.) To make the first EFFECTS statement true, the interpreter simply adds

```
''data(employee-file, (Smith, ID#174, sales))=true''
```

to its state description list. The second EFFECTS statement is also easy to make true, for all that is required is to add

```
universe(Smith) = true
universe(ID#174) = true
universe(sales) = true
```

to the list. The net effect is that the ''employee-file'' relation is created, and one n-tuple is entered in the relation table.

Now suppose that one executes ''list(employee-file).'' After looking up the specification for ''list,'' the interpreter assigns R the value ''employee-file'' and then examines the EFFECTS statements. The first three statements make the function call return a list without repetition of exactly those expressions X, such that "tempdata(R, X)=true" gets added to the description list. And why are such assertions added? Because of the EFFECTS statement that says that the "tempdata" and "data" functions must agree on relations lacking definitions. In the present case, the equation

```
tempdata (R, (X(1), . . . , X(N))) = 'data'
         (R, (X(1), . . . , X(N)))
```

is satisfied already for all values of R and $X(1)$ through $X(N)$ except when these are bound to "employee-file" and "Smith," "ID#174," and "sales," respectively. The single quotes around "data" indicate (as in Parnas modules) that the old value ("true") of this function must be used so the only way that this equation can be satisfied is to add

```
''tempdata(employee-file,(Smith,ID#174,sales))=true''
```

to the state description list. The function value returned by the interpreter is thus "(Smith, ID#174, sales))."

It is evident from this illustration that the interpreter is imitating the steps taken by designers when simulating their designs by hand. The state of the system is represented by a list of facts. All possible substitutions into the specifications are made to deduce, whenever possible, which facts must be added and which deleted to satisfy the specifications. If there remains a choice, such as the alternatives in a disjunction ("or") statement, each alternative is assumed in turn until one is found that allows satisfaction of the specifications.

Quantified statements present the interpreter with a more difficult problem. Universal statements are considered to be pattern-action rules that are continually applied to the list of facts. (There are actually two lists; the old list of facts and the update list. After all changes have been added to the update list, it is combined with the old list to make it ready for the next function call.) Existential statements are handled like disjunctions of indeterminate length. If an object, which has already been mentioned, can be found with the necessary properties, an existential statement is just ignored. Otherwise, a new object is created to serve the role of the one that is asserted to exist. It is essential that the specifications be sufficiently detailed so that only a finite number of new facts or objects be created; otherwise, the interpreter will not terminate.

Besides direct execution of specifications, the interpreter must provide symbolic execution. That is, it (the interpreter) will provide a facility for deducing global facts about a design in the form of theorems. This facility will be used to verify implementations and to derive some performance estimations. The immediate purpose of the execution facilities is to verify that a system design accomplishes the required task and knows how well the design performs.

7 CONCLUSION

The design approach advocated in this chapter is one of successive refinement and evaluation of a working or prototype model of the desired system. The refinements cause the model to gradually satisfy the design requirements, one by one, until all are satisfied. It is similar to the process of sculpting a block of stone, which is done by chipping it away gradually as the finished sculpture takes shape. To do the refinement steps effectively, the designers require tools to measure how close they are getting to their goal, but until now, few of these tools were readily available.

A comprehensive package of tools to help designers in refining their prototypes is proposed. It is based upon a specification and design language for describing a model as a set of modules and a language semantics that considers the model to be an abstract machine. The D interpreter gives the designers the ability to watch the machine run, while the symbolic evaluator helps them draw conclusions about the machine's general behavior. The various performance evaluation facilities provide information for deciding which of several refinements should be pursued. Finally, the tool set provides designers with some ability to determine the quality of their design; this kind of feedback will stimulate superior work.

REFERENCES

1. Astrahan, M. M., *et al*, "System R: Relational Approach to Database Management," *ACM TODS*, Vol. 1, No. 2, 1976, pp. 97–137.
2. Baker, J. and R. T. Yeh, "A Hierarchical Design Methodology for Data Base System," TR-70, Dept. of Computer Science, University of Texas at Austin, Austin, Texas, 1977.
3. Balzer, R., N. Goldman, and D. Wile, "Informality in Program Specifications," *IEEE-TSE*, Vol. SE-4, No. 2, 1978, pp. 94–103.
4. Bayer, R. and E. McCreight, "Organization and Maintenance of Ordered Indexes," *Acta Informatica*, Vol. 1, No. 3, 1972, pp. 173–189.
5. Boehm, B., "Software and Its Impact: A Quantitative Study," *Datamation*, Vol. 19, No. 5, May, 1973.
6. Brown, R., J. Browne, and K. Chandy, "Memory Management and Response Time," *CACM*, Vol. 20, No. 3, 1977, pp. 153–165.
7. Chester, D. and R. T. Yeh, "Software Development by Evaluation of System Design," *Proc. Int. Conf. Software Applications*, 1977, pp. 431–441.
8. Codd, E. G., "A Relational Model of Data for Large Shared Data Banks," *CACM*, Vol. 13, No. 6, 1970, pp. 377–387.
9. DeRemer, F. and H. Kron, "Programming-in-the-Large Versus Programming-in-the Small," *Proc. Int. Cong. on Reliable Software*, Los Angeles, 1975, pp. 114–121.
10. Dijkstra, E. W., "Notes on Structured Programming," *Structured Programming*, (Eds. Hoare, Dahl, Dijkstra), NY: Academic Press, 1972, pp. 1–82.
11. Elcock, E., J. Foster, P. Gray, J. McGregor, and A. Murray, "Abset, A Programming Language Based on Sets: Motivation and Examples," *Machine Intelligence*, Vol. 6, 1972, pp. 467–492.
12. Ferrentino, A. B. and H. D. Mills, "State Machines and Their Semantics in Software Engineering," *Proc. Int. Conf. Computer Software and Applications*, 1977, pp. 242–251.

13. Fikes, R., "REF-ARF: A System for Solving Problems Stated as Procedures," *Artificial Intelligence*, 1, 1970, pp. 27–120.
14. Good, D., R. London, and W. Bledsoe, "An Interactive Program Verification System," *IEEE-TSE*, Vol. SE-1, No. 1, 1975, pp. 59–67.
15. Goodenough, John B., "Exception Handling: Issues and a Proposed Notation," *CACM*, Vol. 13, No. 6, 1975, pp. 377–387.
16. Hewitt, C. and A. Yonezawa, "Symbolic Evaluation Using Conceptual Representations for Programs with Side-Effects," *A.I. Memo 399*, Artificial Intelligence Lab., M.I.T., 1976.
17. Hoare, C. A. R., (1970), "An Axiomatic Approach to Computer Programming," *CACM*, Vol. 12, No. 5, 1970, pp. 76–80, 83.
18. King, J., "Symbolic Execution and Program Testing," *CACM*, Vol. 19, No. 7, 1975, pp. 385–394.
19. Kraegeloh, Klaus-Dieter and Peter C. Lockemann, "Hierarchies of Data Base Languages: An Example," *Information Systems*, Vol. 1, 1975.
20. Lauriere, J., "Un Langage et un Programme Pour Enoncer et Resoudre des Problemes Combinatoires," These de Doctorat d'Etat, Universite Pierre et Marie Curie, Paris, May 1975.
21. Parnas, D., "A Technique for Software Module Specification with Examples," *CACM*, Vol. 15, No. 5, 1972, pp. 330–336.
22. Parnas, D., "On the Criteria to be Used in Decomposing Systems into Modules," *CACM*, Vol. 15, No. 12, 1972, pp. 1053–1058.
23. Parnas, D. and G. Handzel, "More on Specification Techniques for Software Modules," Forschungsbericht BS I 75/1, Fachbereich Informatik, T. H., Darmstadt, February 1975.
24. Parnas, D., "On A Buzzword: Hierarchical Structures," *Proc. IFIP*, 1976.
25. Robinson, L. and K. N. Levitt, "Proof Techniques for Hierarchically Structured Programs," *Current Trends in Programming Methodology: Program Validation*, Vol. 2, (ed. R. T. Yeh), Englewood Cliffs, NJ: Prentice-Hall, 1977.
26. Wegbreit, B., "Verifying Program Performance," *JACM*, Vol. 23, No. 4, 1976, pp. 691–699.
27. Yeh, R. T. (Ed.) *Current Trends In Programming Methodology: Software Specification and Design*, Vol. 1, Englewood Cliffs, NJ: Prentice-Hall, Inc, 1977.
28. Yeh, R. T. and J. Baker, "Toward a Design Methodology for DBMS: A Software Engineering Approach," *Proc. 3rd Int. Conf. on VLDB*, Tokyo, Japan, October, 1977.
29. Yeh, R. T. (Ed.), *Current Trends in Programming Methodology: Program Validation*, Vol. 2, Englewood Cliffs, NJ: Prentice-Hall, Inc, 1977.

Chapter 9

Requirements for Database Support in Computer-Aided Software Engineering

BOB STRONG
Technical Vice President
Ontologic, Inc.
Billerica, MA

ABSTRACT

This Chapter will discuss the functions of a database in a Computer-Aided Software Engineering (CASE) environment and the requirements to be met by such a tool. Currently available tools only begin to scratch the surface of the possible uses of a database in CASE. Indeed, outside of the research laboratory, there are few examples of good tools using database techniques. The requirements for a design database to support CASE are drawn by analogy from the experience of other engineering disciplines. The data to be managed is discussed. The intimate linkage between the nature of the tools and the nature of the product is explored, particularly in terms of the demands placed on the data management tools in support of the application itself. The use of a storage system to provide an interconnection mechanism among the tools of the environment is analyzed, as is the impact of reasoning tools and object-oriented techniques on the data management system.

1 INTRODUCTION

Although the software engineering community has used its tools, computers and their information management capabilities, for many years to store and edit the text and executable forms of programs, it is only recently that the rich possibilities available from the use of databases have become apparent. Editing environments which are supported by a database, databases to support compilers and tool integration software based on database mechanisms are now being explored, and in a few instances, being brought to market. The Trellis programming environment[1] demonstrates the power of a database to support editing, compilation, and debug phases of programming. The use of a database as a code library manager to support software reuse is discussed by Burton, *et al.*[2]

The utility of a database as an integration platform is explored by Paseman.[3] These efforts build upon a history of successively more sophisticated use of data and text management tools and, in many products, supporting aspects of the software development task.

The number of commercially available tools which make good use of data management technology is small. Careful analysis of the uses of data management in CASE tools is fairly recent. The analysis given by Bernstein[4] is perhaps the best from the point of view of the technical details. Bernstein also gives a rather extensive bibliography. The goal of this Chapter, however, is not to review the literature concerning this technology, but rather to view the problem from a very practical standpoint. The author explores the range of things for which one may want to use data systems in CASE environments. The author then examines what can be done with the data management technology available, and where the technology is found lacking.

The author examines the software engineering process beginning with the information it generates and the information it uses. The objective is to explore the requirements placed on tools to manage program design and maintenance information. The role of database technology in the software design process has been the subject of much recent interest in both the design research community and the database community.[5,6] The state of development of information management systems to support CASE is somewhat behind the state of tools in other engineering disciplines. The author is, however, perhaps on the verge of breakthroughs in a number of significant areas.

This Chapter will approach the problem of information management in CASE environments by comparing the tasks and results of CASE activities with the corresponding aspects of the other Computer-Aided Design (CAD) tool sets and exploring the role of information management tools in the engineering process. By examining the specific nature of the information on which CASE is based, it is possible to explore the requirements for information management systems to support it.

A review of some critical characteristics of current Data Base Management System (DBMS) models makes possible a test of the fit between the capabilities of these systems and CASE requirements. The limitations of most currently available general purpose database systems, and the possibilities offered by some recent advances in data management technology are explored in the latter part of this Chapter. Specific support for object-oriented approaches and AI techniques is dealt with in the last Section.

2 A VIEW OF THE ENGINEERING PROCESS

The process of design can be viewed as an iterative process of information capture, analysis of the captured information against criteria for a good design, and either return to the first step for refinement or release of the design for reproduction. To elaborate one might say that first a requirement is captured. Next a design is proposed to meet the requirement. The design is analyzed for compatibility with many different kinds of constraints, including cost, manufacturability, and extent to which the requirements are satisfied. Designs which meet the constraints may be permitted to go on to manufacture and ultimately to use. Other designs are returned for modification.

This process is shown in Figure 9-1, which also identifies several points in the process where a representation of the design is needed. In a CAD process, some portion of the process is computer supported. This is done by allowing the computer to store the relevant representations of the design and possibly a statement of the requirements, and by providing computer tools to support various phases of the process. In some narrowly defined areas of application, it may be possible to perform all of the work after the capture of the requirements in an automated way, but this is seldom possible. Indeed it is more often the case that a designer or analyst gets involved and either performs or supervises each stage of the process.

A look at a mechanical design task might give some useful insights. The designers of an automobile might start with requirements on the cost, weight, top speed, handling, gas mileage, and time-to-market for a new model. There is a generally accepted framework for the design of cars which leads to a simplification of the design space. For example, five wheeled vehicles are generally not considered as a starting point. There is also generally a body of old designs, built to meet different but similarly stated requirements. Designs are normally approached by decomposing the problem along familiar lines, using existing designs for components where the requirements can be met, and modifying rather than re-inventing components when the requirements dictate something new.

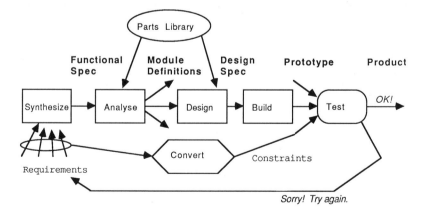

Figure 9-1. The basic design cycle.

The requirements stated at the outset are translated into analyses to be performed on the design and criteria for success. The structural relationships representing the decomposition of the problem and corresponding decomposition of the solution, are captured, along with information to support the management of the design process. The representations of designs for the various components are now built, or borrowed from the past, and linked to the overall product description. Designs for an individual component may in fact have several different representations, reflecting the analyses which are to be performed.

As the design process proceeds, the representations are refined or replaced until a set is found which meets the requirements. When a suitable set of component designs is found, a single representation is generated and passed from the design process to the manufacturing process. This representation defines how the design is to be manufactured and assembled into a usable automobile.

The data which must be captured to support this process includes not only the decomposition of the design into manageable sub-designs, but possibly several representations of each component. New representations are often introduced to support the efficient execution of an analysis. The output of the design process will be another representation, possibly quite different from the working representations of the design process, keyed to the requirements of the manufacturing process. This "output" from the design process may also contain information which summarizes the results of the analyses and provides criteria for testing the manufactured product.

Of course, this is a much simplified description of the actual process, and the intrusion of human-mediated or human-implemented steps is significant. Mechanical design is one of the easiest CAD disciplines to describe. Indeed, because the distinction between the CAD tools, the manufacturing facility, and the end-user's framework is so blurred in software engineering, it is hard to identify the boundaries and correspondingly difficult to discuss the process. However, there is mounting evidence that the fundamental process and the support that automated tools must provide are fundamentally analogous between the two disciplines.

In the corresponding description of a software design process, a set of requirements would be captured, a functional specification written and an architecture generated. The process of design itself would begin by modularizing the task into a set of sub-tasks, each with its own specification and requirements. Unlike the mechanical design task described, an element is missing in the software world—there is generally no body of "old code" through which one can browse looking for designs to reuse. So new designs are generated for all components, tests are prepared, and the whole package goes off to the "analysis" stage. At this point, one runs headlong into another anomaly: the analysis for code modules generally consists of running a small number of tests on the "real thing," and the tests are often carried out by the designer as part of a tightly coupled debug cycle. Formal testing, simulation prior to coding, and formal reviews of various kinds are gaining in popularity, and require formal documentation of the modules at this stage. Finally, if it is really broken, it goes back to the designer for re-work. If it is robust enough to survive in the target environment, the code and design documentation move on to a process of formal testing, product documentation, etc.

In the real world, the design process does not stop with the manufacture of the product. Seldom is a product shipped with no defects, and even if it is defect free, changing user requirements will soon lead to the realization that the design process is embedded in a larger process of maintenance and evolution. A simplified version of this effect is shown in Figure 9-2. The effect is that the demands of the market place produce feedback which cause review of the design, possible redesign, and consequent altered design representations. In software development, we usually make a major distinction between a maintenance task (sometimes called continuing engineering) and the development of a new design.

The engineering process model, which has been outlined, can be summarized as follows. A set of requirements is generated and captured by the designer. The first step in the design process is to rephrase these requirements in a form that can be used to test the viability of a design, that is, into constraints with which an acceptable design must meet. The second step is the generation of a suitable starting point for the design process; this requires decomposing the problem into manageable pieces, and capturing the decomposition, then retrieving from historical storage a starting point for the design effort. The process continues by generating a suitable sub-design for each element from an existing design or as a new design. The sub-designs are represented in a form which the computer can support, and then subjected to analyses. The analysis programs may require that additional representations be provided for, or derived from, the basic representation. The results of the analyses are used to modify the designs until the analyses show that the requirements are met. With all requirements satisfied, the design may be represented in the form required by the manufacturing process. Re-design is triggered by the modification of the requirements, which might be caused by the discovery of problems with the original design, or by evolution of user-needs.

There is a fairly large body of research work, and many *ad hoc* tools addressing the support of mechanical design. The research efforts along this line are documented for example by Atwood,[7] Ketabchi[8] and Su.[9] Some sort of database, often "homegrown," underlies almost every tool for computer aided mechanical design on the market.

One significant factor in the previous scenario is that designs are re-used. Designers in most engineering disciplines reuse designs because it is usually cheaper and less error-prone to modify an existing design and its associated manufacturing process than it is to create a new design. Old designs are also modified when problems are identified with them and when it is necessary to

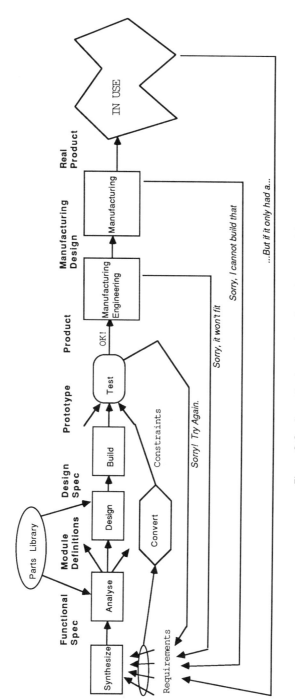

Figure 9-2. A continuing engineering schema model.

repair existing copies or to make sure that copies manufactured in the future do not contain the same problem. Software engineering recognizes this last kind of reuse but thinks of it as repair rather than reuse.

Software engineering is essentially similar to mechanical engineering in the process followed. The essential differences are related to the fact that in software, the normal representation of the design is often indistinguishable from the final replicated product, and to the fact that one has a mistaken tendency to respond to new requirements by creating a new design when modification of an existing design would be much more efficient. One tends to see the process as a one-time process and to be oblivious to the outer environment, which is at least as important for software engineering as it is for other design disciplines.

3   AN HISTORICAL PERSPECTIVE

The use of the computer as a tool in the software preparation process has been an accepted practice since the economics of interactive computing and magnetic storage have permitted. One of the first steps taken in support of this, has invariably been the storage and retrieval of the code itself, but many other kinds of support have often quickly followed. Source code management facilities, cross-reference listers, search-and-replace editors, and may other tools have been built up over the years.

In the "early days" of computing, merely a few years ago, there was almost nothing upon which to build these tools. One turned to the file management systems, which managed the storage space of the magnetic medium, and added structure to the files. Commercial source code management tools now come with many basic computer systems and are available from many independent sources. As CASE technology develops, these tools become more effective and more demanding of the mechanisms on which they are built. The use of databases is a natural continuation of the development of these tools.

The evolution of tools to support programming can fall along two related paths: the evolution of the tools, and the evolution of the environments in which the tools are used. These paths are now converging with the development of Integrated Programming Support Environments. While development and implementation of tools to assist with software development has been quite successful, the interactions required among those tools are hampered by the need, as existed in the past, to build a unique information management facility for each tool.

Database systems, a generalized information management tool, offer the opportunity to overcome this limitation.

4   WHAT'S IN A DATABASE?

There are many ways of building support facilities for software development. These range from building interface programs, which use the file system of the working environment, to the construction and use of special purpose storage systems. These extremes are the opposite ends of a spectrum of possible tools. Somewhere in the middle of the possibilities lies the class of tools called General Purpose Database Management Systems (DBMSs).

General purpose database management systems, are characterized by the following:

- support for shared access to large bodies of data,
- flexible definition of the structure of the data of interest to the specific application area, and
- the ability to attach a wide range of general purpose tools for manipulating and analyzing data.

Of course, the appropriateness of the tools and the range of the data definition facility significantly influence the utility of this class of tools for CASE applications.

Data Sharing: database systems, at least most of the DBMS tools on the market as general purpose systems, emphasize the sharing of data. This usually means the sharing of data among many users, often geographically distributed, and competing for short term access to small segments of a very large body of stored material. This emphasis may lead the reader to dismiss the use of such tools, thinking that their problems are different. Specifically, one may already have thought that a program is often not "small," and the collection of programs and other supporting material in a CASE application is seldom "large." At least a CASE database does not fit this model in the sense that the granule of data-sharing is seldom a few bytes out of many megabytes for a few seconds, but is more likely to be several thousand bytes for up to several hours. One may also have heard of databases of several gigabytes and that they were considered small databases, yet a few megabytes of source code indeed represents a large software system.

The criteria for the use of a DBMS in support of CASE applications will not be the same as those for the use of a similar tool in a banking transaction system or similar application. Nonetheless, data sharing is an essential component of the reason for using a DBMS. In addition to the need to support multiple developments, and to provide management tools for multiple-developer projects, a single user may properly demand "multi-user" support. Perhaps the best illustration of this need is the debugging situation, where an execution of the application (or a simulation) is using the database at the same time as the debugging environment, which provides the ability to control program execution and to edit the database content, and perhaps a compiler or other translation tool and the source code editor also may be running.

In the personal computer (PC) world, a new class of DBMS has been developed which supports an individual user without the overhead and complexity of the DBMS tools of the mainframe and mini-computer environments. It is hopeful that in a similar fashion DBMS tools suitable for CASE applications will become available in the PC space, the mini/workstation space and the mainframe space. For the moment, the best tools available will be found in the mini/workstation space.

4.1 Data Types and Flexibility

The primary characteristic of a DBMS seen by a CASE tool developer will be the types of data which it can support. Most DBMSs will support a variety of numeric values and text strings up to some reasonable length. Thus it is almost always possible to capture management information, such as the number of lines of code in a program, the name of the program, or the name of its author. Each DBMS has a characteristic set of data types which can be stored, interpreted and manipulated; that is, the DBMS provides a type system to the client applications, which must match the type system of the clients.

Some systems limit the set of types to a well-chosen few to get a better grip on the problem of managing storage. Many of these will require the database designer to specify a fixed length for storage allocation for such types as strings, for a similar reason. Some DBMS designers, having made very different assumptions about the applications for which their tool will be used, have arranged that all data will be stored in the form of variable-length strings. The performance characteristics of these two choices can be very different. Unfortunately, neither choice is entirely satisfactory for CASE system implementation. Computer Aided Software Engineering applications must be able to store, retrieve, and manipulate both long and variable length text, the programs, and short, fixed or limited length values representing the description of the program.

There have recently appeared a few DBMSs which allow the user a choice. One of a fixed set of built in types can be used, or the developer can specify an appropriate alternative. In addition to text, such alternatives may include things like bit-maps representing sampled images.

Another useful capability in the data type system of a DBMS is the ability to parameterize a field so that its type depends on the requirements of the specific instance. For example, the eighth descriptor of a program interface in a CASE system might specify a vector of initialization data. The data types of the elements of that vector depend on what the program is supposed to do and on the types of its internal variables. The dimensionality of the vector may also differ from program to program.

Obviously, the amount of flexibility required and the specific data types needed will vary among CASE applications. Each DBMS should be examined to determine what forms of data it will support, and what forms of flexible extension to the basic data types are supported.

4.2   Metadata—The Data Dictionary

A DBMS usually maintains a description of the data it stores. This data, which describes the data the user deals with, is called metadata. The metadata is useful to the DBMS in structuring its manipulation of storage. It is also useful to the tools of a CASE system as a guide to the handling of the stored data.

Metadata is commonly stored in a facility called a data dictionary, and the data dictionary may in turn be either a separate tool with its own storage or an integral part of the database. One of the more encouraging trends in DBMS in the past few years has been the dominance of data dictionaries stored in the database that they describe. The obvious advantage of this is that the tools which create and use the database can get access to the metadata at run-time and may do so through the same interface used to gain access to the CASE data itself.

In the previous Section, there is a discussion of the problem of data types. The data dictionary is where the data type information is recorded along with two higher levels of information about the stored information.

The highest level of information which a data dictionary supports is the notion of ''a kind of thing which will be described in the database.'' Normally it is assumed that many specific things of each kind which the database understands will be recorded. Thus, if a CASE database records information about software products, about the programs which make up a product, and about the programmers who implement the programs, each class of thing, product, program and programmer, would have a description in the data dictionary.

At the second level, one for each class of thing, a listing of the parameters which describe the class. Perhaps, for instance, programmers are described as having a name, an age, a degree, a set of specific skills, and a set of active tasks. This level of description is still generic in that all programmers recorded in the database would be described by an identical collection of attributes.

At the third level, each attribute is described by the data type(s) allowed and by any further restrictions on the range of a value which an attribute may take. It may be known, for instance, that the company has a fixed maximum retirement age and that the age of a programmer cannot exceed that limit.

At the third level, information about relationships among things may be found. Database management systems often provide ways for the database designer to record how, given an entity of class A, to find a related entity of class B. For instance, one may wish to find the author of a program, given the identity of the program. In some DBMSs this amounts to allowing the data dictionary to record that in field x of a descriptor for an entity of class y, the value is expected to be an identifier for another entity from class z. In some systems, it will also record which field of the descriptor for class z is to be compared with the identifier. In some data management systems the identifier field can be interpreted by the data manager without resort to searching for a match, a distinct advantage when data containing complex structures must be managed.

The form of the data descriptions supported by a DBMS, called the data model of the DBMS, is a major distinguishing characteristic of the different kinds of DBMSs. This issue is discussed in a later Section.

4.3   Generic Tools — Query Languages

The availability of general purpose tools—tools which can manipulate the data of an application even though they are not specifically built with the application in mind—is a major attraction of the DBMS solution. Programmers are forever performing tasks like ''find all references to data object zzxyw.'' The similarity of such tasks to the classic role of the DBMS in answering questions like ''who has blue eyes?'' should not be ignored.

Generic tools of this type are made possible by the availability of the data dictionary, and their capabilities are limited primarily by the information recorded in the data dictionary.

The most common general purpose tool is called a ''query system'' and has as its primary purpose the identification and retrieval of ''interesting'' instances in the database by the examination of their content, a process sometimes called ''associative retrieval.'' A query language is a means of describing what to look for and what to report back from the instances found. Query languages typically try to provide a simplified view of the world, based on the structure provided by the data dictionary.

A standardized query language, called SQL (Structured Query Language), has been defined and is offered with many DBMS packages. In the databases focused on the management of text, a second form is common, one in which the writing of string-matching expressions is relatively easy. Generally, the most critical aspect of query tools for CASE environments will be that all data is reachable, even data whose description may be unique to the CASE tool. If the DBMS stores programs, the query facility should be able to compare stored programs (or program fragments) with a test case and return the programs which match.

A second class of generic tools, closely related to the query system, is a report writer. Tools of this sort are normally used to format and display the material retrieved by a query. Their formatting capability and ability to deal with odd data types, such as bit-maps, is usually very limited. In conjunction with a query tool, a report writer is often used as a quick way to accomplish a simple task which will not be repeated. Both query systems and report tools have much lower performance than an equivalent program built specifically for the task.

Another group of generic capabilities is related to the fact that the primary role of the DBMS is to act as a storage manager. These tools are directed toward the management of the stored information: to protect it from un-authorized access; provide long term protection against major damage by maintaining backup copies, journals of activity, etc. In CASE applications, it seems likely that the CASE tools might want to implement specific solutions to many of the problems addressed by these generic tools since the evolution of the data of a CASE environment will differ significantly from the evolution of the data types for which these facilities were designed.

4.4   Integrity and Internal Consistency

One of the important characteristics of a database for a banking application or airline reservation system is that its content always reflects the state of the external world. In a CASE application, there is often no real world to emulate. Furthermore, in CASE, as in most design applications, it is important to record multiple possible realities—multiple possible solutions to the problem at hand, only one of which may ultimately meet the requirements.

Whereas in most applications of databases, the intent is to keep the database both internally consistent and consistent with the real world at all times, it is inherent in design applications that the designer will take a piece of the design, which may be consistent with other pieces when he or she starts, and make it inconsistent for long periods of time, possibly only returning to a state known to be consistent at the very end of the design process. Databases which support design must behave very differently than banking databases.

In the commercial databases, which shadow the real world, the common discipline is to assume that the database is consistent when an activity is started, then to group together into an atomic unit all of the changes to the database required to take it from one consistent state to another. This grouping of activities, called a transaction, all must be applied to the database safely and completely, or none must be applied. The integrity of the system in these commercial applications relies on trusted programs which act through the defensive shield of the transaction.

In design databases, it is required that the database permit inconsistent states but that it never advertise a state as consistent if it is not. To accomplish this, one may either test for consistency from the outside, or build the consistency checks into the database itself.

It is useful to be able to deal with consistency issues in a "hard" fashion, as in the case of a limitation on allowed values, or in a "soft" fashion, as in a test attached to the data, but only applied when requested. Very few DBMSs today provide an adequate constraint mechanism for the implementation of CASE applications, so the criterion must shift: the DBMS tools must be tolerant of inconsistency, and at the same time allow consistency to be tested and recorded.

As a result, the focus in support of CASE applications is currently based on the alternative view of keeping track of the evolution of the design objects, programs and program fragments in this case; and keeping track of the individual programs, fragments and collections of programs or fragments which are consistent. The former is referred to as the maintenance of versions and alternatives, the latter as the configuration management problem. Both capabilities could be provided internally if a suitable constraint facility existed, but they are most often supported externally, at present with special tools running as part of the CASE application.

5 THE DATA OF SOFTWARE ENGINEERING

The ability of a DBMS to support a particular activity depends in large part on the ability of the metadata mechanisms of the database manager to capture and make use of a suitable description of the data to be managed. In this Section, the author discusses the data associated with a CASE application to learn what a DBMS would have to manage.

It should be noted that there are many possible levels of detail at which management of CASE data would be useful. The purpose of this Chapter is to open possibilities. Therefore, this Section will explore its subject matter rather than define it.

5.1 Programs

The central objective and the central object of a CASE environment is the program. Fundamentally, the CASE environment is present to support the design, construction, and testing of programs. Programs, over their lifetimes, will have numerous different forms and representations. The most often thought of, however, is the "source code" form.

Source code, at the most basic level, is simply text—one or more strings of characters, possibly humanly readable, hopefully following the syntactic rules of a well defined programming language and hopefully implementing a semantically meaningful function within the goals of the programming effort. This high level view of source code treats the program or program fragment as a whole. It has a function and a mechanism for interpreting its meaning, but it can be described, stored, and manipulated at this level as an indivisible unit.

In database terms, programs at this level constitute large stored values. A database operating at this level would be able to capture descriptive information about the programs but would not be able to distinguish sub-structure within the program nor provide any capability based on the sub-structure. Manipulation of the internal representation of a stored program unit would be left to the CASE tools, which might retrieve the program from the database, manipulate it and return it as a unit to the database.

The important observation here is that the database stores, examines, and retrieves chunks of data. The smaller the chunk, the more effectively the database and the associated DBMS tools will be able to assist the CASE application tools. Generally, the larger the chunks, the greater the responsibility taken by the CASE tools.

5.2 Program Structure

In fact, a program fragment, at almost any level of detail, is a highly structured entity. Syntactic structures in the language invariably provide for the identification and invocation of sub-programs and functions. Syntactic structures at a lower level identify data elements and data structures manipulated by the program, and provide for the combination of these into expressions of various kinds. The relationships among the chunks allow the reconstruction of the chunks into larger program units, etc.

One extreme level of detail in the decomposition of a program is the parse tree produced by a syntax sensitive editor or the front end of a language processor which might operate on the program. At this level, the chunks stored are usually quite small, but the complexity of the relationships to be managed becomes very large. The microscopic detail becomes evident at the cost of obscuring the larger picture. For instance, in the larger picture, finding a function call with particular arguments is straightforward, a string matching problem, but interpreting the meaning of an overloaded operator is difficult. In the extreme of the parse tree, the exact meaning of the operator is easy to determine but the function call hard to find.

The observations one might draw from this discussion are two: it is important, for various tasks, to have a representation at a level of detail which is appropriate to the task at hand—no one representation is efficient for all tasks; and for some tasks a very detailed representation is important. On the other hand, most of the value of data management support will be achieved if the data system is capable of storing code fragments at the procedure, function, or sub-routine level, along with the appropriate relationships, and capable of storing interface descriptions for the stored fragments.

It is particularly important to pay attention to the issue of structure and its representation. The preceding discussion comments on the need to represent the static structures of the program, as might be captured in a parse tree. In software engineering, however, the dynamic relationships represented by control-flow and data-flow graphs are equally important. They capture important aspects of the behavior of the program and allow one to reason about it. The DBMS must be capable of capturing all of these relationships at once, and must be able to accommodate to the fact that the fundamental units of program appropriate to one structure may be inappropriate to another structure and another purpose.

5.3   Alternative Representations of Programs

The issue of alternative representations for programs deserves more examination. It was observed earlier that in most engineering disciplines the process begins with a requirements specification. In a sense, a hypothetical software element which meets a particular requirement list is perfectly well represented by the requirements, as an interface definition, for the purposes of system simulation at a higher level. Indeed, such a representation may be essential to the task of validating the requirements.

The process of software development may proceed bottom up, top down, or more commonly from both directions simultaneously. The elements of a design, at any stage of the implementation, may be connected in a data-driven or in a control-flow fashion. In the true spirit of engineering design, there may be several contending designs, competing to be the ''proper'' implementation for a particular set of requirements. The DBMS must accommodate a wide range of development disciplines.

There may be several different implementations appropriate to different tasks. For instance, one frequently ''sees'' the source code form augmented by one (or more) compiled forms of a program package. In environments supporting an interpreter, incremental compiler, or similar tools, these extremes augmented by an intermediate form are found. If we understand that an interpreter is a form of simulation engine, simulating the behavior of the program in an environment similar to that in which the compiled code will execute on some hardware platform, it is understandable that numerous other forms of simulation may exist, ranging from symbolic execution to machine simulators capable of inferring the timing of a real-time process.

In a sense, this image of alternate representations can unify the concepts of versions and alternative designs by adding the concept of an executable engine for an alternate one. Each of these forms of alternate representation for a program fragment, however, has much in common with its source code cousin. The same interface specification applies, no matter how it is implemented. Implementations differ, however, in terms of what it means to generate an alternate representation, and what effect(s) this might have on the question of whether a particular configuration is consistent or not.

5.4   Descriptions of Programs

In the previous Section one observes that for some purposes the requirements to be met by a program can serve as a sufficient description of the program itself. This is an example of the description of the interface to a program. There are, of course, significant defects in the interface specified by most requirements statements, and an interface specification alone is seldom sufficient to support all of the interesting possibilities in a CASE environment. It is, however, an essential element in support of many goals of CASE systems.

The description of the interface to a functional element implemented in software is slightly different from the description for any other sort of implementation. It must specify exactly what interactions are allowed with the object, how the object can be expected to respond and what the "visible" characteristics of the object are, that is, anything which can be known about it without interacting with it; for example, a program might export a variable or the result of a computation for reference by other programs.

The description of a program must address administrative issues as well. Who designed it? Who implemented it initially? Who has modified it since and why? How is it related to other programs, as consumer of their output, sources of information for them to process, or dependent on their interfaces? The majority of the information required for these functions amounts to interface specifications, short pieces of text (at least by comparison with the size of programs), and the identities of other programs, data paths, etc. Except for the interface specifications, there are no surprises here.

Stepping up to the highest level at which software is described, a different problem arises at the level of user's manuals and programmer's guides. Text becomes a dominant factor again. Since this book is not concerned with documentation systems nor with the support of the writing process, the comments here will be limited to a few observations: program text often gets used in the documentation; the pictorial representations used in user documentation are frequently derivable from the information about program structure stored in the CASE system for other reasons. Thus the CASE database, even if it is not used also as a document database, should support the documentation process by producing suitable textual, graphical, and pictorial representations for use in the documentation.

5.5 Interfaces and Reusability

The capture of interface specifications in the database is key to the reusability of software. The specification allows both the designer and the CASE tools to make and validate interconnections of program fragments. The form of an interface specification which must be stored depends on the way the program pieces will be connected.

An interface has two sides—outside and inside, source and sink, client and server. In the environment of a CASE system, a program is an implementation of some functionality. The program has a number of interfaces. For some of those interfaces it is a client, for some perhaps a server. In many current programming languages, the program itself specifies the interface it serves and to some degree what it expects of the interfaces upon which it calls. Unfortunately, these specifications are seldom complete. They may cover most of the syntactic issues but seldom describe constraints on information to be passed either in or out, and typically attempt no description of the semantics of the interface other than through the code itself.

In order to reuse a piece of code, the designer must be able to find it and associate it with the semantics he or she desires. A major role of the DBMS in this process is the task of searching for a match between the desired semantics and the semantics of the available pieces. Unfortunately, the proper level of description to support such a search is not at all clear. Software has the peculiar properties that it can embody rigid semantics or be re-interpreted fairly freely. For example; consider two programs, each of which accepts a list on integers and returns an ordered list of the same numbers. To know which program is appropriate to use to sort a list of medical record numbers for retrieval from the shelves, it is important to know that the first sorts directly on the input integer, and the other performs a hash function and sorts on the hashed number but returns the original. The programmer would know that medical records are stored in "terminal digit order" on the shelves. Using the program, which includes a hash function, would allow the programmer to confine his modifications to the replacement of the hash function by a decimal-digit-reversal. This approach not only reduces the likelihood of introducing a bug but structures the code so that future changes in retrieval mechanism can be made easily.

Many pieces of code are difficult to reuse because they have side-effects. Yet it is sometimes those side-effects which are important in selecting a piece of code for reuse. A programmer who wants to display a plot of a data set is concerned whether the result will appear on the display screen, on a plotter which he/she does not have or as a data structure to be displayed by some other program. Side-effects are an important characteristic of the description of a program. If side-effects have side-effects, as well they might, it would be important for the DBMS, in processing a query, to be able to trace all of the secondary effects of executing a piece of code.

Frequently, when a piece of code, which is of interest to the programmers is found, it refers to another piece of code. Thus reusing a program requires that we reuse all of the program fragments on which it depends. As with side-effects, the DBMS must record the dependencies among program elements and accumulate them so as to present a true picture of the consequences of using a piece of existing code.

5.6   Requirements and Constraints

In the initial discussion of the engineering processes, which opened this Chapter, there was discussion of requirements and the translation of requirements into constraints. This conversion and the imposition of the constraints which result normally take place at the interfaces of programs. In large measure, it is the imposition of an evaluation of constraint specifications which allows using a DBMS as a tool in the validation of a software system.

A constraint on the type, representation, and range limit of an input variable is matched against the type, representation, and expected range of an output variable to determine that a particular connection is permissible. Thus these characteristics of each input and each output must be recorded in the interface specification of each program module.

The invocation of a particular program or function may be permissible only under certain conditions. For example, the compilation of code may be permissible only after an interface validation has been performed.

These and other constraints can be supported in a CASE environment through the use of either a special constraint language or the query language of the DBMS. Query and constraint mechanisms have much in common: the role of a query system is usually to answer questions of the form "does there exist anything in the database with these characteristics?" The role of a constraint mechanism is to answer the question "Does this item in the database have these characteristics?" The difference, to a first order, is that the system knows that it is to test only one case, "this one," when processing a constraint. In the more general query situation, it is expected to look for, find, and evaluate all possible candidates.

Thus the existence of a high quality query facility can serve as a mechanism for implementing constraints, particularly if the database is capable of storing query specifications, and the query processor can be invoked programmatically with a stored specification.

5.7   The Data of the Program

A DBMS can be a useful adjunct to a CASE system if all it does is describe programs and their interfaces. If it is capable of storing and managing the code itself, so much the better. Even better is a DBMS with the ability to capture, and even impose constraints on its content, thus guaranteeing a level of semantic integrity within the database. But what happens when it comes time to test the programs that have been built with the CASE system?

5.8   Design Environment and Run-Time Environment

The CASE environments previously used tended to focus on the end of the process—on what we do after the implementation of a program is "finished." They have focused on the testing of programs and have had as a primary function the provision of an environment for testing which controlled the program during the test.

In the past, one usually managed this by building their CASE tool, the "debugger," for the expected run-time environment of the application being built. Occasionally, for instance, when building the operating system for a not-yet-extant machine, one would simulate that run-time environment. When the database used for the CASE system coincides with the DBMS environment expected by the program to be tested, or when the DBMS can emulate that environment, one has a particularly powerful situation.

As will be discussed in the next Section, the various forms of DBMSs available offer different levels of capability for emulating a run-time environment. There are significant issues concerning the construction of programs which influence the viability of this technique as well.

If it is to be possible to use the database to emulate the run-time environment of the program, the database and the CASE tool applications must provide for the storage and retrieval of data consistent with the interface specifications of the program under test. This can get to be a rather demanding requirement in extreme cases, such as programs which manipulate seismic data or satellite images, where the 'emulation' is at least as hard as the management of the 'real' data, but for ordinary situations, it can prove quite workable.

The interfaces of most programs involve not only data values transferred but also procedural components. These may take the form of functions, procedures, or whole programs to be invoked, or various sorts of requests to the program under test. While most database systems would be unable to provide all of these interfaces directly, they can often support the simple creation of dummy or stub implementations, through the storage of input-output data sets, precomputed to provide suitable test examples.

5.9   Testing and Test Evaluation

This raises the subject of tests and test evaluation. One of the major values of a DBMS is the availability of tools for the extraction and analysis of the data contained in the database. Whether the database is intimately connected to the testing process or not, it can be used effectively by recording the results of the tests in the database. Once recorded, they can be analyzed for conformance with the requirements, restated of course as constraints or queries, and may be compared against earlier executions of the same tests to determine whether a particular set of changes improved compliance or not. This use would, of course, represent a traditional use of a database.

The interface specification of the program under test again plays a significant role in the use of the DBMS. The interface specification of the program, at least in so far as it addresses the type, representation, and constraints applicable to the input and output values of the program, maps directly to the data definition for the test data and the results of the test to be stored in the database.

An Observation on Coincidences

At this point in the discussion, before leaving the characteristics of the problem domain to examine the characteristics of available DBMS models, it is worthwhile taking a step back to examine what has been presented. There are a number of coincidences and ''unholy'' alliances in the presentation.

The first observation is the frequency which the interface specification for the program being developed appears in the requirements for the database system. This should not be surprising; after all, the interface specification was a way of defining legal matches between the elements of a software system. The metadata stored in the data dictionary of a DBMS is, in fact, the definition of the vast majority of the interface to a DBMS and its stored databases. The DBMS gets its flexibility by allowing the user to describe an interface that the DBMS is to provide, precisely the capability required in the CASE application, where the interface to a program under development and test are to be described.

The second observation is that this interface modeling is in large measure why general purpose databases exist. By allowing for the definition and redefinition of interfaces, DBMSs foster the integration of otherwise unrelated applications which share data to implement a larger and broader whole. It is now understood that CASE environments have a special character: they are built of software as tools for the construction of other software, and they share data with the software built under their control.

6 DATA MODELS AND MODEL LEVELS FOR CASE

The characteristic of a DBMS, which most distinguishes it from other software systems, is the mechanism it supports for describing data. This mechanism usually assumes some fairly specific characteristics about the world it is to describe and the objects which populate that world. The term DATA MODEL is used to identify the abstract descriptive mechanism, and DBMSs fall into a relatively small set of categories according to the data model they support. In this Section, the author will explore the data models of several types of DBMSs, which are currently of interest, and compare their capabilities in the context of the requirements of CASE applications as previously examined.

In the DBMS, there is a mechanism for describing data, the data to be stored. The description provides an abstraction—a model—for the stored data. The stored data may in turn be a model for some external object and its behavior. In the CASE environment, the stored data may include one or more models for a software system and finally the software system itself.

All CASE applications are unique among design support tools in the requirement that the tools be able to represent and manipulate objects which may use similar or even identical tools in performing their assigned tasks. At times the following discussion may become confusing because of a DBMS to be addressed that stores and manipulates an entity which in turn may implement a DBMS or use one in the course of its activities.

6.1 Criteria for Evaluating Data Models

In the previous Sections, we have taken a careful in-depth look at the data storage requirements of CASE systems and the uses which we might expect to make of the data. In order to evaluate specific DBMS models, we need to narrow the discussion to a few criteria which are easily discussed. To get to a set of manageable criteria, we will revisit the preceding discussion from a more abstract point of view.

The Atomic Unit of Data—Levels of Model

The first question, which must be answered in examining a DBMS, is what is it able to model? What is the unit to be described, and what forms of description apply? If one is modeling blocks of wood as seen by a child, each block would be described by a small set of values, perhaps a characteristic shape and two or three dimensions appropriate to the shape. The manufacturer might also be interested in the wood used and the price and date manufactured. In any event, however, the description is simple and one dimensional: it consists of at most an ordered list of values taken from an ordered list of domains.

To a plant biologist, however, the wood block is not simple at all: it has substructure. The grain of the wood reflects the growth history of the tree from which it was cut. The grain structure may reveal the age of the tree, if something is known about how the block was cut from the tree. Perhaps the structure of the fibers, and even their chemical content, would allow a curious biologist to understand from what diseases the tree suffered, and what nutrients were prominent in the soil in which it grew.

A CASE database should include the following criteria:

1. It must describe and store simple entities, such as program text units, programmers, and projects. To this end, it must handle numeric, string, and date values, and store and retrieve text without limitation on its content.
2. Store multiple values for a single attribute; for example, a list of modification dates, or input parameters might be required.
3. Entities stored in the database must be identifiable as distinct, in spite of the possibility that one may have attribute values identical to another.
4. Store and refer to complex objects; that is, objects composed of other objects. Thus the identifier of another entity must be a legitimate attribute value.

It is necessary to be concerned with the ability to describe data at many different levels of detail and to create models at several levels of abstraction in various parts of the CASE application. Many of the entities to be described will be built up by describing smaller elements. The descriptions may be in the form of text, traditional data values, such as numerical parameters or selections from an enumeration.

Modeling Dependencies and Relationships

Seldom will it be sufficient for the system to store only the descriptions of the basic entities. Many applications will require that linkages be maintained among loosely related entities—a program and its author. Finally, there is the problem of storing program structures: data-flow graphs and control-flow graphs, cross-reference structures and dependency graphs all must be accommodated if the database is to capture the essential elements of the software design process.

To simplify the evaluation of the data models as they handle relationships, two basic paradigms to be examined are: the decomposition of a program as might be seen in a top-down design process, and the relationship between a program and its authors. The first, sometimes referred to as a parts decomposition, is characteristic of many forms of graphical relationships. The latter is characteristic of list or set-valued relationships.

Further criteria for a CASE database include the following:

5. The DBMS must be able to store arbitrary relationships among the entities it describes.
6. Retrieve sets of related entities. It must be possible to define the concept of a related entity either inside the object, by its direct relationships, or externally, by specifying a collection of entities directly.
7. Where a group of entities is related implicitly via a set of attribute values, it must be possible for the database system to construct an explicit collection when required.

There are a number of pitfalls in this portion of the requirements list; for example, graph structures with cycles are likely to cause difficulty for all but the most sophisticated retrieval mechanism. It would be of interest to attach attributes to a relationship between objects.

Where database systems handle the storage and retrieval of data about a single entity, its representation, more or less identical at the lowest level, they handle the matter of relationships very differently. Each data model has a method of dealing with relationships, but the performance implications for the methods employed are very different.

Interfaces and Constraints

The representation of an interface is a key element of the description of a piece of software. An interface characteristically consists of two pieces, the set of exported data values, and the set of entry points, each with its associated sets of input parameters, possible returned values and error conditions. When constraints are used, they usually identify a condition which must be met at an entry point for the entry point to be used or a condition that the remainder of the system may rely upon when an entry point returns. Less commonly, constraints may be stated in such a way that they can be relied upon only under limited circumstances. In CASE applications these "occasional" constraints will often be validated by a tool under the control of the user.

Unlike the usage which is common in database tools supporting constraints, the constraints required in CASE applications are dynamic rather than static. It is not so much that some state of the database be met whenever one is able to "see" that state, rather when an interface element is accessible during execution of the program, the constraint be satisfied.

The last three criteria for the evaluation are the following:

8. It must be possible to associate either with entity types or with their data values one or more constraints. It must be possible to evaluate the constraint, when an attempt is made to modify the entity to which it is attached, and the failure of the constraint must be able to prevent the update to the database.
9. It must be possible to access, during the processing of a constraint, entities other than the one which triggered the constraint.
10. The combination of the manner in which interfaces are described and the manner in which constraints are implemented must permit constraint specifications to check that interface specifications are met.

These criteria are less explicitly defined than preferred for the following evaluation. The reason is relatively straightforward: while a few constraint systems and a few interface validation mechanisms have been built, there is by no means a consensus about how to describe or implement such mechanisms in most of the models which will be discussed. Thus most of this discussion will be based on the availability of conceivable solutions.

The Relational Model

The Relational Model[10] is the most common model being sold today. It has largely replaced the older hierarchical and network models in the sales of new database tools, though as with most new technology, replacement of the older models will not occur for some time. The model dates from research done at IBM in the early 1970s and has, as its major claim to fame, the simplicity of its model of the world.

In a relational database, all entities are assumed to belong to groups of entities, and within a group, it is presumed that the description of an individual is the same for all individuals.

Individuals are presumed to be identifiable, and distinguishable from all other individuals, by one or more sets of values in its description. Within a group of entities, the appropriate description is an ordered list of values drawn from an ordered list of domains. The simplicity of this model allows a mathematical treatment of the abstract structure; one of the reasons it was originally attractive.

The usual visual representation of a relational database is as a collection of tables, called relations. Each table represents a different type of entity, perhaps one for programs and another for their authors. An entry (row) in a table, sometimes referred to as a tuple, represents a unique individual of the type described by the table. Each column in a table represents a descriptor, and its associated domain of values. All entities described by a particular table have the same set of descriptors and the same domains for the descriptors. Relationships between individuals in different tables are represented by values stored in the descriptors. Figure 9-3 shows a simplified schema, such as might be used in a CASE system.

In this model, an object is found by searching the relation to which it belongs, looking for records whose content matches the value(s) given as its identifier. Looking for ''Sam'' is essentially identical to looking for ''green eyed people.'' A relational system will usually support one or more methods of indexing, and some concept of linkage between the relations. The database designer can take advantage of these bits of knowledge embedded in the database system to speed up access, such as access by name, or to provide the system with ways of finding efficient linkages. Generally speaking, an attempt is made in the relational model to concentrate the information about the meaning of the data, and in particular the relationships among stored elements, in the applications program or in the head of the user, rather than in the data itself.

In relational systems, the integrity of the data depends on the completeness, accuracy and integrity of the programs operating on it. For example, suppose that a PERSON record has attributes which are the identifiers of the person's parents. If a parent record is deleted, and the child record is not properly updated, a dangling reference is created. This problem, commonly called the ''referential integrity problem,'' has recently been attacked by adding to the data dictionary a form of constraint which warns of or forcibly corrects some forms of this error. In general, however, the formal definition of the relational model does not include support for constraints or other integrity enhancement mechanisms.

Relative to our criteria for utility, we find the relational model quite compatible with the requirements for the storage of case data (criterion 1), except for the storage of the program text. Some recent relational implementations and extensions of commercial relational-model systems, have supported a ''data type'' which is large and unstructured. This is one solution to the text problem. Perhaps a better solution though is to adopt the technique used in a number of source-code control and configuration management systems in the past ten years—to use a ''private'' portion of the file system of the local storage environment to store program text and to store in the database the file names under

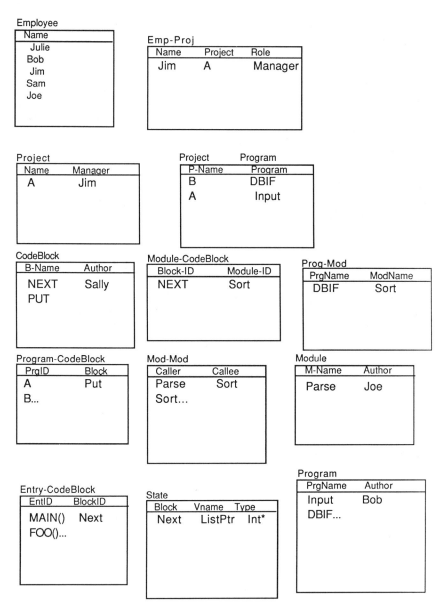

Figure 9-3. A simple relational schema for CASE.

which the text has been "hidden." Because this imposes more burden on the programmer of the CASE tools than the basic relational model does, it is an acceptable solution.

While multiple-valued attributes are not properly supported in a relational model (criterion 2), they are frequently provided. This is often the result of trying to move users from older models, the CODASYL network model in particular, where the multiple-valued attribute is the basic model. Since this capability is central to the ability to store complex, structured entities (criterion 4), it is essential that this mechanism be available.

In general, relational systems do not provide directly for an explicit identifier (criterion 3). However, many implementations of relational systems are built upon older methodology and, therefore use an identifier internally. Furthermore, in the worst case, it is simply necessary to allocate one field to a unique identifier, and the system will usually provide support for maintaining uniqueness.

Criterion 4, support for complex entities, can be restated as support for part/ sub-part decompositions. While a suitable data structure can be built up through a "cell" concept with two to four identifiers, the availability of "set valued" attributes, a "sub-parts" attribute whose references point to other "parts," makes the task of the programmer much easier. Parts are, of course only one kind of relationship of interest (criterion 5). The key-field mechanisms of the relational DBMS are sufficient.

The query language of the relational world, of which the *ad hoc* standard is SQL, is excellent at allowing the retrieval of arbitrarily defined collections of related entities. Criterion 6 is satisfied.

One of the major deficiencies of the relational model is the need to search recursively in order to generate a "parts explosion" for any given assembly. In the CASE world, that means that the problem of finding all of the code which might be executed as a result of invoking some high level function can be arbitrarily complex. Unless performance is of no consequence, the relational model fails on criterion 7. This problem with relational systems effects the utility of the DBMS for a wide range of tasks. The prevalence of these tasks led at least one researcher[11] to add a "transitive closure" operation to the relational query language. This operation computes a closed collection of objects that (under some criteria) refer to each other, do not refer to objects outside the collection, and do not include any object which is not referenced by another object in the collection.

Constraint mechanisms do not fit directly into the model provided by relational database systems. Relational systems, as indicated above, usually assume that all of the procedural "knowledge" required by the user is associated with the application program. Some commercial relational DBMS packages are now providing a form of constraint mechanism, often aimed specifically at the maintenance of referential integrity. In general, however, relational systems are very weak in this respect.

Since the constraint mechanism must be associated with application code, it cannot generally be any more secure and correct than the application code and clearly cannot be relied upon to provide an independent enforcement mechanism. However, since there are no restrictions on things which general applications code can do, the letter of the criteria can be met even though the spirit cannot be. In many systems it may be easier to use the system query language to implement constraints than to use a procedural language interface to the database. This does not, however, make the data any more secure or improve the conclusion that relational systems are weak on the Criteria that address constraints.

Although the use of constraints to enforce interface specifications is limited by the weak constraint systems available, the modeling of interfaces is possible. Whether the target programming language supports abstract data types or not, the goal in a CASE tool environment is to make code reusable and verifiable by encapsulating modules in the descriptive envelope of an abstraction. The interface specification will have two components, one describing the state exported by the module, and one describing the procedural interfaces of the module.

The description of the exported state is fairly straightforward in a relational system. Any state variable will be described by its name, its underlying data type, and possibly a range restriction or other constraint. This fixed number of descriptive attributes fits the relational model's table format well—so long as the constraints are described elsewhere and only referenced in the interface specification.

The description of the procedural interface is somewhat more complicated. The hope in any database environment is that the description of a class of things, procedural interfaces in this case, will be common to all members of the class. Unfortunately, while there are a small number of common elements to the description of an entry point, there is much variation as well. Each entry will have a name, and a calling convention or similar specification of how the service requestor is to communicate with it. It will also include the identification of all formal parameters, state modifications, and returned values.

There are two problems here: it is absolutely necessary that sets of arbitrary size be available for listing the parameters, and it is necessary as a practical matter that the description allow the type, and therefore the appropriate description, of some parameters to depend on the value of other parameters. All of this is possible in most relational systems at the cost of using four or more tables in the descriptions, and the cost of doing the associated JOIN operations (to link the appropriate elements of an interface together) when an interface check is to occur. Sets in relational systems can be implemented by the user by giving the set an identifier, placing the set members in a table (with the members of all other sets of the same kind), and using the set identifier to retrieve the members when they are needed.

Modeling software module interfaces using a relational database system is possible, but painful. The resulting model will be expensive to use because of all of the table linkages which are required. Furthermore, because the definition of an interface is scattered far and wide through the database, the user of the CASE tool must rely on the tool to gather together the information. The database provides little assistance.

6.2   The File System Model

File systems have been the mainstay storage mechanism of CASE tools in the past. A small diversion is appropriate here to place them in perspective. File systems, and their associated directories, can be viewed as a database which supports the storage and retrieval of large, usually unstructured objects. Sometimes they also support the structuring of the stored objects as a collection of "records." For whatever grain size(s) they support, they provide for the identification, storage, and retrieval of the objects, and also for the maintenance of support information: time of creation or modification, owner identity, and access control information. They may also support a limited amount of descriptive text, provide concurrency control via a lock system, etc.

A great deal of success has been achieved at the level of source code management and configuration management with commercially available tools based on files. All of these tools, of course, are achieved by the addition of significant capability in the application program layer. Recent explorations of the problems posed by using a file system and its supporting directories as a basis for CASE efforts have included work by Nestor[5] and Leblang.[12]

In terms of the evaluation criteria, Criteria 1, 2, and 4 are not met for the simple reason that there is no direct support for sub-structure at the levels required: there is no concept of an attribute within a stored object. Criterion 3—identification—is met at the level of granularity supported, and most directory systems provide a sufficient level of support for finding the stored entities. Except for the possibility of mapping a hierarchical decomposition of an entity onto the hierarchical structure of a directory system, relationships among the stored entities are generally not supported. Thus Criteria 5, 6, and 7 are not met. Similarly, there is no support for constraints, so criteria 8, 9, and 10 cannot be satisfied except by transferring responsibility for constraint management to the application program.

Nonetheless, the level of success, which has been achieved with file based tools, is remarkable.

6.3   The Entity-Relationship Model

The entity-relationship model was introduced by Peter Chen.[13] It has a number of manifestations as modeling tools for the design of databases and as tools which provide the model as the interface to the database user. This model and the Object Model described in the next sub-Section are examples of a class of models called "semantic models" because of the way they capture information about the meaning and use of the data as well as its structure.

The intent of the entity-relationship model is to model the relationships among database entities directly and to provide a way to associate information with the relationships themselves. Thus in an E-R model it is possible to note that the price paid for a car is an attribute of the relationship between the car and its owner and not properly an attribute of either the car or the owner. E-R models are most often built upon an older database model, often a relational model. Because of this implementation choice, they will inherit the limitations of the underlying data model except where the modeling extensions are a dominant factor. Figure 9-4 reproduces the schema for our CASE example in an entity-relationship diagram.

An E-R model provides a significant benefit over the relational models in the maintenance of set-valued attributes (viewed as 1 to N relationships) and in the modeling of complex objects (using relationships as a structuring paradigm for the objects). Thus Criteria 2, 4, 5, and 6 are better met with an E-R database. This is true in essence, because the E-R interface takes care of recognizing and taking advantage of the relationships defined among database entities. It hides from the user and application all of the task of identifying and retrieving the collection of related entities.

Because the relationship is a first class entity in the model, E-R models are also better able than relational databases to maintain referential integrity, to maintain inverse relationships, and to place constraints on the cardinality of a relationship. This enhances the ability of the model to deal with Criteria 8 and 10. The existence of the relationship as a place to attach constraints and the possibility of using the relationship and its attributes, as the description of an interface, greatly enhances the utility of the E-R model for CASE applications.

On the other hand, E-R model databases will not solve the problems inherent in text management. They will carry through the vices of the underlying storage manager, particularly performance limitations. Unless a query facility built specifically for the E-R environment is provided, access to the data for nontool uses (for example, management purposes) will have the behavior and limitations of the underlying model, not of the E-R model. The E-R model, although semantically richer than many other models, is still essentially a record-based DATA model. The limitations of record-based models have been explored in detail by William Kent.[14]

6.4   The Object Model

The Object Model is very new in database terms. E. F. Codd's first papers on the principles of relational systems appeared at the end of the 1960s and early in the 1970s. The first papers on E-R models appeared in the mid 1970s. The first papers on object-based models for databases appeared in the early 1980s. The heritage of object models is long, dating to at least the Simula-67 effort in mid-1960s, and varied, including efforts in the language research community, the AI community, and the database community. Far from arising as a point solution to a particular problem, object concepts appear to arise as a common solution to a very wide range of problems. Knowledge representation, office systems, and programmer productivity have all led to object concepts, but no

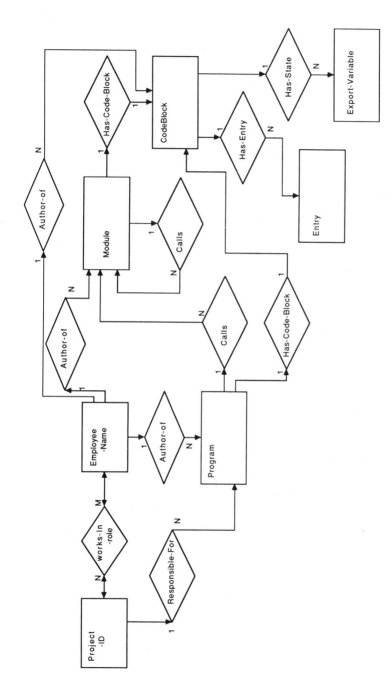

Figure 9-4. The CASE schema as an entity-relationship model.

portion of the software community has recognized a need for object techniques more than the community building software tools to support design applications.

Object systems (see P. Wegner[15] for a discussion of the key characteristics of an object system) combine the characteristics of abstract data type systems, a strong model of identity for things represented (hence "objects"), and a concept of extensibility through inheritance from one abstract data type to another. The abstract data type concept allows the programmer to encapsulate the state of an object within a procedural interface. Inheritance provides a way to reuse both the procedural and state portions of previously defined types in the definition of new types, and often allows the state the procedural interface or both to be modified ("refined") as they are inherited.

Because of the abstract data type character of an object system, an object model database has some fundamentally distinct characteristics. A procedural model is added to the data model, and a procedural interface to the data, even the visible data, is introduced. This greatly expands the level of support for constraints and for the introduction of new basic data types.

In an object model database, the conceptual structure is one of a graph of related objects, where each arc in the graph represents a relationship in the database and each node, or object in the graph is represented by a body of visible state, the attributes or properties of the object, and a collection of allowable operations which may be applied to the object. Both properties and operations are defined in an interface specification for things of that type. This structure is used for referring to and manipulating the stored objects, both programmatically and during interactive *ad hoc* query access. Figure 9-5 shows the CASE schema example in object form.

Historically, the first major coalescence of object concepts occurred in Smalltalk. As a result, there is an unusual terminology associated with some object systems; for example, the term CLASS is sometimes used where TYPE is more appropriate, and instead of "operating on" an object, the phrase "send a message to object x" is used. There are some technical differences between the message paradigm and the operation paradigm, but they are not material here. It is important here to note the implication, embedded in the phrase about messages, that the database is an active entity. The mere fact of touching an innocent looking piece of data causes code to be executed, and that code can be used to do nearly anything which is appropriate.

There are several ways in which the basic facilities of an object database can be implemented. By far the largest group of existing implementations has been achieved by extending an existing database, often a relational system. As indicated in the previous Section, this tends to carry forward both the virtues and the vices of the original. Another group of implementations has occurred in the LISP community. Due to significant limitations in communicating from LISP systems to non-LISP systems, the LISP-based tools have not been widely

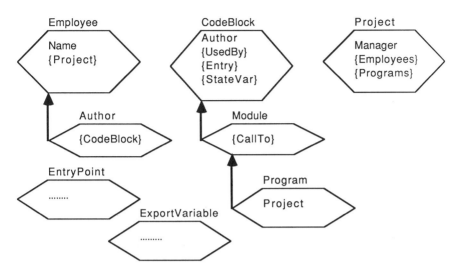

Figure 9-5(a). An object model for the CASE schema.

used. In the last two years, products have become available which implement object system behavior directly. These latter products provide more of the value discussed here than do the other solutions. Main-stream technology and LISP-based object systems are commercially available. Object systems built upon relational databases exist in a number of research laboratories and will become available from many database vendors over the next three years. Many software houses supporting the design community have built partial implementations of object databases for internal use.

To maintain a consistent view, a main-stream object system will be used for comparison against the criteria for database support for CASE. It should be noted, however, that there is a wide variation among the few object systems currently available. Object systems based on non-object storage systems will have limitations which can be inferred from the nature of the underlying model. A full object model is capable of directly implementing all of the other data models discussed in this Chapter. Because of the fundamental character of an object system as an active system, other models can support partial emulation of an object system but cannot subsume them. The object model appears to be an extensible superset of all other models generally available.

Object models support the usual array of base data types, numbers, strings, etc., and in addition support a range of aggregate types, such as sets, lists, queues, etc. They support the relationship directly and can support relationships as first class objects if the relationship must have attributes. Since aggregates are treated as objects, allowing an object, say a person, to have a set-valued property, perhaps the set of children of that person, is straightforward. Thus Criteria 1, 2, 3, and 5 are met directly.

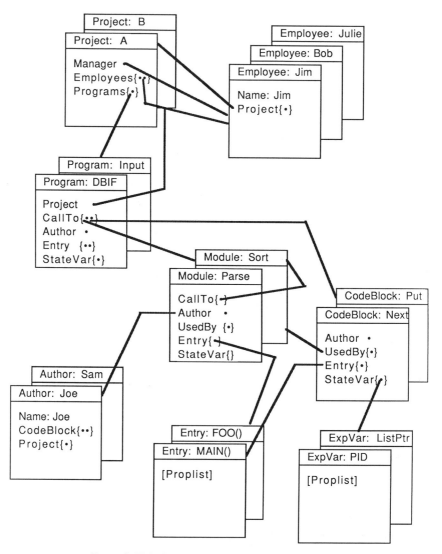

Figure 9-5(b). The data in an object model for CASE.

Object models deal with complexity very easily. When the programmer holds the identifier for an object, the amount of storage required for that object is generally not known nor is it material to the programmer. The fact that an ''F-15 Fighter Aircraft'' object is associated, via its sub-parts property, with a parts breakdown of more than 585,000 parts, associated into numerous sub-assemblies and each with its own description, specifications, etc., is not material to the programmer. The F-15 is an object and is no harder to handle than a single screw from its parts breakdown. The object representing the NASA Space Station On-Board Software System is no harder to handle than the portion of that software which controls the temperature in the commander's office—each is simply an object. Criterion 4 is satisfied.

Criteria 6 and 7 are related to the problems of aggregation and associative retrieval. Since explicit aggregates are supported in all object systems, the first level requirement for retrieval of related objects is met. However, it is also important, in an environment characterized by nested decomposition, to be able to generate the transitive closure of the parts of an assembly. This facility is rarely available. Where needed, the user must implement a graph-walking program. The user may be required to maintain an explicit aggregate or configuration representing the closure. On the other hand, since the database is active, it is easy to automate the maintenance of such aggregates when they are appropriate.

An object system implements its active behavior by maintaining a relationship between the type of an object and the code which may manipulate such objects. This relationship is typically represented in the form of a dispatch mechanism, which given an object and a requested operation or message finds the code which implements the operation. This dispatch mechanism provides a natural place to attach triggers, constraints, assertion enforcers, and all manners of other code which need to be sensitive to what data is touched, what operation was requested or who is requesting the action. Most object databases directly provide for the attachment of code to implement triggers or constraints. In all cases, the trigger code or constraint code is at least as free to manipulate objects and the environment as ordinary application code would be, thus Criteria 8 and 9 are satisfied.

Criterion 10 raises some interesting points about object systems. The description given earlier in this Chapter for the critical aspects of the specification of an interface to a code module looks suspiciously like the description of the interface to an abstract data type in the object system. Well it might, because the two are essentially identical in basic form. Indeed the type-checking system of the object environment is performing the same tasks, both statically and dynamically, that the interface verification mechanism of the CASE tool is doing. This suggests two methods by which Criterion 10 can be satisfied: one might use TYPES to describe and provide an implementation for code modules, or if the type system of the object system is sufficiently different from the type system of the target environment, the object system can be used to implement the conceptual elements of the target type system and its interface specification (entry points, arguments, argument specifications, etc.).

With respect to the ten basic criteria proposed, the object model appears almost complete.

6.5   The Hypertext Model[16]

The hypertext model is based on the concept that much information can be organized according to levels of detail. The classic example might start with the table of contents of a book. A user would identify a topic of interest, allowing the system to descend a level to the summary for a Chapter. When the user selects an entry in the summary, the text of the Chapter appropriate to that topic might be brought up and then a graph providing elaboration on the topic, or a photograph of a person mentioned in the text, etc.

This model has a great deal of appeal due to its relationship to the top-down design methodologies and to the composition mechanisms associated with bottom-up methodologies. In general, if all, or nearly all, of the structure of a complex object in the CASE domain were hierarchical, the hypertext paradigm might be appropriate. Certainly it may be appropriate as an interaction metaphor where the metaphor fits the structural aspects of the design methodology of the tools.

While the hypertext methodology clearly has an advantage over a file system methodology in providing structure and navigational retrieval, it lacks many of the basic facilities for which we sought database methodology. Think of the graph which is traversed by the interactions described. Unless the hypertext nodes are augmented by information about the ''text'' at that node, Criteria 1 through 3 are not met. In general, only one form of relationship is supported, limiting the utility of the methodology and compromising Criterion 5.

There are other severe limititations inherent in a pure hypertext solution, but there are many advantages to a hypertext solution in conjunction with a traditional database. The database is augmented by a system capable of storing and manipulating the text which is so difficult in a pure database. The database and its associative retrieval mechanisms can be used to create alternative relationships in the hypertext system, to annotate the connections with interface specifications, and the like. The hypertext mechanism provides a structural framework to which one can attach many kinds of other information. The key to making this marriage of hypertext and DBMS work would be the possibility of passing information from the hypertext environment to tools invoked ''in context'' at user direction.

6.6   Older Models

There are a number of older data models which might be considered, including hierarchical and network models. All of the record based models, including IMS and IMS-like hierarchical and CODASYL network models suffer from the same basic limitations as the relational model. Network models are sometimes seen at the core of homegrown design databases because of the rich structuring mechanisms they provide. Some vendors have elected to retain the network-model underpinnings when implementing their relational products, and most network model vendors are now providing relational style query systems as interfaces to the older facilities.

In general, since the best of these older models are equivalent to the E-R models in expressiveness and support for the requirements of CASE, and since in most cases E-R models are better, there seems little point in reviewing the older models in detail. The extent to which these older models force the application to take over the semantic interpretation of the data they store argues for leaving them behind as far as CASE applications are concerned.

6.7 Levels of Modeling Revisited

A look back at the discussions of the specific models reviewed will reveal that there is a wide variation in the level of modeling supported. The hierarchical, network, and relational data models support the description, storage, and manipulation of most data needed in a CASE environment but fail to support the critical aspects of structural relationships, the storage and manipulation of structured text and the management and imposition of constraints well enough to be effective. The E-R model captures the structural concepts well but still fails to support text or constraints well. Hypertext, by itself is not very helpful. In conjunction with one of these data models and supported by a good interface to the tools which will manipulate the text, can provide a significant improvement. Object systems, at least at this level of analysis, meet the major needs of a CASE system.

The record-based data models support the storage and manipulation of information about the entities with which CASE works and can store most of the basic data types supported by the languages which CASE tools will manipulate. They do not, however, manage well either the subject matter of CASE, program text, and executable text, or the procedural aspects of maintaining a safe CASE environment.

The addition of a hypertext framework to the capabilities of a record-based model enhances the ability of the management environment to handle the subject matter of CASE. Since hypertext is largely about the interactions between users and structured text, the hypertext framework may provide other useful forms of support to the CASE system designer.

The object model, apparently flexible and extensible enough to meet all of the basic requirements, models and manages not only the subject matter (text) and its structure but also deals with the description and constraint problems as well. Object models of course have their negative side: more work may have to be done to get started, since existing object-model products tend to come from the vendor in an "empty" form, devoid of any useful CASE-oriented concepts.

6.8 Some Additional Issues

There are a number of issues beyond the modeling issues that have been addressed in this chapter. Many of these issues are current topics in the research community and not beneficiary of any reasonable consensus at this point in time. This Section will try to point out the issues and to identify the important characteristics in a CASE context. Specifically, the problem of concurrency control, the use of the database to support simulation, and the use and capabilities of query facilities will be addressed.

Transactions and Concurrency Control

The transaction models supported by most current DBMSs are derived to serve the requirements of either the on-line data entry and edit application or a decision support application. In the former, transactions involve very little processing, typically less than a few seconds, and are based on user interactions with the system which last at most a few minutes. As a result, the systems are tuned for low rates of interaction between transactions and assume that a transaction can be backed out and retried with impunity. In the latter, the interaction is primarily a retrieval and formatting function, and while a session may last an hour or more, database updates are infrequent and relatively simple.

In a design environment, the length of time devoted to a session is often many hours and sometimes days. The conceptual transaction extends from the time the first element of a design is picked up from the database, to the time the last change is committed. The transaction will involve numerous changes to the design, all of which must succeed for the session to be successful. In some design settings, such a transaction will last a week or more and involve thousands of high level, perhaps hundreds of thousands of low level, changes to the data. It is simply not acceptable to tell a designer after a week's work that the system was not able to complete the transaction in a consistent manner. For this reason, most design systems operate on a pre-reservation or "check out" mode. The designer reserves the material he or she requires prior to beginning work and may acquire additional portions of the design as the task progresses.

Under this discipline, there is a premium on allowing the designer to control the level of granularity of the reservation. Sharing designs with other workers is effectively accomplished by breaking the design down into small enough pieces so that maximum progress can be made but keeping the granularity large until a need arises so that there is a very high probability that any portions of the design which might need to be added to the critical set for a particular transaction have a high probability of being already under the control of the designer. Although transaction models like this have been discussed in the literature, and although check-out/check-in algorithms are in common use for custom design-management software, they are generally absent from the commercial database market.

An alternative, which has been explored in a number of experimental systems and is used in a number of configuration management tools, is to use the history of modifications to a design as a control mechanism. In this paradigm, the designer picks up the elements to be worked on as of some specific time and is allowed to complete work no matter what competing changes occur in the database between start and finish. This is accomplished by recognizing each revision to the database as an independent entity and allowing a set of revisions to become the *de facto* new state of the database only if no conflict occurs. If there is conflict, the new set of changes becomes an alternative reality, an alternative design.

In such a scenario, based as it is on an object having a number of possibly valid states, each possible state of an object, each possibly valid configuration of object states, and each sequence of changes must be distinguishable. While it is usually possible to achieve this effect at the application program level, it is much easier to use the tool environment if the proper choice can be made without human intervention, at least most of the time. This in turn requires that the DBMS support a naming structure which allows access to the default "current" version when no qualification is given, yet retrieves the correct version when asked. The system must also support the elimination of extraneous branches of the tree through merger of two "conflicting" designs. The latter may of course require human intervention. Although there has been considerable use of such versioning systems in code management tools and configuration management systems, there appear to be no commercial DBMS products that support this facility directly. Both a better transaction model and version support at the DBMS level are necessary for the success of DBMS tools in design environments, especially in support of CASE.

Modeling Run-time Data

One of the principal functions of a CASE environment is the management and support of the process of finding and removing defects in the software. A number of techniques have been developed, ranging from a control and observation mechanism in the target run-time environment—the traditional debugger—to symbolic execution in an artificial environment. In many cases, the run-time environment is simply not available or cannot be instrumented. In those circumstances, some form of artificial environment is required, and the database has a role to play in that environment.

The obvious function of a DBMS during the testing process is as a surrogate for the run-time environment of the program under test and, in particular for its database component. Since the run-time environment is chosen, or imposed, independent of the choice of tools environments, the user is required to adapt the CASE environment to simulate the run-time environment, and cannot dictate the run-time environment.

In general, any system providing but not imposing, a greater semantic richness should be able to emulate any less rich tool at the level of data structures. In particular, the data structures of a relational world can be modeled by a network or entity-relationship database, and all three can be modeled by an object database. From a different perspective, so long as the primitive data types of the underlying DBMS cover or can be composed to form the types required by the application, a procedural interface can be built which emulates the target run-time database.

At the procedural interface—the point of contact between the application and the data system—the situation is not so rosy. With the exception of standard interfaces, like the SQL query language discussed in the next sub-Section, there is little commonality among the available products. An interface layer will be required to map almost any database interface into the form expected by the application under test. This places a premium on the ease of implementing interfaces and will bias the selection of a database technology for CASE toward the object technology.

Object systems, being active systems, have another advantage and uncover an additional method for addressing the problem of test environments. Many object systems will be able to reach outside their own confines to retrieve information from a foreign database, such as the target database for the application, thus allowing a harness to be built for a controlled and measured test environment, yet allowing the target database to be used for the test process.

Standards

The issue of standards, and the value they add to a tool from the perspective of a user, is particularly important in the CASE field. Both the environments for which a CASE system builds applications, and the environment of the CASE system itself are highly varied. Users will typically not be able to specify for the tool developer a single target application environment nor will they be satisfied with restrictions that all tools come from a single vendor. The following section will address the latter subject.

Database interface standards are of two types: the interactive facilities for specifying retrieval and update to the database called "query languages," and the programmatic interface equivalent. There have been only two significant standards, the CODASYL standard for programmatic interfaces to network databases, and the SQL standard for access to relational databases and databases with a relational interpretation. Since network model databases appear to be of limited use in CASE environments, SQL will be focused.

Structured Query Language grew out of the work which led to relational databases. Its initial definition was essentially established by IBM at the end of the 1970s and has been adopted not only by the relational database community but by almost every database vendor. It has been the subject of a standardization effort by the American National Standards Institute. Many database tools, Fourth Generation Languages (4GLs) and Decision Support System (DSS) tools are being built using SQL as an interface to the data management system. Structured Query Language has a number of clear deficiencies which prevent its use as the primary interface between the CASE tools and their data support system, but it is now a necessary adjunct to the CASE environment.

7 THE IMPACT OF PROGRAM STYLE AND EXECUTION DISCIPLINE

A database should be thought of as capturing, at any given point in time, the state of a world. A database is not very effective at the representation of dynamic behavior. As a result, the way a piece of software and its data structures will be modeled depends upon, and strongly influences the form of a procedural component of the CASE environment which provides the dynamic element. These aspects are in turn closely coupled to the design methodology implemented by the CASE system, if it imposes a methodology.

In both the traditional control-flow or call-return model and in a data-flow model, the elements of program which are represented in the CASE database have aspects of private and public data and aspects of invocation and event management. Where hardware execution environments may have truly asynchronous behavior, however, the database effectively synchronizes the interactions among the elements of a program by synchronizing and serializing the updates to the data visible to them. Although database systems are usually built to support concurrent execution of programs, it is very difficult to simulate much beyond a single-threaded execution discipline because the database cannot effectively simulate the signaling of a waiting process that data has changed or that has become available.

On the data side of the problem, however, there appears to be little difficulty. The construction of buffers, queues, and other structures to hold dynamic information is no harder in an object system than the representation of the static or quasi-static state of the software system. In other data models, the addition of code external to the database, which can maintain the required dynamic discipline, is not too difficult.

The methodology for software design and the execution discipline of the application built with a set of CASE tools does not have a significant effect on the choice of a data management facility to support the CASE environment. Such issues influence the form and complexity of the CASE tools built upon the data system, and the form of the data system does indeed influence the complexity of building such tools. The richer the data manager is in modeling capability, and the greater its facilities for active behavior, the easier will be the task of the tool developer.

8 THE DATABASE AS A TOOL PLATFORM

There has been significant interest lately in the use of a database as an integration platform for design tools. In this view, the database, and its modeling capabilities become a glue which holds the tools together and allows them to exchange information. Several research efforts in the direction of tool integration are under way, including the Esprit program in Europe, the Software Engineering Institute at Carnegie Mellon University, and the efforts to build programming support environments for Ada software. Paseman[3] describes a commercial effort in this direction.

The integration of disparate tools can place rather severe requirements on the data management system. Each tool may have, or assume, a distinct type system, a distinct representation, and a distinct subset of information, or view of the common data. Each tool may assume, or insist, that certain constraints are met by the data. The database must adapt to these requirements and assumptions and to provide each tool with the data it needs and a way to pass information to other tools.

Inherent in the database viewpoint are a type system, the sharing of information, and the persistence of storage. To succeed as a tool platform, a database must provide a type system which subsumes the type systems of the tools to be used. In addition, it must be able to provide an interface which allows flexible control over the ''external'' representation of those types so that each tool can receive the data in a form corresponding to its own representation. Of course, there is an assumption here that the platform, the DBMS and its adjunct services, is more adaptable than the tools themselves. That is a reasonable assumption, since the database has at its core a modeling capability designed for flexibility and because the goal must always be to allow the incremental addition of tools to the environment.

The platform concept imposes another task, however, which has not previously been observed. Each tool will most likely expect to see slightly different information, packaged slightly differently; for example, tool A might maintain a header on the source code text file which is incompatible with tool B. The platform must provide each tool with an appropriate and different representation of the source code module. The data management system, composing appropriate data when exporting a module to each tool and stripping appropriate data for independent storage when the module is returned, must flexibly model the interface of each and every tool in the environment. Furthermore, it must be possible to add to the modeling facilities whenever it is necessary to bring in a new tool.

Many data management systems have historically provided a means by which the schema of the database can be modified as it is seen by different users. These mechanisms are called VIEW facilities. They are typically capable of reformatting and subsetting the available data within the paradigm of the underlying data model. Relational systems offer relational views. One cannot, however, depend on all of the tools subscribing to a single data model. To accommodate tools requiring different interpretations of the same information, one is forced either to use a data model which subsumes the others or to build an interface layer over the DBMS which can provide the necessary mapping facilities. In either case, an object system appears to have an advantage. Being semantically richer than its competitors, it is able to cover the requirement for emulation of other data models and being an active rather than passive component, it offers the tools to implement many of the required mapping functions. Because a DBMS is designed to tolerate the modification of its schema over time, the introduction of a new tool can usually be accomplished without reworking the old interfaces.

Although it would appear that the use of a database as a tool platform provides an ideal solution, there can be problems. It is neither certain that the integration is possible nor certain that it is appropriate. The most difficult problems will arise from type system incompatibilities. The simple things, such as incompatible number ranges, can be very difficult to deal with and sometimes even harder to recognize as the cause of problems. The modeling power of the database may be great, but it cannot overcome fundamental differences in every case.

9 THE IMPACT OF AI AND OBJECT-ORIENTED TECHNIQUES

Two trends in software development deserve attention before this Chapter is brought to an end. Artificial Intelligence (AI) techniques and object-oriented methodologies are rising in importance. Both of these methodologies are based on efforts to raise the level at which software is created. Both depend on the ability of the software system to capture and make use of abstractions. To do an effective job of supporting the development of AI and object-based software, the tools must support the same level of abstraction.

The object database technology reviewed here is derived from the efforts to represent knowledge in the AI world and from efforts in the programming language world to find structuring paradigms for software which are rich enough to encourage the reuse of software. While the object database systems that result are likely to be sufficient to support development of all sorts of traditional software systems—when the software under development reaches the level of abstraction of the tool environment—the ability of the tools to provide a satisfactory framework is strained. Thus it is important when considering tools to support these new forms of software, that the tools be based on a paradigm similar to or compatible with the target environment. When examining AI systems or object systems closely, there are significant differences, most often differences in their type systems, which must be taken into account.

10 SUMMARY

Database technology has a great deal to offer to CASE. A database system is fundamentally a modeling mechanism that provides a type system, persistent storage, sharing of information, and a host of lesser services to its clients. Many of those services are required to build efficient and effective CASE environments. The database can provide not only a storage medium for the subject matter and management data of the software engineering discipline but also a platform for linking together the tools which form the environment. With a little work, it can emulate the environment of the application programs as well and, thus provide an effective environment for software test and repair.

The fundamental character of a database system is defined by the type system it provides for modeling. The selection of a modeling mechanism must be based on an examination of the modeling requirements of the applications being built and the modeling requirements of the tools.

While significant results can be achieved with tools as simple as a file system and its directory structure, current record-oriented database technologies, including network, relational and entity-relationship approaches, offer significant additional capabilities. The object databases now entering the market have greater advantages. Object systems are built to support abstraction, extensibility, and active behavior, all of which combine to enhance the ability of the CASE tools to support the user in his task.

Current object technologies are not, however, a total solution. One is forced to use data technology from the same family as the application technology, when the application type system approaches the database type system in complexity and semantic level.

Databases represent essentially static worlds. Many forms of dynamic behavior are difficult to model with database technology: especially difficult are execution environments and dynamically applied constraints. These limitations should not, however, deter one from seeking the many advantages which database technology can bring to CASE.

REFERENCES

1. O'Brien, P. D., D. C. Halbert, and M. F. Kilian, "The Trellis Programming Environment," *Proc. OOPSLA 87,* ACM Press, New York, 1987, pp. 91–102.
2. Burton, B. A., R. W. Aragon, S. A. Bailey, K. D. Koehler, and L. A. Mayes, "The Reusable Software Library," *IEEE Software,* Vol. 4, No. 4, IEEE Computer Society Press, New York, July 1987, pp. 25–33.
3. Paseman, W., "Architecture of an Integration and Portability Platform," *Proc. COMPCON Spring 1988,* IEEE Computer Society Press, New York, 1988.
4. Bernstein, P. A., "Database System Support for Software Engineering—An Extended Abstract," *Proc. 9th Intl. Conf. on Software Engineering,* IEEE Computer Society Press, New York, 1987, pp. 166–178.
5. Nestor, J. R., "Toward A Persistent Object Base," International Workshop on Programming

Environments," *Lecture Notes in Computer Science, Number 244,* New York: Springer-Verlag, 1986.

6. Dittrich, K. R., and R. A. Lorie, "Object-Oriented Database Concepts for Engineering Applications," *Proc. COMPINT* 85, IEEE Computer Society Press, New York, 1985, pp. 321–325.

7. Atwood, T. M., "An Object-Oriented DBMS for Design Support Applications," *Proc. COMPINT 85,* IEEE Computer Society Press, New York, 1985, pp. 299–307.

8. Ketabchi, M. A., "Modeling and Managing CAD Databases," *IEEE Computer,* Vol. 20, No. 2, IEEE Computer Society Press, New York, February 1987, pp. 93–102.

9. Su, S. Y. W., "Modeling Integrated Manufacturing Data with SAM*," *IEEE Computer,* Vol. 19, No. 1, IEEE Computer Society Press, New York, January 1986, pp. 34–49.

10. Codd, E. F., "A Relational Model of Data for Large Shared Data Banks," *Communications of the ACM,* Vol. 13, No. 6, ACM Press, New York, June 1970, pp. 377–387.

11. Glagowski, T. G., "Using a Relational Query Language as a Software Maintenance Tool," *Proc. Conference on Software Maintenance-1985,* IEEE Computer Society Press, New York, 1985, pp. 211–220.

12. Leblang, D. B., and R. P. Chase, Jr., "Computer-Aided Software Engineering in a Distributed Workstation Environment," Proc. *SIGPLAN Notices,* Vol. 19, No. 5, ACM Press, New York, May 1984, pp. 104–112.

13. Chen, P. P. S., "The Entity-Relationship Model: Toward a Unified View of Data," *ACM Transactions on Database Systems,* Vol. 1, No. 1, ACM Press, New York, March 1976, pp. 9–36.

14. Kent, W., "Limitations of Record-Based Information Models," *ACM Transactions on Database Systems,* Vol. 4, No. 1, ACM Press, New York, March 1979, pp. 107–131.

15. Wegner, P., "Dimensions of Object-Based Language Design," *Proc. OOPSLA 87,* ACM Press, New York, 1987, pp. 168–182.

16. Conklin, J., "Hypertext Systems for Nonlinear Organization of Text; Introduction and Survey," *IEEE Computer,* Vol. 20, No. 9, IEEE Computer Society Press, New York, September 1987, pp. 17–41.

Part II

Sample CASE Tools and Perspectives in CASE

The gross architecture of a CASE environment is shown in the Figure II-1. There are two key components to such an environment; a User Interface Manager (UIM) and a design database. The UIM consists of a number of subsystems to manage different types of objects a user might need. Ideally, user interface can be customized for different users with a user interface generator. The design database is the heart of any CASE environment, and it usually will contain several layers of data: for example, the layer of reusable components, such as code, specification, and design rules, will be a key part of the DB in any future CASE environment. Not only is it desirable to capitalize on existing specifications so that new specifications can be designed by utilizing or combining these conceptual components, but it is also important to allow existing domain specific applications, routines, etc., to be incorporated to provide an open-ended environment for users. Often a general CASE environment can be customized by incorporating specific domain knowledge into its design DB: this will assist the user to use appropriate application concepts when developing a specification. The domain knowledge can also be used for semantic and quality validation of the resulting specification because more advanced validation can usually be done only in the context of specific domain.

A good CASE environment usually provides services to accept several kinds of specifications; and usually can analyze, transform, or even synthesize the specifications and maintain a large, growing set of interrelated specifications and applications. To provide such services, a CASE environment should have at least the following domain independent functionalities:

1) User Interface Support—the system must allow a user (analyst, designer, specifier) to work with iconographic notations often in multi-window mode. Several attributes of such a support subsystem are described as follows:

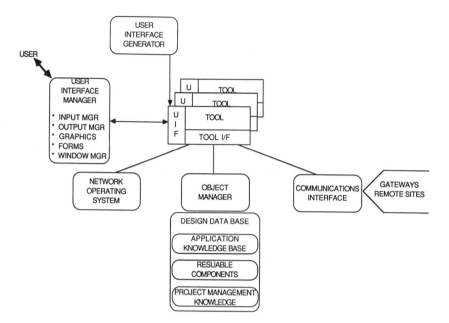

Figure II-1. The gross architecture of a CASE environment.

- It should be easy-to-use in the reuse that simple things are simple to do. The learning curve should be incremental rather than a step-function;

- Applications could be specific and incremental; i.e., one can begin with a framework or skeleton and add details when appropriate;

- When appropriate, browsing or hierarchical navigation of specification should be possible;

- Design documentation based on specification can be generated automatically; and

- Specifications could be displayed simultaneously in different formats or media (via data/concept dictionary), and skeletons of specifications can be selectively outputted.

2) Design Support—the primary functionality here is semantics preserving transformation of specifications; for example, the mapping of one specification to an executable specification for prototyping purposes or the restructuring of a specification to improve its performance.

3) Verification and Validation Support—the goal of verification is to ensure that a specification is complete and correct; for example, making sure that no syntax error is contained in a specification. Validation, on the other

hand, is concerned with the consistency of one level of specification with respect to the next higher level of specification; for example, does the specified application meet its intended purpose as stated in its requirements document?

4) Project Management Support—in this category, there is a variety of functionalities, which include version and configuration control, maintenance of design decisions and design histories, tracking of changes, etc. These features are crucial for any CASE environment to be effective in large projects.

The purpose of this note is to present a general framework when evaluating any CASE tools. Clearly, tools presented by selected papers in Part II do not have all the features described above. The challenge of future CASE environments not only lies in providing the described functionalities but is also to integrate existing tools so as to provide a migration path from the current system to the new system.

The section begins with a survey of CASE tools. In Chapter 10, Pieter R. Mimno discusses the major components of CASE products; namely, diagrammer, design analyzer, code generator, and central repository. Most CASE products are designed to support a particular methodology. Buying such a product may mean the commitment of the organization to that particular tool's methodology. The author provides a detailed discussion and a checklist of the four classifications of CASE products; i.e., products that support information engineering, structured engineering, developments, and COBOL generation.

In Chapter 11, M. Alford presents an overview of the concepts of Requirements Driven Design (RDD) and illustrates the application of the concepts of RDD with an example.

In Chapter 12, Michael D. Konrad and Terry A. Welch introduce a functional prototyping system called "Proto." The Proto consists of four critical components; namely, a functionally specific language, a library of reusable software, a set of interactive tools, and a methodology that guides an analyst in constructions, analysis, and validation of functional specifications. A procedure is outlined on how to use Proto to build and evaluate functional prototypes.

In Chapter 13, Yoshihiro Oki, et al., describe SPDTOOLS, which are a set of software tools that support program design, coding, and documentation based on SPD (Structured Program Diagram). An example is used to illustrate the functions of the three components of SPDTOOLS; namely, SPD Editor, Translator, and SPD Documentor. The user interface supported by the tools is demonstrated.

In Chapter 14, D. Tajima, et al., describe the hardware configuration and software architecture of SKIPS/SDE system. The design decisions of the system and its major characteristics are detailed. The functions of the filing system are discussed: in particular; the multi-key search method that provides alternate ways of searching for an object. The chapter concludes by describing and evaluating the tools that have been developed and are targeted for business application software written in COBOL.

In Chapter 15, L. Markosian, *et al.*, describe a knowledge-based software development system. The chapter begins by describing the distinction between a knowledge-based approach from the traditional approach in software development: in particular; REFINE is used to illustrate the three main components of a knowledge-based software development subsystem, specifically representation knowledge, implementation knowledge and tools, and process and policy knowledge.

In Chapter 16, Y. Matsumoto describes the tool environments of the Toshiba Fuchu Software Factory (TFSF). A software development life cycle is described as a network of processes. To develop a project, the project manager selects a set of unit processes and defines the interconnection and the design interface. Project management in TFSF is a look-forward type of management. The author discusses the flow of the project management and describes the procedures which are required to accomplish a unit process. The tools that are available in the design environment are described.

In Chapter 17, R.T. Yeh introduces MicroSTEP, a software system that automates the coding and testing phase of the software development cycle. The MicroSTEP Design methodology is illustrated with a detailed example in this chapter.

Chapter 10

Survey of CASE Tools

PIETER R. MIMNO
High-Productivity Software, Inc.
Marblehead, MA.

1 TRENDS IN CASE TECHNOLOGY

Rapid advances in personal computer technology are ushering in a new generation of front-end software development systems based on Computer-Aided Software Engineering (CASE) techniques. The most advanced CASE tools incorporate features, such as graphical design aids, automated design analyzers, expert systems, and integrated code generators. The tools are oriented toward the support of systems analysts, system designers, application developers, programmers, engineers, and system builders. Computer-Aided Software Engineering tools are fundamentally altering the way systems are specified, designed, implemented, and maintained.

Computer-Aided Software Engineering tools are designed to operate on personal workstations, which are rapidly becoming the standard environment for the development of software. This new generation of tools applies rigorous engineering principles to the development and analysis of software specifications. The CASE technology represents a new approach to the implementation of complex systems. The tools have the potential to automate all phases of the life-cycle process and to tie application development more closely to the strategic operations of the business.

A CASE workbench should implement a complete software development environment that supports the entire life-cycle process, customization for each workstation user, powerful graphics, project-level coordination, and intelligent operation.

Relative to current fourth-generation language (4GL) tools, the major advantages of CASE products can be summarized as follows:

- **automation of the entire development life cycle process,** including the critical, early analysis, and design phases with an integrated family of software tools;
- **interactive development environment** characterized by rapid response time, intuitive system operation, and on-line error checking;

- **automatic analysis of specifications** for logical completeness and consistency, using design analyzers that incorporate expert systems; and
- **generation of efficient code** that does not impose a run-time performance penalty. This may be accomplished through the close integration of a front-end CASE product coupled to a back-end COBOL generator.

A major objective of CASE technology is to bring the same benefits to software development as CAD/CAM has brought to manufacturing. Both CAD/CAM and CASE technologies enforce a disciplined engineering approach to the development of systems. Both use interactive graphical design techniques, design analysis and checking facilities, repositories of design elements, and prototyping techniques. These processes are applied and enforced throughout all phases of the design, development, manufacturing, testing, deployment, and maintenance process.

The CASE products evaluated in this chapter are being driven by advances in technology that are fundamentally changing the life-cycle process. Significant changes are occurring in the following:

- Human Factors: Major improvements are being made in human interfaces, including the use of simplified, intuitive command interfaces, elimination of alien syntax, extensive utilization of graphics, etc. The use of these techniques in well-designed CASE tools encourages much closer end-user involvement.
- Intelligent Workstation Orientation: Many CASE products are available as intelligent desktop workstations that utilize IBM PC or PC-compatible microcomputers. The workstation environment provides dedicated processing capability, deci-second response time, superior graphics, and access to thousands of MS-DOS- or OS/2-compatible software support packages.
- Graphical Design Techniques: An important new technology incorporated into many CASE products is the utilization of front-end graphical design techniques that are amenable to automatic analysis. Systems are specified in graphical form, the diagrams are analyzed automatically for design errors and inconsistencies and, in some integrated products, the specifications are converted automatically into code.
- Artificial Intelligence: CASE tools are making increasing use of artificial intelligence techniques, including the incorporation of expert system shells and a knowledge base of rules of inference.

These trends in technology are converging to produce a whole new generation of tools that are fundamentally different from previous technology. An important function of this chapter is to indicate how individual CASE products best incorporate these new ideas in technology.

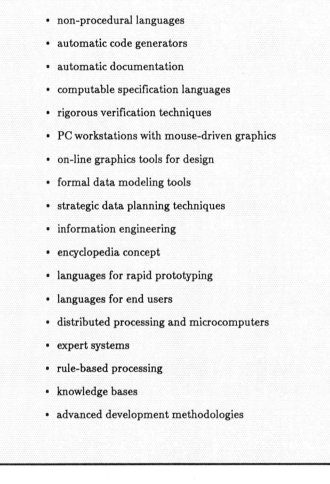

- non-procedural languages
- automatic code generators
- automatic documentation
- computable specification languages
- rigorous verification techniques
- PC workstations with mouse-driven graphics
- on-line graphics tools for design
- formal data modeling tools
- strategic data planning techniques
- information engineering
- encyclopedia concept
- languages for rapid prototyping
- languages for end users
- distributed processing and microcomputers
- expert systems
- rule-based processing
- knowledge bases
- advanced development methodologies

2   KEY COMPONENTS OF CASE PRODUCTS

Computer-Aided Software Engineering provides both the process and the tools for every part of the software development life cycle. Major emphasis in CASE technology is placed on the early phases of the life cycle, i.e., feasibility studies, requirements analyses, and system design. Numerous studies have shown that the majority of errors occurring in the software development process may be traced back to the analysis and design phases. Errors caught in the early design phases are much less expensive to detect and correct than errors uncovered during later stages of development. CASE products are evolving in the direction shown in Figure 10-1. This figure illustrates the key functions provided by

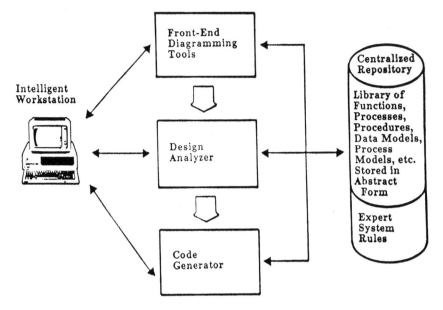

Figure 10-1. Key components of CASE products.

technically advanced CASE products. Descriptions of the key components of CASE products follow.

CAD / CAP Diagramming Techniques

Most CASE tools utilize computer-aided design and programming techniques to create diagrams of the system design. Analysts are able to interactively create, verify, and revise drawings on the screen. CASE tools support diagramming techniques associated with a variety of development methodologies, including modern techniques based on formal information models and older, manually-oriented structured engineering techniques (e.g., Yourdon-DeMarco, Gane & Sarson, Jackson, Warnier-Orr, etc.).

Design Analyzers

The function of the design analyzer is to detect internal inconsistencies, ambiguities, and incompleteness in the design specifications. To provide rigorous consistency and completeness checks, the analyzer must be based on an underlying formal information model. Design analyzers in current CASE tools are rapidly being improved to incorporate smart editors, intelligent assistants, and expert systems.

Code Generators

Many CASE tools are moving toward integration with a code generation module to automatically generate code from consistent design specifications. To generate efficient code, a simple import/export link between the front-end and back-end is not sufficient. A very tight coupling is required between the front-end CASE tool and the back-end code generator.

Repositories

The heart of a well-designed CASE system is a central respository (or encyclopedia) used as a knowledge base to store information about the organization, its structure, enterprise model, functions, procedures, data models, data entities, entity relationships, process models, etc. Sufficient detail is maintained about the design of a procedure so that program code for that procedure can be generated automatically. As shown in Figure 10-2, the repository should contain a database of pure specifications, stored in abstract form, that can be viewed in a variety of consistent graphical formats, including data-flow diagrams, structure charts, entity relationship diagrams, navigation charts, action diagrams, etc. It should be possible to translate automatically from one view to another while maintaining consistency between all views. Relative to a data dictionary, a repository or encyclopedia is a higher-level knowledge base that coordinates and analyzes information as well as stores it.

Expert Systems

A few CASE tools are beginning to incorporate expert systems. These apply inference processing to a knowledge base containing data and rules. Currently, expert systems are used in a narrow domain to detect inconsistent or incorrect database actions. However, the use of expert system techniques is likely to be extended to support all phases of the development life-cycle process. Ultimately, most CASE products will be knowledge-base-driven.

Methodologies

CASE tools are moving toward the incorporation of a disciplined methodology to guide the analyst, step-by-step, in the application of the tool. The specification of a comprehensive, well-defined development process ensures a more standardized approach to the design and implementation of systems and enables management to gain better control over the development process.

All the products compared in this chapter are evaluated in the context of the trends in technology described earlier. The components of each product are also matched against the evolving CASE structure presented in Figure 10-1.

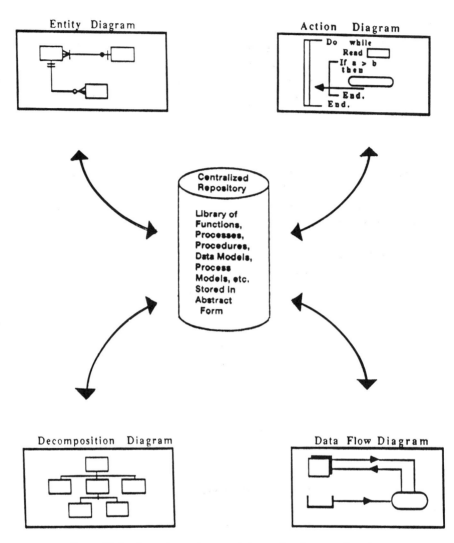

Figure 10-2. Central repository and alternative diagramming views.

Support of Life-Cycle Process

Data-Processing (DP) professionals are faced with the major challenge of designing and implementing the increasingly complex systems required to support strategic use of computers. Traditional techniques, such as hand-coding applications in COBOL, are entirely inadequate for highly complex applications. It is simply impossible for analysts to keep track of all the links and interconnections in large, complex systems. Applications developed by hand are extremely inefficient in terms of productivity and are, generally, full of inconsistencies and design errors.

Highly-integrated 4GLs, such as ADS/OnLine from Cullinet Software, Inc., APPLICATION FACTORY from Cortex Corporation, IDEAL from Applied Data Research, Inc., MANTIS from Cincom Systems, Inc., MODEL 204 from Computer Corporation of America, and NATURAL from Software AG were introduced to aid DP professionals in the development of complex systems. Each of these tools provides a wide variety of integrated functions, including a database management system (DBMS), non-procedural functions (screen and report generation, database queries, decision support, graphics, etc.), as well as a high-level procedural language. Many organizations have demonstrated that 4GL tools can be used effectively to achieve a major improvement in productivity—in many cases, a 10:1 improvement in productivity over COBOL.

Despite their potential for productivity improvements, 4GL tools designed for use by DP professionals have not replaced COBOL as the language of choice for the implementation of complex systems. This is attributed to many factors, including the following:

- Perceived lack of performance in an on-line transaction-processing environment. 4GLs impose a performance penalty in machine resources and processing speed relative to hand-generated COBOL programs. Although it varies greatly, this performance penalty can be as high as 100%. For many applications, particularly heavily loaded, on-line trans-action-processing applications, a performance penalty of more than 10% is unacceptable. However, for many organizations, the ability to generate applications five to ten times faster than with hand-coding techniques is more important than run-time performance.
- Lack of support for the entire development life cycle process, particularly the critical analysis and design phases.
- Reluctance on the part of DP professionals to use a tool that appears to lack the flexibility and functional capabilities of third-generation languages such as COBOL.
- Lack of a well-documented life-cycle process for 4GLs.

Those CASE tools which are not linked to code generators and support only the analysis and design phases do not overcome the limitations of current 4GL products. They are used primarily to enter specifications in graphical form and check the logical consistency and completeness of the specifications. The resulting set of specifications must then be converted by hand into program code. Due to the inefficiency of the programming process, some current CASE tools offer only limited gains in productivity.

Integrated-Case (I-CASE)

A major challenge for all vendors of CASE products is to implement an integrated architecture that provides a tight linkage between a CASE tool and an associated code generator. *I-CASE* describes such an environment in which the CASE product and the code generator are very closely coupled.

Several vendors (KnowledgeWare, Texas Instruments, Cortex, Index Technology, and CGI) have taken steps to develop tightly integrated interfaces between their CASE products and an associated code generator. Their objective is to generate code automatically from logically consistent and complete graphical specifications.

An alternative approach, pursued by Index Technology and other vendors, is to provide flexible linkages between CASE tools and a variety of code generators and application generators. This approach would be facilitated through the adoption by the industry of a standard electronic data interchange format governing the transmission of text and graphic data. In the near future, CASE products are likely to be interfaced to a wide variety of code generators and 4GL application generators.

All CASE tools, coupled with COBOL generators (e.g., APS, GAMMA, PACBASE, TELON, THE INTELLIGENT ASSISTANT, or TRANSFORM), offer the potential of overcoming the limitations of current 4GL products. Figure 10-3 illustrates the use of a front-end CASE tool to enter and check specifications, while a back-end generator converts these specifications directly into COBOL code. Initial products may use import/export file facilities to link the CASE tool's repository to the data dictionary facilities of the code generator on the mainframe.

A simple import/export file facility has not proven to be an adequate interface between a CASE product and an associated code generator. Much tighter coupling between these components is necessary to generate efficient code.

The combination of a front-end CASE tool and a back-end COBOL generator supports the entire life-cycle process and generates highly efficient code that may be used without performance penalty in a heavily loaded, transaction-processing environment. Some IS organizations still committed to COBOL are choosing to skip over the current 4GL technology and move directly to the next generation of tools—CASE front ends coupled to efficient code generators.

Many CASE products are likely to provide a generalized and customizable interface to a variety of code generators. These products will extend support to the *entire* life cycle and will leverage the investment made in mainframe code generation facilities.

CASE tools may also be interfaced to more traditional 4GL products, such as ADS/OnLine, APPLICATION FACTORY, IDEAL, MANTIS, MODEL 204, and NATURAL. APPLICATION FACTORY from Cortex Corporation is the first traditional 4GL application generator to be interfaced to a CASE front end.

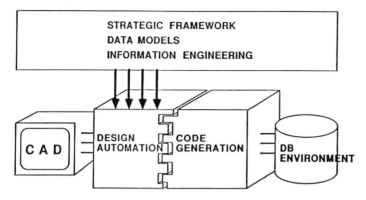

Figure 10-3. CASE product as front end to COBOL generator.

As illustrated in Figure 10-4, the Cortex product is an integrated application generator that provides support for all phases of the application development life cycle. The front-end CASE product, called CorVision, incorporates a graphical user interface that supports several diagramming techniques. CorVision interfaces with APPLICATION FACTORY, which runs in the DEC VAX/VMS environment. APPLICATION FACTORY supports a central

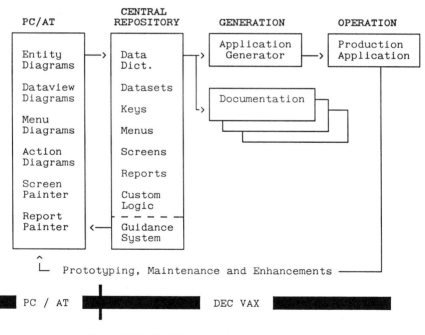

Figure 10-4. CorVision development environment.

repository for application specifications and a 4GL code generator that generates FACTORY applications. The vendor refers to the development approach provided by the combination of CorVision and APPLICATION FACTORY as "picture programming."

Vendors of CASE products are aware of the necessity of supporting the entire life-cycle process, including the automatic generation of code from logically consistent and complete specifications. At present, most CASE products support only low-level code generation facilities, such as the ability to generate screen maps and data layouts for external programming languages such as COBOL, C, BASIC, and PL/I.

Using the import/export facilities of tools such as Excelerator, organizations have developed interfaces to external mainframe and microcomputer software systems, such as IMS DB/DC, IDMS/IDD, Data manager, dBASE III, Telon's Design Facility, MFAS, and IBM's GDDM Graphics Display Manager.

The next step for these vendors is to build integrated interfaces to code generators, such as GAMMA from KnowledgeWare, TELON from Pansophic Systems, TRANSFORM from Transform Logic Corporation, NATURAL from Software AG, PowerHouse from Cognos Corporation, DEC VAX COBOL, and Micro Focus VM COBOL, etc.

Several CASE vendors have announced the near availability of interfaces to COBOL generators. These include KnowledgeWare, Inc., which has developed an interface between Information Engineering Workbench and GAMMA; Index Technology, which is developing an interface between Excelerator and TELON; CGI Systems, which has released a proprietary CASE front end to PACBASE and Texas Instruments, which has developed an integrated code generator for its product Information Engineering Facility.

Some tools may utilize an open CASE architecture based on the use of a relational DataBase Management System (DBMS), such as IBM's DB2 as a standard system repository. As shown in Figure 10-5, the approach employs a relational DBMS as a centralized corporate repository that can be interfaced to a variety of front-end CASE tools and back-end code generators. At present, application generators that provide read/write interfaces to DB2 include Application System and CSP from IBM, FOCUS from Information Builders, Inc., NOMAD2 from MUST Software International (formerly D&B Computing Services), ORACLE from Oracle Corporation, and INGRES from Relational Technology, Inc. IBM is encouraging vendors of CASE tools and code generators to standardize on the use of DB2 as the source of system-wide data and process definitions. This approach would provide a great deal of flexibility since customers could select both the front-end CASE product and the back-end application generator from a variety of options.

3 COMPARISON OF PRODUCT FUNCTIONALITY

Attempting to compare and contrast the wide assortment of CASE products can easily become confusing. It is difficult to evaluate the functionality of the avail-

IBM Mainframe

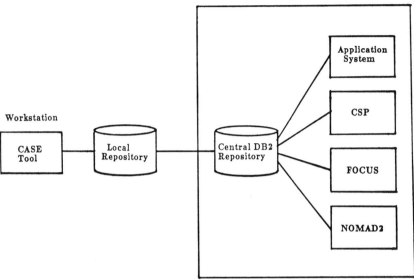

Figure 10-5. Use of DB2 as a centralized repository.

able competing products. For example, does a large number of supported diagramming techniques outweigh the provision of an integrated project management system? Should the lack of a code generator disqualify a product from consideration? Must an organization adhere to a specific development methodology (such as information engineering) to realize significant gains from a product?

The tradeoffs that these questions entail reflect the diversity of functionality in current CASE product offerings. To properly assess the tradeoffs requires a framework for evaluating CASE products. The proposed framework establishes a process whereby the requirements or commitments of the organization are understood in relation to the functionality of a CASE product.

Table 10-1 lists representative CASE products divided into four categories that reflect their primary range of functionality, e.g., support for information engineering, structured engineering, development methodologies, and COBOL generation.

As shown in Table 10-1 the four distinct functional classifications of CASE products are the following:

- products that support **information engineering techniques** (i.e., a life-cycle process derived from the strategic plans of the enterprise and that provides a repository to create and maintain enterprise models, data models and process models);
- products that support **structured diagramming** techniques (i.e., Yourdon-DeMarco, Gane-Sarson or Jackson development methodologies) and that

Table 10-1. Representative CASE Products.

Products Supporting Information Engineering

CorVision	Cortex Corp.
Information Engineering Facility	Texas Instruments
Information Engineering Workbench*	KnowledgeWare, Inc.

Products Supporting Structured Engineering

Adpac Productivity Tools	Adpac Corp.
Analyst/Designer Toolkit	Yourdon Software
CASE 2000	Nastec Corp.
Design Graphics System	CADWARE Group, Ltd.
Developer (The)	ASYST Technologies
Excelerator	Index Technology Corp.
Manager Family (The)	MSP
Multipro	Cap Gemini Software Products
Teamwork	Cadre Technologies
TIP	Technology Info. Products
vsDesigner	Visual Software, Inc.

Structured Development Aids for System Analysts

Appl. Systems Development Env.	Digital Equipment Corp.
CASE Software Factory	Tektronix, Inc.
Data Resources Leverage	D. Appleton Co.
Design Machine	Ken Orr & Associates
DESIGN/1	Arthur Andersen
ER-Modeler Package	Chen & Associates
IDMS/Auto-Mate Plus	Cullinet Software, Inc.
InfoModel Software	Info-Model, Inc.
MAESTRO	Softlab Systems, Inc.
Meta Systems Toolset	Meta Systems
Netron/CAP	Netron
ProKit* Analyst/Workbench	McDonnell Douglas ISG
ProMod	ProMod, Inc.

COBOL Generators

APS Development Center	Sage Systems, Inc.
GAMMA	KnowledgeWare, Inc.
Intelligent Assistant (The)	On-Line Business Systems, Inc.
PACBASE	CGI Systems, Inc.
TELON	Pansophic Systems, Inc.
TRANSFORM	Transform Logic Corp.

*also supports Structured Engineering

support at least the three basic structured software engineering diagramming types (i.e., data flow, control flow, and entity-relationship);
- products that provide **structured development aids** for the systems analyst; and
- products that generate **application code** using a COBOL generator.

These four categories of CASE tools reflect the following four distinct types of commitment that organizations may make to technology:

- commitment to an **Information Engineering** systems development methodology;
- to a **Structured Engineering** systems development methodology;
- to the support of the **analytical requirements** of systems analysts; and
- to the **automatic generation of COBOL code** for new application systems.

In the following section, each of these categories of technology is summarized briefly.

Products That Support Information Engineering

Information Engineering is a new life-cycle process that is based on a top-down view of the information processing strategy of the organization. It is a set of formal techniques in which enterprise models, data models, and process models are built up in a comprehensive knowledge base managed by an encyclopedia or repository. The models are used within a clearly-defined life-cycle process to create and maintain DP systems.

A primary objective of information engineering is to provide an enterprise-wide set of automated disciplines that link the development of applications to the top management goals and strategic plans of the enterprise. The top-down strategic view embodied in information engineering is specifically designed to support the development of the strategic systems of the 1990s.

The top-down nature of the life-cycle process for information engineering is illustrated in Figure 10-6. In this Figure, the life-cycle process is depicted in the form of a pyramid. Each layer of the pyramid represents a stage in the life-cycle process; i.e., a **strategy** phase, an **analysis** phase, a **design** phase, and a **construction** phase. The left side of the pyramid represents the portion of the life cycle involved in the specification of data for an application. The right side represents the steps required to specify processes (or activities) for the application.

An engineering-like discipline is used throughout all phases of the life-cycle development process. Computerized tools ensure that all interfaces within the process are seamless; i.e., the information collected at the higher stages of the process are used automatically by analysts as they progress to more detailed phases of the process. A common encyclopedia or repository is used to ensure that all process and data definitions are consistent.

Figure 10-7 illustrates the major functions performed at each level of the pyramid as part of the information engineering life cycle process. These functions may be summarized as follows:

- **Information Strategy Planning (Strategy Level):** The first step in the life-cycle process is to capture top management goals and critical success

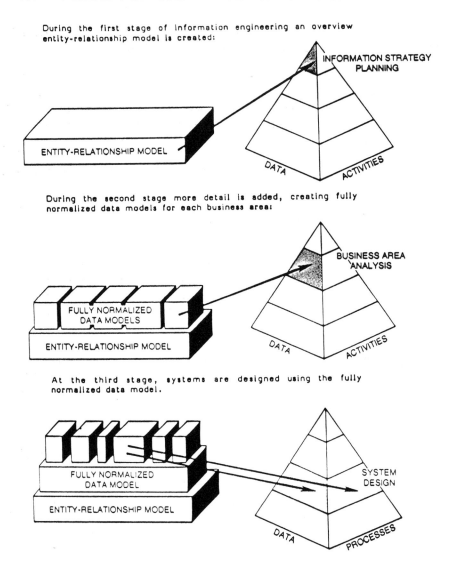

Figure 10-6. Information engineering methodology.

factors in a knowledge base or encyclopedia. The encyclopedia contains a high-level model of the enterprise, its functions, data and information needs. As shown in Figure 10-7, primary outputs of this phase include an enterprise model and entity-relationship (ER) diagrams.

- **Business Area Analysis:** The next step in the life-cycle process is to determine what processes are required to operate a specific business area, how these processes interrelate and what data are needed for these processes.

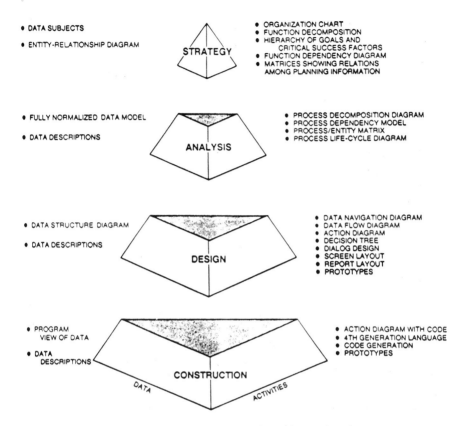

Figure 10-7. Diagrams used in information engineering.

A separate Business Area Analysis is normally done for each business area. Primary outputs of this stage include process decomposition diagrams, normalized data models, and data descriptions.

• **System Design:** At the design stage, direct end-user involvement is usually required to specify how selected processes are to be implemented in the form of user interaction, data flow, and procedures.

The primary outputs of this stage are working prototypes of the application that implement sequences of screens, reports, menu structures, decision trees, and procedural logic. Diagram types produced in the system design phase include data navigation diagrams, data flow diagrams, and action diagrams.

• **Construction:** the final step in the life-cycle process is to construct the application using a variety of code generators, fourth-generation languages and decision support tools. The objective is to accumulate specifications in sufficient enough detail that the system can be built automatically from consistent, computable specifications.

Diagram types supported by information engineering typically include the following:

* decomposition,
* dependency,
* data flow,
* action,
* data analysis,
* data structure,
* entity-relationship,
* data navigation,
* decision trees and tables,
* state transition, and
* dialogue design.

A commitment to an information engineering approach is appropriate for organizations that are interested in using the most powerful techniques available for building strategic systems. Information engineering technology is unfamiliar to most analysts and may require extensive retraining of the technical staff. However, the approach is ideally suited to the development of strategic or mission-critical systems that operate at the heart of the organization.

Figure 10-8 shows a matrix which compares the functionality of the CASE products listed in Table 10-1. A comparison of the functionality of products that support an information engineering methodology is presented in the matrix. Tools which implement an information engineering approach include CorVision and APPLICATION FACTORY from Cortex Corporation, Information Engineering Workbench from KnowledgeWare, Inc., and Information Engineering Facility from Texas Instruments, Inc. Though CorVision spans all phases of the application life cycle and incorporates a fully integrated code generator that produces optimized code for the DEC VAX VMS environment, it provides only partial implementation of information engineering techniques.

IEW from KnowledgeWare and IEF from Texas Instruments are more comprehensive tools aimed at supporting the full range of information engineering technology. Major components of both IEW and IEF are currently available (however, not yet fully integrated into an overall mainframe/workstation environment). In addition to its commitment to advanced information engineering concepts, the Information Engineering Workbench from KnowledgeWare, Inc. also supports the more familiar structured engineering diagramming types (i.e., decomposition diagrams, data flow diagrams, and entity-relationship diagrams).

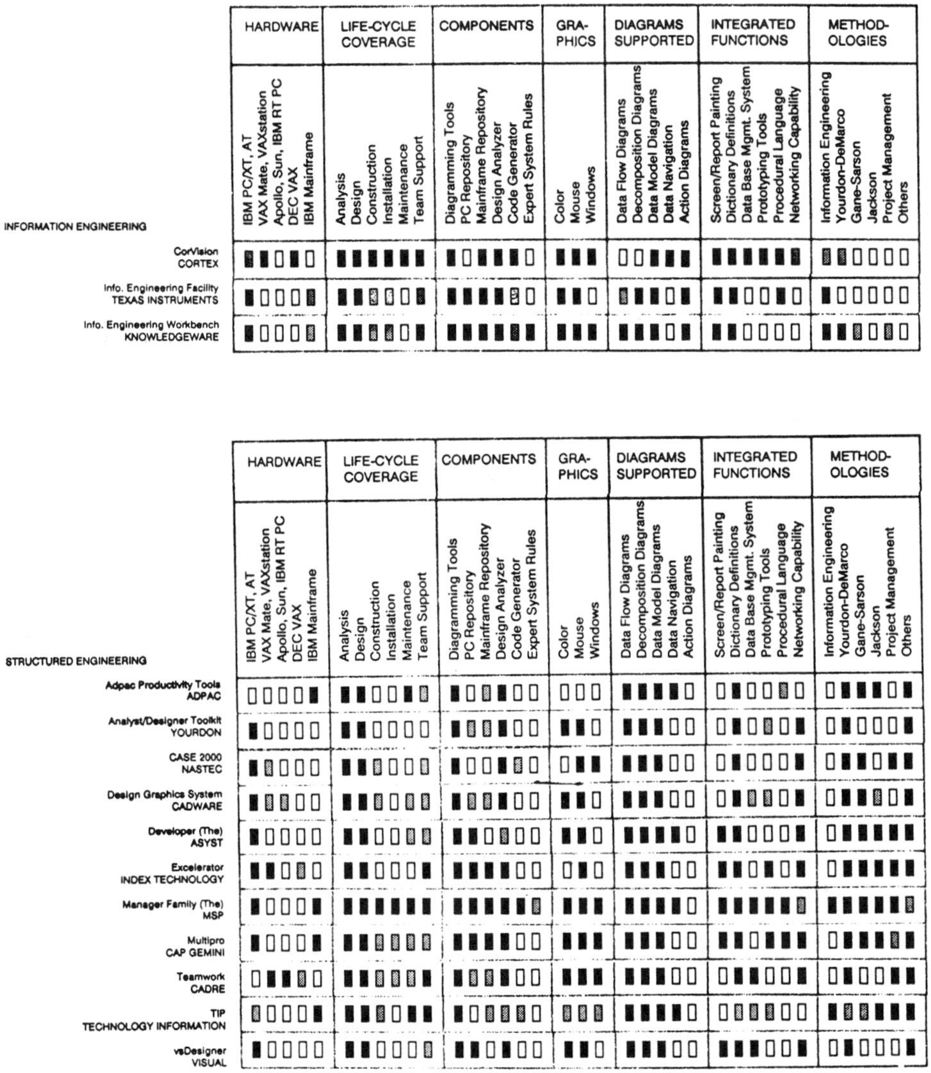

Figure 10-8. Product functionality matrix.

Products That Support Structured Engineering

A large number of CASE products support differing forms of structured engineering methodologies. To provide a clear differentiation, the products are divided into the following two categories, those supporting structured engineering and those supporting structured development aids:

- **Products Supporting Structured Engineering**—defined as products that support all three basic structured engineering diagramming types, i.e., decomposition diagrams, data flow diagrams, and entity-relationship diagrams.
- **Products Supporting Structured Development Aids**—defined as products that support one or more, but not all three, of the basic structured diagramming types.

Structured methodologies, developed in the 1970s, provide analysts with a disciplined representation of the specifications for a system. Representative structured methodologies include those introduced by Yourdon and DeMarco, Gane and Sarson, Constantine, Jackson and others. Structured techniques utilized by these methodologies include the following:

- Hierarchy Plus Input Output (HIPO) charts,
- data flow diagrams,
- structure (decomposition) charts,
- entity-relationship diagrams,
- Warnier-Orr charts,
- Michael Jackson charts,
- Nassi-Shneiderman charts, and
- Structured English and pseudocode.

Structured diagramming techniques (i.e., the use of data flow diagrams, decomposition diagrams, and E-R diagrams) are familiar to large numbers of system analysts and designers. Numerous systems have been specified in the form of leveled sets of data flow diagrams and structure charts.

Early CASE tools, such as Excelerator from Index Technology, were initially developed as computer-aided drafting or diagramming tools to simplify the entry of diagrams on a computer screen. More recent versions of these tools go well beyond simple drafting capability. They generally store specifications in an automated system information repository and incorporate automatic design analysis and checking functions.

CASE products that support a structured engineering methodology usually provide a set of integrated facilities that automate the early phases of the development life cycle, including feasibility studies, requirements analysis and detailed design. Typical facilities include support for a wide variety of structured diagramming techniques, design analysis, screen and report generation, automatic documentation, and facilities for sharing data between distributed PCs and a departmental or central computer. To support the entire life cycle process, most vendors are working intensively to provide interfaces to code generators.

None of these tools incorporates an information engineering methodology. They are useful primarily for project-oriented applications that do not take a global, strategic view of the organization.

A commitment to CASE tools that support structured engineering is appropriate for organizations that do not need the more complex and powerful features of an information engineering methodology. In addition, an orientation toward structured engineering minimizes training requirements because many analysts already understand these widely used techniques. There is a clear tradeoff between the use of structured engineering versus information engineering. Structured engineering tools tend to be easier to learn and employ familiar diagramming techniques; however, they provide only a limited view of the strategic information requirements of the organization. In contrast, tools based on information engineering are more complex and use less familiar techniques; however, they are rooted in a top-down strategic view of the organization that is highly appropriate for the development of mission-critical systems.

Figure 10-8 includes a comparison of the functionality of the CASE products that support a structured engineering methodology (as listed in Table 10-1). These products support all three basic structured diagramming types (i.e., decomposition, data flow, and entity-relationship). Representative tools include Analyst/Designer Toolkit from Yourdon Software, CASE 2000 from Nastec Corporation, Design Graphics System from CADWARE Group, Ltd., Excelerator from Index Technology Corp., The Manager Family from MSP, Multipro from Cap Gemini Software Products, Teamwork from Cadre Technologies, TIP from Technology Information Products, and vsDesigner from Visual Software, Inc. Currently, these products support only the early analysis and design phases of the life-cycle process. However, most vendors are committed to support of the entire life cycle via interfaces to a variety of code generators.

Structured Development Aids for System Analysts

As noted above, the distinguishing feature of structured development aids for systems analysts is that these products do not incorporate all three of the basic structured diagramming types needed to represent a software system (i.e., decomposition diagrams, data flow diagrams, and entity-relationship diagrams). Most of the products in this category provide one or more of these diagram types.

Several products in this category provide support for a particular development methodology such as Yourdon/DeMarco, Warnier/Orr, Peter Chen's Entity-Relationship approach, PSL/PSA, etc. The tool automatically enforces the rigorous procedures of the methodology, maintains an integrated design database, ensures the consistency of the database, and generates automatic system documentation.

Figure 10-8 includes a comparison of the functionality of products that support structured development aids for system analysts. Representative tools in this category include Design Machine from Ken Orr & Associates, DESIGN/1 from Arthur Andersen, ER-Modeler Package from Chen & Associates, IDMS/Auto-Mate Plus from Cullinet Software, Inc., MAESTRO from Softlab Systems, Inc., Meta Systems Toolset from Meta Systems, and ProKit* Analyst/ Workbench from McDonnell Douglas ISG.

COBOL Code Generators

Code generators, such as APS, GAMMA, PACBASE, TELON, THE INTEL-LIGENT ASSISTANT, and TRANSFORM automatically generate COBOL code from user-supplied specifications. System components include a data dictionary, librarian, documentation manager, and application generator. These tools generally incorporate an interactive screen-menu interface for specifying design-level information, such as edit criteria, screen layouts, data base descriptions, data access, and control procedures. Constructs that cannot be specified using the design facility must be implemented with custom COBOL code.

COBOL code generators, generally, do not support the degree of integrated functionality or data base management capability provided by the leading fully-integrated application generators. They are complex products that do not accommodate a user-friendly interface. The primary strength of these tools is that they generate efficient COBOL code, which does not impose a significant performance penalty at run time.

Vendors of COBOL generators are building comprehensive front-end facilities to their products to simplify interaction with the tool. For example, CGI Systems, Inc. has developed a complete CASE front-end for their PACBASE product.

The next generation of CASE products is likely to provide generalized interfaces to a variety of code generators, including COBOL generators. A CASE tool combined with a COBOL generator is capable of supporting the entire life-cycle process while generating COBOL code that is competitive with hand-generated code in terms of run-time performance. This combination of tools is significant because it offers IS managers the opportunity to improve programmer productivity, maintain a commitment to COBOL, and avoid a run-time performance penalty.

A comparison of the functionality of leading COBOL generators is presented in Figure 10-8. Leading tools in this category include APS from Sage Systems, GAMMA from KnowledgeWare, PACBASE from CGI Systems, Inc., TELON from Pansophic Systems, Inc., THE INTELLIGENT ASSISTANT and TRANSFORM from Transform Logic Corporation.

Functionality Matrix

A comparison of all of the CASE products listed in Table 10-1 is presented in Figure 10-8. Each row of the matrix summarizes the functionality of a specific product. Columns of the matrix show the availability of a particular function, such as diagramming tools, design analysis, and code generation, across all products. The functional categories included in the matrix are specific to CASE products.

Categories of functions that are presented in the functionality matrix include the following:

- **Hardware:** hardware environment for the product.
- **Life-Cycle Coverage:** portion of the entire life-cycle development process that is supported by the product, e.g., analysis of requirements, system design, construction (coding) of programs, program installation, and program maintenance.
- **Components of Product:** Key components of CASE products, as defined in Figure 10-1.
- **Graphics:** Use of graphic techniques such as color, mouse, and windows.
- **Diagrams Supported:** Types of diagramming techniques supported by the product, e.g., Control Flow Diagrams, Data Flow Diagrams, Decomposition Diagrams, Data Model Diagrams, etc.
- **Integrated Functionality:** Integrated functions that are available to the analyst in the environment of the product, e.g., screen and report painting, dictionary entry definitions, data base management, prototyping tools, procedural language, and networking capability, etc.
- **Methodologies:** Application development methodologies supported by the product, e.g., information engineering, Yourdon-DeMarco, Gane & Sarson, Jackson, etc.

An explanation of the definition of each column of the functionality matrix is presented in Table 10-2, and each entry in the matrix indicates whether or not a particular function is available in a specific product, e.g., function is available, function is partially available, and function is not available.

The functionality matrix provides a useful "first cut" in determining whether a product meets the needs of a potential user. The matrix provides answers to such questions as the following:

- Does the tool run on an IBM PC/XT, AT, PS/2, Apollo, Sun, or IBM RT PC?
- Is the tool available for a DEC VAX environment?
- Does the tool support the entire life cycle process?

Table 10-2. Questions used to assess product functionality.

Hardware Environment

- **IBM PC/XT, AT, PS/2:** Does the tool run on an IBM PC/XT or PC/AT (or fully compatible machine) in a PC-DOS environment, or on an IBM PS/2 in an OS/2 environment?

- **VAX Mate, VAXstation:** Does the tool run on a DEC VAX Mate or VAXstation terminal?

- **Apollo, Sun, IBM RT PC:** Does the tool run on workstations that are typically used for CAD/CAM, such as Apollo, Sun or IBM RT PC super micros?

- **DEC VAX:** Does the tool run on a DEC VAX or microVAXcomputer?

- **IBM Mainframe:** Does the tool run on an IBM Series/370 mainframe computer?

Life-Cycle Coverage

- Is the tool applicable to the **analysis phase** of the life-cycle process (i.e., feasibility analysis and requirements analysis)?

- Is the tool applicable to the **design phase** of the life-cycle process (i.e., preliminary design, initial prototyping and detailed design)?

- Is the tool applicable to the **construction phase** of the life-cycle process (i.e., final prototyping, procedural logic and coding & unit testing)?

- Is the tool applicable to the **installation phase** of the life-cycle process (i.e., integrated testing, production testing and installation of the system)?

- Is the tool applicable to the **maintenance phase** of the life-cycle process (i.e., modification of specifications, re-engineering of the system, retesting and reinstallation?

- Does the tool support the requirements of a **project team**, i.e., support for a departmental-level repository, consolidation of specifications from all members of a team, global analysis of consolidated specifications and support for project management.

Table 10-2. (*Continued*)

Components of the Tool

- **Diagramming Tools:** Does the tool provide a set of front-end diagramming facilities that enable the analyst to specify an application system in graphical form?

- **PC Repository:** Does the tool maintain application specifications in a centralized repository or encyclopedia? Ideally, the repository should store the meaning of the specification in abstract form, not simply as a graphic image. The repository should be a knowledge-base for the application, rather than only a dictionary.

- **Mainframe Repository:** Does the tool maintain a mainframe or host-computer version of the repository in abstract form to be shared among multiple analysts working on the same project?

- **Design Analyzer:** Does the tool incorporate a design analyzer to detect design errors such as inconsistencies and incompleteness at all levels of the specification?

- **Code Generator:** Does the tool generate 100% of the code automatically from the graphical specifications?

- **Expert System Rules:** Does the tool utilize a knowledge base that contains expert system rules? To qualify as a knowledge-based tool, the system should incorporate an expert system shell, rules of inference and an inference processor.

Graphics

- **Color:** Does the system display graphics in color?

- **Mouse:** Does the system support a mouse pointing device?

- **Windows:** Does the system permit the simultaneous display of multiple graphical windows on the screen? Can each window be used to display a different diagram or view of the specifications?

Table 10-2. (*Continued*)

Diagrams Supported

- **Data Flow Diagrams:** Does the tool support the creation and manipulation of data flow diagrams?

- **Decomposition Diagrams:** Does the tool support the creation and manipulation of decomposition diagrams (i.e., structure diagrams or decision tree diagrams)?

- **Data Model Diagrams:** Does the tool support the creation and manipulation of logical data models and entity relationship diagrams?

- **Data Navigation Diagrams:** Does the tool support the creation and manipulation of data navigation diagrams (i.e., diagrams that show the sequence of data base operations in graphical form)?

- **Action Diagrams:** Does the tool support the creation and manipulation of action diagrams (i.e., diagrams that incorporate both data actions and procedural logic for an application in a graphical format)?

Integrated Functions

- **Screen/Report Painting:** Does the tool provide a user-friendly means of generating screen panels, menu dialogues and report formats?

- **Dictionary Definitions:** Does the tool provide on-line interfaces to enter and modify dictionary definitions for data elements, data records, data stores, data models, data flows, data relationships, processes, functions, etc.?

- **Data Base Management System:** Does the tool utilize an integrated data base management system to manipulate data entities in the repository or encyclopedia?

- **Prototyping Tools:** Does the tool support a prototyping methodology, in which the analyst is encouraged to work closely with end users to build successively more detailed prototypes of the system?

- **Procedural Language:** Does the tool incorporate a procedural language (i.e., very high-level procedural statements)?

- **Networking Capability:** Does the tool support the incorporation of the terminal within a communications network?

Table 10-2. (*Continued*)

Methodologies Supported

- **Information Engineering:** Does the tool support an information engineering methodology (i.e., a set of formal techniques in which enterprise models, data models and process models are built up in a comprehensive knowledge base and are used to create and maintain application systems)?

- **Yourdon-DeMarco:** Does the tool support the specification of diagrams using the Yourdon or DeMarco structured methodology?

- **Gane-Sarson:** Does the tool support the specification of diagrams using the Gane & Sarson structured methodology?

- **Jackson:** Does the tool support the specification of structured diagrams using the Jackson structured methodology?

- **Others:** Are other development methodologies supported by the product?

- **Project Management:** Does the tool support facilities that enable a project leader to manage a project, e.g., calendar and assignment of responsibilities, relationships of activities including time constraints, updated reports of project schedules, and resource and cost accounting (planned versus actual)?

- How technically advanced is a particular tool (i.e., how many of the components illustrated in Figure 10-1 are incorporated in the tool)?
- What types of front-end diagramming facilities are provided by the tool?
- Does the tool support a range of integrated functions such as data-base management, report generation, screen panel painting, decision support, and procedural language?
- What development methodologies are supported by the product?

Desirable Product Features

In summary, software development workstations differ greatly from other powerful, high-productivity tools. The following concepts should be incorporated into development workstations:

- provision of a highly interactive, responsive and dedicated **environment** in which to develop software;
- **automation** of many software development tasks;
- provision of a pictorial view of software by means of powerful **graphics;**
- capability of **rapid prototyping** for creating models of the system to help discover and clarify user requirements;
- collection of information necessary for **automatic code generation** from system analysis and design;
- **automatic, comprehensive checking and analysis** for early elimination of errors;
- utilization of an **encyclopedia** or **repository;**
- **ease of use;**
- appropriateness for use with advanced methodologies such as interactive **Joint Application Design (JAD)** sessions;
- fully integrated with a **code generator** (commonality of architecture with a code generator; i.e., they both use the same encyclopedia).

To provide a major increase in development productivity across a broad spectrum of analysts and end users, managers should seek out products which support most of the following features:

- Support for the entire development life cycle, including the automatic generation of a high percentage of the executable code from graphical specifications. Some products support only low-level code generation functions such as generation of COBOL data divisions. For applications requiring high on-line performance, the front-end CASE tool should be tightly integrated with a COBOL generator such as APS, GAMMA, PACBASE, TELON or TRANSFORM. This combination is called an I-CASE product, i.e., an integrated CASE tool.

- Availability of most of the product components shown in Figure 10-1, i.e., diagramming tools, a central repository of information, a design analyzer based on a formal information model, an integrated code generator, workstation orientation and the use of a knowledge base incorporating expert system rules.
- Use of a repository to store not simply a representation of the form of the diagram but the meaning of the diagram in abstract form. The repository should be a central source of specification information that can be viewed in many graphical forms. Some CASE tools store graphical specifications in the form of data flow diagrams or structure charts. This approach makes it difficult, if not impossible, to convert specifications automatically from one consistent graphical view to another.
- Support for the basic set of diagramming techniques used in a structured software engineering life-cycle process to represent a software system. These include decomposition diagrams, data flow diagrams, and entity-relationship diagrams (i.e., data entities and entity relationships). To provide rigorous consistency and completeness checking, it is essential for the diagramming techniques to be based on a formal information model such as the Entity Relationship Model developed by Peter Chen, an information engineering model or others. Many methodologies support only portions of a formal information model and cannot provide complete consistency checking. A tool may also utilize other diagram types such as decision trees, action diagrams, state transition diagrams, network management diagrams, etc. The tool should permit flexible conversion from one graphical format to another.
- Superb human factor considerations, including subsecond response to on-line interaction, elimination of complex command mnemonics, intuitive system operation, on-line diagnostic, and HELP facilities and elimination of the need for user reference manuals.
- Availability of the tool on widely used workstations, including the IBM PC and DEC Micro VAX series. In the future, support should also be provided for the IBM OS/2 Presentation Manager.
- Networking capability permitting the interconnection of multiple workstations and facilitating access to corporate mainframe data bases. Ideally, the networking capability should support IBM's communications strategy; i.e., a Token Ring approach within a Local Area Network, the OS/2 Communications Manager to control communications and use of the Systems Application Architecture (SAA) to provide a common user interface across multiple architectures.
- Central mainframe or minicomputer repository (or encyclopedia) shared by many developers with version control, project management facilities, global consistency, and completeness checking, etc.
- Open software architecture, including MS-DOS compatibility, to make use

of the thousands of MS-DOS compatible support programs that are available for the work-station environment.

- Compatibility with widely used software facilities that are likely to be available at a computer site, including DBMS, such as IMS, DB2, IDMS/R, DATACOM/DB, ADABAS, etc; utilities such as ISPF and GDDM; application generators, such as CSP, ADS/OnLine, IDEAL, NATURAL, APPLICATION FACTORY, Cognos PowerHouse, etc; and COBOL generators such as TELON, GAMMA, TRANSFORM, PACBASE, APS, Micro Focus VS, COBOL, etc.
- Support for real-time applications.
- Support for prototyping tools that provide a closely integrated family of procedural and non-procedural functions using a common command syntax, including:
  - data-base query and update;
  - report generator;
  - screen painter;
  - graphics generator;
  - decision support and financial analysis functions;
  - project management tools; and
  - well-structured, very high-level procedural language.
- Support for a rigorous, structured methodology that is easy-to-use and that integrates planning, specification, design, and coding.
- Support for more recent methodologies, such as information engineering, that integrate many of the strategic processes of an organization into a single, coherent structure.
- Utilization of a well-defined life-cycle process to guide the analyst, step-by-step, in the specification and implementation of an application system. An objective of the life cycle process (or development methodology) is to assist all analysts in an organization to achieve a significant improvement in productivity with the CASE product.

Chapter 11

Software Requirements Engineering Methodology (SREM) At The Age of Eleven—Requirements Driven Design

MACK ALFORD
Ascent Logic Corporation
San Jose, CA

ABSTRACT

This Chapter presents an example application of the concepts of Requirements Driven Design (RDD) to the home heating problem. The Requirements Driven Design methods for system and software specification and design are currently supported by two sets of tools: the Distributed Computing Design System tools developed by TRW for and distributed by the U.S. Army to SDI contractors; and the RDD-100 tools developed by Ascent Logic Corporation, currently in commercial release.

1 INTRODUCTION

The concepts, principles, and formal foundations of Requirements Driven Design (RDD) are the result of 15 years research and development sponsored by the U.S. Government. An overview of the history of its development is presented in [1], and is summarized as follows.

The concepts of Requirements Driven Design had their origins in a project performed by TRW in 1968–1969 sponsored by the U.S. Army whose purpose was to represent the software requirements for the SAFEGUARD Ballistic Missile Defense System. The concepts were used to successfully develop software for a real time system in 1969–1975, thus demonstrating their fundamental soundness. The concepts were then formalized and refined under a series of contracts sponsored by the U.S. Army and performed by TRW Huntsville Operations during the period from 1973 until 1987.

From 1973 to 1977, research was performed to formalize the software requirements concepts developed for SAFEGUARD and develop automated tools to provide automated consistency/completeness checking and documentation. The result was the Software Requirements Engineering Method (SREM), first published at the First International Software Engineering Conference in 1977. The key to the method was the definition of software requirements at the state machine/stimulus-response level of detail (i.e., for each input transaction, define the conditions under which specific output messages were to be generated, and specific elements of the state were to be accessed and updated) to which performance requirements could be applied (e.g., response times from input to output, and accuracy of outputs and state updates). The key concept of the tools supporting the method was the use of an Element-Relation-Attribute language to express the concepts (e.g., Message Passed by Input Interface, Message Contains Data), and the use of a graph to formally describe the stimulus-response processing. The methods and tools were applied to a number of problems to demonstrate their feasibility and utility.

These concepts were extended between 1977 and 1980 to address the issues of specifying system level requirements (including functional, performance, and nonfunctional requirements, such as reliability) and allocating these requirements to the system components, including specifically a data processing component. The key problem addressed was the representation of behavior at the system level, and the formal definition of decomposition of such requirements which would preserve this behavior by construction. Again, methods for representing both functional, performance, and nonfunctional requirements were developed. Considerable care was given to the development of a smooth transition between the system level requirements, interface designs, fault detection and recovery requirements, and the representation of the software requirements developed in the SREM research. The SREM tools were extended to support the definition and consistency/completeness checking at the system level. The methods and tools were applied to a number of problems to demonstrate their feasibility and utility.

The concepts were extended again from 1981 to 1985 to address the problems of expressing designs for real-time embedded distributed systems in the Distributed Computing Design System (DCDS) project. This project was driven by a critical observation: if one believed that the method for allocating system requirements to components worked, and one believed the axiom that a component could be considered as a system, then the same methods used at the top level should apply to all levels of software engineering. The system level methods were thus applied to the problems of distributed design, real-time design for high reliability, module level design, and the definition of the integration test plans. The results of the research were summarized in Reference 1.

The prototype tools developed during the DCDS project were used on a number of projects and are currently distributed by the U.S. Army to its contractors. In 1987, the Ascent Logic Corporation was formed to commercialize these concepts with highly interactive, high resolution graphics workstation based tools, which would be made available to the Software Engineering community.

Overview of the RDD Concepts

The fundamental concepts of RDD are the following:

- Define requirements in a way which captures desired system behavior, i.e., conditional sequence and concurrency of functions which map inputs into outputs, as well as performance and nonfunctional requirements (e.g., safety, security). Since software reliability is defined as the probability that the software does what the user expects, definition of desired behavior is the foundation for reliability.
- This required behavior should be decomposed and allocated to components in a way which explicitly preserves the desired behavior.
- Interface designs are rigorously derived to implement flow of items between functions allocated to different components. This is performed iteratively to yield a formal derivation of the layers of interface between components. Interface designs preserve the desired behavior.
- This desired behavior should be preserved where possible in the presence of faults, exceptions, and constraints. This means that the functions allocated to each component are subjected to a Failure Modes Effects Analysis, and functions may be added to the system level requirements to detect exceptions and recovered back to the desired behavior. These functions are decomposed and allocated to the components. This provides for an explicit definition of recovery from any exception, and an explicit definition of the layers of defense against component faults. Nonfunctional requirements (e.g., safety and security) are handled in the same way.
- The above process is repeated for each level of system, Data Processor, and software design component. Since each stage of design preserves the behavior allocated to it, the behavior specified at the top level is preserved by construction, thus yielding reliable systems. Traceability to original requirements is thus built into the development process rather than being added on, and this substantially reduces the effort to make subsequent design modifications in response to requirements changes.

The concepts of RDD differ from the traditions of Systems Engineering—the only real difference is that behavior is captured, not just functions, and the same techniques are applied to software development as well as top level system definition. These concepts differ substantially from the more traditional data flow methods by providing a systematic, constructive design approach. Behavior is explicitly defined, rather than just describing data flows or even state machines. Design takes place by formally allocating behavior to components, thus preserving the traceability between system and component behavior, rather than having discontinuities between requirements and design representations. Multiple designs can be quickly created by changing the criteria for allocation. Interface designs are explicitly and formally derived, rather than being added on in an *ad hoc* fashion. Issues of fault detection and recovery are explicitly and systematically addressed, rather than being left to the ingenuity of the developer.

The RDD approach views design as a process of allocating required behavior to components, rather than starting with a clean piece of paper, constructing components, then later trying to map requirements onto them. This can occur at a number of levels of a system:

- allocation of system level functions between the environment and a black box system;
- allocation of black box system functions to components or subsystems (e.g., a data processor subsystem);
- allocation of data processing functions onto software design elements; or
- decomposition and allocation of an algorithm to units of code which will implement it.

In this chapter, the author will focus on the problem of representing system level requirements and allocating them onto first the data processor, then software components.

The basic building block of the description is the **discrete function** which accepts one or more discrete inputs, generates one or more discrete outputs (including state information), and transitions to a new state to receive the next input. When a number of discrete functions are connected by a graph which defines conditional sequencing, one has by defintion a **state machine.** This part of the technology is not new—a number of different researchers use the concept of state machines to represent sequencing conditions (e.g., to represent communication protocols, to represent actions of robots, and even to describe sequencing conditions in some data flow requirements/design approaches). But other methods are stuck with the limitations of the state machine (i.e., systems with large numbers of states cannot be handled effectively, and the representation of concurrent systems causes a state explosion).

To overcome the limitations of the state machine model, the RDD approach provides the ability to aggregate a graph of discrete functions into a simplified building block called the **time function.** By definition, a time function accepts a structure of inputs over some finite period of time and generates some structure of outputs during that period of time, until some **completion condition** is satisfied. In the same manner, a sequence of inputs or outputs can be aggregated into a higher level building block called a **time item.** Much larger behaviors can then be represented using graphs whose nodes are time functions which input and output item streams. Graphs of time functions can be further aggregated into higher level time functions, to an arbitrary number of levels.

In addition to representing conditional sequences of functions, the RDD graphs provide the ability to represent various types of concurrency of the following functions and/or items:

- Concurrent interleaved streams of input items, specifying both partial sequencing and concurrency (e.g., input from each user arrives in sequence but may be arbitrarily interleaved between users);
- Independent concurrent functions, with no interactions—this provides the ability to define independent state machines;
- Pipelined concurrent functions—this provides the ability to represent behavior in which the output stream of one function becomes the input stream of another. This concurrency may be serialized at design time;
- Interdependent concurrent functions, requiring coordination—this provides the ability to describe the desired behavior of concurrent state machines with constraints; and
- Replicated concurrent functions, requiring coordination (e.g., processing inputs from a number of users)—this provides the ability to describe the behavior of many identical concurrent state machines with constraints.

Such graphs of items and functions can be used to express arbitrarily complex system behaviors in a hierarchical manner, which are more understandable than if the behavior was represented at a state machine. For example, the behavior of a set of elevators would be described as the behavior of replicated elevators, where each elevator responded to its button inputs and inputs from a coordination function.

If data processing functions are being described, and the discrete functions are complex, then they can be further decomposed into a stimulus-response level of description. An entire function or path can be allocated to a single task, or the stimulus-response can be subdivided and mapped onto multiple tasks, and these can be allocated to different processors if needed to satisfy response time requirements.

The tools developed to support the RDD approach to system/software design provide the following capabilities to the users:

- aid the user to input the requirements/design information with minimum effort;
- aid several users in coordinating their efforts on a single design;
- provide a reviewers aid for the review process (e.g., show traceability from a requirement to where it is satisfied in the system description);

- perform automated consistency/completeness analyses (e.g., verify that each input to a function is generated before it is used);
- provide automated aids to extract the requirements/design information into required documentation formats required by software development standards; and
- provide support for easily identifying the impact of a requirements change and then making the change.

Many of the features of RDD can be illustrated by its application to the Home Heating Problem. The requirements for the home heating problem appear in Appendix 1. The reformulation of the requirements into a format, which can be used for traceability purposes, appears in Appendix 2. What follows is a brief sketch of results of applying the RDD steps to the home heating problem.

2   DEFINING THE SYSTEM BEHAVIOR

The author starts the definition of the system behavior by defining the home heating system, including its attributes, and defining the highest level function of the system, named HEAT HOUSE AS REQUIRED. This can be done using paper forms or using templates in tools which keep the information in an Element-Relation-Attributed database. An example of such information follows.

```
SYSTEM: HOME HEATING SYSTEM.
        PERFORMS FUNCTION: HEAT HOUSE AS REQUIRED
        EXHIBITS PERFORMANCE INDEX    COST
                                      DATE AVAILABLE
        TRACED FROM SYSTEM REQUIREMENTS PARA_1_0.
        DOCUMENTED BY SOURCE HOME HEATING RQTS

FUNCTION: HEAT HOUSE AS REQUIRED.
        INPUTS ITEM OIL
               ITEM ELECTRICITY
        OUTPUTS ITEM HEAT
        PERFORMED BY SYSTEM HOME HEATING SYSTEM
        EXHIBITS PERFORMANCE INDEX PI1 TEMPERATURES
                      EXTREMES
                PERFORMANCE INDEX PI2 TURN OFF RESPONSE
                      TIME
        CONSTRAINED BY
                CONSTRAINT SAFETY1 RESTART TIME OF 5
                      MINUTES
        COMPLETION CRITERIA: "NO LONGER REPAIRABLE."
```

Note that the SYSTEM has relationships which link it to its top level function, and its top level performance indices, and that traceability to the system requirements document is built in, rather than being added on at the last minute. The top level FUNCTION is defined by its inputs and outputs, the performance indices used to determine whether the system is a "good one," a safety constraint which must be satisfied at all times, and its completion criteria. This completion criteria is not contained in the top level system requirements documents, and thus a design decision was made as to when the system function should cease. As will be seen later, this turns out to be a critical decision.

The components of the system are also defined and linked to the system in the following way:

```
SYSTEM: HOME HEATING SYSTEM
    BUILT FROM SUBSYSTEM TEMP SENSOR
             SUBSYSTEM CONTROLLER
             SUBSYSTEM FURNACE
             SUBSYSTEM MASTER SWITCH
             SUBSYSTEM ABNORMAL STATUS INDICATOR
```

Each subsystem is then defined—in the interest of brevity, only one is shown as follows:

```
SUBSYSTEM TEMP SENSOR
    INPUTS ITEM POOR TEMPERATURE VS TIME
           ITEM TEMPERATURE SETTING VS TIME
    OUTPUTS ITEM DELTA-TEMPERATURE VS TIME
    TRACED FROM SYSTEM REQUIREMENT
             P2 TEMPERATURE CONTROL DEVICE
```

The system function HEAT HOUSE is decomposed in two stages: first, the function is decomposed assuming no faults or exceptions; then the exceptions are identified using these graphs, and functions are added to deal with the exceptions.

If one looks at the system as a whole, and ignores all faults, there are essentially two modes of operation: the master switch is off, and the system is not heating; or the master switch is on, and the system is heating. Since the resident may turn on and turn off the system at will, the system cycles between these two states. This behavior is formalized in the F_NET in Figure 11-1.

In Figure 11-1, each node of the graph represents a function which transforms a time-set of inputs (e.g., on/off switch position versus time, temperature difference versus time) into a time-set of outputs (e.g., time-set of commands to furnace). For example, the FUNCTION CYCLE HEAT ON AND OFF can be described in terms of its inputs, outputs, and completion criteria as follows:

```
FUNCTION: CYCLE HEAT ON AND OFF
  INPUTS ITEM: ROOM TEMPERATURE VS TIME
         ITEM ON_OFF_SWITCH_VALUES
         ITEM OIL
         ITEM ELECTRICITY
  OUTPUTS ITEM HEAT.
```

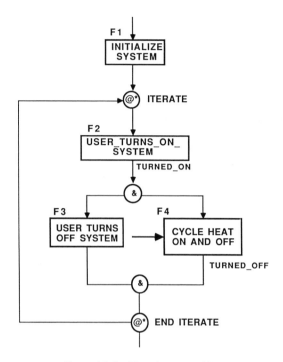

Figure 11-1. First decomposition.

```
COMPLETION CRITERIA: "TURNED OFF."
EXHIBITS PERFORMANCE INDEX PI1 TEMPERATURE EXTREMES
              PERFORMANCE INDEX PI2 TURN OFF
              RESPONSE TIME.
```

Now if this behavior is compared to the definition of the top level system function, one discovers a problem: the completion criterion of the top level function was "NO LONGER REPAIRABLE," whereas the above behavior continues indefinitely. To address this problem, one must modify the decomposition in the following way: first, add an abnormal exit to F4 which enables a function F5 REPAIR AND RESET; if the system cannot be repaired, then F5 will produce an exit from the behavior that the system is "no longer repairable." This is illustrated in Figure 11-2.

Now the number of exits match, and the decomposition process can continue. To further illustrate the process, select F4 HOME HEATING CYCLE for further decomposition. This function is first decomposed to describe its normal behavior.

While the system is in the heating mode, the system is cycling between heating and waiting for the temperature to drop. The normal mode of operation is as follows: when the temperature drops sufficiently, then the system should start

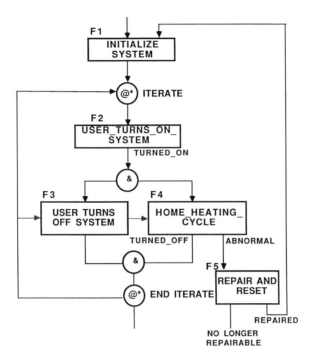

Figure 11-2. Modified decomposition.

the heating cycle; the system prepares for heating by performing a sequence of actions of starting the motor, then "the ignition is activated and the oil valve is opened." The exact wording suggests that the ignition activation and oil valve opening are simultaneous or in parallel—for the sake of safety, a decision was made to require these to occur in the sequence "ignition is activated, and THEN the oil valve is opened."

When the temperature has risen sufficiently, the system shuts the furnace off by going through the sequence of closing the oil valve, then "five seconds later (to allow for valve lag time), the motor and ignition are deactivated: there is a three second lag time before the motor stops." Again, the requirements are ambiguous, so for the sake of safety, first the motor will be turned off, and three seconds later the ignition will be turned off.

Next the behavior when the user turns off the system is addressed. If the system is waiting for a low temp, simply exit. If the system is heating the house, a turned-off exit to the shutdown sequence is necessary. If the system is in the TURN ON mode, then there is a decision to make: should the system have a special turn-off, or take the normal turn-on sequence and then the normal shutdown sequence. If the performance requirements allow it, the latter will be the simplest behavior; if the performance requirements on shutdown response time do not allow it, additional paths of functionality might be required, which are ignored for the moment. The resulting system behavior can be formalized in the F_NET as shown in Figure 11-3.

Abnormal Behavior

When the inputs and outputs of each function are specified, and then compared to those of Function F44, they can be made to match (e.g., Function F44 is the one that actually generates the heat). However, when the number of exits is compared, there is a mismatch. F4 has two exits (i.e., TURNED OFF and ABNORMAL) while the above behavior has only the TURNED OFF exit. This requires that the behavior in the presence of exceptions be defined.

The two abnormal conditions cited in the requirements were INADEQUATE FUEL FLOW and LACK OF COMBUSTION. If either is detected, the system is to shut down and then display the conditions. When the above behavior is analyzed, it appears that the only place where the INADEQUATE FUEL FLOW and NO COMBUSTION exits can occur is in the HEAT HOUSE function F45.

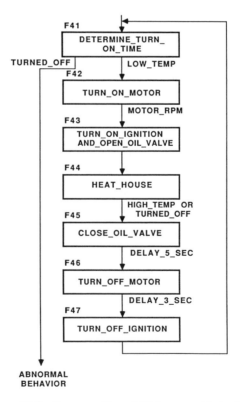

Figure 11-3. Decomposition of F4 for normal behavior.

But, if recovery is defined as getting back to the standard flow, no recovery procedure is defined. One option might be to simply repeat the process of turning on the furnace and hope it will cure itself: another option might be to require for the sake of safety that the furnace be repaired and reset before going back into normal operation. Since the shutdown behavior should be the same as in the normal case, this behavior can be modified by adding an exit to F44 if an exception is identified, and add another exit to F47 to abort. The result appears in Figure 11-4.

If this behavior is compared to the original requirements, one notices that the safety requirements of a 5-minute delay between any shutdown and the next startup are not yet satisfied. These can be addressed in either of two ways: add a function after F47 to delay for 5 minutes, or add a function before F42 to ensure a 5-minute delay. Assume for the purposes of this example that the second alternative is selected.

Next, a Failure Modes Effects Analysis is performed on the specified behavior to determine if there might be any reason why each transformation, and each transition might not be accomplished. When function F42 is reached, the

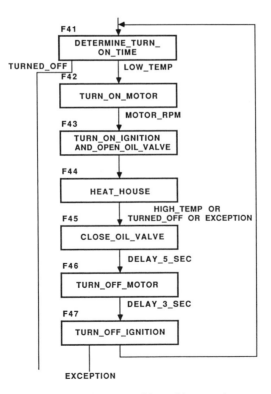

Figure 11-4. Decomposition with exceptions.

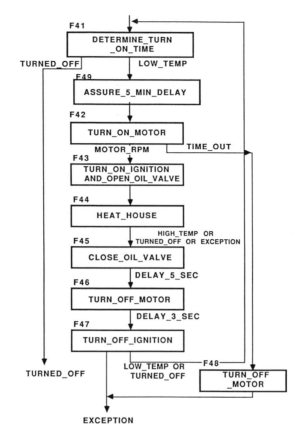

Figure 11-5. Decomposition with exceptions and safety.

problem might be identified of the motor not coming up to speed within a reasonable amount of time. The result would be that the system would hang until the MOTOR RPM signal was received, if ever. Such an exception can be detected by a timeout. Then there are at least two ways of dealing with this situation: go through the normal cycle, and discover that there is inadequate fuel flow, or detect it and abort.

A decision is made to raise the exception "motor_timed_out" from this function, and respond by shutting down the motor and raising the exception "inadequate_fuel_flow." The combination of standard_flow and exception layers is presented in Figure 11-5.

3   DECOMPOSITION AND ALLOCATION

Each of the functions on Figure 11-5 can now be defined and decomposed and allocated to be performed by the various components of the system; for example, the function F41, which determines turn-on time, can be defined as follows:

```
F41_DETERMINE_TURN_ON_TIME
    DESCRIPTION: "This function of the system senses
    the temperature in the house and the state of
    the ON/OFF switch, and exits when the switch has
    been turned off, or exits when a low temperature
    has been sensed. . ."
    INPUTS ITEM ON_OFF_SWITCH_VALUE_VS_TIME.
    OUTPUTS ITEM HEAT_VS_TIME.
    EXITS BY
        COMPLETION CRITERIA: TURNED OFF
        COMPLETION CRITERIA LOW TEMPERATURE
```

This function, F41, can now be decomposed into a collection of concurrent functions, shown in Figure 11-6. Note that the functionality level is down to the point where the functions can be allocated to components. The HOUSE-_LOSES_HEAT function transmits house temperature to the temperature sensor which is allocated the function SENSE_TEMPERATURE, outputting a discrete temperature to the COMPUTE_TURN_ON_TIME function allocated to the controller. Similarly, the value of the master switch is sensed by the function SENSE_SWITCH_OFF, also allocated to the controller.

When this decomposition and allocation procedure is repeated for each function, one will find that the controller has been allocated a structure of functions. The overall required behavior of the Data Processor can be derived by taking Figure 11-5, inserting all of the decompositions, and then discarding all functions allocated to the Data Processor. The result is summarized in Figure 11-7. The functions allocated to the other components, and to the environment, then become requirements for simulation software used to test the Data Processor hardware and software during the integration test phase of software/DP development.

Summary of Issues Identified

The decomposition/allocation activities to specify the required system behavior led to the identification of the following two critical issues:

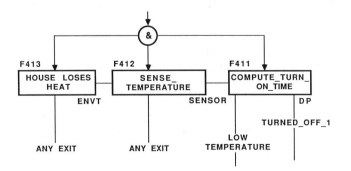

Figure 11-6. Decomposition and allocation.

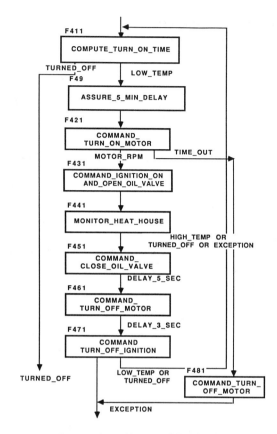

Figure 11-7. Required DP behavior.

- The requirements did not specify how the system recovered when a malfunction was detected; and
- the requirements did not specify what the system should do if the motor was turned on but did not get up to speed within a reasonable amount of time.

In addition, at least two design decisions were made to define behavior which satisfied the following overall requirements:

- The behavior of the system in the turning-on-motor state when the user turned off the master switch was selected (i.e., wait until the furnace was operating to identify the system had been turned off, then turn off); and
- the behavior of the system.

4 DECOMPOSITION TO STATE MACHINE LEVEL

The graph in Figure 11-7 is not yet a state machine because each of the nodes on the graph represent functions which input time sequences of inputs (e.g., temperature difference versus time) and outputs time sequences of commands to the furnace. For example, the function F411

```
COMPUTE_TURN_ON_TIME can be defined as follows:
    FUNCTION F411_COMPUTE_TURN_ON_TIME.
        INPUTS ITEM TEMPERATURE_DIFFERENCE_VS_TIME
               ITEM ON_OFF_SWITCH_VALUES.
        COMPLETION_CRITERIA:
            "Low temperature—when temperature is
            low enough to require the furnace to be
            turned on and master switch is still ON
            Turned-off—master switch has been
            turned off."
```

This function can be decomposed to the state machine level in several different ways which depend in part on the interface design decisions, response time requirements for the transitions, and design decisions on how to satisfy those response time requirements. The interface between the controller and the on/off switch and temperature sensor could be designed to send discrete messages only when something changed; that could result in a design in which the controller simply waited for a discrete event.

A simple design of waiting for the temperature to cross the 2 degree threshold will not work because the temperature sensor has a 1 minute delay time. The simple design which predicts when the temperature will cross the 2 degree threshold and delays until that time will not work either, because this design assumes a constant heat loss, and if someone opens a door, the temperature may cross the 2 degree threshold before it was predicted. A more complex design which combines both of these features might be represented as follows:

- Assume that the inputs from the on/off switch and temperature are discretes which interrupt the processor. Then the function can simply be decomposed into two functions which wait for the arrival of temperature and on/off discretes. The temperature monitoring function exits when either a measurement of −2 degrees or the predicted time for the −2 degree crossing has arrived.

On the other hand, suppose that the sensors send signals continuously; this imposes an interface requirement to sample the signals periodically—the frequency of the period is selected to meet response time requirements. If the sample rates are selected to be the same, then the following design would result:

- Assume the inputs are continuous and to be sampled by the controller. The function can first be decomposed into a single cyclic discrete function which checks values of instantaneous inputs of master switch and temperature, and changes state if specified conditions are satisfied. This decomposition is presented, in Figure 11-8A.

If the different inputs require sampling at different rates because of differing response time requirements, the function might first be decomposed into two concurrent functions, then each decomposed into state machines. This might also be done to preserve modularity. This would result in the following design:

- Again assume inputs are continuous. Since two different concurrent inputs occur, the function can be subdivided into two concurrent functions (one to monitor temperature, the other to monitor on/off switch), and then these are decomposed to a cyclic monitoring function. This will postpone the decision on cycle rates until later, rather than tying them together at design time. This decomposition is presented in Figure 11-8B

5   DECOMPOSITION TO THE STIMULUS-RESPONSE LEVEL

Having reached the discrete function (i.e., state-machine) level of description, the previous decomposition approach can no longer be applied. The decomposition of a discrete function is represented instead as a stimulus-response network of transformations and decisions, which identify flow of data and conditions of processing. This is represented as an R_NET or SUBNET in the Requirements Statement Language of SREM.

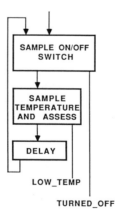

Figure 11-8a. Serialized decomposition.

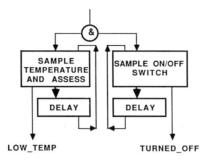

Figure 11-8b. Concurrent decomposition.

Decomposition of the function which monitors the on/off switch is simple—if the switch value is "ON," then no transition occurs and if it is "OFF," then the controller switches to the "OFF" mode. The definition of the transitions for the function SAMPLE TEMPERATURE AND ASSESS shown in Figure 11-8 is a little more complicated. Again, there are a number of ways of decomposing this function. One way is described as follows in terms of the conditions for changing modes and updating the data base:

- If the temperature difference between measured temperature and desired temperature is less than or equal to −2 degrees, then the LOW_TEMPERATURE exit is taken.
- Remember that the temperature sensor has about a 1 minute delay time. The requirement to use previous heat-loss information to determine turn-on time leads to an approach where the time for temperature to cross the −2 degree mark is predicted using previous information, and the LOW_TEMP exit is taken if current time is greater than the predicted time.
- If the temperature has not changed since the last measurement, and the predicted time is greater than current time, then the delay exit is taken.
- If the temperature has changed, then the temperature change should be recorded, and the delay exit taken.
- If the temperature has changed to −1 degree, then a predicted furnace turn-on time should be predicted, and the delay exit taken.

This concept of operation is formalized in the SUBNET presented in Figure 11-9. Note that this decomposition preserves the exits from the discrete function in Figure 11-8. Further, it forces up into visibility the requirement to keep TEMP HISTORY as state information, to be accessed and updated by the processing of temperature information.

This behavior is not unique—the decisions could have been made in a different sequence, the time to turn-on the furnace could be rounded off, etc., which

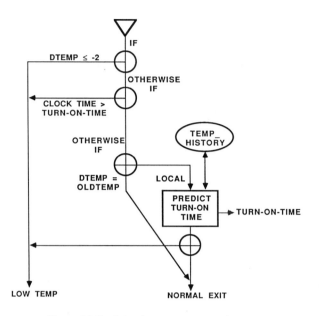

Figure 11-9. Stimulus-response requirements.

would result in a slightly different but equally ''valid'' implementation of the state machine.

6   AUGMENTATION OF THE REQUIREMENTS

To implement Paragraph 5 of the requirements, i.e., to provide a controller for a set of 5 Condos with a limitation of total fuel flow, the previously discussed decomposition can be augmented as follows: first, the top level system function, PROVIDE_HEAT_TO_CONDOS, can be defined; this Function can now be decomposed using a theorem which states that any controller which controls a number items can be represented (without loss of generality) in terms of a set of controllers (i.e., one per condo) plus a coordination function. Figure 11-10 presents such a decomposition.

Note that the function PROVIDE_HEAT_TO_A_CONDO is quite similar to the function PROVIDE_HEAT_AS_REQUIRED identified at the beginning of this chapter. The primary difference is that the function PRO-VIDE_HEAT_TO_A_CONDO has an extra set of outputs (i.e., CONDO_STATUS) and an extra set of inputs (i.e., CONDO_CONTROLS). The coordination function CONTROL_CONDOS accepts the status information from each condo, and uses a set of rules to generate and output the set of control information to each condo. The controller must enforce the constraint that only four heaters be on at a time.

The decomposition of the CONTROL__CONDOS function could follow any one of a number of possible strategies. Consider the following examples:

A) Delay any heater until one of the other heaters naturally turns off. This is simple but would probably result in a CONDO experiencing a temperature of less than −2 degrees while waiting and requires an additional mode for the control system (i.e., waiting for permission to turn on).

B) If a CONDO gets near the −2 degree mark, turn off the heater of the CONDO with the highest current temperature. This would preserve the number of states but would add an additional exit condition for the heathome function (i.e., exit if a control-command is received, and result in a higher data flow between controllers and a more complex algorithm for the coordination controller.

Either of these control strategies can be implemented in a rather straightforward fashion and by augmenting the single-controller state diagrams by adding outputs and some additional states; however, both require the decomposition of the controller function down to the state machine level to complete the definition of the system.

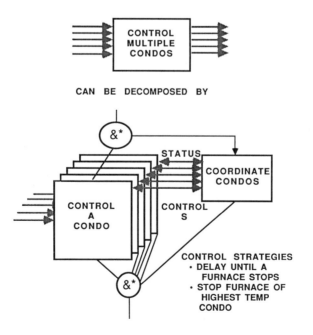

Figure 11-10. Decomposing the control of multiple furnaces.

Consider the diagram in Figure 11-7. To implement strategy A, add a status output to F411, add a control input to F412, and change the completion criterion to the combination (delayed_5_minutes AND permission_received). To implement strategy B add the status output from F411, and add a control input to F451, and change the completion criterion to read (high_temp OR turned_off OR exception OR control_received). In both cases a function must be added to the decomposition to check to see if the control-received condition has occurred. In both cases, the modification to the state transition diagrams is rather small.

7   TRANSITION TO A SOFTWARE DESIGN

Transition of the above requirements into a design occurs by first mapping the required functions and SUBNETs onto processors. There are at least four simple mappings which could be defined as follows:

- Map all processing onto a single centralized processor.
- Map all processing for each condo onto its own processor and the coordination function onto a central processor (this is a master-multiple-slave design concept).
- Map all processing for each condo onto its own processor and the coordination function onto condo 1 processor,
- Map all processing for each condo and the coordination function onto its own processor but only instantiate the controller on one of them. Fail-over logic can now be implemented to bring up the coordination function on another processor if a failure occurs.
- Decompose the coordination function into a set of replicated cooperating communicating coordination functions, and allocate one each to the condo processors. Now agreement protocols are used to agree on which furnace is to be turned-on and turned-off. This is a truly distributed design.

Note that each of these designs can be defined by a set of decompositions and allocations. Note further that each design will have different execution time, memory size, and communication rate combinations than the others. Moreover, each design would have different fault tolerance properties from the others (e.g., survivability, autonomy, robustness to communication failures, reliability, availability, etc.) Note further, however, that each of these designs can be constructed to preserve the sequencing and time delay requirements originally specified.

The design of the processing within each controller continues with the allocation of functions or SUBNETs onto logically concurrent units of code called TASKs. A variety of top-level designs can easily be identified as follows:

A) All of the processing for a single CONDO could be mapped onto a single program which serialized all of the required concurrency. The result would be a program which could be directly written in serial programming languages, such as FORTRAN or PASCAL.

B) Each function in Figure 11-7 could be mapped onto a task; this could be directly implemented in programming languages which have concurrency constructs like C or even Ada.

C) Each function at the level of Figure 11-8 could be mapped onto a task (this would provide multiple concurrent tasks, one for each input source during each mode of operation); this would have many more tasks and thus might result in a higher overhead for scheduling.

D) All processing of temperature inputs could be allocated to a single TASK; this would result in a concurrent-state-machine implementation with a small number of TASKs but with more complex code within each TASK. This type of design could be directly prototyped by using the SREM Simulator Generator functions.

E) All processing of all temperature information for all condos could be mapped into a single task on the central processor.

To show how these designs can be easily implemented with strict traceability using the Distributed Design Language of RDD, consider the design approach B. Referring to Figure 11-7, the following design could be generated to implement the function COMPUTE_TURN_ON_TIME.

```
TASK_COMPLETE_TURN_ON_TIME.
    TRACED FROM FUNCTION F411_COMPUTE_TURN_ON_TIME.
    READS BUFFER B_ON_OFF_SWITCH
         BUFFER B_D_TEMP
         DATA_FILE DF_TEMPERATURE_HISTORY
    UPDATES DATA_FILE DF_TEMPERATURE_HISTORY
    ENABLED_BY: "E_WAITING_FOR_LOW_TEMP"
    SETS EVENT E_TURNED_OFF_1
         EVENT E_LOW_TEMP
         EVENT E_WAITING_FOR_LOW_TEMP
    PDL:"
         "read buffer on-off switch
          if on
               then set event turned-off-1
               else read buffer d_temp
               SUBNET SAMPLE_TEMPERATURE_AND_ASSESS
               (sets event E_LOW_TEMP or)
               (sets event E_WAITING_FOR_LOW_TEMP
               delayed by(an amount SAMPLE_TIME)."
```

Note that this design has mapped processing onto tasks and mapped required data onto data objects. For example, the temperature history data required on

Fig 11-9 is mapped onto a data file (special type of data object) called DF_TEMPERATURE_HISTORY, while the information flowing between tasks is mapped onto data objects called BUFFERs.

Mapping these logical designs onto physical designs of compilable units of code in the programming language leads to even more variability. For example, even if a number of logically concurrent TASKs are identified at the previous level, they could be implemented by using concurrent constructs in the programming language (e.g., mapped directly into Ada TASKs) or by serializing them at implementation time (e.g., by mapping the TASKs into Ada procedures and then scheduling them using a user executive Ada task which calls the procedures when conditions have been satisfied). The latter design requires more user code but provides a more efficient implementation and more control over the execution time characteristics of the design. Similarly, the data objects could of course be implemented with COMMON storage in FORTRAN, while implemented with PACKAGEs in Ada.

8 INTEGRATION TEST CONSIDERATIONS

One of the appreciable benefits of the RDD approach to integration testing is that it identifies functions which must be simulated in order to perform testing of the software. Consider Figure 11-5; to provide an environment for the testing of the controllers, the functions HOUSE_LOSES_HEAT and SENSE_TEM-PERATURE will have to be simulated.

A second appreciable benefit of the RDD approach to integration testing is that it provides for an orderly identification of the integration test cases. Consider Figure 11-6; by examining the diagram, it can be seen that at least the following conditions are necessary to test this top-level system behavior:

- While the system is waiting for a low temperature, turn it off.
- While the system is waiting for a low temperature, feed in a low temperature (at least four subcases will be needed here—see Figure 11-9).
- At least one test case should have no delay required to enforce the 5 minute rule.
- While the system is waiting for a 5 minute delay between last shut down and next start up, turn the system off.
- While motor is coming up to speed, do not input the motor-up-to-speed discrete.
- When the furnace is on, provide an exception.
- When the furnace is on, turn the system off.
- When the furnace is on, allow the temperature to rise above +2 degrees (again, at least four subcases can be identified similar to those in Figure 11-9).
- While the oil valve is being turned off, turn the system off.
- While waiting for the motor to go off, turn the system off.

These different conditions can be integrated into a single scenario or developed in a number of test cases of increasing complexity. This is quite simple to do if the behavior is explicitly specified, but quite difficult to do if the behavior is not explicitly specified.

9 CONCLUSIONS

A sketch of the application of RDD to the home heating problem has been presented above—the complete presentation of results would take more pages than are available. However, even this sketch shows a number of the strengths of RDD:

- Specification of the system behavior surfaces issues which might go otherwise unrecognized which are system level issues; for example, the requirement to represent behavior surfaced the problem of how to recover from a detected failure and the failure modes effects analysis surfaced the problem of what to do if the motor does not come up to speed. Neither of these problems were addressed in the requirements document.
- RDD can be used to define requirements regardless of where the system boundary is drawn. The specification of environment functions is later used to define requirements for simulators to test the controller during integration testing.
- The transition from functions to state machine to stimulus-response representation of the state machine occurs smoothly. Moreover, the continued decompositions and allocations can be made to preserve the data flow and state transitions at each level of description.
- The RDD design approach provides for the identification of a large number of potential centralized or distributed designs; each of these designs preserves the data flow and stimulus-response of the requirements, although they differ in their fault tolerance properties.
- The RDD design approach provides the definition of a large number of real-time designs; each provides the specified functionality, but they differ in their efficiencies.
- The RDD test planning approach uses the system specifications to systematically generate required test conditions and test cases to demonstrate the specified system behavior.
- The application of RDD to this simple problem demonstrates that even simple problems are not simple. Thus, even "trivial" problems could probably profit from the application of the concepts, and even small problems could profit from the use of the tools to help analyze the consistency/completeness conditions and provide documentation support.

REFERENCE

1. Alford, M., "SREM AT THE AGE OF EIGHT: The Distributed Computing Design System," IEEE *Computer*, Vol. 18, No. 4, April 1985, pp. 36–47.

Appendix 1

ORIGINAL REQUIREMENTS FOR THE HOME HEATING PROBLEM

I. Overall Requirements

1. Home Heating Overview

A temperature sensing device compares the difference between the temperature t, sensed in the house, and the reference temperature t_r, which is the desired house temperature. The difference between these two, the error in the temperature, is measured and sent to the controller (see Figure 11-1). The controller signals the furnace; the furnace produces heat, which is introduced to the house at rate Q_i; the house loses heat at the rate Q_o. If insufficient heat is supplied to the house, the temperature t falls: if the amount of heat going into the house exceeds that flowing out by natural means, the temperature of the house rises. The purpose of the feedback mechanism is to keep the difference between the reference temperature t_r, and the temperature of the house within desired limits if possible. A high outdoor temperature with a resultant heat flow into the house is possible, but no air conditioner is present in the current system.

2. Temperature Control Device

A computer system interacting with a temperature sensing device is used to control the desired temperature of the house. A master switch can be set at "HEAT" or "OFF." With a "HEAT" setting, the furnace will operate as in the description: With an "OFF" setting, the furnace will not operate. The homeowner is also allowed to select a desired temperature setting.

For purposes of comfort and furnace efficiency, the total change of temperature allowed in the house will be 4 degrees. If a room temperature of 70 degrees is desired, the furnace must operate so that the temperature never falls below 68 degrees or rises above 72 degrees (unless the outside temperature is greater than 72 degrees).

Note that if the comfort interval (bandwidth) is too small, the frequency with which the furnace oscillates between ON and OFF will be too rapid to be efficient. If the bandwidth is too great, the house will sometimes be too cold and sometimes too warm.

The temperature-sensing device does not have great precision and accuracy. It will detect temperature variations of the order of magnitude of 1 degree. It also has a time lag of the order of 1 minute.

3. The Furnace Subsystem

The oil furnace, which is used to heat the house, has a motor which drives a fan to supply combustion air and also drives a fuel pump.

When the house gets too cold, the motor is activated. When the motor reaches normal operating speed, the ignition is activated and the oil valve is opened. The fuel is ignited at this time, and the furnace begins to heat the water, which circulates through the house.

A fuel flow indicator and an optical combustion sensor signal the controller if abnormalities occur.

The furnace is alternately activated and deactivated by the controller to maintain the temperature within the required limits. When the furnace is deactivated, first the oil valve is closed, and 5 seconds later (to allow for the valve lag time), the motor and ignition are de-activated. There is a 3-second lag time before the motor stops.

4. Controller—Inputs/Outputs for the Controller

Inputs to the Controller include the following:

• Heating system master switch setting which can be "OFF" or "HEAT."
• Error between the house temperature and the temperature setting (t_r-t).
• Motor RPM status, which is a discrete, indicating whether or not the motor is at normal operating speed.
• Combustion status, which is a discrete, indicating whether combustion is taking place or not.
• Fuel flow status which indicates whether adequate fuel flow exists or not.

Outputs from the Controller include the following:

• Valve signal which is a discrete, signaling the valve to open or close.
• Motor[1] signal which is a discrete, directing the motor to start or stop.
• Ignition signal which is a discrete directing ignition to start or stop.
• Signals to indicate abnormal status for combustion and fuel flow.

Controller Requirements
When the master switch is on and outside temperature permits,

```
t_r-2  ⊂  house temperature  ⊃  t_r  +  2
```

where t_r is the temperature setting.

Furnace input control signals shall be generated in a manner compatible with furnace operation. The minimum time for furnace restart after prior "ON" interval is 5 minutes.

Furnace turn-off shall be initiated within 5 seconds after the following:

• master switch is turned off,
• fuel flow rate falls below adequate levels, or
• the optical detector indicates the absence of combustion.

To minimize the extent of house temperature over-shoots and under-shoots beyond the desired limits, the timing of furnace signals initiating or terminating calls for heat shall be based on the rate of temperature change during the corresponding interval.

The controller shall send signals to a status indicator device when abnormal conditions exist—inadequate fuel flow or lack of combustion.

5. A Change of Requirements

The customer wishes to modify the controller so that it can be used for a group of 5 condominiums. Each condo has the same temperature control device, furnace system, abnormal status indicator, and heating requirements previously described. However, all use oil from a single oil tank. It has been determined that the oil flow will allow at most 4 furnaces to operate simultaneously.

Appendix 2
REFORMATION OF THE HOME HEATING PROBLEM REQUIREMENTS INTO SSL

SYSTEM_REQUIREMENT: P1_HOME_HEATING_OVERVIEW— DESCRIPTION

A temperature sensing device compares the difference between the temperature t, sensed in the house, and the reference temperature t_r, which is the desired house temperature. The difference between these two, the error in the temperature, is measured and sent to the controller (see Figure 11-1). The controller signals the furnace; the furnace produces heat, which is introduced to the house at rate Q_i; the house loses heat at the rate of Q_o. If insufficient heat is supplied to the house, the temperature t falls. If the amount of heat going into the house exceeds that flowing out by natural means, the temperature of the house rises. The purpose of the feedback mechanism is to keep the difference between the reference temperature t_r, and the temperature of the house within desired limits if possible. A high outdoor temperature with a resultant heat flow into the house is possible but no air conditioner is present in the current system.

SYSTEM_REQUIREMENT: P1_F1_FIGURE_1—DESCRIPTION
Block diagram presenting subsystems and their relationships. SUBSYSTEMS include the following:

- master switch,
- controller,
- furnace,
- temp sensor, and
- abnormal status indicator

SYSTEM_REQUIREMENT: P2_TEMPERATURE_CONTROL_DEVICE CONTAINS THE FOLLOWING:

```
SYSTEM_REQUIREMENT:
    P2_1_MASTER_SWITCH_AND_TEMP_SETTING
SYSTEM_REQUIREMENT:
    P2_2_ALLOWED_TEMPERATURE_CHANGE
SYSTEM_REQUIREMENT:
    P2_3_TEMPERATURE_TOLERANCE_RATIONALE
SYSTEM_REQUIREMENT:
    P2_4_TEMPERATURE_SENSING_PRECISION.
```

SYSTEM_REQUIREMENT:
P2_1_MASTER_SWITCH_AND_TEMP_SETTING—DESCRIPTION
   A computer system interacting with a temperature sensing device is used to control the desired temperature of the house. A master switch can be set at "HEAT" or "OFF." With a "HEAT" setting, the furnace will operate as in the description. With an "OFF" setting, the furnace will not operate. The homeowner is able to select a desired temperature setting.

SYSTEM_REQUIREMENT: P2_2_ALLOWED_TEMPERATURE_CHANGE— DESCRIPTION
   For purposes of comfort and furnace efficiency, the total change of room temperature allowed in the house will be 4 degrees. If a room temperature of 70 degrees is desired, the furnace must operate so that the temperature never falls below 68 degrees or rises above 72 degrees (unless the outside temperature is greater than 72 degrees).

SYSTEM_REQUIREMENT:
P2_3_TEMPERATURE_TOLERANCE_RATIONALE—DESCRIPTION
   Note that if the comfort interval (bandwidth) is too small, the frequency with which the furnace oscillates between ON and OFF will be too rapid to be efficient. If the bandwidth is too great, the house will sometimes be too cold and sometimes too warm.

SYSTEM_REQUIREMENT: P2_4_TEMPERATURE_SENSING_PRECISION— DESCRIPTION
   The temperature-sensing device does not have great precision and accuracy. It will detect temperature variations of the order of magnitude of 1 degree. It also has a time lag of the order of 1 minute.

SYSTEM_REQUIREMENT: P3_THE_FURNACE_SUBSYSTEM CONTAINS THE FOLLOWING:

```
SYSTEM_REQUIREMENT:P3_1_OIL_FURNACE_DESCRIPTION
SYSTEM_REQUIREMENT:P3_2_FURNACE_OPERATION
SYSTEM_REQUIREMENT:
      P3_3_FURNACE_SUBSYSTEM_SAFETY_CONDITIONS
```

SYSTEM_REQUIREMENT: P3_1_OIL_FURNACE_DESCRIPTION— DESCRIPTION
   The oil furnace, which is used to heat the house, has a motor which drives a fan to supply combustion air, and also drives a fuel pump.

SYSTEM_REQUIREMENT: P3_2_FURNACE_OPERATION—DESCRIPTION
   When the house gets too cold, the motor is activated. When the motor reaches normal operating speed, the ignition is activated and the oil valve is opened. The fuel is ignited at this time and the furnace begins to heat the water, which circulates through the house. A fuel flow indicator and an optical combustion sensor signal the controller if abnormalities occur.

Chapter 12

Functional Prototyping With Proto

MICHAEL D. KONRAD
Software Engineering Institute
Carnegie Mellon University
Pittsburgh, PA

TERRY A. WELCH
International Software Systems, Inc.
Austin, TX

ABSTRACT

Rapid prototyping is pursued as a means to develop and validate functional specifications prior to extensive code development in a large software system. Four critical components of a functional prototyping capability are: 1) a language for specifying the functions being examined, 2) a library of reusable software modules to expedite specification, 3) a set of interactive tools for constructing and analyzing the specification, and 4) a methodology that guides the analyst in construction, analysis, and validation of the functional specification. The authors illustrate how they have realized these four components in Proto, a functional prototyping capability they have developed. In Proto, one creates a specification of the functionality to be examined, augments it to be an executable functional prototype, and validates it via demonstration of system capabilities to potential end-users.

1 INTRODUCTION

Rapid prototyping is pursued as a means to develop and validate functional specifications prior to extensive code development in a large software system. To achieve a functional prototype execution with moderate development effort the following capabilities are desirable:

- a functionality specification language, which minimizes the design decisions which must be provided by the prototype developer when describing prototype functionality;

- a library of reusable software modules to expedite system specification, and a database system to aid in module retrieval and analysis; and
- a set of interactive tools, including a system interpreter with debugging features, which aid in the construction and execution of prototyping experiments.

To these must be added a methodology, guiding one through the construction, analysis, and validation steps.

PROTO is a rapid prototyping system with these capabilities, providing a graphical prototyping language and its support tools. It employs a strategy of component reuse which incorporates object-oriented modules. It provides interactive tools which help users cope with complex system design information by means of graphical presentations.

In PROTO, one creates a functional prototype, which is used to validate the specification of system responses, to determine if the functionality is usable in the target context. This style of prototyping can also be used to verify design decisions, such as algorithm selection, interfaces, etc. This is distinct from behavioral prototyping, which checks the human factors aspects of man-machine interfaces, and performance prototyping which provides response times for a design that implements the target specifications. Both behavioral prototyping and performance prototyping are addressed in Reference 3. Functional prototyping is used to stabilize software requirements via demonstration of system capabilities to potential end-users.

The prototyping language uses a dataflow style of presentation to express precedence relationships between operations. It supports a hierarchical and object-oriented structuring. It supports abstract data type concepts mixed with conventional datatyping but shields the user from data space management concerns.

The prototyping support environment is centered around an object-oriented data management system which is closely coupled to a workstation display. This structure is effective for storing and viewing hierarchical compositions of program graphs, data type definitions, and other design data. The object management system provides better access performance and simplicity of query expression than conventional data management systems do for complex design data.

PROTO capabilities are illustrated via a sequence of screen images in the following sections, which cover the language, reusable library, tools, and methodology.

This work was supported by a Rome Air Development Center contract on rapid prototyping (No. F30602-85-C-0129). References 1 and 4 address the broader topic of what types of capabilities are required to support requirements engineering.

2 THE FUNCTIONAL SPECIFICATION LANGUAGE

A Dataflow Diagram Language

The key features of the PROTO language for functional specification are reviewed in the following section.

The syntax is a refined dataflow diagram syntax, because as a visual form, dataflow diagrams appear to provide ease of understanding for non-programmers, and if used with care, provide a precise description of system functionality. They also serve as suitable inputs to the design process.

Activation Semantics

Proto has adopted a message-passing model for dataflow diagrams, whereby each operation sends its outputs as messages which activate subsequent operations. The message-passing paradigm shields the system specifier from implementation issues of memory space management and operation sequencing. This simplifies the specification of a system relative to doing it in a high-level language such as Pascal. The result is that the prototype may not execute at highest speed, but prototype execution performance is assumed not to be a primary objective so long as it is not unacceptably slow.

Proto specifications are essentially interconnections of components whose functionality can be defined in the following ways:

- as Proto dataflow diagrams,
- selected from a library of reusable components, or
- defined by High Level Language (HLL) source code, including a specialized language unique to Proto called "script."

Target Report Correlation: An Example

Screen images of a session with the Proto tools are used to demonstrate some capabilities of the Proto language and tools.

The application illustrated in these screen images is described as follows: A series of target reports is received from a sensor; for example, it might be satellite observations of tanks. Each target report specifies the position, direction, speed, and size characteristics of a target formation, and specifies the time the report was made. In what follows, each reported target formation is called a "group," and the group which is the subject of the current target report is called "the target."

The software system is to correlate successive reports to determine which reports determine a new position of a previously-reported group or when a new group has entered the view area. This correlation is interactive, with a human analyst making final correlation decisions based on information presented on an Analyst Workstation.

The objective of the prototyping effort is to determine what information is needed by the analyst, called a "correlation analyst," and what operations he/she needs for effective decision making. The system also includes an automated correlation algorithm to aid the analyst, and prototyping serves to determine the benefit of this help.

Figure 12-1 illustrates several levels of the description hierarchy. These are described in turn. At the top left of Figure 12-1 is a data flow consisting of the following operations:

- "gen target rpt"—simulates sensors: produces a fixed sequence of target reports; and
- "correlation center"—software system in which the correlation analyst has a role.

The correlation center (corr center) is defined internally by the data flow, upper right of Figure 12-1. In a data flow the following symbols represent:

- Circles (e.g., "build db") represent operations which produce outputs as a function of explicitly attached inputs.
- Boxes represent persistent (state) data; "DB" is a convenient pseudonym for the database, used to reduce clutter on the diagram. An operation that has access to DB has equivalent access to the central database.
- Small circles on sides represent ports (parameters) by which the component (in this case, correlation center (corr center)) connects to other components externally. Ports are datatyped and labeled (port labels appear in rectangular boxes).

The principal operation, build database (build db), shown at lower right of Figure 12-1, calculates correlations for entry in the database. Internally, it has two logic paths for different types of target reports. Only the correlation of "non-surveillance reports" (nonsrv_rpt) is explored here.

Correlation (correlation) of non-surveillance reports is defined internally, shown at lower center of Figure 12-1, as an automatic correlation (auto correl); for example, the system estimates the identity of the target in terms of the locations of previously seen groups, followed by interactive correlation (interactive correl), where an analyst reviews and possibly modifies the systems's estimate.

Interactive correlation (interactive correl) is defined by the data flow, shown at left in Figure 12-1. It shows that the target report resulting from automatic correlation is displayed (disp_new_target_info). The analyst is given the

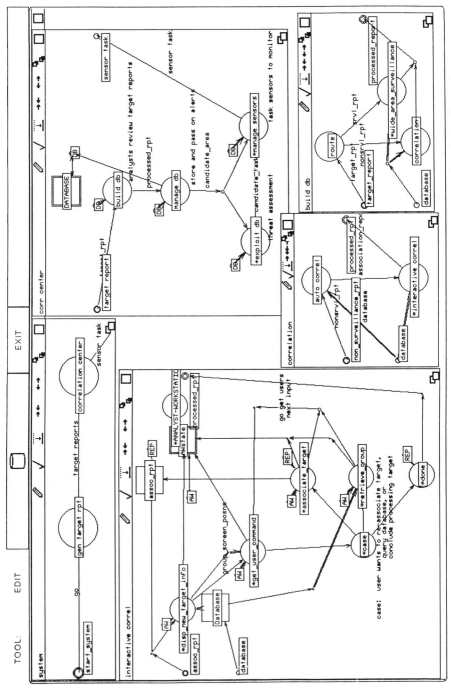

Figure 12-1. The screen during a Proto session—prototyping the correlation analyst's role in the Correlation Center System.

opportunity to alter the automatically-correlated target estimate. Thus, analyst input is queried (get_user_command), and processed via a workstation represented here as object "AWstate."

3 THE PROTO TOOLS

The Interpreter

System enactment is achieved by direct interpretative execution of the dataflow diagrams. This enactment produces the specified system outputs for each set of selected inputs. Thus, multiple "input scenarios" can be applied and the specification reviewed in terms of the results produced. This enables one to exercise a prototype to see how it reacts to particular stressful inputs and to explore implications of "what if" questions.

Interpretation in PROTO produces a graphical animation of the processing and is useful as a debugging aid. Standard debugging support is also provided, such as breakpoints, single-stepping, etc. Interpretation can resume immediately after the re-editing of a specification, allowing timely exploration of user suggestions.

In Figure 12-2, a darkened disk indicates component execution in progress. A component defined by data flow is executed by interpreting the data flow. As a part of executing "correlation center," one executes "build db," which requires execution of "correlation," etc. This shows a snapshot in time of which component operations are in active interpretation.

Figure 12-3 shows the Proto tools display at the right half of the screen; the display has been shrunken to make room for the Analyst Workstation display at the left half of the screen. (Normally, the Analyst Workstation window would appear on a separate end-user screen. They are shown on the same screen here to simplify discussion.)

At right, in Figure 12-3, is the data flow for interactive correlation, prior to displaying the target (disp_new_target_info). At left is the window displaying the Analyst Workstation with the previous target situation. Note the following menu options:

- "associate"—revise identity of target;
- "retrieve"—request information on known group (numbered arrow); and
- "done"—target correctly identified, get the next target report.

In Figure 12-3, note the correspondence between menu options at left and component functions at lower right in the dataflow display. This correspondence makes it easier for the analyst to effect end-user-inspired changes to the functionality.

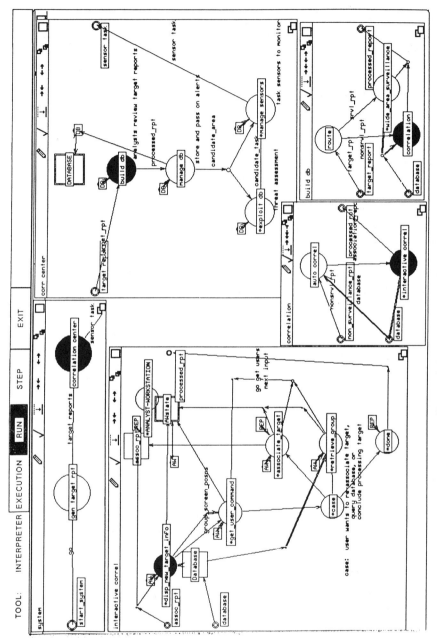

Figure 12-2.   Interpretation in progress.

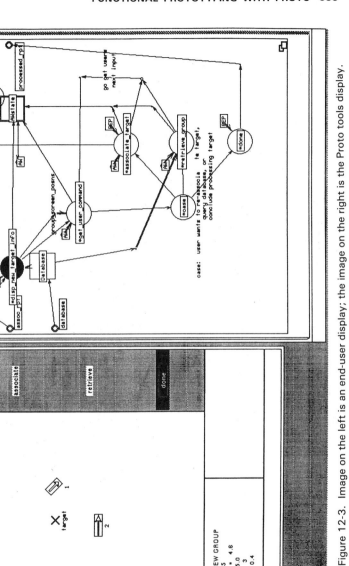
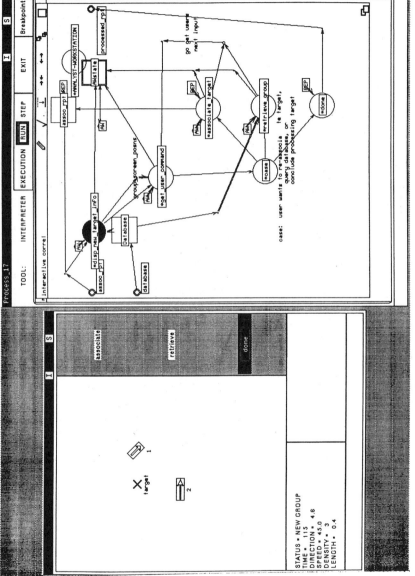

Figure 12-3. Image on the left is an end-user display; the image on the right is the Proto tools display.

If one chooses to look at data values during interpretation, this is done by selecting the appropriate arc. A display is brought up indicating the data. The data can also be modified at this point. This is shown in Figure 12-4.

The Editor

The creation and modification of specifications must be convenient and fast for prototyping to be rapid. Part of the challenge for an editor is meaningful presentation of potentially very complex system specifications in a form that is easily edited.

Presentation of specifications requires extracting views from a multi-level hierarchical specification, in which each level can be described in several dimensions: diagrams, textual specifications, interface specifications, code, etc. The interactive graphical facilities of a workstation provide effective means to let the user navigate and form a view of a specification. PROTO exploits workstation capabilities by a flexible windowing system which allows the user to manage the layout of information on the screen.

Editing of Proto graphs is facilitated by an ''object-oriented'' style of interaction, whereby each icon on the workstation screen corresponds to a database object whose class defines the type of editing available for that object and, thereby defines the content of the ''pop-up'' menu which guides user actions for that object. Modifications are made directly to the database object, for immediate access by other tools.

Component ''route'' is selected by pointing device (mouse) (see Figure 12-5). A pop-up menu lists the following available component-specific actions:

- GRAPH—brings up a window with component's dataflow definition.
- OPEN—access to a components ports and multiple representations.
- CONNECT—arc placement.
- etc.

Selecting an action from the menu is the way to invoke that action.

Selection is the same whether in the Editor or Interpreter. What differs is the list of actions that is displayed.

''OPEN'' on component ''route'' shows its ports and gives access to various types of definition for this component. In Figure 12-6, a text body is selected, and it may be edited at this point with a standard screen editor.

Windows holding a dataflow diagram can be expanded, moved, scrolled, and one can also scale the diagram itself. One invokes these actions through selection of the appropriate icon at top of the window. Figure 12-7 shows two windows holding the same dataflow description. The one on the right has been expanded, scrolled, and scaled.

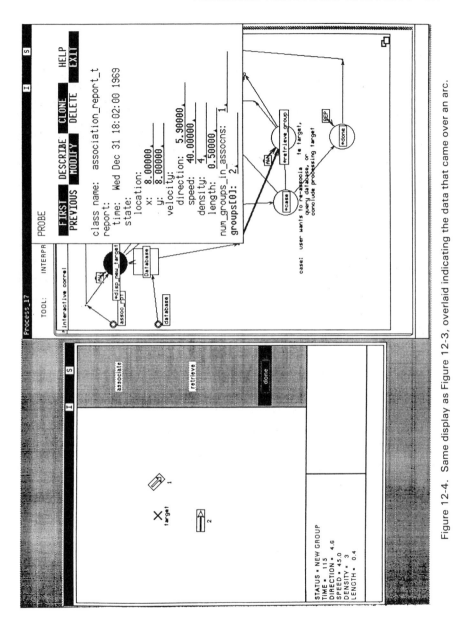

Figure 12-4. Same display as Figure 12-3, overlaid indicating the data that came over an arc.

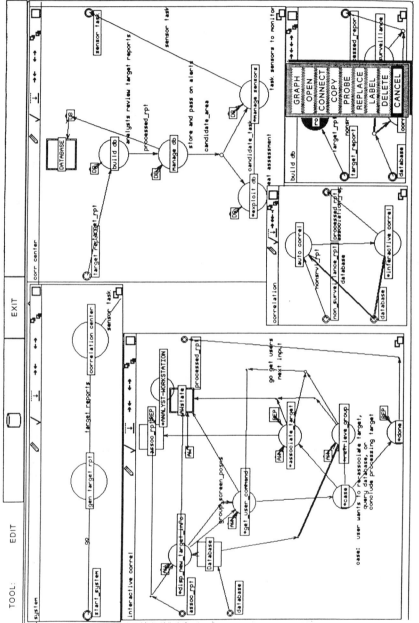

Figure 12-5. A component function is selected by pointing device (mouse). A pop-up menu lists the available actions.

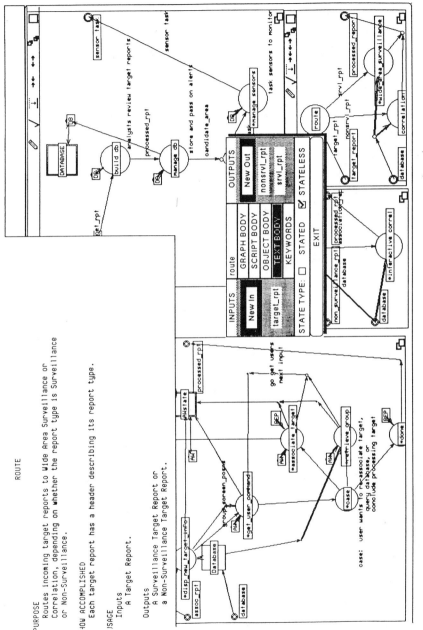

Figure 12-6. Selecting to see the text body of a component function.

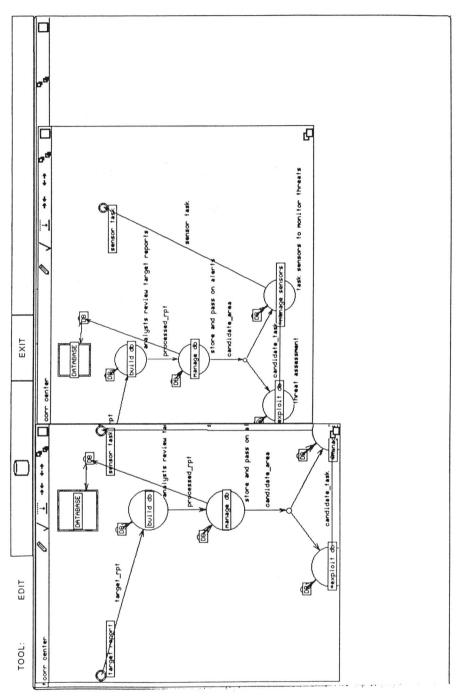

Figure 12-7. Dataflow displays can be scrolled, scaled, and moved.

4 THE REUSE LIBRARY

Prototyping and reuse work well together. The availability of an application-specific library of reusable modules simplifies the construction of prototypes in that application area and reduces the level of computing skills needed by the prototype specifier. Also, the normal impediments to reuse—performance and design robustness—are not critical parameters in prototyping. Prototyping encourages reuse because the system designer can observe the operation of a reusable module in the target system context and, thereby gain better insight into the module's functions.

To facilitate reuse, a prototyping system needs database facilities, which help in selection of candidate modules, out of a reusable library. These facilities support classification of modules, searching for selected module properties, relation of modules to their data types, etc. In addition, the specification language and editing facilities should make it easy to insert (bind) a module into a specification. Figure 12-8 and Figure 12-9 show the typical structure of a reusable module and its incorporation into a Proto specification.

Figure 12-8 illustrates the Analyst Workstation object, exemplifying how a typical collection of reusable modules is documented in Proto. Methods are depicted as components. The message each method expects is indicated by an input arc. Presentation aspects that can be customized (e.g., the fonts and lists of menu options) are indicated as parameters. To use this object, the prototype definer copies the methods needed into the data flow being edited, indicating which workstation, fonts, and menu are being used by providing the appropriate input connections.

Figure 12-9 illustrates the incorporation of Analyst workstation methods into low-level dataflow descriptions. The data flows depicted belong to components shown in the "interactive correlation" data flow (previously shown).

5 METHODOLOGY

This section briefly outlines a procedure for using Proto in building and evaluating functional prototypes of a proposed system. The section concludes with a chart identifying how the major Proto capabilities (editing, interpretation, reuse) might be utilized in this procedure.

The input to the procedure is a vague set of functional requirements. The output is a validated functional specification.

The procedure takes the systems analyst through incremental definition and validation of a functional specification for the proposed system. Each increment deals with the definition and validation of that part of the specification dealing with the needs of a particular end-user role (or interacting ADP system—for simplicity the authors consider an interacting ADP system to be just another type of end-user). The increments are prioritized according to criticality of satis-

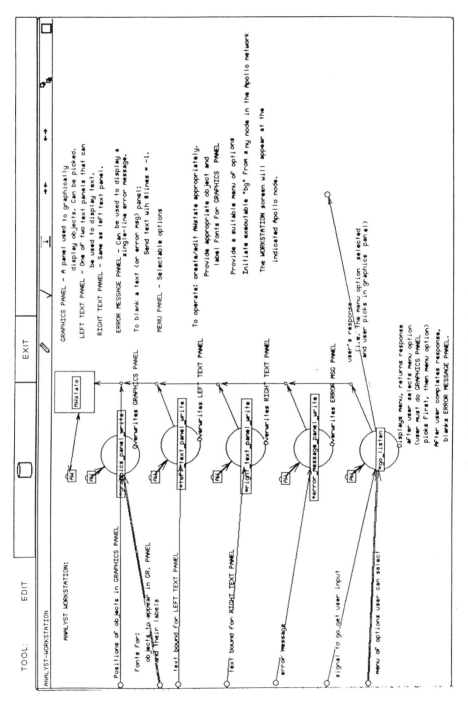

Figure 12-8. The Analyst Workstation object.

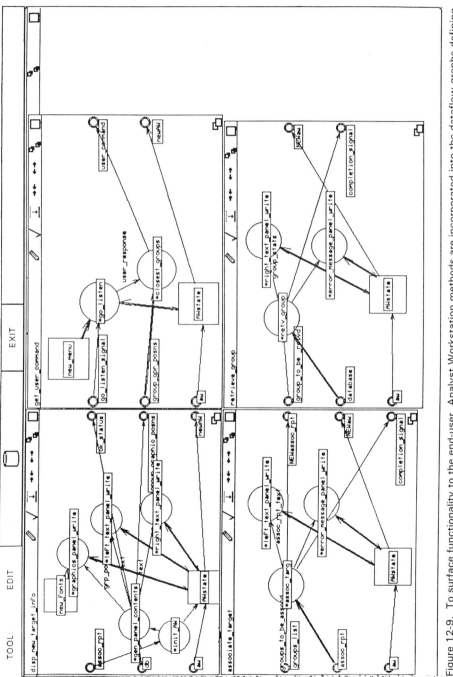

Figure 12-9.   To surface functionality to the end-user, Analyst Workstation methods are incorporated into the dataflow graphs defining component functions of the "interactive correl."

fying that end-user's needs and perceived risk in not being able to do so. Figure 12-10 indicates the major processing steps. If care is taken, the resulting functional specification can be organized by end-user role; a similar idea is employed in Reference 2.

Each increment in the procedure consists of iterations of the following steps,

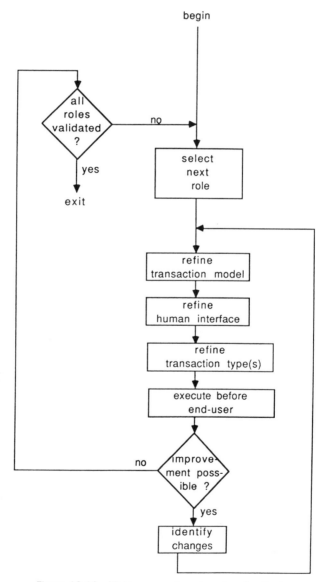

Figure 12-10. Major processing steps in using Proto.

terminated when the representative end-user and the systems analyst fail to find a significantly better way of satisfying that end-user's needs as follows:

(1) specify/modify a "transaction model" of that end-user's interactions with the system;
(2) define/modify the end-user's interface to the system;
(3) specify/modify the transaction types in sufficient detail to be executable;
(4) execute before the end-user evaluates the current set of defined transactions; and
(5) Identify or hypothesize changes that need to be made to the functional specification and begin a new iteration on these steps.

Step (1) consists of specifying a transaction model of the application as seen by the end-user. This means creating a Proto dataflow graph that does the following:

(1a) identifies the sets of entities and relationships the system needs to track in order to respond to the end-user's requests and commands; (each set of entities or relationships of a particular type appears in the data flow as a single "state element" (data store)),
(1b) describes system functions in terms of the types of transactions (i.e., "transaction types") the system must perform, the events that trigger them, the state elements they need to access and/or update, their outputs, the data types, and
(1c) reuses, as appropriate, the state elements characterized in step (1a), and the transaction types and data types identified in step (1b), from previous prototyping efforts (such are obtained through querying the reuse library).

In the case of the "correlation analyst" role in the Correlation Center system we create a dataflow graph that looks like part of the "interactive correl" graph that appears in many of the Figures. The entity is "assoc_rpt" (it appears as a data store). The three transaction types are represented by components "associate_target," "retrieve_group," and "done."

Step (2) consists of identifying all inputs/outputs from/to the end-user and defining overall characteristics of the interface (workstation screen) needed. An attempt should be made to find a suitable interface component that can be parameterized or generated from the reuse library. The intent here is to surface the functionality the end-user needs to accomplish his/her mission; do not address human factors in this functional prototyping procedure.

For the "correlation analyst" role in the Correlation Center system, the

Analyst Workstation object (see Figure 12-8) is reused. Fonts for the groups, target, and labels, as well as the list of menu options must be provided.

To represent this object in the "interactive correl" graph, a data store "AWstate" is place there and appropriately connected to the transactions identified in Step (1). In addition component functions are added to update the end-user screen (disp_new_target_info) and get correlation analyst input (get_user_command).

Step (3) consists of refining the description of each incompletely-specified transaction type from Step (1b) with another level of data flow that correctly computes outputs (and state element updates) from inputs. This means for each transaction type, creating a Proto dataflow graph that includes the following:

(3a) gives a high-level dataflow characterization of how transaction type inputs flow through the required state element queries and updates and whatever transient computations are required;

(3b) expresses each state element update/query identified in Step (3a), with the appropriate method (if the state element is represented as an abstract data type) or data management function;

(3c) expresses each transient computation identified in Step (3a) either directly or in terms of another level of data flow in sufficient detail that when interpreted, produces the correct computation; and

(3d) reuses, as appropriate, methods and data management functions in Step (3b) and application-specific computations in Step (3c), from previous prototyping efforts (such are obtained through querying the reuse library).

For the "correlation analyst" role in the Correlation Center system, this means providing another level of data flow for "associate_target", "retrieve _group", and "done" transaction types. The first two are illustrated by the lower two graphs of Figure 12-9. Note the use of Analyst Workstation methods to surface back to the correlation analyst the results of his/her actions.

Step (4) consists of setting up an experiment in which an end-user is given his/her own workstation (screen) consisting of the interface defined in Step (2). One or more scenarios are defined with the representative end-user that represent typical and stressful usage of the system (Proto is not required to store or manage scenarios). Other devices or human interfaces may need to be simulated. If any high-fidelity simulations are required, the reuse library can be queried for an appropriate parameterizable or generatable simulator (or an appropriate simulator constructed). The systems analyst uses the Proto interpreter to interpret the system through repeated runs of the scenarios, evaluating with the end-user the functional adequacy and correctness of the set of transactions that have been defined.

Processing Steps	Major Proto Capabilities		
	Editing	Interpreting	Reusing
specify transaction model	identify state elements and transaction types, connect to form a dataflow	debug connections between state elements and transaction types	query for data types, and functions that can be used as state elements, transaction types
define (human) interface	bind/connect the appropriate interface component into the transaction model	debug the interface	query for functions that can serve the appropriate communication and interfacing role in a prototype experiment
specify transaction types	define by a new level of data flow with appropriate access and update operations on state elements	debug the dataflow defining the transaction type	query for generic data management functions, application-specific functions that can be bound into the new level of data flow
interpret & end-user evaluates	make changes then resume interpretation	exercise different scenarios	- - - - -

Figure 12-11. Proto capabilities used in the prototyping procedure.

Figure 12-11 shows a chart presenting an overview of how major Proto capabilities (editing, interpreting, reuse) are utilized within the major processing steps identified above.

6 CONCLUSION

A prototyping capability, Proto, was illustrated. Proto provides the ability to create system functionality specifications using dataflow diagrams, with dependence on a library of reusable modules to make prototype construction rapid. Direct enactment of those specifications via interpretation yields a functional prototype, by which those specifications can be reviewed against various input scenarios.

Proto provides tools for building and viewing complex system descriptions, both in terms of hierarchical composition and in viewing multiple dimensions of description. It is a working prototype of a new architecture for software tools systems, where the object-oriented user interface is tightly coupled to an object-managed database. This permits multiple tools to share design data and screen images with consistent interpretations.

REFERENCES

1. International Software Systems, Inc., "RADC Requirements Engineering Testbed Research and Development Program Panel Recommendations," Technical Report, International Software

Systems Inc., 9420 Research Blvd., Suite 200, Austin, TX 78759, December 1987. (Available as an RADC T.R. for contract F30602-85-C-0129.)

2. Mullery, G., "CORE—A Method for Controlled Requirement Expression," Systems Designers Limited, Camberley UK, February 1979.

3. Rzepka, W., and P. Daley, "A Prototyping Tool to Assist in Requirements Engineering," *Proceedings 19th Hawaii International Conference on System Sciences,* Honolulu, HI, January 1986.

4. Rzepka, W., and Y. Ohno, "Requirements Engineering Environments: Software Tools for Modeling User Needs," *IEEE Computer,* Vol. 18, No. 4, April 1985, pp. 9–12.

SOURCE

1. Boar, Bernard H., "Application Prototyping," Wiley-Interscience, (1984).

Chapter 13

SPDTOOLS: A Structured Diagram Based Programming System

Yoshihiro Oki, Hiroyuki Kitagawa, and Kiichi Fujino
Software Engineering Development Laboratory
NEC Corporation
Tokyo 108, Japan

ABSTRACT

Several programming diagrams have been developed and put in use under the
theme of structured programming support. Structured Programming Diagram
(SPD) is NEC's original work for this purpose. SPD was designed about 13
years ago, when the concept of structured programming was proposed and has
been widely used in software development plants. SPDTOOLS are well
organized software tools to support program design, coding, and documentation
based on SPD. A significant feature of SPDTOOLS is the management of
mapping between program design specifications in SPD and executable program
codes. Under SPDTOOLS, a programmer can develop programs in a way
consistent with the conventional development style but more efficiently and
reliably. This chapter discusses: 1) background of SPDTOOLS development;
2) SPDTOOLS overview; 3) SPDTOOLS—components and functions; 4)
program development process examples using SPDTOOLS; and 5) evaluation
of SPDTOOLS. All SPDTOOLS components have been put in use in NEC
software development plants.

1 INTRODUCTION

Since problems in conventional flowcharts were clarified in the structured
programming discussion, several programming diagrams have been proposed
as a result of software engineering research activities[1-13]. SPD (Structured
Programming Diagram)[14] was developed to facilitate the design of well structured programs as a part of system development methodology STEPS
(Standardized Technology and Engineering for Programming Support)[15] in the

NEC Corporation. In SPD, a program designer easily expresses functional structures, control structures, and physical layout for a program on one sheet of paper. Its simple and straightforward notation appeals to both document writers and readers. SPD was developed about 13 years ago and has been used not only by NEC engineers but also by many customers at more than 1200 locations, including government offices, public offices and private enterprises.

SPDTOOLS, the SPD based software tools, have been developed by the NEC corporation. Objectives of SPDTOOLS are the following:

- support program design in SPD;
- support program coding;
- support program maintenance and reuse;
- standardize program specifications and program codes; and
- be usable in average program development environments.

SPDTOOLS are composed of three types of tools: SPD Editor, Translator, and SPD Documentor; The SPD Editor supports program designers interactively in developing program specifications in SPD; Translator translates SPD program specifications into program codes and vice versa; SPD Documentor generates report documents, including SPD, from program codes.

An SPD Editor has the following features, which are keys to its usefulness;

- It provides the user with well devised SPD editing commands.
- The user can oversee the entire SPD structure through SPD skeleton display.
- The user also can input program code segments on the screen referring to the program design specification in SPD.

This chapter is organized as follows: in Section 2, STEPS and SPD are introduced to explain background of SPDTOOLS development. In Section 3, global architecture of SPDTOOLS and SPD/program code mapping schema in SPDTOOLS are explained. Component tools of SPDTOOLS and their functions are described in Section 4. In Section 5, programming process, using SPDTOOLS, is explained following an actual program design scenario. Finally, evaluation of SPDTOOLS and the conclusion are given in Section 6.

2 BACKGROUND

2.1 STEPS: System Development Methodology

STEPS is a software development standard for business application systems (specifying development methodology, documentation system, program modularization criteria, etc.) covering the entire system development cycle.

STEPS was first applied to user system development in 1976. Since then, NEC has improved STEPS every year, and it is widely used at present.

STEPS consists of STEPS System Development Standard and STEPS Programming Standard. The concept of System Development Standard is summarized as follow. As shown in Figure 13-1, STEPS models system development in a multi-stage hierarchical structure. System development is divided into five phases. Each phase is divided into several activities. Project managers can use the end of each activity as a milestone for project management. Each activity is further decomposed into units of work, named work-sets. Specific methodology or technique is given for each work-set and system developers can carry out his/her work according to it.

Each work-set is accomplished by completing standard forms provided in STEPS, referring to the examples. These completed forms are called work documents. Figure 13-2 illustrates system development process utilizing System Development Standard. Documentation activity is done by merging and editing accumulated work documents, at the end of each phase.

Programming Standard handles programs as industrial products and standardizes program patterns and parts and programming methodology. In general, most business application program structures are classified into a number of patterns, such as media conversion and updating/collation of master files. STEPS supplies a standard program pattern library, to standardize program control structure. STEPS Programming Standard defines tree structured diagrams named SPD to specify program design. Standard program patterns are also specified in SPD. When a programmer uses a standard program pattern, what he/she has to do is just to put some pieces of program codes specific to his/her own application to make the program complete. STEPS Programming Standard is designed to bring about the following advantages to its users:

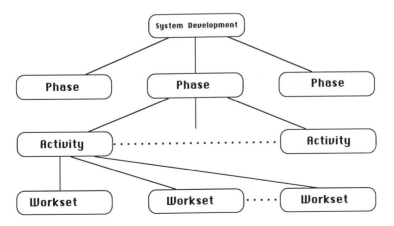

Figure 13-1. Hierarchical structure in STEPS system development process.

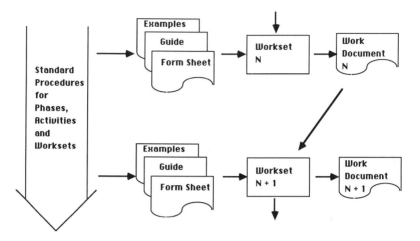

Figure 13-2. STEPS system development process.

- Programs developed on the basis of STEPS program patterns are simple and well structured; therefore, they are easy to modify and maintain.
- STEPS program patterns is used to naturally standardize variable names and labels as well as program structures.
- The user's skill is gradually improved through consciously or unconsciously learning structured programming technique.

2.2 SPD: Program Documentation Technique

STEPS achieved great success in many software development projects, especially program specification in SPD has been widely used not only in business application system development but also in development of other software systems, such as transmission systems, switching systems, operating systems, etc. Though SPD was originally invented as part of STEPS, now it is used as standard program specification method independent of STEPS. In this sense, SPD has replaced conventional Flowchart.

SPD has three important features, which are generically required to most program specification techniques. They are the following:

(1) Clear representation of logical program structures: SPD is well designed to represent functional hierarchy and control structures.
(2) Clear representation of physical program structures: SPD can visualize decomposition of programs into program modules.
(3) Friendliness to its users: SPD notation is simple, and its symbols are easy to understand and remember.

An SPD diagram example is shown in Figure 13-3. As previously mentioned, SPD represents three aspects of program structures on one sheet of paper at once: hierarchical functional structures of programs; control structures specifying program execution sequences; and physical structures representing the way a program is composed of program modules, some of which are often provided in standard libraries.

The functional structure means the hierarchy of functions the program accomplishes. To specify the functional structure, the specification method has to be uniformly applicable both to upper level global structures and to lower level detailed structures. SPD fits well to natural elaboration of functional structures under the discipline of stepwise refinement.

It is well known that program control structures can be developed with only three types of constructs: sequential, selective, and repetitive. In SPD, instances of the basic constructs are represented by SPD nodes. SPD notations for basic constructs are given in Table 13-1. Each SPD basic construct consists of two parts: a procedure part, which contains one or more executable statements; and a control part, which determines the manner in which the procedure part is to be executed. The control part is represented by a symbol placed on the SPD node. The exception is that the sequential construct has no symbol on the node. The procedure part is predetermined to be sequentially executed exactly once. Selective and repetitive constructs have special symbols, the diamond and the circle, respectively, on the SPD node. The diamond has been derived from a flowchart selective symbol. The circle is intuitively associated with repetition. Therefore, these symbols are familiar to software engineers. In selective and repetitive constructs, the control part determines explicitly the manner in which the procedure part is to be executed. In some constructs, the control part is further divided into two sub-parts: a condition sub-part, which is a Boolean expression; and a directive sub-part which would determine the truth value of the condition part. In the following part of this chapter, statements in the procedure part and the control part are generically referred to as phrases.

The physical structure means the program structure at the implementation level. At the very beginning of the program design phase, only upper level major functional modules are defined. Later, these modules are decomposed into a number of detailed modules. In this situation, SPD notations for functional structure representation are of use to keep the parent/child relationship among the modules. SPD sets hierarchical levels where modules belong and specifies their parent/child relationships. As the design activity proceeds, the designer has to decide the implementation of lower level modules. They may be implemented as macros, copy libraries, subroutines, etc. SPD provides a number of symbols to distinguish these implementations of lower level modules. When designing a program using SPD, a designer can elaborate the design step by step rather than give detailed specification from the beginning: for example, first, define upper level modules; second, lower level modules are defined; third,

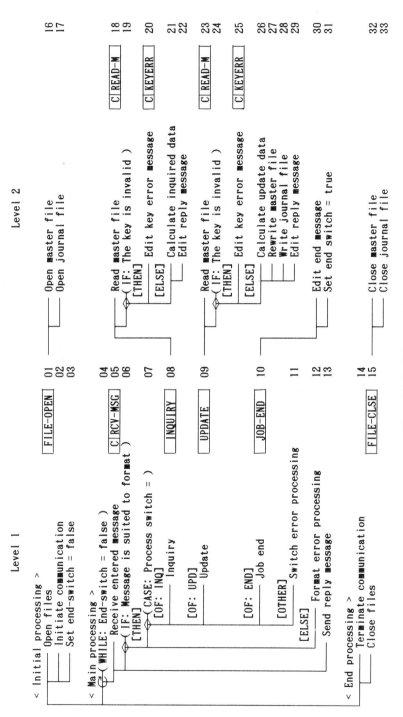

Figure 13-3. SPD example.

Table 13-1. SPD control constructs.

No.	Construct Name	SPD	Flow Chart
1	Imperative	P.P.	P.P.
2	Sequential	P.P.-1 P.P.-2	P.P.-1 P.P.-2
3.1	Iterative loop	(WHILE:Cont.) P.P.	Dir. Cond. P.P.
3.2	Repetitive loop	(UNTIL:Cont.) P.P.	P.P. Dir. Cond.
3.3	Continuos loop	(LOOP) P.P.	P.P.
4.1	Monadic choice	(IF:Cond.) [THEN] P.P.	Dir. Cond. P.P.
4.2	Diadic choice	(IF:Cond.) [THEN] P.P.-1 [ELSE] P.P.-2	Dir. Cond.-1 Cond.-2 P.P.-1 P.P.-2
4.3	Multiple exclusive choice	(CASE:Dir.) [OF:Cond.-1] P.P.-1 [OF:Cond.-2] P.P.-2 [OTHER] P.P.-0	Dir. P.P.-1 Cond.-1 P.P.-2 Cond.-2 P.P.-n Cond.-n
4.4	Multiple inclusive choice	(CASE:Dir.) [OF:Cond.-1] P.P.-1 [OF:Cond.-2] P.P.-2 [OTHER] P.P.-0	Dir. P.P.-1 Cond.-1 P.P.-2 Cond.-2 P.P.-n Cond.-n

Legend: P.P. (Procedure Part)
Cont. (Control)
Cond. (Condition)
Dir. (Directive)

control structure specification is given. Finally, the physical structures of the program are decided.

2.3 Requirements for SPD Support Facilities

Although SPD has a number of features contributing productivity in program development and maintenance, there remain some problems to be solved to make the best use of SPD. For example, one of the most difficult problems for software engineers and managers is the inconsistency between program source codes and program documents sometimes caused in program development life cycle. Generally, in the program design phase, programmers design abstract program structures and specify them in SPD. After that, they give source codes referring to the program design specifications. In these time consuming and tedious works, they often make simple mistakes, such as, violation of data naming or comment rules. Moreover, in the maintenance phase, serious problems occur. Sometimes, requirements for program modification are posted suddenly. In those cases, programmers often change only the program codes but not design specifications. The reason is that they are too busy to spend their time on the correction of documents. As a result, consistency between documents and program codes is violated, and the documents are useless for later maintenance work.

To solve such problems and to facilitate program development and maintenance based on SPD, SPDTOOLS, the computer-based support tools are provided. SPDTOOLS are expected to bring about the following advantages as well as a solution for the above problem:

- Fine printed SPD documents can be readily attained.
- SPD diagrams can be developed and modified easily.
- Standardization of documentation and coding style is promoted.
- Paperless program development is achieved.

3 OVERVIEW

3.1 SPD and Program Abstraction

SPDTOOLS are well organized software tools to support program design, coding, and documentation using SPD. Two types of objects are manipulated in SPDTOOLS; One is program design specification expressed in SPD, and the other is program code.

When designing programs, procedure and condition parts in SPD nodes are written in a natural language. The main objective of drawing SPD diagrams is to specify functional, control, and physical structures of the programs. Detailed descriptions, such as program codes are usually not put into SPD diagrams. In this sense, as shown in Figure 13-4, SPD diagrams are higher level descriptions

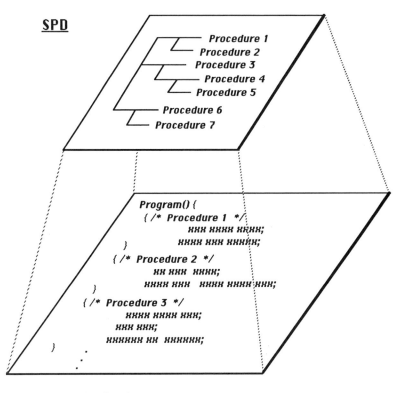

Figure 13-4. Relationship between SPD and program codes.

of programs. In the program coding phase after the program design, programmers give program codes referring to the SPD diagrams.

Higher level design specification is indispensable not only in the design phase but also in the program maintenance and reuse phase. For the program maintenance and reuse purposes, programmers have to understand structures of programs. However, with only program lists, it is very difficult to understand a voluminous amount of program codes. They have to be summarized or illustrated for the purpose of program maintenance and reuse. Therefore, abstract views of program codes usually represented in SPD diagrams have to be supported even after the program coding is completed.

One of the most important features of SPDTOOLS is the concise mapping of program design specifications and actual program codes. In SPDTOOLS, the mapping of program design specifications and actual program codes is done through SPD objects. An SPD object is composed of an SPD diagram and a set of program code segments associated with phrases in the SPD diagram (see Figure 13-2).

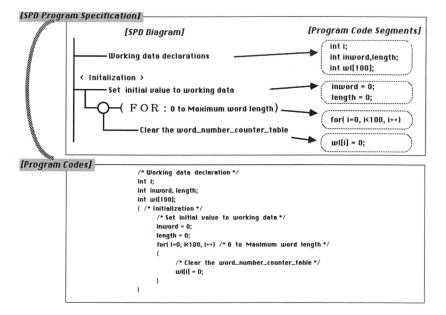

Figure 13-5. Mapping between SPD program specification and program codes.

Several tools and systems that support some types of programming diagrams were developed up to the present.[16-19] However, most of these are capable of handling either only program design specification or only actual program code information in diagram forms. SPDTOOLS features mapping from program design specifications to program codes and vice versa. In SPDTOOLS, the mechanism that manages the one-to-one relationship between SPD objects and program codes is the 'comments rule.' The basic idea is that each phrase in an SPD diagram corresponds to a comment statement in the program code, and the program code segment associated with the phrase corresponds to a series of program codes placed under the comment statement. Of course, this is the basic idea and there are some additional rules to apply it to practical design data. Figure 13-2 shows the mapping with an example. In Figure 13-5, program code segments corresponding to phrases in SPD diagrams are shown in tabular form. All components of SPDTOOLS are developed to assure this mapping under the comment rule.

3.2   SPDTOOLS Configuration

One of the SPD characteristics is the simplicity of its symbols and conventions. In SPD diagrams, there are no slant lines or curved lines. SPD diagrams are composed of only some special node symbols and vertical and horizontal lines. Therefore, they fit well to machine processing and manual processing.

SPDTOOLS configuration is shown in Figure 13-6. An SPD Editor supports interactive development of SPD program design specifications. Forward Translator translates SPD program design specifications into program codes. Backward Translator translates program codes into SPD program design specifications. SPD Documentor generates report documents, including SPD diagrams from program codes.

The main objectives of SPDTOOLS are the following:

- *Support of program design in SPD*—SPD Editor provides the user with powerful facilities for developing and editing SPD diagrams. SPD diagrams are usually revised very frequently in the program design phase. Modification to diagrams, especially insertion or deletion of several basic constructs, causes redrawing of the whole diagram. Automated SPD diagram editing facility is useful for program design. SPD diagrams are internally managed as SPD objects; therefore, the user also can give program code segments to SPD phases with SPD Editor.
- *Support of program coding*—in general, the programmer specifies program

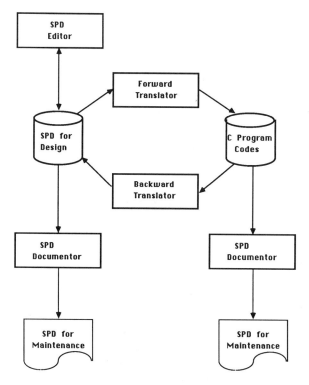

Figure 13-6. SPDTOOLS configuration.

design in SPD diagrams at first and then types in program codes referring to the SPD diagrams. Since SPD diagrams specify functional, control, and physical structures of programs, they include important information for completing program codes. Forward Translator automatically generates skeleton program codes from SPD diagrams. In case program code segments are put with SPD Editor, they are also automatically placed on appropriate positions by Forward Translator.

- *Support of program maintenance and program reuse*—there are many programs in use today. Some of these have no program documents, and some of these have obsolete program documents. To reuse or maintain such programs, much effort is required to understand program functions and program structures. SPD Documentor generates SPD diagrams from program codes and helps the programmer to understand abstract program structures in the program reuse and maintenance phase.

- *Standardization of program specifications and program codes*—using SPD Editor, detailed notations, such as SPD line length and symbol size are naturally standardized. Furthermore, program codes that are generated by Forward Translator have the same program comment style and the same program statement usage. Therefore, SPDTOOLS promote standardization of program codes as well.

- *Fitness to average program development environments*—good documentation and programming tools should be available to any programmer in average program development environments, and such tools should fit well to other tools in the environments. SPDTOOLS are developed on a small personal computer, considering user-friendliness, performance, and connectability.

4 COMPONENTS AND FUNCTIONS

4.1 SPD Editor

The following are features of SPD Editor with session examples from an actual program design work:

- *Well devised SPD editing commands*—through the analysis of program design processes using SPD diagrams, it is clarified that SPD diagrams are often modified by insertion, deletion and replacement of basic control constructs. Therefore, operations required for the modification of control structures greatly influence user-friendliness of support tool. In SPD diagrams, individual control constructs are designated by pointing SPD nodes. Therefore, the structured editing facility, which supports program structure modification by pointing SPD nodes, seems indispensable in SPD Editor. Generally, it is known that there are two ways to interactively edit text or diagram structures. One is a structured or syntax-directed editor approach,[20-23] and the other is a screen editor approach.[24,25] In SPD Editor, advantages of the two approaches are combined and optimized as follows:

- Since, in SPD, one or more basic constructs of programs are often handled as editing units, the structured editor approach is appropriate for the basic editing facility of SPD Editor.
- To decrease complexity of operations and undesirable frequent display redrawing, the screen editor-oriented functions are also implemented in SPD Editor. They include structure independent cursor movement, page based screen management, etc.
- An SPD Editor screen image is shown in Figure 13-7. SPD Editor provides several templates corresponding to basic control constructs in SPD diagrams. These templates are displayed at the lowest display line, and they are input by striking the programmable function keys.
- *SPD skeleton display to oversee the entire SPD structure*—SPD diagrams are suitable for compact program design specifications by nature because individual SPD symbols and their combinations do not require much space for presentation. On average, an SPD diagram extends over only one sheet of paper. Therefore, the entire program structure is easily understandable at a glance. However, in SPD Editor, physical computer display size is limited. Therefore, a facility that can show a compressed SPD skeleton in graphics is implemented in the SPD Editor (see Figure 13-8). The reduction ratio for the skeleton display is 1:6. The present position of the editing window is also displayed and can be moved onto the SPD skeleton display.
- Program code segments input referring to SPD diagrams—SPD diagrams represent abstract program structures as program design specifications. Therefore, while designing programs in SPD diagrams, the programmer does not have to worry about detailed program codes. When the design is finished, the programmer starts coding. SPD Editor has facility to put and edit program code segments referring to the SPD program design specification. SPD Editor provides a sub-window for editing program code segments (see Figure 13-9). The sub-window for editing code segments is opened for each phase in SPD diagrams according to the user demand. Obeying the aforementioned comment rule, the code segments that are input through the sub-window are embedded into program codes generated by Forward Translator.

4.2   Translator

Two kinds of translators are implemented in SPDTOOLS. One is Forward Translator, which translates SPD program specifications into program codes. If code segments to be associated with phases are not yet completed, Forward Translator generates only a skeleton program, composed of program control

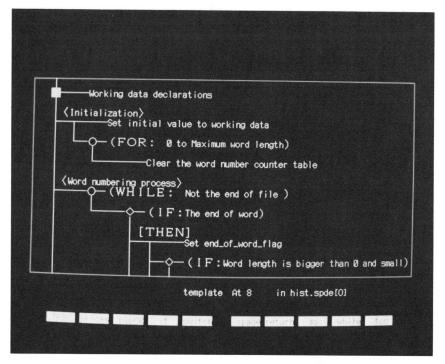

Figure 13-7. SPD editor screen image.

statements, program comments, and partially embedded program codes. If code segments are prepared completely using SPD Editor sub-window, complete program codes are generated by Forward Translator.

The other translator is Backward Translator, which translates existing program codes into SPD program specifications. Using these tools, the programmer can modify programs either at the SPD program specification level or at the program code level.

4.3 SPD Documentor

SPD Documentor generates report documents including SPD diagrams from existing program codes. Generated documents are useful to understand program control structures and functions, especially in the program maintenance and program reuse phases. SPD Documentor has optional functions to control the abstraction level for report generation. According to the selected abstraction level, the following information is included in the report documents:

- level 1: control structures only;
- level 2: control structures + module calls;

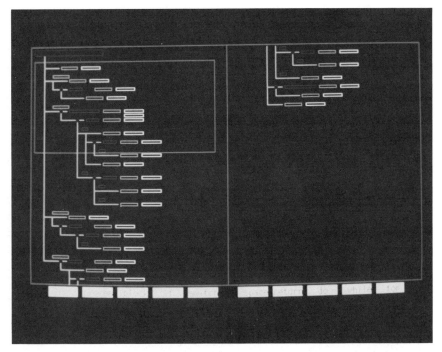

Figure 13-8. SPD skeleton display.

- level 3: control structures + module calls + program comments; and
- level 4: all statements (in detail).

Moreover, the generated documents include useful information other than SPD diagrams. For example, module calling relationships and cross references between data and procedures are reported. Using SPD Documentor, the programmer can obtain SPD diagrams of several description levels easily and quickly.

5 PROGRAM DEVELOPMENT PROCESS USING SPDTOOLS

A sample session of program design and coding process using SPDTOOLS is explained as follows:

Phase 1: Program design—Program module and control structures are designed using SPD Editor, step by step as follows:

- Main modules are listed first. Control structures are not considered at this time, see Figure 13-10. This Figure shows that four main modules are defined.

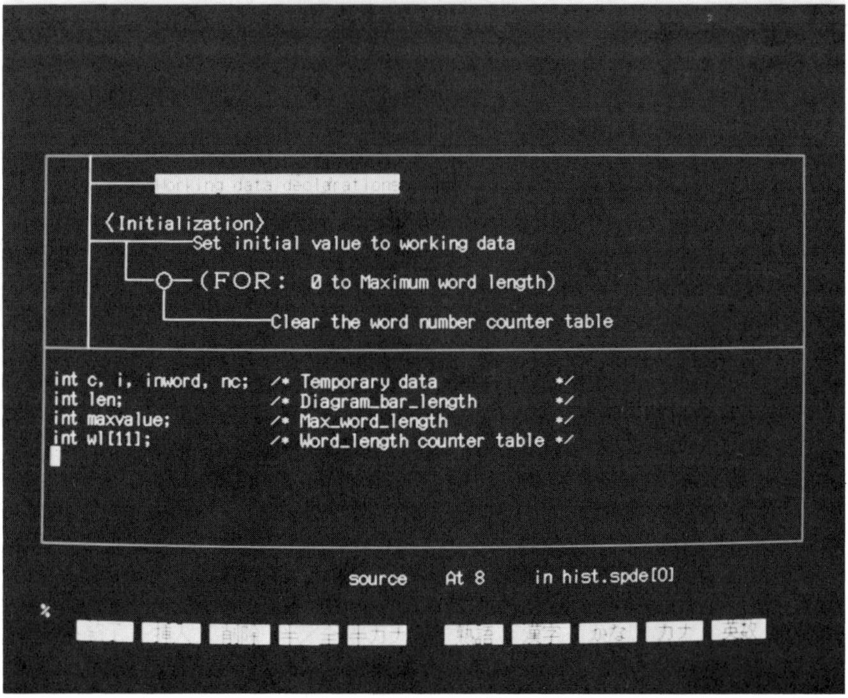
〈Initialization〉
Set initial value to working data
(FOR: 0 to Maximum word length)
Clear the word number counter table
int c, i, inword, nc; /* Temporary data */
int len; /* Diagram_bar_length */
int maxvalue; /* Max_word_length */
int wl[11]; /* Word_length counter table */
source At 8 in hist.spde[0]
%

Figure 13-9. Sub-window for codes segment editing.

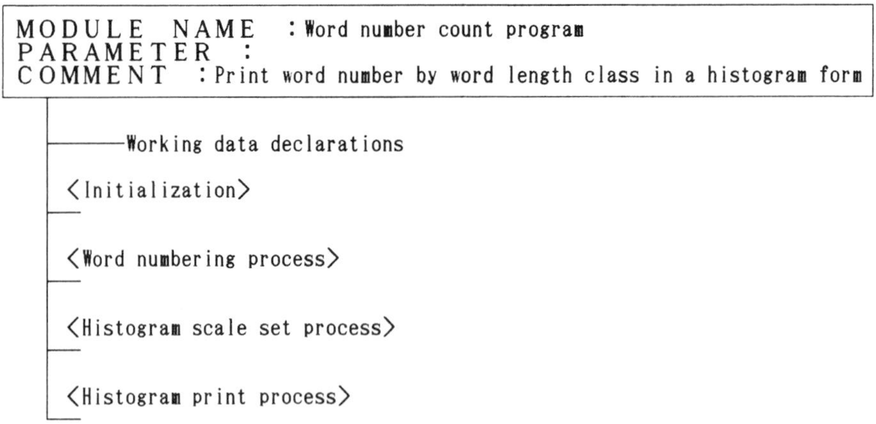
MODULE NAME :Word number count program
PARAMETER :
COMMENT :Print word number by word length class in a histogram form
Working data declarations
〈Initialization〉
〈Word numbering process〉
〈Histogram scale set process〉
〈Histogram print process〉

Figure 13-10. Program design (step *a*).

- The main modules are elaborated, considering the basic procedures for data manipulation (see Figure 13-11). Basic SPD constructs are inserted and deleted at any valid position to elaborate the SPD diagram. In Figure 13-11, "While", "For," and "IF" templates are used, and the whole control structure is roughly designed.
- The entire program specifications are completed (see Figure 13-12). Detailed procedures and control conditions are specified to complete the SPD diagram.

Phase 2: Program coding—Program code segments are inserted partly or completely through the SPD Editor sub-window. Then, program codes are generated from the SPD program specification by Forward Translator (see Figure 13-13). This Figure is a list of program codes generated from the SPD diagram shown in Figure 13-12. Code segments input through the SPD Editor sub-window are directly embedded into the program codes, the phrases in the SPD diagram are transformed into comment statements. If the programmer wants to put more program codes or comments into the generated program codes, he/she can do it using the text editor. Even after that, he can use Backward Translator to get a fresh SPD program specification and edit it with SPD Editor.

Phase 3: Maintenance/Reuse—If the program documents are required in the maintenance/reuse phase, SPD Documentor generates report documents including SPD diagrams from program codes. If a small program change is required, the programmer can modify program codes directly, using a text editor. Next, up-to-date documents should be generated with SPD Documentor. And if a large program change is required, it is more efficient to generate SPD program specifications from program codes with Backward Translator and to modify both SPD diagrams and associated program code segments using SPD Editor.

6 EVALUATION AND CONCLUSION

SPDTOOLS specifically tuned to program development in C language have been implemented. They are running on UNIX[1]. They are used in actual production of switching system software, telecommunication system software, etc. at NEC.

Through practical use, the following effects of SPDTOOLS are clarified:

- Productivity of program design work using SPD has been increased as high as approximately two times.

---

[1]UNIX is a trademark of AT&T Bell Laboratories.

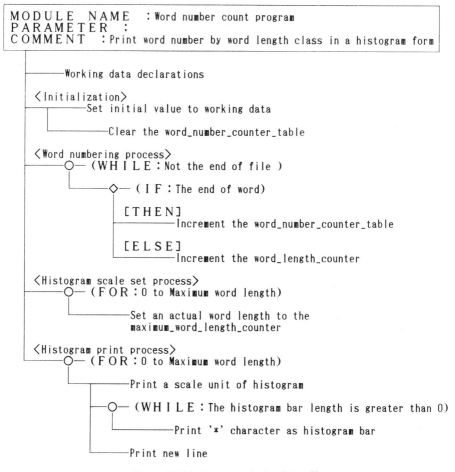

Figure 13-11. Program design (step *b*).

- Standardization of program documents and program codes, especially program comment style has been promoted.
- Novice programmers can develop programs of average quality, if they are carefully trained to use SPD and SPDTOOLS.

The current version of SPDTOOLS intensively supports design and coding of programs. Additional features to support systematic design of relational multiple programs are necessary for further improving software development productivity. The authors have started basic study and development toward extending SPDTOOLS to support such system design.

The authors wish to thank Dr. Y. Mizuno, Senior Vice President of NEC, who made a significant contribution to the initial stage of STEPS and SPD

MODULE NAME : Word number count program
PARAMETER :
COMMENT : Print word number by word length class in a histogram form

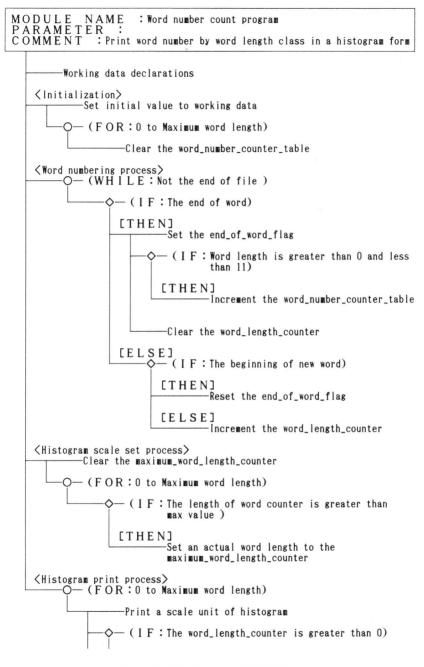

————————Working data declarations

⟨Initialization⟩
————————Set initial value to working data

——O— (F OR : 0 to Maximum word length)
————————Clear the word_number_counter_table

⟨Word numbering process⟩
——O— (WH I L E : Not the end of file)

————◇— (I F : The end of word)

[THEN]
————————Set the end_of_word_flag

————◇— (I F : Word length is greater than 0 and less
than 11)

[THEN]
————————Increment the word_number_counter_table

————————Clear the word_length_counter

[ELSE]
————◇— (I F : The beginning of new word)

[THEN]
————————Reset the end_of_word_flag

[ELSE]
————————Increment the word_length_counter

⟨Histogram scale set process⟩
————————Clear the maximum_word_length_counter

——O— (F OR : 0 to Maximum word length)

————◇— (I F : The length of word counter is greater than
max value)

[THEN]
————————Set an actual word length to the
maximum_word_length_counter

⟨Histogram print process⟩
——O— (F OR : 0 to Maximum word length)

————————Print a scale unit of histogram

————◇— (I F : The word_length_counter is greater than 0)

Figure 13-12. Program design (step *c*).

```
/*Print word number by word length class in a histogram form*/
#include<stdio.h>
main() /*Word number count program*/

{
    /*Working data declarations*/
    int c, i, inword, nc;
    int len;
    int maxvalue;
    int wl[11];
    { /*Initialization*/
        /*Set initial value to working data*/
        inword = 0;
        nc = 0;
        for(i = 0; i < 11; i++) /*0 to Maximum word length*/
        {
                /*Clear the word_number_counter_table*/
                wl[i] = 0;
        }
    }
    { /*Word numbering process*/
        while((c = getchar()) != EOF) /*Not the end of file */
        {
                if( c == ' ' || c == '¥n' || c == '¥t'
                ) /*The end of word*/
                {
                        /*Set the end_of_word_flag*/
                        inword = 0;
                        if(nc > 0 && nc < 11) /*Word length is greater than 0
                                                and less than 11*/
                        {
                                /*Increment the word_number_counter_table*/
                                ++wl[nc];
                        }
                        /*Clear the word_length_counter*/
                        nc = 0;
                }
                else
                {
                        if(inword == 0) /*The beginning of new word*/
                        {
                                /*Reset the end_of_word_flag*/
                                inword = 1;
                                nc = 1;
                        }
                        else
                        {
                                /*Increment the word_length_counter*/
                                ++nc;
                        }
                }
        }
    }
    { /*Histogram scale set process*/
        /*Clear the maximum_word_length_counter*/
        maxvalue = 0;
        for(i = 1; i < 11; i++) /*0 to Maximum word length*/
        {
                if(wl[i] > maxvalue) /*The length of word counter is greater
                                        than maximum value*/
```

Figure 13-13. Generated program codes.

development. The authors are also grateful to Prof. M. Asuma of Waseda University for his contribution to research and development on STEPS, SPD, and SPDTOOLS. Thanks are also due to Mr. T. Saya, Dr. M. Hattori, and Mr. S. Nakata of NEC Software Engineering Development Laboratory for their encouragement and helpful comments during this work.

REFERENCES

1. Nassi, I., and B. Shneiderman, "Flowchart Techniques for Structured Programming," *ACM SIGPLAN Notices*, Vol. 8, No. 8, 1973, pp. 12–26.
2. Chapin, N., "New Format for Flowcharts," *Software-Practice and Experience*, Vol. 6, No. 4, 1974, pp. 341–357.
3. Warnier, J. D., *Logical Construction of Programs*, New York: Van Nostrand Reinhold, 1974.
4. Weiderman, S. H., *et al.*, "Flowcharting Loops Without Cycles," *ACM SIGPLAN Notices*, Vol. 10, No. 4, 1975, pp. 37–46.
5. Stay, J.F. "HIPO and Integrated Program Design," *IBM Syst. J.*, Vol. 15, No. 2, 1976, pp. 143–154.
6. Witty, R.W. "Dimensional Flowcharting," *Software-Practice and Experience*, Vol. 7, 1977, pp. 553–584.
7. Schneiderman, B., *et al.*, "Experimental Investigations of the Utility of Detailed Flowcharts in Programming," *CACM*, Vol. 20, No. 6, 1977, pp. 373–381.
8. Ferstl, O. "Flowcharting by Step-wise Refinement," *ACM SIGPLAN Notices*, Vol. 13, No. 1, 1977, pp. 553–587.
9. Yoder, C. M., "Nassi-Schneiderman Charts: An Alternative Flowcharts for Design," *IEEE Tutorial on Software Design Techniques*, 1978, pp. 386–393.
10. Higgins, D. A., "Structured Programming with Warnier-Orr Diagram," *IEEE Tutorial: Software Design Strategies*, 1979, pp. 60–71.
11. Verdegraal, P. A., *et al.*, "The Warnier-Orr Diagram," *Proc. COMPCON '79*, 1979, pp. 301–306.
12. Futamura, Y., *et al.*, "Development of Computer Programs by PAD (Problem Analysis Diagram)," *Proc. 5th International Conference on Software Eng.*, 1981, pp. 325–332.
13. Hanata, S., *et al.* "Documentation Technology for Packing Hierarchical Function, Data and Control Structures," *Proc. COMPCON '81*, 1981, pp. 284–290.
14. Azuma, M., *et al.*, "SPD A Humanized Documentation Technology," *IEEE Trans. Software Eng.*, Vol. SE-11, No. 9, 1985, pp. 945–954.
15. Azuma, M. and Y. Mizuno, "STEPS: Integrated Software Standards and Its Productivity Impact," *Proc. COMPCON '81*, 1981, pp. 83–95.
16. Petrone, L., *et al.*, "DUAL: An Interactive Tool for Developing Documented Programs by Step-wise Refinements," *Proc. 6th International Conference on Software Eng.*, 1982, pp. 350–357.
17. Alibizuri-Romero, M. B., "Grase—A Graphical Syntax-directed Editor for Structured Programming," *ACM SIGPLAN Notices*, Vol. 19, No. 2, 1984, pp. 28–37.
18. Henderson, P. (Ed) "Software Engineering Symposium on Practical Software Development Environments," *ACM SIGSOFT/SIGPLAN*, Vol. 9, No. 5, 1984, p. 197.
19. Maezawa, H., *et al.*, "Interactive System for Structured Program Production," *Proc. 7th International Conference on Software Eng.*, 1984, pp. 162–171.
20. Donzeau-Gouge, V., *et al.*, "A Structured Oriented Program Editor: A First Step Towards Computer Assisted Programming," *Proc. International Computing Symposium*, 1975, pp. 113–120.

21. Medina-More, R. and P. H. Feiler, "An Incremental Programming Environment," *IEEE Trans. Software Eng.*, Vol. SE-7, No. 5, 1981, pp. 472–482.

22. Teitelbaum, T. and T. Reps, "The Cornell Program Synthesizer: A Syntax-Directed Programming Environment," *CACM*, Vol. 24, No. 7, 1981, pp. 563–573.

23. Allison, L., "Syntax Directed Program Editing," *Software Practice and Experience*, Vol. 13, 1983, pp. 453–465.

24. Irons, E. T. and F. M. Djorup, "A CRT Editing System," *CACM*, Vol. 15, No. 1, 1972, pp. 16–20.

25. Meyrowitz, N., and A. van Dam, "Interactive Editing Systems: Part I, II," *ACM Computing Surveys*, Vol. 14, No. 3, 1982, pp. 321–416.

Chapter 14

Hitachi's Software Factory Tools for COBOL: An Introduction to Skips/SDE for Business Applications.

D. Tajima[1], Y. Usuda[2], F. Tsunoda [2], S. Ebina[2]
Hitachi SK Software, Co., Ltd.[1]
Hitachi Software Engineering Co., Ltd.[2]

1 INTRODUCTION

With the growth of the information society, large scale software systems have become indispensable to our society. On-line real-time application systems for banking and railroad networks are examples of such software products, which have been developed by Hitachi Software Engineering (Hitachi SK). These kinds of systems consist of more than a million lines of code and require hundreds of programmers to complete. Above all, users demand systems with high performance, user-friendliness, high reliability, and fault tolerance, among other requirements.

To meet their requirements, under tight deadlines, Hitachi SK has adopted as their underlying philosophy "the establishment of software development methodology based on engineering approaches." Since the establishment of the company in 1970, an ongoing study of state-of-the-art software production technology, production facilities, software development support systems, and education systems has been under way, and the knowledge acquired has been applied to actual software development.

One of the major contributing factors to the company's production of high quality software has been their five stage productivity improvement strategy.[1] The first stage, concluded in 1975, focused on improving productivity in the coding phase. In the second stage, 1976–1978, structured programming methodology was applied. The third stage, 1979–1981, was the construction of an integrated software development system called SKIPS I based on the traditional waterfall model. In the fourth stage, started in 1982, SKIPS II was developed as an enhanced and refined version of SKIPS I. Both SKIPS I and II were based on TSS (Time Sharing System) running on Hitachi's mainframe computers. At the same time, the effectiveness of tools on personal computers and workstations was investigated.

The following lessons have been derived from Hitachi SK's research and practice on productivity improvement:

- Each project requires its own standards and methodology. Therefore, it is not practical to enforce a single set of standard and/or methodology on every project.
- Tools can be successfully employed on personal computers and workstations and are very effective, unless they require a large amount of computer resources, such as CPU time and disk space.
- It is very important to reuse not only code but also requirement and design documents, since code contains information which is too detailed to analyze whether the code is reusable or not.
- Even though a tool may be effective in some aspects, it may not be accepted by designers and programmers unless it is easy to learn and easy to use.

Using past experiences as a foundation, Hitachi SK started the fifth stage of their productivity improvement strategy in 1986. Its goal is to triple productivity by the end of 1990. In this chapter, Hitachi SK's new software development environment, SKIPS/SDE, is introduced as an example of a software factory approach to commercial software development.

2 BASIC CONCEPT OF SKIPS / SDE

2.1 Purpose of SKIPS / SDE

The purpose of SKIPS/SDE is to triple software productivity through promoting software resource reusability as well as providing assistance in an automation of development activities. Major characteristics of the system are described as the following:

- *Distributed yet integrated environment*—The system provides a distributed software development environment which consists of workstations connected by LANs with file servers and print servers. These LANs can be connected to host computers to form a company-wide network system. Most of the interaction with the system is performed on workstations. As products are developed on this system, they are stored hierarchically. Intermediate products of each project are managed in file servers, and the final products are stored in a company-wide database system.
- *Document reuse*—The system assists in the production and management of documents, such as requirement and design specifications, which are created in the early development phases. These documents usually consist of a mixture of figures, tables, and text (including Japanese text). They can be used in developing support tools for use during the implementation and testing phases. In addition, the system helps accumulate other infor-

mation, such as design memorandums and development activity statistics for reutilization and analysis.

- *Increased automation*—The system helps reduce the time and cost of producing software by assisting early development phases through automated code generation, a facility for reusing source code, including generic algorithms and commonly used subroutines.
- *User-friendly environment*—The system provides a standard human interface that is easy to learn and easy to use by employing icons, multiple windows, and a mouse. Each operation is performed by selecting the desired icon and a command from a pop-up menu. The operation is automatically canceled if the user makes a mistake.
- *Wide applicability*—The system is applicable to a wide variety of development projects such as operating systems, business applications, and embedded systems. In addition, it can be easily customized to a specific project.
- *Extendibility and evolvability*—The system can easily incorporate new features, and it provides a method for installing new development tools. It also has a feature for gathering 'factual data' for system evaluation and improvement.
- *Integration of development and management*—The system can automatically gather various managerial information such as a history of tool usage and product access, as well as programmer activity records. It can process this information and provide reports to managers for evaluation of development projects.

2.2 SKIPS/SDE Design

The SKIPS/SDE design is summarized as the following:

- SKIPS/SDE consists of an application independent resource manager that allows users and tools to manipulate documents as well as source code. On top of the resource manager, common application tools and application specific tools are installed as one of the methods for system extension and evolution. The interface between tools and the resource manager must be logical so that the physical locations of resources are transparent to users.
- The system can manipulate multi-media information, consisting of a mixture of figures, tables, and text (including Japanese text), in a simple and uniform manner.
- Each tool and the resource manager provide a user-friendly interface through multiple windows, icons, and a mouse which are the features of Hitachi workstations, the 2050 series (an MC68010/68020 based UNIX workstation with a high resolution bit map display and multi-window capability). Moreover, the user interface is enhanced by a wide range of colors and figures.

- The resource manager has a feature to automatically obtain programmer activity records so that managers can analyze and make decisions immediately based on this information.
- The system provides features for customizing itself to a specific project, by parameterizing project specific information and localizing modules that provide project specific features. In particular, code generators are designed to localize their language dependent code.

2.3 Development Plan

SKIPS/SDE is evolving according to the following version plan:

V1: Software development using project LANs—the first version of SKIPS/SDE is being applied to model workshops which consist of workstations, LANs, file servers, and print servers. Data transfer from/to host computers is carried out through TSS instead of the LANs. This version has been operational since April, 1988.

V2: Software development using a company-wide integrated network—the second version of SKIPS/SDE will evolve into a company wide integrated network system, based on experiences with V1. It is expected to be completed by April, 1989.

2.4 Hardware Configuration

The SKIPS/SDE hardware configuration is shown in Figure 14-1. The first version of SKIPS/SDE consists of workstations connected by LANs with file

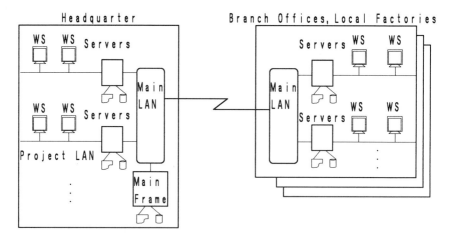

Figure 14-1. SKIPS/SDE hardware configuration.

servers and print servers. In the second version of SKIPS/SDE, these LANs are connected to host computers to form a company-wide network system.

2.5   Software Architecture

The SKIPS/SDE software architecture (V1) is shown in Figure 14-2. SKIPS/SDE consists of various development tools, for example, common tools and domain specific tools, which are integrated through a resource manager called the filing system.
The second version will be designed after V1 becomes operational.

3   FUNCTIONS AND CHARACTERISTICS OF THE FILING SYSTEM

The filing system manages all types of intermediate and final products, such as design documents and source code, which are developed during a software life-cycle. The system makes it possible to register, search, and reuse these products.
   The chief functions of the filing system are shown in Table 14-1. The filing system employs a hierarchical document management method, a multikey search method, and an icon human interface so as to promote reusability in a user-friendly manner.
   Hierarchical Document Management Method—products developed by various tools can be managed in a way similar to the organization of documents in the real world.

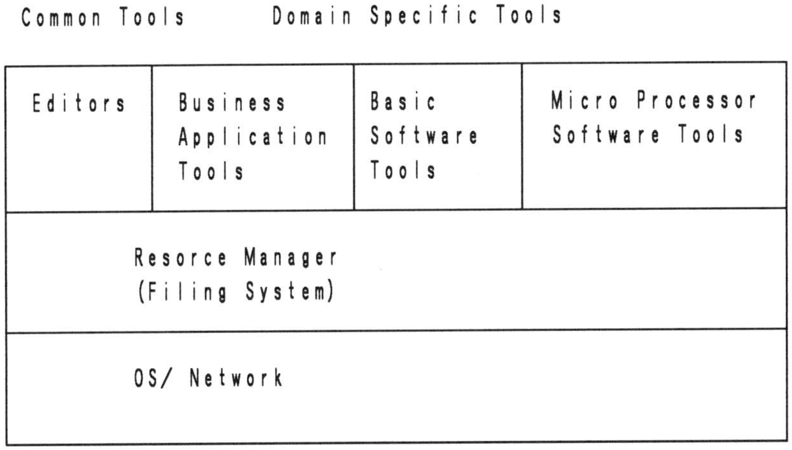

```
Common Tools      Domain Specific Tools
```

Editors	Business Application Tools	Basic Software Tools	Micro Processor Software Tools
Resource Manager (Filing System)			
OS/ Network			

Figure 14-2. SKIPS/SDE software architecture.

Table 14-1. Chief functions of the filing system.

	Function		Meaning
1	Product Management	Product Manipulation	(1) Create cabinets, books and sheets, and set/change their attributes in order to establish the environment for the project and the programmer. (2) Load, store and search products, and prepare a table of contents according to product hierarchy.
2		Access Control	(1) Set/change product access modes. Access modes include read and update, and can be set/changed independently for managers, groups of users, and others.
3	Activity Report	Activity Data Record	(1) Record product access history. (2) Record the sequence of commands entered by each user. (3) Record tool usage history. (4) Record system logging information.
4		Statistics Report	(1) Collect above activity data and report to managers.
5	Document Output Service	LBP Output Request	(1) Request print servers provide product printout. The unit of the request can be either a book, a folder, a sheet, etc.
6		LBP Scheduler	(1) Schedule product output demands for LBP and select an available LBP.

- Objects managed by the filing system are the output of documentation tools (word processors, editors, etc.), and output of development support tools (documents as well as source code).
- Product hierarchy and correspondence to the real world as a

  Cabinet: Each project has a "cabinet," consisting of several "books."

  Book: A "book" represents a document volume, such as a requirement specification or a design specification. A book contains several "folders."

  Folder: A "folder" is similar to a chapter or a section of a book. It consists of a collection of "folders" and/or "sheets."

  Sheet: A sheet is the minimum unit of a product, such as a record specification or a program control flow. Each sheet is output from a certain tool.

Multikey Search Method—products can be searched using an "icon search," "index table search," or "page-specify search." These are defined as the following:

- Icon Search—this searching method is performed along with the hierarchy of cabinets, books, etc., by picking icons in a window until the user reaches the desired object.
- Index Table Search—this method locates a desired object through the user selecting the name or attributes of the object in an index table.
- Page-Specify Search—this method finds an object through the user, specifying the page number of the desired sheet.

Icon Human Interface—the filing system displays icons having shapes similar to the real objects used by programmers, so their meaning is easy to understand (Figure 14-3). In the icon for a sheet, the name of the tool which outputs the sheet is shown.

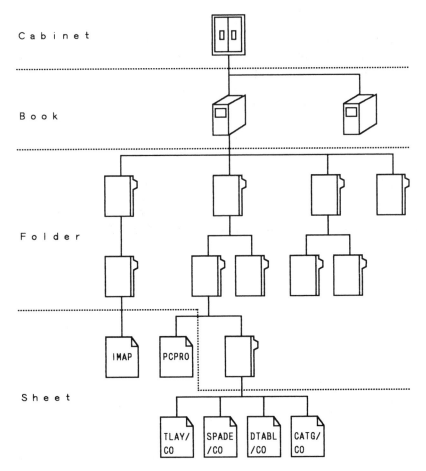

Figure 14-3. Product hierarchy and icons.

4 EXAMPLES OF TOOLS FOR COBOL AND THEIR EVALUATION

In this section, some of the tools which are already operational and have had successful experimental results will be introduced. Although many new approaches for business application software development, such as fourth generation languages (4GL), have become available, COBOL is still one of the major languages for large scale business software because of its standardized language specification and rich set of file and DB/DC facilities. Therefore, among other languages, tools in SKIPS/SDE are primarily targeted for business application software written in COBOL.

For designing tools, the following requirements, derived from past experiences, have been established:

- Each tool must be able to directly manipulate graphic and/or format representation of programs as well as documents with Japanese text.
- Each tool must generate (a portion of) source programs and high quality documents that contain Japanese text.
- Each tool must be easy to learn and easy to use. In particular, help and undo facilities are necessary.
- Each tool must be able to customize itself to a specific project.
- Information generated by a tool during a previous phase must be able to be input into the tool at the current phase without any modification.

The relationships between the various business application tools are shown in Figure 14-4 and their functions are summarized in Table 14-2. Among these tools, five major tools will be discussed. They are: (1) human interface prototyping (PCPRO), (2) form based record definer (TLAY/CO), (3) form based

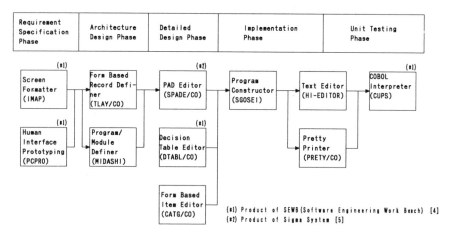

Figure 14-4. SKIPS/SDE for business application.

Table 14-2. Functions of various tools.

Phase	Tool name	Function
Requirement Specification	PCPRO	Simulates transitions of screens and printouts based on the state transition model.
	IMAP	Draws an image of a screen or printout format interactively and generates the corresponding source program.
Architecture Design	MIDASHI	Defines inputs and outputs of a program/module and generates program/module function specification.
	TLAY/CO	Defines a record specification interactively, and generates the corresponding documents as well as the source program automatically.
Detailed Design	SPADE/CO	Draws simplified PAD charts interactively and generates the corresponding document as well as the source program interactively.
	DTABL/CO	Defines a decision table interactively and generates the corresponding source program.
	CATG/CO	Defines an item connection specification interactively, and generates the corresponding document and source program automatically.
Implementation	SGOSEI	Collects a portion of a source program generated by the above tools and constructs program/module.
	HI-EDITOR	Full-screen text editor.
	PRETY/CO	Performs indentation and vertical alignment of COBOL source programs based on a parameterized form of the customer's coding standard.
Unit Testing	CUPS	Interpreter and debugger for COBOL.

item editor (CATG/CO), (4) interactive PAD editor (SPADE/CO), and (5) COBOL interpreter (CUPS). (The suffix "/CO" indicates that the tool is for COBOL. Beside COBOL, the authors are developing tools for PL/I, C, and other languages, by modifying these tools.)

4.1 Human Interface Prototyping (PCPRO)

PCPRO simulates screen transitions of on-line real-time business applications (Figure 14-5). First, the users define the layout and attributes of each screen and/or printout by using the screen formatter (IMAP). Next, they draw a screen transition diagram, as well as screen transition conditions, interactively. The simulation is carried out based on the state transition model generated by the above information. A simulation under the multi-window environment is illus-

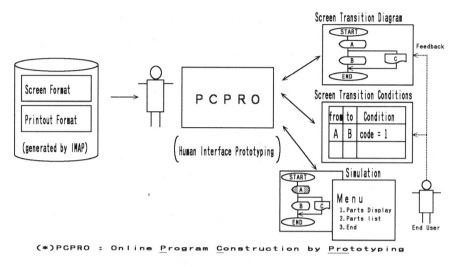

(*)PCPRO : Online Program Construction by Prototyping

Figure 14-5. Human interface prototyping (PCPRO*).

trated in Figure 14-6. The diagram on the left side shows a screen transition diagram. The highlighted symbol indicates the current screen that is displayed on the right side (a ''Menu-Selection'' screen of a purchasing system). At this moment, the user is requested to enter a number indicating which inquiry to make into the purchasing system. If the user enters a particular number, the transition occurs and the next screen is shown according to the previously defined condition.

In the case of business application software development, many problems that are related to human interfacing arise in the later stages of software development. Therefore, this tool is expected to establish user requirements at the early stages of the life-cycle.

4.2   Form Based Record Definer (TLAY/CO)

TLAY/CO is used to define items in a record interactively and to generate several design documents and the corresponding data division source program in COBOL (see Figure 14-7). The generated design documents include a record specification and a record layout chart. An example of a record specification that is generated by TLAY/CO is shown in Figure 14-8. The document defines each item in a record by its Japanese and symbolic names as well as its attributes. The corresponding record layout chart for the above record specification generated by the tool is shown in Figure 14-9. The tool also creates a data dictionary that contains the Japanese and symbolic names of an item as well as its attributes, such as data type, length, initial value, etc. The generated COBOL source program for the corresponding data division is shown in Figure 14-10.

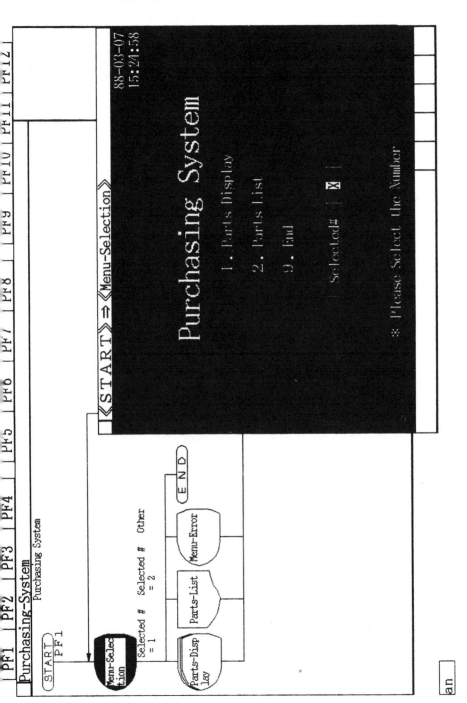

Figure 14-6.   Simulation example.

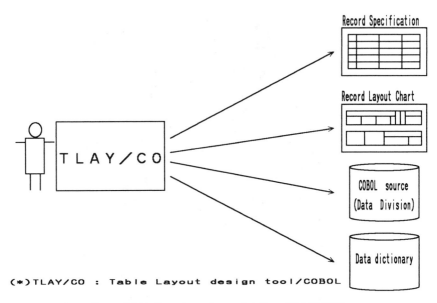

Record Specification

Record Layout Chart

T L A Y ／C O

COBOL source
(Data Division)

Data dictionary

(＊)TLAY/CO : Table Layout design tool/COBOL

Figure 14-7. Form based record definer (TLAY/CO*).

4.3 Form Based Item Editor (CATG/CO)

CATG/CO allows the designers to define how the value of an item in an output record is produced from the values of the items in the input records, by connecting the output item with the input items. It also generates an item connection specification as well as COBOL source code (mostly 'MOVE' statements).

The basic functions of CATG/CO are shown in Figure 14-11. An example of the interaction using a mouse and a pop-up menu, is illustrated in Figure 14-12. If the designer wants to connect an output item with an input item so as to generate a MOVE statement, he or she simply selects those items with the mouse and then selects a command that indicates 'connect' from the menu. If the connection is allowed in COBOL grammar, the color of the items is altered to show that the connection is successful. An example of the item connection specification generated by the tool is shown in Figure 14-13. Each row in the document represents an item in an output record connected to items in several input records. It can contain some supplementary comments, if necessary. The MOVE statements generated by the tool, based on the above item connection specification, are shown in Figure 14-14.

According to our study, more than 50% of the COBOL source statement lines are 'MOVE' statements; this tool is expected to reduce the tedious manual task of writing 'MOVE' statements from item connection specifications.

* * * レコード仕様書 (全税登録データ) * * * 　日付 88-3-7 ページ 0001

Level number　Japanese Item Name　Item Name used in COBOL　Type　Size　Occurs　Location　Others(Initial Value etc)

属性 A:英数字 9:符号無ゾーン S:符号付ゾーン P:符号付COMP-3 B:COMP Z:編集

その他 V:初期値 Z:編集マスク I:INDEX名 R:西定名名 C:コメント

項番	R	レベル	漢字データ名	データ項目名	属性	桁数	配列	位置	その他
1		01	全税登録データ	ALL_DATA				1	
2		03	連番コード	RBN_CODE	X	1		1	
3		03	送付先コード	SOU_CODE	X	1		2	
4		03	調査所在地	SVOZAITT				3	
5		05	漢字禁止サイン	KINSI_S	X	1		3	
6		05	住所コード	ADD_CODE				4	
7		07	新都府県コード	TOFK_C	X	2		4	
8		07	市区郡コード	SKG_CODE	X	3		6	
9		07	大字コード	OZ_CODE	X	3		9	
10		07	字コード	Z_CODE	X	3		12	
11		07	地番号	TI_NO	X	30		15	
12		05	前後の順	BA_BUN	X			45	
13		07	組織コード	S_CODE	X	2		45	
14		07	農事名称	YAGOU	X	35		47	
15		05	開業日	KAI_DAY				82	
16		07	年	NEN	X	3		82	
17		07	月	TUKI	X	2		85	
18		07	日	HI	X	2		87	
19		07	定休コード	TEIKYU_C	X	2		89	
20		05	税目コード	ZEIMOKU_C	X	2		91	
21		05	納税番号	NOUZEI	9	7		93	
22		05	現税担事務所コード	GJIMU_C	X	2		100	
23		05	全税事事務所コード	ZJIMU_C	X	2		102	
24		05	組織コード	SOSIKI_C				104	
25		07	分類	BUNRUI	X	1		104	
26		07	組織番号	S_NO	X	2		105	
27		07	口座情報	KO_DETA	9	7		107	
28		07	口座番号	KOU_NO	9			114	
29		07	預金種目コード	YGSYU_C	X	1		121	
30		07	口座振り有文有無コード	UMU_C	X	1		121	
31		07	支店コード	SITEN_C	X	5		123	

Figure 14-8.　Record specification generated by TLAY/CO.

Figure 14-9. Record layout chart generated by TLAY/CO.

Mar 7 13:00 1988 IN1_MST.cpy Page 1

```
 1      01        ALL_DATA.
 2         03     REN_CODE              PIC X.
 3         03     SOU_CODE              PIC X.
 4         03     SYOZAITI.
 5            05  KINSI_S               PIC X.
 6            05  ADD_CODE.
 7               07  TDFK_C             PIC XX.
 8               07  SKG_CODE           PIC XXX.
 9               07  OZ_CODE            PIC XXX.
10               07  Z_CODE             PIC XXX.
11               07  TI_NO              PIC X(30).
12            05  BA_BUN.
13               07  S_CODE             PIC XX.
14               07  YAGOU              PIC X(35).
15            05  KAI_DAY.
16               07  NEN                PIC XXX.
17               07  TUKI               PIC XX.
18               07  HI                 PIC XX.
19               07  TEIKYU_C           PIC XX.
20            05  ZEIMOKU_C             PIC XX.
21            05  NOUZEI                PIC 9(7).
22            05  GJIMU_C               PIC XX.
23            05  ZJIMU_C               PIC XX.
24            05  SOSIKI_C.
25               07  BUNRUI             PIC X.
26               07  S_NO               PIC XX.
27               07  KO_DETA            PIC 9(7).
28               07  KOU_NO             PIC 9(7).
29               07  YOSYU_C            PIC X.
30               07  UMU_C              PIC X.
31               07  SITEN_C            PIC X(5).
```

Figure 14-10. COBOL source (Data Division) generated by TLAY/CO.

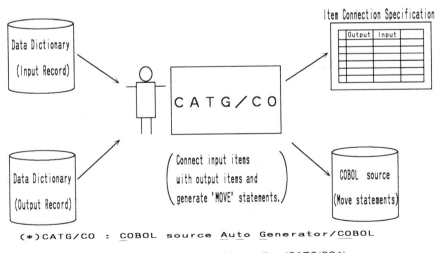

(*)CATG/CO : COBOL source Auto Generator/COBOL

Figure 14-11. Form based item editor (CATG/CO*).

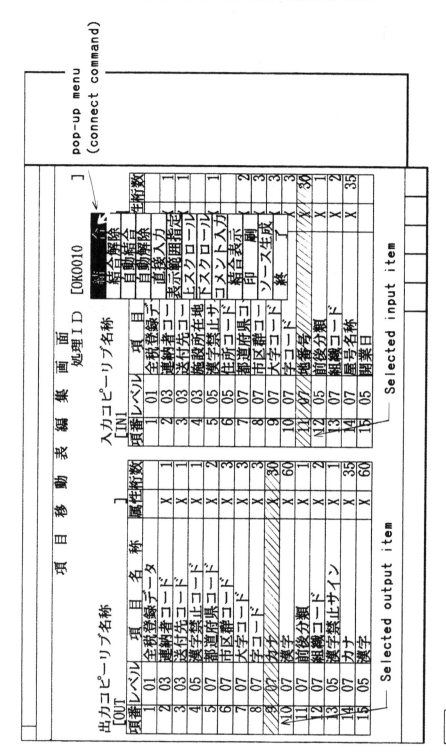

Figure 14-12.   Example of CATG/CO interaction.

Output Record — Input Record1 — input Record2 — Indicate how to edit

プログラム設計	ワークシート	項目移動表編集方法	作成	承認	作成日	P. 1
業務名	項番	プログラム名称		プログラム記号名称	TEST	

項番	受取り側 OUT 項目名称	属性	桁数	送り側 IN1 項目名称	属性	桁数	IN2 項目名称	属性	桁数	編集方法
1	全税登録データ			全税登録データ						
2	連納者コード	X	1	連納者コード	X	1				
3	送付先コード	X	1	送付先コード	X	1				
4	漢字禁止コード	X	1				組織コード	X	2	
5	都道府県コード	X	2	都道府県コード	X	2				
6	市区群コード	X	3	市区群コード	X	3				
7	大字コード	X	3	大字コード	X	3				
8	字コード	X	3	字コード	X	3				
9	カナ	X	30				大字コード	X	3	
10	漢字	X	60				字コード	X	3	
11	前後分類	X	1	前後分類	X	1				入力画面によりセット。 未入力の場合（SPACE）は'380'をセット。
12	組織コード	X	2	組織コード						
13	漢字禁止サイン	X	1	漢字禁止サイン	X	1				法人代表者カナが入力された場合、'1'をセット。 未入力の場合'0'をセット。
14	カナ	X	35				開業日			
15	漢字	X	60							SPACE
16	年	9	4							ZERO
17	月	9	2							ZERO
18	日	9	2							ZERO
19	定休日コード	X	2	定休日コード	X	2				
20	税目コード	X	2	税目コード	X	2				
21	現在	X	2				現県税事務所コード	X	2	ユーザ・テーブル・ファイル（端末管理テーブル）より 仮想端末名称に対応する県税事務所コードを獲得し、セット。
22	変更前	X	2				税目コード	X	2	
23	前後分類	X	1	前後分類	X	1				
24	口座番号	9	7	口座番号	9	7				
25	機関コード	X	4				預金種類コード	X	1	
26	支店コード	X	3	支店コード	X	5				
27	預金種類コード	X	1	預金種類コード	X	1				
28	年	9	4	年	X	3				
29	月	9	2	月	X	2				
30	日	9	2	日	X	2				

Figure 14-13. Item connection specification generated by CATG/CO.

May 27 09:56 1987 TEST.CBL Page 1

```
 1          MOVE TOKUISAKI-M-REC  TO  TOKUISAKI-M-REC.
 2          MOVE TITLE  TO  TITLE.
 3          MOVE TOKUISAKI-CODE  TO  TOKUISAKI-CODE.
 4          MOVE TOKUISAKI-NAME  TO  TOKUISAKI-NAME.
 5          MOVE YUBIN-BANGOU  TO  YUBIN-BANGOU.
 6          MOVE JYUSYO  TO  JYUSYO.
 7          MOVE TOKUISAKI-DATA  TO  TOKUISAKI-DATA.
 8          MOVE SHIMEBI-CODE  TO  SHIMEBI-CODE.
 9          MOVE SHIMEBI-CODE-X  TO  SHIMEBI-CODE-X.
10          MOVE ZEN-SEIKYU  TO  ZEN-SEIKYU.
11          MOVE KON-URIAGE  TO  KON-URIAGE.
12          MOVE KON-HENPIN  TO  KON-HENPIN.
13          MOVE KON-NEBIKI  TO  KON-NEBIKI.
14          MOVE KON-GEN-NYUKIN  TO  KON-GEN-NYUKIN.
15          MOVE KON-TE-NYUKIN  TO  KON-TE-NYUKIN.
16          MOVE KON-NYU-NEBIKI  TO  'KON-NYU-NEBIKI.
17          MOVE KON-NYU-SOSAI  TO  KON-NYU-SOSAI.
18          MOVE DENPYO-MAISU  TO  DENPYO-MAISU.
19          MOVE SYANAI-DATA  TO  SYANAI-DATA.
20          MOVE URIAGE-RUIKEI  TO  URIAGE-RUIKEI.
21          MOVE URIAGE-HEN-NE-RUIKEI  TO  URIAGE-HEN-NE-RUIKEI.
22          MOVE TAIRYU-3  TO  TAIRYU-3.
23          MOVE TAIRYU-2  TO  TAIRYU-2.
24          MOVE TAIRYU-1  TO  TAIRYU-1.
25          MOVE URIAGE  TO  URIAGE.
26          MOVE URIAGE-NEBIKI  TO  URIAGE-NEBIKI.
27          MOVE URIAGE-HENPIN  TO  URIAGE-HENPIN.
28          MOVE GENKIN-NYUKIN  TO  GENKIN-NYUKIN.
29          MOVE TEGATA-NYUKIN  TO  TEGATA-NYUKIN.
30          MOVE NYUKIN-NEBIKI  TO  NYUKIN-NEBIKI.
31          MOVE NYUKIN-SOSAI  TO  NYUKIN-SOSAI.
32          MOVE KARI-URIAGE  TO  KARI-URIAGE.
33          MOVE KARI-URI-SURYO  TO  KARI-URI-SURYO.
34          MOVE KARI-URI-KINGAKU  TO  KARI-URI-KINGAKU.
35          MOVE SONOTA  TO  SONOTA.
36          MOVE YOSHIN  TO  YOSHIN.
37          MOVE TANTOU-CODE  TO  TANTOU-CODE.
38          MOVE EIGYOU-CODE  TO  EIGYOU-CODE.
39          MOVE BUSYO-CODE  TO  BUSYO-CODE.
40          MOVE KAISYU-YOTEI  TO  KAISYU-YOTEI.
41          MOVE LINE-COUNT  TO  LINE-COUNT.
42          MOVE TOKUISAKI-CODE  TO  TOKUISAKI-CODE.
43          MOVE TOKUISAKI-NAME  TO  TOKUISAKI-NAME.
44          MOVE YUBIN-BANGOU  TO  YUBIN-BANGOU.
45          MOVE JYUSYO  TO  JYUSYO.
46          MOVE SHIMEBI-CODE  TO  SHIMEBI-CODE.
47          MOVE NEN-TUKI-HI-CODE  TO  NEN-TUKI-HI-CODE.
48          MOVE KOKYAKU-NAME  TO  KOKYAKU-NAME.
49          MOVE KOKYAKU-CODE  TO  KOKYAKU-CODE.
50          MOVE KOKYAKU-TEL-NO  TO  KOKYAKU-TEL-NO.
```

Figure 14-14. COBOL source generated by CATG/CO.

4.4 Interactive PAD Editor (SPADE/CO)

SPADE/CO is a tool to design the control flow for a COBOL program in the form of a 'simplified' PAD chart. A PAD chart is a graphical representation of structured programming in a tree-structured diagram and was invented at Hitachi's Central Research Institute.[2] Symbols used in the chart include a start symbol, an end symbol, a processing symbol, a selection symbol, and an iteration symbol, which are all allowed in structured programming. The simplified PAD chart is a modified version of the PAD chart which is easier to write than the original version. The symbols in the original PAD chart as well as the simplified one are shown in Table 14-3. An interactive PAD editor based on the original chart was initially developed at Hitachi's System Development Laboratory.[3] SPADE/CO was developed based on the simplified chart because it is more popular than the original one within Hitachi SK. Hereafter, the words 'PAD chart' refer to the simplified PAD chart, unless otherwise stated.

Table 14-3. PAD chart symbols.

Meaning	Symbols		Corresponding Source Program
	PAD Chart	Simplified PAD Chart	
Start	P 1	P 1	P1 SECTION. P1-000. . . .
End	P 2	P 2	. . P1-999. P2.
Processing	P 1 P 2	P 1 P 2	P1 P2 . . .
Select	P 1 C P 2	P 1 C P 2	IF C THEN P1 ELSE P2 END-IF.
Iteration	C — P	U — C — P	PERFORM UNTIL C P END-PERFORM.

This tool allows users to draw PAD charts interactively and to print out the PAD charts as design documents as well as to generate the corresponding COBOL source program. It also accepts a COBOL source program and produces the corresponding PAD chart (see Figure 14-15). An example of the tool's interaction using a mouse, a pop-up menu, and an icon is illustrated in Figure 14-16. PAD chart symbols are defined in the upper part of the window. An icon which represents a pencil (we call it a guidance cursor) shows where the users can edit the chart. In the Figure, the 'undo' command in the menu has been selected: this tool allows users to move, delete, and copy not only a single symbol but also a group of symbols that form 'if statements' and 'until statements.' The layout of the chart is automatically adjusted to minimize space consumption. The PAD chart generated and COBOL source code generated, based on the above chart, are shown in Figure 14-17 and Figure 18, respectively.

4.5   COBOL Interpreter (CUPS)

CUPS is an interpreter and debugger for COBOL programs (Figure 14-19). It executes a COBOL program without compilation. If an error is detected during execution, the user can change from the execution mode to the edit mode and correct the program. The user can then return to the execution mode to continue testing (Figure 14-20a). The tool automatically collects two types of coverage information, C0/C1, to obtain a quantitative measure of the quality of the program (Figure 14-20b). C0 is defined as ''the number of executed statements / the number of executable statements'' and C1 is defined as ''the number of

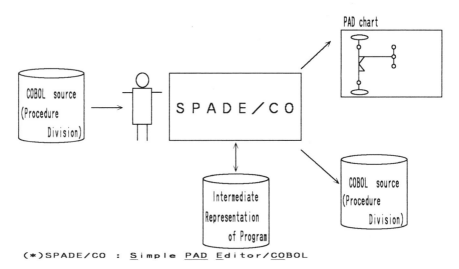

(*)SPADE/CO : Simple PAD Editor/COBOL

Figure 14-15. Interactive PAD editor (SPADE/CO).

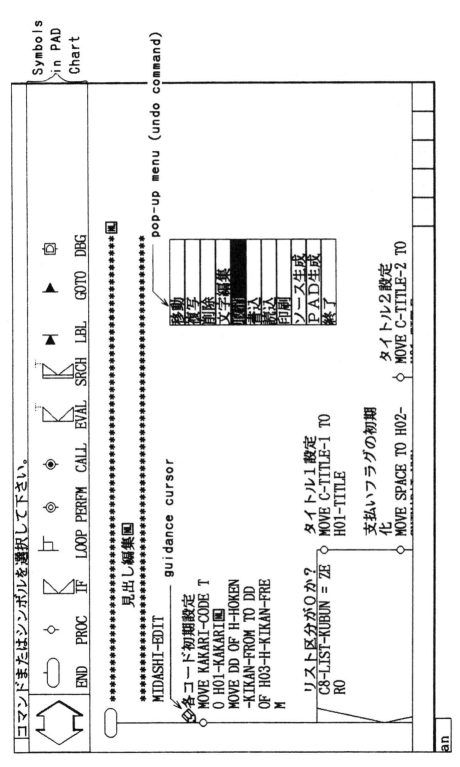

Figure 14-16. Example of SPADE/CO interaction.

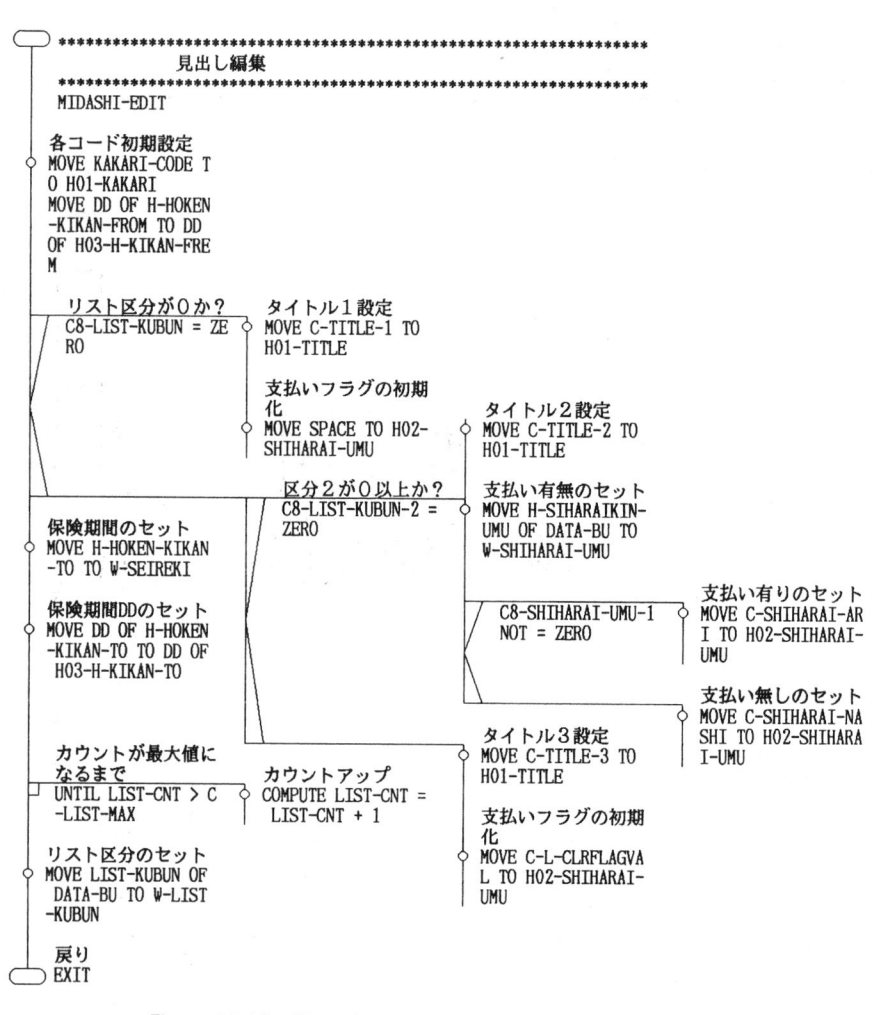

Figure 14-17. Simplified PAD chart generated by SPADE/CO.

executed branches / the number executable branches.'' These two measures are used as exit criteria during the unit testing phase. In Hitachi SK, the quality assurance department will not allow the design and development departments to proceed to the next phase unless every program satisfies the requirement that both C0 and C1 measures are 100%.

4.6 Experimental Evaluation of the Tools

The effects of TLAY/CO, CATG/CO, and SPADE/CO have been investigated. The time to complete the documents and source programs by conventional

```
MIDASHI-EDIT SECTION.
****************************************************************
*              見出し編集
****************************************************************
MIDASHI-EDIT-000.
*各コード初期設定
    MOVE KAKARI-CODE TO H01-KAKARI
    MOVE DD OF H-HOKEN-KIKAN-FROM TO DD OF H03-H-KIKAN-FREM.
*リスト区分が0か?
    IF  C8-LIST-KUBUN = ZERO
    THEN
*タイトル1設定
        MOVE C-TITLE-1 TO H01-TITLE
*支払いフラグの初期化
        MOVE SPACE TO H02-SHIHARAI-UMU
    ELSE
*区分2が0以上か?
        IF  C8-LIST-KUBUN-2 = ZERO
        THEN
*タイトル2設定
            MOVE C-TITLE-2 TO H01-TITLE
*支払い有無のセット
            MOVE H-SIHARAIKIN-UMU OF DATA-BU TO W-SHIHARAI-UMU
            IF  C8-SHIHARAI-UMU-1 NOT = ZERO
            THEN
*支払い有りのセット
                MOVE C-SHIHARAI-ARI TO H02-SHIHARAI-UMU
            ELSE
*支払い無しのセット
                MOVE C-SHIHARAI-NASHI TO H02-SHIHARAI-UMU
            END-IF
        ELSE
*タイトル3設定
            MOVE C-TITLE-3 TO H01-TITLE
*支払いフラグの初期化
            MOVE C-L-CLRFLAGVAL TO H02-SHIHARAI-UMU
        END-IF
    END-IF.
*保険期間のセット
    MOVE H-HOKEN-KIKAN-TO TO W-SEIREKI.
*保険期間DDのセット
    MOVE DD OF H-HOKEN-KIKAN-TO TO DD OF H03-H-KIKAN-TO.
*カウントが最大値になるまで
    PERFORM  UNTIL LIST-CNT > C-LIST-MAX
*カウントアップ
        COMPUTE LIST-CNT = LIST-CNT + 1
    END-PERFORM.
*リスト区分のセット
    MOVE LIST-KUBUN OF DATA-BU TO W-LIST-KUBUN.
*戻り
MIDASHI-EDIT-999.
    EXIT.
```

Figure 14-18. COBOL source (Procedure Division) generated by SPADE/CO.

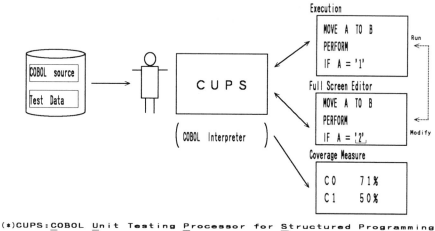

(∗)CUPS:COBOL Unit Testing Processor for Structured Programming

Figure 14-19.   COBOL interpreter (CUPS∗).

manual tasks was compared with the time to produce them using the tools (see Table 14-4). Since each tool only requires entering a minimum amount of data to generate documents and programs, work time to complete these can be reduced by 60% to 90%. In the design phase, about 40% of the work time is spent producing documents and source programs covered by the described three tools; therefore, a work time reduction of about 30% is expected by using these tools.

5   CURRENT STATUS AND FUTURE DIRECTIONS

The first version of SKIPS/SDE is operational and being used by more than 100 designers and programmers for commercial software development. Currently, the real effects of the system are being evaluated to gain feedback for design of the second version of SKIPS/SDE.

Some of the tools in SKIPS/SDE are commercially available in Japan. The screen formatter (IMAP), the human interface prototyping (PCPRO), the decision table editor (DTABL/CO), and the COBOL interpreter (CUPS) are Hitachi products, named SEWB/IMP, SEWB/SIM, SEWB/DTCBL, and SEWB/CUPS, respectively. Here, SEWB (Software Engineering WorkBench) is the generic name for Hitachi's software development tool products running on Hitachi 2050 workstations. SEWB can be integrated with Hitachi's product called EAGLE (mainframe based software development system) to form a distributed software development environment.[4] The interactive PAD editor (SPADE/CO) is among the chart editors for business application in the Sigma Project[5] and will soon become available (Chapter 21 of this book introduces the Sigma Project).

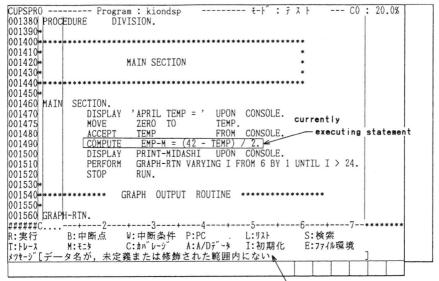

(a) Execution Mode

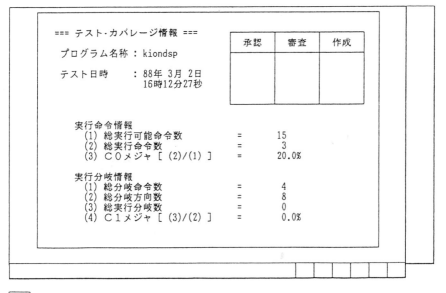

(b) Test Coverage Information

Figure 14-20. Example of CUPS interaction.

Table 14-4. Effects of tools on SKIPS/SDE.

Document Name	Previous Approach	Proposed Approach	Reduced time by each tool (A)	Time Spent by developing the Documents (B)	Effect (A × B)
Record Definition Specification Record Layout Chart	Write Manually. A prototype version of the tool was partially used on PC.	Define record specifications interactively, and generate the corresponding documents as well as source program automatically.	60%	11%	7%
Item Connection Specification	Write Manually.	Define item connection specifications interactively, and generate the corresponding document and source program automatically.	93%	11%	10%
PAD Chart	Write Manually. A prototype version of the tool was partially used on PC.	Draw a simplified PAD chart interactively and generate the corresponding document as well as source program interactively.	79%	19%	15%
Cumulative Effect at the Design Phase					32%

6 SUMMARY

In this chapter, a distributed yet integrated software development environment, called SKIPS/SDE, was first described as an example of a software factory approach to commercial software development. SKIPS/SDE utilizes a local area network of Hitachi's workstations, file servers, and print servers. Notable features of the system include the development of a filing system for document and product reusability and a collection of application domain specific tools placed on top of the filing system. The SKIPS/SDE description was followed by an explanation of a series of tools for business application software written in COBOL, where several tools for business applications were introduced. Those tools are expected to improve productivity by 30% in the design and implementation phases according to the authors experimental evaluation. SKIPS/SDE has been operational since April 1988 and is currently used by more than 100 designers and programmers for commercial software development.

The SKIPS/SDE project has been possible due to efforts of many people at Hitachi SK. In addition to the helpful comments from the associates and the reviewers, the authors gratefully acknowledge Messrs. Maezawa, Tsuda, Hagi, and Ishimoto at Hitachi Ltd. for stimulating discussions during the course of the project.

REFERENCES

1. Tajima, D., and T. Matsubara, "Inside the Japanese Software Industry," *IEEE Computer,* March 1984, pp. 34-43.
2. Futamura, Y., T. Kawai, H. Horikoshi, and M. Tsutsumi, "Development of Computer Programs by Problem Analysis Diagram (PAD)," *Proc. of 5th International Conference on Software Engineering,* March 1981, pp. 325-332.
3. Maezawa, H., M. Kobayashi, K. Saito, and Y. Futamura, "Interactive System for Structured Program Production," *Proc. of 7th International Conference on Software Engineering,* March 1984, pp. 162-171.
4. Tsuda, M., Y. Hagi, H. Maezawa, N. Ishimoto, and M. Takahashi, "Distributed Environment for Software Development (SEWB) Using Workstations," *Nikkei Computer,* August 17, 1987 (in Japanese).
5. Kamijo, F., "Japan's Sigma Project," in *Modern Software Engineering: Foundations and Current Perspectives* (eds. P. A. Ng and R. T. Yeh), NY: Van Nostrand Reinhold, October, 1989, pp. 602-612.

Chapter 15

Knowledge-Based Software Engineering Using REFINE

LAWRENCE MARKOSIAN, LEONOR ABRAÍDO-FANDIÑO, and STEVE KATZMAN
Reasoning Systems, Inc.
Palo Alto, CA

1 INTRODUCTION

Software is currently the major cost in information processing systems. It is estimated to be 13% of the U.S. GNP in 1990. Initial costs of development are considerable, but continuing maintenance and enhancement is disastrous—often consuming 80 to 90% of available programming resources. These costs can be attributed to the inherent weaknesses of the existing traditional software paradigms and their supporting technology.

Software engineering studies have shown that the cost of program definition change during the software process increases with each passing stage; it can run up to three orders of magnitude more on fielded code than at design time. *Bugs* are well known for causing changes in fielded code. Less notoriety, but probably more real cost, comes from the need to modify code before its release to meet a change in requirements.

Producing executable code in a fraction of the time currently required has high inherent value. Doing so in a manner that increases extensibility and modifiability offers an additional advantage.

A new, *knowledge-based* software development paradigm, offering considerable advantages for getting more quickly to the code, has now begun to emerge from research and development laboratories, and earn its way into operations. This chapter discusses the knowledge-based software paradigm with specific reference to Reasoning Systems' **REFINE**[1], one of the first knowledge-based commercial software development environments, and the first to be based on the powerful features of transformational programming.

How does the knowledge-based approach differ from those used for the past several decades? What are its features? Where is its inherent value? What benefits are available immediately? What skills, learning, and procedures does it require of its practitioners? This chapter will address these and related issues.

---

[1]REFINE is a registered trademark and codemark of Reasoning Systems, Inc., Palo Alto, CA.

The Traditional Approach

The traditional approach to software design and maintenance is inherently expensive. In some more or less rigorous fashion, software requirements are identified and specifications for satisfying these requirements are developed. These specifications, if written at all, may be stated in an informal language. As a result, there are only limited ways of manipulating them to ensure correctness, completeness, and lack of ambiguity.

Next, programmers produce code to meet the specifications. As implementation decisions and optimizations are included in the body of code, it becomes larger and more complex. Thus, the more optimized the code, the more difficult it is to understand and modify. Maintaining consistency between code and specifications is often neglected. It is a relatively long process to develop the code from specifications, and not until code is produced can verification and validation testing be completed.

Verification testing assures that code corresponds to specifications. When such tests fail, code must be corrected and rewritten. With validation errors, neither specifications nor code meet the requirements, so specifications and code should be changed. Nevertheless, the code is often changed without the corresponding changes to the specifications: the code becomes the *de facto* specification. Code optimization usually decreases code clarity, making the code a difficult specification to use as the basis for future maintenance. Maintenance is especially costly and frustrating.

The Knowledge-Based Approach

Knowledge-based software development, as discussed, addresses the issues of *what is to be done* (specification) and *how to do it* (coding). Requirements, i.e., *what is the end users' need*, is a so-called upstream process whose challenges are described in this book, Chapter 18 (Belady).

At the crux of the knowledge-based approach lies a simple belief: it is easier to reuse information when it is formally captured and organized.

This is the path for arriving more quickly at code: discover and organize the knowledge that programmers and groups of programmers use in developing code, and make it reusable. Reuse comes via automation of coding and information capture and via effective organization and presentation of information to the software developer. Environments that provide and support reuse of knowledge are *knowledge-based*.

A knowledge-based software development system has the following three main components:

- representation knowledge captured in an extensible, very high level specification language;

- implementation knowledge embodied in a corresponding specification compiler; and
- tools, process, and policy knowledge stored in an integrated, knowledge-based software development environment.

Representation Knowledge

The designer represents specifications in a very-high-level language (VHLL). This language contains constructs whose level of abstraction allows for (possibly) many procedural implementations. The VHLL encourages its own extension by the user to the application domain in a manner far richer than adding macros or other forms for procedural encapsulation.

Implementation Knowledge

Specifications of VHLL are typically a factor of 5 to 10 times shorter and usually much simpler to read than conventional high-order languages or specifications, since the omitted and often confusing implementation details are automatically filled in by a synthesis process. This is the role for the specification compiler. The compiler synthesizes efficient code that implements the specification. Synthesis is by stepwise refinement using transformations that embody programming expertise. Specifications can be validated in a *rapid prototyping* mode, because they are *executable*, they can be tested and analyzed. This clearly supports earlier determination that the specification is as desired. The "design-prototype-assess" process iterates until the design is well understood and error-free. Changes are performed on the specifications, thereby shifting the locus of maintenance activities from code to specifications.

Tools, Process, and Policy Knowledge

The integrated software design environment provides the framework for capture of refinements and enforcement of policies in the process of code development. It provides the basis for automated support for software design, version control, configuration management, test development and management, documentation development and management, and project management.

A major feature of REFINE's software development environment is that programs, specifications, documentation, and development histories are stored in the knowledge base, making it easy for the programmer to query and analyze software. For example, the programmer can easily answer such questions as "What are all the functions compiled by Joe on September 13 that use the transitive closure operator and return a set of symbols?", or "What are all the programs that elicited fatal compiler errors the last time they were compiled?" Finding the answers to such questions in a typical file-based programming environment is a time-consuming and *ad hoc* process, since files fail to capture much of the information that is most important to a programmer.

The REFINE software development environment can be extended and customized to the user's environment, just as for the VHLL. The advantages of knowledge-based programming apply here as well. All the tools in the core environment are available for constructing extensions.

Outline

In this chapter, the features and benefits of the knowledge-based approach will be discussed and illustrated, with special emphasis on the REFINE specification language and compiler. Future articles will focus on applications of the integrated software design environment. It is noteworthy here, however, to point out that Reasoning's development environment is REFINE-based, i.e., that REFINE is the principal tool used for REFINE's own development.

The remainder of the chapter is organized as follows. Section II presents an overview of the REFINE environment: the editor, compiler, documentation system, debugging tools, browser, syntax system, and context mechanism.

Section III presents elementary examples that illustrate some of the significant features of the REFINE language, including set-theoretic data types, the knowledge base, logic assertions for declarative-style programming, pattern matching, and transformation rules.

Section IV contains a more elaborate, though simple example of REFINE's use, transaction processing for a library. Reasoning and REFINE users are currently writing descriptions of applications for commercial operation.

Section V concludes the chapter with a summary of future development directions for the REFINE system.

2 AN OVERVIEW OF THE REFINE ENVIRONMENT

Reasoning Systems' support for knowledge-based programming is embodied in the REFINE knowledge-based programming environment. REFINE's principal features are the following:

- **The REFINE specification language.** The REFINE programming language provides integrated use of set operations, logic, constraints, transformation rules, pattern matching, and procedure.
- **The REFINE specification compiler.** The REFINE specification compiler is implemented as a program transformation system. REFINE programs are compiled into a conventional third generation language (such as C or Common Lisp) by successive applications of program transformation rules, which are themselves written in REFINE. As a result, the REFINE compiler and most of the REFINE system are bootstrapped (written in its own language).

- **The REFINE knowledge base management system.** REFINE provides a powerful object-centered knowledge base that the user can query and modify using the REFINE language. REFINE programs and other software-related objects, documents and test cases, for example, are stored in the knowledge base. This integrated representation makes REFINE ideal for writing programs that manipulate software objects, such as program transformation systems and documentation systems. The programmer can use the knowledge base to represent the objects in the application domain. All the REFINE tools for manipulating the knowledge base can be used by the application—object classes, types, functions, constraints, and grammars are among the objects that the programmer can define and manipulate. The programmer can define domain-specific languages to describe an application domain, complete with surface and abstract syntax, and all the features provided by REFINE for manipulating the knowledge base.

REFINE Tools

The environment for REFINE program development includes several toolsets, here presented in two groups. The first group, language-oriented components, includes the compiler and the syntax system. The second set of development tools includes the command interface, the context mechanism, the documentation system, the browser/editor for the knowledge base, and the debugging system.

The REFINE Compiler

The REFINE compiler is implemented as a program transformation system. The bulk of the compiler is a set of program transformation rules that are used to transform, by successive refinement, REFINE programs into an executable language; currently, the target language is Common Lisp.

The control structure of the compiler is extremely simple: a sequence of passes over the program tree, where an individual pass applies each of a sequence of transformation rules to every object in the tree, with the traversal being done top-down. Each transformation rule encapsulates a piece of programming knowledge; the decoupling of knowledge from control makes the compiler easy to extend. The sequencing of rules within a pass allows a simple method of resolving conflicts when more than one rule could apply: the first rule in the sequence will be chosen. For example, a rule that performs an optimization will typically occur at the beginning of a pass. This ensures that the later rules do not change the program tree beyond optimization recognition before the optimization takes place.

The REFINE compiler is incremental in two senses. First, separate definitions in a program can be compiled independently without need for re-compiling other definitions or re-linking. Second, when compiling a block of definitions, the compiler keeps track of which definitions have changed and will recompile only those that have changed. As a result, file compilation goes very quickly when the programmer has only changed a few definitions in a file.

REFINE is a strongly-typed language, but the burden of declarations and consistency is greatly relieved by the compiler's *type analyzer*. The type analyzer provides more than passive testing. It combines the information from user declarations, the knowledge base, and the use of data structures within the program to deduce the types of undeclared variables when enough contextual information is available to do so. The programmer can therefore omit most type declarations. The type analyzer also checks the consistency of declarations with actual usage and reports all type errors in a program.

The REFINE Syntax System

The syntax system allows the user to define domain-specific languages by defining *grammars* that serve as a mapping between objects in the knowledge base and their textual forms. The syntax system compiles a grammar into a parser, pretty-printer, and lexical analyzer for the domain specific language. The parser can be used to create new objects by parsing text, and the pretty-printer can be used to view existing objects. For example, users have used the syntax system to define the C syntax in REFINE. They then used this grammar to parse and manipulate C programs in the knowledge base. The parser for the REFINE specification language was itself generated using the syntax system.

The syntax system is based on an LALR(1) parser generator[1] sufficient for handling most programming languages. The parsers are interfaced to the environment so that syntactic analysis is performed as the input is entered. This interface allows users to correct errors interactively.

The Context Mechanism

The context mechanism maintains a hierarchy of states of the knowledge base within a session. The state of the knowledge base is the set of all objects that exist and the values of all their attributes at some given point in time. Previous states can be recreated.

The context mechanism is particularly useful for search programs where the state of partial solutions is represented in the knowledge base. A variety of backtracking search algorithms can be implemented easily using this tool. As another example, a scheduling application could use the context mechanism to store several alternative schedules and then run analysis programs to identify the best one. More generally, the space of possible implementations of a specification may be developed to look for an implementation that is optimal with respect to some performance metric.

The Documentation System

The documentation system provides an online browser for the REFINE User's Guide. The online browser allows the programmer to inspect a hierarchy of sections and subsections of the manual, to view the text of any section, and to browse the online index for the document. There is also a facility for keyword-based access to documentation.

The documentation system generates a large portion of the REFINE documentation automatically by computing the text of documents directly from information in the knowledge base. In some cases, the program being described is executed to generate its documentation. For example, the document text used to describe the type-checking rule for a language construct is generated by actually constructing an instance of the construct, running the type checker on the instance, and paraphrasing the results in an English-like notation. This technique ensures that the documentation is consistent with program functionality.

The documentation system can also be used to document user's applications. The structure and means of computing the documentation are defined by the user.

The Knowledge Base Browser/Editor

The browser provides a menu-oriented interface to the knowledge base that allows objects and their attributes to be displayed and edited. Objects can be displayed in a frame format, i.e., attribute/value pairs or printed using a user-specified grammar. Special capabilities exist for viewing REFINE specifications stored in the knowledge base: the ability to view all specifications that reference the current object of focus, view all specifications that the current specification references, and view all subtrees of the current (abstract syntax) tree.

The Debugging System

The REFINE debugging tools let the programmer monitor run-time events. The events that can be monitored are transformation rule firing, function calls, modification of knowledge base attributes, and instantiation of object classes (creation of new objects in a given object class). The debugging tools can be accessed interactively via a menu-oriented *debug options editor* or programmatically via a set of functions.

3 THE REFINE LANGUAGE

This section illustrates, by example, some noteworthy features of the REFINE language and the style of REFINE programming. The complete language is described in the REFINE User's Guide.[6]

The REFINE language supports a variety of different programming styles (set-theoretic, logical, transformational, object-oriented, and procedural, among others); hence REFINE is called a *multi-paradigm language*. The variety and integration of constructs available in REFINE, at both the high-level (e.g., pattern matching) and the low-level (e.g., "enumerate"), makes the language *wide-spectrum*. The multi-paradigm and wide-spectrum nature of REFINE allow the programmer to use a single programming language to solve a variety of problems in the manner most appropriate to each.

Data Types

The types *integer*, *real*, *character*, *symbol*, and *boolean* are supplied, as are the usual operations on these types. In addition, *universal* and *existential quantifiers* may be used in boolean expressions. Thus

$$\exists(x) \; (x \in R \land \forall (y) \; (y \in S \to x < y))$$

is a boolean expression which is true if R contains an element smaller than every element of S.

Set-Theoretic Data Types

Set theory serves the needs of mathematicians as a notation for describing, communicating, and reasoning about abstract objects. REFINE furnishes set-theoretic notation by providing *set*, *sequence*, *tuple*, and *map* as data type constructors; it also supplies operations for binary relations modeled as sets of tuples with two components.

The usefulness of these in data abstraction has been demonstrated by many modern programming languages and systems. For example:

- Relations are the primary abstraction mechanism for relational databases and Prolog.[12,3]
- The versatility of sequences, implemented as lists, has been demonstrated in Lisp[9] and functional languages.
- The SETL language provides a comprehensive collection of set-theoretic types in a single language. The advantages of set-theoretic types are shown by SETL's success for combinatorial programming problems[7] and by SETL's use in constructing the first validated Ada compiler.[4]

Sets and Sequences

The usual way to create a set in REFINE is with a *set former*, for example,

$$\text{primes} = \{x | \; (x) \; x \in [2 \; . \; . \; 100] \land$$
$$\forall \; (y) \; (y \in [2 \; . \; . \; x - 1]$$
$$\to x \bmod y \neq 0)\}$$

defines the set of prime numbers $\leq$ 100. The set former requires from the user only a *description* or *specification* of the elements that compose the set. In this case the description closely reflects the definition of a prime number. It may be read "the set of all numbers x such that x is an integer between 2 and 100 and for every number y between 2 and x $-$ 1, y does not divide x."

The elements of a set can themselves be sets, or any other type, subject only to a type homogeneity restriction. For example, the set former

$$\{\{x, y\} \mid (x, y) \; x \in primes \; \wedge$$
$$y \in primes \; \wedge \; x + 2 = y\}$$

forms the set of all sets of twin primes $<$ 100. (Twin primes are pairs of prime numbers whose values differ by 2, such as 5 and 7.)

REFINE's operations on sets include union, intersection, element addition, element deletion, size (cardinality), difference, subset, and membership. In addition, the reduce operator can be used to apply an operation to each element of a set in order to collapse the set to a single value. For example, given that a perfect number is one whose proper divisors sum to the number (6 is perfect because $6 = 1 + 2 + 3$), the expression

$$\{n \mid (n) \; n \in [1 \; . \; . \; 1000] \; \wedge$$
$$n = reduce \; ('+,$$
$$\{d \mid (d) \; d \in [1 \; . \; . \; n - 1] \; \wedge$$
$$n \; mod \; d = 0\})\}$$

computes the set of perfect numbers between 1 and 1000, where

$$reduce \; ('+, \{d \mid (d) \; d \in [1 \; . \; . \; n - 1]$$
$$\wedge \; n \; mod \; d = 0\})\}$$

forms the sum of the divisors of *n*.

Sequences can be created with a sequence former, which is similar to the set former, and the reduce operator will work on sequences as well as sets. REFINE provides additional operations specifically for manipulating sequences.

Note that the effects of the above-mentioned set and sequence operations are achieved in many languages by explicitly constructed loops or recursive function definitions. REFINE's conciseness results in part from capturing these operations as primitives. Its readability stems from the use of very-high-level data types.

Maps

The map data type in REFINE is used to represent finite maps, i.e., single-valued partial functions from a domain of values to a range of values. Maps may be created with a map former, which is analogous to the set former. Map formers are bracketed by { | and | }; the empty map is denoted by { | | }. For example, we can map each integer from 2 to 100 to the set of all its nontrivial divisors:

divisors = { | x → y | (x, y)
x ∈ [2 . . 100] ∧
y = {d| (d) d ∈ [2 . . x − 1] ∧ x mod d = 0} | }.

With this map, the set of primes may be alternatively defined as

{p| (p) p ∈ domain(divisors) ∧ divisors(p) = {}}

or, taking advantage of REFINE's inverse operator for maps, as

inverse(divisors) ({ })

Control Constructs

Transforms

One of the most novel features of the REFINE language is the transform construct. The power of the construct has abundantly proven its value, both in the development of REFINE and in subsequent software development using the system.

A transform specifies certain kinds of state transformations (side effecting operations) by stating the pre-condition and post-condition of the transformation. The transformation construct frees the programmer from specifying a specific sequence of actions that accomplish the desired transformation. The REFINE compiler generates the required procedure based on the description of the pre-condition and post-condition.

For example, the construct

⟨x, y⟩ ∈ R → x mod y in S

has the same effect as:

enumerate p over R do
S ← with p.1 mod p.2

(here p.1 and p.2 refer to the first and second fields of the tuple p, respectively).

Such transforms have wide applicability and are much easier to write and understand than their procedural counterparts. For example, they allow the compiler to determine which left-hand-side conjuncts are used for enumerating and which for testing, the nesting order of enumerations in the procedure which implements that transform, and the order and manner in which the right-hand side conjuncts will be made true.

Functions

The REFINE function construct is used to define maps whose values are computed rather than stored. A REFINE function captures the concept of a map with an infinite domain. In addition to a conventional function definition style, for example,

function cube (n: integer): integer = n * n * n

functions may be defined with a computed-using clause which, in conjunction with the pattern matching constructs, provides pattern-directed invocation. Consider the following recursive definition of the function prefixes, which computes all prefixes of a sequence:

function prefixes (s : seq(integer)): set (seq (integer))
    computed-using prefixes ([$s1, . .]) = {s1, . .}

If, during program execution, the system wants to evaluate

prefixes ([1,2,3])

it must use the assertion:

prefixes ([$s1, . .]) = {s1, . .}.

In this case it will be able to match s1 (on the left hand side) to [ ], [1], [1,2], and [1,2,3]; the "$" here is a sequence segment marker. On the other hand, because of those matches of s1, the equality to the right hand side asserts that all of the following are true:

prefixes ([1,2,3]) = {[ ], . .}
prefixes ([1,2,3]) = {[1], . .}
prefixes ([1,2,3]) = {[1,2], . .}
prefixes ([1,2,3]) = {[1,2,3], . .}.

In each case, ". ." refers to the minimum elements that will make the set be consistent with all the other cases. For example, the assertion:

prefixes ([1,2,3]) = {[ ], . .}

requires ". ." to include [1], [1,2], and [1,2,3] to be consistent with the other cases. Finally, all cases are determined to have the same set value:

prefixes ([1,2,3]) = {[ ], [1], [1,2], [1,2,3]}.

Language Constructs for Knowledged-Based Programming

Objects

Embedded in the REFINE language environment is an object-oriented knowledge base. The knowledge base contains a finite set of entities called kb-objects grouped into classes. Objects are related by the value of their *attributes*. An *attribute* is just a map whose domain is an object class; the primary difference between attributes and other maps is that attributes are implemented in a distributed way as slots of objects. REFINE provides a set of powerful tools for attributes (browsers, editors, etc.) that are not available for ordinary maps; the knowledge base is an underlying data manager that supports this set of tools. Characteristics of the data manager include the following:

- Classes may be ordered by the inclusion relation so that the knowledge base supports single inheritance.
- Attributes may be defined by assertions. An attribute may be computed in a demand-driven manner: only when the value of an attribute on some object is required, is the value computed. Optionally, the resulting value may be cached.
- Converse attributes may be maintained automatically.
- A context-free language having an LALR(1) grammar and its representation as an abstract syntax tree within the knowledge base, may be specified. With a quotation construct, the pattern matching capability is extended to the user-specified context-free language.
- *Kb*-objects may be created by parsing input strings and printed with respect to the grammar. In fact, alternative grammars may be specified to display objects according to different user views. These objects may be examined or edited using an environmental tool called the *browser*.

Patterns

It is convenient and useful to specify pattern matching transforms in the knowledge base. If one had a program with a high level declarative representation and wants to specify the refinement into a procedure, a pattern matching transform might be used.

The program is begun to be represented as an object with attributes in the knowledge base. Because the values of these attributes can be other objects or aggregates of objects, one can consider the program to be represented by an abstract syntax tree whose nodes are *Kb*-objects.

A pattern quotation was used to specify a structure by quoting user defined syntax, and consider a match to that pattern (i.e., an identification of the sought-after structure) to be the preconditions of a transform. Achieving the postconditions would involve a modification of the initial substructure of the program to that substructure representing a procedural implementation of the declaration.

Pattern matching transforms are just as useful when the graphs to be manipulated are not abstract syntax or part of a programming language. This point is demonstrated in the examples on transformations on red-black trees and library transaction processing.

Two Simple Examples

Tuples, Maps, and Binary Relations

This first problem demonstrates the usefulness of sets, maps, and binary relations (see Figure 15-1). The problem is: given a map (Neighbors) from a point to its neighbors, return the map from a point to all the points to which that point can connect. Assume points are represented as symbols.

A function is necessary which takes a map as an input argument and returns a map (see Figure 15-2). The following function returns the map in which we are interested:

```
function connect (M: map(integer, set(integer)))
       : map(integer, set(integer)) =
       let(connect-relation =
           (tclosure ({⟨x,y⟩   | (x)
               x in domain (M) &
               y in M(x)})))
       {|   x → image (connect-relation, {x})   | (x)
               x in domain(connect-relation)   |}
```

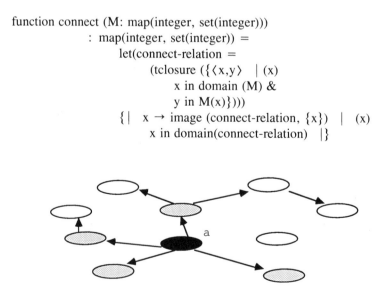

Figure 15-1. Neighbors ('a) returns the neighbors of the point a.

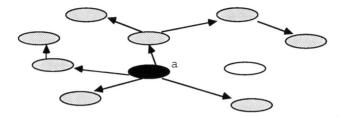

Figure 15-2. Connect (neighbors) ('a) returns the set of all points reachable from the point a.

First, specify a relation corresponding to the input map:

$\{\langle x,y \rangle \ | (x) \ x \text{ in domain(M) } \& \ y \text{ in } M(x)\}$

then name the transitive closure of this relation connect-relation using the let construct, and convert connect-relation back to a map:

$\{| \ x \rightarrow \text{image (connect-relation, } \{x\}) \ | \ (x)$
$x \text{ in domain(connect-relation) } |\}.$

This is the desired map and is what the function returns.

Transformations on Red-Black Trees

The next example demonstrates how REFINE may be used to specify programs that manipulate trees via tree transformation. This type of computation has many important applications including term-rewriting and program compilation. In the example the trees are binary. Associated with each vertex is a color, "red" or "black", and a key, which is an integer.

In REFINE, the tree may be represented by an object class, red-black-tree, having attributes color, tree-key, left-subtree and right-subtree:

var trees: object-class subtype-of user-object

var red-black-tree: object-class subtype-of trees

var color: map(red-black-tree, string) = $\{| \ |\}$

var tree-key: map(red-black-tree, integer) = $\{| \ |\}$

var left-subtree: map(red-black-tree, red-black-tree)
   = $\{| \ |\}$

var right-subtree: map(red-black-tree, red-black-tree)
   = $\{| \ |\}$

To use the pattern facilities, a grammar is defined for representing the trees. A suitable grammar is

red-black-tree : : = ε |
    "(" color ","
    tree-key ","
    red-black-tree ","
    red-black-tree ")"

color : : = string
tree-key : : = integer

The corresponding grammar definition in REFINE is

the-grammar red-black-grammar
    productions
        red-black-tree : : =
            ["(" color "," tree-key ","
            left-subtree "," right-subtree ")"]
                builds red-black-tree
    with-comment-start-charts "*"
    with-brackets "(" matching ")"
    end

Some transformations are displayed graphically. In the Figures a vertex colored red is denoted by a double circle and a vertex colored black by a single circle. Using this grammar (see Figure 15-3) a REFINE transformation that tests whether a tree matches the form on the left of transform 1 and, if it does, transforms it into the form on the right is

p =
    '("black", @p-key, @pl-tree,
        ("black", @v-key,
            ("red", @l-key, @ll-tree, @lr-tree),
            ("red", @r-key, @rl-tree, @rr-tree)))'

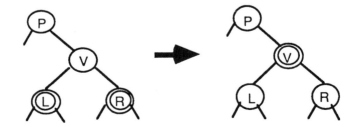

Figure 15-3. Transform 1—a single circle = black, and a double circle = red.

→

p = '("black", @p-key,

    @pl-tree,
      ("red", @v-key,
        ("black", @l-key, @ll-tree, @lr-tree),
        ("black", @r-key, @rl-tree, @rr-tree)))'

This reads "if p is labelled 'black' and p's right child is labelled 'black' and that child's children are both labelled 'red', then reverse the colors of the right child and its children."

The second transformation (see Figure 15-4) is more complicated. Transform 2 is expressed in REFINE as follows:

g = '("black", @g-key, @a, ("red", @p-key, @s, @v))' ∧

a = '("black", @@, @@, @@)' ∧

v = '("black", @@,

    ("red", @@, @@, @@), ("red", @@, @@, @@))'

→

g = '("black", @p-key, ("red", @g-key, @a, @s), @v)'

Observe that after transform 2 is performed the resulting tree matches the pre-condition for transform 1, and so it may be applied.

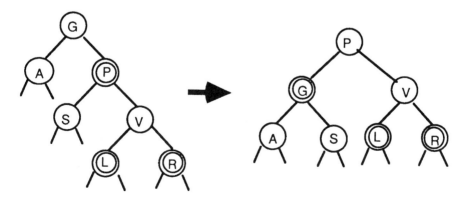

Figure 15-4. Transform 2.

The final transform is 3 (see Figure 15-5). The REFINE code for transformation 3 is

g = '(@g-color, @g-key, @a, @p)' ∧

p = '("red", @p-key, @v, @s)' ∧

v = '("black", @v-key, @l, @r)' ∧

l = '("red", @l-key, @ll-tree, @lr-tree)' ∧

s = '("black", @s-key, @s1, @s2)'

→

g = '(@g-color, @g-key, @a,
        ("red", @v-key,
          ("black", @l-key, @ll-tree, @lr-tree),
          ("black", @p-key, @r,
          ("red", @s-key, @s1, @s2))))'

Observe that after transform 3 is performed the resulting tree matches the pre-condition for transform 2, and so it can be applied. Transform 1 can then be applied to the tree resulting from transform 2.

The reader may be curious about the origin of the above example. Transformations 2 and 3 are called *rotations* and are used to maintain balance in binary search trees. Algorithms that perform these operations are extremely subtle and difficult to understand when written in lower-level languages. The transformations described here are used to balance *red-black trees*. A *red-black search tree* is a binary tree in which each vertex contains a key and is colored either red or black. It satisfies the following constraints:

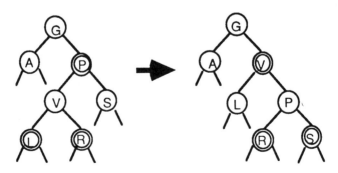

Figure 15-5. Transform 3.

- It is a search tree; thus the key of the left (right) child is $\leq$ ($\geq$) the key of its parent.
- There is a number n such that all paths from the root to a leaf have n or n + 1 black vertices. The leaves and the root are colored black.
- No path contains two consecutive red vertices.

Notice that the discussed transformations preserve these conditions.

To insert a new key into the structure, the tree is descended from the root to the proper position for the new leaf. While descending, certain ''housekeeping'' operations are performed to maintain balance; namely, if during the descent a vertex is encountered with two red children, a modification is made to the tree. The modification is to perform one of the three transformations discussed above. One of the transformations will always apply, by the definition of red-black tree. The goal of the housekeeping is to ensure that when the position for the new leaf is reached it can be inserted without violating the conditions on a red-black tree. (See Reference 8 for details.)

4 A LIBRARY TRANSACTION PROCESSING SYSTEM

This example focuses on transaction processing of books at a library. However, the discussion is valid for most systems whose function is to react to random, sequential events by updating a model of the world, issuing status reports, and perhaps initiating some response. The sorts of transactions that are handled at libraries include borrowing and returning books, adding new books to the library's collection, and sending out overdue notices. The library system must maintain a model of the world, including data on cardholders, books on loan, etc. Indeed, the library will need to maintain several consistent representations of the world—for example, one for accounting purposes, and one for librarians processing book requests. Reports on the status of the library's book collection must be issued on a regular basis. Finally, the library system will need to interact with the world by sending out overdue notices in accordance with library policy.

Object Classes in the Library System

The process of implementing the library system begins by building a knowledge-based model which includes a specification of the classes of objects in the domain. In the library domain, the object classes include libraries, books, borrowers, staff members, and transactions.

Attributes in the Library System

For each object class that has been identified for a particular domain, there are corresponding attributes of interest to the problem solver. For example, for a library one would be interested in the collection of books that belong to the library, the set of books that are on loan, the set of books that are out for repair, the set of overdue books, the set of available books, the set of cardholders, the set of books that a cardholder has borrowed, and so on. Table 15-1 provides a list of principal object classes and their attributes for the library model.

Table 15-1. Principal object classes in the library domain with their attributes and attribute types.

OBJECT CLASS
  Attribute name : Attribute data type

Book

Book-Title	: *string*	
Authors	: *(set string)*	% a book can have more than one author
Subject	: *string*	
Copy-number	: *integer*	
Home-library	: *library*	% library is a user-defined object class
Last-Borrowed-Date	: *date*	
Due-Date	: *date*	
Return-Date	: *date*	
Current-Borrower	: *borrower*	% borrower is a user-defined object % class

Borrower

Name	: *string*
Books-Borrowed-By	: *(set book)*
Cardholder-at	: *(set library)*

Library

Book-Collection	: *(set book)*
Books-On-Loan	: *(set book)*
Books-Out-For-Repair	: *(set book)*
Available-Books	: *(set book)*
Cardholders	: *(set borrower)*
Borrowing-Limit	: *integer*
Circulation-Data	: *real*

Transaction

Transaction-Requester	: *borrower*
Transaction-Library	: *library*
Transaction-Title	: *string*
Transaction-Date	: *date*
Transaction-type	: *symbol* {'borrow, 'return, 'remove, 'add}

Library-world

Transaction-queue	: *(seq transaction)*
Calendar-date	: *date*

However, a difference between the REFINE representation and that used in the database world is that the knowledge-based model is object-oriented, not relation-oriented. As a consequence, the knowledge based approach is capable of easily representing not only the large, simple relations that are typically found in databases, but *complex* relations among objects that exhibit a lot of structure. For example, a more detailed knowledge-based library model might include a specification of the content of each book—say, the chapter/subchapter/section/subsection hierarchy of a mathematics book and the axioms, definitions, lemmas, theorems, and examples discussed in each part.

Once the object classes and their attributes are specified, the domain modeler can proceed to create instances of each of the classes in order to characterize a *particular* library domain. This activity is analogous to the creation of database relations. The REFINE system supports interactive, menu-based graphical definition of object class instances.

Constraints on Attribute Values

The builder of a REFINE domain model can proceed to specify the logical relationships among objects and their attributes. These relationships are specified using the REFINE language, which includes first order logic and very-high-level data types (such as sets, sequences, and mappings). In the example, the following assertion is made relating the Available-Books, Books-on-Loan, and Books-Out-for-Repair attributes of libraries:

- The set of a library's available books is equal to the set of books in the library's collection less the union of the on-loan and out-for-repair books.

This assertion is expressed in REFINE as

Available-Books(library) =
Book-Collection(library) less (Books-on-Loan(library)
∪ Books-Out-for Repair(library))

Similarly, the following assertion could be made relating a library's set of books on loan and books in the library's collection for which there is a person among the library's cardholders who is the book's current borrower:

- The set of books on loan is the set of books in the library's collection for which there is a person among the library's cardholders who is the book's current borrower.

This assertion is expressed in REFINE as

Books-On-Loan (library) =
  { book | (book) book is-in Book-Collection(library)
    and there-exists person
      (person is-in Cardholders(library)
      and Current-Borrower(book) =
        person) }

Note that these relationships are specified declaratively, simply expressed in first order logic and set theory; they are not programmed. They are natural expressions of domain constraints. In particular, they do not require programming using "methods," "message passing," iterative or recursive control constructs, or any of the other procedural language constructs associated with either traditional object-oriented or procedural programming languages. *The relationships are simply stated in the language of mathematics and the application domain.* The REFINE specification compiler can generate programs to implement each specification.

How Can a Knowledge-Based Model be Used?

Because domain knowledge is represented explicitly in a knowledge-based model (instead of being implicitly contained with a program), it is available for use in a wide variety of applications. Some of these applications for our example might include the following:

- a transaction processor;
- a simulator;
- testing/validation environment;
- documentation generator;
- report generator; and
- automated test generator.

Each of these applications would, of course, require its own specification, but they would all access the same library domain model. Examples of REFINE specifications from several of these applications will be given. Some are illustrated in Figure 15-6.

Application No. 1: Transaction Processing

Assume that the domain modeler has now defined the library transaction domain and an instance of that domain—specific libraries, books, borrowers, etc.

Rule Borrow-a-Book-by-Title (tr : transaction) transform

% Here are the preconditions for this rule to be applied:

requester = Transaction-Requester (tr) and

    % Bind the variable requester for convenience in later use.

library = Transaction-Library (tr) and

    % Bind the variable library for convenience in later use.

requester in card-holders (library) and

    % Condition (1)-requester must be a cardholder at the library at which

    % request is made.

library-book in Available-Books (library) and

    % Condition (2)-there must be a book in the available

    % books at the library

Book-Title (library-book) = Transaction-Title (tr) and

    % . . . with the requested title.

size (Books-Borrowed-By (requester)) <

    Borrowing-Limit (library)

    % Condition (3)-the number of books already borrowed by the

    % requester must be less than the library's lending limit

$\rightarrow$

    % Here is the single postcondition for this rule:

current-borrower (library-book) = requester

Figure 15-6. REFINE specification of state transformation rule for processing transactions to borrow a library book.

Looking at an application built using that model—a processor for transactions at a library. The approach in building the transaction processor is to do the following:

- specify what it means to process the various types of library transactions, then
- apply the processor to a time-ordered sequence of test transactions.

In REFINE, we can specify how a transaction is to be processed by writing *state transformation rules*. The *preconditions* of the transformation rule specify the conditions that must be satisfied for a transaction to be processed by the rule. The *postconditions* state what the library model is to look like after a transaction has been successfully processed.

Typical preconditions for processing a *borrow* type transaction would be the following:

- the requester must be a cardholder at the library at which the request is being made,
- there must be a book with the requested title available at the library, and
- the number of books already borrowed by the requester must not have reached the library's lending limit.

The postcondition for this transaction is simply that the current borrower of the book is the requester. The REFINE specification of this transformation rule is provided in Figure 15-6. Note that these preconditions and postconditions have been expressed declaratively in the REFINE specification language; the REFINE compiler will automatically generate a program to test the preconditions and a program to generate a state of the library domain in which the postcondition is met.

Automated Constraint Maintenance

When a book is borrowed by someone, it is often necessary to update several data bases. For example, the library may maintain, for each of its cardholders, a list of books borrowed by that borrower and the set of all books currently on loan from the library. If the transformation rule simply updates the status of the book being borrowed (i.e., its current-borrower attribute), without also updating the other data bases, there will be an inconsistency in the overall state description. On the other hand, it is a burden on the programmer to require code to be written to propagate consequences of changes throughout the knowledge base. Instead, the compiler is preferred to *maintain* certain constraints on the knowledge base. In the following example, it is desirable to assert the following two constraints:

(1) A book has been borrowed by a person if and only if the person is that book's current borrower; this constraint is stated as follows in REFINE:

For-all book,
    person (book is-in Books-Borrowed-By (person)
        if-and-only-if
    person = Current-Borrower (book))

(2) A book is in a library's set of books on loan if and only if the book has a current borrower; this constraint is stated as follows in REFINE:

For-all book
  (book is-in Books-On-Loan (lib)
    if-and-only-if
    there-is person (person = Current-Borrower (book)))

The REFINE compiler allows these and other assertions to be maintained as constraints on the data base automatically. Therefore, the transformation rule that was discussed earlier needs only to specify that the Current-Borrower of a book is updated; the related attributes of other objects will be updated automatically by the compiler.

Application No. 2: Simulation

The transaction processing specification can be used by the REFINE compiler, as previously described, to synthesize an implementation of a real library transaction system on suitable hardware.

However, it can also be used as a simulator—for example, to study the effectiveness of manually following an informal specification of library policy or for predicting the behavior of a manually programmed on-line system that uses standard data bases and COBOL programs to implement the specification. The use of state transformations is a powerful technique for simulation, in which events (such as transactions) are to be processed with consequent changes in the domain state. In a typical simulation, the processing of one event not only changes the domain state but also causes other events to be created and inserted into an event queue. If one were to extend the library example to a simulator, the borrow transaction might cause a book-return event with a randomly selected date during the following 6 weeks to be put into the event queue.

Support for Simulation in REFINE

REFINE supports simulation problems using the same capabilities—domain specification, specification of relationships among objects in the domain, and specification of event processing using state transformation rules—that were used in the transaction processor itself. In addition to VHLL constructs to support these capabilities, REFINE provides lower-level procedural constructs (such as while-do and if-then-else) that allow the user to write programs to control the application of transformation rules to events in an event queue. Figure 15-7 shows the REFINE specification of a top-level algorithm to control the application of transaction processing rules and the updating of a calendar. This algorithm assumes there is a queue associated with an instance of a library world. The set of elements in the transaction queue forms the scenario of events,

Function Simulation-Control (lw : library-world)
  print-message ("Starting simulation at time = ", time);
  while not empty (Transaction-Queue (lw)) do
    (let (trans :transaction)
      trans ← first (Transaction-Queue (lw));
      result-set ←
        { result | (result :boolean)
        result = apply-rule (rule-name, trans) };
      if result-set = {false" then
        print-message (
          "Could not process the following transaction:",
          trans)
      else
        print-message ("Processed transaction", trans);
      Transaction-Queue (lw) ←
        rest (Transaction-Queue (lw)));
  print-message ("Simulation ended at time = ", time)

Figure 15-7. Specification of a top-level control algorithm for simulation control.

such as borrowing a book; each element has a time and date stamp associated with it. Other programs would have been used by the scenario writer to assist in generating the scenario—for example, by time-ordering events in the transaction queue and by running validity checks on the scenario. Note that events other than transactions must be processed in the simulation, such as calendar-updating events, one of which should appear before each transaction for a date different from the date for the preceding transaction. The transformation rule to handle the calendar-update event is specified as follows:

Rule Update-Calendar (lw : library-world) transform

ev = first(Transaction-Queue(lw)) and
Event-Type(ev) = 'update and
Update-To(ev) = new-date

→

Calendar-Date(lw) = new-date

The top-level control algorithm simply applies transaction-processing transformation rules to the top (current) element of the queue. If none of the rules can be applied (because the preconditions for none of the rules are met), the program prints a message and removes the element from the queue. If some rules are applicable, they are applied, a message indicating which rule(s) were applied is printed, and the transaction is removed from the queue.

These lower-level constructs can be used in specifications of relationships among domain objects and in transformations as well, wherever the desired specification is more naturally expressed procedurally rather than declaratively. Thus, unlike expert system shells, REFINE does not enforce a certain style of programming with the only option being to "escape to Lisp" or some other underlying language.

Graphical Simulation Tool

Figures 15-8a and 15-8b show an application of graphical techniques to support model definition and animation of a simulation. In Figure 15-8a, the user has displayed the initial state of a particular library world, Library-World-1, and "elaborated" one of its attribute values—its Libraries. This is a set of library instances and includes both Stanford and Berkeley. The former has also been elaborated, as well as two of its attributes, Book-Collection and Books-Out-For-Repair. The user then processes a transaction in which a borrower, Eric McCarthy, borrows the book entitled *Axiomatic Set Theory* from the Stanford library. (The transaction is processed by applying the state transformation rule in Figure 15-2 to it.) Figure 15-8b shows the new state of the library world: shaded boxes indicate attributes of objects whose values have changed, and these objects have been automatically elaborated in depth so that all changes to the initial state are displayed. Not all the state changes that are shown were explicitly included in the transformation rule that processes the borrow-book transaction. In particular, that rule changes only the Current-Borrower attribute of the book being borrowed; all the other changes are maintained using REFINE's constraint maintenance system.

This tool is one example of a graphical simulation tool of very general applicability, especially at the prototype stage. For many applications more specialized, domain-specific tools will be needed.

Application 3: Validation/Testing Environment

One of the main uses of a simulator is to validate and test a prototype. This use requires collecting and analyzing test data on the behavior of the prototype under realistic operating scenarios. One method of validating the transaction processor is to monitor the knowledge base to be sure that certain requirements on the system are met at all times. Suppose the library sends overdue notices to borrowers with books that are more than 10 days overdue, and makes a record of the overdue notice that was sent. If a book is returned that is more than 10 days overdue, there should be record of an overdue notice associated with this book having been sent out:

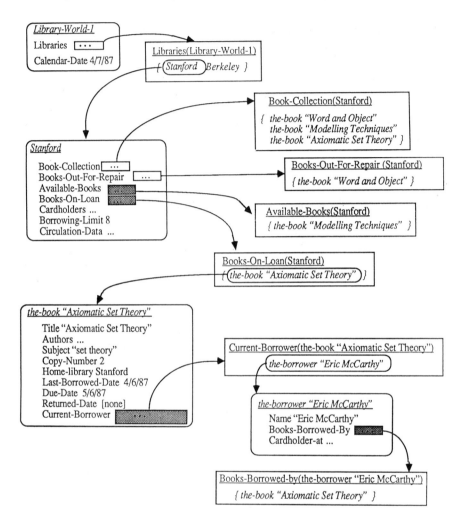

Figure 15-8(a). Graphic elaboration of an initial state of the library domain Library-World-1.

Return-Date(book) = Calendar-date
and Due-Date(book) < Calendar-Date − 10
→
there-is(notice)(notice is-in notices and
                In-Reference-To(notice) = book)

However, the specifications for processing transactions and sending overdue notices do not explicitly state that this requirement will be met. The transaction

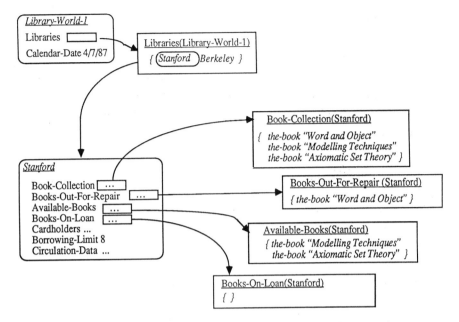

Figure 15-8(b). State following processing of borrow-book transaction.

processing system can be validated with respect to this requirement by evaluating this assertion whenever an overdue book is returned.

There may be several ways of returning a book (for example: returning it directly to the library from which it was borrowed, returning it to a cooperating library that will forward it, mailing it in, etc.). Finer-grained simulations might specify, for each method, a distinct transaction processing rule that, among other things, updates the Return-Date of the book. REFINE enables the user to declare that the above validation criterion is to be checked whenever the value of Return-Date (book) is changed. It is not necessary for the user to insert a function call in each place that Return-Date (book) is referenced. The appropriate code is inserted by the compiler automatically. This is a case where an assertion is checked automatically whenever the knowledge base is changed in such a way that the assertion might be violated.

Clearly, in a more complex simulation (or in a real transaction processing system) many more subtle validity tests must be performed.

Application 4: Report Generator

The knowledge based model can support report generation using the REFINE specification language as a query language. For example, in the library transaction domain, it might be required to issue a daily report listing such information as the following:

- the set of books on loan from the library that are more than 10 days overdue;

{ book | book is-in Books-On-Loan(lib) and
            Due-Date(book) < Calendar-date-10 }

- the set of borrowers that have a book on loan from the library that is more
  than 10 days overdue for which an overdue notice was sent at least 5 days
  ago (these are the people the library staff will telephone today);

{ person |
    there-is book
      (book is-in Books-On-Loan(lib) and
      Due-Date(book) < Calendar-date − 10 and
      Current-Borrower(book) = person and
      there-is notice
        (Recipient(notice) = person and
        In-Reference-To(notice) = book and
        Date-Sent(notice) < Calendar-date − 5)) }

As these two examples illustrate, REFINE allows the user to write queries
on the knowledge base using the same language in which the knowledge base
was specified. In particular, first order logic and set theory are supported in the
query language; there are no artificial limitations on the kinds of queries that
can be made. Queries can be written that precisely capture arbitrarily complex
user intentions. Notice that the REFINE query can include not only knowledge
base accesses but arbitrary mathematical and logical operations on the retrieved
values, all in a homogeneous language. In fact, the user could have included
calls to functions defined previously. For example, the boolean-valued function
Notice-Was-Sent-at-least-5 days-ago? could have been previously defined as

Function
Notice-Was-Sent-at-least-5-days-ago? (person, book) :
boolean
    there-is notice
      (Recipient(notice) = person and
      In-Reference-To(notice) = book and
      At-least-5-Days-Old? (notice))

and then the preceding query could have been written more simply as

{ person |
    there-is book
      (book is-in Books-On-Loan(library) and
      Due-Date (book) < Calendar-date − 10 and
      Current-Borrower(book) = person and
      Notice-Was-Sent-at-least-5-days-ago? (person,
book)) }

Some Observations on this Example

In the example, the library domain was modeled at a level of abstraction sufficient to generate prototype of several possible applications: a simulator, a transaction processor, validation environment, and a report generator. If knowledge about libraries was modeled correctly at this level of abstraction, we need not throw away the model or application specification when it becomes necessary to extend or create a finer-grained representation of the library domain. Instead, the extension is added as a *refinement* of the original model: new object classes, more attributes of existing object classes, and more relationships among existing objects. It was not necessary to make a large "up front" investment in detailed model building that would be thrown away later. Note, also, that *validation* of the model (and applications) at a high level of abstraction was achieved. Thus there is increased confidence that further refinements of the model will not reveal high-level errors.

In addition to the flexibility and extensibility afforded by the domain model, it was noted that declarative REFINE specifications are shorter than the equivalent program implementation. Moreover, because the models and specifications explicitly state only the essential domain and application knowledge (and omit implementation details) they are easier to read and understand than program implementations. The ease of readability and understandability translates to sharply reduced maintenance costs later in the software life cycle.

5 DEVELOPMENT DIRECTIONS FOR REFINE

Experience with the REFINE system has set forth the direction for future enhancements to the system. The main areas of improvement will include the user interface to REFINE, improvements to the synthesized code, improvements aimed at programming in the large, and additional tools supporting software engineering.

Many extensions are currently under development or in internal use. One example is a testing support tool. This tool supports the execution and validation of test case results. It may be run after software has been completed or undergone modification. In certain cases, it is possible to partially or fully automate the generation of tests.

Another example is greater optimization of code. The system will allow user directives to specify data type representation. Eventually, REFINE may choose a good data structure representation using proven heuristics. The generation of other target languages, such as C, is also a current effort.

Longer range plans include support for better abstraction and modularization, support for multiple inheritance in the knowledge base, and unification of maps, functions and attributes. Capabilities of the knowledge base (inheritance, logic, and caching, among others) will also be extended to other data types. More sophisticated storage management will improve the performance of the system.

An improved input/output (I/O) facility will greatly simplify the specification of I/O.

6 CONCLUSION

Knowledge-based software engineering using REFINE has proven effective in a number of areas. Users have experienced up to a 10-fold increase in productivity in building compilers and other parts of software development environments. Prototyping of domain models in such areas as communications and project management has also proven to be a good match to the capabilities described in this paper. A variety of successful applications has shown the versatility of this knowledge-based approach.

Knowledge-based software engineering differs from the conventional software development approach in that rather than exploring aspects of an application domain (and its programs) in a way that can be taught or explained to others, analysis of program characteristics is made so that the information gained can be formalized and added to a knowledge-based compiler. By adding this information to the compiler, application of this knowledge can be automated. The user is thus freed from the time-consuming task of applying that knowledge in every program for which the knowledge is appropriate. This approach is inherently valuable because it allows automatic reuse of knowledge, and offloads the user—in an extremely labor intensive environment. Immediate benefits include increased productivity in prototyping and development of application specific environments. The future promises a significant shift toward improved effectiveness in the role of the programmer in software development.

REFERENCES

1. Aho, A. V., R. Sethi, and J. D. Ullman, *Compilers; Principles, Techniques and Tools*, Reading, Massachusetts: Addison-Wesley, 1986.
2. Boehm, Barry W. *Software Engineering Economics*. Englewood Cliffs, New Jersey: Prentice-Hall, Inc., 1981, Ch. 27, p. 18.
3. Kowalski, R., *Logic for Problem Solving*. North-Holland, Amsterdam, 1979.
4. Kruchten, P. and E. Schonberg, "The Ada/Ed system: a large-scale experiment in software prototyping using SETL," *Technology and Science of Informatics*, Vol. 3, No. 3, 1984.
5. Milner, R., "A theory of type polymorphism in programming," *Journal of Computer and System Sciences*, Vol. 17, No. 3, December 1978.
6. *REFINE™ User's Guide*, Palo Alto, CA: Reasoning Systems, Inc., 1985.
7. Schwartz, J., et al., *Programming with Sets: An Introduction to SETL*, New York: Springer-Verlag, 1986.
8. Sedgewick, R., *Algorithms*. Reading, Massachusetts: Addison-Wesley, 1983.
9. Steele, G., *Common Lisp*, Digital Press, 1984.
10. Sufrin, B., ed. *Z Handbook (Draft 1.1)*, Oxford University Computing Laboratory, Programming Research Group, March 1986.
11. Turner, D., "An overview of Miranda," *ACM SIGPLAN Notices*, Vol. 21, No. 12, December 1986.
12. Ullman, J., *Principles of Database Systems*, 2nd. ed., Rockville, Maryland: Computer Science Press, 1983.

Chapter 16:

Toshiba Fuchu Software Factory

YOSHIHIRO MATSUMOTO
Toshiba Corporation
Fuchu, Tokyo, Japan

1 INTRODUCTION

A software factory is defined as an environment which allows software manufacturing organizations to design, program, test, ship, install, and maintain commercial software products in a unified manner. Toshiba Fuchu Software Factory is one of five software factories owned by Toshiba Corporation. Toshiba Fuchu Software Factory (TFSF) is planned to attain specified quality and productivity levels and includes the following items.

- properly designed workspaces;
- software tools, user interfaces, and tool maintenance facilities;
- standardized, baseline management system for design review; inspection and configuration management;
- standardized technical methodologies and disciplines;
- education programs;
- project progress management systems;
- cost management systems;
- productivity management system;
- quality assurance system with standardized quality metrics;
- quality circle activities;
- documentation support;
- existing software library and maintenance support for it;
- technical data library; and
- career development system.

The TFSF was founded in 1977. It is located inside the Toshiba Fuchu Plant which manufactures industrial process control systems for electric power networks, nuclear/thermal power generation, steel industries, city water/gas supply, factory automation and traffic control, as well as the equipment used to control these systems.[4]

The TFSF manufactures application software which is loaded into the process computers or microcomputers used for these applications. Process computers (4/32 MB main memory, 5.6/16 MIPS) are also manufactured in the same factory.

The number of persons housed in the TFSF in 1986 was approximately 2,300, in the areas including system engineering, design, programming, testing, quality assurance, project management, installation, plant-site alignment, and maintenance. The total amount of software accepted (acceptance means contracts completion) and shipped to outside customers is about 8.2 million equivalent assembler source lines (EASL)[3] per month, which includes data declaration lines and executable lines but does not include basic software such as OS, utilities, and language processors.

In the software factory, many projects run in parallel. Each project manufactures different software based on individual customer requirements. Projects are organized under the responsibility of a department, section, or unit manager. There are many departments, sections, and units in the factory. Although each project belongs to a different organization, it follows the same disciplines and management procedures of the software factory once it becomes a part of the factory.

The average size of application software which is manufactured by a project is 4 million EASL (the range is 1 to 21 million EASL). The software manufactured by a project consists of 150–300 real-time tasks associated with common data, common routines, and functions.

2 BASIC CONCEPTS OF A SOFTWARE PRODUCTION ENVIRONMENT

The Software Workbench System (SWB system) and the Hardware Workbench System (HWB system) are the tool environments used in the TFSF. These systems are developed in the factory, based on the factory-members' requirements, and they are used only internally. The life cycles of systems (combinations of software and hardware) that are under production or maintenance are covered within the functional scope of the SWB and HWB systems.

Important concepts underlying the SWB system are described in the following section.

Software production should act in synergy with hardware production. Hardware means programmable controllers, firmware, and logic circuits built with discrete components, gate-arrays, LSIs or VLSIs, which are used to construct interfaces between computer and plant equipments. There are strong needs to find possibilities for utilizing hardware in place of software, especially in the development of microcomputer software.

The HWB system provides computer assistance for engineering, design, manufacturing, and testing of ROMs (read only memories), LSIs, printed circuit boards, chassis, cabinets, and switchboards.

As shown in Figure 16-1, the life cycles for both software and hardware are indivisible both in the beginning and at the end of the life cycle. This fact brought about the principle that the environment should permit design/production of software and hardware to take place on a unified basis.

The engineering activities in the early stage of the life cycle, requirements specification and design of system architecture for software and hardware are supported by the common environment. Hardware and software are combined in the system test phase in which both hardware and software testing is performed under the common environment.

Project process model should be decided prior to the project start. A software producing paradigm is a set of related concepts, disciplines, practices, and techniques applied in producing software. A project process model defines unit workloads (unit processes) and their connections project-by-project based on a paradigm particular to each project.

The waterfall life cycle model is a strict sequence of phases, where no phase may be bypassed. This model has been widely applied in industry but is not completely successful because of many reasons. One of the reasons is that, in a practical industrial production environment, the development project often reuses a number of existing processes and software modules in a nonsequential way. For example, when a software system to control large nuclear power stations is developed, it is found that partial processes and software modules, which are used to control steam turbines (a part of the nuclear power plant), are about the same as those developed by the projects responsible for fossil fuel-type thermal power stations. So, those processes and software modules may be reused, which were developed by some existing or finished thermal power plant projects.

In the author's life cycle model, which may be thought as a class of the process network model, a life cycle is viewed as a network of unit processes. A unit process is similar to a connected series of responsible member's activities, where each activity and the connections between activities are specified in advance. It is called unit workload in the Toshiba Fuchu factory. All unit processes or unit workloads are independently defined. Each unit workload has well defined interfaces to allow connection with other unit workloads which have matching interfaces.

To define a particular project life cycle model, which matches each project, the project manager may select a set of unit workloads, define the interconnection and design the interfaces.

At the early stage of a project, the life cycle model and the paradigm, which will be used by the project, are defined in the design review meetings. It is critically important that all project members attend the meetings and participate in the agreement.

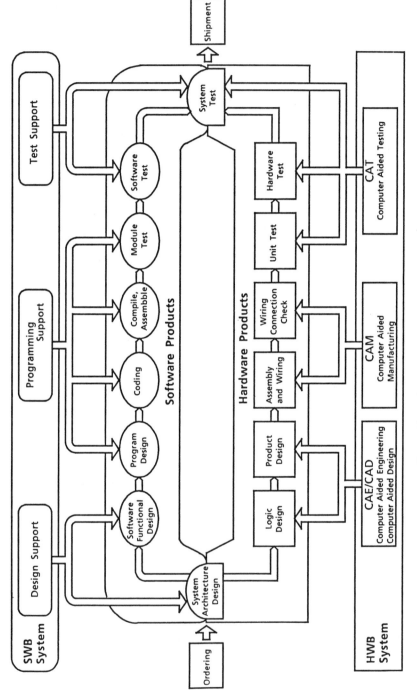

Figure 16-1. System products development lifecycle.

The support for project management, a function included in the SWB system, has its base on the process network model. It stores reusable properties of past unit workloads, such as cost experience and time experience, associated with each unit workload. It assists projects to use existing experiences by retrieving existing unit workloads and to create a new process network model which fits the project.

The environment supports activities throughout defined life cycles in a consistent manner to progress/cost/productivity/quality management, requirements definition/prototyping/operational specification, design, programming, reuse of specification/design/program/test documentation, testing, career development, education/technical transfer configuration management, and maintenance.

Figure 16-2 shows the configuration of the SWB system. Users of the system are classified into two: project members, consisting of designer, programmer, tester, and maintenance personnel; and managers for production control, project control, and quality control. Each class of users uses different tools, however one unique interface is provided to both classes of users.

Configuration items, which are included in the software under development, are stored in the software engineering database under the control of configuration management system. The tools, classified in six subsystems (SWB-I, II, III, IV, P, and Q), access the software engineering database. Functions provided by each tool are the following:

* SWB-I—support for editing program text, source level test, translation, and managing project files;
* SWB-II—support for loading object codes to target computers, test on the target computers, and test analysis;
* SWB-III—support for requirements analysis, specification documentation, and specification analysis;
* SWB-IV—support for maintaining documents and programs;
* SWB-P—support for project management described in the previous section; and
* SWB-Q—support for design reviews, inspections, recording quality, quality evaluation, and estimating residual faults.

The SWB system also provides a support for reusing existing software configuration items which are stored in a reusable resources library.

3 PROJECT MANAGEMENT

Project management is conducted in a manner which is called look-forward type management or objective-based management. In look-forward manner, each responsible member's daily objectives, as well as the deviations between objec-

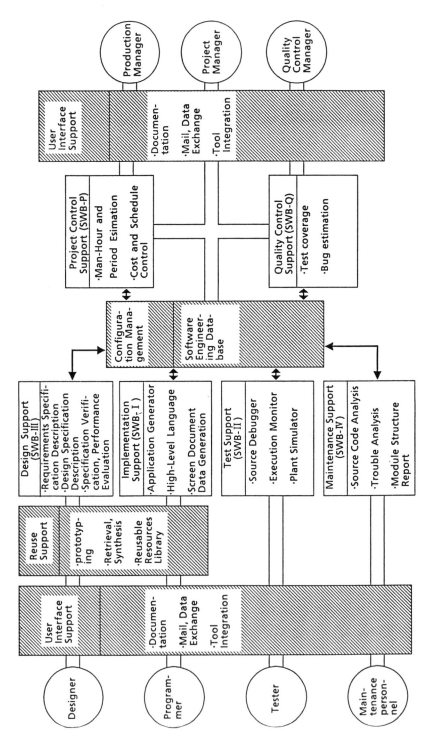

Figure 16-2. SWB system configuration.

tives and accomplishments, are made visible so that every member could work looking forward to go beyond objectives.

The items which characterize look-forward type management are the following:

- Target project cost is established at the beginning of the project.
- Project activity is divided in unit workloads. A unit workload is defined as an activity to accomplish a software configuration item by one person.
- Unit workloads are defined phase by phase at the beginning of every phase. The target cost for each unit workload derived from the target project cost is defined as well.
- The person who is responsible for the unit workload, the number of specification sheets or source lines of program which should be completed in this unit workload, cost or hours allowed in implementing this software configuration item, and the due reusability factor are designed in consideration with the personal performance of the person in charge, characteristic of the objective software configuration item and the project deadline.
- In the course of progress, the amount of product and resource expenditure is entered daily or weekly through terminals into a computer system by each person in charge of the unit workload.
- The computer system analyzes the status of progress and resource expenditure and displays the deviation between current and target status.

The general flow of the project management is shown in Figure 16-3. The flow consists of five major parts: (1) confirmation of project objectives, (2) division of project activity into unit workloads, definition of unit workloads, and assignment of objectives for each unit workload, (3) progress reporting by individuals, (4) analysis of progress in terms of productivity, expenditure, and adherence to the schedule, and (5) quality control.

The first step in the first part is to retrieve responsible persons' personal spectrum characteristics which are saved in the file. This data is used in the cost estimation in the first part of the flow. The project objectives other than the cost (e.g., time constraints) are also defined in this part. Once the objectives have been decided, project planning can begin which is in the second part of the flow. This basically consists of planning the project workload in terms of unit workloads. Software configuration items are also planned at this time and the progress schedule is generated based on the project workload plan.

At this stage, the unit workload order sheets can be generated. Each unit workload order sheet states the objectives for the responsible person to accomplish and technical suggestions to be followed. At the end of every week, each project member must enter work completed. This constitutes the third part of the process flow. This information is valuable in updating the project and schedule. In the fourth part of the process, the computer calculates the deviation

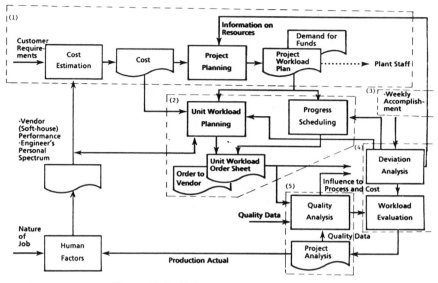

Figure 16-3. Project management system.

from the plan for the use of managers. If the deviation surpasses the allowable limit, the progress schedule must be revised.

Before any unit workload is considered to be completed, a quality analysis must be performed. If it meets the established criteria, it is complete. The final step of the project is to perform an analysis: this provides information on actual productivity and quality for future reference. This information is used to update the personal performance records, including mention of experience gained on the current project.

The unit workload is the major concept used in planning projects. One unit workload represents the process of one individual for implementing one software configuration item. Objectives of a unit workload are established at the beginning of the project. There is, for example, a project productivity objective that corresponds to the total project workload. Likewise, unit workload objectives are established for each unit workload: this means, in effect, that productivity objectives for each individual member are calculated.

What exactly is a unit workload? A unit workload is, in fact, a process. It communicates with many other processes or unit workloads. The typical items which are communicated between unit workloads are shown in Figure 16-4. The inputs to the unit workload include constraints, such as the progress schedule, definition of the products to be manufactured, and specifications. Assignment of resources shown at the bottom of the box includes the tools and time that are available. Output from the unit workload takes the form of resultant productivity and product documents. The description of the unit workload order sheet is the process program[8] which defines all relevant data and the procedural

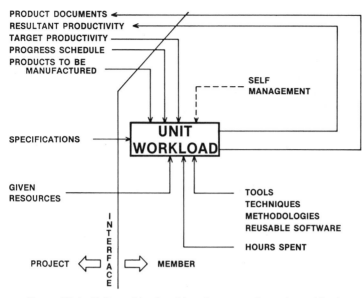

Figure 16-4. Unit workload and interfaces to other unit workloads.

steps to implement the unit workload. This unit workload order sheet is given to the individual who performs the unit workload.

Concerning project management, conventional management is characterized by initiation of corrective actions based on ex post facto reports concerning progress, expenses, quality, etc. The type of project management that the author is practicing, is characterized by advance planning for metrics and objectives for managing the project at the beginning of the project. Daily reports are made on individual progress to allow quick identification of discrepancies between the objectives and actual productivity. This allows quick execution of corrective actions.

4 PROCESS PROGRAMMING

The description of the procedures which are required to accomplish a unit workload is encapsulated in an object. An object is represented by a process program. In the author's process, programming a typical unit workload is represented by a class, while a specialization of that unit workload is represented by an instance which is derived from a class or classes.

An object, or a representation of a unit workload, interacts with many other objects. The interactions, as a whole, form a network.

To show how each process program interacts with the user, an example program is used. The following is an example program:

Instance Creation
[A0 = = [DesignDataLogger ← [: new............................]]]
[A1 = = [DesignAnalogDataRead ← [: new PersonName ResourceName
      ProductName ProductivityValue EndDate ParentName
      BrotherName]]]
[A2 = = [DesignInOutTransform ← [: new ....]]]
[A3 = = [DesignLogOutput ← [: new.........................]]]

An example description of the class: DesignAnalogDataRead follows:

```
01  [ : Class DesignAnalogDataRead
02  ( : ClassVariables              )
03  ( : ClassScripts
04    ( : receive [ : new *ResponsiblePerson *GivenResources *Product-
          ToMake
          *ObjectiveProductivity *ScheduledEnd]
05    ( : var Obj)
06    [Obj := [%Self ← [ : new]]]
07    [Obj ← [ : GivenDefinition *ResponsiblePerson *GivenResources
          *ProductToMake *ObjectiveProductivity *ScheduledEnd
          *ParentProcess *BrotherProcess]]
08    ^Obj))
09  ( : InstanceVariables ResponsiblePerson GivenResources Product-
          ToMake
          ObjectiveProductivity StartTime ScheduledEnd
          ParentProcess BrotherProcess
          InputIdent ScanFreq InputRange ConvFactorA
          ConvFactorB  EngUnit  NoOfInput  PointCompTime-
          Allowed
          ReadInDataMemoryAssignment MemoryAssign-
          DeliveryTime
          SpecificationDeliveryTime CompletionTime Note)
10  ( : InstanceScripts
11    ( : receive [ : GivenDefinition *ResponsiblePerson *Given-
          Resources
          *ProductToMake *ObjectiveProductivity
          *ScheduledEnd]
12    [ResponsiblePerson := *ResponsiblePerson]
13    [GivenResources := *GivenResources]
14    [ProductToMake := *ProductToMake]
15    [ObjectiveProductivity := *ObjectiveProductivity]
16    [ScheduledEnd := *ScheduledEnd])
```

```
17      ( : receive [ : Unit-Workload-Start]
18      [TTY ← [ : princ "Would you start this workload? If you start,
                    please key-in HH/DD/MM/YY"]]
19      [StartTime := [TTY ← [ : read]]]
20      [ParentProcess ← [ : GiveMeSpecification]]
21          ( : receive [ : GiveYouSpecification *InputIdent *ScanFreq
                *InputRange  *ConvFactorA  *ConvFactorB  *EngUnit
                *NoOfInput]
22      [InputIdent := *InputIdent]
23      [ScanFreq := *ScanFreq]
24      [InputRange := *InputRange]
25      [ConvFactorA := *ConvFactorA]
26      [ConvFactorB := *ConvFactorB]
27      [EngUnit := *EngUnit]
28      [NoOfInput := *NoOfInput])
29      [TTY ← [ : princ "Specification has been given. Please key-in
                HH/DD/MM/YY"""]]
30      [SpecificationDeliveryTime := (cons [TTY ← [ : read]]
                                            SpecificationDeliveryTime)]
31      [TTY ← [ : princ "Evaluate input hardware performance using
                the number of inputs(NoOfInput) and scan frequency
                (ScanFreq). Then determine allowable computation
                time for processing a point. Please key-in the result"
                ]]
32      [PointCompTimeAllowed := [TTY ← [ : read]]]
33      [TTY ← [ : princ "Assign the terminal number(hardware) for
                each input point and key-in the assignment"]]
34      [InputPointAllocation := [TTY ← [ : read]]]
35      [TTY ← [ : princ "Are you ready to design program logic and
                memory allocation?" If yes, please key-in YES"]]
36      [Note := [TTY ← [ : read]]]
37      (if (eq Note 'YES)
38          then
39              [TTY ← [ : Princ "We will request memory allocation for
                    storing converted data"]]
40              [BrotherProcess ← [ : GiveMeMemoryAssignment]])
41          ( : receive [ : GiveYouMemoryAssignment *A]
42      [ReadInDataMemoryAssignment := *A]
43      [TTY ← [ : princ "Memory assignment has arrived. Please
                key-in HH/DD/MM/YY"]]
44      [MemoryAssignDeliveryTime := (cons [TTY ← [ : read]]
                                            MemoryAssign-
                                            DeliveryTime)]
```

45   [TTY ← [: princ "Start design of input conversion program:
Y = ConvFactorA∗X + ConvFactorB, where
X : raw input, Y : data in engineering unit which should be passed to InOutTransform.
While you design, please consult reusable programs listed in the following:
. . . .
If the design has been completed,
please key-in COMPLETED. If anything wrong, please
key-in INCOMPLETE]]

46   [Note := [TTY ← [: read]]]
47   (if (eq Note 'COMPLETED)
48   then
49   [TTY ← [: princ "You have completed the unit workload.
Please key-in HH/DD/MM/YY"]]
50   [CompletionTime := [TTY ← [: read]]]
51   else
52   [TTY ← [: princ "What has happened?
Please key-in the name of inadequate items"]]
53   [InadequateItems := [TTY ← [: read]]]
54   [TTY ← [: princ "Please key-in the name of the unit workload by which the adequate items has been delivered"]]
55   [Note := [TTY ← [: read]]
56   (if (eq Note ParentProcess)
57   then [ParentProcess ← [: GiveMeRevised-Specification]])
58   (if (eq Note BrotherProcess)
59   then [BrotherProcess ← [GiveMeRevisedMemory-Assignment
60   ]])))))]

This example is a simplified process program which is used in the design of industrial data logger software. This data logger only handles analog inputs. One assumes that process A0 or basic design is performed first and then the detailed designs of three concurrent processes A1, A2, and A3 are performed next. A1, A2, and A3 are design processes for input conditioning, input/output conversion and output log respectively. All process programs representing A0, A1, A2, and A3 are instances derived from the classes, DesignDataLogger, DesignAnalogDataRead, DesignInOutTransform, and DesignLogOutput, respectively. The language used for presenting the process program is a Lisp-based object-oriented language called object oriented knowledge based language (OKBL) which was developed by the author's group.[5]

The creation of the instances A0, A1, A2, and A3 from the classes, which are DesignDataLogger, DesignAnalogDataRead, DesignInputOutput-Transform, and DesignLogOutput, is made by executing the first six lines headed by 'Instance Creation.'

The explanation on several important statements in the description of the class, DesignAnalogDataRead is followed. The description from line 01 through line 08 defines class attributes. By executing the second line of the Instance Creation shown previously, line 04 statement is invoked. By executing line 06, instance A1 is created, to which the values of each variable (symbol headed by *) are passed. In this example program, ParentProcess is instantiated as A0, and BrotherProcess is instantiated as A2.

The description from line 09 through line 60 defines the instance. If the project manager wants to start unit workload A1, he/she may send a message [: Unit-Workload-Start] to instance A1. Then line 17 is activated, and the work station owned by ResponsiblePerson displays the statement ''Would you start . . . . '' defined in line 18. The time to start the unit workload is stored in StartTime and used for obtaining cost and productivity. By executing line 20, instance A1 requests ParentProcess or A0 to send the specification. If the specification is sent from A0, the lines from 21 through 28 are executed. In line 29, the work station asks the user to enter the date. The date is stored in the list named SpecificationDeliveryTime. The list is required because the receipt of the specification may be repeated when the processes between A0 and A1 are to be iterated.

In the course of the unit workload progress, the instance interacts with the user in lines 31, 33, 35, and 39. Through those interactions, the instance gives the user guidance on how to advance the design. In line 40, the instance asks BrotherProcess A2 to send the memory allocation for storing converted input data. If the data is received, line 41 is activated. The date of receipt is stored in the list named MemoryAssignDeliveryTime. The list is used to consider repeated arrivals of the memory assignment data when the processes between A1 and A2 are to be iterated. The unit workload finishes by executing line 50. If it is incomplete, it iterates in the following manner. When the given specification is not implementable, ParentProcess A0 is re-invoked by the execution of line 57. When revised specification is prepared, line 21 will be entered again. When given memory assignment is unreasonable, BrotherProcess A2 will be re-invoked by executing line 59. If revised memory assignment is prepared, line 41 will be entered again.

The process programming has the following purposes:

- It is used for performing unit workload planning and project scheduling.
- The execution of the specified project process program assists project

members to conduct their work and decision-making, as well as to select reusable software configuration items.

• Reusing existing process programs is useful for improving the quality of the processes and to increase project productivity.

• Filing existing process programs for the completed projects is useful for the evolution (maintenance) of that software.

5 SOFTWARE DESIGN ENVIRONMENTS

In the design process, the designer is required to make a design model first by considering required functions and constraints. During this process, the designer develops several alternatives, compares them and selects the best for implementation. For the designer to compare and evaluate design alternatives, the SWB system provides Functional Component Connection Diagram (FCD) and Module Connection Diagram (MCD) both of which were developed and used internally. The FCD and MCD provide designers with a means to model design views from various aspects.

The aspects to be applicable are the following:

• Functional model vs. programming model—FCD describes functions and relationships between functions, while MCD describes program/data modules and relationships between modules. The software engineering database in the SWB, previously illustrated in Figure 16-2, keeps the record of dependencies between functions and modules.

• Data, control flow model vs. entity relationship model[2]—FCD describes control and data flows and dependencies between them through the functions with which they are related. FCD also can be used to describe entity-relationship (ER) diagrams, such as semantic data models.

• Program module structure vs. database structure—MCD describes structures between program/data modules, and database structures.

• Standard module configuration vs. reusable module configuration—through the interface of MCD users can retrieve various existing module configurations and view/compare them.

Functional Component Connection Diagram(FCD)

At the beginning of the preliminary design, the designer is required to transform from the "what" domain to the "how" domain. The following models are normally used during this transformation:

• data flow model,
• control flow model, and
• function and data structure model.

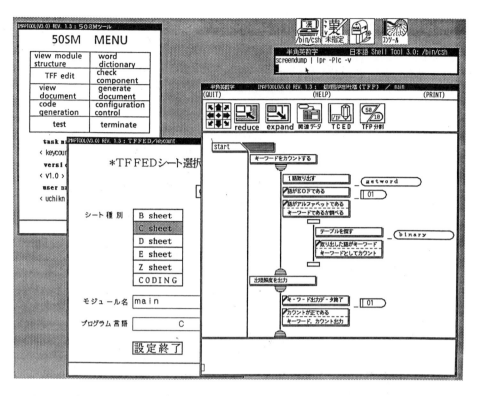

Figure 16-5. Example of CRT pattern to show editor functions in drawing FCD (Functional Component Diagram).

The FCD provides FCD Editor to enable building these models. The FCD Editor, a tool for drawing FCDs, has the following functions:

- interactive editing of the FCD diagram,
- guide for structured design,
- verification of design,
- aid for designing database structure, and
- pretty printing for both diagrams and specifications.

Figure 16-5 shows an example of an FCD. A set of icons, which are included in the small window at the left lower corner, represents the entries to each tool subsystem. There are seven types of icons. Their functions are: access to the cabinets storing documents, access to the folders filing the documents, access to functional component connection diagrams, access to the data structure diagrams, access to the entity/relationship descriptions, the function to create document, and the function to delete document. A cabinet contains folders, while a folder contains diagrams or documents.

If, for example, one needs to select and display the FCD diagram that is to be edited, first access the cabinet or the folder that stores the diagram. When the cabinet is accessed, move the mouse cursor on the cabinet icon and then move the cursor to the pop-up menu and click "display;" then the window shows the list of folders included in the selected cabinet. In the same manner, one can open folders and view the list of diagrams included in the selected folders. When the desired diagram is reached, the silhouette or the rough pattern of the diagram is displayed in a peep sub-window.

To revise or edit the selected diagram, you may click "edit" in the pop-up menu. Then the diagram editor is invoked, and the selected diagram is displayed on the background window. The diagram shown in the background window of Figure 16-5 is an example of FCD diagram.

Notations for major symbols used in the FCD are the following:

- white head arrow = control
- black head arrow = data (input, output, record, transaction)
- box = function
- parallelogram = data set
- hexagon = interface
- a node on control arrow denoted as "p" = parallel begin
- a node on control arrow denoted as "j" = parallel end
  (also used as AND joint)
- a node on control arrow denoted as "m" = OR joint
- a node on control arrow denoted as "c" = conditional select
- a node on control arrow denoted as "g" = generate initiation

The upper right half of the diagram describes control flows. The lower left half describes data flows. Each function box can further be refined and detailed in subsidiary FCD diagrams. The FCD provides designers with a means of viewing functional distributions, control flows, and data flows in the same sheet.

The content of the FCD can be revised, appended, or deleted by using icons. The menu of 14 icons is displayed in the upper end of the screen. If one wants to execute a function, select an icon by moving the mouse cursor to it and clicking the mouse. Then move the cursor to the location that is to be accessed. The FCD includes symbols, nodes, and arrows. Any new item of symbol type, node type, or arrow type can be inserted into the diagram by using either one of three icons on the left end of the menu bar. For example, a new function box can be created by selecting and clicking FUNC icon, followed by moving the cursor to the location needed to access and clicking again. Similarly, one can draw the data arrows, control arrows, and other symbols.

The second pop-up menu shown in the top right corner of the screen in Figure 16-5 lists the functions for doing clerical work. For example, when "c → p" in the menu is executed, the background window changes to display the parent

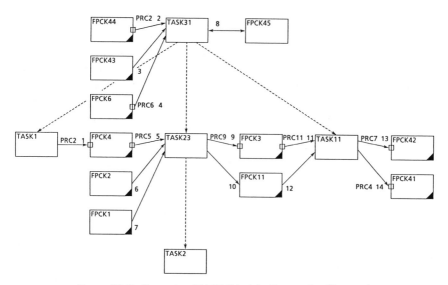

Figure 16-6. Example of MCD (Module Connection Diagram).

diagram for the current display. To see the child diagram for a functional box of the current FCD diagram, point and click that box and select "p → c", then the background window changes to display the child FCD diagram for the box selected.

Module Connection Diagram

The module connection diagram (MCD) is used to design program modules and their structures using data flow and control flow.

Figure 16-6 shows an example of MCD description. The MCD has a similar outlook to that of the FCD. However, MCD defines the detail structure of program modules and data modules.

The elements included in the MCD and their meanings are described in the following:

- box = task
- box with small mark on the right lower corner = package
- small square on the package = interface routine
- straight arrow = data communication path
- dotted arrow = control path

In the example of Figure 16-6, there are five tasks, TASK1, TASK31, TASK23, TASK2, and TASK11. Each dotted arrow connecting tasks represents that there exists a relationship (activates/activated, terminates/terminated, synchronizes/synchronized, or interrupts/interrupted) between the tasks of both ends. The label attached to each arrow describes the semantics of the arrow. The Figure describes that TASK31 activates TASK1, TASK23, and TASK11, while TASK23 activates TASK2 (the labels of the arrows are not shown).

A solid arrow connecting task and package represents data communication. For example, TASK23 calls procedures in package FPCK4 to get data, while it calls procedures in package FPCK3 to output data.

A package, for example FPCK43, is a set of common data, which is directly accessed without using procedure. The case, such as FPCK43 is for special purposes.

Technical Description Formula for Fifty Step/Module Design

The Technical description Formula for Fifty step/module design (TFF) is a diagram for representing algorithms of a subprogram consisting of less than 50 lines of source statements or data lines. Figure 16-7 demonstrates a capability of the TFF editor. The window on the top left corner is the initial window which includes the selection menu for basic functions. By selecting "TFF edit" in the menu, for example, the second menu window on the center lower part appears. It is used for selecting the form of the document to be edited. In this example, "C sheet" for document type, "main" for module name, and "c" for programming language are selected. The selected TFF module is shown in the window located in the right half.

The diagrammatic semantics for representing TFF module are described in the following:

- The vertical straight line starting from the small box in the top with the name "start" and terminating at the small box (not shown in the Figure) with the name "end" represents the scope of the TFF module.
- The vertical straight line with small half circles at both ends represents an iterative block.
- The vertical straight line with small boxes at both ends represents a sequential block.
- The vertical straight line with small triangles at both ends represents if-endif block or case-endcase block.
- The rectangle box represents a unit of action statements.
- The ellipse represents a called module.
- The box with a small triangle at the left upper corner represents exit from the iteration.
- The box which has a dotted line dividing itself and has a small triangle at the left upper corner represents a pair of a condition and the associated action conducted if the condition is satisfied.

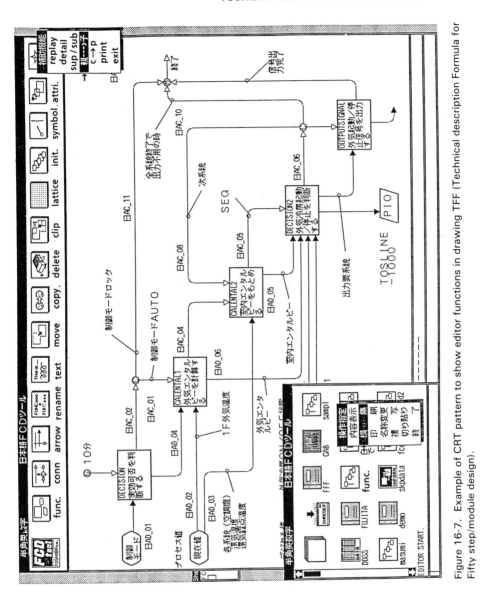

Figure 16-7. Example of CRT pattern to show editor functions in drawing TFF (Technical description Formula for Fifty step/module design).

By using TFF editor, designers are assisted in drawing TFF diagrams in an efficient manner, and the structured design of the algorithmic logic of the TFF module is conducted systematically as the result.

The patterns for window frame, icons, pop-up, or pull-down menu and cursors are designed carefully through experiments.[7]

For example, the properties of new icons are examined, before they are actually applied, by two successive review sessions with more than 20 observers participating. In the first session, the observers reviewed each icon and guessed the true meaning of each icon. One week later, in the second session, the same observers were gathered, and the same procedures were repeated.

After the sessions, the icons were classified into rank A, B, C, and D. The ranks are defined in the following manner:

RANK A   More than 70% of the observers identified the meaning of the icon in the first session.

RANK B   More than 70% of the observers identified the meaning of the icon in the second session, while less than 70% of the observers identified the icon in the first session.

RANK C   More than 30% and less than 70% identified the meaning of the icon in the second session, while fewer observers identified the icon in the first session.

RANK D   Less than 30% identified the meaning in the first and the second session.

As the result of the examination, the icons of rank C and D were not applied.

A computer system shown in Figure 16-8 is used to execute a set of various tools previously described. In the top level computer, the reusable objects are stored and maintained in the central file. At ACOS, a large scale computer, is used. In the second level computer, the Project-Process Administrator (PPA) is located. For each project, one PPA instance is created. The G8000 series, a super-minicomputer, is used. The bottom level computer is a set of workstations. In a workstation, the objects which represent the workloads of the responsible users are stored and executed. The objects in the bottom level computer act in an interactive mode in such a way that execution is made part-by-part in response to each user input. In the end of each partial execution, a guidance message is displayed to the user, then the next execution is held until the user inputs the next response to that guidance message. All messages sent by objects go to the project PPA, and all messages addressed to other objects are sent by the PPA. The PPA maintains information concerning all message transactions and excution status of all objects acting concurrently.

The tools using FCDs, MCDs, or TFFs are executed on the bottom level workstations, AS3000, or Sun-3 workstation with the function to process Japanese documents.

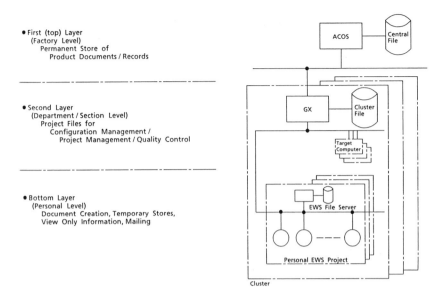

Figure 16-8. Hierarchical computer configuration used in SWB environment.

6 PRODUCTIVITY IMPROVEMENT

Factory-scoped gross productivity is measured every 6-month fiscal term. The gross productivity represents EASLs accepted by the customers during this term divided both by the number of months and by the number of persons. The TFSF has measured gross productivities since 1977. The factory-scoped EASL/person-month including reused codes in 1977 was 1.9 K, while in 1985 it was 3.1 K. The average rate of yearly improvement has been approximately 8%–9%.

The factory-scoped EASL/person-month, not including reused codes in 1977, was 1.0 K, while in 1985 it was 1.6 K. This indicates that reusability was the most important contribution to the productivity improvement.

7 QUALITY IMPROVEMENT

The term ''quality'' is used in this chapter to mean only program reliability. Program reliability has been defined as the probability that a software fault which causes deviation from the required output by more than specified tolerances, in a specified environment, does not occur during a specified exposure period.[9]

The TFSF measures program reliability of all software products before shipment by estimating the number of residual faults by using a method called progressive hyper-geometric.[6]

Reviewing faults records taken over the past ten years, the number of residual faults per 1-K source lines for all projects has been below the level of 0.1. Of all faults found in the factory tests, the percentages are as follows:

* 35% are design faults;
* 20% are program faults;
* 30% are data faults; and
* 15% are hardware and interface faults.

Of all faults found in the plant site tests, the percentages are as follows:

* 45% are design faults;
* 10% are program faults;
* 20% are data faults, and
* 25% are hardware and interface faults.

8 CONCLUSION

The following list summarizes the author's experience on the factors which contribute to the improvement of productivity and quality, and the degrees of their contribution.

• Reuse	0.52
• Improvement of design and programming process	0.18
• Introduction of new software tools	0.09
• Application of new methodologies	0.08
• Optimization of design	
(e.g., to improve functional decomposition)	0.07
• Introduction of new design/programming language	0.06

The software factory and the SWB system are still growing. Additional investment has been made year by year. Improvement of the organizational environments to promote reusability has been the top priority. Approximately 50% of the EASLs shipped to the customers have been the reused codes.

The subject of the next priority is the development of the New-SWB system which will succeed the SWB system. It will be an environment which integrates tools and user interfaces based on a distributed type architecture.

Major subjects to be considered are process programming, the new programming paradigm that applies Artificial Intelligence (AI), and distributed (and parallel) type environments.

REFERENCES

1. Albrecht, A. J., "Measuring Application Development Productivity," *Proceedings Joint SHARE/BUIDE/IBM Application Development Symposium*, 1979, pp. 83-92.
2. Chen, "The Entity-Relationship Model: Toward a Unified View of Data," *ACM Transactions Database System*, Vol. 1, No. 1, 1976, pp. 9-36.
3. Jones, T. C., "Measuring Programming Quality and Productivity," *IBM System Journal*, Vol. 17, No. 1, 1978, pp. 39-63.
4. Matsumoto, Y., et. al., "A software factory," in *Software Engineering Environments*, edited by H. Hunke, New York: North-Holland, 1981.
5. Matsumoto, Y., "Requirements engineering and software development: a study toward another life cycle model," in *Computer Systems for Process Control*, edited by R. Guth, New York: Plenum Press, 1986.
6. Matsumoto, Y., "Software Factory: An overall approach to software production," in *Software Reusability*, edited by P. Freeman, *IEEE Cat. No. EH0256-8*, 1987, pp 155-178.
7. Matsumura, K., et. al., "Visual Man-machine Interface for Program Design and Production," *Proceedings on IEEE Computer Society Workshop on Visual Languages*, 1986, pp. 71-80.
8. Osterweil, L., "Software Processes are Software too," *Proceedings of 9th International Conference on Software Engineering*, 1987, pp. 2-13.
9. "TRW Defense and Space Systems Group," Software Reliability Study, Redondo Beach, Rep. 76-2260. 1-9-5, 1976.

Chapter 17

MicroSTEP: A Business Definition Language System

RAYMOND T. YEH
SYSCORP International, Inc.
Austin, TX

1 INTRODUCTION

Projections show that the demand for applications outstrips society's ability to produce them at this time. A solution to keeping pace with the rapidly growing demand is to enhance the productivity of the individuals developing computer solutions. Another solution is to significantly enhance the ability of individuals, with varying degrees of computer sophistication, to directly solve a wide range of problems. To do so, software development must become a problem definition process rather than a detailed coding process. Users must be able to interact with the computer using abstractions with which they are familiar. MicroSTEP is a software system that aimed to aid users to develop business applications in this way.

As shown in Figure 17-1, MicroSTEP supports a development paradigm that automates two major parts of the traditional software development cycle: coding and testing. With MicroSTEP, the application is maintained by editing the specification as needs evolve; one always has documentation that matches the current application—a rare situation in traditional software development cycles!

Although the analyst still works closely with end-users to determine what's required of the finished application, using MicroSTEP makes it very easy to specify, modify, and maintain the applications.

In addition to preventing most errors during specification rather than simply reporting them during program generation, MicroSTEP also helps eliminate errors by allowing reuse of data that is verified. All data structures and graphic layouts (report and screen formats) can be stored in data dictionaries and reused as needed. Information can be transferred from a data dictionary to a current application with the click of the mouse.

Once an application is generated, it can be easily modified to meet the changing needs of the users. The built-in modularity enables changing one part without producing unwanted side effects in other parts. In the following sections, the author will describe MicroSTEP, and how it is used to specify applications.

502

Traditional Software Development Cycle   MicroSTEP Software Development Cycle

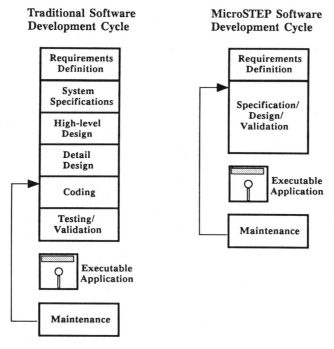

Figure 17-1. Comparison of traditional software development cycle to MicroSTEP software development cycle.

2 WHAT IS MICROSTEP?

Basically, MicroSTEP allows one to build a specification by manipulating graphic icons; check the specification for consistency and completeness; generate, compile, and link the source code; document the design; and validate the application.

MicroSTEP is comprised of the following three basic components:

- a graphics based specification language that supports a graphical specification system;
- a complete application generation system; and
- a sophisticated application run-time environment.

In this section, the conceptual model, which is the basis in the design of the language, the MicroSTEP Design Methodology and an overview of the MicroSTEP system environment are presented.

2.1 The Conceptual Model of the MicroSTEP Language

The MicroSTEP language is designed for those who want to develop business applications; i.e., for system analysts or application programmers. The graphical nature also makes it easy to learn by application specialists, such as accountants who are familiar with the use of microcomputers. For this group, assume that most would not have a solid mathematical background. However, this is not to say that abstraction, formality, and precision are foreign to their normal way of thinking. To develop an interactive graphical language, which is natural to this group for describing their application, it appears that business forms and the notion of information or data flow are very important.

In the MicroSTEP language, the basic idea for representing data is derived from a business form. A generic form consists of two components: the structure of this (printed) form, and the individual data items which are then filled into this general framework. The language must take into account both the definition of a *form*, which handles the structuring of the data, and then knowledge of the structure by asking for legal range in which the values of the individual data items have to fit. Thus, the form corresponds to the printed piece of paper not yet filled-in, on which values correspond to the type definitions of a record, or of an array structure in programming languages like PASCAL. The range definition represents the knowledge of the application specialist about what type of data might be legally filled into this form and, hence corresponds to the definition of a simple type in PASCAL. Form and range definition together are therefore equivalent to the declarations in a procedural programming language.

Business applications are primarily data driven. Data are captures in forms, the flow of data then is to be described by how data is mapped from ''input forms'' to an ''output form.'' In most cases, the mapping is selective permutations of input data, or it may consist of data resulting from simple arithmetic operations among input data elements. For more complex operations, one may utilize a scratchpad to compute intermediate results or to pin down some decision rules, since a scratchpad is nothing but a structured form. Most commercial applications can be described as mappings of the data value from one form to another. Thus, a basic work unit in the MicroSTEP language is an ''activity'' that consists of a ''process'' and its associated input and output form instances as shown in Figure 17-2.

An ''application'' is a set of activities linked together which is called a Form Flow Diagram (FFD). The semantics of an FFD are outlined as the following:

- Data arrives on input queues.
- When inputs are available for an activity, the activity is placed in the mode: ''ready to dispatch.''
- When the activity is dispatched, input data is fetched in a controlled fashion.
- Based on the input, work is performed; output forms are produced and placed into output queues.
- Activity becomes inactive; output queues are released. If directed to more than one subsequent activity, output is replicated.
- When an input is read, it is removed from the queue. If it does not meet selection criteria, it is discarded.

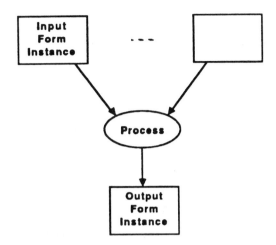

Figure 17-2. An "activity" in the MicroSTEP language.

2.2   The MicroSTEP Design Methodology

MicroSTEP's design methodology eliminates two major parts of the traditional software development: coding and testing as shown in Figure 17-3.
The MicroSTEP specification consists of the following four steps:

1. Create a form flow diagram (the conceptual design) using icons that represent data objects, processes, and links.
2. Describe the fields in each data object.
3. Describe the formats of any data entry screens and reports included in the specification.
4. Describe the way in which MicroSTEP is to process input data objects to produce output data objects.

It is not necessary to complete all the steps in the specification process before one can build a working application. This means that one can use MicroSTEP very effectively to produce prototype applications. One can do the following:

- create a simple specification that focuses on a particular aspect of the total application;
- instruct MicroSTEP to construct default formats for data entry screens and reports;
- generate the partial application from the specification and observe how it behaves;
- demonstrate the program to the users, and solicit their input; and
- modify and build upon the specification to meet the users' application requirements.

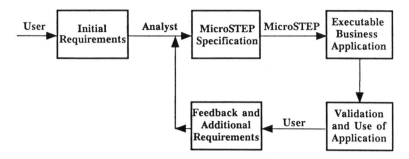

Figure 17-3. The MicroSTEP development cycle.

2.3   The MicroSTEP Environment

MicroSTEP has three underlying components: a graphics-based specification system, an application generation system, and an application run-time environment as depicted in Figure 17-4. A user works primarily with the specification system, choosing a few commands from a pulldown menu to generate and install the application. The components of the specification system are shown in Figure 17-5.

Top STEP is the control point for operating MicroSTEP. One can see the available specifications and data dictionaries and can choose commands for generating an executable application. From Top STEP, enter either the Specification Editor or the Data Dictionary Editor, depending on whether one chooses to create or edit a specification or a data dictionary.

If one chooses to create or open a specification, the Flow Diagram Builder appears on the screen: if one chooses to create or open a data dictionary, the Data Dictionary Editor appears on the screen.

One of the basic differences between a specification and a data dictionary is that a data dictionary has no processes or flow definitions. Therefore, the Activity Builder or the Flow Control Builder cannot be entered from the Data Dictionary Editor. As illustrated in Figure 17-6, data dictionaries are just a collection of data objects, while a flow diagram shows how information flows from data objects to processes.

For each data object one can have definitions of its data structure, and, if the data object is a screen or a report, of its format. This is true whether the data object is from a specification or from a data dictionary.

The primary purpose of having data dictionaries is so data can be reused. MicroSTEP makes it very easy to copy data objects from a data dictionary to a specification and vice versa. When one copies a data object, MicroSTEP also copies its data structure information and, if it's a screen or report, its format. Then, if it's necessary, the information and, if it's a screen or a report, its format can be modified. Then, if it's necessary, one can modify the information as appropriate for the specific application being created.

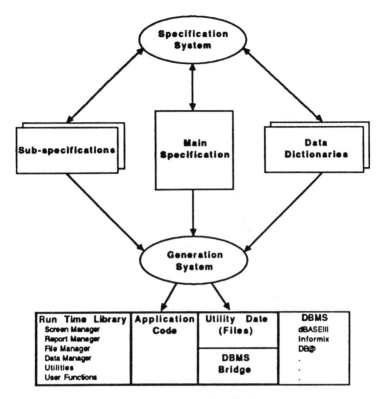

Figure 17-4. An overview of MicroSTEP environment.

MicroSTEP's application generation system is a complex, sophisticated program which makes it easy to build an application from a specification. Components of the generation subsystem are shown in Figure 17-7.

The application generation environment consists of the following features and capabilities, which are available for use when one is ready to actually build the application for which a specification was created:

- a semantic analyzer that automatically checks the specification for completeness and consistency;
- a code generator that automatically produces debugged, executable source code;
- a high-level-language compiler that automatically translates the code into a computer-readable format and then links the various programs comprising the application into one integrated program;
- utilities that automatically control installing and configuring an executable application;

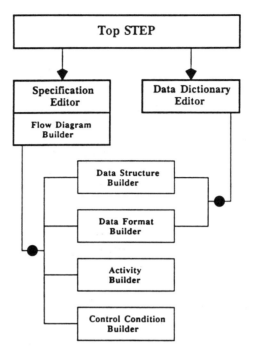

Figure 17-5. User's view of MicroSTEP.

- utilities that allow one to automatically import information from existing data bases and then use this information in the finished application; and
- utilities that automatically create an application on a diskette so one can run it on other computers.

After specifying the detailed design of the custom program through the use of the Specification Editor (the specification development environment), simply instruct MicroSTEP to build the specified application. One can check the specification and then generate and compile the code with a single command.

Components of the application run-time environment are shown in Figure 17-8.

The application run-time environment consists of the following features and capabilities, which are available to be included in the specification so that they appear in the finished application:

- an integrated, full-functions report generator that provides capabilities for formatting and printing reports;
- integrated screen management that provides the following:

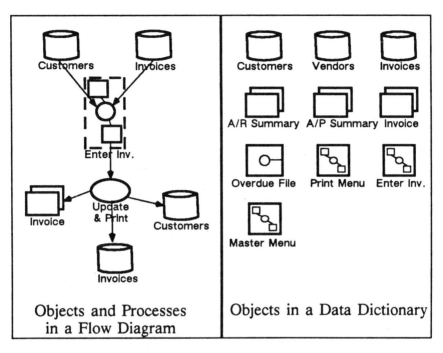

Objects and Processes in a Flow Diagram

Objects in a Data Dictionary

Figure 17-6. Sample contents of a specification and a data dictionary.

- light-bar (highlighted) menus, menu trees, and transactions (exchanges between the user and the program, such as updating files);
- options, or choices, that the user can toggle through;
- scrolling windows for working with or viewing a dynamic list of entries;
- context-sensitive HELP;
- flexible soft key configuration, letting the end-user assign keys of their choice to specific functions you have defined;
- dynamic on-screen computation (if the user changes a value in one place, the change is reflected in any computed fields whose formulas incorporate the changed field);

Guidance System						
Config Mgr.	Run Time Libraries	Install Mgr.	Build Mgr.	HLL Compiler	Code Generator	Semantic Analyser

Figure 17-7. Components of MicroSTEP generation subsystem.

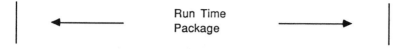

Virtual DB Interface (VDBI)	Data Utilities	Overlay Mgr.	Space Mgr.	Report Mgr.	Screen Mgr.	File Mgr.	Scheduler	Configure (dnyamic)	Generated, Compiled Application Code

Figure 17-8. Components of MicroSTEP run-time environment.

- dynamic data access (data base queries or lookups, to data in major formats, such as dBASEIII, SQLBase, etc)
- editing or constraint checking "on the fly" (the user types a number too large for a given field, and the program displays an error message);

- sequential flat files and extended relational data bases;
- temporary (scratch) files for storing and restructuring data, and computations to map into reports, data entry screens, data bases, and files;
- a virtual data base interface, which creates a generic data base structure that works with an existing Data Base Management System (DBMS) when the user runs the application;
- capability to work with information in standard file formats, such as Lotus, WKS, and DIF files;

MicroSTEP's run-time environment makes it easy for one to create user-responsive (friendly) programs customized for a particular group or site. For example, one can build an application, which includes menus and on-line HELP, that allows users to type information on clear, easy-to-understand data entry screens; to incorporate material from existing data bases; and to generate appropriate reports, to list a few possible functions.

3   HOW TO USE MICROSTEP?

This section provides a guided tour of MicroSTEP, showing how to create a specification from which an executable application can be generated.

A MicroSTEP specification can represent an entire application or a portion of an application. Since specifications can call, or invoke, other specifications, individual modules or programs can be defined as separate specifications. It is somewhat analogous to setting up directories and subdirectories with DOS—one can have a sophisticated tree structure or one can perform all activities from the root directory. To create a specification, the following must be done:

- Draw a flow diagram with icons that represent data objects, processes, and links. While "drawing," MicroSTEP is actually defining much of the specification.
- Provide MicroSTEP with descriptions of the fields for each data object (that is, with information about its data structures).
- Describe the formats of any data entry screens and reports included in the specification.
- Describe how the input is processed to produce the output data.

All the steps don't have to be completed in the specification process before building a working application. And for simple applications, one does not even have to define all of the information listed above. For example, if there's only one input and one output for a process and no special filters or conditions are required, MicroSTEP often can determine how the output data gets its input, and if a particular format is not defined for a data entry screen or report, MicroSTEP will generate one based upon the data structure for that object. In the following sections, the author shows some of the steps required to specify an application.

3.1 Describing The Flow of Data

The flow diagram shows the relationship between the data as it passes through the programs that comprise an application. The way in which one arranges and links the icons of the flow diagram indicates how the information flows from input through processing to output.

To create a flow diagram, the mouse is used to select icons from the icon bar and, then place them in the desired locations on the screen. Since one specification can call or invoke other specifications, a specification or flow diagram can either represent an entire application or a module in an application. Although a single flow diagram can occupy up to 323 pages, it's easier to deal with individual modules when creating a large, complex application. Figure 17-9a shows the high-level flow diagram for the sample application, a Point of Sale/Accounts Receivable/Invoice system, and describes what the icons on the icon bar represent.

This flow diagram indicates that the application begins with a screen activity . This initial screen activity is a master menu that allows the user to choose which module he/she wants to use. A control flow condition, indicated by the symbol ⑦ , is placed on the link that calls each module—SALES, PAYMENTS, REPORTS, POSTING, or INVMAINT. The flow control condition determines which module is called based upon the option the user chooses from the master menu. Except for defining the format, or layout, of the master menu, there are no other definitions required for this specification. For the detailed examples of how one draws a flow diagram, defines data structures, defines formats of screens and reports, and defines the activities, look at the specification for the SALES module. Figure 17-9b shows the flow diagram of the SALES module.

When the application is run and the user chooses the option for entering the SALES module, he/she will be presented with a screen for entering information for an invoice. The screen activity is a unique object in MicroSTEP because it has its own input (keyboard), process, and output (monitor). That is why this icon has three symbols within a dasher boarder. When links flow into the process portion of the screen activity—the circle in the center of the icon—it indicates to MicroSTEP to look up information in the data objects that are linked to it. When the user enters a customer number for a part number on the invoice entry screen, the application will automatically look up and display the remaining customer or part information. After the user enters information for the invoice, the application will print the invoice, write the transaction to the SALES_JOURNAL disk file, and update the INVENTORY data base table.

Also notice the icon in the upper left corner of the screen labeled GLOBAL_DATA. Global Data is data that can be used throughout the application. It has fields for the system date and time, for automatically numbering pages in a report, for giving a status, for storing a commonly used name (such as a company name), for associating a beep with particular data entry fields, for creating menu trees, and for keeping counts. One also can create fields in the Global Data structure for use throughout the application and assign some Global Data fields and initial value.

Now consider how one defines the structure of data objects. To enter the Data Structure Builder, one selects the Enter_Invoice screen activity icon and chooses Structure from the Define menu as shown in Figure 17-10.

3.2   Defining Data Structures

The Data Structure Builder screen has two windows. In the top window, called the active window, the structure is built for the object selected from the flow diagram. In the lower window, called the reference window, the flow diagram can be displayed; then any object can be chosen from the flow diagram and its data structure can be displayed. This lets one easily reuse information because information can be copied from the structure in the reference window to the structure in the active window. Figure 17-10b shows the Data Structure Builder screen with the flow diagram in the reference window. MicroSTEP displays a dialog box to enter information about the first field in the ENTER_INVOICE data structure.

Name the first field "date," specify that it is not a key field and choose Date for the data type. When the OK pushbutton is clicked, the dialog box is removed, and MicroSTEP displays the name of the first field as DATE. (One can enter

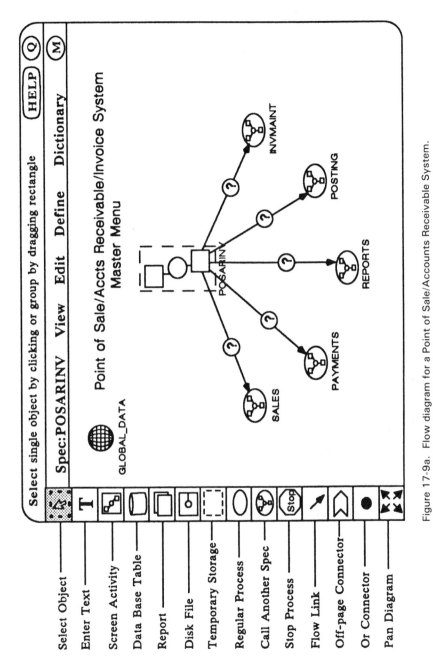

Figure 17-9a. Flow diagram for a Point of Sale/Accounts Receivable System.

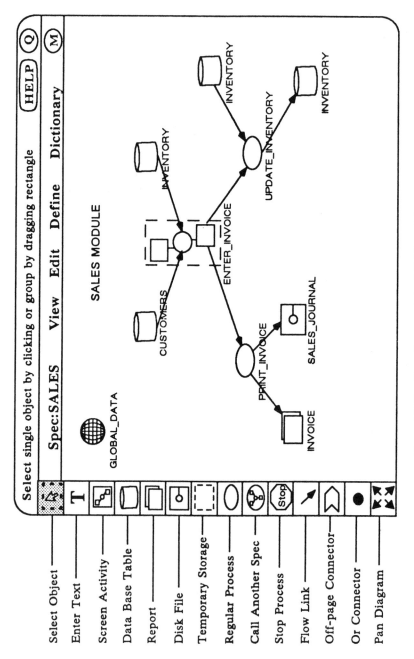

Figure 17-9b. Flow diagram of the SALES module.

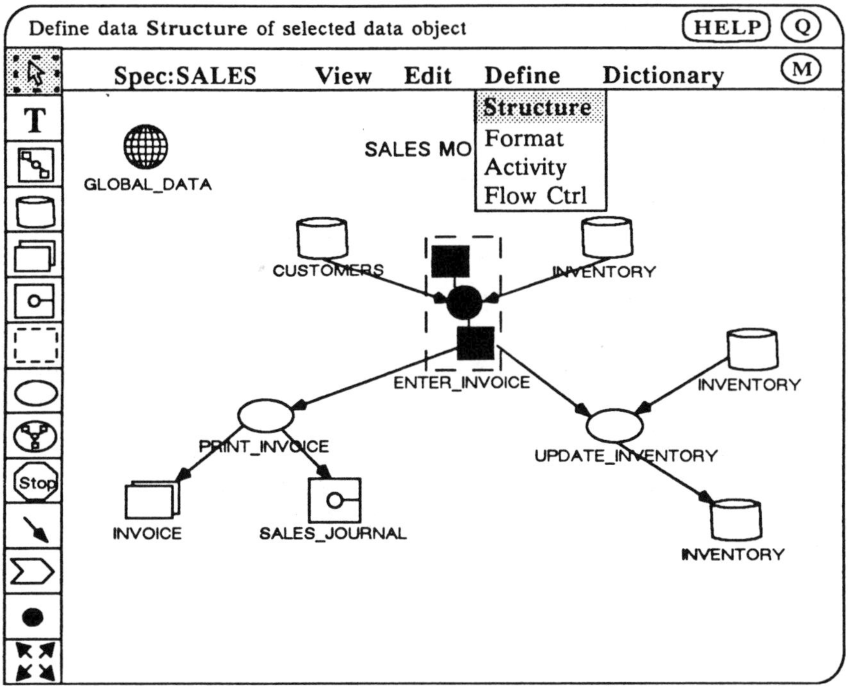

Figure 17-10a. Choosing Define-Structure to enter the Data Structure Builder.

names using all lower case letters; MicroSTEP converts the names entered to upper case letters and adds an underscore wherever blank spaces occur.)

The ⬚ icon lets one select a data object in the flow diagram and display its structure. The same icon can be used to select and copy information from the reference window structure to the structure in the active window. The commands on the Show menu, found on the reference window menu bar, let one control what information is displayed in the reference window (the Global Data structure, the flow diagram, or the structure for a selected data object). Since the data structure for the ENTER_INVOICE screen also contains information about the customer, the CUSTOMER data base table structure can be displayed in the reference window, and the appropriate fields can be copied to the ENTER_INVOICE structure (see Figure 17-11).

Because all the fields from the CUSTOMER.DB structure are required, except the field PHONE copied to the ENTER_INVOICE structure, the copy icon is used to select the entire structure in the reference window (see Figure 17-12) and then to delete the unwanted field.

This results in the data structure shown in Figure 17-13 being created for the ENTER_INVOICE screen activity.

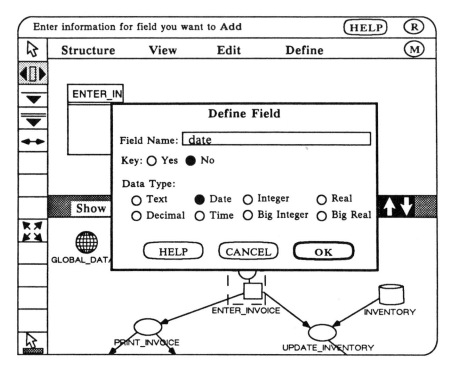

Figure 17-10b. Defining a Field in the data structure.

Now select the PHONE field, using the Select ⌕ icon, and choose Delete from the Edit menu to erase the unwanted field from the ENTER—INVOICE structure. And one could select any other field copied from the reference window and choose Attributes from the Edit menu. This displays the same dialog box as when one first created the field, which allows changing the field name, determining whether it is key, and examining what type data it will contain. For example, one might want to select the NUMBER field and change its name to CUSTO. NO. to clarify what the number represents.

Since the ENTER—INVOICE screen activity also gets information from the INVENTORY data base table, it needs to contain the appropriate fields from that data structure. Figure 17-14 shows how to again display the flow diagram in the reference window by choosing Flow Diagram from the Show menu; then one chooses the INVENTORY data base table icon to display its structure in the reference window (see Figure 17-15).

The data structure resulting from coping inventory data structure to EN-TER—INVOICE Structure appears in Figure 17-16.

Although each invoice will be associated with a unique invoice number and a single customer, the customer may have several purchases on one invoice.

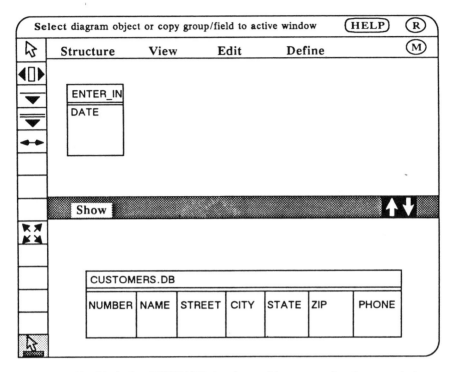

Figure 17-11. Displaying CUSTOMER data base table structure in reference window.

To describe this, a "repeating group" is created to indicate that there can be an unlimited number of occurrences of that data. Repeating groups are represented by a double horizontal line over the group of fields and are created by selecting the repeating group icon (shaded in the icon bar) and dragging the mouse pointer across the fields wanted in the repeating group. When the mouse button is released, MicroSTEP asks the user to enter a name for the group; it will be called PURCHASES (see Figure 17-17). The resulting data structure appears in Figure 17-18.

It is now necessary to add a few new fields to complete the data structure for the invoice entry screen. It needs fields for a subtotal, the tax, total amount of the invoice, the amount tendered, and the change due. When a new field is added, MicroSTEP displays a dialog box so one can enter the field name, determine whether the field is a key, and decide what type data it will contain. (When fields are copied from one data structure to another, all of this information is copied too. However, one can change it by selecting the field and choosing Attributes from the Edit menu.) One uses the Add Field icon ◀[]▶ to add fields to the structure. After this icon is selected, click to the left or the right of the field or group to where the new field is to appear. Figure 17-19 shows how to

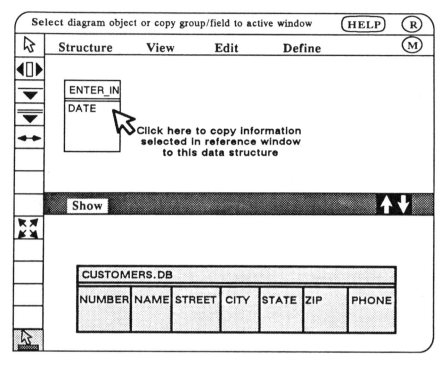

Figure 17-12. Copying all fields from CUSTOMERS structure to ENTER_INV structure.

add a new field. Since one does not want the new field within the repeating group (only one subtotal per invoice_), click to the right of the PURCHASES repeating group rectangle. When the Define Field dialog box appears, enter the field name "subtotal," and click on the radio button next to Decimal because the subtotal will be in dollar amount. A second dialog box appears to ask how many digits the field will contain, and how many should be to the right of the decimal point.

The fields for TAX, TOTAL, AMT_TENDERED, and CHANGE_DUE are added to the structure in the same way as described for the SUBTOTAL field. The finished data structure appears in Figure 17-20.

ENTER_INVOICE							
DATE	NUMBER	NAME	STREET	CITY	STATE	ZIP	PHONE

Figure 17-13. Data structure of ENTER_INVOICE after fields from CUSTOMERS data base copies to it.

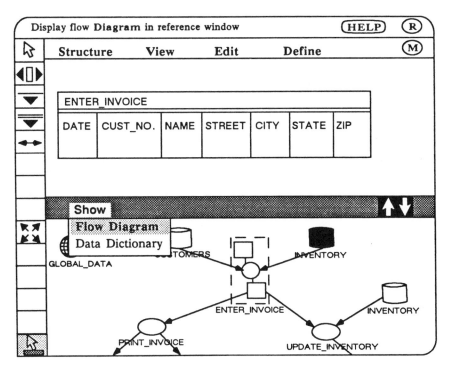

Figure 17-14. Displaying Flow Diagram and then selecting INVENTORY data base to display its structure.

The other icons that help one build and edit data structures are the following:

Simple Group Icon. This icon is used to place a simple group in a data structure. After selecting this icon, click on a single field or drag across several fields to place a simple group above the field or fields. One can create a simple group before or after the fields in the group have been created. In either case, a dialog box appears for entering a group name. Simple groups are just a way of showing that a group of fields are related, but there is only one occurrence of each field in the group. For example, one would create a simple group over the fields STREET, CITY, STATE, and ZIP and label it ADDRESS. A simple group may contain only fields, not any other simple or repeating group.

Move Field Icon. This icon moves a field from one location in the data structure to another. The first click of the mouse selects the field to be moved, and the second click determines its destination position. Clicking on the left half of the destination position places the new field to the left of the existing field; clicking on the right-half places it to the right of the existing field.

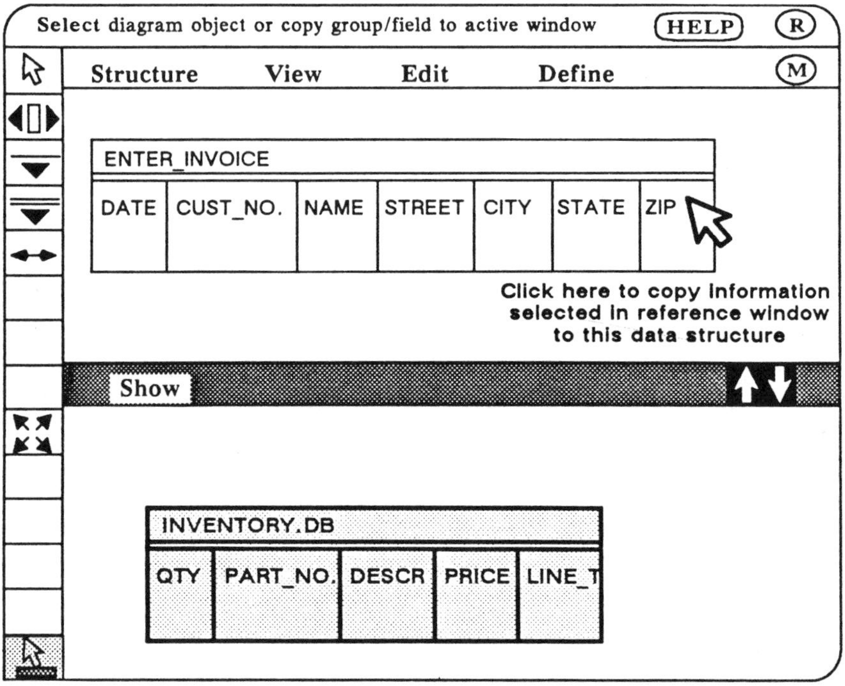

Figure 17-15. Copying the INVENTORY data base structure to the ENTER_INVOICE structure.

Pan Icon. The pan icon scrolls either the data structure in the active window or the information in the reference window. When the screen is split into an active and a reference windows, the Pan icon can be used for either, and it separates the icons that can be used only with the active window (the icons above the Pan icon) and the icons that can be used only with the reference window (the icons below the Pan icon).

In addition to being able to pan the information in either window, the commands on the View menu can zoom out (reduce) and zoom in (enlarge) on the data structure, and display the entire data structure at once (Full View).

ENTER_INVOICE										
DATE	CUST_NO.	NAME	STREET	CITY	STATE	ZIP	QTY	PART_NO.	DESCR	PRICE	LINE_T

Figure 17-16. ENTER_INVOICE data structure after INVENTORY data base fields copied.

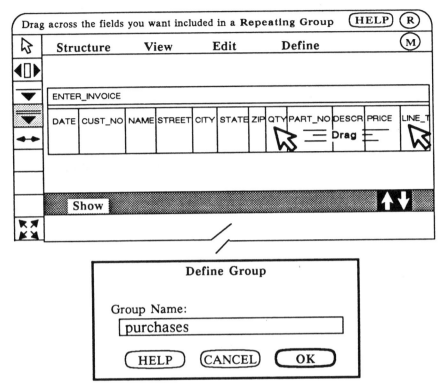

Figure 17-17. Creating a Repeating Group.

If the data object one is defining is a report or a screen activity, the format can also be specified. The format for the ENTER_INVOICE screen activity can be laid out as follows.

3.3   Defining Formats

To define the format, select a report or screen activity icon from the flow diagram, and choose Format from the Define menu or, if one is in the Data Structure Builder, choose Format from its Define menu. Because the data struc-

ENTER_INVOICE							PURCHASES				
DATE	CUST_NO.	NAME	STREET	CITY	STATE	ZIP	QTY	PART_NO.	DESCR	PRICE	LINE_T

Figure 17-18. ENTER_INVOICE structure after Repeating Group named.

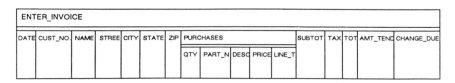

Figure 17-19. Adding a new field to the data structure.

ture for the ENTER_INVOICE screen was just built, move directly to the Screen Format Builder by choosing Format from its Define menu (see Figure 17-21).

3.3.1   Screen Formats

When the Screen Format Builder is entered, the data structure of the screen appears in the reference window (see Figure 17-22). Now click on the desired field in the data structure, and then click on the location in the active window where the field is to be placed.

If one uses the Copy Text icon ⬆xxx , MicroSTEP copies the name of the group or field selected from the structure in the reference window. If the Copy

Figure 17-20. Completed data structure for ENTER_INVOICE screen activity.

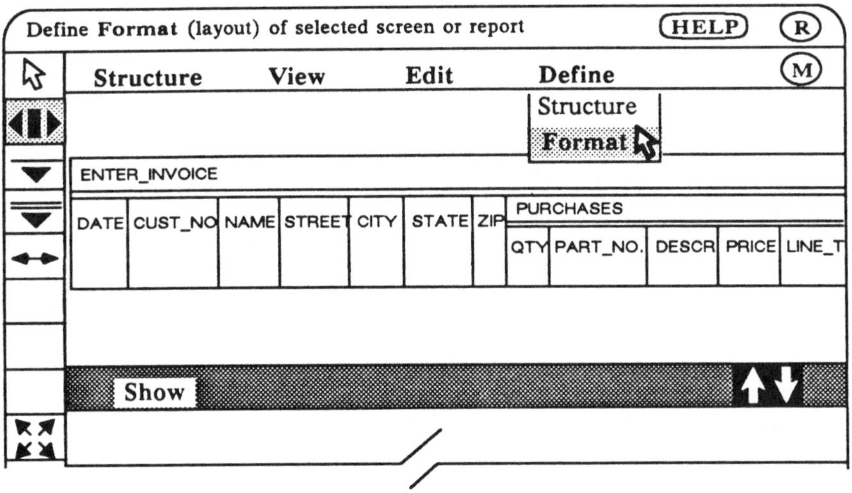

Figure 17-21. Choosing Format from the Define menu to enter the Screen Format Builder.

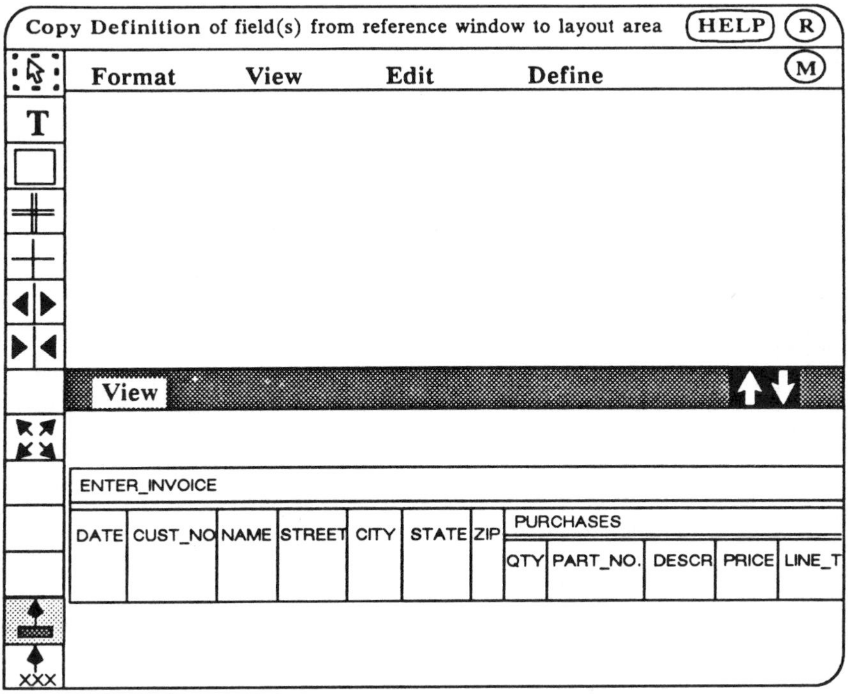

Figure 17-22. Screen Format Builder.

Definition icon ![icon] is used, MicroSTEP copies the definition of the field—type of data, number of characters, and its picture format. From the Flow Diagram Builder, one can choose a command to set default picture formats for display dates, time, decimals, integers, long integers, reals, and long reals. One can also select the currency symbol wanted to display in the generated application, whether a dash (-) or a slash (/) should separate the data components, and whether the integer/decimal separator is a comma/period (9,999.99) or period/comma (9.999,99). This allows one to define the most common formats for displaying different types of data but, of course, one can select any individual field on a particular screen or report and change its display format as appropriate.

One can enter background text or edit text copied with the ![icon] icon by selecting the **T** icon and then clicking to place the cursor, draw boxes by selecting the ☐ icon, or draw vertical or horizontal single or double lines by selecting the ┼ or the ╬ icons. Figure 17-23 shows how the author has used the **T** icon to lay out the background text INVOICE, Customer No., Date, Name, and Address and the Copy Definition ![icon] icon to copy the field information from the data structure to the active window.

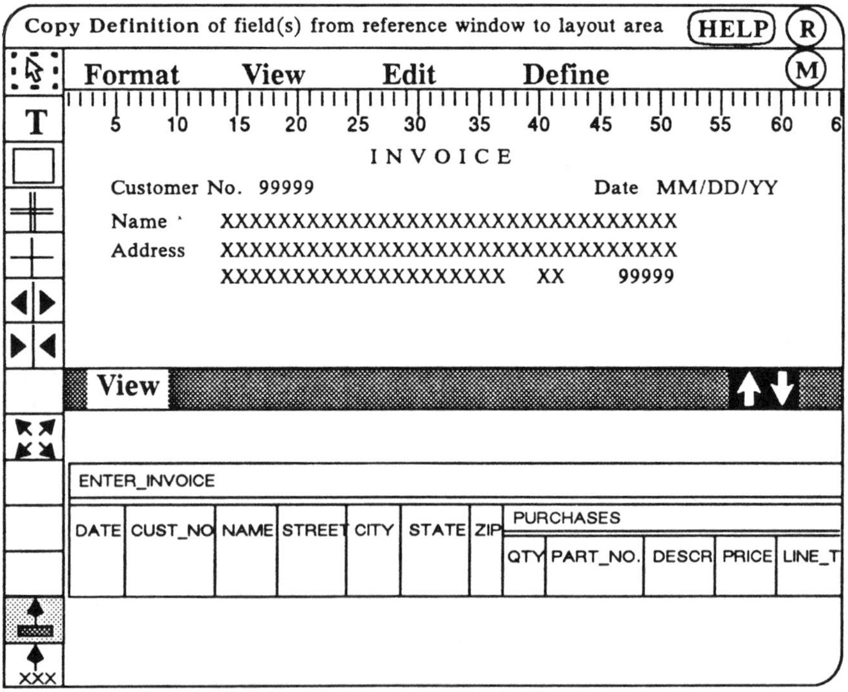

Figure 17-23. Laying out text and field information for INVOICE__ENTRY.

The display format for both the CUST_NO and the ZIP fields were defined as integer fields, so their display format is five 9's. The NAME and STREET fields were defined as text fields with 32 characters, so their display format is 32 X's. Likewise, the CITY and STATE fields were defined as 20 and 2 characters of text, respectively.

MicroSTEP helps one lay out the format by snapping the information—background text, graphics, or field definitions—to character position. Notice that there is also a ruler to help position the information in specific columns. However, it is very easy to select information and move it on the screen until its position is satisfied.

When the user places repeating groups of fields in the format of a screen, MicroSTEP places a single line on the screen. One then selects the group and chooses Resize from the Edit menu. A dotted outline of the group moves down as one moves the mouse pointer down (see Figure 17-24).

Releasing the mouse pointer determines how many lines of data the user will see on the screen at one time when the generated application is run. Three lines of data were chosen to display at one time and a box was drawn around the group so the user would know that this is a scroll window. When the generated

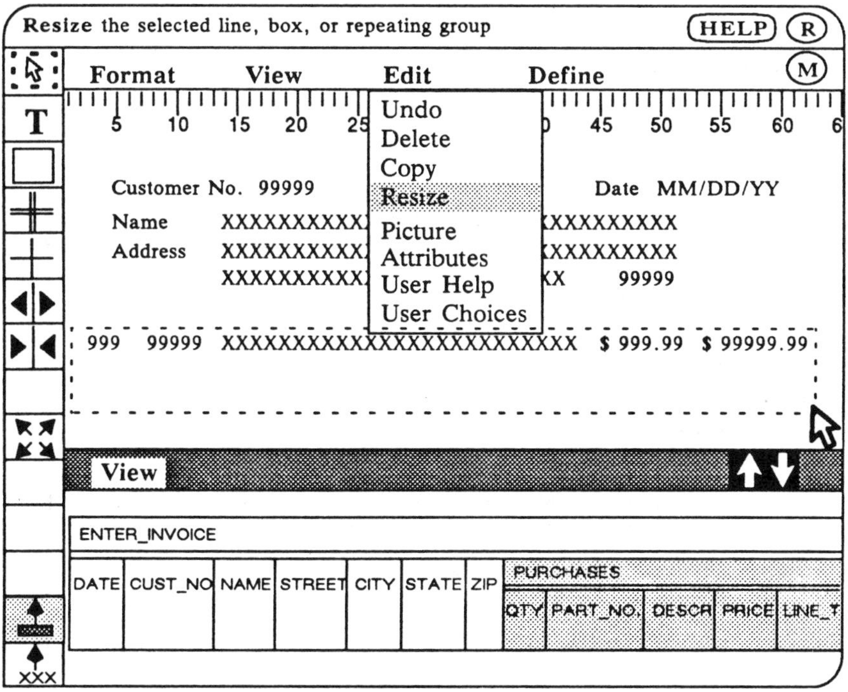

Figure 17-24. Resizing a repeating group of fields.

Draw Rectangle – click, then drag diagonally   (HELP)   (R)

Format   View   Edit   Define   (M)

| | 5   10   15   20   25   30   35   40   45   50   55   60 |

T

I N V O I C E

Customer No. 99999   Date MM/DD/YY

Name   XXXXXXXXXXXXXXXXXXXXXXXXXXXXXXXXX

Address   XXXXXXXXXXXXXXXXXXXXXXXXXXXXXXXXX
            XXXXXXXXXXXXXXXXXXXX XX   99999

99999	XXXXXXXXXXXXXXXXXXXXXXXXX	$ 999.99	$ 99999.99
99999	XXXXXXXXXXXXXXXXXXXXXXXXX	$ 999.99	$ 99999.99
99999	XXXXXXXXXXXXXXXXXXXXXXXXX	$ 999.99	$ 99999.99

Figure 17-25. Drawing a box around the repeating groups to indicate scroll window.

application is run, the information in this window will scroll upwards if the customer has more than three purchases (see Figure 17-25).

MicroSTEP also lets the user select any data entry field and specify how the data should be justified and displayed on the screen. The user can choose to have the data justified to the left or right, centered within the field area, and to

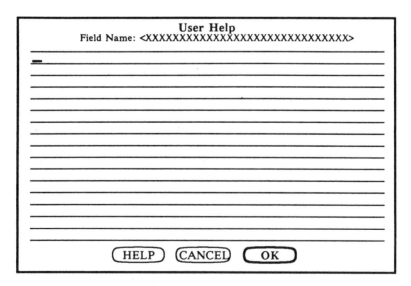

Figure 17-26. Dialog box for entering Help text.

have it underlined, displayed in reverse video, or not displayed at all (such as for entering a password). With any of the display options, it is possible to have the data blink or appear brighter than normal.

To provide Help text for the generated application, the user just selects a field and chooses User Help from the Edit menu. MicroSTEP displays a dialog box in which the user can enter up to 1 kilobyte (about 1023 characters) of text in any format (see Figure 17-26).

When the application is run, and the cursor is positioned in the field, the user can press F1 (or any key specified for displaying Help) to display the Help text entered for that field.

For any text field, the user can enter up to 10 choices that will display when the generated application is run (see Figure 17-27). For example, the user might have a field for entering an employee's sex, with the options Male and Female. The user would be able to toggle between these choices and, when the appropriate one is highlighted, accept it. This can help ensure correct data entry, when there is a limited number of valid responses.

3.3.2   Report Formats

Reports are laid out in a similar manner to screens. However, the Report Format Builder has some additional commands that allow the user to specify headers and footers for each page, for the body of the report, and for each repeating group of data. Figure 17-28 shows the Report Format Builder screen. It has the

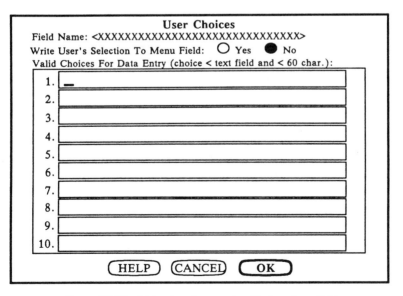

Figure 17-27. Dialog box for entering Choices for a field.

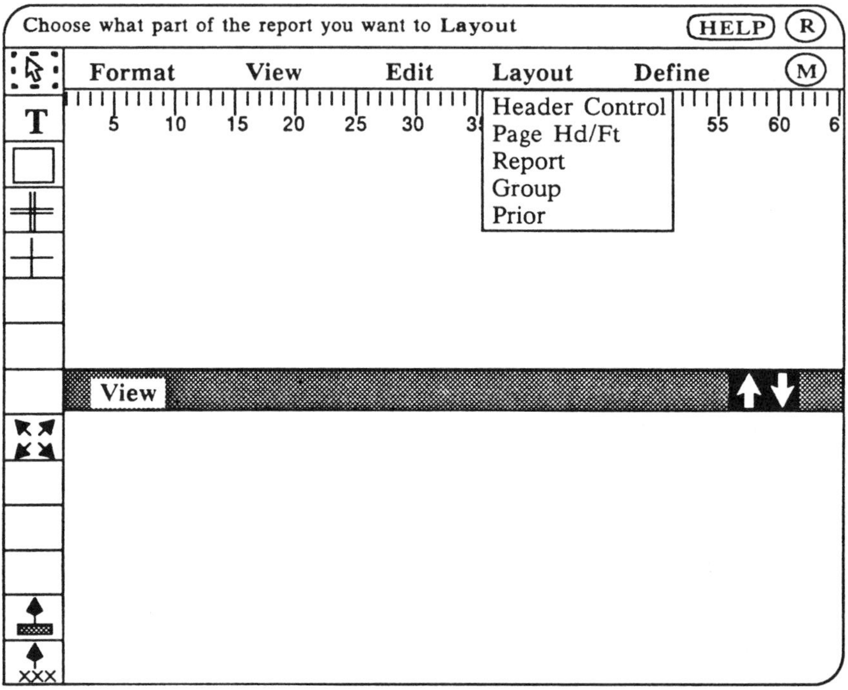

Figure 17-28. Report Format Builder.

same icons as the Screen Format Builder, letting one enter and edit text, draw boxes and lines, and copy field names and field definitions from the reference window to the active window. The Report Format Builder also has a Layout menu, with commands for controlling when the headers print and whether one wants to design the format for the report body or for a repeating group of data.

For each report in the flow diagram, one specifies different parameters for the report width, page width, page length, top margin, bottom margin, and left and right margins. Reports can be designed that have a maximum of 254 columns, and the report width can be larger than the page width that the target printer uses. In this case, MicroSTEP automatically tilts the pages, printing them in sections that can be put together.

3.4   Defining Activities

The Activity Builder is where one defines the business logic of the application. This includes the following:

- how one wants to combine input data prior to its being processed;
- what information one wants to look up and display (screen activities only);

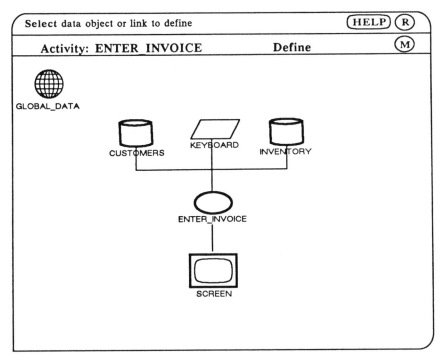

Figure 17-29. Main Activity Builder screen.

- how the fields in the output data are derived; and
- if one wants to filter any data as it flows from the input object through processing to the output data object.

The Activity Builder is entered by choosing a regular process icon ◯ or a screen activity icon from the flow diagram and choosing Activity from the Define menu. In MicroSTEP, an activity is defined as a process with all of its associated input data objects and output data objects. Figure 17-29 shows how the ENTER_INVOICE screen activity appears in the Activity Builder.

MicroSTEP shows the ENTER_INVOICE activity in an "exploded" view; that is, the keyboard is shown along with the input from the CUSTOMERS and INVENTORY data bases, and the screen is shown as the output. This allows one to visualize the details of the activity and also allows one to select the precise point at which data can be filtered. For example, you can filter data from either the CUSTOMERS or INVENTORY data base tables, or you can filter data from all of the input prior to it being processed.

Consider how one would specify that the application will look up the customer's name and address from the CUSTOMERS data base after the user enters a

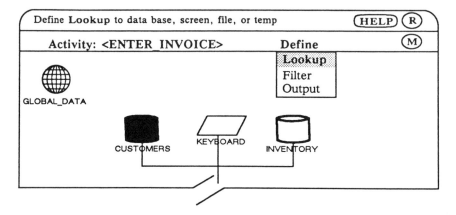

Figure 17-30. Selecting the Define-Lookup command.

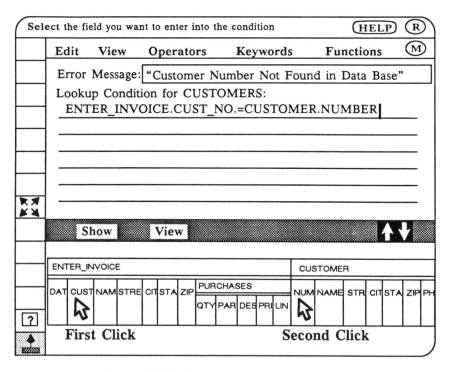

Figure 17-31. Specifying the Lookup condition.

customer number. First select the CUSTOMERS data base icon and then choose Lookup from the Define menu as shown in Figure 17-30.

In Figure 17-31, MicroSTEP displays the combined data structures for the ENTER_INVOICE screen activity and the CUSTOMERS data base table in the reference window. One can use any of the fields from this combined data structure, or fields from the GLOBAL_DATA data structure, to create the lookup condition. However, one needs to use fully qualified names when entering conditions and expressions. A fully qualified name is the name of the data structure (data object name) followed by the name of any higher-level groups, if appropriate, and then the field name. For example, if the data object name is CUSTOMERs, the group name ADDRESS, and the field name STREET, the fully qualified name would be CUSTOMERS. ADDRESS.STREET. Instead of entering names from the keyboard, just use the 👆 icon to click on the fields to use in the condition; MicroSTEP will enter the fully qualified name at the location of the cursor in the active window.

The Operators, Keywords, and Functions menus provide an easy way to enter the entire condition using the mouse. After one clicked on the CUST_NO. field of the ENTER_INVOICE portion of the data structure, he/she just pulled down the Operators menu and selected the equal sign, and then clicked on the NUMBER field of the CUSTOMER portion of the data structure to complete the condition expression. This Lookup condition tells MicroSTEP to generate an application in which the Customer Number entered from the keyboard is looked for in the Customer data base table and, if it is not found, to display the error message "Customer Number Not Found in Data Base." Now look at how

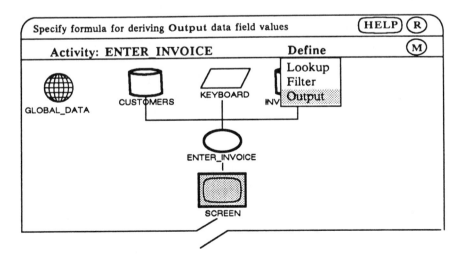

Figure 17-32. Defining Output operations.

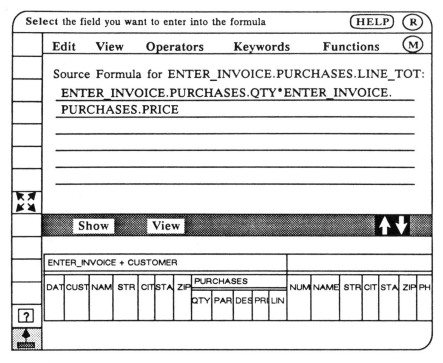

Figure 17-33. Specifying source formulas.

to specify that one wants to calculate a field. First select the screen data object, and choose Output from the Define menu (see Figure 17-32).

MicroSTEP displays the data structure of the ENTER_INVOICE activity and one would click on the LINE_TOT field to indicate that one wants to define the source formula for that field. The next screen that displays lets one enter the formula. When the user enters a quantity and part number, the generated application calculates the line total by multiplying the quantity to the unit price. This is defined by the expression shown in Figure 17-33,

There are a host of other functions available for specifying the business logic of the application. In addition to providing a rich collection of numeric, scientific, and string functions for specifying calculations, MicroSTEP allows one to import functions coded in a high-level language and use them in the specification. And one has many options for matching and merging data, sorting data, and filtering data.

3.5   Generating the Application

Once one has provided MicroSTEP with a complete specification, he/she is ready to generate the executable application. At this point, MicroSTEP will

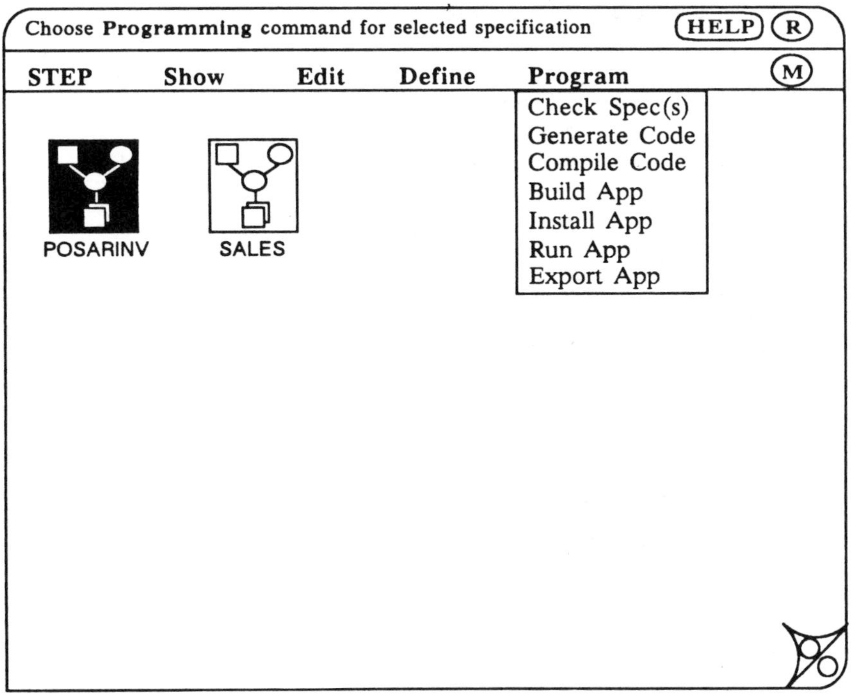

Figure 17-34. Generating the application from Top STEP.

actually write the code from your graphic specification. One chooses commands and the Program menu at Top STEP (see Figure 17-34) to check the specification, build the application, and install it on the appropriate computer.

Notice the two icons that represent the specifications discussed in this chapter. POSARINV is the high-level specification that presents the master menu and then calls the module that corresponds to the user's choice. The module that was examined in detail is the SALES specification. If one selects a specification that calls other specifications, MicroSTEP automatically checks, generates, compiles, builds, or installs the selected specification and any specifications it calls. In this example, choosing the POSARINV specification will also check, generate, compile, build, and install the SALES module. However, one can choose a lower-level specification (one called by another), and execute the Program commands just for that specification.

The commands on the Program menu need to be performed in the order they are listed. For example, one cannot compile code that has not been generated. But any of the commands can be chosen and, if the prerequisite commands have not been executed, Microstep will automatically invoke them.

3.5.1 Checking the Specification

The Check Spec(s) command checks the selected specification and any specification, it calls for consistency and completeness to make certain nothing is forgotten. One can perform this checking operation at any time during the specification process, correcting the errors as the flow diagram is created or activity definitions are specified.

If, for example, a definition is left out, MicroSTEP tells the user so he/she can correct the specification process rather than report it when trying to generate; some cannot be detected. For example, if a format was not specified for a screen or report, MicroSTEP will tell the user that a default layout will be used for that object when one checks the specification. Although one may want to use the default layout, this provides a reminder in case one just forgot to specify the format.

3.5.2 Generating Code

When the Generate Code command is executed, MicroSTEP generated C source code for the specification(s).

3.5.3 Compiling Code

Executing the Compile code command compiles the generated C code.

3.5.4 Building the Application

The Build App command links the compiled code with the appropriate libraries and routines to create an executable application.

3.5.5 Installing the Application

One of MicroSTEP's most useful features is the ability to run the finished application in different environments. This lets the user build the application without having to know or worry about things, such as the specific names of files and data base tables, what kind of printer will be used (see Figure 17-35), what keys the user prefers to use the certain actions (see Figure 17-36), etc. The application can be installed before one distributes it to the end-user or the end-user can install it by typing a command at the DOS prompt prior to running the generated application. The installation routines are designed to run in character mode so the end-user does not need the MicroSTEP programs, graphics card, or mouse to perform the installation; instead one uses the arrow keys, Tab key, and Enter key to move the highlight bar and accepts the choices.

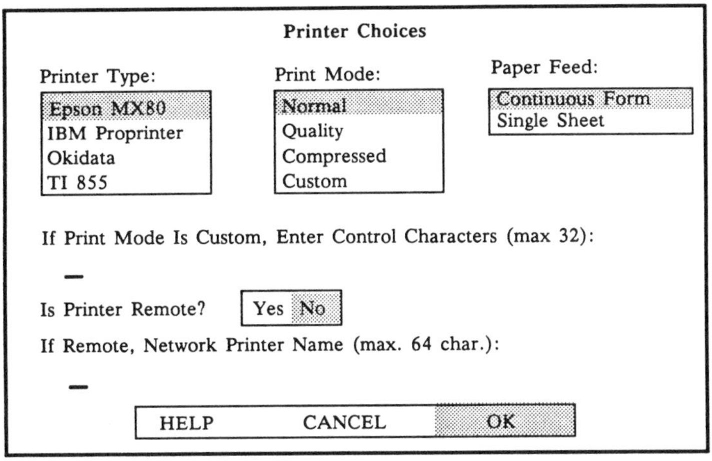

```
┌──────────────────────────────────────────────────────────────────┐
│                        Printer Choices                             │
│                                                                    │
│  Printer Type:       Print Mode:      Paper Feed:                  │
│  ┌──────────────┐   ┌──────────────┐ ┌──────────────────┐         │
│  │ Epson MX80   │   │ Normal       │ │ Continuous Form  │         │
│  │ IBM Proprinter│  │ Quality      │ │ Single Sheet     │         │
│  │ Okidata      │   │ Compressed   │ └──────────────────┘         │
│  │ TI 855       │   │ Custom       │                               │
│  └──────────────┘   └──────────────┘                               │
│                                                                    │
│  If Print Mode Is Custom, Enter Control Characters (max 32):       │
│                                                                    │
│  ▬                                                                 │
│                                                                    │
│  Is Printer Remote?   ┌───────────┐                                │
│                       │ Yes │ No  │                                │
│                       └───────────┘                                │
│  If Remote, Network Printer Name (max. 64 char.):                  │
│                                                                    │
│  ▬                                                                 │
│         ┌──────────────────────────────────────────┐              │
│         │  HELP        CANCEL         OK            │              │
│         └──────────────────────────────────────────┘              │
└──────────────────────────────────────────────────────────────────┘
```

Figure 17-35.   Printer Choices available at installation.

3.5.6   Running the Application

The Run App command runs the generated application so one can verify that it meets the users' needs. This command is provided for convenience, allowing one to test the generated application without exiting from MicroSTEP and to return to the MicroSTEP environment when through.

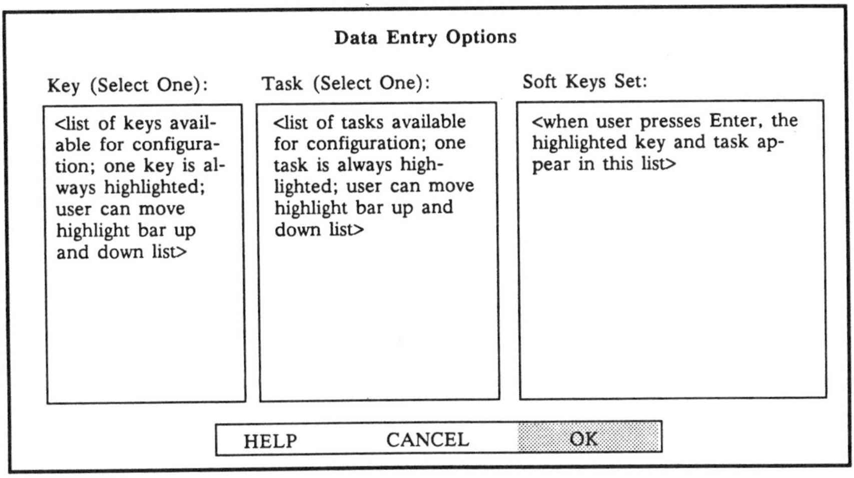

```
┌──────────────────────────────────────────────────────────────────┐
│                      Data Entry Options                            │
│                                                                    │
│  Key (Select One):      Task (Select One):      Soft Keys Set:     │
│  ┌──────────────┐      ┌──────────────┐      ┌──────────────────┐  │
│  │ <list of keys avail- │ <list of tasks available │ <when user presses Enter, the │
│  │ able for configura-  │ for configuration; one   │ highlighted key and task ap-  │
│  │ tion; one key is al- │ task is always high-     │ pear in this list>            │
│  │ ways highlighted;    │ lighted; user can move   │                               │
│  │ user can move        │ highlight bar up and     │                               │
│  │ highlight bar up     │ down list>               │                               │
│  │ and down list>       │                          │                               │
│  └──────────────┘      └──────────────┘      └──────────────────┘  │
│         ┌──────────────────────────────────────────┐              │
│         │  HELP        CANCEL         OK            │              │
│         └──────────────────────────────────────────┘              │
└──────────────────────────────────────────────────────────────────┘
```

Figure 17-36.   Configuring Soft Keys at installation.

4   CONCLUDING REMARKS

In this chapter only some of the features and functionality available with MicroSTEP for building business applications are presented. After seeing the task involved in specifying a small portion of a Point of Sales application, one might already be thinking of the applications one could build. Following are samples of the applications that MicroSTEP is most suited to build:

<table>
<tr><td>Financial</td><td>Administrative</td></tr>
<tr><td>General Ledger</td><td>Payroll</td></tr>
<tr><td>Accounts Payable</td><td>Personnel</td></tr>
<tr><td>Accounts Receivable</td><td>Registration</td></tr>
<tr><td>Billing</td><td>Claims Processing/Analysis</td></tr>
<tr><td>Budget Analysis/Reconciliation</td><td>Student Records Management</td></tr>
<tr><td>Estate Planning/Management</td><td>Contract Control</td></tr>
<tr><td>Loan Processing</td><td>Course Catalog</td></tr>
<tr><td>Bond Analysis</td><td>Travel</td></tr>
<tr><td>Brokerage Systems</td><td></td></tr>
<tr><td>Manufacturing</td><td>Sales and Marketing</td></tr>
<tr><td>Inventory Control</td><td>Sales Analysis/Management</td></tr>
<tr><td>Order Processing</td><td>Lead Tracking</td></tr>
<tr><td></td><td>Sales Forecasting</td></tr>
<tr><td></td><td>Trade Show Registration</td></tr>
<tr><td></td><td>Pricing</td></tr>
<tr><td></td><td>Customer Support</td></tr>
</table>

Part III

International Perspectives

In this part of the book the authors discuss some of the major software projects being developed around the world. Most of the research projects are centered around an integrated environment for CASE, and a system that supports the complete life cycle.

Chapter 18 by L. A. Belady, describes Leonardo—a computer-aided system development environment currently being developed at the Software Technology Program (STP) of Microelectronics and Computer Technology Corporation (MCC). The Chapter first introduces the organization of MCC and the research focus of STP. It then lists the major research efforts underway in STP that are laying the foundation for building Leonardo, specifically studying the possibilities of improving designs, developing a model that can capture the rationale behind design decisions, developing a HyperText system, building a prototype reuse system, developing a team based coordination system, and a language for representing the design of distributed systems. The Chapter concludes by detailing the lessons learned from these projects.

Chapter 19 by W. Royce, describes the two software development environments being developed at Lockheed's Software Technology Center. The first called AdaCraft, is an environment that integrates a set of tools around the Ada programming language semantics and aims to support the complete software development life cycle. The second called Express, is a knowledge-based code synthesis system based on REFINE and Macsyma (see Chapter 15), and the Symbolic workstations, which can produce an executable system from the specification. The Chapter presents a detailed description of the functions provided by the components of the systems.

Chapter 20 by H. L. Yudkin, describes the structure of the Software Productivity Consortium and its technical program. The Chapter details SPC's approach in software development and discusses how prototyping and reuse can be effectively used to increase productivity. It also explains the importance of library management, dynamics assessment, design, traceability, and synthesis.

Chapter 21 by F. Kamijo, introduces the Japan National Project—Sigma system—an integrated software environment. The Chapter describes the goals of the Sigma Project, the hardware architecture and software components of the Sigma system. The Chapter also provides a list of services and tools that are available in the system. It concludes by discussing the sigma application oriented tools for microprocessor based systems, scientific applications, business data processing, and process control systems.

Chapter 22 by W. Schafer and H. Weber, describe the conceptual basis of the European Software Factory (ESF). The Chapter begins by identifying the characteristics of a Software Production Environment (SPE) and claims that a software factory is an SPE that provides full coverage of the production process. The Chapter introduces the architecture of ESF as a multilevel reference model such that new tools can be plugged-in to the most suitable level of the model.

Chapter 23 by F. Sobrinho, describes the Brazilian Software Plant. It is a consortium aiming at creating an environment for the experimentation of research projects and the evaluation of research findings to provide high quality and production cost, to enable Brazil to be competitive with technologically advanced countries, such as the United States, Japan, Germany, and England. The Chapter describes and analyzes the goals, organization, policy, and implementation strategy of such a project, as well as reports on the status and experience learned from the project.

Chapter 24 by F. Liu et. al., describes two areas of software development in China. The Chapter discusses the history of development, establishment and goals of the Software Factory Plan in China, and the initial plan of a national Intelligent Computer System project.

Chapter 18:

Leonardo: The MCC Software Research Project

Laszlo A. Belady
Software Technology Program
Microelectronic and Computer Technology Corporation
Austin, TX

ABSTRACT

An industrial consortium in Austin, Texas, called MCC, is owned by nineteen major U.S. corporations. It conducts long term research in five areas: VLSI packaging, VLSI design, superconductivity, advanced computer architectures, and software technology. While each of the five programs strives for fundamental technological changes, the ultimate goal is to directly transfer usable technologies to the shareholders. To achieve this, the MCC staff built a strong and cooperative relationship with the development organizations of its owners. This results in the MCC consortium working on very important problems and testing and refining raw research results in the tough and realistic environment of the shareholders prior to full-scale use.

The Software Technology Program (STP) is mandated to significantly improve the productivity and quality of the upstream part of the large scale development process. Of particular interest is the design of distributed systems, because of the belief in the strong long term trend that causes isolated, although already complex applications to become integrated into increasingly larger networks. Clearly, in the resulting distributed systems the software is what holds the many hardware and software components together.[1,2]

Research at STP is organized into three cooperative parts. The first is dedicated to the study of the large scale, team based, design process as it is done in industry today—these empirical studies help find the highest payoff areas on which to focus research. The second group invents and develops specific tools to computer-aid development activities currently manually performed—examples are the structuring of early issues in the requirement phase and the reuse of design patterns. The third group is involved in the integration of tools into a common platform which provides a rich graphic user interface and access to an information base organized into shared objects.

The final goal of STP is to deliver the shareholder development organizations prototypes of a comprehensive computer-aided system design environment, called Leonardo. Leonardo contains many tools—either results of MCC research or imported—all supporting the coordinated efforts of customers and software engineers in their pursuit of the definition and design of complex, distributed systems.

1 MCC ORGANIZATION AND OPERATION

MCC is wholly owned by U.S. based corporations. Established in 1983 by eight companies, MCC now has nineteen shareholders. The shareholders are essentially the only source of funding for the research work, which is organized into the following five programs with focus on the design by teams of large, distributed (software) systems:

- Computer Aided Design (VLSI);
- Packaging/Interconnect;
- Superconductivity;
- Advanced Computer Architectures; and
- Software Technology.

Shareholders are free to choose and then support one or more of the programs. In fact, a different subset of shareholders forms the participant group for each of the programs so that each group consists of about six to ten shareholders.

MCC is organized as a flat hierarchy. The highest authority is the Board of Directors; each shareholder is represented on the Board by a senior executive. The Chairman of the Board is also the President of MCC and, thus its Chief Executive Officer (CEO). The first CEO was Ret. Admiral Bobby Ray Inman who played a key role in the site selection of Austin, Texas. The Admiral's reputation and contacts were important in establishing credibility for the new organization. He left MCC in 1986 and was succeeded by Grant Dove, the Executive Vice President in charge of research at Texas Instruments. There is a corporate staff of vice presidents for planning, finance and administration, human resources, and "chief scientist." This staff is small, since the bulk of the personnel is technical, organized into the five research programs mentioned with each headed by a vice president who is the program director. Under the program director, there is another line of management, usually filled by the directors. The organization was designed for low bureaucracy.

Another important characteristic of MCC is its strong and explicit emphasis on technology transfer. The measure of success is the value of MCC-delivered technologies applied to profit making processes in shareholder's shops. To assure success, technical people from shareholders and the MCC research staff must cooperate early in the research cycle. A Technical Advisory Board (TAB), consisting of senior technical representatives, one from each shareholder, helps the CEO guide MCCs research activities and strategic directions. The TAB meets four times a year and also periodically reviews plans and progress. In addition to the TAB, each program has a quarterly meeting with its Program Technical Advisory Committee (PTAC, called STAC for STP where S stands for Software), which has three to five representatives from each of the participating companies. These are people with strong technical backgrounds and involvement in actual development work in their home organization.

Further reinforcement of efficient transfer of research results comes from the liaisons. A liaison is a participant employee on full time assignment with an MCC program. A liaison may spend most of the time on research along with the other staff, but he or she also has another major role, being that of the agent involved with the increasingly intensive exchange of technical information, and in both directions, between the "receiver" organizations back home and the MCC research program. This combination of active research involvement and familiarity with the idiosyncracies of shareholder's internal processes and problems results in one of the great advantages of consortium based research.

Aside from liaisons, the majority of the technical staff has been hired from outside (i.e., academia and non-shareholder companies). All program directors fall into this category. The rest are "assignees": shareholder employees other than liaisons who, for a few years, do research at MCC. In the future, this assignee system may become extended to include shorter periods of stay with MCC, following the growing demands of the transfer of research results.

2 BEGINNINGS OF STP: MISSION, STRATEGY, AND STRUCTURE

Perhaps due to software always being late, the MCC Software Technology Program (STP) started one year later than the other three original programs—as late as January 1985. The program director appointed in late 1984 inherited only a terse message from earlier task forces formed by shareholder experts: mission—extraordinary increase in productivity of development and quality of software.

At this time, the staff was only a few liaisons and a secretary. On the other hand, there were a few strings attached: here is the money, hire the right people, and do the job. While this rarely found freedom looked wonderful, the task of building a high quality organization from scratch, forming a strategy, and constructing a plan seemed formidable.

The first act by the program director, who was previously employed at IBM, was to listen to the "customer." Accordingly, one or two software experts from each participant (at that time eight companies) were invited to Austin for a one day brainstorming session. It was important for the program director to find out whether earlier experience and, therefore, prejudices acquired while being with IBM, were valid in this new setting of a variety of companies in the computer manufacturing, defense contracting, and communications businesses. What was the common problem? What were the shared expectations? Would it be possible to please them all? One must remember, and this is as true today as it was four years ago, that MCC is a great experiment itself, and not all experience gathered elsewhere could be used to maximize its chances of success.

Since the original intent was to launch a sharply focused research effort in the huge software problem domain, the main purpose of the meeting was to help identify the focus. Additional guidance came from the consideration that MCC should exploit its being an industrial organization and should not mimic academia, and that its long term research goals be based on trends of other enabling technologies and of computer applications. Specifically for the software program, trends in hardware technology were also essential.

Rapidly, then, the following was decided:

* Focus: design by teams of large, distributed (software) systems.
* The important issues are design—large, distributed—and that "software" is in parentheses.[1]

In the following section, these issues are considered one by one.

Consider an industrial software project: it is essentially a time consuming and error prone process which must transform rather vague initial customer formulated requirements to the bits and bytes representation necessary for machine interpretation, as indicated by the heavy horizontal line in Figure 18-1. In this Figure, the vertical dotted line, labeled as "blueprint," represents the point at which the project team succeeds in formalizing to some degree the requirements. The "downstream," which starts with this more or less precise specification of the program-to-be, is generally well understood, partly automated, and greatly computer-aided. Computer science research focuses exclusively on this downstream and has already achieved solid results in programming methodology. This helped individuals write quality programs out of well formed specifications. In fact, it is possible that the entire downstream set of activities will be eventually automated, i.e. computer generated.

This is not the case with the upstream activities, which have remained essentially computer unaided. The upstream consists of designing a system of hardware and software functions, which together fulfill the initially vague but gradually certain requirements, with the help of insight gained by examining alternate design solutions.[9] Starting with the dialogue between developer and customer, emphasis is on design, an activity which, judged from the experience gained in other disciplines, should always remain a creative and profoundly human activity—not machinable—but being non-automatable does not necessarily mean not machine supportable. Yet little if any progress in computer aiding the upstream design processes of large projects was made, which explains why most studies of software development concluded that the bulk of total cost

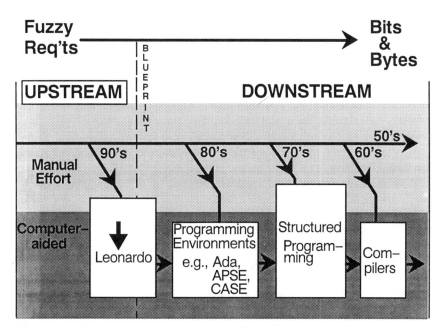

Figure 18-1. Leonardo's role in aiding upstream design efforts.

lies in the upstream.[41] This means that even if the downstream becomes completely automated and thus its cost reduced to zero, total productivity will not even double.

Another important aspect of the upstream is that, again from industry investigations, the really serious and difficult-to-fix software faults are known to come from bad or misunderstood design. Moreover, the impact of design on quality is even greater if the costs of system evolution and maintenance are included: first, the real expensive errors are those made in design; secondly, the cost of finding any error and of the resulting modifications is much higher in badly designed, intertwined software systems.[12]

Consider the "largeness" of software. By this is meant not only the size and complexity of the product but even more importantly the complexity of the process which produces it. This is why large programs must be built by teams or organizations sometimes as large as hundreds of people. Clearly, the computer science model of the solitary programmer writing programs out of precise specifications fails to reflect the reality of industrial software development. In fact, productivity and quality are more related to interpersonal communication, team coordination and the ability to design the system well than to the programming performance of individuals.[8,9,10]

There have been many large complex programs produced in the past: for example, mainframe operating and electronic switching systems. However, most of these have been implemented on single machines. It is believed that in the near future very complex but different types of systems will have to be built as illustrated by the following scenario.

Computer applications developed during the past few decades have been relatively small and developed and operated independently. Nevertheless, the trend has always been the gradual integration of stand-alone applications into larger, common data based software systems. Recently, at many major corporations there is a trend to hook up computer installations and through them a variety of applications into large networks. Moreover, as hardware becomes increasingly cheap—thanks to the microprocessor revolution—new corporate-wide application systems will soon be designed by interconnecting hardware and software capabilities, and thus gradually replacing mainframe computers; most importantly, what "holds" the pieces together is software.

Building large software programs is already difficult enough: add now the extra complexity presented by distributed, asynchronously running systems. Who will build them, and how many software engineers will be needed? The objective is to map all currently manual functions, which all major corporations want to computerize, during the next decades, onto the interconnected set of workstations and other devices. Clearly, without technology to computer-aid the design process this immense task is not possible, yet most computer science research is compartmentalized, such that you either focus on the properties of distributed systems and study parallelism, or are a software engineering scientist, assuming that all programs, even large ones, are always written for single processors. The two subcultures do not even talk to each other! This is why MCC wants to combine the two in STP.

The last issue in focus is that computer-aiding the upstream of software development is at the same time helping the upstream of computer hardware design. As "their" downstream becomes increasingly automated (logic design, circuit placement, etc.) and the number of gates and thus functions on a chip keep increasing, the problem shifts as in softwareland to system design. Design is basically the art and science of making choices from among alternatives based on the analysis of system-wide impact of these choices. It is believed that in the upstream of both software and hardware design the decision of whether a particular system component should be software or be burnt-in silicon will be simply one of the many design decisions. If one succeeds in devising good technology for the upstream of the software process, then the technology will be useful with little change to support the development of any complex system.

Structure

After having sharpened the focus, research policies had to be set. It was thought that these policies should be based on the characteristics of the consortium, exploiting its advantages but also taking into account its limitations. The following was soon decided: the research must be problem driven, its results must form a coherent whole, long term goals must be combined with quick spin-offs, and research must have a healthy empirical component.

The outstanding goal is to improve shareholder's software productivity and quality and not just to develop solutions looking for a problem. Solutions to the stated problem may come from the outside in the form of ideas or prototypes, even products, but some must be developed by MCC because no related effort is being developed. "Not invented here" is banned in STP: it is necessary to rely as much as one can on any excellent results coming from academic or other research institutions, yet it now seems there is probably still more research to do than 50 professionals can handle; even the focused problem domain is very large while its world-wide research coverage is sparse. This is why MCC's research ambition is eventually to establish, and thus become, the world center of the "computer science of the upstream." Part of their results will be the integration of the original results and imported solutions, refined and applied to shareholder problems. This is what is meant by being problem driven.

A group of 50 researchers cannot work on a single problem, because as research progresses, activities become naturally diversified. The resulting technologies make sense by themselves, as individual tools, methods, or subsystems. In fact many organizations, including other programs of MCC, choose to have independent groups producing stand-alone technologies. It was decided to go beyond just a collection of technologies and, rather, spend extra effort on integrating these technologies—whether created by us or imported— into a whole. At MCC, the goal is to deliver to the shareholders the prototypes of a design environment in which individual tools make even more sense together. Figure 18-2 shows the research flow in STP, and how the resources are allocated for the main groups of activities.

MCC is a long term, industrial research organization by design. This does not mean, however, that the waiting time for any result is equally long term. It does mean, though, that instead of working on today's, or even worse, yesterday's problems, MCC must have a long term vision of how the world will look, for example, in ten years when the impact of its research is expected to be strongest. Then, as the work gains momentum toward the long term goal, the continuous flow of by-products of research cannot be stopped, which comes naturally as every seasoned research manager knows from experience. Those at MCC are, therefore, determined to keep focusing on the future, but whenever a potential spin-off emerges and is needed by a shareholder, it is packaged for immediate transfer. In fact, this seems to be the right policy from the viewpoint of the global market where success is tied to the rapidity with which ideas are converted into usable technologies.

One of the advantages of industrial research is the closeness to the "development atmosphere" and the easy access to the development shops—its market. This advantage must be exploited in at least two ways. First, research itself needs a reasonable set of requirements, coming from the "customer." Simply

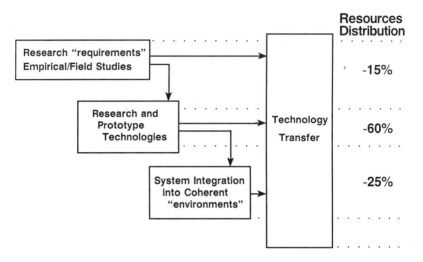

Figure 18-2. STP's research flow and allocation of technical resources.

put, the way software is designed today must be studied if its future is to improve. The study then provides a better understanding of the problems shared by researchers and developers, serving as an excellent preparation for the subsequent transfer of results. Secondly, the initial results of research done in isolation are usually not fully developed and require scaling-up and refinement. This is best done while testing new technologies in the realistic environments of the shareholders. The benefit is thus twofold: understand problem detail, and sharpen tentative solutions.

In the next section, consider how these preliminary efforts led to the outline of an integrated design support environment for the team development of distributed systems.

3   THE EMERGENCE OF LEONARDO

To achieve the extraordinary improvements in software productivity and quality demanded by STP's shareholders, one must introduce revolutionary changes in the methods of large scale software development. For instance, the traditional waterfall model, i.e., the development of software using an assembly-line approach of distinct phases, would certainly not be the appropriate foundation for this research. What then would be the right paradigm of future software development? Can one design, out of unknown components whose supporting research is just about starting, a new development environment? Those at MCC thought not, since research is not the same as development in which many of the technological uncertainties must be resolved prior to overall design.

As stated before, it is also strongly believed that all effort must result in technologies that are not only powerful individually but also make sense in combination with each other. The order is important: first the pieces then integration, because research is basically a bottom up activity, exploring in depth many alternate avenues before choosing one of general validity.[17] Also, early phases of research must be conducted by individuals or small teams; in a larger organization this means concurrent work of more or less unrelated activities, unlike coordinated system development. How does one keep STP research revolutionary and at the same time coherent and converging?

A rather unusual approach, used at MCC, is to let small groups be involved in what is called "component research": examples are the search for better ways of representing and processing issues as they emerge during the early phases of software projects, or the investigation of languages for the design of distributed systems.[8,11] However, MCC personnel also want to spend resources on outlining a framework into which all the technologies, fruits of the component research, ultimately fit. This integration activity serves not only as an "architecture" of a computer-aided environment to help design distributed software systems but also to hold together and help converge the individual research projects. It is believed that without the benefit of this direct experience, STP would eventually fall back to an academic mode in which individual professors with a small staff of everchanging graduate students work essentially independent of each other.

Discussed was both the focused, integrated research effort, and its ultimate manifestation as a coherent computer-aided system development environment, Leonardo. It was thought that Leonardo himself was an early "system man" who could imagine and design solutions out of a variety of components. At the same time the researchers wanted to emphasize that the upstream of software development is as much an engineering activity as it is an art—Leonardo da Vinci was both an engineer and an artist. Leonardo is also an acronym: Low Cost Exploration Offered by the Network Approach to Requirement and Design Optimization.

At present, instead of working toward a comprehensive Leonardo architecture, researchers are integrating research components into a platform called the Design Environment for Leonardo Investigators, Implementors, and Integrators (DELI).[19] The structure and functionality of DELI is described in the following section on System Integration. Listed are some of the major research activities currently underway in STP which are laying the foundation for building Leonardo. Figure 18-1 showed the role of Leonardo in the upstream region of the software design process.

4 SYSTEM INTEGRATION[19]

In 1988, STP researcher's objective has been to define DELI. DELI is a platform built in Common Lisp and network resource tools. It enables STP researchers to work and communicate effectively in a teamwork environment.

The purpose of DELI is to expedite research into the upstream of system development, specifically to increase the following:

1. Efficiency—by enhancing the productivity of prototyping;
2. Synergy—by enhancing the reusability of research results; and
3. Transferability—through easing the process of technology transfer.

DELI will be a computational platform for investigators, permitting rapid prototyping, exploration, and testing of potential Leonardo component packages. For implementors, it will provide for smooth migration of proven component technologies into an evolving, unified Leonardo prototype. For the shareholders, DELI will be a platform for seamless integration of other (non-MCC) products and tools, including those used in downstream development activities.[19]

In summary, DELI will be an apprentice to investigators, a workbench to implementors of new tools and technologies, and a framework to integrators of outside products and research prototypes. Since DELI is the environment that researchers will use to build Leonardo, one can say that DELI itself will evolve into a precursor of Leonardo and eventually into the ultimate system itself.

DELI-88 is designed as a layered system with the following major components:

- Engine layer;
- Language layer;
- DELI layer, and
- Research prototype layer

Each of these layers is associated with a number of attributes. For example, the DELI engine layer is designed to run on a number of networked UNIX[1] workstations. The DELI language layer includes network protocols, such as TCP/IP and the window servers. Finally, at the very top level will be the integrated research prototypes developed by STP such as our issue-based tools. Figure 18-3 shows the relationship of the major software components of DELI.

The Engine Layer—or DELI's machine environment, evolved in 1987 from a mix of Sun workstations and Symbolics Lisp machines to a uniform networked Sun environment. The Sun environment improved over the year in both hardware and the available Common Lisp tools. This improvement led to the decision to make the Sun the main hardware engine.

The Language Layer—comprises imported software that has been integrated into the DELI environment through the development of interfaces. The current

---

[1]UNIX is a registered trademark of AT&T.

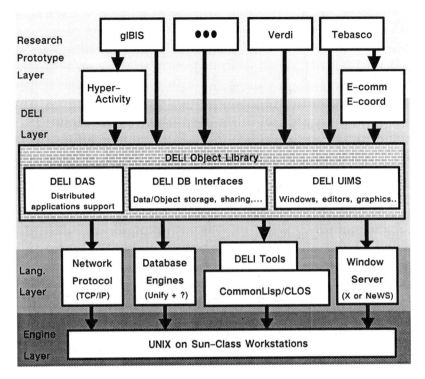

Figure 18-3. The DELI design environment.

list of imported software consists of the X.10 window system from MIT, the Network-extensible Window System (NeWS) from Sun, the public domain GNU Emacs editor, the Unify/Simplify relational data base from Sun, and the UNIX TCP/IP communications protocol.

DELI Layer—is the central part of the DELI architecture. It features internally developed software designed and implemented using an object-oriented paradigm. Its primary goal is to provide DELI applications and developers with a library of classes and methods.

Research Prototype Layer—finally, the Research Prototype Layer, which consists of applications built on and usable in the DELI environment, includes a graphical Issue Based Information System (gIBIS), a distributed systems modeling tool (Verdi), a TEam BASed COordination system (Tebasco), and an Electronic Communication and Coordination (ECC) system. The issue-based system, gIBIS, is currently being developed as the first DELI prototype and will be delivered as part of DELI. gIBIS will be built on top of G-Star (g*), a DELI Hypertext system. ECC is envisioned as a platform for electronic communication. It will provide electronic mail, electronic news, and electronic calendar functions.

4.1   Empirical Studies[17]

The Empirical Studies activity collects data on how design is done to determine where there is the greatest leverage to improve it. The main research of the Empirical Studies activity is in the area of design expertise. The Design Expertise study will assist in the development of workable design tools and environments for Leonardo. Specifically, researchers expect to identify specialized knowledge and design heuristics of skilled designers, such as the following:

- Engineered for use in Leonardo (e.g., in the information base, for intelligent design tools).
- Used to determine what type of tools and environment would best support skilled designers to maximize the benefits from their talents.
- Used to determine what type of training, tools, and environment would elevate the skill of all designers.

In particular, research is being conducted on how superior designers decide to allocate their resources, especially time, to the various activities during design—how designers control their design process. The researchers intend to identify any special heuristics that superior designers possess.

The major goal of the Empirical Studies activity is to explore in collaboration with other STP design groups how the study results can be brought to bear on issues within the technical community.

4.2   HyperText[5,16]

HyperText is an information representation and management system built around a network of multimedia nodes connected together by links. Access is by navigating (i.e., following links) through the network aided by a structural overview.[5,16] From the beginning of the Program, it was realized that a HyperText activity would be important if a distributed set of tools were built which were capable of handling representations of information from the standpoint of multiple views. It was for this reason, that a HyperText system, called PlaneText, was prototyped in 1985. The original version of PlaneText was written in an object-oriented extension of Prolog known as BiggerTalk. Later, in the spring of 1987, a C version of PlaneText was released to the shareholders with a follow-on version in mid 1988.

Hypermedia lies at an interesting intersection of relational data bases, object-oriented information storage and retrieval systems, knowledge representation, and user interface management systems. HyperText is informal knowledge representation used for organizing and manipulating large amounts of irregularly structured information. Figure 18-4 shows the relationship of HyperText representation on the scale from informal to formal.

Figure 18-4. Scale of informal-to-formal representations.

Currently, there are several research projects underway, such as at Brown University (Intermedia), Tektronix Labs (Neptune), and Xerox PARC (NoteCards). There are also some commercially available HyperText-like systems; the most recent announcement being HyperCard on the Macintosh. The architecture of the current generation systems has a number of fundamental limitations that must be resolved in the next generation, such as search and query, composite nodes (structures), virtual structures, computation, versioning, collaborative work, and extensibility and tailorability. It is on the basis of these issues that HyperText research in STP will be continuing.

4.3   Formalizing the Informal (Cellini and gIBIS)[6]

The informal-to-formal activity seeks to develop radically improved methods for developing and capturing the rationale behind design decisions and to support these methods with the appropriate tools. Researchers are interested in early requirements formulation and specification. A model, Cellini, is being developed to accommodate the gradual formalization of system and domain knowledge and the validation of system and environment properties. This model will be based on partial mappings between representations of increasing formality and the exploration of alternate mappings. The result is a representation of the reasoning behind the decisions made in the design to guide further design decisions and to aid the traceability of requirements into the final code.

Making reasonable process assumptions is a significant part of the proposed research and will be based on perceived strengths and weaknesses of current industrial practice among the shareholder organizations. Prototype tools will be implemented to support the capture, display, analysis, modification, and transformation of domain information, requirements, and early design artifacts. Empirical evidence will be gathered concerning the usefulness of the model, methods, and tools. It is also intended that the languages, representations, and prescriptive steps developed be compatible with problem formulation and design strategies identified during the Design Expertise study.

One of the tools under development is the Design Journal, an extension to some basic ideas about issue-based information systems, such as gIBIS.[6] In the near-term, the Design Journal has the following properties:

- Deliberation support for synthesis-oriented methods.
- The design of systems larger than text formatters.

- Constructive design, as opposed to *post hoc* vivisection.
- The design of reactive, as opposed to transformational, systems.

4.4 Design Reuse (ROSE)[3,4,18]

In the area of information reusability, the approach is to build an initial prototype reuse system, ROSE, based on the technology of IDeA and Software Templates. The front end of ROSE reuses software designs expressed in terms of data flow diagrams. It finds specified components based on diagram topology, type constraints, and other criteria. The back end of Rose reuses abstract algorithms. By combining an abstract algorithm with a variety of implementation decisions (e.g., implementation types), a wide variety of customized algorithms can be generated from a single abstract algorithmic seed.

The next generation of reuse systems will be more general than ROSE in that they will handle other representations in addition to data flow diagrams. They will also include a substantial effort aimed at creating reusable components through design recovery (a generalization and extension of the notion of *reverse engineering*) from existing implementations. It is expected that design recovery is to be a major means to populate the reuse library.

What is a design recovery system? Such a system produces abstract design schemas and software templates for the reuse library but, in addition, it produces design artifacts that help developers and maintainers understand the nature, structure, and behavior of an existing software system.

Design recovery must depend on many sources in addition to the source code, including interpretations from an intelligent designer/analyst.[18] An ideal design recovery system must be able to recognize the existence of these conceptual abstractions (perhaps with help from an intelligent user) and establish the associations between them and corresponding elements in the other domains. This work is critically important to solving the problem of populating the reuse library.

4.5 Distributed Systems (Raddle)[11]

The Distributed Systems activity has been based on an improved version of the Raddle language—a language for representing the design of distributed processes. Researchers at STP have used Raddle in several experimental applications and proved its usefulness. One particularly interesting application was the design of an electronic funds transfer system, undertaken with the assistance of one of our shareholders. Our experience in these experiments led to some modifications to the original language, such as the addition of choice and sequence operators. More applications will be undertaken in the future, and additional features to Raddle are expected to be added, such as fault tolerance constructs, and the ability to superimpose two distinct but complementary

Raddle designs. Developing a formal, transformation-based design method is also expected for Raddle.

A second important theoretical advance in Distributed Systems has been the formalization of the notion of superimposition, which allows the formal combination of two separate computational structures into a new single process that performs the computation of both in a unified manner. This idea simplifies the design of complex processes by allowing separate portions of the computation first to be derived independently and then combined in a formal way that preserves the computational objectives of both.

4.6   Visualization (Verdi)[13,14,15]

As a tool in the Distributed Systems research, Verdi was developed as a visual programming environment for Raddle. Verdi permits the user to design distributed systems using a graphical form of Raddle; Verdi also has support for the animation of designs. Verdi is being employed in the design of two real-world distributed applications provided by the shareholders. As new features are added to Raddle, similar functionality to Verdi is also expected to be added.

Verdi was ported from Prolog to Common Lisp and C, and was redesigned to make use of object-oriented concepts. The Verdi editor was enhanced so that it supported a much larger proportion of Raddle, and computer-assisted layout of designs was added. Finally, Verdi was modified to generate a standard internal form shared by other Raddle tools and has evolved to include a greatly improved human interface.

4.7   Coordination Technology[10]

The Coordination Systems activity aims at developing a Coordination System that does the following:

- is fundamentally designed to support the concurrent and coordinated behavior of interrelated organizational tasks, resources and people;
- supplies a uniform and powerful means to establish desired patterns of coordination among design tasks and teams; and
- is subject to on-going adaptable restructuring that is prevalent in any organization.

The Coordination Systems activity is an outgrowth of the work in distributed systems. Therefore, the fundamental approach is based upon the Raddle distributed systems work. Researchers find that the N-party interaction concepts in Raddle encompass both the communication and coordination among the parties involved. Furthermore, these concepts are captured at a sufficiently high level of abstraction so that they can be exploited for coordinating the activities of a design team. To be useful, coordination must be done in a flexible yet integrated manner, with tolerance for unpredictabilities of real life. At STP, the use of graphical languages and highly interactive techniques yields the desired level of flexibility in manipulation of environment artifacts. In the near future, it is intended to extend the use of the prototype to Program-wide applications.[7] The experience gained from such wide use will add to efforts in building a coordination environment integrated within the research platform. In addition, researchers will concentrate on building a library of reusable coordination structures.[20]

5   STP AS AN EXPERIMENT: LESSONS LEARNED

Five years ago no one knew whether a research consortium would work in the U.S. Now there is evidence that shared research is a viable idea, as results in the form of usable technologies flowing from MCC into the shareholder's production facilities. In addition to this basic question of viability, there are some rather technical and technology transfer issues which can be addressed only by large scale experimentation, namely by trying to manage research in a particular way. Although our experience in STP covers a large spectrum of research issues, this chapter elaborates only on the three problems which follow:

- Should a coherent research effort in software environments be conducted on a top down fashion; namely, by starting with the outline of an architecture?
- What should be the end product to be delivered to the shareholders?
- How far should the integration of the individual technologies go?

In the following subsections the researchers experience is summarized in these three areas.

5.1   A Research Architecture?

In the fall of 1985 the first serious attempts were made to supply an overall system architecture for Leonardo. The Design Environments (Integration) Group was asked specifically to come up with an architecture to pull together the technologies that would eventually mature into the complete Leonardo system. In particular, the following were some milestones that were important in the process of attempting to achieve this goal.

- An off-site meeting in September 1985 contributed to the understanding of roles and user scenarios.

- A Requirements and Architecture (R&A) Task Force in late 1985 contributed further to using scenarios as an exploration device. Some experience was gained in the difficulty of writing a requirements document for Leonardo.
- A small researcher/management team in 1986 produced a block diagram visualization of how the components of Leonardo fit together.

The problem of defining Leonardo by taking a top-down approach proved to be exceptionally difficult due to a variety of reasons. The main problem was that although the general ideas of teamwork, multiple views, reuse, representation, and coordination could be expressed in terms of broad generalizations, it proved to be very hard to propose specific solutions and model them in terms of a generalized consistent framework. Getting hold of the very problems proved to be a major problem.

The approach to visualizing Leonardo's functionality through scenarios did not initially lead to anything more than a few interesting experiments. One of these experiments was the R&A Task Force which was constituted in the fall of 1985. The R&A Task Force generated several interesting scenarios for explaining how Leonardo might be used in real-world situations. Despite the apparent usefulness of some of the scenarios, no conceptual framework was provided, nor was there a well defined methodology for dealing with the format and content of the scenarios themselves. Eventually, a technical report on scenario methodology was produced, but not until long after the R&A Task Force had been discontinued.

The next phase of the system architecture effort began a year later in the fall of 1986. An Architecture Study Activity (AS-A) was created, and a major effort was launched to identify a Leonardo conceptual framework. The AS-A effort did not produce the desired result, but it did generate two interesting proposals; one for Team-Based Coordination (Tebasco) and the other for exploration (Columbus). Tebasco eventually became a research activity in its own right and came to be closely associated with the Raddle/Verdi effort. Toward the end of 1986, a new path was chosen to define a system architecture. This effort was focused towards the integration of technologies on a ground-up basis; the activity became known as DELI. With the identification of DELI as a crucial bootstrap platform, the research activities, such as Tebasco, reuse and meeting augmentation began to take on new meaning. It now seemed possible to find ways to fit these technologies together and get maximum benefit and synergy from these seemingly diverse approaches to teamwork and coordination. Also, by the end of 1986, the results of the empirical studies, especially the field studies, began to have an impact. It became possible to map the solutions offered by DELI into solid problem areas that had been identified among the shareholders, thanks to the efforts during 1986, when nineteen separate projects were investigated by visiting STP teams on shareholder sites.

Since the very nature of DELI was such that it could be defined as a focus for all of our research activities, it was possible for STP to make the DELI platform the first major Program deliverable.

In summary, the system architecture that was planned in 1985 has not yet materialized. In its place stands a platform for integration of research into a coherent system, transferred to the shareholders in mid-year 1988. Thus, the research focus has been temporarily deflected from a top-down architecture approach to a more pragmatic method. The DELI method is to build a functioning framework for integration and provide it as an environment that can be used as the bootstrap to build Leonardo itself. In the absence of an overall system architecture, emphasis was placed on research into individual applications which offer good prospects of merging into Leonardo later. At STP, the consensus is that any research activity, including the one into programming environments, must be done iteratively, in an invent-build-observe-correct cycle, which is incompatible with top down architecture of fitting more or less well defined components together. Research results must drive a gradually emerging architecture.

5.2   The Research End-Product

At STP the mission is to introduce, via prototypes, entirely new software technology—coherent techniques and tools—which will bring about extraordinary increases in productivity and quality in the Participants' (i.e., STP shareholders') laboratories in six to nine years. Given this broad set of goals, it was up to the STP management team to define what the model for deliverables should be. Should their research lead to systems that could be used or distributed by the shareholders as products, or should they concentrate on building prototypes that demonstrated proof-of-concept? This issue provided much discussion at MCC among the shareholders and the various research programs.

The model of robust prototypes as deliverables was finally adopted at STP. The most important reason for making this decision was the belief that it would be impossible to productize the deliverables and make them compatible with the needs of all shareholders. Some shareholders are computer manufacturers themselves and have requirements to support a variety of hardware configurations, operating systems, and user interfaces. Other noncomputer manufacturers have diverse equipment and environments already in place. In all cases, the shareholders' have installed systems that represent a large investment, not only in terms of money, but also in terms of the effort put into software applications which provide the backbone of their business. These facts made it unlikely that the shareholders could easily be expected to convert to another hardware/software platform offered by STP.

The understanding, then, of the shareholders' requirements led to the conclusion that software deliverables for such a diverse set of customers could never be effectively produced. The better approach would be to deliver robust, working prototypes built on a generic, widely available set of operating systems, languages, data bases, and user interfaces. Most recently the researchers heard from the shareholders that, in some instances, they would be willing to contract with MCC to provide "productization" services. These contracts will be handled by a separate MCC Support Program that will interface with the MCC research entities, but not be controlled by them. In this way, MCC can preserve its long-term interests in being a research institution while, at the same time, permitting the shareholders to contract for services they may desire in transforming research prototypes into commercial products for specific markets.

From the very beginning, the slogan around STP was "get your hands dirty" by producing working, demonstrable prototypes. In fact, many of the researchers hired were brought on-board because they had a reputation for being able to build. Only academic conceptualizers were not enough to staff the Program (although they do have a good share of them). From the first, creating a balance of researchers and people who could do design and programming was sought. In addition, those at MCC consciously sought out people who were known to be good rapid prototypers. Finally, they now have a small number of good systems people, those who enjoy the complexities of large and distributed networking. It was found that just the right mix of all this talent is needed. STP is not a large organization, nor is there a big parent company to lend support when needed. On the contrary, to a high degree they have learned to be self sufficient in conceptualizing, designing, and prototyping systems without significant reliance on help from the outside.

In summary, their philosophy and method of operation is not only to deliver ideas, concepts, and designs but also working models of software. It is up to the shareholders to determine what they want to do with these prototypes.

5.3 What Does Integration Mean?

From the very first of the major issues that confronted the STP management team was how much integration was desirable? This issue quickly took on the characteristics of a technology transfer problem. As discussed previously in the end product section, the shareholders needs and requirements had to be taken carefully into consideration.

Some consider an "integrated system" to mean a shared set of data objects, information representations, and user interfaces that apply across a large number of modules or built-in applications.

One option available in developing the tools that would eventually go into Leonardo was to use the resources available on Lisp machines to achieve virtually seamless integration among the various software components. Lisp machines offered many attractive advantages in that they had a single address space architecture, supported lightweight processes, and made shared memory possible. Back in 1985, none of these features were operational on UNIX machines, and it was not all together clear when, or if, they might be. Examining the situation more carefully, however, it was decided that the construction of a tightly integrated system, whether or not it was based on Lisp machines, would not be a good idea. What they wanted to achieve with technology transfer was a gradual process whereby the shareholders could take pieces of this research, experiment with these pieces, and slowly build up an expertise with the new methods and platform. As Figure 18-2 shows, the research flow calls for integrating the research results into "coherent environments." By "coherent environments" are meant toolkits in standard window systems for building user interfaces. Tools such as browsers and HyperText systems must be provided which can be used with a variety of different applications running under UNIX. The objective is to make the environment as compatible as possible with other applications, such as CASE tools, that may already be part of the shareholders' software suite.

The choice was to avoid dropping a large, monolithic environment into the shareholder's software operations and telling them to use what was given to the exclusion of everything else. To have done so would have been to follow a recipe for failure. The goal is to build an environment that is capable of *coexisting* and *cooperating* with other tools and systems. It is in, general, an impossible goal to entirely replace what is already available and functioning, and it is not the intention to even try. DELI is engineered to be compatible with standard network window systems running under UNIX. It does not shut any system out or preclude the running of any other applications side-by-side. DELI, being nonmonolithic, allows for smooth change and evolution to a new object-oriented design environment. This approach is what those at STP believe will make technology transfer work.

Finally, DELI's open-architecture approach based on a widely available operating system, means that the shareholders themselves will have the greatest possible latitude in determining what level of integration it is that they need. If they want to build a tightly integrated, proprietary application, then DELI offers them convenient means to do so. If, on the other hand, they want to tap the larger market of software that is tailored for portability and intended to run on a variety of machines supporting UNIX, then they are free to do that also.

In summary, those in STP have always taken the open-ended approach to building their environment. Few possibilities are excluded.

Given this power and extensibility, the temptation to build DELI as a monolith was avoided. Several other research projects are known that were originally started as giant, fully integrated monoliths capable of running by themselves with no coordination or communication with outside systems. Many of these monoliths are now in the process of being rewritten to run on a more generic UNIX platform. Those at MCC think that their approach is right and predict this trend will continue.

6 POSTSCRIPT (FEBRUARY 1989)

Software Technology is a dynamic discipline; its research even more so. Since this chapter was written more than a year ago, much of its content has been adjusted to the changing environment in industry, as well as to the insight gained by the very research conducted in MCC.

Obviously, all the historical passages remain valid and important. Also, most material on empirical studies invariably form the major source of insight to guide the research process.

Nevertheless, it must be pointed out that since the middle of last year several noteworthy changes have occurred: more emphasis on "system design" of mixed, not only software, systems; on design recovery as opposed to reuse; and on design information representation as opposed to improvement of Hypertext technology, which should rather be imported into STP. A strong "Groupware" component has also been emerging, hand-in-hand with coordination technology, as a natural successor to STP's earlier meeting laboratory experiments.[20] Finally, as DELI is becoming commercialized, the bottom-up integration of emerging STP technologies has come to the forefront, to exploit the inherent synergism of the resulting tasks.

REFERENCES

1. Belady, Laszlo, "MCC: Planning the Revolution in Software," *IEEE Software*, November 1985, pp. 68–73.
2. Belady, Laszlo, "Software is the Glue in Large Systems," *Proceedings of the IEEE/National Security Agency Telecom at 150 Symposium*, June 1988.
3. Biggerstaff, Ted, "Reuse of Very Large Scale Components," MCC Software Technology Program non-proprietary technical report, report no. STP-363-88, October 1988.
4. Biggerstaff, Ted, "Design Recovery for Maintenance and Reuse," MCC Software Technology Program Non-proprietary Technical Report, Report No. STP-378-88, November 1988.
5. Conklin, Jeff, "A Survey of Hypertext," MCC Software Technology Program non-proprietary technical report, report no. STP-356-86, December 1987.
6. Conklin, Jeff and Michael Begeman, "gIBIS: A Hypertext Tool for Exploratory Policy Discussion," *CSCW (Computer Supported Cooperative Work) Conference Proceedings*, September 1988.
7. Cook, Peter G., Clarence A. Ellis, and Gail L. Rein, "Meetings Research—A Nick Retrospective," *Book of Articles on Computer Supported Work*, North-Holland, March 1988.
8. Curtis, Bill, H. Krasner, N. Iscoe, "A Field Study of the Software Design Process for Large Systems," *Communications of the ACM*, November 1987, Vol. 31, pp. 1268–1287.
9. Curtis, B., H. Krasner, V. Shen, and N. Iscoe, "On Building Software Process Models under the Lampost," *Proceedings of the 9th International Conference on Software Engineering*, March 1987, pp. 96–103.
10. Curtis, B. and T. Malone, "Introduction to this Special Issue on Computer-Supported Cooperative Work," *Human-Computer Interaction*, 1987, Vol. 3, pp. 1–2.
11. Evangelist, M., V. Shen, I. Forman, M. Graf, "Using Raddle to Design Distributed Systems," *Proceedings of the 10th International Conference on Software Engineering*, April 1988, pp. 102–107.

12. Gerhart, Susan L, "A Broad Spectrum Toolset for Upstream Testing, Verification, and Analysis," *Proceedings of the Second Workshop on Software Testing, Verification, and Analysis*, May 1988, pp. 4–12.

13. Graf, Mike, "A Visual Environment for the Design of Distributed Systems," *IEEE Computer Society 1987 Workshop on Visual Languages*, August 1987.

14. Graf, Mike, "Building a Visual Designer's Environment," *Proceedings of ACM-IEEE Computer Society 1987 Fall Joint Computer Conference*, October 1987, pp. 287–290.

15. Graf, Mike, "The Design of a Distributed System Using a Visual Language," *Proceedings of IEEE Computer Society 1987 Workshop on Languages for Automation*, August 1987, pp. 208–212.

16. Halasz, Frank G, "Reflections on NoteCards: Seven Issues for the Next Generation of Hypermedia Systems," *Communications of the ACM*, 1988, Vol. 31, pp. 836–855.

17. Krasner, H., B. Curtis and N. Iscoe, "Communication Breakdowns and Boundary Spanning Activities on Large Programming Projects," *Proceedings of the Second Workshop on Empirical Studies of Programmers*, December 1987, pp. 47–64.

18. Lubars, Mitchell D. and Mehdi T. Harandi, "Addressing Software Reuse Through Knowledge-Based Design," *Software Reusability*, editors Ted Biggerstaff and Alan J. Perlis, Addison Wesley/ACM, 1989.

19. Marks, P. and Zvi Weiss, "DELI: A Support Environment for Software Engineering Research at MCC." *2nd Israel Conference on Computer Systems*, May 1987, pp. 5.2.1–5.2.5.

20. Rein, Gail L., Clarence A. Ellis, "The Nick Summer Experiment: A Field Study on the Usage of Meeting Support Technology by Software Design Teams," *Human Computer Interaction Journal*, April 1988.

21. Shen, V., H. Krasner, N. Iscoe, and B. Curtis, "A Field Study of the Software Design Process." *Proceedings of the Tenth Software Engineering Workshop, 1987*, Greenbelt, MD: NASA.)

Chapter 19

Lockheed's Software Technology Center

WINSTON ROYCE
Lockheed Aeronautical Systems, Co.
Burbank, CA

1 INTRODUCTION

Lockheed created a Corporate Software Technology center in 1984 to investigate research initiatives in software technology and computer science. The two primary initiatives were concerned with developing advanced software production environments. The goal was to leapfrog the ethernetted current approach to environments, which could be described as bit-mapped graphics workstations ethernetted to mainframe computers with multi-language tools integrated through a project data base or a software configuration management system. All of this was being designed, built, and operated elsewhere in the Lockheed Corporation with considerable success.

Two quite different approaches were deliberately selected to break out of the multi-language, open architecture approach. The first approach was to build an environment which was heavily integrated around a language semantics. Given the existence of a rich language semantics, is there a software productivity benefit in designing all of the tools around the language semantics, integrating the tools around the language semantics and also integrating the tools through this same mechanism? This idea seemed particularly intriguing in 1984 with the imminent introduction of the Ada language for aerospace applications. During the same year, the Rational Corporation had also introduced the R-1000 environment, which provided an existing and powerful foundation for building a high performance environment around the Ada language semantics. Lockheed then elected to build a suite of tools in Ada, for Ada, and integrated by means of Ada, that used the Rational concept as a baseline environment. This suite of Lockheed tools was named AdaCraft. It is described in combination with the Rational environment in the next section.

The second approach for building environments was, in turn, deliberately selected to be different from both the multi-language open architecture approach and from integration around Ada semantics as employed in AdaCraft. The goal of this second approach was to build an automatic programming environment.

The idea was to capture knowledge about how programmers design and code, and install this knowledge within a knowledge base. Then a very high order design language is used in combination with this knowledge base to produce machine language code directly. If the very high order design language has the properties of a problem specification language and is transparent to the application hardware, then an automatic programming environment producing portable code is achieved. The high technical risks of achieving such an environment are self-evident. However, the potential productivity gains are enormous.

In 1984, Reasoning Systems had produced an initial version of such a knowledge-based software development environment called REFINE. Lockheed elected to build a set of software packages, which use REFINE to create a more elaborate environment called EXPRESS, tailored to aerospace applications. The second section following this introduction describes EXPRESS and REFINE.[1]

2 ADACRAFT

2.1 AdaCraft System

The aim of AdaCraft is to significantly reduce software development costs and risks for large military and aerospace projects. To achieve this aim, AdaCraft is designed to support the entire software development life cycle.

The objectives of AdaCraft are to provide Ada software project management, workers, and customers with specific advantages: Ada programming support, lower compilation cost through interactive, incremental compilation; low-cost, high-quality documentation; and an integrated set of tools to support software development.

AdaCraft is an integrated Ada software development environment composed of support components and user tools (Figure 19-1). The AdaCraft approach is to provide integrated support for software development with state-of-the-art facilities that include support for Ada language programming, life-cycle tools with common support components, and a special purpose host computer optimized for Ada software development. The host computer is the Rational R1000, a computer optimized to handle the resource-intensive requirements of Ada compilations.

AdaCraft provides the user with functional capabilities for system and environment support, project management, cost estimating, requirements management, analysis and design support, program generation, integration and testing, documentation support, target support, and operations and maintenance.

---

[1]REFINE is a registered trademark of Reasoning Systems, Palo Alto, CA.

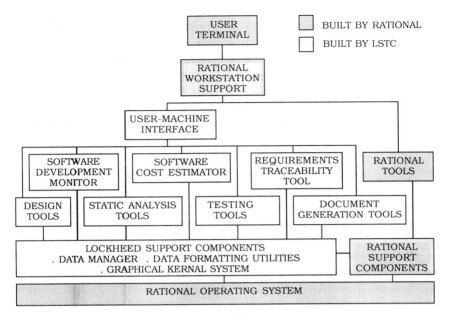

Figure 19-1. The structure of AdaCraft.

2.2 System Support

AdaCraft system support includes the normal range of system functions that support archival procedures and backup of data, restoration of data, protection against data loss, and batch scheduling, as well as hardware support for the resource-intensive tasks associated with Ada compilations.

Preservation of data is supported by six different variations of backup and active procedures. These include the following:

- Full backup of disk images to tape, supporting bulk restore.
- Incremental backup of dirty disk images to tape, supporting bulk.
- Full backup of ASCII images to tape, supporting bulk restore.
- Incremental backup of changed ASCII images, supporting selective restore.
- Full backup of ASCII images to tape, supporting selective restore.
- Incremental backup of ASCII images to tape, supporting selective restore.

Protection against data loss also is provided by regularly scheduled ''snapshots'' of committed changes. This feature is designed to ensure that, should the system fail during the day for some reason, only a limited amount of data would be lost.

The AdaCraft environment offers batch scheduling capabilities that allow users to add, delete, enable, disable, display, or reschedule batch jobs. A disabled job remains in the batch queue but is not submitted unless it is enabled again.

Each R1000 system is configured with hardware and software diagnostics for automated problem reporting, diagnosis, and repair. These diagnostics permit isolation of failed hardware components to the field-replaceable unit. In addition, the R1000 data-link modem enables remote execution of the diagnostics and problem isolation from the Rational Customer Support Response Center. Moreover, through its diagnostic and remote communication capabilities, the R1000 provides automatic notification of system malfunctions to the Rational Customer Support Response Center. This feature enables the R1000 to dial out and automatically submit a support request to the Customer support Response Center without the need for customer intervention.

2.3   Environment Support

The following components provide environment support:

- User-Machine Interface Subsystem (UMIS).
- Bulk-Formatted Input and Output (BFIO).
- Ada Data Manager (ADAM).
- Descriptive Intermediate Attributed Notation for Ada (DIANA).
- Core editor.
- Configuration management.

User-Machine Interface Subsystem

UMIS provides support for the interaction between a user and an AdaCraft tool. The UMIS support component, which can be customized, includes various user-friendly features, such as help, redefinition of key mappings, creation and use of macros, and several modes of interaction. In addition to these capabilities, UMIS is responsible for verifying the syntactic and semantic correctness of all user input.

Bulk-Formatted Input and Output (BFIO)

BFIO provides device-dependent support for input and output of formatted text files by AdaCraft Tools. An AdaCraft tool provides BFIO with textual data and formatting instructions. The formatted text is then output to a device (terminal or disk file). BFIO is also capable of reading formatted text files as input and then providing the AdaCraft tool with unformatted text.

Ada Data Manager

ADAM is an Ada implementation of a rational data base management system (DBMS). The programmatic interface provided by ADAM allows each AdaCraft tool to use ADAM as a repository for and manager of information required by the tool.

Descriptive Intermediate Attributed Notation for Ada

DIANA is a language that provides an internal representation of Ada programs. This language serves as a standard interface language for the tool of the Rational Environment and AdaCraft.

Core Editor

The core editor provides the user with an interface to the Rational Environment and AdaCraft. This editor provides the user with a window-based environment that can be modified and tailored to individual preferences. The two types of windows enable the user to view the objects of the environment, such as Ada specifications, Ada bodies, and text files. Command windows are attached to major windows. In command windows, a user enters declarations and Ada statements that can be immediately executed.

Configuration Management

The Rational Environment provides automated facilities for configuration management. The environment complements the Ada language by enforcing semantic consistency across software components. The environment provides capabilities to manage compilation dependencies, automate the compilation process, and ensure consistency between specification and implementation of software components.

2.4 Project Management

The Development Monitor (DEMON) tracks, maintains, and reports information related to a software development project. It accepts and stores the management approved software structure of the project in a hierarchically structured system. DEMON supports up to five hierarchical levels, with the project representing the highest level and the Ada library units the lowest.

DEMON accepts and stores information of estimated size and effort, work assignments, and scheduling information for products defined in the project software structure. It also automatically records and maintains the date and size of any object when it is created or modified. This information may be retrieved in several ways, including Gantt charts and reports. Manual entry also is supported for information about project effort. Only authorized project personnel may confirm scheduled milestones.

2.5 Cost Estimating

The Software Productivity and Cost Estimator (SPACE) provides the capability to estimate software effort and scheduling. The algorithms are derived from Barry Boehm's Intermediate Constructive Cost Model (COCOMO).

The model incorporates twenty cost-driver attributes covering the following five categories:

* Product size and complexity.
* Host/target environment characteristics.
* Personnel qualifications.
* Project schedule and standards.
* Application-unique factors.

The input to the model is the size, in delivered Ada declarations, and statements of each software component in as many as three levels of system decomposition. The user is also able to override precalibrated default values for all cost drivers. The model generates effort estimates in man-months and schedule estimates in months for all software components.

2.6 Requirements Management

The Automated Requirements Traceability System (ARTS) is a tool that provides the capability to automate the management of requirements over the life of the project. Through a hierarchical structure, which is stored in a data base and supports a top-down organization and decomposition of system requirements, any requirement may be traced to one or more modules that satisfy its specifications. Likewise, all requirements that have not been allocated to a software module can be identified, thus providing a means of checking for completeness.

Every requirement, whether it was extracted from a contractual document or derived from another requirement, may be traced to its originating source. Consistency checking is performed by ensuring that every requirement in the system has a legitimate source and that every requirement has a unique identifier.

Since requirements analysis is an iterative process, ARTS allows the requirements hierarchy structure to expand and reflect changes in the structure. An aid in the assessment of changing a requirement is provided by identifying all the requirements that may be effected by the projected change of a requirement.

Requirements tracking is a significant problem in major software projects. ARTS solves this problem by providing an effective, automated tracking system.

2.7 Analysis and Design Support

Design support consists of a set of tools geared to assist a designer in gathering, organizing, and evaluating detailed information about how a program should accomplish its purpose.

Analysis support provides tools which retrieve, condense, and reorganize information contained in programs. It is useful for purposes of documentation, audit, and configuration control. An example of an analysis support tool is SCAN, which shows data declarations and structures.

N^2 Chart

This tool is concerned with the early steps of the design process: decomposing a system into modules, evaluating the complexity of the interfaces between the resulting pieces, and comparing different approaches. The N^2 Chart is a flexible, high-level notation for expressing design decisions, and the N^2 Chart tool provides a convenient and helpful method for creating them.

Ada Design Language (ADL)

ADL provides the designer with a language for expressing system and module interfaces and algorithms in a preliminary and natural form. It is intended for use before actual code is generated. At that state, a designer is primarily interested in expressing the concepts and ideas necessary for generating code, without being concerned with fine details.

File Compare Tool (FCT)

This tool is used to detect and report the changes between different versions of similar documents or programs for configuration control purposes.

Source Code Analyzer (SCAN)

SCAN is a flexible, general tool for selecting and retrieving information (names, constructs, comments, or counts) from programs. It is useful in performing code audits and generating documentation. Normally such applications require a programmer to write a special-purpose routine for decoding program text or even do the work manually. SCAN provides a quick, reliable, automated alternative.

2.8 Program Generation

The AdaCraft system provides many aids for use during program generation. The Rational environment provides tools for editing Ada units, assisting compilation, and debugging Ada code.

Ada modules are units made up of Ada elements—the keywords, identifiers, statements, and declarations. These elements are built up in a treelike, hierarchical structure to make up Ada objects. The editor knows this structure and uses that knowledge to provide specific operations on these objects. The editor will automatically format the Ada object into some format defined either by the user (project) or by the system default. The editor completes syntax for an Ada object, such as providing an END statement to match a BEGIN statement. While in the editor, a user can incrementally identify all syntax and semantic errors even before producing object code for the object. The editor also provides all common full-screen editing features, such as global replace, word and line insertion, and flexible cut-and-paste operations.

Compiling Ada Units

The Ada language requires ordering rules when compiling an Ada unit that makes calls to, and is, therefore, dependent upon, other Ada units. Because of this requirement, compilation can be a time-consuming operation on most systems. AdaCraft provides compilation management tools that greatly reduce the time spent tracking dependencies between Ada units. The user needs only to specify the order in which all compilation must take place. Conversely, when a change is made to an Ada object that causes other units to obsolesce, the compilation management system brings only those units specifically effected down to a source state to make the change. The system also provides an incremental semanticizer much like the incremental formatter mentioned above. Semantic errors are uncovered while still in the editor, so time spent actually compiling and linking the units is reduced.

Debugging Ada Programs

Rational provides a comprehensive source-level debugger. When the debugger is first activated, a debugger window appears on the screen. The debugger can automatically display the Ada source code for the program being debugged and allows the user to select variables in the source line and request their current value. Common debugging operations—such as breakpoint setting, changing variable values during execution, and viewing the run-time-stack—can be performed on single-task programs as well as on programs that have several parallel tasks running.

2.9   Integration and Testing

Integration in AdaCraft is facilitated by the use of Rational R1000 subsystems. The subsystems are managed as collections of logically related Ada units. They are used to express and enforce the major architectural components of a software system, including their interfaces and interdependencies. The Ada concept of separation of specification from implementation has been extended to subsystems. This allows developers to test and release a baseline subsystem, and then proceed with the implementation of future releases. The released subsystem can easily be combined with various releases of other subsystems for layer- or system-level testing.

Testing in AdaCraft is supported by several tools. The Create_Test Manager tool automatically creates skeleton test drivers based on the Ada specification of the software to be exercised. The driver has a structure predicated on the number of test cases for the test, including calls to all operations exported by the software to be tested. A developer or tester then "fleshes out" the skeleton by adding the necessary logic to each test case. The UMIS and BFIO components can be used to facilitate input and output, and a testing utility library is also available. This library contains random number generators, a debugging aid, routines to generate test reports, and routines to check completeness and consistency of the requirements being tested in the driver with the requirements stored in ARTS.

A set of test coverage instrumentation tools is also included in AdaCraft. These tools collect trace information about a program's run-time behavior and provide summary reports. Reports detail the frequency with which statements or logic branches have been executed and identify statements or branches that were not executed. These reports provide feedback to measure the portions of software exercised by a specific test. A test coverage level can then be achieved by continuing to test until a certain percentage of all statements or logic branches have been executed at least once.

2.10   Documentation Support

The purpose of AdaCraft's documentation support tools is to provide integrated facilities to define and automatically generate documents that incorporate pertinent information from the complete spectrum of AdaCraft data bases, Ada code, and text files.

The user views the system as containing a set of generic document recipes. Each recipe refers to a class of similar documents and generates various documents belonging to that class. Recipes specify document formatting instructions and ingredients. Ingredients are supplied by data bases, code, and text files. A small initial set of predefined, generic document recipes consistent with DOD-STD-2167 will be provided. The user can invoke the predefined recipes or can define generic document recipes to suit a specific purpose.

2.11 Target Support

Rational currently is developing target toolsets for the DEC VAX series under VMS, for Motorola 68000-based computers, and for the 1750A instruction set architecture.

2.12 Operations and Maintenance Support

AdaCraft provides the same support capabilities after system delivery that it offers beforehand. Since support for system operation and maintenance does not differ significantly from the environmental support needed during development, AdaCraft also satisfies the need for this support.

Figure 19-2 shows the relationship between AdaCraft tools and the activities of the software development life cycle. Figure 19-3 shows the same information for Rational components and tools.

3 IMPLEMENTING KNOWLEDGE-BASED (KB) CODE SYNTHESIS

Lockheed's knowledge-based code synthesis system uses an entirely new concept for manufacturing large-scale embedded software systems.

The traditional approach is loosely analogous to Henry Ford's concept of

LOCKHEED TOOL / LIFE CYCLE ACTIVITY	REQUIREMENTS	COSTING	DESIGN	CODE	DEBUG	UNIT TEST	SOFTWARE INTEGRATION TEST	SYSTEM INTEGRATION TEST	CONFIGURATION CONTROL	DOCUMENTATION	REPORTING	STANDARDS, AUDIT	BACKUP AND RECOVERY	LIFE CYCLE MAINTENANCE
ARTS	X	X				X			X	X	X			X
DEMON		X	X			X	X	X	X	X	X			X
SPACE	X										X			X
N-SQUARED CHART (N2)		X								X				X
ADA DESIGN LANGUAGE (ADL)		X	X							X				X
SCAN		X	X	X	X	X				X	X	X		X
FILE COMPARE TOOL							X	X	X	X	X	X	X	X
CREATE_TEST_MANAGER						X	X	X			X			X
COVERAGE TOOL						X	X				X			X
DOCUMENT GENERATOR	X			X	X	X	X	X	X	X	X	X		X

Figure 19-2. Lockheed support mapped against software life-cycle activities.

RATIONAL LIFE CYCLE ACTIVITY / TOOL OR COMPONENT	REQUIREMENTS	COSTING	DESIGN	CODE	DEBUG	UNIT TEST	SOFTWARE INTEGRATION TEST	SYSTEM INTEGRATION TEST	CONFIGURATION CONTROL	DOCUMENTATION	REPORTING	STANDARDS, AUDIT	BACKUP AND RECOVERY	LIFE CYCLE MAINTENANCE
ADA EDITOR/COMPILER			X	X	X	X	X							X
CONFIGURATION MANAGER									X				X	X
TARGET TOOL SETS							X	X	X					X
ETHERNET COMMUNICATIONS							X	X	X		X		X	X
DESIGN FACILITY	X		X						X	X	X	X		X

Figure 19-3. Rational support mapped against software life-cycle activities.

moving an automobile through successive stages of assembly, using specialists at each production station. In software development, the stages are called "life cycle phases," and the manufacturing sequence is called a "methodology." However, a serial sequence using phase specialists is grossly inefficient for software manufacturing because the moving software "automobile" is only a paper entity during the first three-quarters of the assembly process. It is only during the last quarter that people can begin to test and inspect the actual system and make corrections. The current process might be compared to trying to manufacture a new model car by starting the assembly line with a clay model and evolving it in stages into the real vehicle of steel, glass, and plastic.

Lockheed's KB code synthesis methodology will allow the software system to be assembled in a single place by component specialists. These specialists will work on the same software vehicle in such a way that the system itself—not just a paper version—can be tested, inspected, and continuously modified.

This revolutionary methodology requires a large set of supporting technologies. Lockheed's KB code synthesis system is based on three existing advanced hardware and software technologies and a number of inventions to scale up the existing technologies to large aerospace embedded systems, such as Strategic Defense Initiative's battle management problem. Figure 19-4 presents Lockheed's KB code synthesis system architecture. The existing technologies are REFINE, Macsyma, and the Symbolics workstation, while the inventions are represented by the aerospace specification languages and system management component that appear as subsystems within Lockheed's KB code synthesis system triangle.

3.1 The REFINE System

REFINE is the first commercial knowledge-based software development environment. "Knowledge" has two related meanings for a REFINE environ-

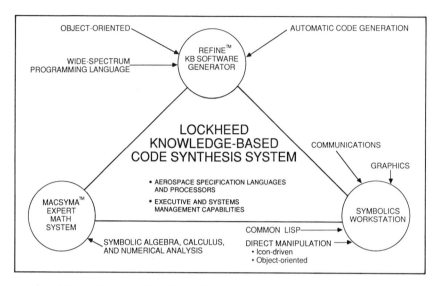

Figure 19-4. Lockheed knowledge-based code synthesis system.

ment: programming knowledge and application knowledge. The storing of both types of knowledge for later reuse provides opportunities for software development productivity gains. Experience has shown that reuse of programming knowledge offers fourfold or greater gains, and reuse of application knowledge should offer equal gains. Overall, the expectation is for an order of magnitude increase in productivity. And the competitive advantages of the future lie in the capture and consistent reuse of basic knowledge.

3.2 The REFINE Language

REFINE's language, also itself called REFINE, is a wide-spectrum, executable, design specification language.

"Wide-spectrum" refers to REFINE's range of language constructs, from low-level procedure to the highest levels of abstraction.

At the low end of this range is straight procedure, including low-level data types, such as numbers, characters, conventional if-then-else statements, loop controls, and assignment forms. In the mid-range transformation rules are logical devices that permit modification of the knowledge base, listing the before and after conditions and letting the REFINE system accurately derive the code to execute what the analyst has specified.

Logic and assertions of fact are at the top end of mathematical abstraction. REFINE also supports quantitative statements, such as "all ships in the port are combat ready," and "there is at least one carrier within range of point A."

3.3   The REFINE Environment

The REFINE system enables application developers to build and use, in software development, a model of their application domain which is the core of their business. For example, aircraft designers concerned with aircraft performance or flying qualities will have Laplace's equation and the Navier-Stokes equations stored as knowledge-based elements, including rules for their solution. The process of software development itself can also be viewed as an application. Modeling this process supports the true integration of program, project, people, and policy information into one environment.

The REFINE environment provides a powerful tool for supporting the software development process. Figure 19-5 shows three components of a customized REFINE environment: program information, project information, and program and policy support tools. These components can be modeled using REFINE's object-oriented language elements and integrated with REFINE's knowledge base management system.

Program information includes the typical elements from the software life cycle: requirements, specifications, code and documentation, and maintenance operations. This information is automatically linked within the basic REFINE system.

Program and policy support tools provide direct support for the programming process. Program support tools assist in: documentation management, test management, version control, configuration management, and so on. Development policies refer to custom guidelines established by each REFINE environment manager to coordinate his software development operations. They can include such things as testing and documentation, constraints, configuration controls, and information access. Each of these tools unburdens humans from what is done by them today, shifting such tasks in the future to computers.

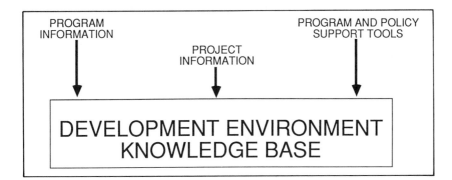

Figure 19-5.   The Customized REFINE Environment.

3.4   How REFINE Works

REFINE is based on a new style of development called transformational programming. To understand transformational programming, it is helpful to know how specifications and programs are represented in REFINE. This representation is easily understood by all who had to diagram sentences in grammar school. One uses the rules of English grammar to find the predicate, subjects, objects, attaching modifiers, and so on in a sentence. REFINE's language parser does the same thing for each specification statement. It creates an entity-relationship (ER) representation of the parsed statement in the knowledge base. This representation has a graphical description, called a tree. The nodes of the tree become objects in the knowledge base and the branches are structural relationships that depend on the grammar of the language.

At the outset, most of the nodes are abstract; that is, declarative describing "what" and not yet fully procedural describing in detail, "how." The REFINE compiler examines nodes of the tree and in each stage determines how to add procedural implementation content to that node. This is done by transforming the structure of that node, usually producing something more complex, since implementation knowledge has been added.

These transformations embody the knowledge used in building a program. Such knowledge includes the means of checking constraints, changing logic into rules, changing rules into procedure, organizing data into memory- or access-efficient structures, deciding the best calculation order, determining whether to store or recompute intermediate results, and many other optimizations.

REFINE itself is implemented using transformation programming; that is, the REFINE system is specified in its own language and compiled into code. To modify the REFINE system, its developers modify the most recent specification, and use the previous version of its code to compile the new specification into a new system. Not only does the REFINE system build itself in code, but its developers also have the benefit of all the tools in the REFINE environment described above.

The use of transformations enables REFINE's developers to add optimization knowledge by adding more transformations. This capability can be compared to that of chess-playing programs whose performance improves when new playing strategies are added. Another benefit of the transformational approach is its potential for producing provably correct programs. Up to this point, most program verification work has been based on very complex theorem-proving and automatic analysis systems. Only very small and elementary programs could be verified. With transformation systems, one need only verify that each of the transformations preserves correctness. The composite of many such transformations also will be correct. Transformation programs can be correct by construction instead of by testing.

3.5 Macsyma[2]

Macsyma is a knowledge-based system originated at MIT and licensed to Symbolics for distribution and enhancement. It encapsulates algebra, calculus, and numerical analysis in the form of expert system rules. Macsyma represents more than 100 years of effort in codifying the rules of algebra and calculus and developing the support environment. To attain a stated goal, such as the integral of an expression in calculus, it develops a search space of alternative trial expressions, computes a measure of ''closeness'' to completion for each alternative, then continues to develop the most promising alternatives until the goal is reached. Algebra rules include the knowledge needed to factor, expand, and simplify. Calculus rules tell how to integrate, solve ordinary differential equations, and differentiate. In the numerical analysis area, computations can be carried out with arbitrary precision arithmetic. All of this unburdens the system analyst and software practitioners from doing critically needed work for which humans are error prone and find boring.

3.6 Symbolics Workstation

The Symbolics workstation provides several advanced hardware and software features. It executes the Common LISP language directly and has a high-performance, bit-mapped graphics interface and corresponding direct manipulation (mouse) interface with the operator. It also provides a high-performance communications capability (over Ethernet) and support object-oriented extensions to the Common LISP standard.

For the purposes of knowledge-based code synthesis, the Common LISP language is intrinsically and conceptually more advanced than C, Pascal, or FORTRAN. Its intrinsic advantages include a larger basic set of language functions and a run-time environment that is defined in the language standard.

The operating system integrates editing, compilation, and loading into a single act. It supports object-oriented programming with a subsystem, called Flavors, that allows users to define abstract data structures (objects) and associate generic processing with those data structures. Flavors provides a unique approach to software reuse in that new object classes can be defined that inherit both the structure and processing capability of existing objects. This inheritability saves the effort of having to define new objects from scratch.

The operation of object-oriented systems is loosely analogous to the rules of genetics. Software is organized as classes, and inheritance is defined for both data structures and associated processes. Genetic engineers can splice a gene segment that has a desirable characteristic—for example, one that produces

---

[2]Macsyma is a trademark of Symbolics, Inc.

insulin—into the DNA of an existing organism and create a living organism with the new characteristic. Using Flavors, software engineers define software segments with desirable characteristics (qualities of data structure and processing, for example) that cannot exist apart from their segments. However, when the engineers designate a complete sequence of software segments to be joined, a "living" software entity is created with all of the characteristics of the component segments (structure and processing). The "direct manipulation" user interface allows high-productivity input by reducing tasks to simpler, easier actions; e.g., selection of input by mouse actions only—no typing. Thus, typing errors are eliminated after the initial entry.

3.7   Aerospace Specification Languages

Our analysis of the labor-intensive tasks in the traditional software development methodology revealed that an enormous manual effort is required to create high-quality paper specifications for an embedded software system. In an ideal world, they would be complete enough to be the sole source of information for a subsequent group of engineers to carry out the next phase of the system's life cycle. They also would concisely communicate what is required of the system by using words with unambiguous, commonly accepted meanings. When acronyms were used, they would be defined fully at their first occurrence. Forward references, pronouns, or vaguely defined words would not appear in ideal specifications. The use of natural, familiar language would enable the specifications to be easily understood by a reader with no specialized knowledge or training.

Finally, and most important, ideal requirements specifications would not include implementation, the description of which might inadvertently preempt the most cost-effective approach to meeting the requirements. Such specifications are called "declarative" and allow the specifier to concentrate on expressing what is to be done rather than how it is to be done. Ideally, only functions to be performed and interfaces to be met are specified, and their contexts are left undefined. Such ideal requirements rarely are achieved today. Knowledge Base code synthesis methods will begin with and help to create such specifications.

From a computer science perspective, ideal specifications can be defined as context-free grammars for which there exists efficient compiler technology, such as that contained in REFINE.

Lockheed's KB code synthesis system has four classes of aerospace specifications languages: objects and policy, symbolic mathematics, displays, and architecture diagrams. Each class of language will have multiple subclasses corresponding to the application areas to which it is tailored.

3.8   Objects and Policy

The Objects and Policy language will be used to express ideal software requirement specifications. Relative to ideal traditional specifications, the objects correspond to the interface requirements, and the policy statements correspond to implementation-independent statements of required functions. The purpose of objects and policy specifications is to defer implementation decisions; that is, not to get involved in implementation until the functional specifications are complete. The Objects and Policy language will unify the three actions of specifying, documenting, and coding into a single act using a vocabulary natural to the application domain in which specifications are being produced. (This unification of these three otherwise separate actions has enormous implications for reduced costs and quicker production.)

As an example, Lockheed has created a language for the handling of military communications messages. In the example messages, quality criteria, and track buffers were defined as objects, and the policy statement was "only messages meeting quality criteria enter the track buffer." The actual code to implement this policy statement is generated without human intervention.

3.9 Symbolic Mathematics

The purpose of Symbolic Mathematics specifications is to provide a natural, more productive form of specification (textbook style) for engineers and scientists. In traditional approaches, this group contributes only peripherally to an embedded system definition. Symbolic Mathematics will make them more productive via automatic differentiation, integration, and algebraic simplification. In addition, this derivation process will be captured for communication to other groups in the development program. Their productivity increase will be realized in their ability to analyze more complex problems and to evaluate more alternative system-level approaches than they can by hand methods.

The Symbolic Mathematics system is based on Macsyma, described earlier. Its main class of problems for application will be environmental modeling, prediction, and error estimation. Lockheed has created a number of examples, including the in-orbit operations of the shuttle robot arm model, which have demonstrated the effectiveness of Symbolic Mathematics, particularly in its ability to simplify the use and understanding of complex mathematics.

3.10 Graphical Specifications for Displays

The third language class, Displays, will make human-machine interface engineers more productive when designing the operator displays for the embedded system. It will allow them to "build" a display graphically. They can select icons, such as graphs, maps, and gauges from stored standard sets.

3.11 Architecture Diagrams

The most common means of portraying computer systems is by means of architectural block diagrams. This essential capability must be included in future systems.

3.12   System Management Capabilities

The knowledge-based Framework will allow specifications written in different languages to communicate with one another by providing a common KB representation. It thus allows a complete embedded system to be specified and executed in a consistent context.

If programs were to be ascribed personalities, then programs written in conventional languages (FORTRAN, COBOL, or Ada) would be considered one-dimensional: they only execute. Programs written in LISP, REFINE, or Lockheed's KB code synthesis system languages would be considered multidimensional: they have the required executable nature and at the same time they have other natures, such as the ability to respond to a variety of requests for information about themselves (interfaces, legal commands, etc.). The self-descriptive nature encourages software reuse and expedites program checkout. The direct-manipulation capability makes multiple-level searches accurate and simple, since the presentation from one query can be directly used in the next with no intermediate confusing results from typing errors as often happens with long type in strings.

3.13   Software Development Using Lockheed's KB Code Synthesis System

Any typical embedded system will be defined using all four classes of aerospace specifications languages. The generation of code for target processors and the addition of performance optimization rules in response to performance bottlenecks in the target processor will be the main activities during the full-scale engineering development phase. Substantial changes to the specification developed during the system definition phase will not occur, thus saving time, effort, and money.

In summary, Lockheed's KB code synthesis system will allow multiple disciplines to develop an ''executable'' equivalent of the software requirement specification, conduct a design review based on the ''executable'' specification and then evolve it into the delivered product. Documentation for the system will be derived from the knowledge base and is, therefore, guaranteed to be in sync with the specification. It will require one-third the time required for traditional Full-Scale Engineering Developments. The concept obviates entire traditional products and activities, including the software design specification, the critical design review, the coding phase, and the design specification.

In the longer term, the underlying technology of Lockheed's KB code synthesis system (the transformational approach) has even greater promise. Lockheed's KB code synthesis system's transformations that underlie the system's operation can be designed as provable mathematical constructs. This attribute directly addresses the question, ''Can the SDI system work?'' or ''Can any large-scale, new software system work?'' This ability to guarantee correctness for all possible modes of operation is, perhaps, KB code synthesis' greatest future potential for improving software construction methodology.

Chapter 20

SPC Software Plan

HOWARD L. YUDKIN
Software Productivity Consortium
Herndon, VA

1 WHAT IS THE SOFTWARE PRODUCTIVITY CONSORTIUM?

1.1 Background

The Software Productivity Consortium is an industry based initiative to accelerate the pace of large scale software development among its member companies and to improve the quality, suitability, and extensibility of their software systems. To do this, the Consortium creates, acquires, integrates, and transfers software products and technology (see Figure 20-1).

Conceptual thinking about the organization dates to the late 1970s. In that time frame, leaders in both government and industry identified a threat not only to the nation's ability to create the very high speed integrated circuits and related hardware technologies necessary for next generation advances in aerospace systems but also a challenge to its ability to generate the software needed to exploit such devices. By 1983, a group of aerospace executives began organizational discussions for a software consortium, culminating in a memorandum of understanding in the following year. The Consortium was incorporated in 1985. Also in that year, the organization developed both its initial technical and business plans and selected a headquarters location in Reston, Virginia. The Consortium's organizational phase ended in June 1986, and it began to assemble a superior technical staff.

1.2 Organization

The Consortium is a private, for profit, Delaware corporation (see Figure 20-2). There are 13 member companies: Allied-Signal Aerospace, Boeing, Ford Aerospace, General Dynamics, Grumman, Harris, Lockheed Missiles and Space, Martin Marietta, McDonnell Douglas, Northrop, TRW, United Technologies, and Vitro. Each holds a share of stock, has equal ownership of Consortium generated technology, and has equal representation on the Consortium's governing board of directors. Each company also belongs to a Software

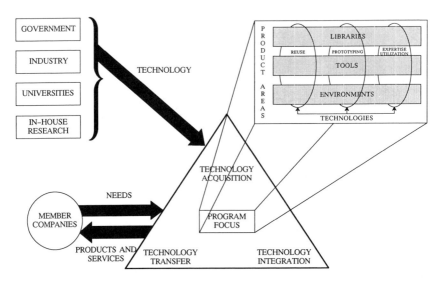

Figure 20-1. An industry initiative for software productivity improvement in practice.

Productivity Consortium limited partnership. The Consortium conducts its program under contracts between the member companies and the limited partnership.

Questions occasionally surface about the antitrust implications of such a joint research and development effort. The Consortium operates in full compliance

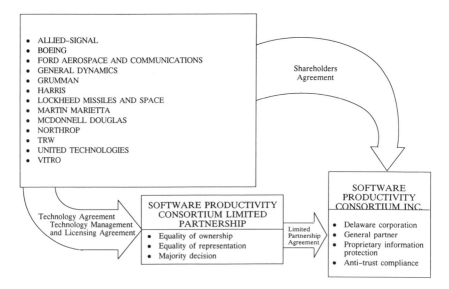

Figure 20-2. A partnership of industry leaders.

with the antitrust laws of the United States. It is afforded limited protection provided in the National Cooperative Research Act, P.L. 98-462. The U.S. Department of Justice has been notified of the Consortium's formation as required. Other agencies of the federal government, including the Department of Defense and the Department of Commerce, have strong interests in the Consortium's success and maintain on-going information exchanges.

At the practical level, the organization has created an antitrust compliance program to avoid antitrust violations. Every employee signs a certificate of compliance with the program. Key points in the Consortium's approach are the following:

- to operate from a single, commonly adopted technical plan;
- to provide all products, technologies, technical documents, and briefings to member companies on an equal and timely basis;
- to maintain equal company representation on the board of directors and technical committees; and
- to counsel employees assigned to work at the Consortium by member companies on the avoidance of information sharing practices which may provide competitive advantage or collusive appearance.

Perhaps the Consortium's single greatest antitrust protection springs from the fact that its activities foster—rather than inhibit—competition. Aerospace companies have been frustrated in their individual attempts to solve a set of fundamental technology questions related to software, either through internal research or through acquisition in the commercial marketplace. Consortium products will make software faster and less expensive to build, thus improving the competitive position of companies who choose to use them.

The Consortium technical program complements the research and development activities of the federal government and academic and private institutions, commercial software companies, and the in-house programs of member companies. The Consortium's technical program has several distinguishing attributes: it creates fully supported software engineering tool products for its members; it transfers these products for use in short term as well as providing support for midterm radical improvement, and it focusses long term technology investigation in high payoff areas with a higher risk than that usually acceptable in the member companies' internal programs.

The Consortium delivery stream begins with its Software Technology Exploration (STE) group. The STE engineers take promising concepts and generate workable software prototypes. A key STE objective is to demonstrate the technical feasibility and effectiveness of a particular tool or technique. The group also has an objective of identifying promising software research in the community and making that information available to the Consortium staff and the member companies.

The results of STE's investigations feed the Software Product Development (SPD) group. The SPD engineers and computer scientists turn prototypes into formal products—fully documented, tested, and quality assured. SPD deliverables will include integrable software engineering tools, capable of meaningful stand alone operation as well as enhanced roles in member company or Consortium defined integrated development environments.

Responsibility for the successful transition of products to member companies belongs to the Software Product Transfer (SPT) group. The SPT group is the Consortium's agency for technology transfer. SPT personnel assure that member companies are prepared to accept Consortium developed technology—and that the technology developed meets member company requirements for functionality, effectiveness, portability, and ease of use.

The Consortium's ambitious development schedule relies on its ability to leverage existing technology. The Development Environment Engineering (DEE) group is the focal point for this activity. The organization provides both the advanced technical computing environment necessary to make rapid progress and the on-going organizational liaison with the commercial marketplace to identify, assess and, when appropriate, incorporate important new products. The DEE group will also operate a test bed for evaluating the Consortium's own product developments.

2 WHY A SOFTWARE CONSORTIUM?

Aerospace and defense systems in the 1990s and beyond will increasingly depend on computer hardware and software for their basic functionality.

The Army, Navy, Air Force, other defense agencies, NASA, and many civilian agencies are planning future systems which rely heavily on embedded software. In a wide variety of applications, from autonomous land vehicles to air traffic control systems, many traditional system control responsibilities are being shifted to software.

The point is vividly illustrated by the changes which have taken place in military avionics: the F-4 fighter used between 1965 and 1974 contained virtually no on-board processing equipment. By 1981, the F-16A featured seven computer systems operating with 135,000 lines of software code. Five years later, the F-16D was introduced with 15 computers and 236,000 lines of code. And the Advanced Tactical Fighter of the 1990s is expected to operate with over 1 million lines of code.

In systems, such as the F-16, software has been used to relieve the constraints traditionally addressed by other elements of a given system, fostering dramatic improvements in total weight, operating maneuverability, combat performance and efficiency. Writing in *IEEE Control Systems Magazine* (April 1987), Jason L. Speyer argues that "Full integration of aircraft design will enable the designer to trade inherent natural stability and control of propulsion, structures, and aerodynamics to achieve efficiencies and performance presently unobtainable.'' In certain experimental applications, such as the forward swept wing X-29 airplane design, software and computers make the airframe structurally stable and the advanced capabilities of the airplane itself feasible.

In DOD parlance, this brand of embedded, distributed processor, real-time software is "mission critical." American military dependence on software is clearly growing, and so is the nation's total dollar outlay for mission critical software. An Institute for Defense Analyses (IDA) study provides ample evidence of the impact of this growth trend. The IDA researchers examined six DOD long-range planning documents with the objective of measuring software dependence in the systems cited. According to the study, 70% of the technologies, functions, and systems discussed in these plans require software to operate. The software performs a wide range of tasks including guidance, sense orientation, trajectory, pattern recognition, and target sorting. In some sense even more important is software's role as the integrating mechanism or "glue" that bonds the different technologies within these systems together. Without reliable software, a majority of the strategic and tactical weapons and weapon systems used in this country's defense simply won't operate.

Clearly large scale software development is a rapidly growing fact of life for aerospace and defense companies, but the transition from electromechanical and electropneumatic to integrated digital electronic systems has created significant technical and business challenges. These include the following important trends:

- implementing system functionality and control in software and instrumentation has brought new competitors into the aerospace industry and blurred the roles played by platform builder, subsystem supplier, and electronic systems integrator;
- the increasing sophistication has contributed to the concentration of government spending in fewer new programs, shrinking the number of major opportunities available to aerospace companies;
- more pervasive systems and complicated software development requirements have generated a shortage of skilled software engineers; and
- the greater use of the fixed price contract in government places a high degree of risk on the systems developer. Unlike less complex technologies which pass through successive prototypes before being "productized," software is judged a failure if it can not fulfill the requirement specifications at the end of a given contract period.

A DOD study team in 1980 looked at the situation in the Command, Control, Communications, and Intelligence arena and concluded, ". . . software development projects rarely meet cost-benefits originally projected, usually cost more than expected, and are usually late. In addition, the software delivered seldom meets user requirements, often times is not usable, or requires extensive rework."[1]

The situation has sparked a critical re-examination of traditional approaches to software development and its place within the systems engineering cycle. Clearly, the issues involved in software development confront aerospace and defense firms with formidable challenges and strategic opportunities. Software is often the highest risk component in mission critical systems and has the longest development lead-times. And while software development costs are high, the costs to maintain and upgrade software are even higher.

A set of leading companies in the aerospace and defense industries has recognized the technology challenges and the market opportunities represented by mission critical software. They have also recognized that today obstacles of a fundamental nature block systems builders from tapping the maximum performance benefits of integrated software. They have formed the Software Productivity Consortium as a highly concentrated, single focus program aimed at improving the software development process.

3 WHAT IS THE CONSORTIUM DOING?

3.1 Strategic Approach

The Consortium is turning software development into a modern engineering discipline. The organization's approach centers around people, their work environment, a specific set of product deliverables based on an integrated set of engineering methodologies, and vigorous plans for transferring its technology into use on actual member company programs.

3.2 Talent

The Consortium has assembled a critical mass of expertise in software engineering. Approximately one-third of its technical staff comes from member companies; the balance has been hired directly from the general work force. The aggregate education and experience levels of these individuals is impressive. For instance, nearly 60% have either masters or doctoral degrees. The average technical staff member has over ten years of experience in the computer industry. Consortium employees have been involved in virtually every software initiative of direct importance to the aerospace industry—from the formulation of the Ada language to the creation of military standards for software development and documentation.

Management philosophy at the Consortium cultivates both professionalism and creativity, teamwork and the individual contributor. The management apparatus is kept purposely flat to avoid excessive bureaucratic procedure and to promote a fluid and dynamic exchange between the senior and junior staff. Within the organization, project teams participate in regular monthly progress reviews to assess compliance with work milestones. Member company oversight takes place in a series of bimonthly board meetings held at the Consortium facility in Reston, Virginia.

To provide a check on excessively inbred thinking and to gain the benefit of alternate viewpoints, the Consortium regularly subjects its activities to review by outstanding professionals from the member companies and from the software engineering and computer science communities at large.

3.3 Environment

The Consortium's technical staff works in one of the most advanced software engineering environments in the country (see Figure 20-3). Here, the objective has been to make the staff productive by providing an environment rich in the best tools, both hardware and software that the current state of the art has to offer. The initial hardware selection was driven by an underlying assumption that graphics have an essential role to play in productivity improvement and that they are best provided by bit-mapped displays. The fast response needed for effective use of the graphics implies the need for considerable compute power on the desk top. This capability is economically provided in the near-term by a workstation-oriented environment. Further, to accommodate the communications needed in the team approach to large software projects, these workstations are interconnected via high-performance LANs that are integrated into a higher-level distributed processing scheme.

The initial Consortium development environment is heterogeneous. In the current state of the art, heterogeneity puts a burden on the user, who generally must be aware of where the various system resources are sited and the varied procedures and protocols needed to access them. The Consortium's objective is to move to an integrated network—a network where all of the system resources are available to the user at a workstation. The user will operate in such an environment without having any specific knowledge of where the system resources are located or procedures to access them. In fact, it should appear to the user that all of the resources are on that individual's workstation. This is essential in distributed systems, where software siting will be a prime technique in performance optimization. Thus the Consortium staff is able to maximize productivity by focusing a relatively higher percentage of time on software design issues—as opposed to the procedural and administrative details of using environment resources.

3.4 Processes and Products

The Consortium provides its member companies with software engineering tools and technology to speed large scale software development and improve results by avoiding redundancy and capitalizing on past work products (see Figure 20-4). The Consortium's products push the state of practice in software engineering, providing software development tools in areas where none exist and both extending and complementing the capabilities of those which do.

Consortium "deliverables" will be software engineering tools and technology

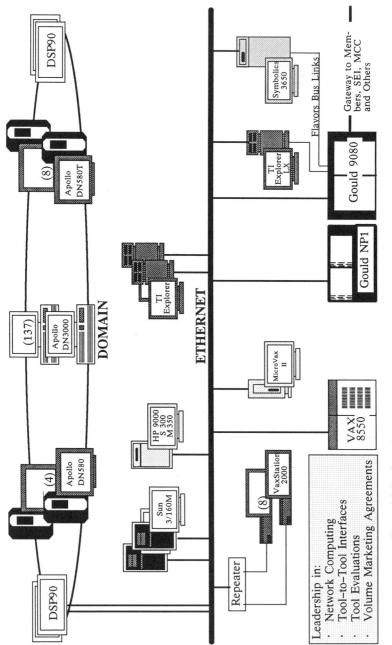

Figure 20-3. One of the nation's most advanced software development environments.

Engineering		Management	
Risk isolation and resolution	Systematic use of standard parts	Planning and control	Satisfaction of contract requirements
(prototyping)	(reuse)	(convergence)	(compliance)
Alternate, consistent representations to match view to viewers needs (physical models)			
Automated use of prior experience (expertise)			

Figure 20-4. Tools and libraries implement a work saving process.

which save work for software engineers, program managers, and administrative personnel. The organization has identified a set of engineering methodologies to accomplish this goal. Two are of key importance: prototyping and reuse.

Prototyping

Prototyping provides a methodology for conceptualizing software in parallel with the balance of a given system. Rather than a ''make it work'' approach, prototyping is performed in the concept stage and allows engineers to explore possibilities and evaluate options without closing doors prematurely. Prototyping tools and techniques allow engineers to synthesize, select, and adapt design alternatives.

Reuse

Reuse further speeds the process by making software development more modular than ever. Rather than start from scratch on every project, reuse proposes a method whereby current work products—requirement specifications, designs, code modules, project management information, test results, and documentation—are categorized into standard parts (i.e. generic components). Candidates for ''decomposition'' into reusable formats include both deployed and prototype systems.

Tools and libraries automate these process steps. Tools which exploit standard components allow the engineering team to avoid unnecessary work. Rather than starting a development effort from scratch, engineers will leverage the results of previous projects.

The use of standard, certified components is a common practice in other engineering disciplines. In software engineering, life cycle objects become the standard components for reuse in new development. This approach allows engineers to rapidly assemble the generic elements of a system, while focusing greater attention on the minority of new design features required. Most often the assemblies will be prototypes to be adapted and transformed to provide the final system.

Standard software components require libraries for storage and management. There will be two basic library structures: reuse libraries pertain to a particular category of application: process control, avionics, navigation and command control are examples; project libraries support a specific project being executed by a member company. Project libraries constitute a central repository and staging area for the software development of major systems. Libraries provide for the preservation of prototype system versions and the retention of information across projects. Libraries will store adaptable objects, including requirements and design specifications, implementation code, assessment information, and project management data as well as the relationships among these objects. By storing both objects *and* relationships, libraries provide a forum for the rapid assembly of reusable components into system prototypes.

Tools that support prototyping reduce risk. First, they allow for early generation of requirement and design specifications. As a result, the tradeoffs between engineering alternatives can be weighed and risks to schedule and cost assessed in the initial stages of development.

Through the integration of software tools and data elements, the Consortium will help bridge the planning and control gap which often develops between project technical and management personnel, resulting in schedule delays and cost escalation. The Consortium tool sets will facilitate closure by making engineering results visible and useful to project management. The tools will also generate outputs which comply with government reporting requirements, thus cutting—and even eliminating—the work needed to ''massage'' end item deliverables.

To facilitate these processes, Consortium tools will generate physical representations of data and procedures which match the needs of the user. Part of this modeling involves the incorporation of visual motifs which speed the engineer's interaction with the system. Consortium human factors specialists are working to assure the appropriateness of product interfaces to the target applications. Software engineering, however, requires more than a well planned set of screens or menus. The ability to move between physical representations of a system at varying levels of abstraction is critical—and missing from tools today. Such a capability will greatly aid the engineer's interaction with the software development process.

Finally, expertise utilization seeks to embed software engineering expertise in the processes, tools, and libraries used to build software. This methodology leverages the benefits of prototyping and reuse by making tools easier and more productive to operate and by directing an engineer's attention towards the most suitable information alternatives.

As noted, all Consortium methodologies target the concept of saved work. How this applies to specific products will be discussed shortly. Note, however, that saved work is also a guiding principle in the Consortium's own tool development processes. The decision to build a software tool is always based on a thorough assessment of other options. In many instances, the Consortium has elected simply to buy commercially available software packages rather than build alternates. Price, functionality, and vendor stability are key considerations here. In other cases, the Consortium works closely with individual vendors in technology sharing partnerships to fit particular products into the organization's software development environment. Where the necessary tools don't exist and can't be produced in an effective and timely manner by an outside supplier, the Consortium builds them. Either way, the Consortium provides its member companies with technology that allows the mixing and matching of tools from diverse sources, including those from the Consortium itself, and those from the commercial marketplace.

The working saving process focusses on design using standard parts. Restricting initial design attention to design based on standard parts allows rapid formulation of prototypes without having to build code from scratch. The restriction provides an early safeguard against unfocused requirements analysis and dead-end design. Instead, initial requirements are stated in terms of the known behavior of standard parts assemblages. When an application is repeated often enough, standard assemblages can also be defined and greater savings can be realized by automating the requirements process along with automatic prototype production. As a result of this process, the applications engineer builds the prototype systems; the traditional hand-off between the applications designer and the software builder—as well as subsequent software engineering activity— is eliminated.

The Consortium estimates that up to 90% of a software development effort can be built with standard components. Consortium researchers have built a mathematical model to explore the relationship between reuse and software productivity. The model lessens the costs to develop reusable software among member companies. For example, assuming an 8% reuse cost relative to building new software, the study shows a 40% productivity gain when engineers use the reuse libraries to extract just 30% of the code in deployed systems (see Figure 20-5).

Productivity rises sharply with percentage increases in reusable work products. Gains reach 300% with 80% reuse from the libraries. While this percentage gain seems large in itself, note that the model applies only to the coding stage of a development. Reuse offers high percentages of saved work in the requirements and design steps as well. Also, this metric is computed against

- Parallels practice in other engineering disciplines

- Accomplishes "most" of the system development through families of requirements, designs, code etc...

- Focuses attention on "new design" ,features

- Facilitates rapid creation of prototypes

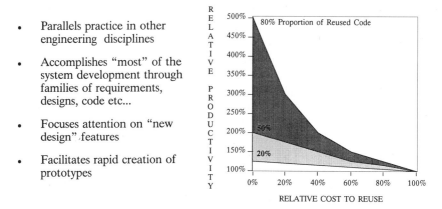

Figure 20-5. Systematic reuse exploits standard components.

best—not most—current practice. Reuse embeds best current practice in the software development process, leading to another source of productivity gains.

Software development in the DOD environment follows a ''waterfall'' methodology specified in Military Standard 2167A. The process begins with a stable set of requirements and passes through design, coding, testing, verification (to assure the code matches the requirement) and validation (to assure that the requirement meets the customer's original demands). But problems in the requirements phase often lead to costly mistakes in subsequent phases. To avoid the possibility of a catastrophic error, best current engineering practice takes a structured analysis approach to requirements, breaking each into finer modules. Each module is engineered as a separate entity with problems flagged as soon as they occur.

Structured analysis is much more difficult to apply in the domain of very large, complex systems. Because of issues such as size, complexity, and concurrency, mission critical systems do not lend themselves to a single iteration through the waterfall model. The problems associated with this approach simply become too big, and the risk of failure too high.

Prototyping offers a method for reducing risk (see Figure 20-6). Prototyping relies on advanced technology to identify and evaluate multiple, partial, or immature solutions to a problem. In this case, software modules pass through several, smaller waterfalls: trial requirements are defined and design alternatives selected. This is a honing process, allowing engineers to weigh and tradeoff various implementations. The prototyping process leads to a production decision—the point at which requirements are completed. Prototyping provides a systematic way to reduce risk.

While prototyping and reuse offer the potential for productivity savings, they require management for control and convergence (see Figure 20-7). Engineers may tend to overbuild a solution. Make/buy decisions still need to be made

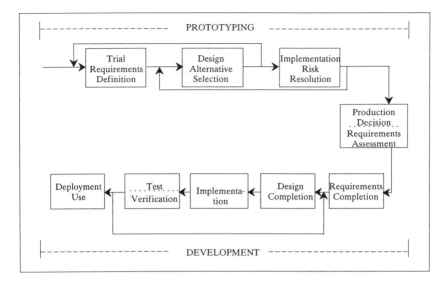

Figure 20-6. Prototyping is a logical way to create an operational software system.

against real project conditions. Project managers cannot stand outside the loop. The Consortium has automated solutions for project management. The convergence of management and technical information will be accomplished in project libraries with the assistance of Consortium built tools and commercially available project management software products.

To this end, the Consortium has already built a project library which integrates the operations of documentation, planning, and configuration management tools. Thus a project manager can use this existing resource to place documents and schedules under configuration control while maintaining basic traceability

- Tie technical and management information together through the project library and traceability tools

- Provide resource estimation and reallocation assistance using project planning and scheduling tools

- Cost improvement depends on above

  - Prototyping can incur extra cost

  - Building for reuse can incur extra cost

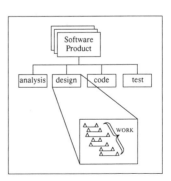

Figure 20-7. Prototyping and reuse require management for control and convergence.

between schedule activities, documents, and work products. Project library technology will evolve so that "real time" engineering data can be used to perform such important management tasks as resource estimation and reallocation assistance.

As a further assist to management control, Consortium tools have been tuned to generate outputs which fully comply with government software standards. The first stage of this automated support has been developed in a series of document preparation templates derived from DOD STD-2167A data item descriptions. As a result, these descriptions can be generated without the time-consuming manual conformance checks normally associated with this activity.

To exploit reuse, new tools are required for the following:

- certification of standard parts;
- management of parts libraries and manipulation of parts;
- synthesis of user applications;
- requirements development based on assembled parts behavior;
- rapid prototyping with reusable components; and
- system analysis for reusable parts extraction.

None of the tools needed to perform these functions are available.

In prototyping, an engineer will view as many alternatives as reasonably possible before committing to one. While this may be a logical approach, automated tools are needed to make it productive. These include tools for the following:

- Assessment to compare requirements and design alternatives and to identify and isolate implementation risks—short of building and testing code.
- Composers/decomposers to assemble prototype systems from prototype components and to analyze systems in terms of their components.
- Traceability to link requirements statements, design decisions, implementation risk resolutions, and associated documentation and planning data.
- User interface prototype generators to assist in requirement definition.

Some of these tools, while not able to interoperate in any meaningful way, do exist, but the needed design, assessment, traceability, and user interface prototype generation tools are not commercially available. Thus the Consortium will concentrate its efforts on building *integrated* tools in these categories.

While the reuse process offers great potential for savings, it also raises difficult questions. For instance, reuse poses a tradeoff between overhead and utility. A standard component must perform enough work to justify the overhead of maintaining it. Conversely, if it performs too much work, it may become too job specific and lose its utility as a standard component. The Consortium is learning how to balance this tradeoff. As a baseline, standard components must be certified to deliver a predefined function—a condition analogous to the certification standards of hardware parts catalogs. Like hardware, software components must function in black box mode, exhibiting externally visible behavior while hiding implementation details. Also like hardware parts, software parts must be flexible and adaptable to meet the needs of evolving products, similar to the way today's microprocessors have been extended to families of mainframe computers.

3.5 Tools for Prototyping and Reuse

Software tools will implement these working saving processes. Among the necessary tools, the Consortium has identified several categories in which it will concentrate its initial tool building activities: library management, dynamics assessment, design, traceability, and synthesis. The other tool categories will be addressed as enough is learned about the underlying technology to make them feasible.

Engineers will need a set of tools to effectively use and manage libraries. The Consortium is building library mechanisms which organize objects by classification, attribute, and relationships to other objects. Rather than search for a specific object, engineers will use reuse libraries to explore alternatives among categories of information. Tools here will support this activity, allowing objects to be cataloged, viewed, and retrieved. Search criteria and results can be saved and supplemented to perform new searches. The tools will support searches for objects of various sizes and provide a mechanism for decomposing reusable components into lower level parts.

Tool sets for dynamics assessment will allow engineers to model the performance of a design before the code is written. Geared for real-time Ada applications, the tools will support the assessment of factors, such as software timing and space requirements.

The Consortium has already built dynamic assessment prototypes with an array of capabilities for modeling system behavior (see Figure 20-8). The scope of these tools ranges from macro level design using queuing network models, to very advanced mathematical models based on stochastic Petri nets for analyzing software level design. The software level assessment tools represent an advance in the state-of-the-art, providing closed form solutions to nonlinear aspects of Ada design. The tools also provide for the simulation of transient aspects of software systems.

The productivity advantage of the dynamics assessment tool set springs from its integration with other Consortium tools and libraries. Because these modeling tools interface directly to the design tool data base, an engineer can quickly simulate a design and display results in useful graphic formats. Through integration with the traceability tool sets, the engineer can not only use the tools to model a design but also perform "what-if" analyses to see the effects of

- Analysis based on mathematical models and simulation for limited class of system architectures

  - Timing

  - Hardware fault tolerance

  - Sizing

- Portray Ada tasking

- Support hardware/software tradeoffs

- Provide graphical interface friendly to software engineer

  - Statistical data

  - Process control diagrams

- Integration with reuse libraries

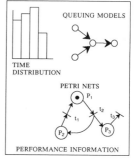

Figure 20-8. Dynamics assessment tools: performance analysis in requirements and design phases.

changes on system performance. Also through integration with reuse libraries, the assessment tools can automatically display the performance characteristics of software components which may be appropriate for adaptation to a new system.

The design tool set will offer engineers the opportunity to work in an Ada-based design environment, using both textual and graphical notations for capturing design ideas. Design representations at varying levels of complexity will be linked to a common, logical data base. Thus changes made at one view will be automatically reflected by transformation in subsequent views (see Figure 20-9). This ability to generate a software design with speed, consistency, and syntactical accuracy—then map back and forth between views of the same design—has many advantages.

For instance, graphics are the preferred notation for representing highly complex systems. This fact is substantiated by the flow diagrams which proliferate in many software development efforts, but today, graphics editors can only depict conceptual information. Few are able to associate abstract diagrammatic representations to actual underlying code—and then only in special cases. Designs created with Consortium built tools will have this ability without restriction. As a result, engineers will work at the level of detail best suited to task requirements and individual expertise. Most important, rapid prototyping of design models can be accomplished. Throughout the process, the tool set will model the ripple effects that design changes in one module will have on others. Because the tool set will integrate with reuse libraries, engineers will be able to rapidly display previously designed software applications. This has obvious benefits for prototyping software, and because the tool set transforms

- Graphical language

- Textual language (PDL)

- All views (graphical and textual) of the design derivable from each other

- Changes made in any view can be reflected in all other views

- Extensive consistency and syntax checking

- Ripple analysis across design

- Integration with reuse libraries

- Rule based composition/ decomposition

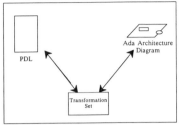

Ada-BASED DESIGN TOOLSET

Figure 20-9. Design tools support Ada-based design with graphical and textual representations.

between text and graphics, software developers can start with its code and reverse engineer a pre-existing application to understand underlying design assumptions. Such an approach will aid in the creation of new software, as well as the maintenance and enhancement of current systems. Extended capabilities will permit composition of full code prototypes to expand on the design model prototype capability already demonstrated.

The engineering community badly needs tools which bring structure and consistency to the hundreds of thousands of life cycle objects which evolve with a project. The Consortium traceability tool set allows engineers to define the relationships between software life cycle objects in a library (see Figure 20-10). After a library schema is defined, the tool automatically infers this set of

- Be able to tailor a library structure to "real world" project needs

- Navigate easily among requirements, design, code, and project management data via the structure

- Provide consistency checks

- Identify relationship test failures

- Generate traceability reports

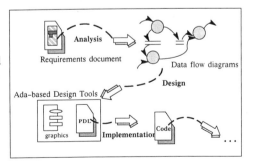

Figure 20-10. Traceability tools: navigation among requirements, design, code, and related data.

relationships so that the library can serve subsequent users. The tool set allows effective navigation among objects. The tools provide a means for decomposing large objects (such as a requirements document) into small objects (such as the associated code). The tool set analyzes constraints placed on the software development team by the team's own software development methodology. As required, it issues predefined reports.

In large scale software development, such a tool set offers numerous benefits. For instance, the number of requirement specifications which need implementation in code can rapidly exceed the abilities of individuals to manage the coding process. As a result, requirements can be overlooked. The Consortium's traceability tool set will analyze such basic constraints and flag errors. Changes in requirements can influence code modules in ways which are extremely difficult for individual engineers to identify and assess. Thus design tradeoffs are made without complete understanding of consequences to other parts of a system. The tool set's navigation and constraint analysis tools will automatically pinpoint the implications of such changes. Because the traceability tools are integrated with the dynamic assessment tools, such changes cannot only be identified but also tested against overall system performance.

A set of synthesis tools will extend the utility of libraries for exploration in specific domains of engineering expertise (see Figure 20-11). These tools are geared for the extraction of application knowledge. The synthesizers have knowledge of standard processes for exploring design alternatives and constraints as well as knowledge about modeling the standard objects in the

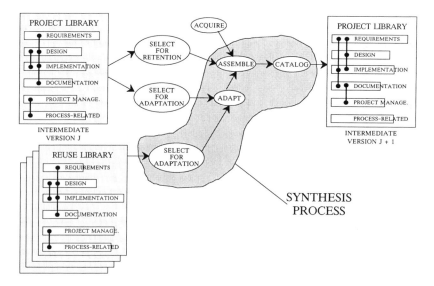

Figure 20-11. Integrated project library is the formum for rapid assembly of reusable components.

particular domain. This embedded expertise helps the engineer build and evaluate prototypes quickly. The tools identify and abort costly and time consuming specification mistakes. The results of preliminary design activities are automatically captured, giving product developers crucial design tradeoff information. Because they integrate with other Consortium products, synthesis tool sets produce results which can be used to originate or supplement project libraries.

The Consortium is currently developing such synthesizers to support the development of cruise missile flight control system software prototypes (see Figure 20-12). This is a model product to demonstrate the feasibility of the synthesis process. Cruise missile flight control domain knowledge provides a context for building and using this tool set, but the tool set concept can be extended to work with a wide variety of mission critical software applications. The missile guidance synthesis tool builds on the CAMP project of the Air Force Armament Laboratory.

Here's a hypothetical example of how the synthesis tool can be used: a control system engineer is working on a navigation and guidance problem. By selectively indicating the form of the control in finer and finer detail, the engineer arrives at a desired set of parameters for a longitudinal autopilot. When the engineer is satisfied that all control parameters have been satisfied, the tool presents an optimization algorithm for design of the autopilot. The engineer modifies the algorithm to meet project needs. At the engineer's command, the tool then pulls the standard parts from the library necessary to realize the design, instantiates them and generates the executable Ada program, using a linear quadratic synthesis process.

- Based on U.S. Air Force "Common Ada Missile Packages" (CAMP) parts

- Initially demonstrates a longitudinal autopilot control system

- Aids understanding of the economics of reuse

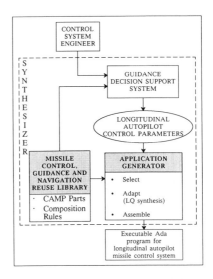

Figure 20-12. A missile guidance synthesis tool has already been prototyped.

The Consortium is packaging its synthesis tool development process into a six stage model for use by member companies in developing business specific applications of the tool set. The Consortium will eventually introduce tools which will decompose library contents into generic subsystems, data structures and related elements, returning them to appropriate reuse libraries for future use. Synthesizers will allow engineers to build application prototypes for given domains from existing components, working in an environment which maximizes use of domain dependent knowledge and minimizes the need for expertise in computers and software.

Configuration technology provides the foundation for prototyping, reuse, and expertise utilization (see Figure 20-13). Each of these methods pose extremely difficult delivery problems for the computer science community—problems addressed by the Consortium's product set architecture. At issue is how to make a common set of software tools and interrelated data available to engineers in a manner which masks the discrepancies between diverse system components; provides uniformity in terms of data definitions, structures and interfaces; and integrates individual tools and data so that the work of one engineering phase can feed subsequent phases. The Consortium is currently building a set of fundamental services to serve as a framework for using its tool sets. Configuration technology tools provide for the mixing, matching, and integration of tools from diverse sources, including Consortium developed, third-party developed, or member company developed software.

The Consortium is building tools which emphasize prototyping and reuse in a series of product sets. These will be transferred to member companies with

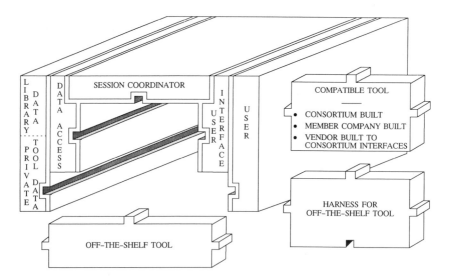

Figure 20-13. A well defined architecture supports environment configurability.

the integration technology needed to add other tools from commercial sources or a company's own development efforts. Product Set 1 includes tools for dynamic assessment, design, and traceability, library management, and synthesis. Although much needs to be done to realize the full potential of the new work saving process, the Consortium's initial tools permit users to begin gaining a work saving advantage.

3.6 Technology Investigations Support Tool Building and Help Set Future Directions

The Consortium's technology investigations feed the product development stream and respond to organization requirements with a variety of technical reports and guides. A majority of this work is conducted by the Consortium's Software Technology Exploration (STE) division. The Consortium's internal technology program concentrates in two principal areas. These are the following:

- software measurement and methodology, and
- certification technology.

Measurement and methodology activities concentrate on understanding the variants in applying the ideas of prototyping and reuse and on how to measure their relative effectiveness. For example, it forms the basis for understanding the technical and economic potential for extensive software component reuse. The measurement research aspect of the work recognizes the critical need to enhance the use of quantitative work measures in the software engineering field. The program addresses the adaptation, application, and validation of measurement technology for use in the current Consortium software development practice.

The Consortium's software certification investigations recognize the need to have standard software parts specifications and performance capabilities captured in highly reliable representations. This includes investigation into various methods of building fault-tolerant software. Quality measurement and estimation research also relate to this concern.

3.7 Mature Technology Transfer Program

The Consortium has developed a multifaceted technology transfer program to provide timely transfer of products to member companies (See Figure 20-14). The SPT Division provides a variety of services to the members, including account marketing and assessment, education and training, and installation support.

In many cases, SPT interacts with a counterpart organization in the member company responsible for software technology transfer. This internal organiza-

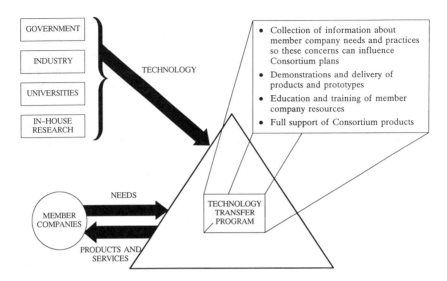

Figure 20-14. A technology transfer program provides timely transfer of products to members.

tion serves as the primary point of contact to accomplish the first step of transfer—the identification and preparation of receiving organizations within the member company. This receptor group also serves as a point of entry into the line organizations. This access is key, providing for early preparation and awareness of Consortium plans and products by member company software managers, program managers and other technical personnel.

This peer to peer linkage between Consortium and member company also supports a necessary flow of information back into the Consortium. Member company needs and practices are a major input to the technical planning process. Such information is gathered by individual Consortium program development managers as they interact with their member company contacts. The Consortium conducts a variety of other activities which generate this crucial feedback, including prototype demonstration workshops, technical program reviews and audits, and product set architecture reviews. Analyzed and assessed in conjunction with technical information from internal and other external sources, this information keeps the Consortium planning process on target, gearing product research and development activities to member company needs.

The Consortium technology transfer strategy provides an incremental payoff stream—one which has already begun to payoff in terms of technical reports, workshops, prototype demonstrations, products, training, and incremental releases.

While technology transfer is an important aspect of the Consortium's technical program, the organization's measure of success is the actual use of its products and technologies in real programs.

4 CONCLUSION

The Software Productivity Consortium is a unified approach to the difficult software development problems facing aerospace companies today. The organization is structured to bring maximum benefit to its members. The Consortium's goal is to make its members more competitive in the systems engineering and integration marketplace. Consortium senior management fully expects to deliver products which will accelerate members far beyond the state of current software development practice.

This will happen in two ways. The Consortium's technical program can either form the basis of an internal software engineering R&D effort or complement its members' existing activities. Either way, the companies which formed the Consortium have invested in the future of software engineering.

REFERENCE

1. *Final Report of the Software Acquisition and Development Working Group*, Assistant Secretary of Defense for Communications, Command, Control and Intelligence, July 1980, pp. 1–3.

Chapter 21

Japan's Sigma Project

Fumihiko Kamijo
Information-Technology Promotion Agency
Shibakoen, Minato-Ku
Tokyo, Japan

I INTRODUCTION

Computer users are aware of the increase of the software inventory that has
occurred while they have accumulated their data processing application. The
inventory of software causes two problems, namely, a delay in the development
of new systems and an excessive workload for maintenance. Both backlogs are
results of a shortage of software engineers, the supply of which is difficult to
increase in a short time because of the complex Japanese educational system.

A possible solution is to improve the code production productivity of the
existing software engineers. Although it was hoped that software engineering
could provide a dramatic solution, it was almost abandoned while experience
in it was being acquired. It is the only technology that is proved to be practical
and usable, but the rate of improvement gained by the technology has been slow
compared to the quick increase rate of the backlog.

Since there is no other candidate, it is now clear that full usage of techniques
of software engineering are a key to solving the backlog problem. The solution
to this technology is software tools. There are many tools applicable in each
phase of the software life cycle, but most of them are not the type of tools based
on a well defined discipline. Some attempts cover a full range of the software
life cycle of locally established standards, others are designed to a specific
application area, but they have never been consolidated into a discipline oriented
and integrated tool system.

The Sigma system (Σ system)[1,2] concept was planned and introduced based
on the observations previously described.

A powerful support to implement successfully the disciplined integration of
software tools is the development environment centered around the UNIX[1]
operating system. The UNIX operating system has been widely accepted by the
academic community, and thus many advanced ideas have been tested and
realized in the form of software tools.

---

[1]UNIX is a registered trademark of AT&T.

Moreover UNIX is independent from other mainframe-supplied operating systems. Its distribution system has a long history; the licensing policy of UNIX System V is also well established by AT&T. It simplifies the complex legal problems associated with operating system licensing to OEM vendors.

The Σ project has borrowed two important features from UNIX: one feature is independence from other software development environments; another is the commonality of interfaces based on the publicity achieved by the policy of source code distribution. These features are valuable because the goals of the project are to construct a comprehensive software environment and to realize a common process for software development.

The software development environment has evolved since the early days of software engineering. One of the most influential advancements of technology is computer networking. The Σ system adopts the excellent controlling capability of a computer network for better management of distributed software development projects; another important advancement is the application of database technology. The sharing of software tools is the most effective method to improve productivity. The software tools in the Σ database are to be propagated using an appropriate means of technology transfer. With all these mechanisms, one can expect a significantly improved, very effective development environment.

Database mechanisms may be combined with application programs: programs may be managed as the machine part storage. It is the important technology toward the reuse of software. The Σ system intends to see through all these objectives.

2 BASIC SYSTEM CONCEPTS

The commonality of interfaces among the tools and engineers is essential to improve the software development productivity and to achieve better training results for engineers. The common interface concept has to be extended to system components, such as the central databases and the distributed workstations.

UNIX System V was selected as the basis for the common operating systems for the Σ center facility and for the Σ workstation. An Σ project team worked out the system software interface standard as the first task and released it to mainframe and workstation vendors. The Σ operating system (Σ OS) definition is a slightly modified version of UNIX System V with a Japanese language option.

2.1 The Architecture of the Σ System Hardware and Software

Hardware for the Σ system consists of three major subsystems. These are the Σ center system, the Σ workstations, and the Σ network. Although the Σ project is responsible for developing an integrated system at a central location, there are plans to set up Σ subcenters as local facilities in many cities.

The Σ center system serves as the central service mechanism for all users. The following are functions of the system:

- collection of candidate software for the software tools (Σ tools);
- appropriate conversion and dissemination of such tools;
- the technical information service;
- the program database service; and
- terminal oriented services using the Σ network.

The Σ workstations are built according to the Σ system software interface definition. The definition was designed and distributed to workstation vendors by the Σ project. They are designed to be connectible to the Σ center via the Σ network, but they may serve as stand-alone software engineering workstations with Σ software tool system.

The Σ network links Σ workstations and Σ center systems. Users may access the common software tools, the application oriented tools, and contributed tools in Σ center databases. They can use any other network services, such as the message exchange facilities provided by the Σ center.

The Σ system software consists of the Σ center software and the user site software (see Figure 21-1). The Σ center software offers various features which will aid the development work. These include the following:

- a set of software tools designed to meet the Σ discipline that realizes the minimal capability of an integrated development environment (the Σ software tool system or Σ tools);

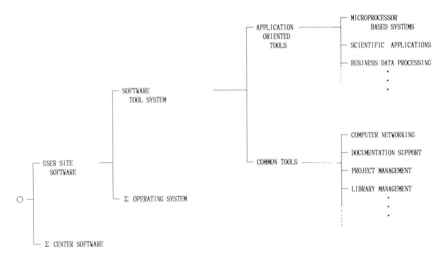

Figure 21-1. Σ system software.

- a software database management service for Σ workstation users;
- a communication network management service using the Σ network definition;
- a demonstration service of the Σ software tool system; and
- a computer center management service for the Σ center.

The user site software consists of a monitor program for Σ workstations (Σ OS) and a set of integrated software tools, the Σ software tool system (Σ tools). Σ OS is the name given to the interface definition among the Σ workstation hardware, the Σ network and the Σ software tool system.

The Σ software tool system is classified in two groups—the common tools and the application oriented tools. In the common tool set there are the computer networking support system, the documentation support system, the project management system, the library management system, and a man-machine interface library. They have been released to workstation vendors so that any Σ workstation may install them as a minimal set of tools common to various applications.

There are four subsystems in the Σ application oriented tools; these are the software development environment for microprocessor-based systems, scientific application, business data processing applications, and process control systems. The following description on some subsystems of the Σ application oriented tools may help in further understanding of the Σ discipline.

Standardization is one important discipline of the software development environment, but effective use of existing tools is also important to improve productivity. The Σ software tool system is designed to accept as many existing tools as possible to fill the needs of customized tools, although modification and/or conversion is necessary. There are tools of various origins that are acceptable by the Σ system; for example, user-owned tools, custom-made private tools, and tools in the market. The Σ tools, for the particular cases, may have to be customized according to the user's specific requirements.

2.2 Development Environment for Microprocessor-Based Systems

The first example of the Σ application oriented tools is the subsystem for microprocessor-based systems.

Software development of microprocessor applications has very specific requirements. The variety of the types of processors causes difficulties. Basic software, such as monitors, language processors, and file systems are not always available. Moreover recent advancement of semiconductor technology has resulted in new processors, one after another. Short life cycles of processors are another cause of difficulty for engineers in this area. One important feature of the development environment for a microprocessor-based system is to introduce hardware independence for the existing development environment. The Σ

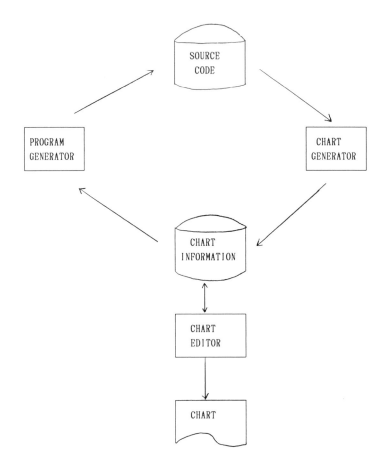

Figure 21-2. Chart-based tools for microprocessor based systems.

project tries to implement more generalized tools, such as editors and test support tools that have the design bases of a higher order language (see Figure 21-2).

An example of the higher order language based tools is the translation system which employs a cross-compilation technique. For example, C is the common language and if a target system has C compiler, then a native compilation process is applicable. Otherwise, a generalized cross-compilation produces programs in the target assembly language, and a native assembler program produces the object modules.

Another example of higher order representation is the chart language. It is one key to improving coding productivity. The Σ chart generator and the Σ chart editor are such tools connect charts and source code. Hierarchical and ComPact (HCP)[2] description chart is selected as the standard chart language for micro-

---

[2]HCP is a registered trademark of Nippon Telephone and Telegraph.

processor-based application. Supported source languages are C (the UNIX System V version) and FORTRAN 77.

When there are few or no high-level language based tools, the testing of large software project is a problem. It is the typical situation encountered in microprocessor application projects. Therefore, a program test support system is another key tool (see Figure 21-3). The Σ project recognized the problem and allocated significant resources to develop the Σ test support system for C, the standard language. It consists of the following tools:

- a C Interpretive Debugger
- an On-line C Symbolic Debugger
- Σ ICE
- a Load Module Debugger
- a Simulator-debugger (planned)
- a Test Case Generator (planned)
- a Test Data Generator (planned)
- a Stub/Driver Generator (planned)
- a Prototyping Tools for Peripheral Device Operation (planned)

2.3   Tools for Scientific Applications

The second example of Σ application oriented tools is designed for users of FORTRAN. Scientific application tools for FORTRAN programmers support all phases of the life cycle of software development. Figure 21-4 shows a tool system supported by FORTRAN 77.

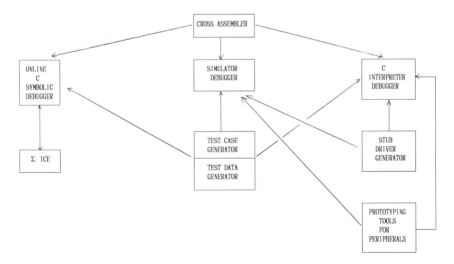

Figure 21-3. Debugging support tools for microprocessor based systems.

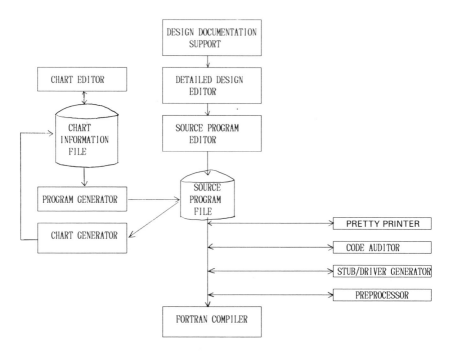

Figure 21-4. Tool system for FORTRAN programming.

Two ways to improve the development productivity are support for automatic documentation in the design phase and interface generation for target machines in the programming phase.

The tools for automatic documentation include Design Documentation Support, the Detailed Design Editor, and the Source Program Editor. Chart-based tools are also supported. Some of the tools to refine source code, such as the Pretty Printer, the Code Auditor, the Preprocessor, and the Stub/Driver Generator are included in the tools for scientific applications.

There are also tools for program testing in a cross development environment: the Symbolic Debugger, the Static Analyzer, the Dynamic Analyzer, and the Side-Effect Analyzer are all effective tools for the cross compilation mechanism.

Since the differences in the FORTRAN languages of many vendors are less significant compared to the COBOL family, an Σ workstation may use the common FORTRAN 77 compiler. Therefore a Σ user may compile his/her source program and test it on different workstations.

Another consideration in a FORTRAN environment is a mechanism to encourage reuse of existing source programs. Scientific applications have better chances in preparation for the well defined algorithm library, and code reuse is an important vehicle to achieve better productivity.

2.4   Tools for Business Data Processing

The third example of Σ application oriented tools is the subset for business data processing. It is designed as a COBOL applications generator (see Figure 21-5). Chart editing, Skeleton editing, Pattern customizing, and interfacing by means of the Σ Data Architecture are the four basic applications.

There are three chart systems supported by the Σ application oriented tools for business applications. They are the YAC II system by Fujitsu Ltd., the PAD system by Hitachi Ltd., and the SPD system by Nippon Electric Corp. Other foreign chart systems may be added to the skeleton generator—that is the main body of the chart-to-source program translator using a template representation. A template is an intermediate mechanism for representing program specifications.

A program skeleton is a custom source text which is generated by the skeleton generator. A skeleton is defined by standard program patterns and customizing parameters. For more detailed adjustments, a program skeleton may be customized using the skeleton editor.

Data Architecture (see Figure 21-6) is the key to source code generation. It defines the interface of the skeleton, the data processing specification, the input/output specification, and program text specification. It consists of the following:

* Program Specification;
* Program Skeleton Definition;
* Generated Source Definition;
* Input/Output Specification;
* Chart Specification;
* Standard Pattern Definition; and
* Program Part Specification.

3   CONCLUSION

The Σ project has a five year development period (1986 to 1990). The results of development will be available, and technology transfer activities will follow as a business activity. Some of the completed tools have been in field testing since the fall of 1987.

The Σ project has tried to follow relevant international standardization activities, for example, the selection of the UNIX operating system as the basis of the Σ system. The choice of System V, instead of the BSD version, was the result of such considerations, although there were some technical difficulties when the decision was made: the expansion of System V for the Japanese language was one of them.

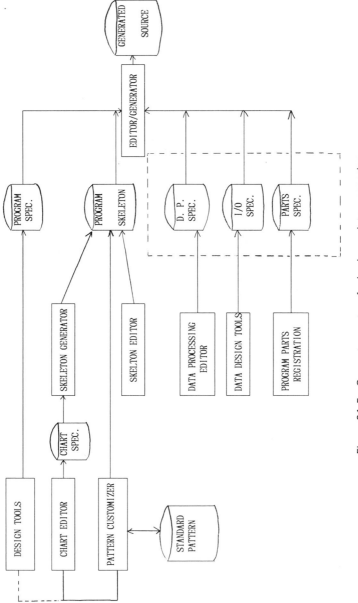

Figure 21-5.   Generator system for business data processing.

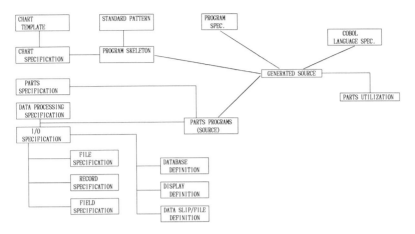

Figure 21-6. Data architecture for business data processing.

Field test activities (Monitoring Test) began in late 1987. The first subsystem in the test field was the tools for microprocessor based applications. The tools for scientific applications are in the test field now, and the business application tools will be next.

The Σ system itself is not a fully completed tool set: rather it provides a minimum subset for development environment. The Σ project expects and encourages users to add as many tools of their own as possible by conversion or interface adjustments. One purpose of the Σ application oriented tools is to provide users with an initial, starting tool set. A user's Σ based development environment will be his/her own customized system. It is the only way a user can evolve an ideal toolset. Custom tools will eventually evolve and be adjusted to Σ OS so that they will become marketable products.

The Σ network may be used as a project management tool in the beginning phase, then as a communication tool for Σ system users, and finally as a method for software propagation.

It is now clear that the Σ project is discipline oriented. There are three issues: standardization, or system commonality; environment independence; and comprehensive integration. The Σ application oriented tools create common access capabilities for Σ workstation users. Independence from hardware and computer networks are achieved by the Σ OS and the Σ network definitions. Well organized integration of the Σ operating system, the Σ software tool system, and the Σ center software offers users a totalized project management capability. The open architecture of the Σ software tool system is particularly important for the users who require a customized environment.

The author is hoping that an integrated software development environment, like the Σ system, would help the improvement of software productivity, software quality, and maintainability not only in Japan but also in any community.

REFERENCES

1. Σ Project: *Proceedings 1st Σ Symposium,* Information-technology Promotion Agency, November 1986 (in Japanese).
2. Σ Project: *Proceedings 2nd Σ Symposium,* Information-technology Promotion Agency, February 1988 (in Japanese).

Chapter 22

European Software Factory Plan—The ESF Profile

WILHELM SCHÄFER
STZ GmbH
Software-Technologie-Zentrum
Dortmund 50
West Germany

HERBERT WEBER
Informatik X
University of Dortmund
Dortmund 50
West Germany

ABSTRACT

The authors present a profile of the EUREKA Software Factory (ESF) after 10 months of work in the definition phase of the project. The ESF project aims at developing flexible concepts for the integration of software development support tools, which have been built at different sites, and the application of those concepts in building customized software factories. The authors discuss the specific characteristics of a software factory in general and of ESF in particular. The latter includes a description of the ESF's basic concepts for achieving tool integration. In particular, this includes the definition of a reference architecture and a reference model which serve as the general framework for tool integration within ESF. This chapter represents the personal views of the authors and does not commit the ESF consortium nor any of the ESF partners to this description of the project.

1 INTRODUCTION—THE ESF PROFILE

The ESF project is a European research effort funded under the EUREKA program. EUREKA is a multinational European research program intended to fund projects in the most important high-tech domains. The ESF project started in September 1986. During the first year, the so-called definition phase, the basic concepts and strategies to be applied in ESF were defined. The project is intended to last for 10 years. The ESF consortium currently includes three research institutions and eleven industrial partners from West Germany, France, the United Kingdom, Sweden, Norway, and Spain.

The term Software Factory (SF) was introduced a number of years ago and has since been used in different ways to denote rather different concepts of the Software Production Environment (SPE)—also called Software Development Environment (SDE)—all to enable a more industrialized production of software. This chapter is intended to characterize a software factory through an analysis of the most important factors of software production environments. This analysis is meant to provide an answer to the question "What is a software factory and what distinguishes a software factory from other types of software production environments?"

The developers of the ESF project chose to propose a number of concepts for a software factory and to develop an architecture proposal for ESF. In this chapter the concepts and the proposed architecture will be evaluated by stating the principal goals to be achieved with ESF and by comparing them with the goals expected to be achieved in other SPE projects. The result of this evaluation will provide an answer to the question "What is specific about ESF, and what distinguishes ESF from other related concepts?"

In addition, an architecture for ESF will be described. Since ESF is not meant to be a single product but a variety of products that conform to a reference model, the architecture, as it is presented here, is called a "reference architecture." An explanation of that reference architecture will then bring about the explanation of how a particular ESF may be built that conforms to this reference architecture.

A delivered software factory that conforms to the reference architecture is called an instantiation of ESF (or ESF instance). Knowledge of this architecture will help suppliers provide components that can be integrated in an ESF instance. The conceptual foundation for producing an instantiation of ESF has been developed in the definition phase and will be described. The interconnection of existing components to ESF is generally important. As tool suppliers may only want to develop tools for particular tasks in the software development process, they must be aware of the constraints that exist for the interconnection of those tools to ESF and for the interoperatability of those tools in the framework of ESF. The development of concepts which support the interconnection and the interoperatability will therefore be explained. The term software factory refers to a system that supports software development for many different application domains and for many different organizational environments.

The chapter is organized as follows: after characterizing a software factory by stating the distinguishing factors to an SPE in the next section, the ESF specifics (i.e., the ESF conceptual basis) are discussed in Section 3. The derivation of a reference architecture from these basic concepts is explained in Section 4. How a certain ESF instance is being built and tailored towards the specific needs of one company is explained in Section 5. Finally, Section 6 includes a summary and a brief description of how future work within ESF will be organized.

2 CHARACTERISTICS OF A SOFTWARE FACTORY

Different types of SPEs (or SDEs) have been proposed and developed (e.g., Gandalf, Mentor, IPSEN, PECAN, etc.)[11,3,5,16] and some of them are in industrial use (e.g., Promod and Prados).[12,10] They differ primarily in the degree of support they provide to software developers—the coverage of the software development process they provide. In many cases, they offer a number of tools which support only a particular task, such as Programming-in-the-Small (e.g., PECAN) or Programming-in-the-Large (e.g., PRADOS).

The types of supports provided by different tools in an SPE and the interoperatability of those tools are the most important discriminating factors of SPEs.

A software factory is an SPE that provides total coverage of the software production process including all technical and managerial tasks. Moreover, it provides a higher degree of automation and permits better resource re-utilization than any other SPE.

To arrive at a more profound characterization of a software factory, the main distinguishing factors of SPEs in general and of an SF in particular will now be discussed.

Characterizing Factors of an SPE

Degree of Coverage

The development of SPEs began with the development of individual tools for the support of software developers in one particular task. A tool, therefore, provides only a partial support in the development of a software system. According to the structuring of the software development process into a number of steps or phases, a tool is supportive in one or only a few of those steps and provides, consequently, only a partial coverage of the production process.

Diversity of Development Methods

The development of software is conventionally enabled through the application of a variety of styles and methods applied at the different stages of software development. Some of these methods are supported by tools. This creates a diversity of styles, methods, and tools that support the software production process. The difficulties arising from the application of different methods, such as the need to learn them all, to apply them in an intertwined mode, the selection of appropriate methods for the respective stage of development, etc., are very often prohibitive in achieving a full coverage of the software development process. A trade-off can therefore be seen between the full coverage of the development process and the selection of a minimal set of methods and tools to achieve that full coverage. A good balance between the number and type of methods and a reasonable degree of coverage is thus crucial in the development of an SPE.

Degree of Integration

A number of different tools integrated into an SPE can be used by software developers in different modes of operation. This usage mode is primarily determined by the degree of integration of tools provided by the SPE. The degree of integration also determines the type of interoperatability between tools in the SPE. To interoperate without human intervention, tools must be able to "understand" each other: they must be able to reuse each other's knowledge with little or no human intervention.

Degree of Expert Knowledge Support

SPEs were first developed to provide data acquisition, data management, and data retrieval capabilities that aid the software developer in his/her task to produce machine readable documents, manipulate those documents in a manner preserving consistency, and provide powerful access capabilities to these documents for their continuous use. These types of SPEs behave in a definite fashion, since all reactions of the SPE to an outside stimulus are determined by the set of programs that constitute the SPE.

In recent attempts to develop next generations of SPEs, expert system concepts which are capable of using expert knowledge to generate new expert knowledge through the existence of deduction capabilities are being exploited. Those deductions are based on a given set of facts and rules that can be stated about a knowledge domain. The deduction mechanism is capable of verifying that facts are compatible with one another, and other facts are implied by the given facts and rules: an example could be the automatic monitoring of consistency between related documents. The SPEs that provide this type of expert system can be expected to react in a nondefinite manner to user stimuli.

Division of Labor Support

Some SPEs may be developed to support an individual software developer. These SPEs do not provide any help in the coordination of work of a number of software developers working on the same software system.

Those SPEs that support many developers, on the other hand, must then be capable to support the division of labor in large software development projects and to relieve management of some coordination functions.

Distribution Support

Since software development requires, in most cases, a division of labor between many—maybe geographically dispersed—developers, the support systems are often needed to be decentralized to provide aid at the location of the software developer. Both locally distributed systems, exploiting the benefits of LAN-type interconnections of host computer systems, as well as widely distributed systems that enable the widely distributed work of software developers are in demand.

Extensibility Support

An SPE can be developed to exist in its original form with minor changes taking place during its lifetime, or it may be developed to enable its upgrading with new functionalities and tools. This extensibility of an SPE is then based on a number of provisional measures that must be taken at the design time. Consequently, nonextendable SPEs may be simpler to produce but are rather inflexible with respect to later changes of requirements. Extendible SPEs require more effort for the development of the proper extension concepts, but later on they are more adaptable to changes of requirements. The extensibility of an SPE also plays an important role in the gradual introduction of SPE supported software development in an organization. It enables an incremental investment and familiarization of the organization with computer supported software production.

User Interface

A uniform User Interface (UI) is a very basic characteristic which is provided by almost all SPEs. It includes a uniform screen layout as well as a uniform command language for all tools of an SPE. From the user's point of view, an SPE could be characterized as one single very sophisticated tool to support software development activities in different stages depending, of course, on the degree of coverage it provides (as previously discussed).

The discussion of the concept of an SF dates back to the late seventies. Many concepts that have been presented over the years are not different from what has been previously termed an SPE. At one stage in that discussion the notion of an SF primarily referred to tailorization of the software production into a great number of very specific and narrow-minded tasks. In other instances the term was used more to refer to any type of industrialization of the production that was meant to overcome the more crafts-oriented software production.

However, one paramount discriminating factor in the separation of an SF and an SPE is that the previously given characteristics could be more or less achieved by an SPE but have to be guaranteed by an SF. In particular, an SF always provides full coverage of the software development process, does not allow a diversity of development methods, provides a very high degree of integration,

Table 22-1. Characterization of
an SPE and its distinction from
an SF.

Factor	SPE	SF
Full coverage	possible	yes
Diversity	possible	no
Integration	low or high	high
Expert knowledge	no	yes
Division of labour	possible	yes
Distribution	possible	yes
Extensibility	possible	yes
Uniform user interf.	yes	yes

provides expert knowledge support, supports many developers, enables a distributed realization of the SF, and provides a high degree of extensibility. Furthermore, the more crafts-oriented software production is overcome within an SF by emphasizing the industrialization and the automation of software production. In the understanding of the ESF project, industrialization depends on the existence of a proper conceptual basis for software production that may then aid in the automation of as many production tasks as possible. In that sense, automation depends on the capability of tools to interact in an SF and to "understand" each other. The possible understanding and meaning of information is related to the degree of integration that has been achieved by the tools of a particular SF. An SF is therefore considered to be a coordinated set of activities (constituting the software development process) supported by an integrated set of tools (constituting the SPE itself). An SF is a very sophisticated version of an SPE with respect to the automatic interoperation of tools in accordance to a given software development process. The characterization of an SPE and its distinction from an SF is summarized in Table 22-1.

The particular importance of integration of tools will be given credit in a description of the integration concepts provided by ESF in the next section. It will become clearer that ESF requires the integration of tools at least on the basis of a proper understanding and thereby formal model of the software development process.

3   THE ESF CONCEPTUAL BASIS

Key Concepts that Form ESF

A priori Integration

A number of projects conducted in recent years have tried to develop an integration concept by starting with existing tools that were integrated through a later developed integration framework.[13,14,15] The results of these projects were systems that provided a rather low degree of integration and were—despite the low degree of integration—rather large and cumbersome. This "a posteriori" integration approach has, for its deficiencies in the ESF project been rejected already in the first proposal. Instead, the ESF project was to become more successful with an "a priori" integration concept.

The difference between the two may best be explained by referring to the respective deficiencies and virtues.

In an a posteriori integration, the integration is essentially the search for the common properties of a number of existing tools: the integration will always rest at a level that is determined by these common properties. The residual differences between tools are ultimately the cause for human intervention in the use of the integrated system. A posteriori integrated systems also lack flexibility for the indirect fixing of the production process with the selection of the tools that will be integrated. The required instantiation, adjustment, and extension capabilities that were to be very important for a software factory cannot be achieved.

A posteriori integrations, however, are attractive for certain reasons. This type of integration provides for the continuous use of existing tools and, hence, for the preservation of investments into their development. For more commercial reasons, the approach is promising since it supports an evolution of a factory out of individual components with a limited investment risk taken with each step in that evolution.

The a priori integration, on the other hand, is a postulate about the most reasonable common properties of tools in a software factory and the development of a kernel that materializes these common properties. In this integration, provisions can be built into that kernel to cope with instantiations, adjustments, and extensions to the utmost degree, and guarantee use of the already existing and available tools and hence a loss of valuable investments.

Based on the experience the ESF partners developed with many projects, the consortium decided to develop an a priori integration concept. This concept has been termed "top-down-conceptualization." The concept suggests that the ESF development starts out with a company's perception of the requirements of a software factory (the top) that will be transformed into a detailed design of such a system (the down). As a result of that procedure, the ESF first exists in the form of a complete specification of the system. That specification may later be implemented in a "bottom-up" fashion with the implementation of individual components, which will later be integrated in accordance to the a priori specification of the system.

Degrees of Tool-Integration

As mentioned in the previous section, each SF provides a very high degree of industrialization and automation. Furthermore, a single instance should not

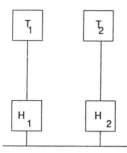

Figure 22-1. Machine-integrated tools.

include a diversity of development methods. To provide the high degree of integration, a number of integration concepts of lower degree must be provided to arrive at that goal. Therefore, an ordering of so-called "integration levels" is introduced and the respective mechanisms explained that are supposed to enable that degree of automation. Furthermore, this precisely defines the ESF-concept of tool integration.

The lowest degree of integration will be achieved by the interconnection of tools that exists on different computer devices via a communication infrastructure (i.e., some type of network facility). That infrastructure only overcomes heterogeneities in hardware and basic software. It enables the user to invoke different tools on the same machine. Hence, tools which are integrated in that sense are called "machine-integrated." The respective integration mechanisms are not of concern in ESF since it is expected that those mechanisms will be provided through standardized computer communication [for example, the International Organization for Standardization/Open System Interconnection (ISO/OSI) reference-model]. Figure 22-1 illustrates this type of integration.

The next higher degree of internal integration is achieved if all tools share a common object-store that stores all objects produced and used by any of the integrated tools. Additionally, tools have to share a common I/O manager who is responsible for the presentation of any information on the screen. Tools that are integrated in that sense are called "object-integrated" (see Figure 22-2).

The common syntactical standard for object descriptions provided by an object storage system or an I/O manager may differ depending on the used object store or I/O manager. The authors explain this more carefully with some examples.

A very simple standard for an object store is provided by the UNIX[1] file system which only offers an alpanumeric string as a syntactical standard. Analogously, the Graphical Kernal System (GKS) as an I/O manager offers only polygons, polymarks, characters, etc. as syntactical standards for representing objects on the screen. A much more sophisticated syntactical standard is provided by an Object Management System (OMS), such as PCTE-OMS[8] or a

---

[1]UNIX is a registered trademark of AT&T.

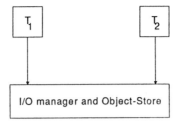

Figure 22-2. Object-integrated tools.

window manager like Sun View.[17] Certain SDE projects concentrate on the development of even more sophisticated object stores, which provide a syntactical standard especially developed for a special SDE (e.g., annotated abstract syntax trees in MENTOR[3] or attributed directed graphs in IPSEN).[6] In such cases the standard provided by these object storage systems enables efficient storage and retrieval of complex objects and particular relations (e.g., static semantics information) between objects.

The next higher degree of integration is achieved if the proper selection of tools that is to be integrated is based on the specification of a software development process. In this case the specification of the software development process (e.g., a certain phase model) determines not only the types of tools that are to be integrated but also the ordering of their application according to a development process. How the specification of a software development process will look will be explained in the next section. Tools integrated in this way are called "process-integrated," as shown in Figure 22-3.

It should be noted that this type of integration does not automatically require that tools are object-integrated. Consider, for example, an SADT-editor,[(2)] an editor used to describe the module architecture of a software system, and a Pascal-editor. Those tools could be ordered and used according to a phase model. However, they must not be able to exchange information via a common storage mechanism. The information represented by the SADT diagram could possibly be transferred to the module architecture editor by the user without any machine support.

The benefits of object-integrated and process-integrated are combined by the next higher degree of integration which is called "method-integrated." It requires a proper selection of tools, according to a certain development process and a proper specification of their interoperation. The latter means that either tools share information via a common object store or a common I/O manager (see Figure 22-4). In addition, transformers are provided which enable the automatic reuse of information assembled with the aid of one tool by another; for example, the derivation of a first coarse-grained module architecture from

---

[(2)]Structural Analysis and Design Technique (SADT) is a registered trademark of Softech.

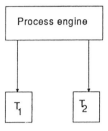

Figure 22-3. Process-integrated tools.

the SADT-description of a software system. This type of integration is, for example, provided by systems like MENTOR, IPSEN, or PROMOD.

This is also that type of integration required from any SF and, particularly, has to be achieved by any ESF instance.

The ultimate degree of integration is achieved if only one single development method exists that will be applied in the development of only one type of object that in turn will be used to uniformly represent all information about a software system. In this case, as shown in Figure 22-5, one single language is used which enables the description of all documents in all stages of software development. The ideas and consequences of such a software development paradigm are described in more detail in References 7 and 18. Tools that are integrated in that sense are called ''method-uniform.''

As already indicated, one may achieve a certain degree of integration only if other lower degrees are already assured. The ordering of these different degrees of integration is summarized in Figure 22-6. The arrows refer to the lower degree of integration that must be provided to achieve the respective higher degree of integration.

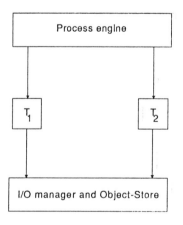

Figure 22-4. Method-integrated tools.

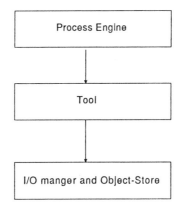

Figure 22-5. Method-uniform tools.

In stating the ESF goal, the tools of any ESF instance must be method-integrated. This requires object-integrated as well as process-integrated tools. How this goal is intended to be achieved and supported by the ESF reference architecture is explained in the next section.

The Role Concept

According to the previously explained a priori integration approach, ESF started out with a requirement analysis of the functionality of an SF (i.e., a careful

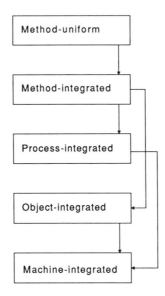

Figure 22-6. Dependencies between degrees of tool integration.

description of the tasks which have to be performed during software development). To describe those tasks in a structured and comprehensive manner, the role concept was introduced—the description of which is based on an Entity Relationship (ER) diagram. It gives a precise definition of the functionality of an SF from the user's point of view.

In more detail, ESF allows various users to play different roles (e.g., a project manager, designer, or programmer) and thus perform different tasks during software development. Particularly, a user performs a task to produce a certain deliverable; a designer uses a certain specification method to produce the module architecture of a certain software system. Those deliverables are produced by one or more tools; for example, editors, compilers, or analyzers, which aid to perform the corresponding task. The most general user view of ESF is displayed in Figure 22-7.

It is worth mentioning here that the supported roles may vary from one ESF instance to another; e.g., one ESF instance may separate the roles of a programmer and a designer, whereas another one combines the two into one role. However, the concept of describing the functionality of any ESF instance by roles is uniform to any ESF instance. Thereby, the required division of labor support provided by any ESF instance is defined by roles.

Reusability

The ESF consortium wanted to tackle the problem of reusing software according to the a priori integration concept. In particular, the ESF consortium wants to

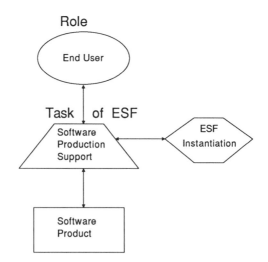

Figure 22-7. General user's view of ESF.

develop methods and techniques for supporting the reusability of prefabricated software components.

A popular term frequently used to describe the goal to be achieved is "software components from off the shelf." It hints at the same parts and components market that exist in many other engineering fields. However, this type of a software component market is far from being existent. For its development, software components must be specified to fulfill precise requirements and thus have a precisely defined "functionality." The development of those software property specifications depends on the existence of formal specification techniques with which one may fully specify all the outside observable properties of those components. One such attempt to develop such a formal specification technique is investigated within the PEACOCK project which is partly carried out at the University of Dortmund.[1]

In addition to the appropriate specification techniques, tools are needed to store reusable components, to search for reusable components in the component store on the basis of the properties descriptions for components, and to validate and verify the interconnectability of components. To provide those tools is to develop a EUREKA Software Factory—for the benefits expected from the re-use of components—as a factory that supports the re-use of components in the production of software to the utmost extent.[9] The ESF itself will be a sample system heavily constructed of such reusable components. Only with the re-use of components and with proper provision for the interconnection of prefabricated components, will the ESF project be able to achieve its goal, which in later discussions is shortly called the "plug-in" property of ESF.

As more companies take part in ESF, which have already invested a considerable amount of effort into the development of tools, ESF also has to take care of the integration of already existing tools. Therefore, the integration techniques (described in the following two sections) offer a degree of flexibility which will minimize the necessary changes of existing tools when including them in a particular ESF instance. However, there exists, of course, the usual trade-off between integration and extensibility. As the degree of integration increases, the extensibility of the SF becomes more difficult.

4 THE ESF REFERENCE ARCHITECTURE

Figure 22-8 shows a first, rough description of the ESF reference architecture. Each box represents a basic component; i.e., a subsystem which is, of course, in a more fine-grained architectural description, subdivided into modules. Each subsystem can be regarded as an encapsulation of an object type. It consists of an export part, its interface, and an implementation part, its body. The interface describes the provided resources; i.e., the (possibly complex) object type together with its operations. Any arrow in the diagram represents a use-relation between subsystems.

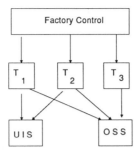

Figure 22-8. ESF reference architecture.

The service provided by the components UIS (User Interface Service), OSS (Object Storage Service), and Factory Control and their interrelation using certain communication mechanisms form the ESF-support. The ESF-support is the interface between an existing operating system and the individual tools of a certain ESF instantiation. Therefore, the tools depicted in Figure 22-8 can be regarded as an arbitrary collection as a certain instantiation is not being described here, but rather the reference architecture is. The above given subsystems are now explained in more detail.

The components UIS and OSS provide the means to achieve object-integration for tools in any ESF instance (see Section 3). UIS provides a common interface for the man–machine dialogue within ESF. All other components use the operations of this interface for reading user inputs or presenting information to the user on some output device (screen, printer, etc.). Operations which are provided by this interface handle, for example, window management which includes the manipulation of special purpose windows, such as forms or menus. However, this does not imply that the implementation of this interface has to be done by building a special ESF-UIS: it could also be done by building adapters to existing windows or I/O-systems for printers, etc. Existing I/O systems could also be used within an ESF instance. Of course, such an interface must be easily extendible. It is then possible to add more sophisticated I/O devices later which allow, for example, speech I/O.

Very similar to the UIS, the OSS provides a common interface to enable the storage and retrieval of objects and relations between objects in a central data repository (or global storage). All other components use that interface if they use the central data repository of an ESF instantiation for storing or retrieving information. The OSS realizes the ESF data model. However, this does not imply that the implementation of this interface has to be done by building a special ESF-OSS (or ESF-OMS). This implementation could also be done by building adapters to existing storage services or OMSs; for example, existing storage services (such as PCTE) could be used within an ESF instance by implementing the ESF-storage service interface on top of the operations of an existing storage service.

In addition to the exchange of information via an OSS, any ESF instance could contain special adapters for the direct exchanges of data between tools. This strategy can be chosen if the exchanged data does not require permanent storage. For example, a syntax-directed editor using an abstract syntax tree representation of a program and a compiler expecting an ASCII-file as input could communicate via an adapter which flattens the tree into a text file. This text file, however, does not have to be stored permanently, as it is never used again. This point-to-point connection is not mentioned explicitly in the architecture, because its existence always depends on the specific tools contained in a particular ESF-instance.

The last subsystem to be explained is the Factory Control. ($T1$, $T2$, and $T3$ are just examples for arbitrary tools.) It provides monitoring capabilities of different tools within one instance.

Monitoring allows the use of different tools only in a certain order or by special users who have the proper access to these tools. For example, certain user roles, such as a project manager, designer, implementor, or secretary are entitled to use certain tools and have certain access rights; for example a project manager is only allowed to use management information tools, an implementor uses only editors and compilers, and the secretary uses only an editor and the mail system. A certain order of tool activations could be necessary to fulfill a certain task, such as updating all project management information in all documents for informing all team members about changes of the design. All these dependencies are implemented and thereby monitored by the component Factory Control. This means that this subsystem realizes the chosen software development process model of one instance—it guarantees method-integrated tools (see Section 3).

In a more advanced ESF instance, smarter techniques could be applied to provide a more powerful factory control. The idea of a rule based expert system is introduced to provide more sophisticated user support; i.e. the Factory Control not only monitors the correct use of tools (as described) but supports a user in choosing the appropriate tools to fulfill the task to be carried out. It could even be described that the factory automatically executes certain tasks (without being triggered by a corresponding user command) because the knowledge acquired by the factory during its use implies to carry out that task. Furthermore, certain user profiles, such as novice, advanced, or experienced are described using the notion of facts and rules, and thus a profile could thereby dynamically change when a certain user is actually using the factory. In this way, it is possible to realize the automatic adaptation of the external behavior of the factory to the knowledge of a certain user. One can say that such a factory not only reacts (i.e., not only carry out user's commands) but gives active support during the software development process. Thereby expert knowledge support becomes part of any ESF instance as required in Section 3. The introduction of such techniques requires the enhancement of the underlying OSS such that it evolves into a knowledge base. The rules and facts expressing the knowledge about the just mentioned sophisticated user support have to be stored and interpreted as well. By enhancing the OSS, those services are provided.

A more detailed description and an example for describing the software development process by rules is contained in a forthcoming publication which examines the subject of expert knowledge support within an SF more thoroughly.[4]

After having given a brief overview of the ESF reference architecture, it is now described in more detail, thereby clarifying the notion of the ESF reference model. It has already been mentioned that ESF heavily emphasizes the extensibility aspect. Therefore, a very central and specific issue of ESF is the way of defining interfaces between the basic architectural components, the UIS and OSS. In other approaches such as PCTE or CAIS[2] just one single interface is provided for these components. Any tool has to be adjusted to that single interface. This of course, heavily restricts the flexibility and does not ideally support the aforementioned plug-in property (Section 3). ESF provides more flexibility in defining different interfaces on different abstraction levels. This so-called ESF Reference Model[(3)] is now explained in more detail.

The key feature of the ESF Reference Model is the aforementioned "plug-in" capability. To enable the plug-ins, standardized "sockets" are needed for the standardized plugs attached to the tools to be integrated into an ESF instance. The ESF Reference Model provides those standardized "sockets" for different types of tools. Therefore, "sockets" will exist at different integration levels. It is assumed in the ESF Reference Model that a level enables the exchange of objects that are specific to that level. Components that are integrated via that level can only exchange objects of the respective type. To enable the plug-in of a great variety of tools, the ESF Reference Model provides for a number of levels at which those plug-ins can take place. The resulting structured integration framework may then be depicted as in Figure 22-9.

Each level L_i foresees the exchange of a number of different types of objects $O_{i,k}$. The levels are ordered in a hierarchic fashion with relationships between the different levels that describe the mappings M_i, M_{i+1} between all the objects at level l_i and the objects at level l_{i+1} as well as the mappings M_i, M_{i-1} between all objects at level l_i and those at level l_{i-1}. Objects at level l_i may be represented by objects at level l_{i-1}.

For any set of tools that may be integrated via level l_i, these tools may be either of the following:

- Horizontally integrated—they exchange objects of the types provided at level l_i and they do not encompass a mapping capability for the represen-

---

[(3)]The name "ESF Reference Model" has been chosen to refer to the similarities between the ESF Reference Model and the ISO/OSI Reference Model. In fact, the ESF Reference Model may be understood as a natural extension of the ISO/OSI model towards a particular application domain.

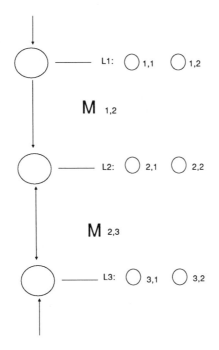

Figure 22-9. ESF reference model: integration levels.

tation of objects provided at level i in terms of objects provided at another level. For example, in Figure 22-10, C_1 and C_2 are integrated via level l_i that provides for the exchange of objects of type O_i, C_1, C_2 could be plugged into an ESF instance via level l_i. As an example, Figure 22-11 shows the horizontal integration of two tools which support manipulation of petri-net diagrams.

• Vertically integrated—different tools adjacent to different integration levels exchange different types of objects provided at the respective level. They must encompass mapping capabilities for the representation of objects provided at level i in terms of objects at level $i+1$ or at level $i-1$ (see Figure 22-12). As an example, the Reference Model is applied to the

Figure 22-10. Horizontal integration.

O ᵢ : Petri Net representation objects

Figure 22-11. A sample horizontal integration.

definition of interfaces for an OMS (see Figure 22-13). A more elaborate description of this example together with its specific benefits is given in Reference 9.

The ESF Reference Model has been introduced as a multi level schema for the integration of tools. Each level has been characterized so far by the types of objects that are subject to exchange on that level.

With the definition of the type of objects that are exchanged between tools, the ESF Reference Model also specifies the kind of operations that can be invoked from tools on objects of the type provided at the respective level. These operations are then the ones that determine the kind of interaction that can take place between tools. For a full specification of that interaction, an additional specification will be given for each level that determines the permitted ordering

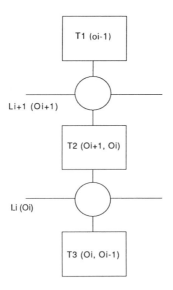

Figure 22-12. Vertical integration.

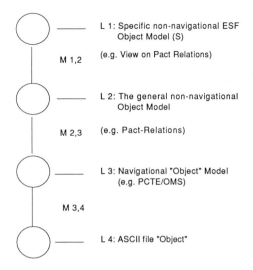

Figure 22-13. A sample vertical integration for OMSs.

of operation invocations at the respective level to guarantee a disciplined inter-action of the integrated tools.

Since the specification of objects together with the permitted operations and with the permitted ordering of operations determines the discipline for interac-tion of tools, these specifications have been called interaction protocols (or sometimes communication layers). Those protocols are intended to be standard-ized within ESF.

A tool can then be integrated into an ESF instance at a particular level of the ESF Reference Model if it obeys the respective interaction protocol. This is the basis for the previously discussed plug-in capability of ESF, since it is intended in the ESF project to develop these protocols and propose their standardization. Note however, that plugging a tool into a lower level usually requires more effort in building the tool than plugging it into a higher level, because the latter one provides already many operations which have to be provided by the tool in the first case. Additionally, using adaptors, of course, results in less efficiency with respect to runtime.

Since many tools can be integrated that all comply with the interaction protocol, these protocols have been given the illustrative name ''Software Buses'' (SWBs). This term refers to the same plug-in capability provided for hardware systems through standard hardware bus systems. This illustrative view is also supported by Figure 22-14, the refined drawing of the reference archi-tecture. It now shows that different possible levels exist where tools could be plugged into an ESF instance.

In the next section, what the procedure looks like that enables the plug-in of a tool is described, and how the instantiation process is supported within ESF.

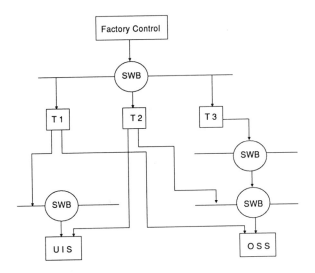

Figure 22-14. Refined reference architecture.

5 INSTANTIATION AND CUSTOMIZATION

In addition to the reference architecture, ESF also provides more detailed concepts for configuring an ESF instantiation. The two orthogonal concepts used in such a configuring process are called customization and implementation.

Customization refers to two possibilities in configurating an entire ESF instance (i.e., creating an ESF instance including all the tools in that particular instance as well as the control of these tools). These include the following:

- The selection of existing appropriate tools such that the resulting instantiation fulfills a particular type of needs and requirements given for a special instantiation.
- The actualization of formal parameters when using generic tools. Here the term ''generic'' is meant to refer to a concept similar to the parameterization concept now available in modern programming languages, such as Ada. Generic tools are instantiated to specific tools by the actualization of the formal parameters of the generic tools with proper actual parameters at actualization time. A parser generator or the generator of a syntax-aided editor, such as MENTOR are examples for such generic tools.

Such a generation is not only possible for individual tools but, however, should be applied to the instantiation process of an entire ESF instance. The generic approach is well suited and should be applied when building an initial ESF instance, whereas the selection of particular tools, in general, should be used when extending an existing instance. Figure 22-15 depicts the customization concept.

Figure 22-15. Formal customization.

In Figure 22-15, the generic ESF is a model (i.e., a conceptual schema in DB-terminology) of an ESF; the ESF instantiation is a specifically tailored model for a particular ESF instance. The customization depicted in the Figure refers to the formal mapping between the two models; therefore, it is called formal customization. Both the generic ESF as well as the ESF-instance may also exist as real implementations, as indicated in Figure 22-16.

The formal customization mapping, existing between the models of the generic ESF and an ESF instantiation, corresponds now to an actual customization mapping between an implemented generic ESF and an implemented ESF instantiation. The implemented generic ESF could be regarded as an environment to support the generation of ESF instances. This will now be explained in more detail.

A meta-model (i.e., a meta-language) as shown in Figure 22-17, is provided to precisely specify the generic ESF (i.e., the model of that generic ESF), the set of permitted ESF instantiations (i.e., the set of models of permitted ESF instantiations), and the mapping between the two models.

It is now important for the application of the instantiation concept to provide answers to the following questions:

- How to arrive at a generic ESF (i.e., a model / a conceptual schema of the generic ESF)?
- How to arrive at an implemented generic ESF?
- How to arrive at an ESF instantiation, and how to arrive at an implemented ESF instantiation?

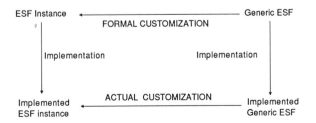

Figure 22-16. Customization and implementation.

Meta Model	Specifications language for specifying
	The generic ESF
	The ESF instances
	The formal customization

Figure 22-17. The meta model.

The answers to these questions are the following:

- The ESF project is aimed at the development of the model of a generic ESF on the basis of the accumulated knowledge and experience of the ESF partners about the production processes that must be supported for the production of different types of software (e.g., commercial software, distributed systems software, real-time software) and for different organizational environments (e.g., hardware manufacturers, software houses, system houses).
- The implementation of the generic ESF will be achieved by a selection of tools that support in the production process as previously defined. The selection may be a selection from the market of existing tools or may be a selection from the wide range of tools to be developed. The generic nature of the implemented generic ESF—either selected or developed—will be established through provisions for parameterization. On the basis of this parameterization concept the implemented generic ESF may be used to derive an implemented ESF instantiation. To enable the derivation of implemented ESF instantiations, the implemented generic ESF must provide the aforementioned actualization capabilities or even generation capabilities. At any rate, both the generic ESF and the implemented generic ESF as well as all possible derived implemented ESF instantiations must conform to the respective interaction protocol(s). For the support of the implementation process, tools may be developed in the ESF project that enable a (partial) automation of that implementation. These may once again be tools that are capable of transforming (i.e., generating) an implementation from the model (i.e., the conceptual schema) of the generic ESF. This is shown in Figure 22-18.
- The derivation of ESF instantiations was already mentioned in the previous paragraph. Since the generic ESF and the implemented generic ESF both provide actualization or generation capabilities, an ESF instantiation and an implemented ESF instantiation can be derived through the application of these mechanisms or through additional manual tailoring. For the support of the customization process, the ESF project will identify—and possibly develop—tools that enable a "mechanization" of that customization process. At both the model level and the implementation level, a "mecha-

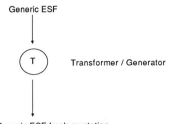

Figure 22-18. Supporting the instantiation process.

nization'' can be achieved with tools for the validation and conformance testing. Those tools aid in the process of ascertaining that an ESF instantiation is in conformance with the generic ESF or that an implemented ESF instantiation is in conformance with the implemented generic ESF.

After having built an ESF instantiation using the concepts of customization and implementation and following the reference architecture (explained in the last section), such an instantiation could now still be extended by adding further tools.

When adding a new tool the following aspects must be considered: first, the degree of integration intended to be achieved requires method integration for any tool to achieve one coherent software production support method within one ESF instantiation; second, at which level the new tool can be integrated must be checked. The easiest way is to integrate horizontally and be able to communicate with the other tools by using the objects provided on that level. In a more difficult situation a vertical integration may be necessary; then it must be checked whether the software bus providing the appropriate mapping from the objects of one level to the objects of a lower level is already available in the instance or is yet to be implemented. Note, however, that adding a new tool does not require that this tool has to communicate with already existing tools in that particular instance. Communication is only enforced in a way that the development methodology within the particular instance is adequately supported.

In summary, tool integration is guided by the reference architecture, because an instantiation that is built following the reference architecture is automatically an open system. This is illustrated in Figure 22-19.

The components of an ESF-architecture are categorized into three different classes. The basic services include ESF-OSS and ESF-UIS, whereas tool services include the already available tools within a particular instance, and interaction services include all the monitoring facilities within a particular instance. The lines visualize the proposed ESF-standards. Figure 22-19 shows that adding a tool to an instance is easy when a tool uses these standards; therefore, tool integration should be done this way. More work has to be done when

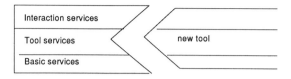

Figure 22-19. A summary of ESF-tool integration.

a certain standard is not matched. For example, when the tool has to be adapted to the ESF-OSS then a special adapter has to be written; i.e., a new software bus has to be implemented.

6 CONCLUSIONS

This chapter describes the conceptual basis of ESF. The ESF model provides a new approach to build software factories. Software factories differ from software production environments in that they heavily emphasize industrialization and automation of the software production.

The ESF approach provides a reference architecture, a reference model, and an instantiation procedure, which altogether allow ESF instances to be derived. Such instances are tailored towards the specific needs and requirements of one company by using a mixture of existing and newly developed tools. In particular, the ESF reference architecture fixes the spectrum of possible ESF instances, whereas the reference model defines different interfaces on different abstraction levels for the different architectural components. The result is that any new tool can be plugged-in on the most suitable level and does not have to be adopted to one specific standard interface. Furthermore, ESF investigates the use of expert knowledge within software development and develops concepts to enable reusability of software components.

Presently, ESF is at the end of its definition phase. The described concepts have been developed in different working groups and are yet under discussion. For the end of 1987, a consolidated report was planned for release which describes the technical basis of ESF.

The main phase started at the beginning of 1988. This phase will be organized in a different way to avoid too much administration overhead. A centralized technical team will define and coordinate different subprojects which are carried out in a decentralized manner. The central team is also responsible for the quality assurance of the subprojects and for the development of ESF-standards.

In the first five years of the main phase, it is intended to build ESF support components—some possible software buses—and use them for building different ESF prototypes. In the next five years, different members of the ESF consortium will build their ESF-instances customized toward their specific needs according to the ESF Reference Architecture.

The authors are indebted to W. Deiters, U. Kelter, and K.-J. Vagts for many fruitful discussions and comments on earlier versions of this chapter. Furthermore, many issues described in this chapter arose during intensive discussions with the other ESF members. The authors also thank Miss E. Denkler for support in typing the manuscript.

REFERENCES

1. Bull, G.M., et. al., "The PEACOCK Paradigm of System Development," *Proc. ESPRIT '85, Status Report of Ongoing Work,* North Holland: Elsevier, 1985, pp. 343–348.
2. "Common Ada Interface Set (CAIS) 85, Requirements and Criteria for CAIS II," *DOD report,* 1985.
3. Donzean-Gouge, V., G. Kahn, B. Lang, and B. Melex, "Document Structure and Modularity in MENTOR," *ACM SIGPLAN,* Vol. 19, No. 5.
4. Deiters, W., W. Schäfer, and K.-J. Vagts, "Formal Models for Describing the Software Development Process," *Technical Report,* University of Dortmund, Dortmund, West Germany (in press).
5. Engels, G., C. Lewerentz, M. Nagl, and W. Schäfer, "On the Structure of an Incremental and Integrated Software Development Environment," *Proceedings of 19th Int. Conf. on System Sciences,* Hawaii.
6. Engels, G., and W. Schäfer, "Graph Grammar Engineering: A Method Used for the Development of an Integrated Programming Support Environment," *LNCS,* Vol. 186, Berlin: Springer-Verlag, 1985, pp. 179–193.
7. Ehrig, H. and H. Weber, "Programming in the Large with Algebraic Module Specification," *Information Processing 86,* (Kugler, ed.), North-Holland: Elsevier, 1986.
8. Gallotz, F., R. Minot, and I. Thomas, "The Object Management System of PCTE as a Software Engineering Database Management System," *SIGPLAN,* Vol. 22, No. 1, 1987.
9. Gasch, B., U. Kelter, H. Kopfer, and H. Weber, "Reference Model for the Integration of Tools within the EUREKA Software Factory," *Proceedings of Fall Joint Computer Conference,* Dallas, October 1987, pp. 183–189.
10. Hirschmann, L., "PRADOS—A Software Development System Supported by a Database," (in German), *UNIX/Mail,* April 1985.
11. Habermann, A. N. and D. Notkin, "Gandalf: Software Development Environments," *IEEE Trans. on Software Engineering,* Vol. 12, No. 12, 1986, pp. 1117–1127.
12. Hruschka, P., "Promod—in the Age 5," *Proc. of ESEC '87 (European Software Engineering Conference), LNCS,* 1987.
13. Merbeth, G., "Report on German Joint Venture Tool Integration Projects," *Proceedings of Fall Joint Computer Conference,* Dallas, October 1987, pp. 214–218.
14. Project POINTE: Private Communications, Software Laboratory, Munich, West Germany.
15. Project RASOP: Private Communications, University of Dortmund, Dortmund, West Germany.
16. Reiss, S. P., "PECAN: Program Development that Supports Multiple Views," *Proceedings of the 7th International Conference on Software Engineering,* March, 1984, pp. 324–333.
17. SunView (Sun Visual/Integrated Environment for Workstations), *Programmer's Guide,* Part Nos. 800-1345-10, Sun Microsystems, Inc., 1986.
18. Weber, H. and H. Ehrig, "Specification of Modular Systems," *IEEE Trans. on Software Engineering,* Vol. 12, No. 7, 1986, pp. 784–798.

Chapter 23

The Model for the Brazilian Software Plant

FUAD GATTAZ SOBRINHO
Software Plant Project
Campinas, SP-Brazil

1 INTRODUCTION

The Brazilian Software Plant Project (SPP) was proposed in 1984 and started in 1986 as a consortium with the purpose of positioning Brazil at the current technological level of other countries (such as the United States, Japan, Germany, England, etc.) in software production technologies. The current participants are the Centro Tecnologico para Informatica (CTI), Empresa Brasileira de Pesquisa Agropecuaria (EMBRAPA), and Banco do Brasil S.A. This chapter is a brief description of the goal, organization, policy, and implementation strategies of the Project.

Before describing the SPP, it is worthwhile to examine the impact of the market place and the production process on the implementation of a software plant.

1.1 The Marketplace

A software product is understood here as something whose value is determined by its properties of satisfying needs when automating human activities.

The priority, at present, is not to compete in the area of software research, where the necessary assets—well equipped schools, skilled labor, and wide distribution of funds to objectives which may be even conflicting among themselves—are inevitably large. On the contrary, to compete in the production area—producing the best quality for the lowest price—through the maximization of the technological opportunity is desirable. This term is here understood as the incorporation of R&D results into commercial products in the shortest span of time possible. Some features of such products can be practically analogous to those of products already available, except for cost and quality differences.

1.2 Production Process

The optimistic view which is held of software products cannot be applied to the program production process. The process of a product engineering, i.e., software engineering—is still undecided between some characteristics typical of craftmanship where there is an absence of a systematic structure that allows for approximations, and simplifications within the real world requirements.

Why is software engineering so far behind other engineering branches? Why are its results so poor in relation to the economic potential (approximately $100 billion a year in the U.S.) that it represents? Because, as a human endeavor, it deals in an area of study absolutely unique in terms of complexity (i.e., variety and quantity). The correct approach to such complexity will still demand much research effort geared towards the identification of the basic components of the software (as in the case of hardware), its composition rules, and the control mechanisms required for a task.

Naturally, this process of evolving from craftwork to engineering is not easily measurable. In many areas it is possible to identify, from the start, the cycle of specification modeling—synthesis as well as the typical assessment procedure for any engineering product. The theory of languages and compilation is the best elaborated theory in all computations in this respect—there is an established theoretical basis, methods for projecting and rehearsing well known compilers (even for making them automatically in some cases) and a teaching process of this theory that is so well placed in a hierarchy that it is possible for an intermediate student to go from beginner classes to a pre-operational compiler within a period of four months. As an illustration, one could compare this to the area of program tests generation.

Also found in this evolution process is the opportunity to compete with those it would be unthinkable to compete with if the production process had already been established and, consequently, automated.

2   THE GOAL OF SPP

The process of maximizing the technological opportunity is a facet of production engineering that needs to be studied, established along operational lines, and continually worked upon. This is the role of the software plant: the creation of an environment where production processes are examined, where research findings are evaluated, where innovations are tried out with the goal of lowering production costs with better quality, and where promising processes are sequently spread out.

The rapid absorption of a research finding into the making of a product is also economically important. Of course, there are findings that are not disclosed and can only be seen in the actual products. This is particularly true of military products. Another function of a structure, such as the one underlying the SPP, is the capacity to emulate successful products, in the shortest possible period of time, whenever those products represent an issue in terms of market. The reverse engineering of software products requires the structuring of the organization in terms of recycling components previously developed, controlled experimentation and so on, as well as the differentiation in the inclusion of specific functions or differentiators. To be number two in the opening of a sales campaign does not mean to be second in terms of profits, as is now widely known.

The establishment of a project, such as the Software Plant, does not mean giving up on basic software research. This would be a price much too high for what today could not be easily afforded. Rather the purpose of implementing such a project would be an effort to gather resources for the area that can turn out competitive products to compete with those produced by whomever is prepared to spend millions of dollars in R&D. In this sense the SPP is a fearless enterprise, which despite being backed by only a small structure (a staff of 150–200) is still capable of competing with companies that require a vast amount of resources.

3   IMPLEMENTATION STRATEGY

3.1   Sharing

Every enterprise that aims at generating software technology—methods, techniques, and tools—is a risk enterprise. Risks present in software projects are not easily quantifiable and require a correct approach in order to minimize their effects. The best way to reduce risk of this kind is to share among various institutions. Some interesting examples can be found in Japan (NEC, Toshiba, etc.), U.S.A. (SPC, MCC), and Europe (ESPRIT), etc. There are countless examples of associations to reduce risks in expensive technological projects (as, for instance, the AIRBUS Project) and the results are not always secured as a consequence of the strategy (as in the case of the Concorde, for example). The sharing scheme allows some beneficial collateral effects in the investment participation. These include the following:

- multiple views on the expected outcomes and, therefore, some constant criticism of products to be developed; and
- demand for an organization that is capable of meeting the expectations of all participants and which is, therefore, pure at the sources—it does not have to, and could not, have idiosyncrasies.

The sharing proposed should make possible participation by companies bearing diverse objectives, imposing discipline to each other in the various related areas, that is, not allowing for the introduction of processes that favor a single co-participant.

3.2   Applied Research

The core idea of a Software Plant Project is to bring together companies to develop applied Research and Development (R&D) on short and medium terms (2–5 years). Further reaching research should be conducted by institutions with this purpose. The attempt to act in R&D outside the major area narrows down the range of possible participants, or else, to lessen the number of participants who are not active in the area of research. R&D groups tend to be naturally formed, each around a main area of research and around a less valued area of development, when they do not pursue the same objectives. Having the same objective means taking part in common activities and sharing a schedule agreed upon by all.

A project like the Software Plant cannot rely solely on itself as a small community of researchers devoted to clarifying and developing the plant on technical and scientific grounds and providing proper training within its boundaries. Rather, the team must be prepared to transfer problems (and resources) to other institutions, when the goal of refining the production process cannot be identified.

3.3 Input

3.3.1 Logistics

One basic type of input for an SPP is the existence of a market that can use the product produced by the Project: methods, techniques, and software tools. Thus, it is necessary that an investigation be made to establish the state-of-the-art technology; identify producers of software who will use the technology generated by the plant; and develop with this technology the software objects required by the plant, establishing in this way, a strong software industry. No process to be introduced into a software house, for example, can suddenly break off its modus operandi or demand sudden change from the body of its professionals.

3.3.2 Human Resources

A software plant can only be feasible if its strategy includes the resources locally available in time and space: in time because the preparation of groups (through courses, talks, etc.) is an expensive and long activity; in space because one way to increase the risks of a software project is the fragmentation of a team into several sites.

The preparation of human resources deserves special attention. Normally, a multi-institutional project has a greater setting time as a result of background and information differences among the teams at the various institutions. It is not usually feasible to submit the teams to a long training period when aiming at bringing up all members to a desirable performance level. Thus, the creation of projects that enable in-service training should be initially carried out wherever the practice of configuration management (and not technical expertise) is stressed. Having obtained a body of professionals with critical capacity, the normal day-to-day evolution of the project should then take place. It is necessary to keep the continuous development of training profiles under strict supervision to facilitate or make possible the spread of knowledge accumulated by new participants or new groups of participants, besides the initial ones.

It is undeniable that the formation of qualified human resources is a key activity to improve the quality of both the process and the product on a short or medium term. This requires the encouragement of a strong interaction, in training and selecting, with the institutions normally linked to this activity—the universities. The correct apportionment of this interaction is a strategic concern of project leaders and will be discussed at a later stage.

3.3.3 Technological Base

The technological base is a state machine that can recognize products already developed as belonging to distinct technological stages and that makes it possible to generate products through more promising technologies than at a given stage.

The specification of the initial technological base of the Project, i.e., its technical facet is a function of product receivers (software producers), of the logistics of Human Resources (quantity and quality), and of the availability of the several technological tendencies. It is essential that the initial base should remain an evolving base provided it ensures recognized maturity. Typical symptoms of maturity are products at their release stage to the market, articles of the 'review' type in well known scientific journals, and publicity articles in technical magazines for the general public. The maturity allows the placement of the project on its real bases (not as research in computer science, for instance) at the time of its disclosure to the public for using jargon already familiar. On the other hand, the technological base must be clearly coherent with the most recent products; if not, there would probably be a risk of rejection from those who would consider the project as trying to reinvent the past.

3.4 Technology Diffusion

The diffusion of technology among participants, at the company level, and among others concerned at a more global level, is one economical justification for upholding a project like the Software Plant Project.

Among participants considered for open channels of communication are those groups in each institution that cooperate in the project site and also development groups housed in the company. These channels are more effective to the extent that there is preparation in the company to welcome new technical output. This demands a learning strategy among manager and overseers to abandon the conventional attitudes of rejecting the utility or the importance of projects generated outside the company.

It is among the other groups concerned where the multiplication factors can be found that are required of a project for the achievement of success. To the supplementation strategy one should add the possibility of engaging the participation of other companies at varying levels of technological growth, regardless of the amount of contribution it can provide. It is important that the project seek the participation of individuals who are willing to promote the success of the project.

The diffusion of the technology generated in the shortest period of time that is possible is one of the main concerns of the Software Plant, not only through the methods and tools internally generated (at a slow pace), but also, and principally, through training in these methods and processes.

3.5 Deliverables

A project such as the Software Plant requires a long maturing period (5–10 years) to show any notable results. Unfortunately, projects of this type are not well taken by the majority of companies not linked to the base structure—typically the government and large companies. Therefore, it is essential that the project is organized around deliverables within short periods of time, even if this amounts to interim changes in orientation in relation to the final goal.

The concept of deliverables associated with the analysis of failure at every stage of the Project's existence is an absolute condition for obtaining financial backing for a long-term project.

All of the project phasing must envision the output of visible and quantifiable products after an initial incubation period which typically lasts about one year. At the finish of every period or phase, a particular result or product must be identified to justify investment, in case the project has to be discontinued. This set of principles must be inserted into the Project's master plan which will be periodically reassessed.

4 ORGANIZATION AND POLICY

To ensure the operating success of the Software Plant over a long period requires an organizational structure where all participants have equal say. In addition, the governing bodies of the plant must have members from each of the participants. These governing bodies must separately decide on policy and technical matters.

An organization based on equal say by each participant will force the governing bodies and management of the Software Plant to resolve conflicts among the participants by forcing the decisions that must be made to be for the good of the entire group.

It is strongly recommended that the Software Plant be located in one place, and have all of the people who work for the Plant be in the same building. The Software Plant should report to a neutral organization, that is not a participant.

This organization must take into account the three primary objectives. These include the following:

- To install and keep operational a Pilot Software Industrialization Line;
- To set up a group of experts in software engineering research to support software industrialization activities; and
- To create a framework for the development of qualified personnel for software industrialization and software engineering research activities. The structure of an SPP is described in Figure 23-1.

The Policy Committee, with one member from each sponsor, will provide top level policy decision making for the Software Plant. Its chairperson is the President of the Software Plant.

The Technical Board, which has one member from each sponsor, will provide technical direction and will resolve technical requirement conflicts among the

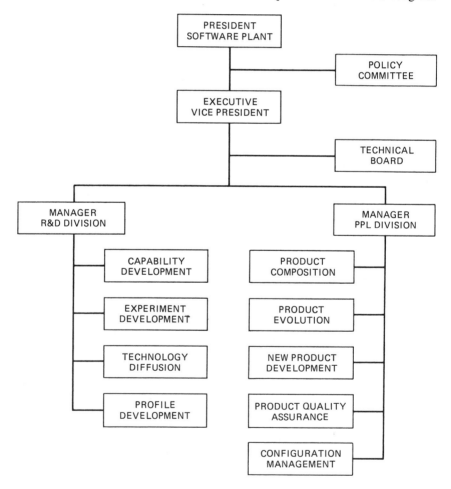

Figure 23-1. The structure of a software plant project.

participants. Its chairperson is the Executive Vice President of the Software Plant.

The President of the Software Plant is the chairperson of the Policy Committee and has final responsibility and authority for all projects within the Plant including technical and financial objectives and accomplishments. His/her primary responsibility is policy, interfacing to sponsors, and general administration.

The Executive Vice President, who is the chairperson of the Technical Board must report to the President and has primary responsibility for all technical decision making within the Software Plant. He/she approves the Technical Requirements document and all changes to it. He/she is the top operating manager in the Plant—complete responsibility and authority for financial and hiring decisions that are within authorized budgets.

Managers of R&D and PPL (Pilot Production Line) divisions must report to the Executive Vice President of the Software Plant. He/she has complete responsibility and authority to execute the projects assigned to their organization. Changes in technical direction consistent with the Technical Requirements document can be made without approval of the Executive Vice President.

The environment of the PPL, is shown in Figure 23-2. This is the production site of the SPP and is composed of the following assembly lines:

- *New Product Development Line*—this line will use as input the requests to develop new software products (i.e., software products not available in the software base). Any software product produced by this line will have the same high level of quality. In this fashion, if a request already involves documents representing views of the required software products (i.e., specification, design, code, or part of any of these), the request should comply with the requirements of the methodology used on the line. Therefore, any new software product produced by the Software Plant will have passes through the specification, design, and test beds.
- *Product Composition Line*—the function of this line is to produce software products derived from the composition of those products already in the Software Base. If new components or modules are required in the line composition process, the New Product Development Line is activated to produce them. Similarly, with the New Product Development Line, if a request involves products not pertaining to the Software Base of the plant, then those products must comply with the PPL product requirements; otherwise, the input products would have to receive evolution treatments (see Product Evolution Line).
- *Product Quality Assurance Line*—this line handles requests on quality assurance for software products. It performs quality assurance services which involve measurements of the quality engineering attributes of flexibility, performance, and verifiability of software products. The software

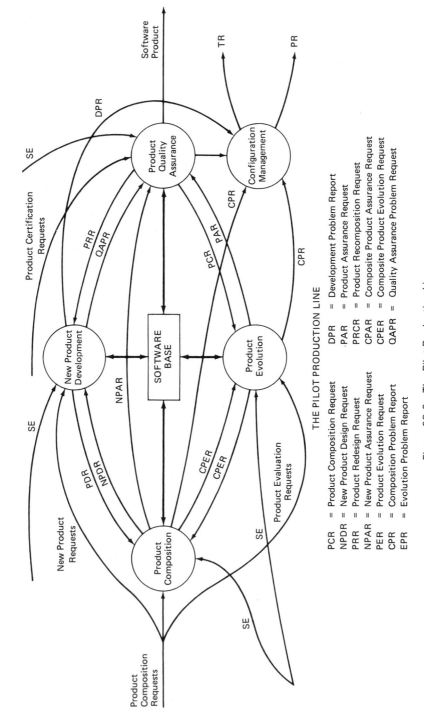

THE PILOT PRODUCTION LINE

PCR = Product Composition Request   DPR = Development Problem Report
NPDR = New Product Design Request   PAR = Product Assurance Request
PRR = Product Redesign Request   PRCR = Product Recomposition Request
NPAR = New Product Assurance Request   CPAR = Composite Product Assurance Request
PER = Product Evolution Request   CPER = Composite Product Evolution Request
CPR = Composition Problem Report   QAPR = Quality Assurance Problem Request
EPR = Evolution Problem Report

Figure 23-2. The Pilot Production Line.

products input to this line may come from outside the Software Plant and from the other industrialization lines. When the requests originate within the production site and the level of quality does not meet the plant's standards, the Product Evolution Line is activated to evolve the product up to the desired quality level.

- *Product Evolution Line*—the configuration of this will provide such evolution services as enhancements, corrections, adaptations, and engineering improvements of software products. Any software product input to this line will receive preparation treatments through the Preparation Bed to assure that the product possesses the formality required by the other beds within this line. Also, this line shall constantly alert the other lines about their production quality, since it will perform all the engineering changes required by the other lines, besides the implementation of the evolution of the production site itself.

- *Configuration Management Line*—the function of this line is to enable the configuration management staff to follow up the industrialization of software products at the production site. The nature of this line is somewhat different from that of the other lines for it neither produces nor evolves software products. It gathers quality, productivity, and standards; it produces information at different control points within the lines on which various managerial decisions are made; it extracts reports on the utility of tools, workbenches, and beds in the industrialization of software products; it broadcasts critical information to alert and motivate the software engineers and managers within the different industrialization lines; and, among other functions, it assures the effectiveness and efficiency of the security and privacy procedures being followed by the production site staff, as well as providing feedback to the configuration management staff of the PPL.

5 THE BRAZILIAN EXPERIENCE

The Brazilian SPP effort was started in 1985 with an international workshop, where the participants were constituted by representatives of existing software initiatives around the world (e.g.: MCC and DOD from the U.S., ESPRIT from Europe, and NEC's Software Factory from Japan), ABICOMP (Brazilian Computer Industry Association), ASSESPRO (Data Processing Services Enterprises Association), SEI (Special Secretary of Informatics), Brazilian universities and internationally known consultants for the evaluation of the SPP Master Plan. The contributions produced in this workshop were incorporated in the Master Plan to get consensus, and the initial set of recommendations proposed by the International and Brazilian Committees is being implemented. The context in which the Brazilian SPP is being implemented is a consortium as shown in Figure 23-3.

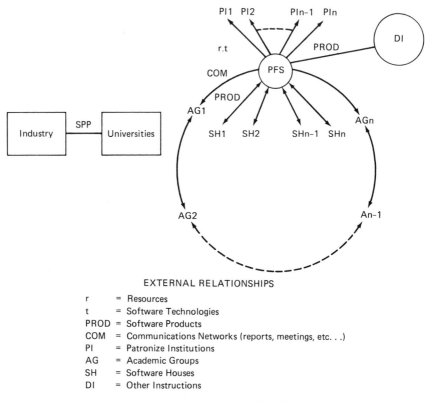

EXTERNAL RELATIONSHIPS

r   = Resources
t   = Software Technologies
PROD   = Software Products
COM   = Communications Networks (reports, meetings, etc. . .)
PI   = Patronize Institutions
AG   = Academic Groups
SH   = Software Houses
DI   = Other Instructions

Figure 23-3. External relationships.

The consortium was formed by the participating institutions to trigger and maintain the linkage between industry and universities for technology development. While the research groups at the universities develop research projects for problems on software production found within the R&D/SPP, the software houses incorporate and use the software production technology developed by the PPL/SPP to help SPP build software tools with the goal of improving their own productivity.

The state of the Brazilian Software Plant Project is described according to the principles contained in its implementation strategy.[1,2]

Given that the Project is still at an early stage, it was not possible to initiate the applied research effort. This was due to the fact that there is not an operating assembly line at present, nor have there been evaluations in terms of deliverables.

5.1   Sharing

The implementation of the Software Plant Project in Brazil involves, at the moment, government institutions sharing among them costs and risks. These institutions are the Centro Tecnologico para Informatica—CTI (Center for Computer Technology), under the Ministry of Science and Technology; Empresa Brasileira de Pesquisa Agropecuaria—EMBRAPA (Agricultural Research Company), under the Ministry of Agriculture; and the Bank of Brasil, attached to the Finance Ministry.[3]

The Project organization is being conducted to comply to the structural guidelines previously formulated and it works as a virtual organization.

All of the resources available for the Plant come from the participating institutions on an equal basis, and each member of the board of directors representing its participating institution has equal participation in the decision making process.

Beside the many and important advantages that the consortium has amassed for the Project, mainly to make it feasible, it was observed that this convergence of efforts has also met with several problems. At the managerial level, owing to the existing differences among the parts involved, the decision making process has suffered as a result of the lack of both administrative and financial autonomy. At the level of personnel concerns, worrying profile differences of the technical staff of the institutions was observed, as well as salary inequalities for equivalent jobs within the plant.

5.2 Inputs

In terms of the market for the products put out by the Software Plant Project, fellowship grants have been contemplated in the plan as incentives to software employees to enable them to participate in the SPP effort.

As for the strengthening of human resources in general, scholarships will also be granted to individuals in the universities across the country for the development of research projects within the software production area.

A group of ten highly qualified technical people from the participating institutions were sent to a software company to get a "fine tuning" on the state of the art technology in the U.S., with the goal of building the initial technological base for the New Product Development and Composition Lines of the PPL/SPP.

5.3 Diffusion of Technology

The technology generated will be transferred, maximizing its diffusion multiplication factor, to the concurring entities through the participation of their staff in projects linked to the Software Plant Project. Thus, at the end of a project, the guest technical staff will return to their original workplaces having observed the methods, techniques, and tools existing in the Plant. In addition the diffusion process has the role of being the external diffusion agent for the sector it represents in the market.

5.4 Deliverables

Within the second year, the SPP will have delivered the kernel of a comprehensive integrated development environment for the New Product Development Line with Object Oriented Technology, the kernels of an Object Manager and User Interface Manager, and a written methodology including Quality Control. With respect to human resources, the SPP will meet with 35 technical staff people trained in its current technological base.

REFERENCES

1. Sobrinho, F.G., *Proposta para implantacao de Fabricas de Software no Brasil*, Washington/DC, March 1984.
2. Sobrinho, F.G., M.D. Ferraretto, K. Techima, G. Bressan, and L.E. Rocha, "The Software Plant Project Master Plan," SEI/CTI, SERPRO; EMBRATEL & EMBRAPA, Campinas/SP, (1985).
3. Sobrinho, F.G. and M.D. Ferraretto, "Software Plant: the Brazilian Software Consortium," *Proc. 1987 Fall Joint Computer Conference,* IEEE, Dallas, Texas, 1987.

Chapter 24

Software Technology Research and Development in China

FENGQIAO LIU
China Software Technology Development Center
Beijing, China

CHENGWEI WANG
Beijing Institute of System Engineering
Beijing, China

FELICIA CHENG
Institute for Integrated Systems Research
Department of Computer & Information Science
New Jersey Institute of Technology
Newark, NJ

1 INTRODUCTION

During the last three decades of worldwide technological revolution, China was behind many countries in technological research. As a developing country, China is unable to undertake full-scale development of high technology in the immediate future. Yet, it is of paramont importance for China to take full advantage of modern science and technology to achieve the strategic goal of quadrupling its national industrial and agricultural output by the year 2000.

Over the last five years, China has done much to keep up with other countries. In 1982, the State Sciences and Technology Committee of China proposed and later established a software factory which promoted the software industry in China. In 1987, the High Technology Development Program was established to expand technological research. One of the seven research areas included in the program is the research on Information Technology, which focused on the development of intelligent computer systems.

In this chapter, the authors provide a status report of the software factory plan and describe the overall structure of the intelligent computer system. The software factory plan began four years ago, and what has been accomplished is described and also, what is hoped to be achieved in the research on the development of intelligent computer systems.

2   SOFTWARE FACTORY PLAN

2.1   Background

In 1982 and 1983, to encourage the development of the software industry in China, the State Sciences and Technology Committee of China (SSTCC) organized several meetings and symposiums to discuss issues relating to software research, development and production. The meetings were attended by over 100 software experts from industries, academies of science and universities. The following ideas were communicated:

- The worldwide technological revolution provides an opportunity for China to modernize. Learning from technologically advanced countries can aid in the development of sciences and technology in China. To avoid the software crisis experienced by other countries, software development should be switched from manualized to industrialized. Software engineering methodologies should be introduced and promoted nationwide.
- Standard software development practices and tools should be developed to improve the quality of software and to increase the productivity of software developers.
- A software factory should be established as a model to demonstrate software engineering practices in China.

In 1984, the SSTCA initiated the China Software Technology Development Center (CSTDC) to implement a Software Engineering International Cooperation (SEIC) Project. The following are the major components of the project:

- Set up a software factory in Beijing as a model in China.
- Set up a training center at Beijing University to train software engineers for the Beijing Software Factory (BSF).
- Develop a standard software development methodology and an integrated software development environment for the software factory.
- Organize a software company in the United States to support the implementation of the SEIC project.

Since the Spring of 1984, over 100 researchers from thirteen institutions have been involved in the project. The leaders of the sub-projects are visiting scholars with expertise in software engineering in advanced countries. A general group, which specifies the common design goal, was also set up. The project is expected to be completed by the end of 1989.

2.2   The Software Factory Plan

The software factory plan is a four year plan. Organized by the CSTDC, it is aimed at setting up a software factory in Beijing. The software factory will be used as a model for industrializing the production of software. Its main functions are as follows:

- Design software development methodologies to produce high quality, low-cost software products for domestic and international markets.
- Cooperate with universities and research institutions to develop an integrated software development environment for the software factory.
- Gather information on the application of software development methodologies for improving the quality of software and increasing the productivity of software engineers.
- Transfer the technologies developed to other companies throughout the country to enable software development methodologies to be moved from R&D to a practical applications setting.

It is expected that 400 people will be hired, and the plan is projected for completion by the end of 1989.

2.3   Training Center

To carry out the software factory plan, a large number of qualified software engineers are needed. To meet the competition in future markets, it has decided that software engineers should come from the younger generation. Computer science education has not provided sufficient practical experience for the students. Therefore, SSTCC decided to set up a training center in Beijing University. It was designed to train qualified software engineers for the software factory. The following approaches were adopted by the center:

- The center will cooperate with international researchers. Major instructors will be hired from United States. Every student entering the center must already possess a degree of higher education and pass an entrance examination.
- The duration of study is two years. In the first six months, the emphasis is on spoken English, the next twelve months for software engineering principles and methodologies, and the last six months on the practical application of the software principle and methodologies.

The following courses are currently offered by the center:

- software specifications, environment, and tools;
- systems software: database management systems, compilers, operating systems, and networking software;
- scientific calculations;
- CAD/CAM;
- management information systems;

- Chinese character processing; and
- graphics and image processing.

Currently, the BSF has already designed and implemented documentation standards for its software development process. A partial listing of other developments include:

- structured editors, cross-compilers, and other software tools;
- quality control and management systems for Chinese factories;
- CAD system for simulating detonation construction techniques;
- CAD architectural system design;
- Chinese character terminal cards for displaying and editing Chinese characters;
- material management system used by the Ministry of Coal Industry; and
- satellite I/O processing system for the Bureau of Atmospheric Science.

The BSF has also developed working relationships with other factories, companies, and government institutions throughout China, as well as with over 30 companies from other countries. Current joint projects include the implementation of an electronic CAD system to develop tools for designing computer chips and other related hardware, compiler design, the development of a new version of the RBASE Relational Database Series, and the porting of software from one machine to another.

2.4   Integrated Software Engineering Environment (ISEE) Project

It was recognized that to improve the quality of software and increase the productivity of software engineers, an integrated software engineering environment is necessary. The ISEE was initiated in parallel with the software factory plan and aims at establishing an integrated software development support environment and is designed to support all phases of software development and management processes.

The project will be carried out in two steps: in the first step, a set of tools, which are guided by common design principles, will be developed; in the second step, the integration of the set of tools will be completed in the software factory.

The design of the ISEE project is guided by the following principles:

- support software development methodologies that are proven to have significant beneficial effects on the software development process;
- provide an integrated set of tools that will enhance the development process at each phase of the software life-cycle;
- allow future expansion;
- consist of a common information base and a uniform user-friendly interface;

- practical and economical to implement; and
- adapt to new techniques such as artificial intelligence and fourth generation language.

The following are chosen as the basic building blocks in the first step:

- The UNIX[1] system is adopted as the basic system, and the C programming language as the development language.
- All the software tools will be developed on a host machine and transferred to the target machine using cross-compilers.
- Yourdon's structured design methodology is used as the design methodology.

Currently, the ISEE project provides software developers with a set of tools which include the following:

- DSE (Design Structured Editor)—a set of tools which support requirement analysis, general design, and detailed design. It consists of textual and graphic editors and can be used to create data flow diagrams and structured charts.
- CSEL (C-based Syntax-directed Editor)—a syntax-directed editor for the C programming environment. It is user friendly, easy to use, and easy to learn.
- C-cross (C cross-compiler system)—a general-purpose software tool which has the capability of converting a C program to any given assembly code so that programs running on a host machine can be transfered to any target machine.
- DMSS and CMS (Decision-Making Supporting System and Configuration Management System)—DMSS is a general decision-making supporting system for project managers. It consists of five subsystems:
  - model building system,
  - scheduling network system,
  - data collecting system,
  - reporting system, and
  - project management base.
- It can be used by managers for controlling cost and schedules. CMS is a configuration management system, the functions of which are to manage and trace source code, data, and documents.
- EASYCODE—the kernel of this tool is a program generator that transforms concept-based specifications into target programs.

---

[1]UNIX is a registered trademark of AT&T Bell Laboratories.

- USE (Universal Structured Editor)—a versatile, language independent structured editor. USE can be used to edit programs written in different languages. It provides a uniform user-interface and an identical set of editing commands.

The ISEE is a national project, that involves ten universities and academic institutions. They include the following:

- Beijing Institute of Aeronautics and Astronautics;
- Beijing University;
- Qing Hua University;
- Huazhong University of Science and Technology;
- Northwest University
- East China University of Chemical Technology;
- Beijing University of Poly Technologies;
- Software Research Institute of Academia Sinica;
- Automation Research Institute of Academia Sinica; and
- China Printing Technology Research Institute.

It has been three years since the project's start in August 1984, when the project was started. In the first year and a half, four review meetings were held in China to inspect progress of the project, and experts from abroad were invited to attend and give comments.

Now the first step has come to an end. All the tools are near completion, and several have actually been finished. So far, 250 man-years were spent on the project. In the near future, it will be time to move on to the second step, and the final integrated version will be implemented either on a AT&T 3B5, a Pyramid, or a VAX 11/785 computer systems.

3   INTELLIGENT COMPUTER SYSTEM

3.1   Background

In the spring of 1987, the High Technology Development Program was established in China. It is a component of the Seventh Five Year Plan (1986–1990) which plans to serve economic development at the turn of the century. The High Technology Development Program consists of seven research areas. These include the following:

- biotechnology,
- space technology,
- information technology,
- laser technology,
- automation technology,

- energy technology, and
- advanced materials.

Over the next 15 years, the projects outlined in the program aim to pool the best technological resources in China to keep up with the high technology development internationally, to bridge the gap between China and other countries in the most important technological areas, and, wherever possible, strive for breakthroughs. The program also aims to provide technological backups for economic development and to train a large number of qualified personnel for future needs.

In the information technology area, the emphasis is on intelligent computer systems. In what follows, the overall structure of the intelligent computer system is discussed and what is hoped to achieve is described.

3.2 Structure of the Intelligent Computer System

The aim of the development of an intelligent computer system in China by the year 2000 is to explore a computer's ability to understand certain aspects of human intelligence. Therefore, research efforts will be concentrated on developing "intelligent" computers with knowledge processing capability; implementing advanced human-machine interfaces, such as natural language processing and vision abilities; and enhancing the likelihood of software automation. Artificial Intelligence (AI) will be promoted to lay the foundation for the intelligent computer system.

To attain these goals, an overall structure of the intelligent computer system which includes the four generic areas of research is needed. These four areas are; basic theory of the intelligent computer system, the architecture of the intelligent computer system, the intelligent interfaces, and intelligent software and its supporting environment. It is expected that achievement of those generic areas of research will support other important applications.

The study and applications of the intelligent computer system will be closely linked to other projects in the High Technology Development Program (e.g., Automation Technology). The structure of the development program of the intelligent computer system in China can be shown as a pyramid (Figure 24-1), and a brief explanation will be given.

3.2.1 Basic Theory of an Intelligent Computer System

What is the basic theory of an intelligent computer system? To answer this question, the question: "What is an intelligent computer system?" must be addressed. The simplest answer can be "an AI oriented computer system." A detailed and widely accepted definition of AI is also hard to come by. The author's definition is as follows:

> AI: the information processing and computer simulation of human intelligence and behavior.

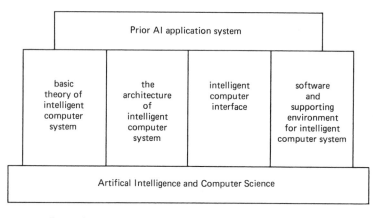

Figure 24-1. Artificial intelligence and computer science.

Through this definition, the study and investigation of the basic theory of an intelligent computer system can be initiated in two areas: first, from a micro view, e.g., the study of the structure of human brain and the process thinking in nerve cells, the study of the structure of human eyes, and the process of vision in visual cells; second, from a macro view, e.g., the study of the procedure of thinking and vision in a general manner, and the processing of information and knowledge. In the authors' opinion, both studies are essential, but the macro view deserves more attention, as it is more relative to the development of intelligent computer system. For instance, a large portion of human intelligence is believed to be based on rules of thumb although it may appear as instinct, reasoning, or common sense.

To explore the essential mechanism and to create a solid foundation of an intelligent computer system, the authors focus on the study of cognitive science. The human thinking process is explored, not only the logical thinking process, but also the image processing process. The authors enhance their study of cognitive psychology to include the study of the psychogenic process of human thinking and memory. Also considered is the biophysical process of human vision, hearing, memory, and thinking as an inseparable part of the basic theory study.

For the same reason, and from a global point of view, using the principle of graphic topology, image and pattern recognition is studied, and the computer's approach of representing and processing images is explored. Since no exact algorithm and representation are known, or for which the known algorithms and representations fail to reproduce and simulate the characteristics or process of human intelligence and behavior, also included are the basic scientific research of mathematical logic, fuzzy theory, and linguistics in the study.

Attempts will be made to add a computational domain to linguistic theory, to develop a mixed symbolic and numerical computation in computer representations and reasoning mechanisms, to construct an effective scheme for manipulating knowledge, and to create fuzzy representations used in data or information base systems.

3.2.2 The Architecture of An Intelligent Computer System

The main problems facing the architecture of an intelligent computer system are the thinking mechanism and the speed of processing. The final goal of the project is to build an intelligent computer system which can simulate human thinking and behavior. There are many different approaches to explore the cognitive process and reflect it in a computer architecture, but in the initial stage, a knowledge processing oriented architecture will be designed that has parallel distributed processing ability.

Since acquisition, storage, processing, and application of knowledge are all dependent on the performance of the knowledge base, and since symbolic manipulation is a memory-intensive and time-consuming process, the knowledge base and the effective method of symbolic manipulation and parallel processing are considered to be the core of the architecture of the intelligent computer system and are critical to the computation mechanism. The performance of an intelligent computer system should be realized in the following aspects:

- Various Representations of Knowledge—both condition-conclusion and reduction forms of knowledge can be represented properly. The knowledge representation can be used for specifying facts as well as uncertainties.
- An Efficient Scheme of Knowledge Base—in future AI applications, flexible and fast retrieval of knowledge is the kernel of any knowledge-base system, because in the process of reasoning and the acquiring of knowledge, searching for the correct rules and subsystems will be the most frequent operations. The knowledge base used in future intelligent computer systems is expected to have a hierarchical structure with different control rules for different layers.
- The inductive learning and the automatic acquisition of knowledge—an acceptable and practical AI application system must have the ability to induce rules from facts, to modify and supplement existing rules, to delete incompatible rules, and to create new rules automatically.
- Highly parallel and distributed processing ability—the intelligent computer will have highly parallel and distributed processing elements performing different levels of parallel processing. And the architecture of an intelligent computer will be expected to provide high accessibility and decentralized decision making ability: it means that the system can be applied to a broad scope of an AI application and can be assigned for decision making at different levels and at different sites.

To implement the requirements mentioned above, improving the current Von Neumann's computer architecture and developing a non-Von Neumann's computer architecture oriented to AI applications are both encouraged.

3.2.3   Intelligent Computer Interface

One major difference between intelligent computer systems and traditional computer systems is that intelligent computer systems relate more closely to human analytical characteristics. Using different types of human-machine interactive working mode, more human intelligence and knowledge can be explored, and a harmonic human-machine environment can be created. To achieve this goal, the traditional computer interface is merged with concepts from cognitive psychology. It is expected that an intelligent interface will play a key role in the success of future intelligent computer systems.

Two aspects in this area will concentrate on the following: natural language processing, especially on Chinese language processing; and a graphics supported human-machine interface.

3.2.3.1   Natural Language Processing   Experience has shown that Chinese language processing is difficult because it has very special features. Chinese is not an alphabetic system but a type of pictograph, it cannot be represented by a finite set of characters and handled by the computer keyboard in an easy and uniform manner. Unlike English and other languages in which a sentence is composed of words, and words are separated by blanks, words in Chinese have no such deterministic and specific boundaries. Words in Chinese are more context-sensitive than other languages. Semantic analysis is essential, and has to be done with the assistance of syntactical analysis and inference rules. In Figure 24-2, there are seven Chinese characters. The meaning of the seven characters is "computer system architecture." But a 2/3/4/5/6 character combination also provides different meaning. As Chinese computer scientists, it is their duty to contribute to the research and success of Chinese language processing.

计	算					—— computing
计	算	机				—— computer
计	算	机	系			—— department of computer science
计	算	机	系	统		—— computer system
计	算	机	系	统	结	—— the node of a computer system
计	算	机	系	统	结	构 —— computer system architecture

Figure 24-2.   Chart with Chinese characters.

3.2.3.2 Graphics Supported Human-Machine Interface In the area of graphics supported human-machine interface research is conducted in both theoretical and practical aspects by studying formal and informal models, such as problem-oriented descriptive models (the frame models and the semantic network models), the interaction-oriented control models (the models which simulate human logical thinking and image thinking), and the knowledge association models (the models that use association methods to combine the descriptive models and the control models). These models will be studied individually and are relative to each other. Some psychological issues will be studied, such as what effect the computer will have on society and humanity.

It must be emphasized that during the research, process models are often studied according to a particular type of knowledge which is relatively independent from others. In the real application, a number of models have to be considered as a single unit to fully understand and utilize this knowledge.

3.2.4 Software and Supporting Environment for Intelligent Computer Systems

During the past 50 years, the data which was manipulated and processed by computers are mainly numerical data which was represented as a set of discrete numbers and symbols. As information technology evolves, the object of computing is shifting from data processing to knowledge processing. In the latter case, some questions about supporting the environment of intelligent computer system arise. For example: What is the impact of the software supporting environment on AI software development? How widely will traditional tools be used in AI software development and maintenance? Will the life-cycle concept remain to be important in the future? And are there any new ideas and performance requirements on CASE (Computer-Aided Software Engineering)?

To answer these questions the essential difference between data processing and knowledge processing will be discussed from the point of view of software programming and maintenance.

From the view point of computer science, knowledge is organized data. If one continues to call the next generation of computers data processors, the data to be processed and manipulated by a computer is generalized data: formal representation of facts, concepts, and rules.

In knowledge-based programming, a problem is solved by inferring from knowledge which is predefined, acquired, generated, revoked, and/or changed in the course of execution. This is quite different from the conventional programming methods which are based on predefined algorithms. In knowledge-based programming, the inference mechanism and the mechanism to dynamically change knowledge are most important (Figure 24-3).

There are several reasons to claim that computing is knowledge programming. These include the following:

DATA PROCESSING   ———   KNOWLEDGE PROCESSING

(discrete numbers   (formal representation

and symbols)   of facts, concepts,

                                 and rules

CONVENTIONAL   ———   KNOWLEDGE-BASED

PROGRAMMING   PROGRAMMING

(algorithm)   (algorithm,

                                 inference mechanism,

                                 knowledge change

                                 mechanism)

Figure 24-3. Chart.

- Computers are machines for manipulating knowledge.
- Programming languages are formalized knowledge which consists of structures, in which knowledge can be expressed, and inference systems, which are able to use that knowledge to solve specific problems.
- Programs are sets of knowledge.
- Programming is a knowledge-intensive activity.

According to these assumptions, the life cycle concept is considered still valid and will follow the CASE principles as a guideline in the development and maintenance of AI software. Since more man power will be required during the requirements and maintenance phases, and since software requirements—mainly done manually—will be done in a computer-assisted environment, and software maintenance, which was only associated with those activities that were performed after the development process, will now be an inseparable part of the development process, the rapid prototyping approach will be used to develop the system.

In summary, effort is concentrated on the following aspects:

- To provide a powerful language environment for different AI applications, such as those for Prolog, Lisp, OPS5, and Smalltalk80, etc.
- To study a "base" language that will be able to support existing programming languages and can be implemented in a parallel architecture efficiently.
- To invent AI programming languages that can support multiple programming paradigms and AI applications.
- To provide a set of integrated tools as part of the software development environment that aims to support the complete life-cycle of AI software.

- To study automatic programming focusing on the following two aspects:

  - to build a set of tools that enables a user to obtain formal specifications from informal requirements; and
  - to develop tools that allow software to be directly generated from its specifications.

4   CONCLUSION

Although there has been a great effort to apply the new scientific results into real applications, there is still a large gap between academic research and industrial production. Currently, this problem is more profound in China. This chapter has presented recent work on computer science research and development. During the past three decades, the development of computer science and technology has produced a profound impact on the progress of Chinese society. It can be predicted that the development of an intelligent computer system will push human intelligence to a new level and will greatly enrich human knowledge. There will be a new technological revolution. Chinese computer scientists would like to have more close and deep contacts, and to cooperate with researchers in other parts of the world, and to give their contributions to the research and development in software technology.

Index